VAN GOGH AND GAUGUIN

DOUGLAS W. DRUICK AND PETER KORT ZEGERS

IN COLLABORATION WITH BRITT SALVESEN

WITH CONTRIBUTIONS TO THE TEXT
BY KRISTIN HOERMANN LISTER

AND THE ASSISTANCE OF MARY C. WEAVER

VAN GOGH

AND GAUGUIN

THE STUDIO OF THE SOUTH

THE ART INSTITUTE OF CHICAGO

 Thames & Hudson

VAN GOGH MUSEUM, AMSTERDAM

This book was published in conjunction with the exhibition "Van Gogh and Gauguin: The Studio of the South," co-organized by The Art Institute of Chicago and the Van Gogh Museum, Amsterdam.

Exhibition dates:
The Art Institute of Chicago,
22 September 2001–13 January 2002
Van Gogh Museum, Amsterdam,
9 February–2 June 2002

The exhibition and the book that accompanies it were made possible through the generous support of Ameritech (Chicago) and ABN AMRO (Amsterdam). Additional support was provided by: An indemnity from the Federal Council on the Arts and Humanities.

Edited and produced by the Publications Department, The Art Institute of Chicago, Susan F. Rossen, Executive Director of Publications
Edited by: Britt Salvesen, Associate Editor, assisted by Lisa Meyerowitz and Katherine Reilly, special-projects editors, and Faith Brabenec Hart, independent editor
Produced by: Amanda W. Freymann, Associate Director of Publications, Production, assisted by Stacey Hendricks, Production Assistant, and Karen Gephart Altschul, Photo Editor

Designed by studio blue, Chicago
Color separations by Professional Graphics, Rockford, Illinois
Printed by Arnoldo Mondadori Editore, S.p.A., Verona, Italy

For photography credits, see p. 417
Front of cover and jacket:
Paul Gauguin, *Self-Portrait Dedicated to Vincent van Gogh (Les Misérables)* (detail), 1888, cat. 33; and Vincent van Gogh, *Self-Portrait Dedicated to Paul Gauguin (Bonze)* (detail), 1888, cat. 64.
P. ii: Paul Gauguin, *Sunflowers on an Armchair* (detail), 1901, cat. 144.
P. iii: Vincent van Gogh, *Sunflowers* (detail), 1889, cat. 110.
Back of cover and jacket; and p. xiii: Vincent van Gogh, *The Yellow House* (detail), 1888, cat. 66.

First published in hardcover in the United States of America in 2001 by Thames & Hudson Inc., 500 Fifth Avenue, New York, NY 10110
First published in the United Kingdom in 2001 by Thames & Hudson Ltd, 181A High Holborn, London WC1V7QX

Library of Congress Catalog Card Number 2001087364
British Library Cataloguing-in-Publication data: A catalogue record for this book is available from the British Library, London
ISBN 0–500–51054–7 (hardcover)
ISBN 0–86559–194–6 (softcover)

Library of Congress Cataloging-in-Publication Data
Druick, Douglas W.
Van Gogh and Gauguin : the studio of the south / by Douglas W. Druick and Peter Kort Zegers in collaboration with Britt Salvesen ; with contributions to the text by Kristin Hoermann Lister and the assistance of Mary C. Weaver.
p. cm.
Published in conjunction with an exhibition held at The Art Institute of Chicago, Sept. 22, 2001–Jan. 13, 2002 and the Van Gogh Museum, Amsterdam, Feb. 2–June 2, 2002.
Includes bibliographical references and index.
ISBN 0-500-51054-7 (alk. paper) —
ISBN 0-86559-194-6 (pbk. : alk. paper)
1. Gogh, Vincent van, 1853–1890—Biography. 2. Artists—Netherlands—Biography. 3. Gauguin, Paul, 1848–1903—Biography. 4. Artists—France—Biography. 5. Artistic collaboration—France—Arles. I. Zegers, Peter. II. Salvesen, Britt. III. Lister, Kristin Hoermann. IV. Weaver, Mary. V. Art Institute of Chicago. VI. Van Gogh Museum. VII. Title.

ND653.G7 D76 2001
759.9492—dc21
[B]
2001037695

JAN   2002

CONTENTS

viii
Sponsor's Statement

ix
Directors' Preface

x
Acknowledgments

1
PROLOGUE

4
CHAPTER 1
ORIGINS
1848–1885

50
CHAPTER 2
ENCOUNTERS
October 1885–February 1887

94
CHAPTER 3
SOUTH VERSUS
NORTH
February 1887–October 1888

156
CHAPTER 4
THE STUDIO OF
THE SOUTH
23 October–23 December 1888

161
Opening Gambits
23 October–28 October

170
Settling In
29 October–3 November

182
Assigning Roles
4 November–10 November

196
Memory
11 November–17 November

206
Threat of Success
18 November–24 November

221
Family Portraits
25 November–3 December

234
Artists' Portraits
4 December–17 December

244
Denouement
18 December–23 December

262
CHAPTER 5
CORRESPONDENCE
24 December 1888–29 July 1890

332
CODA
THE STUDIO
OF THE TROPICS
June 1891–May 1903

354
APPENDIX
Tracing an Interaction:
Supporting Evidence,
Experimental Grounds
by Kristin Hoermann
Lister, Cornelia Peres,
and Inge Fiedler

370
Notes

401
Selected Bibliography

404
Checklist of the Exhibition

410
Lenders to the Exhibition

411
Index

417
Photography Credits

Through its sponsorship of the arts, ABN AMRO seeks to make a beneficial contribution to society as a whole. This philosophy is reflected in our regular involvement in a range of fascinating and prestigious artistic projects. We are very proud, therefore, to act as partner to the Van Gogh Museum, Amsterdam, for the exhibition "Van Gogh and Gauguin."

The story of this legendary and intriguing relationship is retold through 120 outstanding works. Although Vincent van Gogh and Paul Gauguin were very different characters, each with his own specific ideas about art, the two men exerted a significant and undeniable influence on each other and provided mutual inspiration. This fact is clearly evident in the marvellous paintings that, thanks to the generosity of numerous lenders, are included in the exhibition. The quality of the exhibition is also reflected in the catalogue, which offers fascinating insights into the eventful lives, critical dialogue, and path-breaking work of these outstanding artists.

The once-in-a-lifetime opportunity to view all of these works together, whether in Amsterdam or in Chicago, is sure to appeal to many people throughout the world. As one of the world's leading financial institutions, we aim to put our extensive know-how and experience together to work to our customers' benefit. To achieve that goal, we focus on our customers' financial needs, while creating maximum economic value for our shareholders.

We hope and trust that many people will enjoy "Van Gogh and Gauguin," both in Amsterdam and in Chicago, and that all who see it will be inspired by this unique event.

Rijkman W. J. Groenink
ABN AMRO
Chairman of the Managing Board

The friendship and rivalry between Vincent van Gogh and Paul Gauguin formed the backdrop for one of the most compelling episodes in the history of modern art. The story of two great talents brought together by circumstance and mutual respect has many of the elements of great drama: harmony and conflict, shared ambitions and disappointments, admiration and contempt, and most famously rage and even bloodshed. Pieced together from fragmentary sources and exaggerated in the telling, it is a saga that has at times taken on the quality of myth, capturing the imagination of generations of historians, writers, and filmmakers.

Yet if the human drama of the encounter between van Gogh and Gauguin might seem familiar, the full history of their artistic relationship has not yet received the attention that it deserves. This book and the exhibition it accompanies set out to explore that relationship in full. From the beginnings of their awareness of each other's art in the mid-1880s, through the brief, frenetic period of collaboration in Arles to the end of their respective careers, their complex interaction is traced, revealed, and analyzed. Drawing on a vast array of sources and with the benefit of extensive technical studies of the works of art themselves, the scholars involved in this project have brought new depth and insight to a fascinating dialogue. Biographical details have been painstakingly reconstructed, and the dating and sequence of van Gogh's and Gauguin's art has been re-examined to provide a framework for the painters' evolving ideas and artistic intercourse. It now becomes clear how each man played a vital role in the other's search for a personal manner and expressive content, as collective endeavor sharpened personal intention and ambition. Together, van Gogh and Gauguin's contribution to the history of art was a formidable one. Through this study, we gain a greater understanding of their aims, achievements, and the underlying meaning of their work.

In contrast to the relationship that is the subject of this book, the partnership between The Art Institute of Chicago and the Van Gogh Museum, Amsterdam, has been harmonious at every stage. With the respective strengths of our collections and the expertise of our curatorial teams, the two institutions are logical partners for this undertaking. But although both our institutions are accustomed to mounting international exhibitions, this project has been of an order and scale that falls outside the realms of our normal experience. It could only have been realized thanks to the total commitment of our respective staffs; and we would like to pay tribute to all our colleagues for their dedication, enthusiasm, and effort.

Particular acknowledgment is due to the authors of this book: Douglas W. Druick, the Art Institute's Searle Curator of European Paintings and Prince Trust Curator of Prints and Drawings, and Peter Kort Zegers, Rothman Family Research Curator at the Art Institute. Their inspired vision and impressive scholarship has been at the very heart of this project. It is a tribute to their achievement as authors and researchers that the drama and excitement of the artistic encounter they describe are enhanced and intensified for being uncovered in all their complexity. In Amsterdam this project was directed by Andreas Blühm, Head of Exhibitions at the Van Gogh Museum. The specialists at the Van Gogh Museum, led by Chief Curator Sjraar van Heugten, Curator Louis van Tilborgh, and Leo Jansen, Director of the Van Gogh Letters Project, provided invaluable support. In addition to these individuals, we wish to express our deepest gratitude to the staffs of both The Art Institute of Chicago and the Van Gogh Museum, whose professionalism and dedication were significant in this challenging undertaking.

In some ways, it is not surprising that this is the first major exhibition that reunites the art of Van Gogh and Gauguin, since the obstacles to realizing such a project are formidable, not least in terms of loans and logistics. Works by these artists are, understandably, highly-prized possessions, but the nature of our theme meant that choices and options were severely restricted. Success depended on obtaining enough of the pictures that are the most relevant and revealing of the unfolding dialogue between the two artists. Inevitably, there are works that we have not been able to secure for this show, but the outstanding support of private collectors and of our colleagues in the museum world has meant that we have been able to display many more (or rather combinations of related ones) than we ever dared to hope when this project began, in the mid-1990s. We would like to give our special thanks to all the lenders for their trust and generous support.

The exhibition benefited greatly from an indemnity from the Federal Council on the Arts and Humanities and from the Dutch Government. For all her help and support, we are grateful to Alice Whelihan, Indemnity Administrator, Museum Program, National Endowment for the Arts, and Ceef Kovtleve. Finally, we would like to thank our sponsors—in Chicago, Ameritech and Ameritech Foundation; and, in Amsterdam, ABN AMRO bank—for enabling us to make this exhibition for the enjoyment and enlightenment of our publics. Van Gogh could paint sunflowers as, in his words, a symbol of gratitude. We can only say thank you.

James N. Wood
Director and President,
The Art Institute of Chicago

John Leighton
Director, Van Gogh Museum,
Amsterdam

ACKNOWLEDGMENTS

The organization of the first extensive exhibition devoted to the collaboration of Vincent van Gogh and Paul Gauguin has been an international effort requiring the cooperation of many colleagues. Our focus on not one but two major artists, and on the particular works through which their dialogue is reflected, has brought with it unique challenges. Fifty-two museums and a significant number of private collectors from more than seventeen countries generously have agreed to participate by making works in their collections accessible for technical study and for loan. Other colleagues in museums, universities, libraries, archives, government agencies, galleries, and auction houses have contributed to this project. To all who have worked in helping us realize the exhibition and its accompanying publication, we would like to extend our deepest gratitude.

We are acutely aware of the debt we owe to scholars who have devoted their energies to both artists over the past century. This publication cannot be the place for a complete bibliography that would include each valuable contribution. As much as possible we have attempted to acknowledge the sources most pertinent to our argument; but endnotes alone cannot adequately recognize the formative influences that over time have shaped our thinking about these highly complex artists. Therefore we take this opportunity to recognize both the original pioneers and their successors who have continued to shape our understanding, bringing new primary documentation to light and fresh interpretations to bear on the works. The first half of the twentieth century witnessed the foundational contributions of, among others, Jo van Gogh-Bonger, Charles Chassé, Raymond Cogniat, J.-B. de la Faille, Marcel Guérin, Jean Loize, Maurice Malingue, John Rewald, Jean de Rotonchamp, and Meyer Schapiro. The expansion of the field of inquiry, beginning in the 1950s, involved such talents as Merete Bodelsen, Douglas Cooper,

Bengt Danielsson, Bernard Dorival, Henri Dorra, Christopher Gray, Jan Hulsker, Sven Lövgren, and Marc Tralbaut. Since Mark Roskill's groundbreaking study of both artists appeared in 1970, the literature has been enriched by Ziva Amishai-Maisels, Wayne Andersen, Gilles Artur, Martin Bailey, Jean-Louis Bonnat, Richard Brettell, Françoise Cachin, Elizabeth Childs, Carol Christensen, Denise Delouche, Roland Dorn, Stephen Eisenman, Walter Feilchenfeldt, Richard Field, Claire Frèches-Thory, Vojtěch Jirat-Wasiutyński, Tsukasa Kōdera, Eberhard Kornfeld, Sjraar van Heugten, Cornelia Homburg, Naomi Maurer, Victor Merlhès, H. Travers Newton, Jr., Bronwen Nicholson, Fieke Pabst, Ronald Pickvance, Griselda Pollock, Debora Silverman, Susan Alyson Stein, Chris Stolwijk, Charles Stuckey, Judy Sund, Jehanne Teilhet-Fisk, Belinda Thomson, Richard Thomson, Louis van Tilborgh, Evert van Uitert, Kirk Varnedoe, Robert Welsh, Bogomila Welsh-Ovcharov, Johannes van der Wolk, and Carol Zemel.

Like all those seeking a deeper understanding of van Gogh and Gauguin, we have relied on the writings that each left behind. Therefore we also owe our thanks to those individuals who helped us negotiate the complexities of the primary documentation: Victor Merlhès of the Centre National de la Recherche Scientifique, France, and the authority on Gauguin's writings, generously shared unpublished material with us and unfailingly responded to our inquiries. Leo Jansen at the Van Gogh Museum answered innumerable questions and guided us in our navigation of the vast van Gogh correspondence, in addition to providing valuable original research.

Also to be thanked for specific contributions are Rosemary Crill, Véronique de la Hougue, Vojtěch Jirat-Wasiutyński, Fred Leeman, Audrey Léger, Joachim Pissarro, Dieter Schwarz, and Belinda Thomson.

An exhibition of this scope would have been impossible without the assistance of colleagues in the art market who located works, helped to secure loans, and provided essential research and photographic materials. We are particularly indebted in this regard to Alexander Apsis, William Aquavella, David Nash, and Martha Parrish in New York; and to Desmond Corcoran, Thomas Gibson, and Libby Howie in London.

We are also grateful to many individuals at the auction houses Christie's and Sotheby's, particularly Charles Moffett, David Norman, and Benjamin Dollar at Sotheby's New York, and especially Franck Giraud at Christie's New York, who generously provided valuable assistance at several crucial moments in the project. For additional help in facilitating loans of works central to our exhibition, we wish to thank Rupert Burgess, Léonard Giannada, Paul Josefowitz, Sophia McAllister, Yutaka Mino, and Sadao Ogawa.

Conservation research was an essential part of our project from the beginning. We are grateful to the directors of the institutions who authorized access to the works in their collections. The many conservators and scientists and other colleagues to whom we are indebted include: Thomas Becker, Lucy Belloli, Karoline Beltinger, Barbara Berrie, René Boitelle, Mette Bjarnof, Henrik Bjerre, Annetje Boersma, David Bomford, Elisabeth Bracht, Karin Breuer, Didier Brunner, Barbara Buckley, Christian Bührle, Andreas Burmester, Aviva Burnstock, Derrick Cartwright, Dorothy Catling, Patrick Le Chanu, Carol Christensen, Barbara Cisterina, Jim Coddington, Isabelle Collet, Herman Degel, Michele Derrick, Caroline van der Elst, Eugěnia Giorini Esmeraldo, Debra Evans, Cristina Ferreyros, Joe Fronek, Michael Gallagher, Liudmila Gavrilenko, Muriel Geldof, Melanie Gifford, Joseph Godla, Carl Grimm, Karin Groen, Charlotte Hale, Paul

Haner, Bruno Heimberg, Ella Hendriks, Christoph Herm, Ann Hoenigswald, Jan Jedlicka, Piet de Jonge, Peter Klein, Steve Kornhauser, Alexander Kossolapov, Konrad Laudenbacher, Gary Laughlin, Luuk van der Loeff , Christian Marty, Hans Peter Marty, Lucy McCrone, David Miller, Mary Miller, Helen Mikolaychuk, Elizabeth Mention, Richard Newman, Britta Nilsson, Roorda Pappenheim, Eineda Parreira, Paul Pfister, Leif Einar Plahter, Renate Po, Gillian Poulter, Virginia Rasmussen, Antony Reeve, Mariantonia Reinhard-Felice, Christopher Riopelle, Walter Rossacher, Ashok Roy, Ana Sánchez-Lassa de los Santos, Mary Sebera, Suzanne Siano, Julie Simek, Maartje Skare-Hessels, Hubert von Sonnenburg, Suzanne Stangier, Dave Stoney, Mark Tucker, Tim Vander Wood, Raymond White, Jim Wright, Martin Wyld, and Jasja Yff. Michael Bayard, Research Microscopist, deserves our extra thanks for providing critical analysis and interpretation.

A variety of public institutions around the world displayed remarkable generosity in making their objects available for loan to the exhibition. For their essential cooperation and enthusiastic support, we extend our thanks to the directors and also to other colleagues: Christoph Becker, Cynthia Burlingham, Maria Coctakis, Philip Conisbee, Andrea Czére, Nanne Dekking, Eugênia Gorini Esmeraldo, Yasuo Goto, Ernest Haverkamp, Sidsel Helliesen, Hiroshi Hirano, Cornelia Homburg, Masaru Ijarashi, Toshihiko Jshii, David Jaffe, Robert Flynn Johnson, George Keyes, Albert Kostenevich, Marit Ingeborg Lange, Thomas Lederballe, Ellen Lee, Tomás Llorens, Henri Loyrette, Patrice Marandel, Steven Nash, Patrick Noon, Meira Perry-Lehmann, Ursula Perucchi-Petri, Eliza Rathbone, Christopher Riopelle, Joseph J. Rishel, Kevin Sharp, George Shackelford, Susan Alyson Stein, Charles Stuckey, Gary Tinterow, Kirk Varnedoe, Tomas Vleek and Koki Yokuu. Deserving of special acknowledgment are the private collectors who have so generously made their treasured works available.

Our partnership with the Van Gogh Museum, Amsterdam, began nearly a decade ago, with our first collaboration, the exhibition and publication "Odilon Redon: Prince of Dreams." We could never have realized "The Studio of the South" without working together on every aspect of the research, planning, and securing of loans. We are grateful to all of the dedicated staff at the Van Gogh Museum for their enthusiasm, generosity, and support through these many years of preparation. In Amsterdam the project was directed by Andreas Blühm, Head of Exhibitions, supported by Ruth Kervezee, Director of Finance and Administration, with the assistance of Jelle Sybrandy, Project Manager. Crucial to the project were specialists at the Van Gogh Museum, led by Chief Curator Sjraar van Heugten, Curator of Paintings Louis van Tilborgh, Curator of Drawings Marije Vellekoop, and Leo Jansen, Director of The Van Gogh Letters Project. René Boitelle and Ella Hendriks (Conservators), Ton Boxma (Director, Van Gogh Museum Enterprises), Monique Hageman and Fieke Pabst (Documentalists), and Hans Luijten (Editor of the Van Gogh Letters Project) provided valuable assistance. We are also grateful to Rianne Norbart, Heidi Vandamme, Arda van Dam, and Saskia Beukers (Publicity, Public Relations, and Development); Marie Baarspul, Caroline Breunesse, Melanie Verhoeven, and Berber Vinckemöller (Education); and Aly Noordermeer, Martine Kilburn, and Sara Verboven (Registrars). Ton Hoofwijk (Security) and Jan Samuelsz (Services) supervised all technical aspects of the exhibition in Amsterdam. Marion de Vries (Financial Comptroller) kept a skilled and wary eye on the budget. The Van Gogh Museum's installation was designed by Martien van Goor of Greiner van Goor Architecten, assisted by Piet Beckers, and was executed by Bart van der Linden. Pieter Roozen was responsible for the exhibition's art direction. Manfred Kausen provided valuable advice.

The Van Gogh Museum also extends special thanks to the chairman and members of the board of the Vincent van Gogh Foundation for making this project possible by allowing generous loans from the foundation's collection and for their unfailing support in many other aspects of this project. Special mention is due of Chairman of the Board Willem van Gogh, and to Frans de Haas, Manager, BV't Lanthuys, the foundation's daughter company, for their enthusiastic contributions.

At The Art Institute of Chicago, we wish to thank the members of the "Van Gogh/ Gauguin" research and exhibition team. This includes Britt Salvesen, Associate Editor in the Publications Department, who not only sensitively honed our text over many months but became our collaborator, enriching our endeavor with her own understanding of the field and clear and intelligent writing style. In the Department of European Painting, Mary Weaver worked imaginatively and relentlessly along with us in our research, contributing to it in many ways. With efficiency and exemplary attention to detail, Barbara Mirecki handled the myriad challenges of exhibition coordination. Cornelia Peres (formerly Head Restorer at the Van Gogh Museum) and Kristin Hoermann Lister, conservator, in collaboration with microscopist Inge Fiedler (both of the Art Institute) investigated technical questions in a productive collaboration that was invaluable to our enterprise. The publication has greatly benefited from Ms. Lister's ongoing contributions and suggestions. Jennifer Paoletti and Rebecca Glenn contributed their research efforts and organizational skills at critical moments during the exhibition planning.

We wish to thank the entire staffs of the Departments of European Painting and Prints and Drawings, who not only assisted us with many aspects of this project, but also shouldered much responsibility over the period when we were researching and writing this book. In Prints and Drawings, we acknowledge Suzanne Folds McCullagh, Martha Tedeschi, Mark Pascale, Laura Giles, Barbara Hinde, Harriet Stratis, David Chandler, Margo McFarland, Caesar Citraro, Chris Conniff-O'Shea, Elvee O'Kelly, Julie Houghton, and Chris Buoscio. In European Painting, we thank Martha Wolff, Larry Feinberg, Gloria Groom, Adrienne Jeske, Darren Burge, and Sandra Jaggi. A special debt of thanks is owed Geri Banik. We would also like to signal our appreciation for the assistance of interns Nell Andrew, Joshua Ellenbogen, Christine Hahn, Ulrike Meitzner, Tania Ralli, Kate Reid, and Ana Maria Reyes.

The Publications Department brought great energy and dedication to realize this book and others related to the exhibition. In addition to Britt Salvesen, we wish to thank, on the editorial side, Lisa Meyerowitz, Katherine Reilly, Faith Hart, Cris Ligenza, and Silva Tokatlian. On the production side, we are grateful to Amanda W. Freymann, Karen Gephart Altschul, Stacey Hendricks, and Ruth Williams. Susan F. Rossen, Executive Director of Publications, and Ms. Freymann, Associate Director, Production, coordinated the project with the Van Gogh Museum and our publishing partners worldwide: Thomas Neurath and Susan Dwyer of Thames and Hudson, Ltd., and Stefano Peccatori at Electa Editore. We are especially fortunate to be able to work with Pat Goley, of ProGraphics, Inc., and his dedicated staff, as well as with the design team at studio blue, Chicago: Kathy Fredrickson, Cheryl Towler Weese, Erin Lyons, Garrett Niksch, and Matt Simpson. Studio blue met the challenge of presenting a great deal of textual and visual information with a clarifying and engaging format. The illuminating maps and diagrams are the creations of cartographer Tom Willcockson, Mapcraft, Woodstock, Illinois.

Other staff members at the Art Institute to be acknowledged are Dorothy Schroeder, Assistant Director for Exhibitions and Budget; Neal Benezra, Deputy Director; and Vice Presidents Robert Mars (Administrative Affairs) and Ed Horner (Development). Supporting our research from the outset were Jack Brown and the dedicated staff of the Ryerson and Burnham Libraries: Marcy Neth, along with Peter Blank, Michael Donovan, Lauren Lessing, Natalya Lonchnya, and Susan Perry. We are grateful to Donna Forrest and the Copy Center staff: Sanna Evans, Melanie Lieb, Molly Riess, and Christian Serig; and to Frank Zuccari and the following members of the Conservation Department: Cynthia Kuniej Berry, John Mancini, Steve Starling, and Kirk Vuillemot. Special acknowledgment is due Tim Lennon, Bonnie Rimer, Eva Schuchardt, and Jeanine Wine as well as apprentices Neil Jezierski and Stacy Wollmering. We are indebted as well to Bernd Jesse (Asian Art); Lisa Key, Greg Perry, and Karin Victoria (Development); Ian Wardropper and Ghenette Zelleke (European Decorative Arts and Sculpture); Lyn DelliQuadri, Joe Cochand, Susanna Kim, and Jeff Wonderland (Graphic Design and Communications); Alan Newman and his staff (Imaging); Elizabeth Grainer and her staff (Marketing); Daniel Schulman (Modern and Contemporary Art); Jane Clarke, Robert Eskridge, Miranda Hofelt, Clare Kunny, Jean Sousa, and David Stark (Museum Education); Mary Solt and Tamra Yost (Museum Registration); Eileen Harakal and John F. Hindman (Public Affairs); Robert Koverman (Security); and Anders Nyberg (Visitor Services).

We are very pleased to collaborate with John Vinci and his staff at Vinci-Hamp, Architects, who provided the Art Institute with yet another intelligent and cohesive, exhibition design. We offer additional personal thanks to Edward McCormick Blair, Steve Fearon, Theo de Klerk, Sarah Peabody, Manava Teena, and Irene Zegers.

Last, but not least, we would like to thank James N. Wood, Director and President, The Art Institute of Chicago, and John Leighton, Director, Van Gogh Museum, Amsterdam, for believing in this project and giving us encouragement, sound advice, and support at every turn.

Douglas W. Druick
Peter Kort Zegers

PROLOGUE

theo, Merci de t...
que je viens de rec...
...en que Gauguin...
...norais qu'il était...
...il a passé par...
...s il a été vrai...
et vrai matelot.
...our lui un ter...
...a personne enco...
confiance. il a...
à quelque chose
...s d'Islande de Loti...
...a le meme effet qu...
...t nous avons...
...illé il a une
...n grand paysage
...raconte de la B
...fant et ... l'on...
...épatant. ...ux ici d'entrer dan
...x plus g...
qu'ici. D'u...
et surtout plus...
...e la petite natur...

...y manquait -
...e de l'éclairer ce q...
...s riche et fécond...
...yées au sceau de...
...ainte du voisin et...
...mon Van Gogh p...
...revoir tout ce qui...
...oleils sur Soleils...
...le portrait du poète
...cheveux jaune de c...
...une de chrôme...
...e de chrôme 3 avec
...aune de chrôme N°...
...sait un peintre Ital...
tout est jaune : je
...us informer que Va...
...inalité a trouvé...
...e jour il m'en é...
...grand il écrit à s...

a
Vincent van Gogh
Letter to Theo, [27 or
28 October 1888]
(letter 719/558b)
Van Gogh Museum,
Amsterdam
(Vincent van Gogh
Foundation)

b
Paul Gauguin
Extract from *Avant
et après*, 1903, p. 12
Private collection

The "Studio of the South" began as an undefined set of ideas in the mind of Vincent van Gogh, informing his decision in 1880, at age twenty-seven, to become an artist. Rethought and refined over the following years, the concept involved a vision of art as a potential source of hope amid the challenges of modern life; of the artist as missionary prophet; and of a brotherhood of painters joined in the pursuit of shared beliefs. For less than a year, the Studio of the South (*L'Atelier du Midi*) existed as a physical place: the yellow house that van Gogh rented in May 1888 on a sunny square outside the old town walls of Arles in southern France. His ambition was realized for a period of nine weeks, beginning on 23 October 1888, when Paul Gauguin, at van Gogh's invitation, joined him in Arles. The two painters lived and worked together, constantly discussing their past experiences, future goals, and definitions of art and the artist's role in a dialogue carried out in conversations and in pictures. The collaboration proved pivotal for each, in different ways. For van Gogh the Studio of the South was a destination, the personal and professional haven he had sought for years; for Gauguin it was a point of departure, instrumental in helping him chart his future course.

In preparing the house as a site for collaboration, van Gogh painted many of the canvases— such as the *Sunflowers*, *The Bedroom*, and *The Yellow House* (ch. 3, figs. 57–58, 78, 71)—that would prove central to his legacy. In the aftermath of the events that brought his dream of a permanent studio and an enduring partnership with Gauguin to an end on 23 December 1888, Vincent continued to look back at this period of interaction while attempting to move his art forward, sustaining the dialogue at a remove—actually (through correspondence) and imaginatively—producing works like *The Starry Night* (ch. 5, fig. 45).

For Gauguin as well, the Studio of the South was a turning point, marking his professional life into a "before" and an "after." *Avant et après*, the memoir he drafted in 1903 on the Marquesan island of Hiva Oa, hints as much (see Coda). Accepting and preparing for the leadership role that van Gogh attributed to him, during the summer of 1888 in Brittany Gauguin produced breakthrough compositions such as *Vision of the Sermon* (ch. 3, fig. 59) in response to ideas proffered in letters. Though he subsequently denied van Gogh's influence, the Arles experience was critical to Gauguin's devising the project that led him to the South Pacific.

This publication and the exhibition it accompanies focuses on the relationship between van Gogh and Gauguin from the time they met in Paris in 1887, through the weeks spent together in Arles, and beyond to van Gogh's death in Auvers in 1890. The first chapter summarizes the formations that conditioned their responses to each other, and a Coda reviews Gauguin's final years from the perspective of the Studio of the Tropics, the outgrowth of the Studio of the South and the time with van Gogh. These extended perimeters reflect the premise that, by re-examining the artists' interaction in light of recent scholarship, scientific analysis, and close reading of primary documents, it can be posited that van Gogh and Gauguin were critical to each other's articulation and enactment of artistic mission in ways that are more far-reaching than have been apparent.

From this broadened perspective, various enabling factors become evident: First, van Gogh, his expectations nurtured in large part by a lifetime of reading, immediately recognized in Gauguin and in his recent paintings certain qualities that fulfilled his particular conception of the artist and ideal of modern art. Second, the initial conversations in which van Gogh shared these ideas with Gauguin afforded the latter a new way of thinking about his life and work. Though Gauguin had dismissed, as recently as 1886, the possibility of relocating to the French colony of Tahiti as

detrimental to a career in art, he now began seriously to consider the mythic potential of his past experiences and future prospects. Third, the long-distance correspondence in which the two artists engaged during the five months between the initial invitation and Gauguin's arrival in Arles fostered a false sense of mutuality, which, when they finally joined forces, both reinforced and undermined their project. Thus their time together—unrelieved by distractions and experienced far more intensely than its measure in days might indicate—resulted in a productivity all the more remarkable since each was consciously attempting to move his art in new directions while processing the influential presence of the other. Finally, the legacy of their time together served as a mutual reference that continued to motivate both artists after the Arles experiment ended.

Arles remains central to our account, the point at which the protagonists' pasts came together and their futures unfolded. The sixty-three days that they spent together there have often been represented—beginning with Gauguin's own account—as a dramatic narrative of embattled and battling genius, of new beginnings and tragic endings. Notable attempts to uncover the history behind popular myths include Mark Roskill's pioneering study of 1970.[1] Since then new methodological and interpretive approaches, together with an expanding body of primary source materials, including the letters and writings of both van Gogh and Gauguin and those close to them, have made possible new perspectives on their interaction.

It was while we were researching Gauguin's response to the Universal Exposition of 1889 that we found ourselves facing issues which we ultimately realized could be productively addressed with reference to the relationship between Gauguin and van Gogh.[2] Our outlook has of course been shaped by the many ways of thinking about these artists presented by scholars over the past two decades. In studies specifically addressing the van Gogh-

Gauguin relationship, Evert van Uitert, Griselda Pollock, and Debora Silverman have each offered new insights and raised challenging questions; drawn upon a wide range of sources; and demonstrated the considerable breadth of this field of inquiry.[3]

Our intention here is to complement the above-mentioned, recent investigations with a view that is at once close up and slowed down. First and foremost are the pictures that van Gogh and Gauguin painted while together. To date there has been no consensus on precisely what comprises the Arles oeuvre, and still less on the chronological order in which the artists realized their canvases. This has naturally impeded an understanding of the way their relationship evolved: what the issues were, when they came into play, how they were expressed in works of art. Each time that the two men painted side by side can be seen as one event in a sequence; the history of the Studio of the South changes depending on how these events are ordered. *What* and *when* are therefore critical to understanding *why*, to appreciating the intricacies of the give-and-take between the two artists, and to perceiving both the motivating forces and later outcomes of the partnership.

To address this challenge, we have marshaled resources that the museum has to offer. One of our first priorities was to gather technical information on works known or presumed to have been executed in Arles. The data gathered by a team of conservators from The Art Institute of Chicago and the Van Gogh Museum, Amsterdam—through means including microscopic study, x-radiography, thread counts, fiber- and paint-sample analysis—has made it possible to establish the parameters of van Gogh's and Gauguin's Arles production more definitively. Technical examination has also revealed specific connections between specific works, shedding light on various key questions, including how, precisely, the two painters launched their collaboration.

For example until now we have known only half the story of the artists' first excursion to the plains around Arles on circa 26 October: van Gogh made explicit reference in a letter to his brother Theo to the two canvases he executed (ch. 4, figs. 6, 9), but he described his friend's concurrent efforts only generically. We have now identified one of two works that Gauguin made (ch. 4, fig. 11; the other is lost) by matching the canvas of what had been a variously dated work to the pre-primed linen support used by van Gogh during this initial campaign. Van Gogh must have given the canvas to Gauguin, a theory that not only establishes the work in question, but also suggests the Dutch artist's impatience to begin. When the paintings' subjects and handling are taken into account, the nature of debates already under way becomes clear. During the rest of their time together, the artists worked primarily on a coarse jute support purchased locally. Initial characterization of the jute through thread-count comparisons definitively dates twenty-seven canvases by both artists to Arles. Analysis of these works reveals that the painters experimented with ground preparations, according to which the jute paintings can be grouped into three subsets (see App., fig. 3). These results, together with the signposts in contemporary correspondence that provide some secure dates, have yielded a more exact chronology of the Arles oeuvre, a skeletal structure that serves as a basis for imagining the dialogue. From this new sequence of making, we have inferred new patterns of meaning.

An internally coherent idea of the Arles period—approximating a day-to-day picture of the artists' collaboration—also takes into account specific factors such as weather conditions, topography, current events, and personal literary and aesthetic interests, as gleaned from newspapers, maps, letters, and other sources. More importantly it depends on an understanding of the pasts that van Gogh and Gauguin brought with them to Arles. In this regard the full range of the writings left by both artist has been key: van Gogh's vast correspondence, numbering some nine hundred letters, many of them up to ten pages in length; and Gauguin's significantly smaller correspondence and many essays and memoirs, a good number as yet unpublished.[4] These texts cannot, by any stretch of the imagination, be considered transparent documents. Gauguin admittedly manipulated his largely retrospective accounts, and van Gogh did so as well, if less consciously, in his virtually daily reports (most sent to his brother Theo) on his life, art, and feelings.

Their inherently mediated nature notwithstanding, these primary sources contain provocative repetitions of words, ideas, and associations that point to recurrent concerns, habitual ways of thinking, and densely layered personal and professional investments and identifications. We attempted to extrapolate the major themes at issue in Arles in part by continually submitting our various hypotheses to an indexical test of the large body of documentation that we had scanned into a database. In this way, for example, we found that Vincent's 1889 characterization of the failed Studio of the South as a shipwreck carried multivalent meanings, due to his frequent employment, long before meeting the ex-sailor Gauguin, of this otherwise commonplace metaphor in times of trial. Such emblematic usage and relational circuitry emerged from our close reading of van Gogh's correspondence in the original Dutch and French. If van Gogh's earlier correspondence contains the seeds of later preoccupations, in Gauguin's writing the echoes tend to reverberate in the other direction. Writing after Arles, he rehearsed without attribution discussions (about Delacroix, Rembrandt, Wagner) that clearly seem to have been initiated by van Gogh in the Yellow House.

The artists' writings of course elucidate the broader contexts within which they were produced, contexts that have been profitably addressed by recent scholars. Debora Silverman has tied the divergent expectations that van

Gogh and Gauguin brought to their collaboration to differences in their respective mental frameworks, in turn rooted in the cultural, religious, and educational formation of each man. Their "creative competition," as Evert van Uitert has called it, is illuminated when considered against the backdrop of the fragmentation of the late nineteenth-century art world. After the last Impressionist exhibition, held in 1886, the cultural field came to resemble a game board, requiring strategic responses from its participants. As Griselda Pollock has argued, artists had to produce work that demonstrably engaged with the avant-garde, by referring and deferring to what was current and by demonstrating at the same time a clear difference in order to signal progress and thus originality. With his deliberate creation of a persona to complement the aspirations of his art, Gauguin can be seen as prototypical in this dynamic, and his oeuvre "a specific narrative of it."[5]

Acknowledging these shaping forces, the study undertaken here adjusts the focus to consider how the van Gogh–Gauguin relationship evolved, responding and ultimately contributing to key modernist debates. What Pollock and others have termed a masculinist discourse, in which Gauguin figures as a paradigm, was actively fostered by both artists in Arles: van Gogh admired Gauguin's confident prowess in life and art, and Gauguin responsively indulged in his propensity for posturing. This concern with virility paralleled an engagement with colonialist fantasies of escape from the modern city and rejuvenation in exotic territories, implicit in van Gogh's Studio of the South and explicit in Gauguin's tropical transplant.

While certainly propelled by larger cultural forces, the van Gogh–Gauguin narrative very much depended on characteristics specific to each man and on the timing of their meeting; their interaction was determined in part by the particular possibilities that they perceived in and offered to each other. Misapprehension and misunderstanding, while obviously prob-lematic at one level, also proved catalytic, making the alliance differently productive for both. As in any relationship, similarities and dissimilarities fostered the attraction. Van Gogh and Gauguin shared an investment of identity in the profession of artist: they were largely self-taught, had committed to art relatively late in life after personal and career-related trials, and felt attendant pressure to prove themselves through their production. But these likenesses could not mask profound differences in experience and worldview. Though acknowledging himself as Dutch to the core, van Gogh had, over the course of his adult life, come to feel himself a misfit in the culture of his upbringing. He had decided to become an artist in the hope of finding a truer homeland, where his beliefs and idiosyncrasies would be normalized. Rejection, failure, and doubt had prompted him to protracted self-analysis, which led him to see himself as the protagonist in a scenario woven from the strands of cultural predisposition and temperamental inclination. Impelled by a complex mix of humility and ambition, he chose to sign himself Vincent rather than van Gogh (and we follow him in this hence-forward).[6]

Vincent eventually enacted his quest by going to Arles and transforming a modest house in a Provençal outpost into the Studio of the South. The inventor of the story assigns the roles. For reasons involving Gauguin's art as well as his personality and life experience, Vincent considered him the ideal, senior partner he had long sought for his voyage; for reasons both of circumstance and character, Gauguin lent himself to the project. If Gauguin provided Vincent with imaginative stimulus to realize his long-held goals, Vincent in turn helped Gauguin to formulate his own aims, until then relatively amorphous. Lacking Vincent's singular intellectual focus and seamlessly interwoven conception of personal and professional identity, Gauguin was engaged in the process of redefining himself in both arenas at the time of their meeting, and he was intrigued by the mythic dimen-sion of Vincent's understanding of artistic destiny. Vincent's perception and articulation of Gauguin's heroic lineaments directly addressed the latter's immediate requirements, fostering and sharpening his predisposition to a larger-than-life persona.

The influence that Vincent and Gauguin exerted on each other, even during the time they worked side by side in Arles, does not manifest itself in the kind of stylistic similarity seen in the early works of founding Impressionists Monet, Renoir, and Sisley; nor does it begin to approach the near-merging of pictorial identity with which Braque and Picasso experimented while developing Cubism. From a formal perspective, Vincent and Gauguin looked to different models: the former to Jean-François Millet and Adolphe Monticelli, and the latter to Edgar Degas and Paul Cézanne. To be sure, the two artists exchanged ideas about materials and techniques, but the impact that they had on each other extended far beyond these parameters. While occasionally acknowledged formally and iconographically, it is more often than not covert; emulation and resistance forming part of the fabric rather than marking the surface of the works they produced in dialogue.

Theirs was an exchange between evenly but differently matched artists, who apprehended each other in accord with their individual histories of processing the experiences that fed their creativity. This and the exceptional circumstances of their partnership—the comparatively extended time they lived and worked side by side, the wealth of primary documents—afford unique opportunities for investigating how influence can operate. Viewing the works of art against the many other variables in play elicits glimpses into an interaction that manifests itself in ways at once oblique and profound. While the dialogue between van Gogh and Gauguin can never be reconstructed literally, it can be reconstrued, thus offering new insights into the formations, aims, and achievements of two key figures in the history of modern art.

1
Van Gogh and Gauguin
emerged from very dif-
ferent cultural milieux.

a Church of San
Marcelo, Lima,
Peru, on the corner
of Calle Mirones
and Calle Sacristia
San Marcelo, two
blocks from the
Echenique residence,
where Gauguin lived
between 1849 and 1854

b Dutch Reformed
Church, Zundert,
the Netherlands,
where the Reverend
Theodorus van Gogh
preached between
1849 and 1871

Central to the creative dynamic between Paul Gauguin and Vincent van Gogh was the way each (however inadvertently) addressed the needs and stimulated the development of the other. Their exchange involved an imperfect understanding fostered by a potent combination of similarities and differences. In certain respects their personal histories were alike. Each was self-taught, having resolved on a career in art relatively late in life and only after professional failures and personal ruptures. Both expected, with remarkable clarity of purpose, to refashion themselves, to construct new identities, through this newly chosen vocation. And they found that they could converse in an aesthetic lingua franca about related admirations and ideas. But belying these points of contact were profound dissimilarities in background, temperament, and experience, all of which conspired to inflect differently the way each man saw life, read art, construed the artist's mission, and presented himself to the world. When they met, Gauguin was thirty-nine, his achievements to date including world travel, a business career, family life, and association with the practice and politics of vanguard art. Lacking comparable experience, Vincent at thirty-four was ready to defer to his friend's seniority. But Gauguin had not invested years—as Vincent had—in what amounted to a course of self-examination, and he lacked the younger man's deep-rooted sense of origin, identity, and purpose. In this regard Gauguin had much to learn from Vincent.

Two remarkable still lifes provide points of access into an understanding of their respective artistic formations. Each was an attempt at pictorial self-representation; each was painted in 1885, a year that marked a turning point in both careers; and each can be read as a kind of valediction of the preceding years. Both still lifes function within and disrupt art-historical tradition; both mobilize public and private symbolism; both are about con-

structing identity. The works that Vincent and Gauguin went on to produce may bear relatively little outward resemblance to these early statements, but they retain the same core concerns.

Vincent's canvas features a modern novel, an open Bible, and an extinguished candle (fig. 3). These ingredients proclaim the composition's roots in seventeenth-century Dutch still-life practice, specifically the tradition of so-called *vanitas* imagery, designed to convey the moralizing message of life's transience, the precariousness of earthly human achievement, and its emptiness apart from God (see fig. 2). This genre gained legibility through its continuity with the emblem books of popular culture, which present memorable, edifying combinations of simple images and short texts (see figs. 9–10, 13–14, 18–19).[1]

Despite the relatively fixed significance of the staple ingredients of *vanitas* still lifes, the combination of elements can produce ambiguity. Such is the case here. Vincent drew upon the painterly skill that he had painstakingly achieved in the four years of independent study since his momentous decision to become an artist, as well as a much more recent interest in color. Deliberately, he established oppositions between large and small, open and shut, monochromatic and brightly colored—and between the depicted texts. Given their specificity, these initially suggest the explanatory function of the emblematic tradition. The Bible is opened to the Old Testament book of Isaiah, chapter 35, a narrative familiar to a Bible-literate culture as the most frequently cited of the poet-prophet's "Servant Songs." Its protagonist—"despised and rejected of men, a man of sorrows, and acquainted with grief"—suffers for the sins of others; he thus functions as a prototype for Christ and the New Testament's promise of eternal life. The other text that Vincent portrayed is Émile Zola's 1884 novel, *La Joie de*

vivre (*Joy of Life*). Its presence here would seem to reinforce the traditional message of the *vanitas* genre: the Bible is the enduring truth against which all else is measured and found wanting; life's fleeting pleasures pale when set against the fact of death and the transcendent significance of God's word, the only means to salvation.[2]

But is the message of Vincent's still life so straightforward? The Bible's size and heft suggest its authority, but the bright yellow novel threatens to outshine it, vying for the viewer's attention. Moreover, the extinguished candle—commonplace metaphor of the ephemeral nature of existence—here functions as a questionable symbolic signpost, insofar as it is associated more directly with the Good Book than with the novel. Ambiguity deepens with the recognition that the yellow volume's significance cannot be judged by its cover. *La Joie de vivre* was not, as here, a closed book for all viewers in 1885; those who were familiar with the issues that Zola raised regarding faith in an age of science could have detected the potential subversive-

3

2
Jan van der Heyde
(Dutch; 1637–1712)
Still Life with Bible
1664
Oil on canvas
27 x 20.7 cm
Mauritshuis, The
Hague
The Bible is open to
the Book of Jeremiah.

3
Vincent van Gogh
*Still Life with Bible and
Zola's "Joie de vivre"*
October 1885
[F 113, JH 946]
Oil on canvas
65 x 78 cm
Van Gogh Museum,
Amsterdam
(Vincent van Gogh
Foundation)
Cat. 3

4

5

6

4
Paul Gauguin
Still Life in an Interior
Early 1885 [W 176]
Oil on canvas
60 x 74 cm
Private collection

5
Diego Velázquez
(Spanish; 1599–1660)
*Kitchen Maid with the
Supper at Emmaus*
c. 1618/19
Oil on canvas
55 x 118 cm
The National
Gallery of Ireland,
Dublin

6
Gustav Wentzel
(Norwegian;
1859–1927)
Breakfast
1882
Oil on canvas
101 x 137.5 cm
Nasjonalgalleriet,
Oslo

ness in the pairing. At stake in Vincent's quiet picture was nothing so much as a battle of the books.

Since *La Joie de vivre* would become a leitmotif in the thinking that Vincent shared with Gauguin, as the latter acknowledged (see Coda), its plot bears repeating. In this darkly philosophical novel, Zola asked whether it is possible, in the absence of traditional religious belief, to accept life's miseries and lead a good, meaningful existence. His robust heroine, Pauline, embodies the case for the affirmative. Enduring relentless hardship, she retains a vivid enthusiasm, finding a sense of purpose in helping the poor and the sick. The chief recipient of her ministrations—and the primary challenge to her worldview—is her spoiled cousin Lazare, who like his biblical namesake requires resurrection. Country born, Lazare goes to the city to become a doctor but succumbs to a fatalism born of the spectacle of human suffering, the materialism of science, and the pessimistic philosophy of Schopenhauer. With the loss of his Christian faith, Lazare becomes transfixed with despair, caught between terror at the prospect of death without the promise of salvation on the one hand, and disgust at life's apparent meaninglessness on the other. Only fleetingly can he glimpse the truth of Pauline's life: that "Joy lies in action," and that the consolations afforded by Nature, the healthy satisfaction of carnal appetites, and love for humanity permit a positive response to the question "Isn't living enough?"[3]

Even for a reader familiar with both Isaiah and Zola, Vincent's pairing of texts remains cryptic. At a fundamental level, it signified privately rather than publicly. The Bible shown here belonged to the artist's father, the Reverend Theodorus van Gogh, who had died suddenly just months before the picture was painted and whose relationship with his son had been turbulent for years. Vincent, having

attempted to follow in his father's footsteps as a preacher as part of his long battle with doubt, was acutely responsive to the story of Pauline and Lazare, which dramatizes precisely these conflicts. Having found traditional religion inadequate to his needs and goals, Vincent had opted to become an artist. His still life proposes that literature like Zola's is modernity's true gospel, supplanting the New Testament. Moreover it announces Vincent's own intention to emulate Zola's achievement in the medium of painting, and thus to perform his father's mission in terms relevant to the present age. Recognition of these layers of reference, however, requires familiarity with a book not on the table— that of Vincent's life and letters.

Public and private meanings likewise coexist in Gauguin's contemporaneous still life, set in the apartment that he and his family rented in Copenhagen from December 1884 to late April 1885. The remarkable complexity of the composition—large objects arrayed on a table that extends across the entire foreground, furniture looming in the middle register, and a grouping of figures silhouetted against windows in the background—reflects the experience gained through more than a decade of part-time painting. The texts it references are exclusively visual. Cézanne's presiding artistic influence is evident in the modeling of the vegetables and cloth, and in the blue, leaf-patterned wallpaper recalling that in a Cézanne still life Gauguin owned (see fig. 57). But Gauguin's picture disrupts the protocol of still life insofar as its interest lies as much in the figures in the background as in the foreground objects, so that the work flirts with crossing over into genre. This kind of juxtaposition has art-historical precedents, notably early seventeenth-century compositions contrasting homely kitchen scenes, seen close up, with views into a different space, where episodes in the life of Christ, such as the supper at Emmaus, can be glimpsed (see fig. 5).

Put to a purely secular purpose by Gauguin, the device becomes provocative.[4]

The picture's spatial organization is initially puzzling, even suggesting a game played with mirrors or windows. Comparison with a contemporary picture by Norwegian artist Gustav Wentzel, which depicts an apartment such as that of the Gauguins in more conventional terms (fig. 6), suggests some clarifying possibilities. Arguably, Gauguin's still life is set on a dining-room table, like the one in the foreground of Wentzel's painting, beyond which an opening leads to a windowed room containing a high bed, a somewhat lower cloth-covered table, and five figures, summarily defined, backlit, and in unclear relation to one another. Conversely, Gauguin could have adopted the reverse point of view, in which case the figures occupy a windowed dining room, with the artist looking in from a space corresponding to the one in which we glimpse a seated man's back in the Norwegian's canvas. In any case Gauguin thwarted the easy apprehension of spatial continuity. The table supporting the still-life elements, dominated by an imposing Scandinavian tankard of reddish wood, appears to press up against the opening to the next room. Its apparent proximity to the wall behind it misleadingly suggests that the scene beyond the table is a mirror reflection, an impression countered by the fact that it includes neither the still life nor the painter. As it is, the assembly of objects appears to block access to the room beyond, maintaining the effect of two separate spheres.

And so, even when thus "explained," the picture remains ambiguous. What are we to make of the insistent compositional disjunction, the decision to emphasize inanimate objects while relegating the scene of domestic sociability to the background? The traditional role of still life within artistic practice—as a means for the painter to apply his craft to subjects he selects, disposes, and controls—is suggestive here. Possibly the contrast Gauguin represented involves the difference between the realms of the professional and the personal, the trope of art versus life.

The very question is colored by our knowledge of the biographical circumstances surrounding this picture. The figures represent Gauguin's family, gathered in a Danish apartment far from the French capital, where he had begun practicing his art. It is a composition in which the artist referred to his own particular experience of life in this place and time. Gauguin had committed to being a full-time artist less than two years earlier, and his utter lack of financial success accounted for his family's being in his wife's native Copenhagen, near her relatives. Desperately unhappy there, he found the country, its people, and the local artists' community unsympathetic, and he felt offended by the perception, held by his wife and her circle, that he had

put his family at risk in the pursuit of selfish aims. After twelve years of marriage and five children, he was discovering that the spaces of art and domesticity were discontinuous. The tankard—an object that Gauguin had represented in earlier works and carried with him from place to place—is a symbolic stand-in for the artist (see figs. 51–52, 58). The painting starkly states the choice he was facing and intimates which side he would fall on.

Within months of completing their respective still lifes, both Vincent and Gauguin had left their families behind and set out for Paris with the intention of establishing themselves as artists. Vincent's *Still Life with Bible and Zola's "Joie de vivre"* and Gauguin's *Still Life in an Interior* can be seen as self-portraits, statements of the identity they sought and the choices that entailed. How did these two artists arrive at the point of making such statements? However comparable the still lifes seem in intent, the answer is different in each case. As

we shall see, with Vincent the primary considerations include his sense of location, of Dutchness, more specifically of the Dutch Reformed Church; his thorough acquaintance with the Bible, inculcated by a close-knit family that included several preachers; his attraction to literature and to correspondingly narrative visual imagery; a near-mythic sense of himself learned at what he called the University of Sorrow. With Gauguin by contrast the leitmotifs are a sense of dislocation and rootlessness, beginning with his sojourn in Lima, Peru, as a young boy; an education derived here and there, on land and sea; a love of spectacle and the exotic, fostered by a mythologized family history. Vincent imaginatively recalled his childhood home as a nurturing nest; Gauguin's earliest memories were more of life in a gilded cage. With such notions of their pasts conditioning their perceptions, Vincent and Gauguin set about forging their careers as modern artists.

7

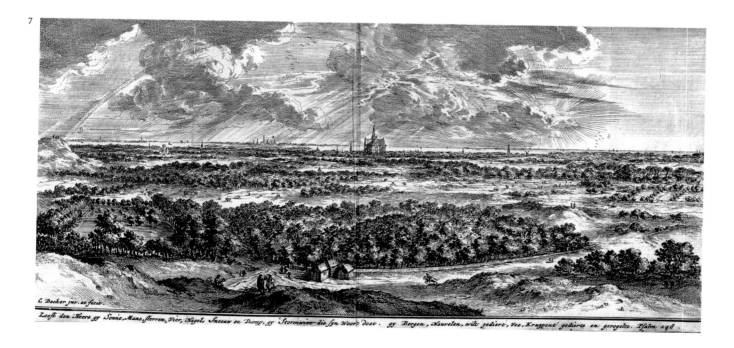

Praise the Lord ye sun and moon, stars, hail, snow, vapors; ye stormy wind fulfilling His word; ye mountains, hills, beasts, cattle; creeping things and flying fowl. From Psalm 148

GRONINGEN
FRIESLAND
DRENTHE ● Assen
Nieuw-Amsterdam ○
Hoogeveen ○
NORTH HOLLAND
Zuider Zee
OVERIJSSEL
● Haarlem ● Amsterdam
GELDERLAND
Scheveningen ○ SOUTH HOLLAND UTRECHT The Netherlands
● The Hague ● Utrecht
Rotterdam Rhine ● Arnhem
Waal Nymegen
North Sea Maas ● Dordrecht
NORTH BRABANT
Etten ○ Breda ○ ● Helvoirt Düsseldorf ●
ZEELAND Zundert ○ ● Tilburg ○ Nuenen
Schelde Eindhoven Rhine
● Ostend Antwerp BRABANT
● Antwerp ○ Gheel Cologne ●
WEST FLANDERS Ghent ● Maastricht
EAST FLANDERS LIMBURG
Brussels ● ● Louvain ● Aachen Germany
Lille ● BORINAGE Liege ●
Wasmes Mons Namur Meuse LIEGE
● Courrières ○ ● Cuesmes NAMUR
● Arras France ● Dinant
HAINAUT ARDENNES
Lux.
35 miles
35 kilometers

ing conformity and an emulation of Jesus that took the form of humility and service. This doctrine of Christ's humanity gained immediacy through the Groningen preachers' use of visual imagery in their sermons and books. Indeed the boundaries between devotional literature and art criticism became blurred in this era of the *dominocratie*—the intellectual leadership of the clergy—as exemplified by publications known as *bijschriften-poëzie*, or poetic commentary. Aimed variously at children and adults, these books consisted of images paired with edifying texts provided by clergymen. The best-known authors of this genre were J. J. L. ten Kate and Eliza Laurillard, whose volumes feature photographs and reproductions of paintings by diverse international contemporary artists and by Old Masters, and have titles such as *Art Jewels for the Parlor Table*. Vincent was only one of thousands of middle-class Dutch who came into contact with a particular strain of contemporary art—and learned a particular moralistic way of thinking about that art in terms of texts—through these books.[6]

The visual practices mobilized by Groningen School preachers and writers had two important antecedents in Dutch culture. The first was the custom of intense typological reading of the Scriptures, an interpretive strategy through which prefigurations of Christ and his Passion are discovered in the Old Testament. The second was the northern emblematic tradition, a verbal-pictorial art form dating back to the sixteenth and seventeenth centuries that finds the revelation of the infinite in the finite, God-given meaning in the book of nature (see fig. 7). Along with allegorists such as John Bunyan (see fig. 11), emblem writers read symbolic significance in every natural fact, human action, and product; ordinary items and events could thus impart moral lessons. The nineteenth century saw a revival of this genre, with its diffused piety and cross-class accessibility. New editions of

Vincent's Youth

Vincent Willem van Gogh was born in 1853, the first surviving child of the Reverend Theodorus van Gogh and Anna van Gogh-Carbentus, who went on to have two more sons, Theodorus (Theo) and Cornelis (Cor), and three daughters, Anna, Elizabeth (Lies), and Willemina (Wil). The van Gogh family was steeped in the practices of the Groningen School, the nineteenth-century reform movement within Dutch Calvinism to which Vincent's father and maternal uncle the Reverend Johannes Stricker subscribed. Seeking to assert emotional piety over dry dogma, Groningen theologians rediscovered Thomas à Kempis's fifteenth-century classic of devotional literature, *Imitation of Christ*. Uncle

Stricker summed up the modernized version of this creed in his most popular book, *Jesus of Nazareth, Drawn According to History* (1868), and in various articles:

Many Christians are wandering, like aimless pilgrims on the wrong path. They accept everything that is said in the Bible, and faith becomes a matter of intellect and memory. This kind of belief is belief on Jesus, but not belief in Jesus.... Belief in Jesus is absolute submission to the Son of God.[5]

For all its emphasis on subjective experience, Dutch Reformed tenets remained profoundly social in nature, demanding a kind of consent-

7
Coenraad Decker
(Dutch; 1651–1685)
*View of Haarlem
from the Dunes* from
Jan van
Westerhoven, Jr.,

*Den Schepper verheer-
lijckt in den Schepselen*
(*The Creator Praised
by All Creation*)
(Haarlem, 1685)
Rijksuniversiteit,
Algemene
Bibliotheek, Utrecht

8
Map of the
Netherlands and
Belgium

One who pinches candles with a snuffer / has to be careful not to grab too far /
Because when you snuff the flame too fiery / you extinguish large torches too /
and you have nothing to be grateful for / But black smoke and dirty stench.
Jacob Cats, *Complete Works* (Amsterdam/The Hague, 1712), p. 127

It is all right to extinguish the candle, but when you put the snuffer on the candle
prematurely, there will be no result.　Vincent to Theo, [c. 21–28 March 1883]

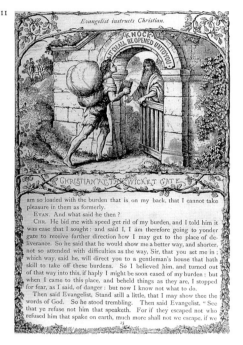

the works of its key original proponents such as Jacob ("Father") Cats and Jan Luyken, with updated illustrations (figs. 9–10), continued to serve as a "second Bible," their memorable text-and-image combinations invested with threefold relevance to love, social interaction, and religion. The cycles of the seasons thereby overlapped with the Christian pilgrim's progression through the joys and trials of life toward celestial Jerusalem.[7] Although Vincent made no explicit references to either Luyken or Cats, his Dutch letters are replete with colloquialisms and metaphors rooted in this heritage, which was central to the sermonizing practice of his father and uncle. In the same spirit the Reverend van Gogh hung a reproduction *Funeral Procession through a Field* (fig. 12), by a contemporary Dutch artist, in the parsonage, and he evoked the image in a sermon to explicate the New Testament parable of spiritual growth and human life as a cycle of sowing and reaping (Mark 4:26–29).[8] To this same image, Vincent would later add other passages from the Bible as well as lines

from a poem by Longfellow. A product of his culture, he developed the habits of thought that it inculcated, seeing the world emblematically, as an enormous network of analogies that enabled multivalent metaphorical discourse. Such was his mental universe.

Dominant as this thinking was in Vincent's upbringing, the beliefs of the Dutch Reformed Church were not in fact widely shared by the populace of North Brabant, the southern province where he grew up. The faith that Theodorus van Gogh preached from 1849 to 1871 in the village of Groot Zundert—less than a mile from the recently redefined border separating the Protestant Netherlands from Catholic Belgium—was espoused by a decided minority. The parsonage, situated on Zundert's main thoroughfare, directly opposite the town hall and main square (see map, fig. 15), was a Protestant outpost in a predominantly Catholic region. At the time of Vincent's birth, Protestants comprised only about three percent of Zundert's four thousand inhabitants.[9]

Situated on a heath, Zundert was critically positioned as a coach stop on the route leading from Breda to Antwerp, a string of buildings on either side of the thoroughfare surrounded by vast, largely uncultivated areas of land (see map, fig. 16). Though of sober beauty, these tracts afforded only meager existence to the farmers who attempted to raise rye, oats, and potatoes. The reverend's job was to swell the Protestant ranks not through conversion of resident Catholics but by importing new souls. As an administrator of the local welfare society, he recruited Protestants from the north to the south with agricultural rather than theological inducements, providing farmland to those willing to relocate and struggle against the unyielding soil. He screened, supervised, and evaluated candidates, and— when necessary—evicted those who failed.[10] These responsibilities gave him a status and power in the community belied by the small size of his flock. With his caring ministrations, the reverend won admiration from the locals and instilled an ideal of service in his

9
"Keep Hope Alive"
from Jacob Cats, *Alle
de Wercken (Complete
Works)*
(Amsterdam/The
Hague, 1712), p. 127

10
"Keep Hope Alive"
from Jacob Cats, *Alle
de Wercken (Complete
Works)* (Zwolle,
1862), p. 157

11
"Christian at the
Wicket Gate"
from John Bunyan,
Pilgrim's Progress
(London, 1874–75),
p. 25

12
After J. J. van der
Maaten
(Dutch; 1820–1879)
*Funeral Procession
through a Field*
1863
Lithograph, anno-
tated by Vincent
van Gogh
26.1 x 33.6 cm
Courtesy Van Gogh
Museum,
Amsterdam
(Vincent van Gogh
Foundation)

13
"The Pilgrim: Hope
Is Solace" from Jan
Luyken, *De Zedelijke
en Stichtelyke
Gezangen (Moral and
Edifying Hymns)*
(Amsterdam, 1709),
p. 82
Leiden University
Library,
The Netherlands

14
"The Reapers: Proud
Today, Dead
Tomorrow" from
Jan Luyken, *Vonken
der Liefde Jesu
(Sparks of Jesus' Love)*
(Amsterdam, 1696),
p. 190

12

13

14

eldest son, who occasionally accompanied him on his missions.

Vincent's golden memories of his early years in Brabant contain little hint of the complex social forces with which his father contended. Instead he and his beloved brother Theo (four years his junior) recalled their youth in "our Brabant" as a magical time of edenic oneness with nature, spent roaming through fields of grain and heather, swamps, and thickets of firs surrounding the one-street town. Their response to the flat stretches of landscape, little changed in its essentials over the centuries, was colored by a deep-seated sense of nation and by a feeling of reverence and wonder before God's creation (see fig. 7).

Vincent's feelings of nostalgia and loss set in early, precipitated by the cataclysmic "exile" he endured in 1864, when, at age eleven, he was sent away to boarding school by his parents. He began his secondary education in 1866, in nearby Tilburg, where he boarded with a family. He did well but was not happy, and abruptly left the school in his second year. The reasons for this remain unclear; no sources indicate that the adolescent manifested any signs of the epilepsy with which he was later diagnosed.[11] After Vincent spent more than a year at home, it was decided that he should pursue a career in the art business, a profession in which his father's three brothers—Vincent (known as Cent), Hein, and Cornelis (Cor)—had achieved success. Through Cent's influence, the sixteen-year-old Vincent began to work at the Hague branch of the Paris-based international art gallery Goupil et Cie, which sold reproductions and original works of art by well-known, largely French and Dutch artists. He served as junior clerk under manager Herman Gijsbertus-Tersteeg, trusted assistant of Cent, who was by now living in Paris.

Vincent tried to present a brave face, but this initial foray into urban commerce proved

During my illness I saw again every room in the house at Zundert, every path, every plant in the garden, the views of the fields outside, the neighbors, the graveyard, the church, our kitchen garden at the back—down to a magpie's nest in a tall acacia in the graveyard. Vincent to Theo, [23 January 1889]

15
Map of Zundert

difficult for him, and time did not ease his discomfort. Snippets of family correspondence from the years 1873–75, when Vincent moved from The Hague to London and then to Paris, not only outline the chronology of this peripatetic period, but also map Vincent's struggle with depression and speak volumes about the complex dynamic of ambition, disenchantment, devotion, and dependency that bound parents and siblings together:

Never lose sight of your goal, namely to become independent.
　—Father to Theo, January 1873

Don't lose heart; it is very difficult at times; everything will turn out all right. Nobody can do as he wishes in the beginning.
　—Vincent to Theo, 28 January 1873

I am going to [Goupil's branch office in] London.… It will be a different life.… I shall probably have to live alone in rooms.
　—Vincent to Theo, 17 March 1873

Make yourself indispensable … and you will remain our crown and our honor and our joy, just like Vincent, who has great satisfaction [from his work].
　—Mother to Theo, 31 May 1873

How I should like to have you here [in London].… I think so often of that walk on the Rijswijk road, when we drank milk at the mill after the rain.… That Rijswijk road holds memories for me which are perhaps the most beautiful I have.
　—Vincent to Theo, 20 July 1873

Everything is not so beautiful as it seemed to me at the beginning. Perhaps it is my own fault, so I shall bear with it a little longer.
　—Vincent to family friends, 7 August 1873

If one really loves nature, one can find beauty everywhere. But still I sometimes long for

Holland and especially for home.
　—Vincent to Theo, 30 April 1874

He has withdrawn from the world and people.… Don't you think it very sad that Vincent does not write to us? … He thought that Father had brought about his transfer [from London to Paris].
　—Mother to Theo, 28 October 1874

He is *eccentric* and that's why we think we have to *wait* and be *patient*. But it's very difficult for us.
　—Father to Theo, 28 October 1874

Do you sometimes hear from Vincent? I never do. It seems to me that he has illusions about people and judges them before he knows them, and then, when he finds out how they really are and that they don't come up to the expectation he had formed *too soon* about them, he is so disappointed that he throws them away like a bouquet of wilted flowers.
　—Anna to Theo, 25 April 1875

I hope and I trust that I am not what many people think I am just now.… *Pour agir dans le monde il faut mourir à soi-même. Le peuple qui se fait le missionnaire d'une pensée religieuse n'a plus d'autre patrie que cette pensée* [To get along in the world one must die to oneself. People who make themselves the missionaries of a religion have no other homeland than that religion.]
　—Vincent to Theo, 8 May 1875[12]

By 1875 Vincent was clearly concerned with matters other than securing his future at Goupil's. As the French quotation—taken from the writings of Ernest Renan—suggests, literature, along with art, had assumed growing importance for Vincent as a source of both instruction and consolation when facing the feelings he invoked with the metaphor of a lost homeland.

In Search of a Homeland

What had gone wrong? Vincent would refer to himself as "the man whose little boat capsized when he was twenty … and sank." Through the image of the sea voyage (which would become his abiding figure for his life's progress), he apparently referred here to events of 1873–74, specifically to the discovery that a young woman to whom he had become attached did not reciprocate his feelings. Vincent's difficulty in accepting this points toward a larger problem. His own writings and the observations of acquaintances testify to his shyness and awkwardness in social situations. His earnest intensity hampered his ability to establish and sustain relationships, as did his demand that friends share his interests and beliefs and his tendency, hinted at by his sister, to idealize and then become disillusioned. At work and in life, Vincent increasingly sensed that he did not fit in.[13]

Around this time Vincent began to seek solace by sharing his feelings in letters to his brother, who in 1873 followed him into the art business and would remain his sole lifelong friend. And increasingly Vincent would try to understand his emotions and chart his course with reference to the books and images that he gathered around him in the rented rooms he likened to a ship's cabin. Early formative navigational texts included *Les Musées de la Hollande* (*The Museums of Holland*; 1858–60) by Théophile Thoré (Willem Bürger) and *L'Amour* (*Love*; 1858) by Jules Michelet. Vincent derived mutually reinforcing messages from these ostensibly disparate books, using ideas gleaned from them to reinforce and expand his own thinking in a manner that typifies the associational interpretive strategies that he would practice all his life.

Thoré's groundbreaking study of seventeenth-century Dutch painting made a daring claim for the Northern tradition of realism in the face of French prejudices that deemed this art

lacking in nobility, idealism, and expression. The unique achievement of the Dutch School, Thoré contended, was to express life and ideas in palpable, incarnate form, rather than "abstractly," as in the mythological and history painting favored by Latin cultures. This was the result of the Protestant Dutch republic's unique history and spirit of democracy. In stating that art had mirrored society in this past golden age, Thoré revealed his agenda for present-day France: realism could be linked with revolution, monarchy replaced by democracy. In the Netherlands, *Les Musées de la Hollande* read somewhat differently, of course, but no less tendentiously. Resurgent Dutch nationalism found its artistic figurehead in Rembrandt van Rijn, while Belgium extolled Peter Paul Rubens. Thoré validated this opposition by insisting on the essential differences between the Dutch and Flemish schools as exemplified by these two giants.[14]

Thoré's construction pitted Rembrandt, with his art of and for the people, against Rubens, who, in the art historian's view, had been enslaved within the power systems represented by religion and mythology. Rather than pursuing vague "mystic ideas," Rembrandt began with the natural world, apprehending it imaginatively and suffusing his depictions of ordinary people with the mystery of transcendence: everyday life intimates eternal life. Rembrandt was "the great revelator." But landscape too, in the hands of the great Dutch masters of the genre, could exude the latent symbolism—what Thoré called the irresistible melancholy—of great poetry.[15] Dovetailing in this way with the emblematic tradition, Thoré's exegesis struck a chord with Vincent. Though he had been raised in a primarily Catholic community virtually within sight of Belgium, Vincent considered himself and his natal countryside essentially Dutch. Landscape paintings of the national school thus confirmed his sense of identity, just as Thoré's interpretive strategy justified his life-

long preference for reality over abstraction (as he put it) and for humility over grandiosity.

Michelet's *L'Amour* struck Vincent as both a "revelation and a gospel," and not only because it offered insights into the psychology of the opposite sex woefully absent from his education. He was particularly taken with a chapter entitled "Les Aspirations de l'automne," in which the author vividly recalled an experience of three decades earlier, when he glimpsed an elegant, older woman walking in a garden. Her demeanor prompted his curiosity about her life, which in turn led him to associate her with portraits that she resembled, remembered from museum visits. And these paintings, by extension, prompted fantasies about the lives and woes of the sitters, one of whom had an unfocused expression that the author read as a sign of years spent scanning the barren wastes of the North Sea. Michelet's suggestive metaphors and richly allusive way of thinking about life and pictures captured Vincent's imagination and provided an inspiring example for the use of works of art as touchstones for emotional experience. More and more readily, he responded to the world—nature, people, pictures, and books—through an associative network constantly enriched by accrued experience. As he practiced his own analogical thinking, Vincent found resemblances in Rembrandt's figures to people he knew and vice versa. He habitually saw books and read pictures, perceiving no distinction between verbal and visual imagery or (arguably) between the observed and the represented.[16]

Michelet's bittersweet evocation of seasonal and emotional cycles also appealed powerfully as a lesson in accepting life's hardships, as is evident from the lines that Vincent appended to Michelet when, several years later, he copied passages from "Les Aspirations de l'automne" into one of the albums he made for his brother and friends: "As sorrowful yet always rejoicing."[17] This was the spirit in which Saint Paul

Town Hall

Van Gogh Parsonage

4 miles

4 kilometers

Wooded

Fen and Heath

THE NETHERLANDS

Rotterdam

NORTH BRABANT

Etten   Breda   Helvoirt

Zundert   Tilburg   Nuenen

Eindhoven

Antwerp   Gheel

Ghent

BELGIUM

Brussels   Louvain

enjoined those who worked in Christ's ministry to live (2 Corinthians 6:10), a phrase that became a kind of credo for the equanimity Vincent sought in the face of difficulty. Vincent's conjunction of Paul and Michelet, like his references to the latter's writing as a "gospel," suggests how art and literature complemented and in a sense explicated the Bible's message.

This openness to new ideas and new authorities called into question the teachings of Vincent's youth. He was by no means exceptional in questioning the doctrines he had been brought up to respect; throughout industrializing Europe, the ethos of critical inquiry strained the faith-reason relationship to the breaking point. The Reverend Stricker's book devoted to a historical Jesus reveals the shift within the ranks of the Groningen School toward an investigative revisionism. But Vincent's uncle had also observed that if faith were an illusion, then "I pray you, let us keep the illusion."[18] By 1875 Vincent questioned his ability to continue to do so.

A picture of Vincent at this moment in his life is provided by the several albums he filled with favorite passages copied from his wide-ranging reading. Self-portrait collages motivated (as, later, his art would be) by a desire for self-expression and communication, they reveal a young man well acquainted with grief, struggling with doubt and belief. German and French Romantics such as Heinrich Heine, Ludwig Uhland, and Alfred de Musset, together with later French writers Émile Souvestre, Joseph Autran, and Jules Michelet, gave Vincent the words in which to articulate both his nostalgic memories of the happiness and security of childhood and his present pain of loneliness and unrequited love. These borrowed voices speak of hope alternating with despair, figure life as a perilous journey on rough seas, and occasionally call on God and Christ for protection or rescue.[19] But the sav-

It was so beautiful on the heath; though it was dark, one could distinguish the heath, and the pine woods, and moors extending far and wide. . . . The sky was overcast, but the evening star was shining through the clouds, and now and then more stars appeared. It was very early when I arrived at the churchyard in Zundert; everything was so quiet. I went over all the dear old spots, and the little paths, and waited for the sunrise there. You know the story of the Resurrection—everything reminded me of it that morning in the quiet graveyard.   Vincent to Theo, 8 April 1877

ior who emerges in the pages of Vincent's albums is not the Jesus of the Reverend van Gogh's religious preaching, but rather the Jesus imagined by Ernest Renan and by Scottish philosopher Thomas Carlyle.

As his album transcriptions testify, Vincent was drawn to Renan's highly controversial portrayal of a historical Jesus, the greatest of the sons of man, an individual who conquered the demons all men fight and who, on the eve of his ultimate trial, faced his agony in the Garden of Gethsemane alone—without angels and sustained only by strength of character. This Jesus refused the trappings of organized ecclesiastical practice, instead preaching a religion of humanity; in his actions and words, he had rehabilitated the Bible's message and thus revealed himself an "incomparable artist." Renan's construction of Jesus as existential artist-hero dovetailed in Vincent's mind with the thinking of Carlyle, which he initially encountered through a French publication.[20]

One of Vincent's albums provides a condensed guide to the Carlylean tenets that appealed to him most strongly. Carlyle believed in the need for belief, a position that Vincent found useful to adopt as he confronted doubts about traditional religion. In the past, Carlyle wrote, people felt and acted in accord with a faith that did not suffer from doubt, but religions rise and fall over the cyclical course of history, and the symbolic trappings through which each creed reveals the transcendent, unchanging Truth become worn out through use and familiarity. Such was the case with traditional Christianity, "The Worship of Sorrow": it was now an essentially threadbare garment, insufficient to the capitalist age. Modern man was experiencing the pain—as Vincent transcribed—of having "lost the soul out of him." The old verities needed to be clothed in the newly woven cloak of a new religion. Carlyle identified the agent of past and future renewal as the Hero who defines his age and restores its knowledge of, and faith in, eternal Truth. Christ was perhaps the greatest of the breed, but there had been others throughout history: prophets such as Saint Paul, Martin Luther, and Muhammad, and poet-prophets Dante, Shakespeare, and latterly Goethe. Their works, revelations of the divine, remained imperishable.[21]

The albums reveal Vincent's developing equation of art and religion, artist and pilgrim, and his identification with the premise that sorrow in one form or another is the artist's lot, the price of the consolation that his work affords to others. He copied out lines from Musset's poem "La Nuit de décembre"—carried lifelong in his head (see ch. 4)—identifying Solitude as the artist's constant companion. Committing to paper Michelet's reiteration of the Romantic claim that "sorrow is the better part of the great artist's genius," Vincent included his memorable analogy of the artist to a caged nightingale whose song, beautiful precisely because of its melancholy, expresses its ongoing internal struggles and yearning for freedom; and who is by nature solitary, subject to nervous attacks and epilepsy.[22]

The literary passages and art reproductions that Vincent collected (see fig. 17) show him identifying a community of kindred spirits, seeking both the expression and reassuring echo of his own feelings. But in contemplating the great existential question raised by Heine and Carlyle alike—"What is the meaning of Man? Where does he come from? Where is he going?"—Vincent strayed perilously far from his parents' teachings. As Theo would later explain, Vincent was waging a "battle … against doubt. It was like a violent storm breaking above him." When it struck, in 1875, Vincent responded by heading toward the seemingly safe harbor of certainty, the "homeland" of his parents' religion. Embracing the authority of his father and of the Bible, Vincent foreswore the German Romantics as dangerous, and advised Theo to follow him in destroying his volumes of Michelet and Renan. Over the

17

18

19

next three years, the Man of Sorrows (see fig. 20) would be his model, "sorrowful but always rejoicing" his mantra.[23]

Far from being pleased by their son's return to the fold, Vincent's parents worried that he was suffering from a physical or mental illness, or at the very least an inappropriate indulgence in melancholy. They hoped that the phase would pass, but it did not. In early 1876 Vincent lost his position at Goupil's. In mid-April he left for England, where he took first one teaching post and then another, the second at a school run by the Reverend Jones, a Methodist minister under whose guidance Vincent began to teach less and work more in the parish. After speaking at several prayer meetings at the Methodist chapel in Richmond, on Sunday, 5 November, Vincent delivered his first sermon.[24]

It was his second creation, after the albums, and the first work in which his own voice emerges directly. The theme is *vanitas*—the transience of the world and its glories—expressed through the dominant metaphor of Christian pilgrimage:

Keep yourself as a pilgrim and a stranger on earth, a person to whom the affairs of the world mean nothing apart from Christ.[25]

Vincent studded his sermon with the stock-in-trade emblems—the pilgrim's journey, the storm at sea, casting the nets, sowing, and reaping (see figs. 13–14, 18–19)—that served as signposts throughout his life. Drawing on the rhetorical strategies practiced by his father and uncle, he described a painting by English artist George Boughton (fig. 21), reading it allegorically in terms of Bunyan's *Pilgrim's Progress*, misremembering the woman whom the pilgrim addresses as dressed in black, and identifying her as "sorrowful yet always rejoicing."[26]

Vincent's text departs from the conventional models on which it clearly depends in its lack of moderation: the insistently reiterated metaphors, the palpably heartfelt autobiographical references, the urgent emotional timber. His abiding concerns come through in the sermon's basic premise that sorrow is our existential lot, that life is akin to a voyage in a small bark on waters that become ever more turbulent as the "golden hours of our early days" recede into the past and we experience the loss of loved ones and separation from home and the charmed security of childhood. Regret, Vincent professed, is compounded by a sense of personal failure that we are not what we once were nor what we dreamt we should be. Buffeted by the "great storms of life," we despair, longing for guid-

ance and "a Father, a Father's love and a Father's approval," and seeking the peace we have lost. At this point in the sermon, Vincent shifted from the congregational "we" to the "I" of personal experience and example. His parents, he shared with his listeners, had inspired him in his moment of darkness, when he had embraced a faith that was not dead, but only dormant. With this affirmation, the feeling of "eternal youth and enthusiasm" supplanted "unbelief." Thus Vincent demonstrated how "the seed of His word that has been sown in our hearts" can flourish. "Born again," we look to Christ and derive "consolation … in this life" where we are "strangers": our faith in ultimate peace enables us, in the perennially heartening words of Saint Paul, to be "sorrowful yet always rejoicing."

Vincent's suggestive blurring of divine and parental authority—the identity of the capitalized Father is occasionally unclear in contemporary correspondence—informed his own identity. It was around this time that Vincent recalled his agony at being left by his father at boarding school, using language that echoes the call that Christ made to his Father in Gethsemane. At the same moment, he pasted in his employer's visitors' book a reproduction of Delaroche's painting of the subject (fig. 17), one of a number of interpretations by artists past and present that were among his favorite images. Similarly Vincent paraphrased Christ's lament for the city that stoned its prophets, bemoaning to Theo the lost happiness of their youth: "Oh Jerusalem, Jerusalem! Or rather, oh Zundert, oh Zundert!" This he followed with the remark: "The nature of every true son does indeed bear some resemblance to that of the son who was dead and came back to life."[27]

Such outbursts illuminate Lies's remark that Vincent "would be quite different were he to see himself as an ordinary person."[28] But he clearly did not, apparently harboring both a keen sense of his misery as well as a somewhat grandiose sense of purposeful destiny. His desire to embark on more serious evangelism in England suggests a desire to emulate Christ as well as to throw himself into work, ministering to himself by ministering to others. But his father and uncles deferred this ambition.

Vincent spent Christmas 1876 at home, where it was decided that he would not return to England. First he took a job, arranged by his uncle Cent, in a Dordrecht bookstore, but his "heavy depression" and longing to become a "preacher of the Gospel and sower of the Word" made this an untenable solution.[29] The Reverend van Gogh insisted that Vincent prove his seriousness by undertaking the necessary study for the ministry in Amsterdam, which, since he had never completed secondary school, would take at least seven years, followed by a state examination. Though temperamentally

and academically unprepared for this challenge, Vincent submitted to his father's will.

Vincent would remember this period as one of the worst in his life. Paralyzed by fear that he would disappoint his father and increasingly certain that he would fail, he coped as best he could. Attending sermons by luminaries such as the Reverends ten Kate and Laurillard, he took comfort in their references to familiar works of art; by extension he saw these preachers (and his father and uncle Stricker) as artists themselves. But while he struggled to keep the hierarchy of his enthusiasms in check in order to focus on his studies, he found himself again in need of Rembrandt, Michelet, and, among others, the French peasant painter Jean-François Millet, all of whom prompted the heartfelt exclamation "dat is het"—that's it, the real thing. He asked Theo to send him Michelet's "Aspirations de l'automne," which he had discarded. "I need it again," he confessed, giving Theo a photograph of Christ as the Man of Sorrows, an image that he clearly felt expressed his own beleaguered condition (fig. 20).[30]

Vincent looked to art not only as a source of personal consolation, but as a means to share his innermost feelings with others, a vehicle through which to understand and be understood. He dreamed of using images to bridge the misunderstanding that existed between himself and his father. Would not the reverend, who traveled through the night to comfort the sick and dying, recognize how the chiaro-

scuro of Rembrandt's nocturnal biblical scenes (see ch. 3, fig. 32) conveyed Christ's essential message, "I am the light of the world"? Vincent summoned a still more complicated chain of associations around the picture *A Young Citizen of the Year V* (fig. 22), a reproduction of which he wanted to share with his father. The image of a youth wearing the *bonnet rouge* of the French revolutionaries, his expression "marked by those cataclysmic times," called to mind Vincent's knowledge of this rebellion against authority, gleaned from Dickens's *Tale of Two Cities* and from Michelet's and Carlyle's histories. The boy reminded Vincent of himself, perhaps literally, in terms of physical resemblance (see fig. 23), and certainly symbolically, in that he seemed to embody "sorrowful yet always rejoicing." The fantasy was that the reverend—who complained that Vincent "knows no joy of living"—would understand.[31]

Vincent could not restrict his reading to the Bible nor his looking to Delaroche's *Christ in the Garden of Gethsemane* and the like. He kept despair at bay by reading biographies of painters; musing upon images like *A Young Citizen*; and copying maps, including a chart of Saint Paul's travels. Naturally his studies continued to suffer, and at the end of 1877, he felt nothing but panic: "Where am I? What am I doing? Where am I going?"[32]

Not to university, as soon became clear. His parents, their financial resources strained along with their understanding, considered

22

23

his behavior perverse and defiant, a source of embarrassment. Vincent emerged from the humiliation with some measure of independence, viewing himself as a shipwreck survivor like Daniel Defoe's fictional hero Robinson Crusoe, tested by life. In a letter to Theo tantamount to a manifesto, Vincent proposed continuing his quest to understand God through knowledge of history and the great men who defined it; he would approach the Bible as one source alongside the classics and moderns such as Charles Dickens, Michelet, Rembrandt, Millet, or Georges Michel. Rather than restrict his scope, he would embrace as many ideas and models as possible in a spirit of independence—and he would act. If the hallmark of great art was its ability to "cheer you and feed your inner life," Vincent aimed at a similar achievement through the practical work of evangelism. Though he would never again, after this letter, explicitly cite Saint Paul's dictum linking sorrow and joy, he continued to aspire to its spirit.[33]

Freed by failure to pursue his dream, Vincent began a three-year course of preparation at a mission school outside of Brussels with his parents' grudging support, but inevitably his impatience got the better of him, and he did not survive the ninety-day probationary period. He managed to obtain a position ministering to miners in the Borinage region of southern Belgium, a task he approached with full determination to live in literal imitation of Christ. Modeling himself on Saint Paul's example, Vincent envisioned himself working in this

capacity for three years before undertaking to preach. In Wasmes, the community he reached in January 1879, Vincent soon became wholly absorbed in caring for the sick and those wounded in accidents, denying himself even the basic comfort of a bed. The organization that employed him, disturbed by this extreme behavior, dismissed him the following July; for the next year he stayed in the Borinage on his own, living from hand to mouth. At this point the Reverend van Gogh, alarmed and frustrated, apparently threatened to have Vincent placed in a facility widely renowned for its innovative and humane treatments of its mentally ill patients, who, under state medical supervision, lived and worked with peasant families. The complex was located just south of the Dutch border, in the Belgian town of Gheel (see fig. 24). Phonetically and orthographically, the town's name is the same as the Dutch word for "yellow."[34]

The Borinage experience occasioned a rupture between Vincent and his family that silently echoed in a year-long cessation of correspondence. A letter that Vincent wrote to Theo from Belgium in July 1880 was the product of prolonged, thoughtful stocktaking. In it he announced his new project, insisted on its consistency with his prior aims, and enlisted his brother's support. Wrestling with despair and feelings of worthlessness during the preceding months, he had again sought consolation in literature (adding a wide range of authors, including William Shakespeare, Harriet Beecher Stowe, Victor Hugo, and evidently more Carlyle to his repertoire) and art, asking himself again and again: "What am I good for; could I not be of service or use in some way."[35]

He had, he wrote, become "homesick for the land of pictures." Having not recovered his homeland, or sense of belonging, by following in his father's footsteps, he now determined to seek it in art: to replace passive despair with "active melancholy" and become a painter. Lest Theo think that this constituted a renunciation of previous beliefs, Vincent emphasized that only the objects and means of his veneration would change, and these he outlined in a series of intertextual comparisons between writers and artists whom he regarded as sharing the message of the Bible:

There is something of Rembrandt in Shakespeare, something of Correggio in Michelet,

24

Geel. Rijkskolonie

and something of Delacroix in V. Hugo, and there is also something of Rembrandt in the Gospel or, if you prefer, something of the Gospel in Rembrandt, it comes to much the same thing … and there is something of … Millet in Bunyan, a reality that, in a manner of speaking, is more real than reality itself.…

The love of books is as sacred as that of Rembrandt.… I think that everything that is really good and beautiful, the inner, moral, spiritual, and sublime beauty in men and their works, comes from God.… The best way of knowing God is to love many things.…

Try to grasp the essence of what the great artists, the serious masters, say in their masterpieces, and you will find God in them.

New influences certainly pervade this profession of faith, including Hugo, with his aphorism that *religions pass away, God endures,* and especially Carlyle, who presented the same idea in writings Vincent had read years earlier. But a more recent and extensive encounter with the Scottish philosopher illuminated Vincent's new credo, beginning with the metaphor he used to introduce it: "What the molting season is for birds," he explained to Theo, "… hard times are for us human beings. You can cling on to the molting season, [but] you can also emerge from it reborn."[36]

With this same image of painful molting, Carlyle described the spiritual crisis from which the philosopher-hero of his *Sartor Resartus* (1833–34) emerges with revived faith. For ample reasons Vincent recognized the fictional Professor Diogenes Teufelsdröckh—a "Stranger … Pilgrim, and Traveller" who spends his life seeking answers to the existential queries "Who am I; what is this ME? … Whence? How? Whereto?"—as a kind of brother. Before embarking on his quest, Teufelsdröckh had delighted in an idyllic childhood, secure in his family's love and in his simple Christian faith; sent away to board-

ing school, he had experienced bitterness and betrayal affectively associated with Christ's Agony in the Garden. At his father's death, he learns that he was adopted, a loss of identity at once exhilarating and terrifying. An attempt at a university career fails; intensely shy but longing for friendship and love, Teufelsdröckh is betrayed by his sole comrade and spurned by the woman he desires. He becomes a Wanderer, staff in hand, seeking truth and sailing over unknown seas. Conventional religion proves hollow, and nature alone cannot sustain him. But investigation of "evidences" of religious faith plunges him into paroxysms of doubt that darken into "Unbelief." In the chapter entitled "The Everlasting No," Teufelsdröckh finally confronts all the negative forces assailing him. In a revelatory moment, he discovers untapped strength within himself as his "whole Me" rises up to proclaim "The Everlasting Yea": he realizes that truth resides in subjective experience authenticated by the feeling self, and that one must force oneself to undertake "useful Activity"—however seemingly pointless and unreasonable—in order to discover one's unique capacities and inner talent. "Self help," Teufelsdröckh concludes, is the highest of all possessions. Having found "a whole earth and a whole Heaven" in books, he takes up writing.[37]

By recasting traditional religious experience in psychological terms, Carlyle hoped to restore a sacred dimension to secular modern existence. Symbols surround us, prompting a recognition of the divine in the everyday, but they must first be re-presented by the hero whom Carlyle described in *Sartor Resartus*'s nonfictional complement, *On Heroes and Hero-Worship* (1841). Here Carlyle acknowledged that history's noblest artist-heroes, with Christ at their head, had created works that transcended time, but asked for how long? Looking at the present era, the philosopher wondered whether it was not time "to

embody the divine Spirit of that Religion in a new Mythus, a new vehicle and vesture."[38]

Hoping to be reborn, and inspired by Carlyle's vision, Vincent echoed Teufelsdröckh's belief that he was capable of activity and had "something inside him." In the summer of 1880, he returned to live with his parents, now settled in Etten, but embarked on a journey of self-realization through work as an artist. Carlyle wrote of the inarticulate consciousness, residing in each of us, that we can only recognize and express through our works; he translated the injunction "Know thyself" as "Know what thou canst work at." Vincent, outlining his project to Theo, rephrased Carlyle in terms of his chosen profession:

What is your final goal you may ask. That goal will become clearer, will emerge slowly but surely, much as the draft turns into the sketch and the sketch into the painting through the serious work done on it, through the elaboration of the original vague idea and through the consolidation of the first fleeting and passing thought.[39]

The picture that can be drawn of Gauguin's life up to his mid-twenties is sketchy at best in comparison with the richly nuanced portrait that can be constructed of Vincent. Not only is the documentation meager—and a diaristic correspondence charting intellectual and emotional development nonexistent—the available information is suspect to a considerable degree. What little we know about Gauguin's childhood experiences comes from reminiscences he drafted toward the end of his life.

Subject to the inevitable distortions of time, these were also strategic myth-making efforts in which the artist presented a highly selective and, when necessary, revised account of his early formation. Seeking to nuance and commit to history the identity he had been refining for almost two decades, Gauguin wanted to control an image of himself that he preferred to present suggestively and mysteriously.

The purportedly factual statements that Gauguin made about his early years are fragmented and in some cases seem fabricated or at least inconsistent with what can be inferred from the documents that do exist. His discussion of his maternal grandmother, author and activist Flora Tristan, provides a particularly revealing example. Extant letters reveal Gauguin's knowledge of her work, but later he adopted an ignorant attitude, deferring the question of her achievement to others and venturing only that she was a pretty and noble lady. "Between Truth and Fable I have never been able to distinguish, and I offer you this for what it is worth."[40] A disengenuous rhetorical strategy consonant with his desire to position himself mythically, the disclaimer suggests some insecurity underlying the breezy uninvolved stance that Gauguin adopted in recalling the events of his youth, whole chunks of which get scarcely a mention. Given the demonstrable truths Gauguin wove into his tale, complemented by other sources, we are left to speculate about how a fatherless boy responded to short residences in various places and continents; to moving between different cultures and classes, at home in none of them; to the discovery that his pretty widowed mother depended on the protection of powerful men; to her death when he was nineteen; to many years of world travel at sea; to negotiating different social milieux as a young man while relying on his mother's protector. Gauguin's silences on such scores, like his misrepresentations on others, point toward a portrait he did not intend to paint: of a young man lacking deep roots and exhibiting a fluid, shifting personality that allowed him to move with the tide and, to a degree, to be defined by outside forces; a young man who deferred the conscious construction of an identity until this activity became his life's project.

Born in Paris in the revolutionary year of 1848, Eugène Henri Paul Gauguin was the second

25
Map of Peru

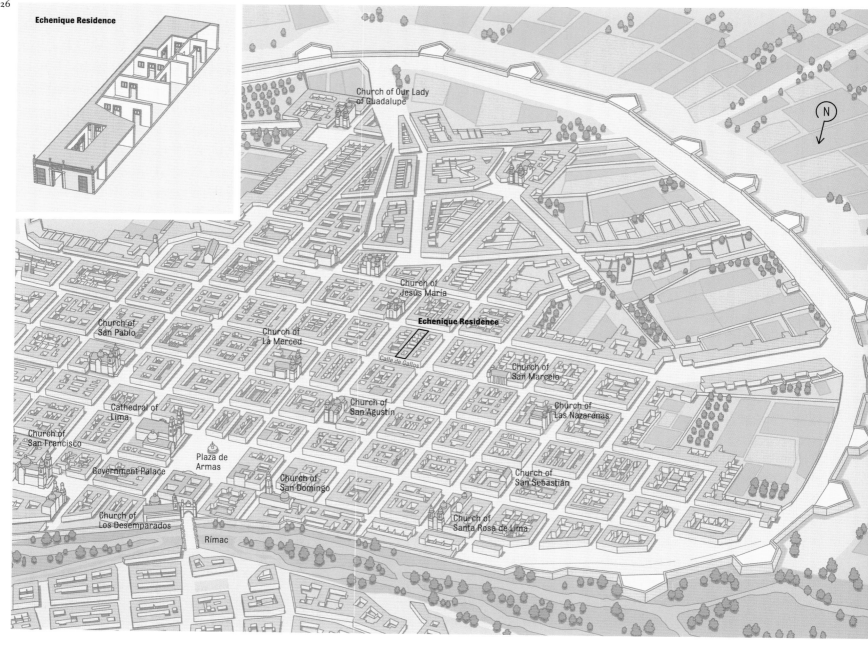

Echenique Residence

Church of Our Lady of Guadalupe

Church of San Pablo

Church of La Merced

Church of Jesús María

Echenique Residence

Calle de Gallos

Church of San Marcelo

Cathedral of Lima

Church of San Agustín

Church of Las Nazarenas

Church of San Francisco

Plaza de Armas

Government Palace

Church of San Domingo

Church of San Sebastián

Church of Los Desemparados

Rímac

Church of Santa Rosa de Lima

N

child and only son of Clovis Gauguin and Aline Marie Chazal. Clovis Gauguin was professionally involved with unfolding political turmoil, for he was an editor of a radical, anti-Bonapartist newspaper, *Le National*—or such was the case on 8 June 1848 when he registered his son's birth. The baptismal certificate, signed a month later, lists him as unemployed. Events had evidently conspired to encourage the Gauguins to leave France. On 8 August 1849 the family left the port of Le Havre bound for Lima, Peru, an arduous four-month journey.[41]

Gauguin would suggest that his father, fore-seeing the coup d'état through which Louis-Napoléon would transform himself from president to emperor, chose his moment to escape with the idea of founding a newspaper in the Peruvian capital. Whether Clovis in fact possessed the financial resources Gauguin intimated, the language skills, or even the intention to attempt such an enterprise is unknown. It seems more likely that he was still without work and possibly in poor health. And indeed Clovis Gauguin died of a rup-tured aneurysm on board ship in the Strait of Magellan, two months into the crossing.

Responsibility for the two infants, Marie and Paul, thus fell to twenty-four-year-old Aline, left alone to confront relatives she had appar-ently never met.[42]

That Aline and her husband had set out for Lima suggests desperation, given the com-plexities of Aline's mother's history with the Spanish kin she claimed through her father. (Flora Tristan was the natural daughter of Thérèse Laisnay, a Frenchwoman, and Don Mariano de Tristán y Moscoso, a descendant of a long-established Spanish colonial family in Peru.) Flora escaped the confining shackles of her marriage to engraver André Chazal through a messy divorce that involved her accusing Chazal of molesting Aline, and his nearly successful shooting attempt on Flora's life. Determined to redress wrongs, Flora placed Aline in a boarding school in 1833 and left France for Peru, where she intended to claim her inheritance. She had been only three when her father died, but she was well aware of the reputed wealth and prestige of his South American relations, and with a sense of real purpose she contacted Don Mariano's older brother, her uncle Don Pio de Tristán y Moscoso.[43]

The trajectory of Don Pio's career corresponds to the turbulent history of Peru, a country that saw thirty-two changes of regime between 1824, when the four-year war of independence led by Simón Bolívar concluded, and 1845, when Ramón Castilla consolidated power as the republic's first legitimately elected president. A royalist and for a few weeks in 1824 nominal viceroy of Spain's last South American bastion, Don Pio had ensured his position within the unstable republic by prudently surrendering his hometown, the southern city of Arequipa, to Bolívar's forces; rewarded with the governorship of Cuzco, the ancient Incan capital, he went on to hold a number of positions. He was installed as the prefect of Arequipa when he received Flora's impertinent demand from France. He had ignored her mother's inquiries over the years, and when Flora resumed the correspondence, he deigned to offer her payment but continued to deny that she was a legal descendant of his family. Flora ultimately extracted very little in the way of money from the man she called the personification of avarice and cunning, but she later published an account of her fifteen months' adventure as *The Peregrinations of a Pariah* (1834), a volume that achieved considerable success in France and that Don Pio burned publicly in Arequipa's Plaza de Armas.[44]

The resilient colonial probably thought he had heard the last of his late brother's French family; Flora Tristan died in 1844, and Aline, her only child, married Clovis Gauguin two years later and seemed destined to settle down to a middle-class life in Paris. Don Pio was in any case distracted by his own subsequent rise in the republican government, thanks in part to his son-in-law General José Rufino Echenique, who had held various ministerial offices, was currently vice president of Peru, and would be elected president in March 1851. What could have led Aline—surely aware not only of Flora's story, but also of Don Pio's bitter response to her published version of it—to imagine that against all odds she could prevail where her forceful mother had failed? Possibly she operated under the same naïve optimism that would later lead her son to continue imagining a carefree existence in the tropics even after his own life's experience should have taught him otherwise.

In November 1849 Aline and her two young children made their way to Echenique's residence on the Calle de Gallos (see map, fig. 26), where the now-septuagenarian Don Pio resided. The house, which still exists, is a one-story structure with a narrow façade, the entrance adorned only by fluted pilasters, linked by a carved garland and each surmounted by a grotesque head (see fig. 30); a balustrade runs along the roofline. Somewhat modest in contrast with the dilapidated grandeur of the hispano-moorish buildings that then dominated the city, the building extends back an entire city block, with rooms arranged around inner courtyards (see inset, fig. 26, and fig. 31). Access to the out-of-doors is afforded by grilled windows and by the rooftop terrace.

Somewhat improbably welcomed into this typical upper-class Peruvian household, Aline ended up staying for four and a half years, until Paul reached his seventh year. He would later state:

I have a remarkable visual memory and I recall this time of life, our house, and ever so many things that happened; the monument at the Presidency, the church the dome of which was entirely of carved wood. . . . I still see the *petite négresse* who, as the custom was, carried to church the little rug on which we knelt to pray. I also see that Chinese servant of ours who was so clever at ironing.[45]

It appears that Aline fared no better or worse than her mother. She would come away with no legal recognition or financial entitlements, but while she resided with her great-uncle, she and her children apparently led a privileged life, despite their irregular status. Given the elevated position of the Echenique household, Gauguin's recollections of being attended by servants ring true, supporting the inference that he enjoyed the cosseted upbringing of a genuine *patroncito* of that society's upper echelons, a race-inflected rank reflected in contemporary imagery (see fig. 28). Daily life was doubtless colorful and stimulating for the boy. On supervised outings to church and other places, he would have taken in the vivid spectacle of mid-nineteenth-century Lima, a city of 85,000 people that, though run down after so many years of political instability, nonetheless retained a certain exotic splendor. Founded by Spanish conquistador Francisco Pizarro in 1535, Lima was a fortified oasis in the midst of Peru's coastal desert. Situated on the slopes of the valley of the Rímac river, it is surrounded by plains and rocky outcroppings. The snow-capped, glacier-covered Cordilleras, or Andes mountains, lie immediately to the east; and to the west is the Pacific Ocean and the country's principal port, Callao, where the Gauguins disembarked.

From April to October, the city is covered in a canopy of gray mist or coastal fog, which yields gradually to the sun in the following months. Earthquakes are not uncommon. Offset by the Andes beyond, the towering bel-

26
Map of Lima, c. 1850s, with an inset of the Echenique residence on Calle de Gallos, Gauguin's childhood home from 1849 to 1854, now 253 Avenida de la Emancipación

27
Daguerreotype of
Church of San
Agustín, Lima
1847

28
Benjamin Franklin
Pease (American;
1822–1888)
El Patroncito
c. 1855
Daguerreotype
13.5 x 10.2 cm
McElroy Collection,
Tucson

29
Lima cityscape with
the church of Santo
Domingo
from Mariano Paz
Soldán, *Atlas
geográfico del Perú*
(Paris, 1865), pl. 28

30
Grotesque head on
the façade of the
Echenique residence,
Calle de Gallos, Lima

31
Léonce Angrand
(French; 1808–1886)
*House on Calle de
Gallos*
9 May 1838
Chalk on paper
26.5 x 17 cm
In *Lima Sketchbook*,
folio 24
Bibliothèque
Nationale, Paris

32
Johann Mortiz
Rugendas
(German; 1802–1858)
*Plaza de Armas
Looking toward the
Cathedral*
1842/44
Watercolor on paper
Museo de Arte de
Lima

33
Johann Moritz
Rugendas
Tapadas
n.d.
Graphite on paper

fries, steeples, and domes of the cathedral and other major churches dominated the skyline, dwarfing all other edifices. In the 1800s Lima counted some sixty-seven places of worship, serving parishes, monasteries, and convents. These ornate, polychromed churches, many of them Spanish Baroque in style, dotted the cityscape (see figs. 27, 29), complemented by equally multicolored, stuccoed buildings of varying styles, often featuring doorways, portals, grilled windows, and projecting latticed balconies of carved wood.

The city's squares and streets were paved only partially or not at all. Gauguin and his family would have strolled around the lively Plaza de Armas, Lima's main square and site of shopping arcades (see fig. 32); the cathedral, with a red and yellow painted façade and three green doors; the government palace housing the president's offices and apartments; the palace of the archbishop; and the sixteenth-century tiered bronze fountain that Gauguin referred to as "the monument." He would have negotiated the scavenging buzzards attracted by the refuse on rooftops and by the open sewers that

disfigured the streets. Frequent processionals marking Catholic saints' days and holidays added to the local color and attracted mixed audiences including noisy street vendors, ambulant musicians, and the upper-class creole women known as *tapadas*. These distinctive figures had adapted the Moorish tradition of covering themselves in the street, drawing their *mantos* (shawls) over their heads so that only one eye could be seen (see fig. 33).[46]

Gauguin's memories of how pretty his young mother looked when thus costumed served to support his view of her as a "very noble Spanish lady"; he also described his maternal grandmother in these terms. But the fact remains that Flora had failed to establish her lineage. An anecdote related by Gauguin about a prank played by Aline in the government palace points toward her sense of her own uncertain social position and hints at an awareness of the complex hierarchies of class and race that inflected his formative years in Lima. According to the story, Aline arranged for a dinner guest, a high-ranking officer, to be served food that had been spiced "with a

vengeance." The man, "who had Indian blood in his veins," had become her target by boasting of his fondness for pimento.[47] It remains unclear whether the boasting alone, or the additional fact of his mixed heritage, prompted Aline's practical joke.

To be sure, centuries of interconnection between the Spanish colonialists and the Peruvian native peoples had produced many offspring, including Castilla, Echenique's predecessor as president. Nonetheless, the country's ruling classes defended their elite identity and racial purity, which they felt to be threatened by the negative image of the Peruvian national type that had gained worldwide currency. Romantic European perceptions, fostered in articles and books, represented the people with their Incan heritage as "savage denizens of primeval forests, half covered with feathers, who shoot down foreigners with bows and arrows" and then eat them. The native populations, as well as the descendants of African slaves and the Chinese workers who had been brought in to replace them, were all denied Peruvian citizenship and largely excluded from the ruling classes'

34
Paul Gauguin
Self-Portrait
1877 [W 25]
Oil on canvas
46 x 38 cm
Fogg Art Museum,
Harvard University
Art Museums,
gift of Helen W.
Ellsworth in
memory of
Duncan S.
Ellsworth '22

vision of the country's future.[48] Indigenous peoples were clearly regarded with ambivalence by those of European descent, a growing interest in pre-Columbian cultural artifacts (pottery and metalwork) notwithstanding.

Gauguin's own later assertions of mixed Incan-European ancestry had nothing to do with the reality of Aline's claims, and those of her mother, to the Tristán de Moscoso family. Flora Tristan had made a point of the family's pure Spanish blood, though she allowed that Don Pio's physiognomy had been altered by life in a foreign climate. Gauguin likewise declared his mother's noble, Castilian background. The only connection to Indian Peru that Aline could provide was through the pre-Columbian vases and massive silver figurines that Gauguin said she owned and which he claimed disappeared in the last days of the Franco-Prussian War of 1870–71. But this lineage, even if established solely through material artifacts, appears to have been fictional: no such objects appear in either Aline's 1865 will or the detailed inventory of her estate that was prepared after her death in 1867.[49]

The Gauguins occupied a precarious position in a turbulent country. Peru's increasing involvement with the international economy—mainly through the trade of guano, which was dug up by a conscripted labor force—may have brought prosperity, but it did not produce political stability. Just the opposite. Echenique's government, perceived as self-serving and corrupt, became increasingly unpopular, and discontent led to open revolt. In June 1854 former *caudillo* Castilla became the leader of the anti-Echenique forces. As in 1848 Aline found herself carried on the tides of political change. In early August 1854, when Echenique was on the battlefield, Aline applied for and obtained a passport from the French embassy. She and her children departed none too soon. In early January 1855, Castilla emerged victorious from the battle of La Palma,

exiled Echenique to Chile, and resumed the presidency.

Back in France, Aline experienced an exile of a different kind. Without resources, she turned to her husband's father, Guillaume Gauguin, who lived in Orléans and had offered to divide his estate between her and his surviving son, Isidore (Zizi), currently serving a sentence in an Algerian penal colony for his involvement in the 1851 protest staged in Orléans against Louis-Napoléon's coup d'état. The senior Gauguin died within months of Aline's arrival, naming Isidore—who was allowed to return to France on 20 April 1855—the deputy guardian of his grandchildren. Paul, at seven, had to learn French, which he initially spoke with a Spanish accent.[50] He was registered as a day student in a local school.

What Aline did over the next years is unclear. Money was evidently an issue, leading her in 1859 to liquidate part of the children's inheritance from their grandfather. That year Paul, now eleven, entered the Petit Séminaire de La Chapelle-Saint-Mesmin, run by the well-known bishop of Orléans, Félix-Antoine-Philibert Dupanloup, as a sort of laboratory for the educational reforms he advocated. Gauguin remembered this period as one of "theological study," and indeed Dupanloup inculcated his pupils with a particular interpretation of Catholic catechism meant to sustain faith in an era of skepticism, one that mobilized students' imaginations to make belief vivid. Renan, like Gauguin a pupil of Dupanloup's, recalled the way in which the seminary program encouraged self-examination to the point of abstract dreaming.[51]

Gauguin would claim: "It was there I learned … to distrust everything that was contrary to my instincts, my heart, and my reason." Typically, this statement is open ended: does it confirm or condemn Dupanloup's deeply antipositivist, antinaturalist ideology? Gauguin's additional contention that he imbibed a Jesuitical casuistry, which allowed him to reconcile conscience, passion, and self-interest, suggests a certain ironic antipathy.[52] More positive memories of his three years' instruction at the seminary may have served Gauguin when he came to articulate an antimaterialist aesthetic position that relied on the resources of the imagination and aspired to mystery. But then many other tributaries were to feed into this development—notably his tutelage with Vincent.

In 1861 Aline relocated to Paris, where she worked as a dressmaker. This represented a decided fall in social rank for someone who, according to her son, found the word "trade" offensive. The profession Aline now joined was, like many open to women, popularly associated with the bartering of sexual favors; and in fact it was possibly a liaison that brought her to Paris. That year she became friendly with Gustave Arosa, a wealthy businessman of Spanish descent whose father had made a fortune in the Peruvian guano trade. His brother's mistress, also a dressmaker, lived near Aline's shop, and while this is circumstantial at best, the role that Arosa would take as protector to Aline and her children suggests close ties. Whether this in turn affected her relationship with her son, who joined her in the capital in 1862, is open to speculation. Aline had sold another portion of Paul's inheritance to pay for his tuition at the Institut Loriol in Paris, where he was to prepare for the entrance examinations for the naval academy. But two years later, he was sent back to Orléans to board at a *lycée*. The will that Aline drafted in 1865 hints at his difficult behavior: she appended to her provisional bequest to her son an admonition that he "get on with his career, since he has made himself so disliked by all my friends that he will one day find himself alone."[53] The friends in question were doubtless Arosa, named the children's legal guardian in the will, and his circle.

In December 1865, the naval academy no longer an option, Gauguin enlisted as an officer's candidate in the merchant marines. His subsequent travels would take him around the world—even back to Peru. During a stopover in India in 1867, he learned that Aline had died on 7 July, following an illness. The following year he entered the French navy for obligatory military service. Released after the Franco-Prussian War, Gauguin returned to Paris in 1871, twenty-three years old and with five years' experience at sea behind him, a considerable inheritance at his disposal, and—having become accustomed to a very structured life and to following orders—apparently no plans for the future. He followed his sister into the orbit of Arosa, who took the rough-edged but now apparently more malleable Gauguin under his wing, getting him a job as a stock-exchange agent and welcoming him into his social circle. Through Arosa, Gauguin became acquainted with Mette Gad, the outspoken Danish woman whom he would marry in 1873. Also through Arosa he developed an interest in art, for his former guardian's extensive collection ranged from various ceramics to paintings of Eugène Delacroix, Camille Corot, Gustave Courbet, and founding Impressionist Camille Pissarro. Arosa's tastes, like Arosa's friends, became Gauguin's. The young man's skill as a stockbroker is not documented, but the harebrained business schemes that he would later concoct suggest that his imagination outstripped his acumen. Apparently, however, under Arosa's mentorship he benefited from the speculative post-war economy, his steadily rising salary adequate to support his growing family (he and Mette had five children by 1883) and to allow him to dabble in art as practitioner and patron.[54]

There is no evidence—even from Gauguin's own lips—of any serious youthful inclination toward art, and his rather sudden and, as it turned out, persistent interest can at least in part be attributed to Arosa's example as col-

lector and to the ambition of one of his daughters to become a painter. Gauguin started painting in the summer of 1873, just months before his wedding, which took place in November with his boss and Arosa in attendance. The following year Mette gave birth to their first son, Emil. Gauguin, in his avocation of Sunday painter, began to manifest the personal ambition evidently lacking professionally. In the spring of 1876, he successfully submitted a competent landscape to the Salon, the large, juried, state-sponsored exhibition of contemporary art held annually in Paris. Subsequently he changed jobs and moved to bigger quarters in time for the birth of their second child, Aline, in late 1877. Their new landlord, Jules Bouillot, was a sculptor, as was fellow tenant Jean-Paul Aubé.[55]

The absence of Gauguin's name in Salon catalogues after 1876 indicates that he either was rejected or stopped submitting works. In any case the art he had begun to collect reveals a taste that departed from the conservatism that reigned among the Salon jury. A self-portrait that Gauguin painted in 1877 (fig. 34) presents a rather callow, full-faced individual, with a soft, complacent demeanor at odds with the somewhat theatrical flourishes of small goatee and rakish cap. The first of a lifetime of such statements, it is a portrait of the young man as an artist.

Vincent's momentous resolution of 1879–80 was only the first step along a difficult road to establishing his artistic skills and identity. The next five years would take him back to his parents' home in Etten; to The Hague, artistic capital of the Netherlands; to the moors of Drenthe; and back to his family, now relocated in Nuenen. It was a difficult and complicated pilgrimage.

From the outset Vincent invested all-encompassing expectations in his new career. He anticipated that the identity of "artist" would normalize what had seemed outlandish: his neglected appearance, coarse manners, and inability to support himself, as well as the perceived strangeness of his behavior. Commonplace tropes of marginalization and eccentricity—"relatively few people know why an artist acts as he does"—allowed Vincent to imagine those who had criticized his actions finally conceding, "Your work demands it, and we understand why it is so." Throughout the rest of his life, Vincent pursued his craft in hopes of regaining the confidence and respect of his father, uncles, and former boss Tersteeg.[56]

Vincent did not wait long to test the acceptance of those close to him. During the summer of 1881, he fell in love with his cousin Kee Vos, daughter of his uncle Stricker, and a widow seven years his senior. Perceiving her as the muse necessary to his artistic future, Vincent tenaciously refused to accept her "no" for an answer. The family closed ranks against him, criticizing his persistence and demanding that he give up. In a final attempt to win Kee, Vincent went to Amsterdam, interrupting the Strickers' dinner and demanding to see her; he put his fingers in a blazing lamp, declaring: "Let me see her for as long as I can keep my hand in the flame." His uncle promptly extinguished his hopes, sending Vincent home to a difficult period of soul-searching.[57]

Vincent interpreted this rejection as ultimate proof that the religion practiced by his uncle and father was essentially hollow, dominated by the rigid convention of Pharisees rather than the heartfelt compassion and love of humanity he recognized in the work of Michelet and Hugo. His parents, deaf to these modern gospels, seemed increasingly alien, and the objects of his admiration more real. In the fall of 1881, he took to speaking of "Father Michelet" and "Father Millet." Finally signaling his apostasy by refusing to attend church on Christmas Day, Vincent precipitated a blow-up with his father and abruptly left the Etten parsonage for The Hague. Over the next two years, he worked on sharpening his skills and sense of mission, constructing the independent identity that led him to sign his works "Vincent," a gesture corresponding to the growing feeling that "essentially I am *not* a 'van Gogh.'"[58]

Issues of independence, identity, and control had figured largely in Vincent's choice of profession. "If I can only continue to work somehow," Vincent wrote in the fall of 1880, "it will set me right again." He found art-making to be restorative, and over the years he often referred to the calming effect that drawing and painting had on his nervous constitution. But art also served as a vehicle for expressing himself according to his character and temperament, as well as the means of one day making his living. Contemplating ways of reaching his goal, he rejected the kind of formal training and obedience to standards set by others that had scuttled his attempts to pursue a career in the church. Instead he opted to teach himself, beginning by copying from instruction manuals such as Karl Robert's *Fusain sans maître* (*Drawing without a Master*). This genre—together with the example of "fathers" like Millet, who could be idealized and interpreted without threat of constraint, influence, or censure—afforded Vincent the requisite cre-

ative freedom to regulate and shape his own progress. He naturalized and emblematized his approach by associating it with the image of the sower laboring in rhythmic harmony with natural cycles: "You must wait for the natural season, and that is not here yet.... I shall not run after art lovers or dealers.... In due time we shall reap."[59]

Vincent pursued the metaphor in talking about his initial studies as the seed for further sowing that might produce a harvest of saleable work, and in describing his relentless attempts to master drawing in terms of improving the quality of the seed. And he gave it literal expression by launching his career with drawings after a reproduction of Millet's famous *Sower* (figs. 35–36), five of which he had finished by September 1880, and periodically revisiting the theme over the coming years to measure the progress made through relentless application and, when possible, study from the model. Surviving examples spanning 1881 through 1884 (figs. 37–39) illustrate—in a kind of freeze-frame sequence—Vincent's slow but steady

35

35
Jean-François Millet
(French; 1814–1875)
The Sower
1850
Oil on canvas
101.6 x 82.6 cm

Museum of Fine
Arts, Boston, gift of
Quincy Adams
Shaw through
Quincy A. Shaw, Jr.,
and Mrs. Marian
Shaw Haughton

36
Paul-Edmé LeRat
(French; 1849–1892)
after Millet
The Sower
Etching, squared for
transfer by Vincent
van Gogh
12 x 9.5 cm
Van Gogh Museum,
Amsterdam
(Vincent van Gogh
Foundation)

37
Vincent van Gogh
The Sower
(after Millet)
Early 1881
[F 830, JH 1]
Pencil, ink, and
paint on paper
48 x 36.5 cm
Van Gogh Museum,
Amsterdam
(Vincent van Gogh
Foundation)

38
Vincent van Gogh
Sower
December 1882
[F 852, JH 275]
Pencil, brush and
ink on paper
61 x 40 cm
P. and N. de Boer
Foundation,
Amsterdam

39
P. H. van Bemmel
(Dutch; 19th century)
Sower
1884
Photograph of a lost
painting by Vincent
van Gogh
Van Gogh Museum,
Amsterdam
(Vincent van Gogh
Foundation)

progress in coming to grips with the human figure and gaining mastery of his materials, first in drawing, then painting.[60]

More than a benchmark, the figure of the sower was central to Vincent's larger symbolic construction of his chosen profession as a calling. In one sense a life in art fostered the illusion of family connection, involving him in what he saw as the same line of work as his paternal uncles and Theo, now working at one of Goupil's Paris branches. The sower also represents Vincent's earlier ambition to be a Christian laborer and sower of God's word, not any longer through emulating the Reverend Theodorus van Gogh, but by a parallel path, following the example of "Father Millet," whose *Sower* embodies his "evangelical tone." The motif enjoyed widespread currency as a symbol of evangelism (see fig. 40). Relevant to Vincent in this regard was Carlyle's discussion of any true vocation as "apostolic work," an "acted Gospel of freedom"; and his description of great books as tilled fields and of writing as "sowing in the seedfield of public opin-

ion." Likewise Vincent would come to analogize his artworks as "seed … sown in the field of public opinion."[61]

The "sublime, almost religious emotion" that Vincent admired in Millet arose from the painter's ability to treat ostensibly real subject matter in such a way as to intimate the "quelque chose là-haut" ("something transcendent" or "something on high"), arousing consciousness of the "existence of God and eternity." Millet's art was one of great consolation. The love for humanity demonstrated in his work as well as in that of Carlyle, Hugo, and others led Vincent to define the painter's "duty to put an idea into his work." His goal was the kind of art that Thoré, in *Les Musées de la Hollande*, described Rembrandt as practicing—a realism that pointed toward the infinite, that Vincent termed more real than reality, and that was in effect symbolic. Vincent aspired to be a "true Realist," in the sense of Carlyle's heroes, who disclosed the "awful Reality which lies at the bottom of all Appearance."[62] Painting was, in other words, a spiritual mis-

sion, an existential pilgrimage, and a mythic enterprise that Vincent approached with characteristically idealistic expectations.

Shortly before leaving Etten for The Hague in 1881, Vincent had called on Anthon van Rappard, an artist friend he had met in Belgium, to join him in becoming a fisherman on the "sea that we call the Ocean of Reality." This echo of Christ's call to his disciples reveals the reach of an ambition that only occasionally shows itself between the lines of Vincent's voluminous correspondence. Turning thirty in 1883, Vincent would take heart, despite his belated start and continued financial dependence, by recalling that Jesus had been an ordinary carpenter until that age. Having earlier expressed the desire to draw using a carpenter's pencil (albeit with reference to Dürer and Michelangelo), Vincent mused on how Jesus raised himself into something else.[63]

By this time Vincent had been in The Hague for a year and a half, and his original optimism

36

37

38

39

about the city had waned. Disappointment had resulted from unrealistic expectations, played out in his different interactions with would-be friends, mentors, and lovers: the first with van Rappard; the second with Anton Mauve, a successful Hague School painter and Vincent's cousin by marriage; the third with Clasina (Sien) Hoornik, a prostitute with whom he established a household shortly after his arrival. Vincent's relationship with Sien reveals his tendency to filter his experience through the lenses of different associations. He felt ill at ease with people of his own social background, and Sien fulfilled his fantasy of getting along better with common folk. Clearly, however, he was more attuned to his own needs than to his companion's individual subjectivity; he would remark, while he and Sien were still living together, that "books and reality and art are alike to me . . . If I didn't look for art in reality, I should probably find her stupid." She appeared to him the picture of suffering, "a pale face, a sorrowful look like an Ecce Homo on a dark background" (see fig. 20). Having walked a thorny path of tears, this scorned person served as both mirror and ideal muse—a Woman of Sorrows.[64]

Sien posed for *Sorrow* (fig. 42), Vincent's powerful image of a naked, pregnant woman with her head buried in her folded arms, which he considered his best figure drawing to date. The artist's expressive aim was twofold. First, he wanted to preach what he called the "good sermon on resignation," the one he had never heard in his father's church but had discovered in Michelet, whom he acknowledged in the quotation he inscribed below the image. Second, he hoped to show the world that music existed inside him, though he recognized that he was seen as a "nonentity, eccentric, [and] unpleasant."[65]

In *Sorrow* Vincent made a conscious attempt at what he called the English style of drafts-manship, as seen in the London-based periodical *The Graphic*, which had published wood engravings representing the poor and downtrodden in the 1870s, images that Vincent specifically connected with Sien and valued as another modern gospel. In addition to the virtues of sobriety and simplicity, he discerned in the illustrations of Luke Fildes, Frank Holl, and their colleagues the same quality that he now discovered in the controversial novels of Émile Zola: a compassion for marginal figures (like the fallen woman he himself had rescued), accompanied by understanding of the social forces complicit in their situation.[66]

A single impulse led Vincent to collect wood engravings from *The Graphic* and to take in Sien: he consciously strove to understand art and life simultaneously. Both the prints and the companion functioned as a kind of litmus test that Vincent administered to friends and family. His parents, following the precepts of their church, failed, for they saw sin in his "respecting a whore," and the liaison revived the threat of Gheel. Vincent expected better of his artist colleagues. In friendship as in art, he drew a strict distinction between the real and the conventional. The former involved shared belief and the testing of convictions through the interrogation he referred to as *wrijving* (friction). Greatness of any kind could only result from the exercise of will—according to Carlyle, from thought shaped by action and not merely by emotion. Vincent extended this precept to his relationships: "Friendship must be primarily *action* not simply feeling." Understandably, few could withstand Vincent's intensity for long. While working at Goupil's in Paris in 1876, Vincent had conscripted Harry Gladwell, a teenaged newcomer to the firm, to join him for Bible readings in his "cabin," relieved by instructional museum visits. But Gladwell had soon jumped ship to fall in with more fun-loving companions. Vincent's need for "a friend of whom we might say: *dat is het*"

only increased with his embrace of the artistic vocation.[67]

Despite the change of direction entailed by that decision, Vincent continued to navigate by the same metaphoric coordinates. "I have a firm *faith* in art," he would write in spring 1883, "a firm confidence in its being a powerful stream which carries man to a harbor." His vocation was a voyage. He likened his love of

40

41

42

that one must lose life in order to find it. Half measures were no measures, painting was a gospel, and the cost of discipleship was complete submission to its demands. Vincent, tireless in articulating these requirements, kept his friend on a kind of extended probation. Though van Rappard passed an important test by finally confirming *The Graphic*'s importance, he incurred Vincent's condemnation by considering enrollment in the academy in Brussels and by accepting certain types of commissions that Vincent considered a waste of precious time. The friendship lasted as long as it did because the two men conducted it primarily through correspondence. Van Rappard would describe their rare get-togethers as oppressive, confessing that he felt respect rather than affection for Vincent.[69]

Vincent's interaction with Mauve shows that he had just as much difficulty when the roles were reversed. The established painter initially showed considerable generosity toward his wife's kinsman, arranging for his access to models and tutoring him in the practice of watercolor. Vincent was both grateful and heartened, but he could only follow where he wished to be led. When he asked questions, he did not welcome wrong answers, like those he received when he asked Mauve and Tersteeg how to make his work more saleable. Their practical counsel went contrary to his convictions, and he would not budge on matters of faith. Mauve further offended Vincent by disdaining the *Graphic* illustrations as too literary.[70] Finally, Vincent's choice of female companion, together with his ingrained resistance to authority, led to an awkward, resentful estrangement from Mauve and Tersteeg.

Vincent's rereading of Carlyle's *Sartor Resartus* in the summer of 1883 underscored his sense of having arrived at a critical juncture in his pilgrimage. Tersteeg and the world of commercial art that he represented would hence-forth embody "the everlasting no," a negativity extending to the artists' community at large. Vincent had imagined a homeland of mutually supportive individuals united by common purpose and beliefs, a warm and harmonious society. Instead discussions became fierce quarrels, his work was received unsympathetically, and he himself was the subject of gossip. He had determined that painters as a group were no better than a family, a combination of self-interested people who united only to gang up at another's expense.[71]

Setting aside—though by no means relinquishing—his dream of a brotherhood of painters such as he imagined had existed at *The Graphic* in its heyday, Vincent attempted to live in isolation, like the shipwrecked Robinson Crusoe, and focus on his work.[72] But this strategy left him alienated, with a growing sense of being out of step with the present. In letters to Theo and van Rappard, he began referring to the decadence of contemporary art, attributable in part to the denigrating effects of city life; and he experienced intense nostalgia for the fields of Brabant. Finally in September 1883, he left The Hague and Sien for Drenthe, the region of vast moors and heaths in the northern Netherlands.

drawing to that of a sailor for the sea, and talked of venturing into the new media of oil and watercolor as seeking the open waters; he spoke of turning adversity to his advantage like a pilot using a storm to make headway, and of ridding himself of painful memories by throwing them overboard like useless ballast. He imagined himself launching a boat when he set up his Hague studio, which he tried to fit out like a comfortable barge, came to love as a sailor loves his ship, and imagined as the long-sought harbor or refuge.[68] But Sien did not fulfill the role of the fellow traveler Vincent required.

He had already extended the invitation to van Rappard and would continue to attempt to engage him in his mission. "Life means painting to me," he confided in 1882, in the same breath recalling Christ's words to the effect

40
Jean-Baptiste-
Etienne Marchais
(French; b. 1818)
after Émile Signol
(French; 1804–1892)
Christ Laborer
Lithograph
Bibliothèque
Nationale, Paris

41
T. B. Wirgman
(British; 1848–1925)
Some "Graphic" Artists
from *The Graphic*
(Christmas 1882),
annotated by
Vincent van Gogh
Van Gogh Museum,
Amsterdam
(Vincent van Gogh
Foundation)

42
Vincent van Gogh
Sorrow
c. 10 April 1882
[F 929a, JH 130]
Pencil and chalk
on paper
44.5 x 27 cm
Walsall Museum
and Art Gallery,
Walsall, England

Vincent's descriptions of Drenthe (and of its inhabitants' "healthy melancholy") tell us much more about his own interior landscape than about the region's. He mediated his experience through associative filters, perceiving a series of "just likes." Indulging his fantasies of escape and regression, and referring to his extensive mental image bank, Vincent declared himself transported in time to art's golden ages. He looked around him and saw van Goyens, de Konincks, Ruysdaels, Michels (see fig. 44), Rousseaus, Duprés, Daubignys. Layering the past onto the present served to insulate him; one could be tranquil, he wrote, having "miles and miles of Michels between oneself and the ordinary world."[73]

Though Drenthe supported some artists' colonies, Vincent clearly had little inclination to seek them out. Instead he nursed the hope that Theo, who had admitted to difficulties at Goupil's, might give up art-dealing and join him as brother-painter. Theo must, Vincent insisted, leave the sinking ship, exercise his willpower, and realize his true nature by committing to life as an artist. In pressing his argument, he revealed the ambivalence about the market that had thwarted his desire for financial independence (and would continue to do so): making art was noble; selling it was not.[74]

But Vincent's proposal to his brother had nothing to do with financial practicalities. Working together, he and Theo would join a lineage including Adriaan and Isaäk van Ostade in the seventeenth century and more recently Jules and Émile Breton; their larger mission would mirror that of the Puritans, about whom he had read in Carlyle's *On Heroes and Hero-Worship*. The van Gogh brothers not only resembled the Puritans physically (with their "reddish hair … and square foreheads"), but could emulate them philosophically by founding a sheltering homeland of painters. The fantasy was informed by Vincent's idealized notion of the "family life" enjoyed by the

Barbizon painters; evenings would be spent together looking at and discussing art. But camaraderie—*gezelligheid*—was not the only goal, as attested by Vincent's reference to the pilgrim fathers, victims of religious persecution. He spoke of saving Theo from degenerative urban life, of effecting a renewal of body and soul. Millet served as model, for the peasant-painter had believed in a higher power and had become an evangel of its gospel; the goal was rescue from existential despair. Vincent imagined them together recapturing their youthful sense of idyllic immersion in nature and freedom from the need to "obey," but also in so doing becoming less self-engrossed and troubled by the problem of God's existence. Subsuming ego in missionary purpose, he and Theo would find themselves "feeling, thinking, and believing so exactly alike" that their work would "merge."[75]

Three months' worth of letters from Vincent on this subject—increasingly excited, insistent, and finally overwrought—did not have their intended effect. By the end of November 1883, it was clear that Theo's answer was no. Precipitously deflated, lonely, and in need of money, Vincent regretfully left Drenthe and returned to live with his parents, now installed in Nuenen. Somehow Vincent had hoped their attitude toward him might have changed, but he found his father still implacable; moreover, his suspicions of betrayal aroused, he also included Theo among those who refused to understand him. Though he felt he should break decisively with his father, he literally could not afford to do so. Instead he persuaded Theo to consider the monthly sum he provided a payment for work rather than charity. Despite his brother's concession, Vincent felt beleaguered, likening himself to a weaver with "tangled threads and a pattern gone to hell."[76]

The metaphor was a significant one, derived from such sources as Dickens's preface to *Little Dorrit*, George Eliot's *Silas Marner*, and of course Carlyle's *Sartor Resartus*, and brought

to life in Nuenen by the hand-loom weavers who labored in the vicinity. The weaver, like the sower, came to symbolize artistic aspirations, maintained in the face of adverse social, economic, and spiritual conditions; Vincent identified with these workers in his desire to equate art-making with wage-earning craft.[77] Addressing this meaningful motif, Vincent began to pull together strands of Romantic subjectivity and New Testament mission into a design with outlines provided by Carlyle, who spoke of weaving "new vestures" for old truths currently clad in threadbare "church clothes." Finally, Vincent's numerous sketches and paintings of the Nuenen weavers (see fig. 43) speak to the shift in his ambition from drawing to painting, and to a new interest in color that led him to the theories of Delacroix as recorded by Charles Blanc and other art historians.[78]

Van Rappard's criticism of the figural disproportions in the weaver images led Vincent to explain his intention: to privilege expressive force and the "idea" over accuracy and technical polish. Comparing his pictorial style to language, Vincent claimed to speak the native tongue of a non-specialist audience whose response to the "awakening power" of pictures depended not on their content or execution, but rather on what shone through them: the artist's soul.[79] This argument again echoes Carlyle's idea that each age requires a new dialect (like new clothes), comprehensible owing to its sincerity and freedom from convention.

Vincent similarly marshaled his arguments in response to Theo's suggestion that he might do well to look at living artists other than Millet's followers. Dismissive of debates about creative priority—who is first and who is second—Vincent took another page from Carlyle to argue the virtue of following in the footsteps of a true leader. Édouard Manet, whom Theo admired, might be "original," but that in itself was insufficient: to qualify as "essen-

43
Vincent van Gogh
Weaver near an Open Window
1884 [F 24, JH 500]
Oil on canvas
68 x 93 cm
Neue Pinakothek,
Munich

44
Georges Michel
(French; 1763–1843)
The Storm
1814/30
Oil on canvas
58.7 x 73 cm

The Art Institute of
Chicago, Wilson L.
Mead Fund, 1935.374

43

44

45
Vincent van Gogh
Sketch of *Still Life
with Vase and Honesty*
(*"Judaspenningen"*),
Pipe, and Tobacco in
letter to Theo
[5 April 1885]
(letter 493/398; JH
726)
Pen and ink and
watercolor on paper
Van Gogh Museum,
Amsterdam
(Vincent van Gogh
Foundation)

46
Vincent van Gogh
Lane of Poplars
Late October 1884
[F 122, JH 522]
Oil on canvas,
mounted on panel
99 x 66 cm
Van Gogh Museum,
Amsterdam
(Vincent van Gogh
Foundation)

45

46

tially modern," the artist must open new spiritual horizons as Millet had. Despite his scant knowledge of Manet and ignorance of Impressionism, Vincent felt confident that no contemporary painter measured up to this standard. But he was ready to concede that a writer had: Zola.[80]

Vincent felt increasingly convinced that Zola had produced an exemplary modern gospel in works like *Au bonheur des dames* (*The Ladies' Paradise*; 1883), a novel that presents the department store, a recent innovation, as social microcosm. Zola captured Vincent's imagination with his contrast between the world-view of the scrappy protagonist, Octave Mouret, and that of his well-born school friend, Paul de Vallagnosc. The latter has adopted pessimism and irony as a defense against the challenges of modern life, but Mouret thinks his friend a fool for trying to protect himself at all costs against suffering. Living intensely is what counts, Vincent copied out for Theo: "Action is its own reward—to act, to create, to fight against the facts, *to conquer them or be conquered by them*, all human joy [*joie*] and health *consists in that*."[81]

This was Carlyle's philosophy of action, dramatized and rendered compelling through art. In Vincent's correspondence with Theo, "Mouret" became a code name for the passionate engagement he required. Zola's more overtly philosophical *Joie de vivre* confirmed Vincent's belief in the author's essential modernity. Pauline's resilience, healthy distrust of "abstract" religious thought, and unstinting ministry to others inspired him to recognize and transcend his Lazare-like fear that "all is vanity."[82] Such were the symbolic underpinnings of *Still Life with Bible and Zola's "Joie de vivre,"* which Vincent would paint in October 1885, seven months after the sudden death of the Reverend van Gogh, at age sixty-three.

The loss of his father represented the decisive break that Vincent could not effect on his own with the figure who, more than anyone, embodied the everlasting no, who had remained unshakeable in beliefs that ran counter to his son's. Writing to Theo about the impact of their father's death, Vincent included a sketch of a just-completed still life featuring the reverend's tobacco pouch and pipe beside a vase of the flowers called *Judaspenningen* in Dutch—literally, Judas-pennies (fig. 45). Juxtaposing the plant named after the silver coins that Judas received for betraying Christ with items associated with his father, Vincent alluded to his own private Gethsemane.[83] He had second thoughts about this still life (soon thereafter burying it under another), but he remained committed to the resolutions prompted by Theodorus's death: to seize the opportunity to make something of his life; to try to be true to himself; to remember that whatever the chances for happiness in "'la joie (?) de vivre,' as it is called, one must work and take risks if one wants to live." This determination grew out of the sense of liberation he now felt. Tailoring Mouret's speech to his own life experience, Vincent observed how change—freeing oneself from the influence of upbringing and parental expectations—came at great cost.[84]

Corresponding changes in his painting were immediately apparent. To be sure, during the preceding months, Vincent had been making strides, extending his expressive range by exploring the theory of complementary colors. He put what he learned from books into practice in pictures such as *Lane of Poplars* (fig. 46), an autumn landscape structured around the opposition of blue and orange (see ch. 2, fig. 8).[85] Featuring a lone figure in black, the scene is infused with a sense of loss that recalls the artist's early attachment to Michelet's "Aspirations de l'automne." But within days of his father's death, Vincent moved into an entirely new realm, tackling his most ambitious painting to date, *The Potato Eaters* (fig. 47).

Completed in a scant three weeks and immediately sent to Theo in Paris, the picture can be regarded as a belated coming of age. Vincent, in typically metaphoric terms, considered it to have been harvested from many years of studies, a pattern woven from many disparate threads. With his choice of subject, he declared his intention to follow in the footsteps of quintessential peasant painter Millet; with his earthy colors and deliberately coarse draftsmanship, he hoped to demonstrate the authenticity of his approach. Yet the result—an assembly of low-browed, gnarled figures in a disconcertingly confined, darkly lugubrious space—thwarted contemporary genre expectations. Far from a reassuring image of an unchanging, contented peasantry, it is imprinted with the irresolution resulting from Vincent's contradictory treatment of the peasants as both subjects (with whom he felt "at home") and objects (different from "us civilized people").[86]

Theo, while he admired his brother's avoidance of idealization, had major reservations about *The Potato Eaters*. For him the torsos were inadequately realized and the palette was far too dark. Van Rappard, upon receiving a lithographic version of an earlier version of the composition (fig. 48), proffered an unequivocally negative response. He captured the disruptive impact of the work by stating baldly that it "terrified" him; adding several technical criticisms, he called into question Vincent's claim to lineage with Millet. Vincent did not take this attack in stride. He felt pressed to defend his authenticity: "I want to paint what I feel and feel what I paint." In response to the criticisms, which felt like physical blows, Vincent railed against van Rappard's pharisaic academic values and demanded a recantation.[87] The friendship did not survive the ensuing exchange, and indeed Vincent never again attempted a figure picture as ambitious or as attentive to the social conditions of modern life.

47

48

49

47
Vincent van Gogh
The Potato Eaters
Early May 1882
[F 82, JH 764]
Oil on canvas
82 x 114 cm
Van Gogh Museum,
Amsterdam
(Vincent van Gogh
Foundation)

48
Vincent van Gogh
The Potato Eaters
Mid-April 1882
[F 1661, JH 737]
Lithograph
26.5 x 32 cm
Van Gogh Museum,
Amsterdam
(Vincent van Gogh
Foundation)

49
Vincent van Gogh
Country Churchyard
c. 11 May 1885
[F 84, JH 772]
Oil on canvas
63 x 79 cm
Van Gogh Museum,
Amsterdam
(Vincent van Gogh
Foundation)

Vincent felt somewhat more inclined to listen to Theo, who made some of the same points in a more constructive manner. Vincent applied himself anew to certain fine points of figure drawing, and more importantly he evaluated and articulated his expressive aims. Foreswearing an aesthetic based on literal truth and technical exactitude, he embraced the "truer" truth revealed in the "incorrect" draftsmanship of Daumier or Michelangelo, who painted things not as they are but as they felt them. While Vincent's embrace of subjectivity echoes Zola's famous description of art as "nature seen through a temperament," it includes the critical qualifier that resulted from his early schooling in emblematics, reinforced by his reading, from Thoré through Carlyle. The painter must be a thinker; he must intimate that "all reality is at the same time symbolic" and produce an art at once true to nature and revelatory of the infinite. For Vincent, exemplars of this symbolic realism included not only Rembrandt and Millet, but also Delacroix.[88]

The presence of the Romantic master in Vincent's pantheon points to an important new concern with color. Theo had been

telling him for months that his paintings were too black, but Vincent had stubbornly insisted: "I shall become darker rather than lighter." In the wake of *The Potato Eaters*, however, he realized that color could help him achieve his goals. As in the past, he set himself an assignment. Since deciding to become an artist, he had formulated his ideas about art with reference to his memories of paintings seen years earlier and to black-and-white reproductions he had at hand. So in October 1885 Vincent made a trip to Amsterdam's just-opened Rijksmuseum, to analyze the collections from the perspective of his current interests. His view inflected by what Theo had told him about Impressionism, he now noticed how quickly the seventeenth-century Dutch masters, such as Hals, must have worked, and wondered whether Ruysdael had not pioneered *plein-air* painting. In other words acquaintance with the works of these long-venerated artist-heroes seemed to confirm Vincent's sense that they, together with French painters of the Generation of 1830, provided sufficient instruction. In the face of Theo's suggestion that he look to Manet, he stuck to Hals, whom he now aligned with Delacroix among the colorists, as opposed to

the tonal tradition of "harmonists," exemplified by Rembrandt and Millet.[89]

On his return to Nuenen, Vincent responded to Theo's discussion of Manet with a picture that he painted "in *one rush*, in one day" to demonstrate the progress he had made in mastering his craft (fig. 3). He described it as a "still life of an open, thus broken white, leather-bound Bible, with a yellow brown foreground and just a hint of lemon yellow." The simple characterization suggests an exercise in form and color; in fact the picture is a manifesto. Vincent's reticence on this score is not exceptional. Though his massive correspondence brims with avowals of his intentions in and for his work, Vincent often remained silent about his deepest feelings and their expression in his art. This had been the case when, in June, he had painted an old church tower under demolition and the adjacent burial ground, with its black wood crosses (fig. 49). The subject had long interested him, as he explained to Theo: evoking the lives of the peasants who work the land that is also their final resting place, it symbolized transience and cyclical continuity. But for Vincent the meanings ran deeper, and the buried significance of this image of a religious structure in ruins surfaces only obliquely in his reference to a favorite aphorism: "'Religions pass away, God endures,' is a saying of Victor Hugo's, whom they also brought to rest recently."[90] The "also" refers to the Reverend Theodorus van Gogh, who had been buried in this same peasants' cemetery on 30 March—coincidentally, Vincent's thirty-second birthday.

Similarly invested, *Still Life with Bible and Zola's "Joie de vivre"* not only intimates the passing of the reverend's religion, but specifically takes issue with his failure to understand that for Vincent painting was a faith, and with his refusal to recognize what his son saw in modern gospels by Hugo, Michelet, and Zola. The juxtaposition of old and new gospels relates to the contrast Vincent had already drawn between good and bad sermons on dealing with life's sorrows, but goes still further. For the picture is also the artist's programmatic attempt to deploy color according to his own understanding of its capacities, so that it "expresses something in itself." That Zola's books were actually published in bindings like the one Vincent recorded does not take away from the fact that yellow—*gheel*—resonated with the misery and betrayal Vincent had endured in the aftermath of his attempt to preach in the Borinage. Following this episode, Vincent had set out to craft an identity through making art—an identity here suggestively linked with the novel via the color that became (as Gauguin would later note) his signature. In referencing Zola, whom he now understood to be a poetic romantic in realist's clothing, Vincent signaled his ambition to parallel the author's achievement in his own work, to fill a void by becoming an essentially modern artist, preaching the good sermon in a dialect that would resonate with the present age.[91]

Still Life with Bible and Zola's "Joie de vivre" announced both a new receptivity and a new resolve. Vincent started to talk of leaving Nuenen for Antwerp, where he could study the nude at art school and rejoin "the painters' world" he had abandoned; he felt sufficiently independent, thanks to ripened powers, to withstand its common intrigues. He was, in short, sufficiently secure in his own identity to risk influence:

As I have been working absolutely alone for years, I imagine that, though I want to and can learn from others, and even adopt some technical things, I shall always see with my *own eyes*, and render things originally.[92]

Within days of making this statement, Vincent was on his way to Belgium.

In the winter of 1878–79, while Vincent toiled in the Borinage and on his way to choosing life as an artist, Gauguin found himself in circumstances that, though quite different, likewise led him finally to declare himself an artist. Still working on the stock exchange, he formed a friendship with Camille Pissarro, a founding member of the Impressionist group, whom Arosa had begun to patronize in the early 1870s. In a mutually advantageous relationship, Gauguin bought work from Pissarro, who in turn gave the Sunday painter advice on art. Thanks to this new connection, in April 1879 Gauguin received a last-minute invitation to join in the Impressionists' fourth group exhibition, where he participated as lender (of three Pissarros) and exhibitor. His modest contribution—a conventional marble bust of his son Emil—was insufficient to earn him privileges of membership in the form of critical recognition or respect from other artists. In any event he was not the first amateur-collector to show with the group, and his fellow exhibitors probably valued his qualifications as patron above his skills as an artist.[93]

At the time of Gauguin's joining, the group was increasingly plagued by internal dissent; an initial idea to have the billing of the 1879 show reflect the presence of "impressionists" and "realists" within the group acknowledged the distinctions (evident to critics and core participants alike) between Monet's experiments with the decomposition of light in landscape motifs and Degas's focus on draftsmanship and urban subjects. Such diversity had not been a problem in 1874, when the group first formed; indeed it was part and parcel of its rhetoric of innovation and independence. As the decade drew to a close, however, ideological differences, exacerbated by changes in membership, complicated the issue of stylistic heterogeneity. Nonetheless the 1879 exhibition was a success.

In attaching himself to Pissarro, Gauguin found a mentor unwavering in his commit-

50
Paul Gauguin
*Apple Trees,
Hermitage, Pontoise*
1879 [W 33]
Oil on canvas
65 x 100 cm
Aargauer
Kunsthaus, Aarau,
Switzerland

ment to collective endeavors and a model of probity. However, loyalty did not prevent Pissarro from wishing the Impressionists to be more disciplined in their work—to exhibit fully realized pictures (*tableaux*) and not just the spontaneous sketches or studies (*esquisses* or *études*) that, from the outset, had made their achievement difficult to assess. Gauguin evidently bore this concern in mind as he painted under Pissarro's direct influence during the summer of 1879 in the village of Pontoise. A group of works depicting apple trees reveals his quick absorption of Pissarro's stylistic hallmarks and his readiness to acknowledge his indebtedness. Treating one of the older Impressionist's signature motifs, familiar to him from a work in his own collection, Gauguin first made a sketch from nature, to which he then referred when elaborating two larger, more finished versions in the studio (see fig. 50). They can be read as demonstration pieces, "masterpieces" in the traditional sense of skill attained in the course of an apprenticeship, and as attempts at producing an authoritative Impressionist *tableau* suitable for exhibition.[94]

Yet when Gauguin showed this and other works at the fifth Impressionist exhibition, in 1880, they met with indifference. Critics paid little attention to the experiments of a junior member, concerned instead with diagnosing the demise of Impressionism. Among the symptoms they discerned were a lack of shared vision and quantity at the expense of quality—specifically, the desertion of former leaders including Monet and Renoir and the inclusion of too many less-talented followers, such as Gauguin. When mentioned at all, Gauguin was identified as a heavy-handed recruit under Pissarro's banner. In an interview Monet himself volunteered that the original "little clique has become a great club which opens its doors to the first-come dauber."[95]

Nonetheless Gauguin persisted, at the expense, it appears, of his marriage. During the spring of 1880, Mette spent some months with her family in Copenhagen; on her return to Paris she left their firstborn, Emil, to be raised in the home of Danish friends. Gauguin proved himself even more focused on his art. He changed jobs and in the summer relocated the family to the Vaugirard district of Paris, where he sublet a house with a studio—his first. There he set to work on paintings that reveal his desire to incorporate the lessons of Impressionism in a more personal manner. The still life he entitled *Pour faire un bouquet* (*To Make a Bouquet* or *The Makings of a Bouquet*) (fig. 53) assimilates the color and brushwork of Monet and Pissarro in the service of a composition that recalls—with its abrupt croppings and exaggerated contrasts of near and far—Degas's representations of modern urban life. Fusing two different and seemingly incompatible strands of vanguard practice, Gauguin sought originality.

Gauguin played with the juxtaposition of opposites in another way in another contemporary still life, which features a wood tankard and a metal pitcher (fig. 51). A sharply defined negative space separates the markedly disparate objects, emphasizing the absence of any mediating forms, such as would be seen in a more abundant still life. Here Gauguin disrupted the genre's conventions by borrowing from another: caricature. For the sturdy

51

52

53

51
Paul Gauguin
*Wood Tankard and
Metal Pitcher*
1880 [W 47]

Oil on canvas
55 x 65 cm
The Art Institute of
Chicago,
Millennium Gift of
Sara Lee
Corporation,
1999.362
Cat. 1

52
Norwegian tankard
1740
Rootwood
H. 26 cm
Courtesy Trafalgar
Galleries, London

53
Paul Gauguin
To Make a Bouquet or
*The Makings of a
Bouquet (Pour faire un
bouquet)*
1880 [W 49]
Oil on canvas
55 x 65 cm
Private collection

Norwegian rootwood tankard appears strikingly ill-matched to the graceful if modest pitcher; the pairing is at once humorous and slightly sinister in its awkwardness and disproportion. Wittily—with seeming artlessness—the composition evokes the odd-couple narrative and, given the circumstances, may refer to the strains in Gauguin's relationship with Mette. Certainly it is provocative.[96]

The tankard and the textile (apparently North African) hanging behind it on the wall indicate—along with other fabrics, fans, ceramics, and carvings that decorated the family home—Gauguin's abiding attraction to the so-called folk arts (see fig. 52). While these items appear, prop-like, in several paintings, in sculptural experiments this interest assumed more than representational significance. Possibly, as his debut with the Impressionists suggests, Gauguin regarded sculpture as the vehicle in which his efforts would be evaluated more on their own terms, rather than in comparison with the work of the senior Impressionists, who were almost exclusively devoted to painting. Degas, currently sculpting in wax, was the notable exception. As Gauguin now pursued his own three-dimensional work, he abandoned marble, with its high-art connotations, and cannily elected to work in wood, a medium bypassed by Degas. He later claimed to have carved in his youth, and presumably during his years on board ship, he would have been exposed to sailors' whittling.[97]

Carvings such as *Woman Strolling* (figs. 54–55) clearly allude to Degas prototypes, but Gauguin's deliberately rough execution and choice of homely material constitute an overt challenge to notions of finish, as if in defiant misconstrual of the debate about Impressionist painterly practice as lacking in rigor. Degas had been the model for adopting an unorthodox medium; Pissarro provided an example of conscious simplification, derived in part from study of the "primitives"—a blanket category embracing the art of the early Italian and Northern schools as well as Egyptian and Gothic sculpture.[98] These very terms emerged in critical responses to Gauguin's latest work, shown in 1881 at the sixth Impressionist exhibition: one writer likened *Woman Strolling* to the "elegant figures in Egyptian frescoes and papyrus paintings"; another called the same piece "gothically modern."[99]

Finally achieving some individual recognition, Gauguin had also gained insight into the shaky dynamics of the group on which his identity as a painter depended. During the show's planning, bitter internal debates arose around newcomers invited by Degas. Caillebotte tried to persuade Pissarro to join him in keeping their group "exclusively artistic," by which he meant rejecting Degas's crowd. Unsuccessful in imposing this standard, Caillebotte withdrew, and Gauguin ended up assisting Degas with the organization of the exhibition. Featuring Degas's *Little Fourteen-Year-Old Dancer* together with work by his perceived adherents, the show raised—more explicitly than ever before—the question of the connection between vanguard painters and the writers of the Naturalist school, led by Zola.

As Gauguin recognized, the perception of such a link threatened to taint a self-consciously independent pictorial agenda with literary bias. This he considered dangerous. "Impressionism" was gaining a mythic currency, the successive exhibitions cumulatively serving to establish it as a "movement" within the evolution of modern styles. Its original leaders, supported by sympathetic professional art critics and by dealers specializing in contemporary painting, were gaining in influence and reputation. Gauguin, who had yet to make his name and was increasingly intent on doing so, felt vulnerable to any attack on the group endeavor, and in particular did not want to be associated with a descriptive Naturalism.[100]

Actively involving himself in art-world politics, Gauguin took to proprietarily talking of protecting "our movement" and "our future." Somewhat riskily (given his still-marginal status), he voiced the opinion that Monet and Sisley were flooding the market with sketches at a moment when the Impressionists should be demonstrating their ability to realize *tableaux*, and he accused senior members, their reputations made, of selfish disregard for the fate of their juniors. Yet at the same time, he did not wish to be categorized with the newest members, whom he felt diluted the group's message of independence. In 1882, when plans for a seventh exhibition again stalled over a Degas recruit, Gauguin grandiloquently tendered his resignation to Pissarro.[101]

Others would have been only too happy to see him disappear. Monet and Renoir found Gauguin's manner aggressive and his behavior dictatorial and presumptuous, given that his talent did not qualify him for inclusion in Monet's idea of an exhibition "entre nous" (among us), featuring artists of equal talent (Durand-Ruel's recent purchase of two pictures by Gauguin notwithstanding).[102] Monet's and Renoir's elitism was firmly rooted in economic considerations—they feared that showing with lesser lights would exacerbate a market position already compromised by the stock-market crash of January 1882. Pissarro's firm democratic stance saved Gauguin from being excluded on these grounds, but Gauguin in turn rationalized his own continued opposition to some of Degas's followers.

Ultimately Degas withdrew from the 1882 exhibition, and Gauguin was widely blamed

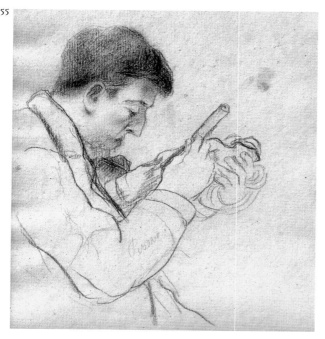

for the absence of one of the group's founding masters (Monet, like Renoir, appeared solely through the machinations of Durand-Ruel). Reviews characterized Gauguin as pretentious, the "independent who has the most to do to earn his name." Even more damagingly, critics stated that his work had failed to advance—a very serious charge in the current climate. The critics who called for more rigorous progress and individual authenticity were in tacit complicity with of commercial realities. The recession had placed new demands on all interested parties: recently established artists sought to safeguard their status by showing in flashy new venues such as Georges Petit's gallery; Durand-Ruel, who had helped to establish these artists' reputations, sustained them through the innovation of the one-person retrospective exhibition.[103]

The eighteen months following the April 1882 closing of the seventh Impressionist exhibition were difficult for Gauguin. Approaching thirty-five, he faced a dilemma. He was increasingly frustrated to find himself still confined to the position of amateur painter, knowing full well that the greats had started young and devoted all their resources to art; he was unable to follow the advice he gave Pissarro, to work more in the studio and attempt more *tableaux*. He could, however, still add to his collection of pictures by Cézanne, an artist whom (as he explained to Pissarro) he admired for the forceful construction of his works, a remarkable and fully developed example of which Gauguin already owned (fig. 57). Correspondingly, his attention to his job at the stock exchange flagged at precisely the moment when the sluggish market put his financial future in serious jeopardy.[104] This internal conflict was enmeshed with those he confronted in the art world.

Though he professed his dedication to "preaching" the gospel of Impressionism, Gauguin

54
Paul Gauguin
Woman Strolling
1880 [G 4]
Tropical laurel,
stained red and black
H. 25 cm
Private collection

55
Camille Pissarro
(Danish; 1831–1903)
*Paul Gauguin Carving
"Woman Strolling"*
1880
Black chalk on paper
29.5 x 23.3 cm
Nationalmuseum,
Stockholm

56
Photograph of Paul
and Mette Gauguin
in Copenhagen
1885
Musée
Départemental
Maurice Denis, Le
Prieuré, Saint-
Germain-en-Laye

57
Paul Cézanne
(French; 1839–1906)
*Still Life with Bowl,
Glass, Knife, Apples,
and Grapes*
c. 1880
Oil on canvas
46 x 55 cm
Private collection

was not included in the inner circle's communal dinners. As the spirit of group endeavor
eroded on all sides, senior figures looked to new
venues and solo careers—Monet, Renoir, Sisley,
and Pissarro all had one-man shows in 1883—
and even junior players took a stand against a
shared style and argued for personal vision as
the hallmark of true art. Gauguin recognized
that without the stage provided by the Impressionist exhibitions, it would be very difficult
to build a reputation through continued demonstration of progress.[105]

By the fall of 1883, Gauguin's increasingly desperate efforts to organize an eighth group
exhibition met with little enthusiasm, even
from Pissarro, and with outright hostility from
Monet and Renoir. To make matters worse,
it was clear that he would soon be losing his job,
had no prospects for another, and felt little
motivation to find one. The decision had been

made for him: he would become a painter. The
prospect of having to make a living as a full-
time artist lent even more urgency to his analysis of the market, leading him to take the
hasty and ill-considered step of leaving Paris
for Rouen. His expectation of finding ready
patronage among the bourgeois of the provinces quickly proved false. His financial straits
becoming desperate, Gauguin sold paintings
from his collection (retaining his treasured
Cézanne), cashed in his life-insurance policy,
and hatched fruitless schemes involving colleagues and dealers. Fed up, Mette returned
with the children to Denmark, where her
proficiency in French allowed her to earn an
income as a teacher and translator.

Gauguin now had the time to be more productive, but his work had suffered as a result of
his obsession with selling. Pissarro bluntly said
as much, and Gauguin accepted the criticism.

In a sketchbook purchased in Rouen, he outlined his conception of art under the rubric
"Notes synthétiques." Gauguin's idea of an
art of synthesis, linked to his conversations
with Pissarro and admiration of Cézanne,
implied opposition to the analysis of light and
atmosphere practiced by Monet. These terms
would, in the coming years, accrue much
more specific aesthetic and formal connotations than Gauguin was yet capable of articulating, let alone demonstrating pictorially.
Nevertheless the "Notes synthétiques" contain some ambitious claims, using piecemeal
references to current theories such as those of
Delacroix and Blanc. Conceived as a traditional
paragone, or comparison of the various arts,
the text defends painting over music and literature through an incomplete exploration of
analogies that Gauguin would mobilize more
coherently years later. The "Notes synthétiques" do clearly reveal Gauguin's predisposi-

58
Paul Gauguin
Sleeping Child
1884 [W 81]
Oil on canvas
46 x 55.5 cm
Private collection

59
Paul Gauguin
Decorated Wooden Box
1884 [G 8]
Pearwood, stained
red, with iron, leather,
and inlaid wood *netsuke*
H. 32 cm
Uno Wallmann

60
"Graves with human
remains and various
objects" from
Alexandre Brongniart,
*Traité des arts
céramiques* (Paris,
1877), pl. 2, figs. 1 and 3

58

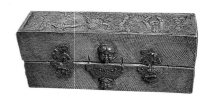

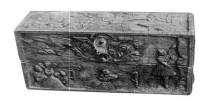

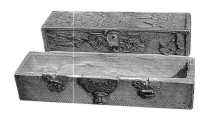

59

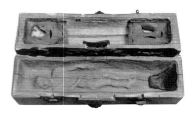

60

tion both to theorize and to hold forth; however, the word was in advance of the deed.[106]

Recognizing that his attempt to produce works expressly for the market had been a failure, Gauguin now determined to paint less hastily and more searchingly. His stated goal: to learn to know himself and find out "how far one can go." This resolution can be seen in several works of 1884, including a bizarre double portrait of his son Clovis and the Norwegian tankard (fig. 58). The disproportionate scale of the sleeping child and the object he appears to grasp, together with the indeterminate setting, conspires to create a mysterious atmosphere enhanced by the background, a blue field scattered with bird motifs that could be a wallpaper pattern but suggests a dream state. In this image personal symbolism looms large. The tankard's dominant form and emphatic relationship to the child—seen in the context of the earlier and later still lifes in which the same object appears (see figs. 4, 51)—point to its metaphoric function as surrogate for the artist, a crafted rather than human presence.[107]

Gauguin's identification with this roughly hewn object is of a piece with the sculptural impulse that had led to *Woman Strolling* and, in 1884, to a strange and perplexing carved box (fig. 59). In terms of its possible function, the object can be compared to containers such as sewing cases, tobacco boxes, and seamen's chests. Its iconography presents still other possibilities. The motifs on the front and top derive from Degas's images of the ballet and café-concert, while the back features, beside the box's hinges, two inlaid Japanese *netsuke* representing the goddess of mirth. Their proximity suggests Impressionism's indebtedness to these foreign muses, still categorized as primitive. In the vein of *vanitas* imagery, however, the sophisticated, playful exterior conceals grim evidence of human mortality, for the box—in fact a coffin—contains a prostrate

figure, inspired by a recent publication on the history of ceramics (see fig. 60).

The box's juxtapositions are provocative but obscure. With the theme of laughing on the outside while dying on the inside, the artist may have intended a statement about his professional and personal situation—a statement he could perhaps formulate only in the medium of sculpture, which allowed him access to distant cultures and folk traditions. For despite his strenuous defense of painting in the "Notes synthétiques," Gauguin remained inhibited by the presence of competing vanguard models and by the increasingly ill-defined expectations associated with "high art." In this admittedly unresolved carving, Gauguin took steps outside the European tradition to attempt the kind of cross-cultural assemblage that would eventually, through artistic experimentation and intellectual interrogation, become his hallmark.

Still far from capitalizing on these nascent innovations, Gauguin could not yet chart his own course. In the fall of 1884, he took a job as a salesman on commission with a Roubaix-based canvas-manufacturing firm, Dillies et Cie; assigned Denmark as his territory, doubtless at his request though he did not speak the language, he prepared to rejoin his family. The ambition and naïve optimism he brought to Scandinavia only made the reality harder to accept. Though Mette had connections in the local art community, Gauguin disdained its conservatism and blamed this provincial mindset for his inability to sell either the canvases he painted or those of the firm that employed him.

Hungry for news of Paris, he kept in touch with Pissarro, fellow Impressionist Armand Guillaumin, and an amateur painter he knew from his early days at the stock exchange, Émile Schuffenecker. Pissarro continued to play the role of mentor to Gauguin, who

welcomed the older artist's critique of recent work and began his sojourn in Copenhagen attempting to achieve greater luminosity and simplicity by following his advice. Schuffenecker served as an audience, allowing Gauguin to rehearse his theoretical musings on the nature of visual experience; informed by a heady mixture of aesthetic and graphological theories, he pondered how color, line, and form convey complex information and stimulate emotional response.[108] As in the "Notes synthétiques," however, ambition continued to outstrip achievement.

By January 1885 the future looked bleak. But Gauguin demurred when Schuffenecker proposed that he join him in sending work to the second exhibition held by the Groupe des Artistes Indépendants, which had formed the previous year. His reservations centered around the inclusiveness of the Indépendants—its membership was totally open and its exhibitions unjuried—and its pragmatic refusal to define any unifying aesthetic goals. Gauguin saw that he had little to gain and much to lose by walking onto this particular stage. In the wildly democratic environment of the Indépendants, where he would be surrounded by hundreds of aspirants, he risked such status as he had achieved during the past six years by riding Pissarro's coattails.

Durand-Ruel's involvement in the formation of a Société de Saint Luc, named after the patron saint of painters, struck Gauguin as ironic, given the fact that the dealer had conceived it as a venue for educating amateurs and potential clients while refusing to help artists like Gauguin himself. So from a distance, Gauguin continued to lobby Pissarro, declaiming on the evils of the Impressionists' favoring personality and privilege over cohesion, and suggesting that they make places at their exclusive dinners for juniors of less experience but comparable faith. His reference to his own "republican philosophy,"

61
Paul Gauguin
Self-Portrait at the Easel
c. 1 May 1885 [W138]
Oil on canvas
65.2 x 54.3 cm

Kimbell Art
Museum, Fort
Worth, Texas
Cat. 2

couched in the rhetoric of his more politically astute mentor, was clearly calculated to mask self-interest, but his confident façade sometimes revealed fissures, as when he admitted to embarrassment at offering himself like a whore to the market and finding no takers.[109]

Gauguin's deteriorating domestic situation intensified his feelings of alienation. In May 1885 he confided to Schuffenecker that he had endured total isolation for months. Mette was angry, reproachful about his painting, and ashamed by the change in their standard of living. In the eyes of her family and friends, Gauguin was a monster whose wife put bread on the table while he played at art. He now realized that he could no longer balance painting and working at something else. At around this same time, he told Pissarro that were it not for his art, he would go up to the attic and hang himself.[110]

In a somber self-portrait, probably painted only weeks earlier, Gauguin represented himself as a painter in a garret, seated, brush in hand, before his easel, uncertainly scrutinizing his image in the mirror (fig. 61).[111] The handling, like the gaze, is tentative; the hand grasping the brush appears atrophied. This, the first self-portrait he had essayed in eight years, stands in marked contrast to its predecessor (fig. 34). Here Gauguin assertively displays the tools that proclaim his professional identity, but he wears a less complacent expression. An aura of anxiety results from the way the light falls, dividing the face; and from the impossibly shallow, claustrophobic space in which the painter—sandwiched between the wooden beam and chair back on one side, and the canvas stretcher and easel on the other—seems scarcely able to move. The attic setting is a staple element in the romantic image of the suffering artist, but Gauguin's depiction is a literal one: he worked in the

attic of a Copenhagen apartment building, a stranger in a foreign city, practicing his craft while members of the family below condemned him for not earning money. In such circumstances the portrait was an act of defiance and resolve.

Emotional distance and competing commitments are expressed differently—less melodramatically and more innovatively—in Gauguin's *Still Life in an Interior* (fig. 4). The artist provided a suggestive gloss for this picture in a May letter to Pissarro. Committing himself to the use of purposeful exaggeration in his art, Gauguin argued that "salvation lies only in the extreme." This was the seed of the new identity he was forging, intimated in his unusual still life and enacted in June. At that point he left Copenhagen, taking his son Clovis with him, and returned to Paris.[112]

468. PARIS — Boulev
vu à vol d'oiseau

1
Paris, c. 1900. The broad streets of this chic, right-bank district—the *grands boulevards*—were lined with financial institutions, shops, restaurants, and high-end art galleries.

a Boussod, Valadon et Cie, no. 19, boulevard Montmartre (managed by Theo van Gogh from early 1881)

Gauguin and the Last Impressionist Exhibition

Gauguin returned to France from Denmark in June 1885, accompanied by his six-year-old son, Clovis. Leaving the boy with his sister, Marie, Gauguin went to Dieppe, the seaside resort on the Normandy coast, where he stayed through the fall. If he hoped to be invited to join the coterie of well-heeled artists—Degas among them—who summered there, he was disappointed. Paying the price for fomenting the intrigues that had provoked Degas to withdraw from the 1882 Impressionist exhibition, Gauguin received the cold shoulder.[1] Left to himself, he painted coastal scenes of boats and bathers as well as landscapes of the hinterland (see fig. 2).

In August he made a brief trip to London, to the headquarters of the exiled Manuel-Ruiz Zorrilla, a former prime minister under the Spanish monarchy now intent on republican revolution. Two years earlier, when Zorrilla's organization was based in Paris, Gauguin had undertaken a secret mission on its behalf to northern Spain. Now as then, his motives were mixed: through his mother and Arosa, he had longstanding Spanish allegiances; he relished the cloak-and-dagger secrecy; and he hoped that he might come out of it with a little money.[2] His politics were more revolutionary than his painting, but with similarly inconsequential results.

Money was now an enormous problem. Returning to Paris in early October, Gauguin rented an apartment and brought Clovis to live with him. By December the situation had deteriorated. Durand-Ruel was unwilling or unable to offer support, his paintings were rejected at a Danish exhibition, and Clovis contracted smallpox. Gauguin, having sought employment at the Bourse (stock exchange) in vain, was forced to take a job working for the railroads, first as a poster hanger, then as an inspector, and finally as an administrative secretary. The art market, deadened by an ongoing economic slump, offered no prospects

for sales. But there was a beacon on the horizon, as Gauguin informed Mette just after Christmas:

In March we will put on a very comprehensive exhibition with the new impressionists who have talent…. This exhibition will probably cause a great uproar; perhaps it will be the starting point of our success.[3]

The show in question was the eighth in the series of Impressionist group initiatives and the first essayed since 1882. Organized by senior figures Pissarro and Degas, it would indeed be a turning point—but Gauguin could not have been more wrong about its impact on his own career.

Enormous changes had taken place in the art world during the twelve years since the first, groundbreaking Impressionist exhibition of 1874, as Degas acknowledged in the conditions he set for participating in the 1886 event. His old rule—that no one who displayed work in the Impressionist exhibition could appear in the Salon—still applied, but a new rule also prohibited participants from sending work to the exhibition of a dealer.[4] The rhetoric of inde-

pendence formerly guaranteed by taking distance from state-sponsored institutions now required an equidistant positioning vis-à-vis influential dealers such as Petit and Durand-Ruel, who—with their speculative strategies and marketing of reputations through exhibitions, retrospectives, publications, and public relations—had altered the market's structure and power relations.

In any event the independent Impressionism still imagined by Degas and Pissarro was by now an illusion. Although most of the veteran exhibitors supported the project of an eighth group exhibition at one point or another in the fall of 1885, by November Monet had accepted Petit's invitation to participate in his International Exhibition of 1886 on the condition that he would not take part in an Impressionist exhibition, should one take place. Renoir joined him, and Sisley too absented himself from the exhibition that opened in May 1886. Moreover, all three of these core Impressionists—plus Morisot, a disillusioned but desperate Pissarro, and other artists including Whistler—would appear in Petit's 1887 International Exhibition. This commercial venture outdid the 1886 independent show insofar as it constituted the most representative display of Impressionist painting mounted in the capital in five years. The group's identity, and the rhetoric of revolution and independence associated with it, had been breached.

The expansion of the ranks had the effect of blurring distinctions between the founding Impressionists and those artists who absorbed (through affinity or expediency) their innovations to invest their otherwise conservative, palatable art with an up-to-date cachet. Increasingly, "impressionist" was a lowercase term, lacking in descriptive specificity and used expansively to designate a wide range of modernist practice—whether that of Monet, Whistler, or Jean-Charles Cazin. At the same time, Impressionism was entering the ranks of history. The 1886 group exhibition—the

last "independent" venture—marked its passing.

But it also signaled the emergence of something new, as seen in the works of the "new impressionists" to whom Gauguin referred in his letter to Mette. Georges Seurat and Paul Signac, sponsored (like Gauguin) by Pissarro, came from the ranks of the recently formed Société des Artistes Indépendants (see ch. 1), as did fellow newcomer Odilon Redon. Guillaumin, the only veteran Impressionist to join the Indépendants, had introduced Pissarro to Seurat in October 1885, with immediate consequences. So taken was Pissarro with the younger artist's ideas and scientific technique of color juxtaposition that he was immediately converted to the method of applying unmixed dabs of color and persuaded his

son Lucien and Signac to adopt it as well.[5] Pissarro lobbied early and successfully with Degas for the inclusion of Seurat and Signac in the 1886 exhibition. But in early May, he engaged in a dispute with Morisot's husband (Édouard Manet's brother, Eugène), whom he believed echoed the opinion of the Impressionists now aligned with Petit, over the new technique exemplified in Seurat's *Sunday on La Grande Jatte—1884* (fig. 3) and in large canvases by Pissarro (see fig. 4) and Signac. Pissarro vigorously defended Seurat's radical picture of modern leisure. With its distinctive application of paint and hieratic figures, he believed that it represented progress—stylistic innovation supported by scientific and theoretical acumen—that the older Impressionists had a vested interest in opposing.

3

4

2
Paul Gauguin
Resting Cows
1885 [W 160]
Oil on canvas
64 x 80 cm
Boymans-
van Beuningen
Museum,
Rotterdam

3
Georges Seurat
(French; 1859–1891)
*A Sunday on La
Grande Jatte—1884*
1884–86
Oil on canvas
207.6 x 308 cm
The Art Institute
of Chicago,
Helen Birch Bartlett
Collection, 1926.224

4
Camille Pissarro
(Danish; 1831–1903)
Apple Picking
1882–86
Oil on canvas
128 x 128 cm
Ohara Museum
of Art,
Kuranshiki, Japan

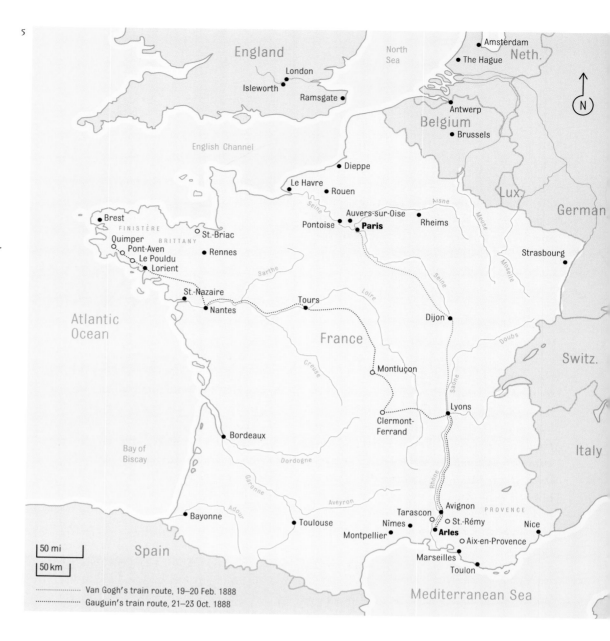

5

The exhibition did not attempt to reconcile the dueling camps: the practitioners of Seurat's technique shared a room by themselves, apart from the larger space of the gallery. The partition had long-term implications as well. Amid the fragmentation of the Impressionist enterprise, a distinct new direction announced itself. Within weeks of the 15 May opening, it was clear to some that the Impressionists had successors. While established critics focused on Degas's pastel series of nudes as the show's controversial centerpiece, younger writers who were affiliated with more marginal, progressive publications saw the *Grande Jatte* as initiating a new direction in art and criticism.

In June Félix Fénéon, an art critic and clerk at the war ministry, published a review in the Symbolist periodical *La Vogue* outlining the issues that would inform subsequent debate. His argument, despite its complex presentation and use of mathematical equations, was simple: the Impressionists conveyed luminosity by intuitively decomposing color, while the new group achieved the same end more successfully and less arbitrarily with a technique based on the science of optical mixture—instead of combining pigments on the palette, they applied small touches of pure color that mix in the eye. This scientifically justified technique seemed, in Fénéon's and Pissarro's view, to be the culmination of Impressionism.[6]

Coincident with the emergence of the Neo-Impressionists (as Fénéon baptized them in fall 1886) was Zola's version of the story of Impressionism, *L'Oeuvre*, an art world roman à clef.[7] Conflating two different landmark events in the recent history of vanguard painting—the 1863 Salon des Refusés, where Manet had displayed his notorious *Déjeuner sur l'herbe* (1863; Musée d'Orsay, Paris), and the 1874 inaugural Impressionist exhibition—Zola presented an assessment of the contemporary vanguard scene consis-

tent with the views he had expressed as an art critic during the previous two decades. Though an early defender of Manet, since the 1860s Zola had deplored the fact that the "new school of painting" represented by Manet and his followers had yet to produce a "genius," had yet to yield a "masterpiece" that could measure up to the achievements of a Delacroix or an Ingres. While gifted analysts of visual experience, they had not progressed to an art of ideas; they produced an endless series of preliminary studies (*études*) but deferred tackling the full-fledged picture (*tableau*). Against the backdrop of a rapidly changing art world in which reputations were made overnight rather than earned over a lifetime, Zola introduced a series of characters representing a spectrum of interests and positions. At the story's center is Claude Lantier, a pioneering genius of *plein-air*

painting. His work, though ridiculed in the marketplace, is pillaged by less scrupulous painters who, supported by equally opportunistic dealers, convert innovation into commercial success. Unable to follow through on his initial discoveries with a conclusive statement, Claude loses his way and perishes. Though the venal marketplace contributes to Claude's downfall, Zola located the true cause elsewhere. The "stain" of Romanticism—the lingering hold of imaginative subjectivity—rendered Claude's generation constitutionally incapable of pursuing the implications of their daring experiments to their logical conclusion. Claude had initiated a "passion for reality pushed to the point of scientific analysis," but it had been checked in its evolution because the man to bring it forward had yet to be born.[8]

L'Oeuvre caused a sensation in the art world; everyone saw himself portrayed in its pages, and not positively. Monet and Manet were mentioned in connection with Claude; Cézanne, offended by a perceived resemblance, broke with Zola, his childhood friend.[9] Even those too junior to have possibly served as models felt implicated. The responses of Theo van Gogh, Gauguin, and eighteen-year-old art student Émile Bernard (soon to become a close friend of Vincent and, subsequently, of Gauguin) sound three of the various chords that the novel struck.

Though only six at the time of the first Impressionist exhibition, Bernard—who, employing the new terminological equivalence to signal his vanguard ambitions, styled himself a "moderniste impressionniste"—had by July 1886 read *L'Oeuvre* three or four times. He took its message to heart, characterizing the challenge he faced as that of realizing "the modern" when one is "steeped in romanticism."[10] Theo, when he first heard of the book, imagined (perhaps apprehensively) that his brother Vincent had much in common with the hero. Upon reading it he concluded otherwise: Claude "was looking for the unattainable, while Vincent loves the *things that exist* far too much to fall for *that*."[11] Gauguin, for his part, immediately had to confront the personal implications of Zola's indictment of Impressionism's misplaced ambitions, self-deception, and failure. Back in Copenhagen, Mette had taken on the assignment of translating *L'Oeuvre* for serialization in the prominent newspaper *Politiken*. In a letter of late June, Gauguin expressed his chagrin at Mette's involvement in what he called Zola's "worst book from every point of view."[12] By then it was painfully clear that the last Impressionist exhibition had not yielded the success he had counted on, making it all the more likely that Mette and her family would connect him with the protagonist who sacrificed his wife and family for art with disastrous results.

The few comments that Gauguin's canvases provoked were devastating. Despite his past association with the group, he was frequently misidentifed as a newcomer; his work was deemed pale in comparison to Guillaumin's, evidencing shortcomings and riven by diverse influences.[13] For mainstream critics his newcomer status was that of apprentice rather than innovator. Though Fénéon identified Gauguin as an old hand—a representative of "Impressionism as it has been interpreted in prior exhibitions"—he did not number him among the leaders of the original Impressionist revolution. Certainly with his "oppressive atmosphere" and "muted harmonies," Gauguin did not figure among the leaders of the new revolution, who achieved luminosity with a scientific approach and more dispassionate application.[14] Doubly marginalized as a new follower of an old movement and a non-follower in a new movement that would soon discredit its forebears, Gauguin risked being written out of the evolving vanguard scenario.

In that scenario Neo-Impressionism seemed to provide a new chapter, and a happier ending, to *L'Oeuvre*. Seurat boldly declined to produce mere *plein-air études*, instead realizing highly mediated *tableaux* in the studio. His *Grande Jatte* seemed to satisfy Zola's call for a masterpiece. Advocates of Neo-Impressionism hailed the movement for overcoming the insufficiencies of Impressionism by privileging science over subjectivity, artistic conception over bravura brushwork, synthesis over analysis. Even before the exhibition's opening, Pissarro, in the context of discussions of *L'Oeuvre*, attributed the Impressionists' failure to appreciate the progress represented by Seurat to their romantic bias.[15] By the fall Pissarro had formulated a distinction between *romantic* and *scientific* impressionism, using language that implicitly set a retrograde, emotional, unsystematic movement against a progressive, rational, theoretical one.

Gauguin shared Pissarro's and Zola's view that Impressionism had become overly invested in the sketch (see ch. 1); he had recognized the problem but had not devised a solution. Now he found himself at a crossroads. He had been friendly enough with Seurat that winter to share with him a text that treats the importance of painting from memory after grounding oneself in the study of nature, endorses the silhouetting of figures, and encourages the painter to be more concerned with harmony than with contrast. Attributed to a Persian aesthetician, this work has recently been posited as Gauguin's own fabrication.[16] It is nonetheless difficult to assess his opinion of Seurat's art. Gauguin's love of Cézanne's deeper intuition—his "mysterious *écriture*" that transcends rationality—suggests his temperamental disinclination to experiment with Neo-Impressionism. (Only in 1889 would he essay the technique he disparaged as "petit point" in a still life, and then as a joke sign the diminutive composition "Ripipoint.")[17]

Gauguin's reservations were practical as well. The prospect of reprising the role he had played since the mid-1870s—accompanying Pissarro as he in turn followed a new leader—promised only further deferral of success, which he could ill afford. Now relying on a career in painting, at age thirty-eight and with a reputation still to make, Gauguin could not risk embracing pointillism. Instead he determined to find a style of his own. The impetus that Seurat had not provided would come from an unlikely quarter: the van Gogh brothers.

Vincent arrived in Paris just weeks before the opening of the 1886 Impressionist exhibition. The previous three months, spent in Antwerp, had been brutally difficult—his letters to Theo tell of his grinding poverty and physical exhaustion—but adversity did not check the drive to advance his art that had prompted him to leave Nuenen. In Antwerp Vincent visited museums, made the rounds of galleries, spent some weeks in an academic studio, and went to dance halls in search of modern subjects. All of these activities fueled his ambition to improve his figure drawing and to concentrate on color—and to do so in dialogue with other artists. Although his experience in the institutional setting of Antwerp's academy had its frustrations, Vincent relished the interaction after almost two years of isolation and unspoken reproach in Nuenen: "I find here the friction [*wrijving*] of ideas I want," he stated to Theo. "I get a fresh look at my own work, can judge better what the weak points are, which enables me to correct them."[18]

Stimulating though he found Antwerp, Vincent soon set his sights higher. In letters from January 1886 onward, he discussed the possibility of going to Paris. He was seemingly encouraged, up to a point, by Theo, who was anxious about his brother's deteriorating health but who suggested waiting until the summer, when his own financial circumstances might enable a move to a larger apartment. Vincent cared little for such practical considerations. From a vague possibility, the idea soon took on the shape of a full-fledged scheme, at the center of which was a studio that he imagined setting up with Theo—a meeting-place for artists that would be a sort of sanctuary from and alternative to the hostile environments of the academy and the marketplace.

Vincent strove to maintain realistic expectations; his current immersion in Naturalist literature, as well as his own desperate circumstances, taught him that city life was far from easy. He predicted that he and Theo might have some difficulties living together, and he knew that artists could be petty and competitive. But filled with determination to make his way in an art world that even he could see was undergoing a transformation, he once again became fixed on the idea of joining hands with his brother and with fellow artists: "It is such a splendid idea that, working and thinking together. And every day I

6
Rembrandt van Rijn (Dutch; 1606–1669)
Self-Portrait in Front of the Easel
1660
Oil on canvas
111 x 85 cm
Musée du Louvre, Paris

7
Vincent van Gogh
Self-Portrait with Dark Felt Hat at the Easel
Spring 1886
[F 181, JH 1090]
Oil on canvas
46.5 x 38.5 cm
Van Gogh Museum, Amsterdam (Vincent van Gogh Foundation)
Cat. 8

8
Color star from Charles Blanc, *Grammaire des arts du dessin: Architecture, sculpture, peinture* (Paris, 1867), p. 598

find new proof of the theory that the main reason for much misery among the artists lies in their discord, in their not cooperating, not being good but false to each other."[19] Paris would confirm this observation, but it would also crystallize the dream.

When his hints, and then harangues, had prompted no definite invitation from Theo by the end of February, Vincent took action. He arrived in Paris, unexpectedly, at the beginning of March, sending Theo a note at Boussod et Valadon (the name since 1884 of Goupil's) telling him that he would be waiting at the Louvre's Salon Carré, near the gallery featuring Delacroix's celebrated Apollo ceiling. A self-portrait painted soon after his arrival (fig. 7) reveals the resolve that had brought him to the capital, and something of the dilemma he faced. Despite his ambition to be a figure painter and his chronic need for models, never before had Vincent taken the expedient course of painting his own image. He now did so, fully aware of the symbolic import of his act. He appears as a working professional, standing before an easel with pigment-laden palette in hand. His somewhat formal jacket, tie, and dark felt hat bear little resemblance to the stained worker's clothes and general dishevelment that had made him an object of ridicule and criticism in the past.[20]

The change of clothes corresponded to a shift in attitude. Vincent's readiness to accept his "mistakes" had brought him from the country he knew to the city, where he put aside his habitual insistence that the world accept him as he was and took a hard look at himself. What he saw was a man who appeared as if he had been in prison for ten years, his bad teeth and careworn aspect making him look much older than he was. Theo soon reported that Vincent was so changed his mother would not recognize him: he had purchased new clothes, trimmed his beard, and visited a dentist. This overhaul reflected his new sense of identity grounded in his profession and a new belief in his real potential "to produce and to be something."[21]

In the self-portrait he visualized this identity, and he set his sights high, as is evident in his choice of model: Rembrandt's celebrated self-portrait at the easel (fig. 6), which hung in the Louvre together with the "Lacaze Rembrandt" (ch. 4, fig. 136), which had remained a vivid memory from his Paris stay twelve years earlier.[22] By adopting the Dutch painter's moody, tonal palette along with his composition, Vincent, though aspiring to the colorism of Delacroix, acknowledged his continuing admiration for the great harmonists, among whom he also included Millet and the Hague School painters. These affinities in turn conditioned his initial experience of the vanguard Parisian art that he knew only through Theo's descriptions.

Within weeks of his arrival, he had the opportunity—at the eighth Impressionist exhibition and at Petit's fifth International Exhibition—to encounter the spectrum of current styles, from Monet's to Seurat's. Thus confronted simultaneously with "romantic" and "scientific" impressionism, Vincent would absorb them all at once in a way that a seasoned veteran like Gauguin could not. Impressionism

in any event was not what Vincent had imagined. He later admitted, in a letter to Horace M. Livens, an English painter whom he had befriended in Antwerp, that prior to his arrival in Paris, he had not known what it was, going on to assure Livens that the terms in which the two of them had discussed developing their color differed from vanguard theories. Later still, he would recall how "bitterly, bitterly disappointed" he had been on his initial exposure to the progressive French style: influenced as he was by the ideas of Anton Mauve and Josef Israëls, he found it "slovenly, ugly, badly painted, badly drawn, bad in color, everything that's miserable." Over the course of his first year in Paris, Vincent came to terms with Impressionism (and Neo-Impressionism), but when he professed sincere admiration to Livens for Degas's nudes and Monet's landscapes, he provisionally spoke as one who was not yet a member of that "club."[23]

Vincent also reported to Livens that he had completed several months of study at the Atelier Libre (Free Studio) run by Salon painter Fernand Cormon. George Breitner, an acquaintance from The Hague, had studied there, and Theo had also heard positive reports about the professor and his students. Despite Cormon's reputation for tolerance, Vincent found, as in Antwerp, the programmatic courses in drawing and working after plaster casts less useful than anticipated. Though he soon abandoned the atelier to work alone, he was not isolated, for he had formed friendships with several young painters at Cormon's, including Henri de Toulouse-Lautrec, Louis Anquetin, Frank Boggs, A. S. Hartrick, and Bernard, the last of whom, at eighteen, was just over half Vincent's age (thirty-three). With his new colleagues, Vincent visited dealers and exhibitions and exchanged works, assembling the beginnings of what Theo considered a fine collection. According to Theo, Vincent got along with his fellow artists, regularly visiting the studios of well-known painters and receiving their visits in turn at the larger apartment the brothers now occupied in Montmartre. While he had yet to sell a work, a dealer had taken four pictures on consignment, and there was talk of an exhibition in the coming year.[24]

The tremendous progress that Theo reported by early summer was the result of what Vincent termed a rigorous regime of gymnastics, according to which he exercised his ability to "render *intense* colour and not a *grey* harmony" through floral still lifes.[25] He based his commitment to color not on the Impressionists' example but rather on that of Adolphe Monticelli, the recently deceased Marseilles painter whose richly colored, thickly painted still lifes (see fig. 10) and *scènes galantes* Theo started to buy for Boussod et Valadon and for himself. Such works by Monticelli may indeed have resembled what Vincent had imagined Impressionism to be. Building as they did on the achievement of an artist he admired, Barbizon master Narcisse Diaz, they could be situated in the lineage linking the Generation of 1830 with the present. Vincent's *Bowl with Zinnias and Other Flowers* (fig. 9), with its similar arrangement

of pale blue, red, yellow, orange, and predominantly white flowers set against a greenish ground, is one of several canvases that take their cue directly from the Monticelli still life the brothers owned. The subtle color, varied brushwork, and highly textural surface—the blossoms seem almost sculpted with paint—bespeak a confidence that is also reflected in Vincent's prominent signature; while he conceived these still lifes as experiments, he nonetheless believed that the more ambitious examples might be marketable.[26]

Another still life, painted somewhat later in the summer and featuring sunflowers and roses in the same green ceramic bowl (fig. 11), shows Vincent's aim, articulated by Theo, to realize more lively color in each successive picture.[27] A bold essay in the contrast of complementaries—the predominant greens and reds of the vase and background are relieved by the whites of the roses and enlivened by the orange-yellow sunflower petals—the painting also displays more lively brushwork; the loosely applied, broad strokes introduce a sense of movement and a suggestion of urgency, particularly in the rising forms of the harried sunflowers.

These flowers grew in Vincent's new neighborhood (see fig. 14) at the city's northern edge adjacent to the hilly landscape of the Butte Montmartre. The area was dotted with abandoned limestone and chalk quarries, kitchen gardens, and three surviving windmills—traces of the quickly receding rural past that Georges Michel had painted between the 1810s and 1830s (see ch. 1, fig. 44). Vincent had cherished the proximity of town and country in Brabant and in The Hague, and in Montmartre he could still see the countryside virtually across the street (see fig. 12). He soon began to execute *plein-air* studies of the Butte, in which the brushwork recalls Michel, as does the palette of earth tones also seen in the work of the Hague School artists and characteristic of Vincent's Dutch period. The color manifest in Vincent's floral still lifes had yet to infuse his landscapes. Painted late in the year, *Terrace and Observation Deck at the Moulin de Blute-fin, Montmartre* (fig. 15) witnesses Vincent's rather tentative application of the vibrant color pioneered in the still lifes to an outdoor scene. The complementaries blue and orange, introduced with restraint in the fence, lamps, and wooden observation platform, provide the composition's overall structure. The underlying charcoal drawing, revealed by infrared

Gauguin: New Directions

reflectography (fig. 13), shows the persistence of past habit; lines indicate that Vincent used a threaded perspective frame which he had built in The Hague in 1882 to establish proportion and spatial recession. But the paired figures (which first appeared in his Nuenen works) symbolize the new concern with complementarity. Just as he experimented with chromatic pairings in his painting, he became preoccupied with the possibility of finding a mate in life. As he later explained to his sister, "There are colors which cause each other to shine brilliantly, which form a couple, which complete each other like man and woman."[28]

By the end of 1886, Vincent had begun to move his art in new directions. But although he viewed vanguard examples with an open mind, his approach to color and brushwork was still largely informed by earlier generations of realist artists.[29] Moreover, in focusing on chromatic gymnastics, Vincent had for the moment put on hold his aim, formulated prior to arriving in Paris, to invest his realism with a symbolic resonance.

Gauguin, in his own confrontation with current trends, did not have the luxury of gradual immersion. Vincent had the freedom of anonymity, but Gauguin had a past to overcome, as an amateur Impressionist and, in the eyes of some, an over-reaching hanger-on. He inevitably became embroiled in conflicts that revealed the increasing polarization of the vanguard community. In early June, when Pissarro wrote to his son Lucien about the upcoming second Indépendants exhibition, he expected Seurat, Signac, Gauguin, and Guillaumin to participate. When, by the end of July, Gauguin and Guillaumin withdrew

9
Vincent van Gogh
Bowl with Zinnias and Other Flowers
Summer 1886
[F 251, JH 1142]
Oil on canvas
50.2 x 61 cm
National Gallery
of Canada, Ottawa
Cat. 9

10
Adolphe Monticelli
(French; 1824–1886)
Vase with Flowers
c. 1875
Oil on canvas
51 x 39 cm
Van Gogh Museum,
Amsterdam
(Vincent van Gogh
Foundation)

II
Vincent van Gogh
*Bowl with
Sunflowers, Roses, and
Other Flowers*
Summer 1886
[F 250, JH 1166]
Oil on canvas
50 x 61 cm
Städtische
Kunsthalle,
Mannheim

12
Henri Daudet
(French; 1850–1896)
Le Vieux Montmartre
Photograph of the
Moulin de la Galette
seen from rue Lepic
1886
Bibliothèque
Nationale, Paris

13
Infrared reflec-
togram of fig. 15,
showing charcoal
underdrawing.
Diagonal lines were
made based on the
perspective frame.

14
Vincent van Gogh
*Moulin de Blute-fin,
Montmartre*
Summer 1886
[F 274, JH 1115]
Oil on canvas
46 x 38 cm
Glasgow Museums:
Art Gallery and
Museum,
Kelvingrove
Note the sunflowers
growing at the lower
right.

15
Vincent van Gogh
*Terrace and
Observation Deck at
the Moulin de Blute-fin,
Montmartre*
Late 1886
[F 272, JH 1183]
Oil on canvas,
mounted on
pressboard
44 x 33.5 cm
The Art Institute
of Chicago, Helen
Birch Bartlett
Memorial Collection,
1926.202
Cat. 10
This is a close-up
image of the same
viewing platform
seen in fig. 14.

16
Jean-Paul Aubé
(French; 1837–1916)
Vase
1879
Earthenware
H. 33 cm
Musée Nationale de
Céramique, Sèvres

17
Paul Gauguin
Sketch of vase with a
figurine of a nude
woman
1884/88
Graphite and crayon
on wove paper
16.9 x 22.8 cm
In Sketchbook
no. 16, p. 73
National Gallery of
Art, Washington,
D.C., The Armand
Hammer Collection

14

12

13

15

(but submitted works to an exhibition in Nantes), Signac branded them as cowards for deserting the front, lumping them with conservative Salon favorites and accusing them of denying progress. Pissarro, equally astonished that Gauguin would not be following the new movement to the Indépendants, also regretted his former colleagues' refusal to join the struggle, convinced as he was of the successful outcome of "our optical blends."[30]

A contretemps between Gauguin and Seurat that occurred in mid-June exacerbated the obvious tension. Leaving Paris for the summer, Signac had offered Gauguin temporary use of his studio, unaware that Pissarro would store his recent canvases there. Gauguin went to Signac's studio, intending to copy one of his own wooden reliefs, which he had given to Pissarro and which was now in the studio together with Pissarro's work. He found Seurat there. Ignorant of Signac's invitation and irritated by Gauguin's recent behavior, Seurat denied him access, apparently fearing that Gauguin would take an unauthorized look at Pissarro's most recent innovations. Gauguin strongly protested. Informed of the goings-on by Seurat, Pissarro accused Gauguin of displaying the "tactlessness of a sailor." When the growing consensus regarding his bad manners came back to him, Gauguin wrote to Signac, sarcastically excusing himself as "a badly brought up, tactless man."[31]

A new opportunity that would provide an outlet for Gauguin's defiance had presented itself just before the close of the last Impress-ionist group show. Aware of Gauguin's financial distress, Félix Bracquemond, who had earlier exhibited prints with the Impressionists, purchased one of his paintings. Head of the Auteuil design studio established by the Haviland porcelain manufacturers from 1873 to 1881, Bracquemond introduced Gauguin to his former Haviland colleague the ceramicist Ernest Chaplet. In January 1886 Chaplet had taken over a studio, formerly under the auspices of Haviland, on rue Blomet, in the Vaugirard neighborhood of Paris. Gauguin responded enthusiastically to joining forces with a ceramicist; he had long appreciated the medium, well represented in Arosa's collection (see ch. 1), and he knew several artists like Bracquemond who supported themselves in this way. As he reminded Mette, their old neighbor and friend, sculptor Jean-Paul Aubé, had for years made his living working with the professional ceramicists at Haviland, including Chaplet, fashioning figures in white plaster to decorate their vases (fig. 16). Aubé's fully plastic figures, large in scale relative to the pots on which they perch, informed Gauguin's initial approach to ceramics, as revealed in a sketchbook page including an Aubé-like vase (fig. 17).[32]

Pursuing this direction, Gauguin produced his first work in ceramics, the fully three-dimensional figure of a faun seated atop a small rounded hillock (fig. 18). The choice of subject was significant. In ancient Greek mythology, fauns, satyrs, and the god Pan embody the self-perpetuating vitality of nature in its elementary form and symbolize free sexuality and unbridled lust. Classical representations of these hybrid beings range from almost completely human figures who sport only goat ears and a pair of small horns to more caprine creatures who are equal parts animal and human, and from the sexually reticent to the overtly priapic. Revived in the art of the Renaissance, the image of the faun remained current through the eighteenth century, when it became a staple of the playful, small-scale terracotta and marble sculptures produced by Clodion and his followers.[33]

The iconography proved adaptable to nineteenth-century artistic priorities as well, the faun's identification with human desires serving the caricatural impulse of an Honoré Daumier and the sexual diabolism of a Félicien Rops. From mid-century onward, the darker, carnal nature of the faun took on new meaning when seen through the lens of Charles Darwin's theories of evolution. Half man and half beast, the classical creature seemed to embody new ideas about humanity's emergence from the animal realm. In a culture increasingly ambivalent about modernity, the faun came to embody the uninhibitedness, intuitiveness, sensuality, and rich imaginative connection with nature attributed to primitive man (and children) and considered irrevocably lost to progress. Like the centaur, the faun assumed fresh cultural currency, both as a complex emblem of energy and creativity and as a nostalgic symbol of the passing—the dying off—of an old order, of a tradition finally rendered impotent.[34] Sculptors alert to the ancient figure's new relevance included Rodin, whose

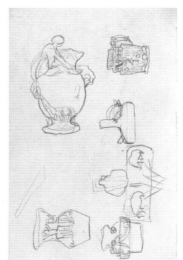

Faun and Nymph (fig. 19) celebrates life in homage to Ovid, and Jean Carriès, whose *Sleeping Faun* (fig. 20) represents this past as a kind of dress-up, fraught with anxiety, at once touching and ridiculous. Both were contemporary with Gauguin's *Faun*, which plays with the same thematic strains.

While modeled in clay in the eighteenth-century tradition, *The Faun* is very much of its time. Seated on a mound, with head cocked and body twisted, the figure appears to be looking for something that is not there. The cowherd's horn held in its right hand signals a pastoral guise—Pan was the god of herdsmen in ancient Greece—but initially the piece included no sign of a flock (Gauguin fashioned the four-legged arched base incised with sheep and cows at year's end). By virtue of its physiognomy, Gauguin's figure recalls the tradition of Romantic demonic imagery—notably Delacroix's images of Mephistopheles in his *Faust* lithographs (1828) (see fig. 21)—yet it exhibits none of Mephistopheles' tense passion, instead appearing rather doleful and distracted. Although the figure's sagging breasts call its gender into question, clearly it is not a fauness but rather a faun that is past its prime; it boasts a carefully crafted, potentially phallic tail, but parted legs reveal the absence of the

19

20

18
Paul Gauguin
The Faun
Winter 1886
[not in B or G]
Unglazed stoneware
with touches of gold
gilding
H. 47 cm

The Art Institute of
Chicago, Estate of
Suzette Morton
Davidson; Major
Acquisitions
Centennial
Endowment, 1997.88
Cat. 6

19
Auguste Rodin
(French; 1840–1917)
Faun and Nymph
1885
Bronze
H. 33.2 cm
Rodin Museum,
Paris

20
Jean Carriès
(French; 1855–1894)
The Sleeping Faun
1885
Patinated plaster
H. 34.5 cm
J. Paul Getty
Museum,
Los Angeles

21
Eugène Delacroix
(French; 1798–1917)
*Faust and
Mephistopheles in
the Harz Mountains*
(detail) from *Faust*,
1828, pl. 14
Lithograph
The Art Institute
of Chicago

22
Photograph of
Edvard Brandes
c. 1880
Brandes
Familiearkiv,
Copenhagen

21

22

often flaunted sign of a faun's virility, resulting in an aura of impotence.

Gauguin evidently linked this iconography to
his failing relationship with Mette. Despite
the fact that the decisions bringing the marriage
to an end were entirely his, he would long
nurse feelings of rejection at what he considered his spouse's coldness, which apparently
included her prohibition of conjugal relations
between them. Insisting that he would not
tolerate such a situation, he worried about—
and cautioned her against—the crime of adul-
tery. His suspicions were fueled by the fact
that Mette's sister Ingeborg had separated
from her husband, painter Fritz Thaulow, and
soon thereafter announced her intention to
marry prominent writer Edvard Brandes.
Gauguin knew Brandes from Copenhagen,
where he was a founder and editor-in-chief
of *Politiken*, the newspaper that serialized
Mette's translation of Zola's novel about artistic impotence.[35]

Gauguin had bumped into Brandes at the Paris
Salon in May, and the Dane had pretended
not to recognize him, spending more time
ogling the ladies than looking at pictures, as
Gauguin pointedly informed Mette. He kept
up the harangue in a subsequent letter, sarcastically invoking Ingeborg's virtue and transcribing Arthur Rimbaud's poem *Tête de faune*
(*Head of a Faun*), substituting "Brandes" where
the poet had written "le faune." Gauguin
wrote this letter at the very moment that he
was firing the sculpture, the face of which
incorporates Brandes's features (see fig. 22):
deep-set eyes, prominent nose, and a wide
mouth that recalls the broad line of his moustache.[36] Giving lust the face of Brandes was a
manifestation of the prim attitude toward sexual rectitude that Gauguin would adopt—with
increasing hypocrisy—with Mette for years to
come. But to complicate this, the faun also
bears a certain resemblance to the artist himself, who would emphasize his strong nose

and chin in self-portrait renderings (see ch. 3,
fig. 74). Certainly the aura of impotence and
melancholy pertains more closely to Gauguin
than to the highly successful Brandes.

The Faun's ambiguous meanings are as conflicted as its maker. The work can be regarded
as a vehicle for the personal expression of feelings of loss. But if it addresses an ending, it
also suggests beginnings. Gauguin's fixation
on Brandes's lechery and on the dubious
morals of Ingeborg (conflated with Mette)
points to his own fantasy of reinventing himself as the independent, bohemian artist, full
of creative energies and in touch with primal
urges. His sculpture intimates the emergence
of a new persona that is literally inscribed in
the clay mound: "P Go," the monogram he
used for the first time in ceramics of 1886–87
and in paintings beginning in 1888. More than
simply an abbreviated form of his signature,
"P. Gauguin," the monogram (pronounced
"pay-go") seems to be a deliberate phonetic
evocation of "pego"—"penis" in the English
slang that the artist would have picked up
during his years as a sailor.[37] Here, apparently
the object of the faun's gaze, the monogram is
intimately connected with the artist's complex, personal iconography.

In mid-July, his first ceramic essay complete,
Gauguin left Paris for Brittany. He planned to
get out of the city and, as he told Bracquemond,
to make art in a backwater. The impetus was
largely financial. In need of money, he had considered venturing further afield, informing
Mette of an offer of an agricultural job in
Oceania. But he could only view the prospect
of work in Tahiti as the renunciation of any
future as a painter; still believing in the possibility of a viable career in art, he could not
imagine resigning himself to life in the French
colony.[38] For the short term, he opted for
Brittany, its principal attraction being the low
cost of living.

He settled in Pont-Aven, a town of some twelve thousand in the department of Finistère (from the Latin *finis terrae*, "land's end") and the site, since the mid-1860s, of an artists' colony numbering more than one hundred French and foreign residents who filled establishments like the Pension Gloanec, where Gauguin installed himself (fig. 23). Contemporary guidebooks represented Pont-Aven and its inhabitants as picturesque or quaint. These characterizations conformed to the "place-myth" of Brittany, in place since the 1830s, as a remote and savage site, home to an ancient culture that could be encountered in the present alive and unchanged. The distinctive Breton costumes—the men's dark wide-brimmed hats; the women's dramatic coiffes—seemed evidence of this timelessness. In fact these garments were modern in origin, and Brittany was experiencing rapid growth in commerce and industry, including the tourism that the region's mythic reputation had stimulated and that the coach service linking Pont-Aven with surrounding towns facilitated.[39]

The costumes and religious pageants of mythic Brittany fascinated the impressionable Bernard—also visiting the region for the first time that summer—more than they did Gauguin. Breton signifiers appear only incidentally in the roughly two dozen works that Gauguin produced during his fourteen-week stay there. But for the distinctive hat worn by the boy at the far right in *Young Breton Bathers* (fig. 25), the scene might be a generic depiction of outdoor summer pastimes. To some observers its handling seemed generically Impressionist as well. Vincent's

friend Hartrick recalled seeing Gauguin, shortly after his arrival, returning one day to the Pension Gloanec for lunch carrying this canvas of "some boys bathing...painted brilliantly with spots of pure color in the usual Impressionist manner."[40] Worked in bright colors and broken strokes, with paired complementaries that create sunlight effects, the canvas indeed typifies the *plein-air* Impressionist aesthetic. Though he had partially executed it on the spot, however, Gauguin had in fact plotted the site details of the Moulin Neuf in a sketchbook drawing (fig. 24).

The increasing importance of drawing to Gauguin emerges in his approach to two figure paintings undertaken later in the summer (figs. 28, 34). The most ambitious of his stay, they mark a decided departure from the Impressionist preoccupation with transcribing momentary atmospheric effects, as well as an embrace of more overtly Breton subject matter. For these works the artist subordinated on-the-spot sketchbook notations to more elaborate drawings from the model executed in the studio (figs. 26–27). The bold contours, simplified planes, and strange figural deployment in these larger drawings, as well as the way they are pieced together in the final paintings, reveal the importance of Pissarro's example in Gauguin's attempt to advance his art in a new direction (figs. 29–30). In his drawing of the seated Breton girl, Gauguin typically appropriated Pissarro's long-practiced strategy of fashioning figures that bend and move in ways so deliberately and painfully awkward that they seem almost unnatural and thus disrupt narrative expectations for a

scene of daily life. For Pissarro such studies were part and parcel of his effort to give his work the "cachet of a modern primitive"; in emulating the simplification that he admired in the art of the early Italian masters, the Egyptians, and the Persians, he achieved in his drawings a synthetic effect that differentiates them from *plein-air* sketches.[41] Gauguin explored this style in works such as *Breton Shepherdess* (fig. 28), in which the deliberately constructed aspect of the figure extends to the surround: the setting is more schematic than illusionistic, composed from individual parts that are assembled one atop the other so as to create a radically tilted space that disobeys perspectival logic.

Breton Women Chatting (fig. 34), a composition featuring women in distinctive regional costumes gathered at a boundary wall, takes this stylistic primitivism further by coding the subject matter as likewise primitive. The breakthrough picture of this period, it is so much more monumental and decorative than any of Gauguin's previous paintings that, despite being clearly dated 1886, it has often been assigned to 1888, where it seems to fit better into a developmental progression. Perhaps responsive to the *Grande Jatte*, *Breton Women Chatting* may be seen as the first expression in Gauguin's painting of the kind of hieratic primitivism that had previously manifested itself only in carvings, such as the *Woman Strolling* (ch. 1, fig. 54). Following the procedure he had learned from Pissarro, Gauguin began with sketches on paper, progressed to a blue-wash drawing on canvas, and finally filled in the wash outlines with paint.[42] But

23
Photograph of artists
posed in front of the
Pension Gloanec
Pont-Aven, Brittany
c. 1890

24
Paul Gauguin
Site drawing, with
color notations, of
the Moulin Neuf
and Aven River
1886
Graphite on paper
In Album RF 29877,
folio 41 verso
Musée d'Orsay,
Paris, Département
des Arts Graphiques

25
Paul Gauguin
*Young Breton Bathers
(Petits Baigneurs)*
Summer 1886
[W 272]
Oil on canvas
60 x 73 cm
Hiroshima
Museum of Art
Cat. 4

the compositional idea was also indebted to Pissarro, who, in the early 1880s, had explored comparable effects in paintings of peasant women gossiping over a fence (Gauguin owned one such example: fig. 35). Degas had adopted the same device, transposing the scene to the racetrack and transforming the figures into elegant urban types (see fig. 36).

Breton costume hides Gauguin's reliance on such models by effectively producing what we read as modernist attention to surface and patterning. In costume illustrations, the figures' various poses and proximity to the picture plane serve a practical purpose, displaying the details of Breton regalia (see fig. 31). The inclusion of several such costumed figures, tightly framed within a shallow pictorial field, almost automatically produces abstract, decorative effects, as in a painting by Salon favorite Pascal-Adolphe-Jean Dagnan-Bouveret (fig. 32). In close-up the motif assumes a concentrated decorative impact that is largely dissipated when incorporated into an ambitious, panoramic view of a traditional Breton pardon (fig. 33).

Its relationship to various models notwithstanding, Gauguin's *Breton Women Chatting* is a remarkable achievement, in which the artist's working process, subject, and framing abet a harmonious, patterned, rhythmic—synthetic—result. But it would be some time before he could apply its animating principles to scenes presenting a deeper landscape. In the meantime he pursued a larger stylistic enterprise that summer: the active development of a particular persona. Costuming was as intrinsic to this process as it is to the contemporaneous painting. Drawing on his nautical past and on his current location, Gauguin took to dressing, as Hartrick would recall decades later, "like a Breton fisherman in a blue jersey … a beret jauntily on the side of his head"; this outfit, together with his rolling swagger, gave him the appearance of a "Biscayan skipper of a coasting schooner" (see ch. 4, fig. 105). In practicing this kind of role-playing, Gauguin followed predecessors such as the American expatriate Whistler, who—with his carefully cultivated mannerisms and keen instinct for publicity—had recently perfected the idea of the artist himself as a work of art. Such performance demanded an audience, which

Gauguin found in Pont-Aven. Although most people were afraid of him, as Hartrick remarked and as Gauguin himself boasted to Mette, he nonetheless felt liked and respected, and fellow artists eagerly sought his counsel. In contrast to the competitive Paris scene, there was little serious challenge to Gauguin's dominance within Pont-Aven's artistic community. Acknowledged, according to his own report, the strongest painter in Pont-Aven—the biggest fish in this small pond—Gauguin felt rejuvenated.[43]

26
Paul Gauguin
Sketch of seated
Breton woman
1886
Graphite on
wove paper
16.9 x 12.6 cm
National Gallery of
Art, Washington,
D.C., The Armand
Hammer Collection

27
Paul Gauguin
Seated Breton Woman
1886
Charcoal, brush
and watercolor
30.5 x 42.2 cm
Musée des Arts
Africains et
Océaniens, Paris

28
Paul Gauguin
Breton Shepherdess
Summer 1886
[W 203]
Oil on canvas
60.4 x 73.3 cm
Laing Art Gallery,
Newcastle upon
Tyne (Tyne and
Wear Museums)
Cat. 5

29
Camille Pissarro
Weeders, Pointoise
1882
Oil on canvas
63 x 77 cm
Private collection

30
Camille Pissarro
Study for *Weeders,
Pointoise*
c. 1881
Black chalk on paper
45.7 x 61 cm
Courtesy Christie's

31
François Hippolyte
Lalaisse
(French; 1812–1884)
Breton Woman from
*Galerie Armoricaine:
Costumes et vues pit-
toresques de la Bretagne*
(Nantes, 1845–46),
pl. 14
Bibliothèque
Nationale, Paris

32
Pascal-Adolphe-Jean
Dagnan-Bouveret
(French; 1852–1929)
Breton Women
1887
Oil on canvas
54.6 x 40.7 cm
Courtesy Christie's
Images New York

33
After Pascal-
Adolphe-Jean
Dagnan-Bouveret
*Breton Women at
a Pardon*
Lithograph
1889
From Albert Wolff,
Figaro—Salon (Paris,
1889), p. 46

34
Paul Gauguin
*Breton Women
Chatting (Bretonnes
causant)*
Summer 1886
[W 201]
Oil on canvas
72 x 91 cm
Bayerische
Staatsgemälde-
sammlungen, Neue
Pinakothek, Munich

35
Camille Pissarro
*Peasant Women
Chatting*
c. 1881
Oil on canvas
35 x 27 cm
Private collection

36
Edgar Degas
(French; 1834–1917)
*Three Women at
the Races*
c. 1885
Pastel on paper
70 x 70 cm
The Denver Art
Museum

31

32

33

34

35

36

Returning to Paris in mid-October, Gauguin re-entered the fray, a player in the continuing hostilities that divided the various vanguard camps, whom Pissarro now identified as the most vocal spokesman of the romantic Impressionists. This said less about those whom Gauguin supported—at this time he had renewed ties with Guillaumin and Degas—than it did about those whom he rejected—Seurat and the Neo-Impressionists. When in early December Gauguin snubbed Pissarro and his new colleagues in the Café Nouvelle-Athènes, Pissarro defended his former student but concluded that his attempts to form new allegiances would come to nothing: "The Impressionists are passé, whatever Gauguin, the sectarian, might say."[44] Gauguin must have realized this as well, for, harnessing the energy of this charged dialogue, he now began actively to seek a means of establishing his own identity.

Throughout his stay in Pont-Aven, Gauguin had held fast to the idea that on returning to Paris he would support himself and Clovis (who was in boarding school while Gauguin was in Brittany) by collaborating with Chaplet to sculpt pots as had Aubé: that is, he would produce "ceramic sculpture" to decorate vessels conceived by others. Back in the capital, Gauguin began his work at Chaplet's rue Blomet studio by adopting Bracquemond's pictorial variation on Aubé's sculptural approach (see fig. 37). The technical exigencies of working in this medium—which required incised outlines to prevent zones of color from mixing during the firing process—encouraged Gauguin to simplify his drawing and render his motifs in a still more synthetic form, fostering the direction in which his Brittany paintings and drawings show him moving.[45]

Almost immediately, however, Gauguin tired of simply embellishing vessels made by others. He abandoned this approach to ceramic decoration as well as Aubé's, along with the high-art sculptural tradition imprinted on *The Faun*. Instead he began to create objects remarkable for their merging of the arts of the potter, sculptor, and painter. Modeled freely by hand out of coils of clay (*colombins*) rather than thrown on the wheel, Gauguin's selectively glazed and roughly executed ceramics display highly idiosyncratic shapes and applied motifs that invoke Western folk-art traditions like the pre-industrial pottery of regional France (Brittany included) and Renaissance Italy, and also such non-European models as Peruvian and Asian pottery.[46]

Many of Gauguin's pots assume the forms of traditional rustic models; others are pointedly fantastic, with big handles and naïvely applied decorative clay motifs (see fig. 38). His willful conjoining of disparate forms in such pieces is reminiscent of Peruvian prototypes but defiant of any utilitarian purpose. A sketchbook page presenting ceramic recipes and drawings of pottery motifs and vessels from ancient Peruvian, Mexican, and Roman sources, copied from the same treatise on ceramics that had informed one of his earlier wooden sculptures (ch. 1, fig. 59), reveals the range of Gauguin's interests. In that carving, he had borrowed from Degas, playing with dissonance by introducing elegant, urban dancers into a rough-hewn formal field that is

37

38

39

worlds removed from the Paris Opéra. While Gauguin quoted Degas in one ceramic, his strategy usually involved using motifs that signify a cultural and geographic distance and that complement rather than contrast with the other elements. And though he once incorporated the image of a North African horseman under a blazing sun apparently inspired by Delacroix, for the most part Gauguin relied on his own Breton figures.[47]

Nonetheless, the hand-modeled pots, like Gauguin's earlier carving, were self-consciously transgressive. He reported to Bracquemond, soon after initiating them, that he was laboring like a slave with Chaplet on "my *colombins*." Possibly he was playing off a slang meaning for *colombin*, which in addition to designating the potter's coil of clay, connotes "turd."[48] With similarly colloquial language, Gauguin invited Bracquemond to come to Chaplet's studio to see his "fifty-five … monstrosities" just emerged from the furnace. Clearly pleased with the small products of his grandiose schemes, Gauguin recognized that they were not the marketable objects he had originally intended, being too "artistic" to be commercial. He nonetheless believed that Bracquemond, a fellow artist, would find them interesting, as had Schuffenecker, and he imagined the success they might meet in

an exhibition like that held by the Union Centrale des Arts Décoratifs.[49] He did not in fact participate in this exhibition, and it is difficult to imagine how his works would have been received there. Deliberately and expressively crude, the more extreme of Gauguin's ceramic sculptures evoke the pre-industrial, even the pre-linguistic, with their emphasis on tactility and their associative—and occasionally formal—suggestions of bodily functions and orifices (see fig. 39). Not only do these works distinguish themselves from the modern refinement of practitioners like Aubé, but they are equally at odds with the modern primitivism of Pissarro and Seurat. Indeed they constitute a strategic response to the latter in that Gauguin capitalized on recent criticism by giving formal as well as personal expression to what they perceived as his sailor's crudeness.

Yet there was no clear venue in which to make such a statement. Traditionally ceramics occupied a low position in the hierarchy of media (not until 1890, with the establishment of the Salon de la Nationale, would the so-called decorative arts be exhibited alongside sculpture and paintings). In the medium of painting, the models, old and new, that crowded the field could not be disregarded, and concerns about invention and originality

were paramount. Only weeks earlier, Pissarro had raised such questions in conversation with Schuffenecker at the Indépendants exhibition. When Schuffenecker (distorting the truth to maintain the peace) told Pissarro about the immense strides that Gauguin was making in Brittany along the lines of the Neo-Impressionists, Pissarro replied sharply that it was too late for Gauguin to sneak back into place. Invoking *L'Oeuvre*'s chief opportunist, a painter named Fagerolles, he put Schuffenecker on notice that "we will certainly make a breakthrough and will not let the 'Fagerolles' pillage us."[50]

Gauguin remained unsure how to pursue in painting the direction he explored in his ceramics. His attempt to absorb and transcend the available alternatives provides the witty subtext of a remarkably strange picture that he executed after firing the ceramics (fig. 40). The mise-en-scène pays explicit homage to Cézanne: a table placed in the corner of a room with walls papered in a pattern reminiscent of the Provençal artist's still lifes (see ch. 1, fig. 57) supports a rumpled cloth and a number of fruits modeled with firm contours and directional brushwork. The respectful mood is disrupted by two quite different intrusions: the strange object on the table that seems to face into the corner, and the head of a bespectacled

young man, abruptly entering the pictorial space at the right. The position of the model—Charles Laval, a young painter whom Gauguin had befriended in Brittany—is indebted to Degas, who had used a similar compositional device in a pastel shown in the sixth Impressionist exhibition (fig. 41).[51] Laval's attention appears to be engaged not by the carefully positioned fruit, but by the oddly shaped ceramic object looming above it—one of the "monstrosities" of which Gauguin was particularly fond.[52] Laval wears a quizzical expression, as if he is trying to make sense of what is before him.

The failure of pictorial elements to combine into a coherent whole in *Still Life with Profile of Charles Laval* is arguably the intention. Gauguin brought together two genres—still life and modern life—and their most prominent contemporary practitioners—Cézanne and Degas—but deliberately declined to resolve them. The ceramic, parachuted into this contested field, introduces a third personality—Gauguin—incarnated as an "authentic," independent entity. Ironic and pointed, this was the first of a number of canvases thematizing the challenges of creativity. Through the figure of Laval, who acts as the viewer's surrogate, Gauguin here seems to have invited us to speculate on his next move.

His options were limited. Bracquemond had taken some paintings—despite finding them, as he confided to Pissarro, strange and a bit confused—because he thought they had something that might interest prospective buyers. He was proven wrong, for the pictures apparently offended those to whom they were shown. As for the ceramics, even Bracquemond, who had encouraged and enabled the venture, considered many to be failures: "Some of the pieces he has made are good enough, but others are of no interest." Between the lines, Pissarro interpreted Bracquemond

as describing "a sailor's art, picked up here and there."[53]

This persistent reading of the art through the man revealed a particular personal bias. Pissarro was relatively unconcerned with the unsystematic execution of Gauguin and other opponents to Neo-Impressionism. Of far greater significance to him were the issues of sincerity, truth of expression, and authenticity. He reserved his harshest scorn for those who staked a claim to these qualities while in fact strategically "pillaging" from other art.[54] The synthesis of various primitivisms was not itself at issue. In his own current production (see fig. 4), Pissarro drew on Japanese,

French Gothic, and contemporary vanguard precedents. It was the nature of the assimilation that troubled Pissarro, who suspected that Gauguin, rather than working through styles and obtaining a profound understanding of them, was just opportunistically passing through and passing on: a *pasticheur* of different aesthetics picked up in various ports. This type of expedient, eclectic borrowing is precisely what Pissarro would later explicitly accuse Gauguin of doing in Tahiti (see Coda).

Pissarro now essentially closed the books on his relationship with Gauguin with a final judgment of his basic character as "anti-artistic…[like] *bibelotage*"—bric-a-brac.[55] Gauguin's

40
Paul Gauguin
Still Life with Profile of Charles Laval
Late 1886 [W 207]
Oil on canvas
46 x 38 cm
Indianapolis
Museum of Art,
Samuel Josefowitz

Collection of the School of Pont-Aven, through the generosity of the Lilly Endowment Inc., the Josefowitz Family, Mr. and Mrs. James M. Cornelius, Mr. and

Mrs. Leonard J. Betley, Lori and Dan Efroymson, and other Friends of the Museum
Cat. 7

41
Edgar Degas
Behind the Scenes
1882/85
Pastel on paper
66 x 38 cm
Private collection, courtesy Pyms Gallery, London

next move was as if calculated to reinforce this perception. Oppressed by financial need, he considered a number of outlandish schemes and finally settled upon traveling to Panama, where his sister's husband, Juan Uribe, was in business. Having persuaded Laval to accompany him, Gauguin sailed for Central America in April. What he found fell far short of his expectations. The local economy was in disarray as the Panama Canal Company was on the verge of bankruptcy; Uribe, basically the keeper of a general store rather than the prosperous financier that Gauguin had assumed him to be, had nothing to offer in the way of jobs or accommodations. The two artists took jobs on the canal, but Laval contracted yellow fever, and Gauguin was laid

off after just two weeks. Hoping initially to settle (and paint) on Taboga, an island sixteen kilometers off the coast from Panama City, they found it to be a tourist trap. They then set their sights on the French colony of Martinique, in the Lesser Antilles, and in early June left their hotel for a small hut on the island.[56] This seemed to be the paradise that Gauguin had sought, and he began to produce some drawings and paintings of the colorful local vegetation and populace. Before long, however, he too fell ill with fever and dysentery and, with Schuffenecker's financial help, returned to France in mid-November. There he would attempt to recover his health and formulate his mission for the future.

41

Just as Gauguin left the Paris scene, Vincent arrived and entered the vanguard circles. He met Signac in the beginning of 1887, when the latter was preparing works for the annual exhibition held by the international society of contemporary artists Les Vingt (The Twenty), held in Brussels. Signac was an eloquent spokesman for Neo-Impressionism, explaining it as a natural development from Impressionism; under his influence Vincent's palette lightened considerably, his brush stroke became more varied, and his subject matter expanded. He took on Impressionism and Neo-Impressionism directly and simultaneously, as seen in *Fishing in Spring* (fig. 44), a picture of the Pont de Clichy where it crosses the Seine at Asnières that recalls the work of Monet (see fig. 42). Theo began dealing in the work of the older artist, as well as of Seurat, that April. Seurat depicted a nearby site in *Fishermen* (fig. 43), possibly a direct response to the 1883 Monet, and a work he included in the 1886 Impressionist exhibition. Vincent's modest contribution to this dialogue even includes a complementary painted border, a Neo-Impressionist innovation.[57]

Theo reported in May that his brother was "trying very hard to put more sunlight" into his paintings.[58] It was around this time that Vincent again turned to self-portraiture, portraying himself in a stylistic guise, that of a practicing pointillist, that was radically different from that of the previous year (fig. 45). However orthodox his Neo-Impressionist technique may appear to be in this portrait and in other works produced at the time of his closest association with Signac, Vincent was neither as theoretically rigorous nor as painstaking and meticulous as Signac, Seurat, and Pissarro. His touch was more gesturally assertive, and he eschewed ostensible neutrality for a surface that is expressive as well as decorative. The rational surfaces of Neo-Impressionism could not satisfy his desire to plumb the depths of character. In this self-portrait, he dutifully juxtaposed the complementaries red and green, but applied them in strokes that seem to radiate with centrifugal force from the composition's center. Swirling like magnetized color filings about the head of the artist, these strokes suggest energy and turbulent feeling, an inner life only hinted at by the artist's baleful stare.

Vincent professed faith in color, but—with his dislike of dogma and theoretical abstraction—he was not cut out to be a strict adherent of Neo-Impressionism. Unlike his precocious friend Bernard, however, he did not set himself against it. The two men had kindred temperaments: both were volatile, prone to strong enthusiasms, fiercely independent, and brusquely outspoken; and they shared a hagiographic view of art history as a moral battleground between "heroes and zeroes." But Vincent wished to remain independent of the sectarian fighting within the Paris vanguard.[59] He clearly saw himself as pursuing what he would later describe as a "regular course in impressionism," preliminaries he believed to be as necessary to a career as it

was formerly to have a course in a Paris studio. He set the assignments himself and felt at liberty to experiment, remaining catholic in outlook and trying different approaches, as a self-portrait painted later that summer suggests (fig. 46). With its combination of feathery and striated brushwork, this sketchy image of the artist is more Impressionist in handling and sunnier in feeling than the earlier example (fig. 45). In effect the self-portrait professes different allegiances, referencing iconographically a portrait that Vincent remembered having seen of Monticelli (see ch. 3, fig. 6) wearing an enormous yellow hat.[60]

Having figuratively donned the hat of Monticelli, Vincent next tried on the shoes of Millet, whom he had long viewed as a "guide and counselor." A large, state-sponsored retrospective devoted to Millet's work that opened in May 1887 provided a provocative counterfoil to Vincent's present aesthetic preoccupations. Black-and-white reproductions had been the primary source for his understanding of—and reverence for—the Barbizon master, a fact that helps to explain the surprise that Vincent now experienced upon discovering that Millet's

painting featured "hardly any color."[61] For this very reason, Millet would play no part in Signac's (1899) construction of the history of French art since Delacroix in terms of a linear, progressive evolution of colorism. Seurat, however, evinced an enduring interest in Millet, whose drawings, with their mysterious blacks, had such an impact on his own.[62] And it was Millet's drawings that Pissarro, on visiting the retrospective, found to be a hundred times better than the paintings, which he believed had aged badly. Specifically Pissarro decried the sentimentality of Millet's representations of a stoic and faithful peasantry—notably the celebrated *Angelus* (1857–59; Paris, Musée d'Orsay)—as essentially conservative. When he saw fellow exhibition-goers brought to tears by such imagery, Pissarro complained that they had probably never experienced "love at first sight" before the real thing, exemplified by Delacroix's frescoes in Saint-Sulpice (see ch. 3, fig. 65).[63]

What Pissarro scorned in Millet, Vincent revered as profoundly spiritual and humanist. His struggle to reconcile his old admiration with new interests informs the suggestive can-

42

43

44

42
Claude Monet
(French; 1840–1926)
*Fishermen on the Seine
at Poissy*
1882
Oil on canvas
60 x 81 cm
Neue Galerie in der
Stallburg, Vienna

43
Georges Seurat
Fishermen
1883
Oil on wood
16 x 25 cm
Musée d'Art
Moderne de Troyes,
gift of Pierre and
Denise Lévy

44
Vincent van Gogh
*Fishing in Spring,
the Pont de Clichy
(Asnières)*
Spring 1887
[F 354, JH 1270]
Oil on canvas
49 x 58 cm
The Art Institute of
Chicago, gift of
Charles Deering
McCormick, Brooks
McCormick, and
Roger McCormick,
1965.1169
Cat. 18

45
Vincent van Gogh
Self-Portrait
Spring 1887
[F 345, JH 1249]
Oil on artist's board,
mounted on
cradled panel
41 x 32.5 cm
The Art Institute of
Chicago, Joseph
Winterbotham
Collection, 1954.326
Cat. 19

46
Vincent van Gogh
Self-Portrait with Straw Hat
Summer 1887
[F 526, JH 1309]
Oil on canvas, mounted on wood panel
34.9 x 26.7 cm
The Detroit Institute of Arts, City of Detroit Purchase
Cat. 20

vas *A Pair of Boots* (fig. 47), seemingly a response to one of Millet's small drawings of peasant clogs (fig. 48) published in Alfred Sensier's biography and included in the retrospective. Millet's humility and commitment to eat, drink, and live like his peasant subjects—characteristics symbolized by these *sabots*—had been very much on Vincent's mind in 1885, when he painted *The Potato Eaters* (ch. 1, fig. 47). This was the picture in which he had attempted to follow Millet's example,

and despite the direction toward strong, intense color that he since had taken in his art, he still looked back on it as his best to date. His preoccupation with color had distracted him from the path announced by his first masterpiece.[64]

Chief among these distractions were Japanese color woodcuts, which Vincent first began to collect in Antwerp and avidly continued to acquire in Paris. As he had done in the 1870s with illustrations from *The Graphic*, he sought to

convert Bernard and other friends to his enthusiasm. Even a display of Japanese prints that he organized in March at Le Tambourin, a café on boulevard de Clichy owned by his (possibly intimate) friend Agostina Segatori, echoed a never-realized plan in The Hague to bring the English illustrators to the attention of the artists' club Pulchri. But there was a great difference. The *Graphic* images addressed a culture and social issues that Vincent understood, experienced, and cared about. By contrast his interest in Japanese prints was primarily formal—he was attracted to their brilliant flat color, simplified forms, incisive drawing, and compositional daring. His ignorance of their cultural context helped foster an idealized conception of Japan as a repository of superior emotional, moral, and aesthetic values.[65]

It was at the moment of the Tambourin exhibition that Vincent began worrying about the collection of prints he had left behind in Nuenen.[66] He was evaluating his life, comparing (as he wrote in a letter to his sister Wil) a past when he "gave myself up to religious and social concerns and considered art holier than I do now" with a present in which love affairs, however impossible, seemed more important—and arguably more sacred—than art or religion. But at the same time, he was ambitious for his painting and dissatisfied with the present scope of his pursuits; he anticipated a future when, having mastered color, he would create "something other than little green landscapes or flowers." This more significant "something" that he hoped to produce was precisely the consoling art that addressed the contemporary experience of melancholy and pessimism. As he had already learned from Carlyle, for the Christian message to regain its original potency to transform society and remain the light of the world, its essential truths had to be re-presented to modern audiences. Zola had achieved this in *La Joie de vivre* and *L'Assommoir*, as had Maupassant, Goncourt, Daudet, and Richepin, authors of books read more recently: they fulfilled "our need for being told the truth [about] life as we feel it ourselves" but leavened their depictions of life's "most poignantly tragic" aspects with "a great richness and a great gaiety."[67]

Holding fast to his view of Naturalist literature as providing a gloss on the biblical message of sorrowful yet always rejoicing, Vincent now stated his aspiration to follow the Naturalists—and Millet—in taking "action in our own time." The image of worn shoes gives

expression to his current predicament. As in a still life featuring workingmen's shoes that he painted shortly after arriving in Paris, the subject is a kind of urban translation of Millet's wooden clogs, a renewal of the vow Vincent made in Nuenen to live like Millet, who maintained that "because I go about in wooden shoes, I shall be able to manage." But the motif's emblematic import also depended on Carlyle. From early on, Vincent had appreciated worn clothing as "bearing the imprint of life," and he is said to have purchased these shoes, as he had earlier obtained garments for models, at a flea market.[68] London's flea market irresistibly draws Carlyle's Teufelsdröckh, *Sartor Resartus*'s philosopher of old clothes, who goes there to revere "those Shells and outer Husks of the Body" and worships the "hollow…Garment with equal fervour as when it contained the Man." Reading Carlyle had alerted Vincent to the expressiveness of these "past witnesses and instruments of Woe and Joy." Worn shoes have metaphoric associations with the pilgrimage and trailblazing imagery that Carlyle used so effectively to describe the emergence and propagation of revitalizing artistic movements: the "inventor …poet" struggles to pace out the "beginning of a 'Path'"; a "second man travels naturally in the footsteps of his foregoer, yet with improvements, with changes where such seem good;…with enlargements," widening the path until it becomes a broad highway that others can follow to the "City or Shrine, or… Reality," the glimpse of the transcendent truth at its end.[69]

Shoes could be quite literal indices of the difficulties of the artist's path, as an anecdote concerning Vincent's vanguard contemporaries reveals. In the late spring of 1887, pressed for money to support his family, Pissarro had attempted to persuade the shoemaker down the street from the van Goghs' apartment to provide shoes for his son Lucien in exchange for a painting. But Lucien reported that while Signac had successfully bartered art for shoes,

the cobbler was less taken with Pissarro's work and declined the offer.[70]

Painting the shoes in the vividly contrasting complementaries orange and blue, Vincent translated his earlier monochrome versions of the subject into strong, intense color. This translation suggests that he was contemplating enlarging the path that Millet had forged, of expressing something transcendent by using an idiom meaningful in his own time. With its varied technique, carefully considered color harmonies, and flourishes such as the lively highlights of the hobnails and the decorative arabesque of the lace, *A Pair of Boots* was apparently of special importance to Vincent. Not only did he prominently sign it, he contradicted his usual practice by dating it, as he did several other canvases that year. Among these are two studies of dried sunflower heads that he painted in the summer (figs. 49–50).[71] One of the sunflower studies is comparable in color, composition, and flourish with the shoes; all three still-life paintings are linked by the theme of following.

The sunflower—*tournesol* in French; turning toward the sun—is rich in traditional symbolism. From the time of its introduction into Europe from the New World in the early sixteenth century, its responsiveness to the sun's movement was seen in terms of lowly nature's attraction to the divine. Emblematically, it thus came to be associated with humanity's love of God, specifically of Christ, the light of the world (see figs. 51, 55–56). With its connotations of worship, devotion, respect, gratitude, and admiration, the sunflower came to be used in imaging different varieties of secular love relationships as well: that of subject for sovereign, child for parent, lover for beloved, friend for friend. This iconographical tradition also embraced the artist's love of nature, as expressed in a poem by seventeenth-century Dutch national bard Joost van den Vondel—a figure doubtless familiar to Vincent—celebrating the artists' confraternity

48

LES SABOTS.

47
Vincent van Gogh
A Pair of Boots
(Les Souliers)
Summer 1887
[F 333, JH 1236]
Oil on canvas
33 x 40.9 cm
The Baltimore
Museum of Art,
The Cone Collection,
formed by Dr.
Claribel Cone and
Miss Etta Cone of
Baltimore, Maryland
Cat. 21

48
Jean-François Millet
(French; 1814–1875)
Wooden Shoes from
Alfred Sensier,
La Vie et l'oeuvre
de J.-F. Millet
(Paris, 1881),
p. 183

49
Vincent van Gogh
Two Sunflowers
Summer 1887
[F 375, JH 1329]
Oil on canvas
43.2 x 61 cm
The Metropolitan
Museum of Art,
New York, Rogers
Fund, 1949
Cat. 23

of Saint Luke: "Just as the sunflower turns its eyes in love toward the vault of heaven, and follows with its face the all-nourishing light of the sun…so the Art of Painting, from inborn inclination, kindled by a sacred fire, follows the beauty of Nature."[72]

The sunflower's multifaceted symbolism endured in the nineteenth century, employed notably in the art and writings of the German Romantics and through the Victorian emblematic revival. The republication and translation of illustrated texts such as *De sonne-bloeme* (fig. 55) helped propagate the flower's traditional Christian symbolism and facilitated its appearance in the visual arts, where it became widely understood as an emblem of faith owing to its "resemblance to the God of Day and its supposed homage to the rising sun."[73] An example is James Tissot's title-page

design for his opulent *Life of Our Saviour Jesus Christ* (fig. 53).

By the early 1880s, the longstanding associations of the sunflower with art and religion had merged. Increasingly employed as a motif in architecture and the decorative arts, it came to symbolize the Aesthetic Movement in England, adopted by Oscar Wilde (see fig. 54) as the emblem of the so-called English Renaissance of art in his efforts to spread the Evangel of Aestheticism. Though this was an evangel at odds with Vincent's—representing the cult of the beautiful and the sheer pleasure of aesthetic contemplation rather than a consoling poetry—his schooling in emblematics made him fully conversant with the flower's metaphoric currency. In a small but affecting drawing featuring a couple walking arm in arm amid tall sunflowers before a rising sun (fig.

52), Vincent brought together the flower's established symbolism and the personal significance he attached to the pair of lovers as representing an ideal of companionship. Later he would observe that sunflowers "also symbolize 'gratitude.'"[74]

Vincent's two sunflower canvases are studies in decorative color, form, and texture. One (fig. 49) is based on contrasts—yellow and blue, front and back, pitted and smooth—recalling the idea Vincent had had in Nuenen to represent the seasons by means of complementaries, with blue and orange indicating summer.[75] The other (fig. 50), depicting frontally facing flower heads in a closely related gamut of yellow, orange, and brown, explores variety within sameness. In both, however, the sunflowers are so insistently monumental, animated, and decorative that they seem to

49

be bursting with symbolic significance and expressive urgency.

The studies of shoes and sunflowers, together with a third floral image depicting four blooms (1887; Kröller-Müller Museum, Otterlo), were apparently included in a large exhibition organized by Vincent and installed at the Grand Bouillon, Restaurant du Chalet, at 43, avenue de Clichy, in November–December 1887.[76] Located in Montmartre, some distance from the Grand Boulevards and the high-end commercial galleries like Boussod et Valadon, the Grand Bouillon was a fitting venue for the group styled by Vincent as the "Impressionists of the Petit Boulevard." Vincent enlisted the participation of Bernard, Anquetin, Lautrec, and the Dutchman A. H. Koning to mount a kind of successor to the Impressionist exhibitions. Two years later Bernard would describe the room as large enough to accommodate about one thousand pictures. The installation was dominated by roughly one hundred of Vincent's recent canvases—a virtual retrospective of his Paris production—including his sun-filled Asnières landscapes and a portrait of the dealer Père Tanguy against a backdrop of Japanese prints. Vincent and his colleagues were united less by stylistic similarity than by their marginal status with respect to institutions of officialdom and to new gallery networks in which senior Impressionists were now ensconced. Regarded as a manifestation of Vincent's desire for communal effort, this exhibition of younger vanguard talent also set the stage for new allegiances.[77]

I am the light of the world: he that followeth me shall not walk in darkness, but shall have the light of life. John 8:12

50
Vincent van Gogh
Two Sunflowers
Summer 1887
[F 376, JH 1331]
Oil on canvas
50 x 60 cm
Kunstmuseum,
Bern, Switzerland,
gift of Professor Dr.
Hans R. Hahnloser
Cat. 24

51
From Zacharias
Heyns, *Emblemata:
Emblèmes chrestiènes
et morales*
(Rotterdam, 1625)
Leiden University
Library,
The Netherlands

52
Vincent van Gogh
*Couple Strolling
amongst Sunflowers*
Summer 1887
Graphite
13.5 x 23.1 cm
Van Gogh Museum,
Amsterdam
(Vincent van Gogh
Foundation)

53
James Tissot
(French; 1836–1902)
*Behold, He Standeth
behind Our Wall*
1886/94
Gouache
14.5 x 17.6 cm
Brooklyn Museum
of Art

54
Charles Kendrick
(American; 1841–1914)
Cover design for Ye
Soul Agonies in ye Life
of Oscar Wilde, 1882

55
From Jeremias
Drexel, *De sonne-
bloeme...[The
Heliotropium]*
(Antwerp, 1687),
illus. facing p. 169
Leiden University
Library, The
Netherlands

56
Alfred Bell
(English; 1832–1895)
"Vocavi et renuistis"
from Jeremias Drexel,
The Heliotropium
(London, 1863),
pl. IV

This separation of the human will from the Divine is further represented by the sun of God's grace being obscured by a cloud, so that its rays cease to fall on the heliotropium, which now droops and withers. Drexel, *The Heliotropum*

Le rayon d'en haut [the light from on high] does not always shine upon us and may well be hidden behind clouds, but without that light a man cannot live and is worth nothing and can do no good. Vincent to Theo, 3 April 1878

The shapes and forms of the people are most appealing to me, and every day there are constant comings and goings of negresses in cheap finery, whose movements are infinitely graceful and varied....They chatter constantly, even when they have heavy loads on their heads. Their gestures are very unusual and their hands play an important role in harmony with their swaying hips.   Gauguin to Schuffenecker, [early July 1887]

We've got a second painting of his, too, which he exchanged for one of my studies, a dried-up river with purple mud and puddles of water reflecting the pure cobalt blue of the sky, green grass. A negro boy with a white and red cow, a negress in blue, and some green forest.   Vincent to Wil, [31 July 1888]

57
Paul Gauguin
Les Négresses (Among the Mangoes [Tropics])
(Aux mangos [Tropiques])
Summer 1887
[W224]
Oil on canvas
89 x 116 cm
Van Gogh Museum,
Amsterdam
(Vincent van Gogh
Foundation)
Cat. 11

58
Paul Gauguin
Martinique (At the Pond's Edge)
Summer 1887
[W222]
Oil on canvas
54 x 56 cm
Van Gogh Museum,
Amsterdam
(Vincent van Gogh
Foundation)
Cat. 12

It was at precisely this moment, mid-November 1887, that Gauguin returned to France from Martinique. Staying temporarily with Schuffenecker in Paris, he was ill and his prospects were poor. Having fallen out with the Neo-Impressionists, he was effectively excluded from vanguard activity. Degas, though better disposed toward Gauguin, remained essentially aloof from the struggles of the younger generation; Guillaumin had always been a follower; and Schuffenecker, while he attempted to act as a bridge between factions, was a lightweight in the eyes of Pissarro and his circle and certainly

was valued by Gauguin more for his support than his talent.[78]

While in Martinique Gauguin had received word that an enthusiast was interested in backing a major joint enterprise in ceramics with Chaplet, but this came to nothing as the potter had since retired. There was one bright spot on the Paris horizon: Boussod et Valadon, Gauguin claimed in a letter to Mette, had become the "center of the impressionists" and was resolved to force their work on its conservative clientele. For once Gauguin's wishful thinking contained a good deal of truth. Since

the spring of 1886, Theo had been transforming the firm's boulevard Montmartre branch, supplementing its staples—works by the Barbizon School and Salon favorites—with pictures by the Impressionists, including Gauguin's friend Guillaumin, with whom the van Gogh brothers had recently become acquainted.[79]

Gauguin met Theo and Vincent in November, at either the Montmartre gallery or the Petit Boulevard exhibition, or both.[80] In December the brothers visited Gauguin at Schuffenecker's, where they saw a selection of work.

58

Theo decided to take some things on commission, and later that month he installed them in the gallery along with works by Pissarro and Guillaumin. On view were Dieppe and Brittany pictures from 1885–86, including *Young Breton Bathers* (fig. 25); one of Gauguin's recently completed Martinique canvases (fig. 61) featuring a lush, sumptuously colored landscape; and a group of five ceramics.

Decisive as it would be in their subsequent careers, the meeting between Gauguin and van Gogh was of consequence for both in the short term, if for different reasons. For Gauguin the van Gogh brothers were a godsend; Theo, an influential dealer who was interested in promoting his work alongside that of established artists, seemed the answer to his prayers. Within weeks, Theo had paid Gauguin a total of nine hundred francs for three works. Only two, including *Young Breton Bathers*, were intended for sale; Theo purchased the third, the most ambitious of Gauguin's four Martinique figure pictures, *Les Négresses* (*Among the Mangoes* [*Tropics*]) (fig. 57), for the collection he was forming together with Vincent. The most expensive purchase they would ever make, it occupied pride of place in their apartment, over the sofa in the sitting room.[81] Finally the better future that Gauguin had envisioned for himself seemed to have arrived.

Vincent factored in Theo's manifest interest in Gauguin, for he shared it with equal or greater intensity. Perhaps aware of this, Gauguin agreed to the suggestion—made before by Vincent to artists whom he admired—that they exchange works. Gauguin received the two studies of cut sunflowers (figs. 49–50) that Vincent had exhibited at the Grand Bouillon; Vincent received a Martinique canvas featuring two women conversing beside a pond (fig. 58), which Gauguin listed as *Négresses* in a later inventory.[82]

Vincent regarded the paintings acquired from Gauguin to be of singular importance.

Although he admired such contemporaries as Bernard and Lautrec, there is nothing to suggest that their work had a comparable effect on him. Gauguin's paintings seem to have produced the shock of recognition that in the past Vincent had often acknowledged with the simple exclamation "Dat is het" ("that's it"). It was an art that moved the van Gogh brothers in a way that brought Millet to mind. It was inspirational, a beacon.

What captivated them in the Martinique canvases, especially in the large picture they consistently referred to as the *Négresses*, was what Vincent extolled to Bernard as "high poetry," the "gentle, astonishing character" in Gauguin's work that he assumed his colleague likewise intuited. Fuller insight into his meaning is provided by Theo, whose instructional letters to his sister and to his future wife—written in early 1889 and reflecting the cumulative impact of the Martinique, Pont-Aven, and Arles paintings—communicate clearly and succinctly the aesthetic position and high esteem for Gauguin he shared with his brother. Theo had acquired, through years of discussion, Vincent's reverence for Zola and Carlyle, as well as his habit of viewing art through these lenses. Both brothers believed that works of art should provide something more than optical pleasure: heartfelt sincerity counted for more than execution, form mattered less than the "philosophy of life" expressed, and notions of beauty were subordinate to the "world of ideas the subject opens up." Zola's novels satisfied the requirement that art provide its audience a foundation on which to build, a "symbol of what is humane" in depictions of sordid contemporary realities that, however foreign to a reader, nonetheless touch the soul. "That," Theo stated with the certainty of religious faith, "is art."[83]

In Theo's view the great artist does not strive to imitate or transcend nature, but rather communicates what the world reveals to him in a way that moves us and gives us "a glimpse of ourselves," in other words, existential

awareness. For, like Vincent, he believed that the "noblest poetry [is] born of suffering." The human condition is art's greatest subject, and the artist's biggest challenge is to give historically specific expression to life as we live it, authentically conveying its sorrows and joys in such a way that offers hope.[84]

Both brothers agreed that Millet had accomplished this for his generation; for them the Barbizon master's work remained a benchmark.[85] But when measuring their contemporaries, they were not always in accord. Vincent apparently did not share Theo's belief in the "genius" of Degas, the acknowledged master of the figure among the Impressionists. Theo thought that Degas understood life in its fullness—that he was a great poet on a par with Millet and a powerful mind comparable to Carlyle and Zola. Not so for Vincent, despite his appreciation of Degas's talent. As for Seurat, Vincent acknowledged his innovations, but was coming to the conclusion that Neo-Impressionism had failed to yield an art that he could consider either personal or original.[86]

On Monet, Vincent and Theo tended to agree: they admired his brilliantly executed landscapes for (as Theo put it) casting a ray of light that many must find reassuring and uplifting in these pessimistic times, but felt that the painter lacked the "impact of…other geniuses." As Zola had so trenchantly pointed out in *L'Oeuvre*, contemporary art still awaited the artist who would lead it to greatness, who would be to "figure painting what…Monet is in landscape."[87]

Theo would later explain the profound impact that Gauguin's "strange poetry" had on them by using Monet as a foil:

Monet…painted those wondrous scenes from nature but one must oneself be happy and healthy to be able to enjoy it for otherwise the thought may occasionally arise "O, I should be happier if only I were there." Whereas

Gauguin whispers words of comfort, as it were, to those who are not happy or healthy. With him, nature itself speaks, while with Monet one hears the maker of the paintings speak.[88]

Monet's virtuosic, feel-good vision of a smiling nature, conjuring up a vacation from life's problems, could appear cruelly indifferent and teasingly inaccessible to those excluded from it. By contrast Gauguin's pictures seemed more emotionally complex and nuanced, reflecting the artist's different moods. Whereas Monet's pictures at best evoked the "sentiments that nature itself would inspire," Gauguin managed to translate the effects of nature on him and so convey them to those unable to distill its poetry for themselves. He nurtured what Theo called "our inner life."[89]

Gauguin's talent promised a great future—possibly the greatest. "Things may go with him," Theo speculated to his sister, "as they went with Millet before him, who is now understood by all for the poetry he preached, it is so mighty that all, young and old alike, find pleasure in it."[90] For the van Gogh brothers, there were few greater accolades. Despite recent perception that Millet's paintings were sentimental, their belief in the profundity of his thought was unshaken, and their search for a successor who might lead a "new movement" continued. It was in terms of the hero—specifically an artist-hero—and with a sentiment tinged with almost messianic longing, that Theo reflected on the inability of scientific progress to mediate irreconcilable human passions and on the role of art: "One day when a man of exceptional stature emerges, he will be able to create the great movement that will be another step forward for centuries."[91]

Because he shared Carlyle's view of history as the history of great individuals, Vincent remained fully persuaded by the model of authorship that conjoined the artist's life and work, exemplified by Sensier's biography of Millet and by retrospective exhibitions cele-

brating the formation of artistic individuality. He and Theo differed from many of their vanguard contemporaries, whose preoccupations ranged from the political to the formal, in their interest in reading the artist's work through the lens of his life. Thus Theo would discover existential meaning in Gauguin's landscapes: "In the main…calm fills his innermost self with resignation, but sometimes also the wild uprush of all his pain and struggle, which he declaims in the deepest, most powerful tones."[92]

Learning the outline of Gauguin's biography, Vincent recognized him as belonging to the company of "true poets." He had suffered incomprehension and financial distress, hardships that corresponded to the core discourse on martyrdom and the struggle to remain true to one's nature found in the monographs devoted to Barbizon School painters and reiterated in *L'Oeuvre*.[93] But it was the additional emblematic associations that could be attached to Gauguin that made him so singularly compelling. Vincent's time in Paris had not affected the essential metaphoric coordinates by which he navigated. He still described himself as "an adventurer [not] by choice but by fate," a "stranger" even to his family and in his homeland; and he would continue to feel like a figure out of Bunyan or Carlyle, "a *wanderer*, going somewhere and to some [possibly nonexistent] destination."[94]

Vincent, however, often longed for companionship on his journey through life, as evidenced by the nature of the attachments he attempted to form with men such as Harry Gladwell and Anthon van Rappard, with women like Kee Vos and Sien Hoornik, and most enduringly with his brother Theo. None of these individuals had led a life that so closely mirrored his expectations as Gauguin, who appeared to Vincent as a member of the confraternity of wanderers that included Bunyan's Christian, Carlyle's Teufelsdröckh, and Vincent himself. Here was a man who had traveled around the world without reach-

ing his destination; a pilgrim who had left his wife and children behind in order to embark on his quest; a fearless adventurer who had enacted the voyage in which Vincent had tried to engage van Rappard in search of a new form of artistic expression; and a seeker of truth who, like the Pilgrims, had fled the oppression of his own country.

The tales of his Caribbean experience that Gauguin shared with Vincent and Theo—no doubt embellished versions of the accounts he wrote in letters to his wife and friends—fostered this mythic apprehension of his life and character. In his own construction, Gauguin had fled "a boring and enervated life" in the "desert" that was Paris in order to "reinvigorate [himself] far from all humanity" in a healthier climate, to cure himself of the maladies brought upon him by "misfortune, lack of affection, a worn-out life lacking all hope." He and Laval had anticipated "an easy and inexpensive life," living "like savages."[95] After initial disappointments and hardships in Panama City, they discovered in Martinique an island "Paradise" where nature was beneficent and Europeans were pampered by the native population—especially the women. Feeding on fish and fruit, ensconced in a "negro cabin," bathing on a sandy beach, and gazing upon "coconut palms and other fruit trees wonderful for the landscape painter," they believed that they had hit upon an untapped vein of subject matter for art: "The natives offer the most boundless picturesqueness that we could desire. There is enough to observe and create, in a direction yet unexploited, for many generations of artists." Only the martyrdom of fever, pain, and stress forced them to foresake this apparent arcadia and return to civilization.[96]

Gauguin's immersion in another culture satisfied Vincent's view that the most touching things from the brushes of the Old Masters were rooted in "life and reality itself."[97] When he himself had attempted in 1885 to represent the Brabant peasantry, he had considered it essential to associate with his subjects and visit their cottages. Similarly Gauguin, by living among natives in a hut on a plantation, had produced an art out of genuine experience. Moreover the setting that Gauguin portrayed, together with his subject matter—dark-skinned natives at work—conjured associations in Vincent's mind with Harriet Beecher Stowe's classic, *Uncle Tom's Cabin*, a book that he revered as offering "one of the strongest proofs" of the existence of "something transcendent in which Millet believed"—in other words, proof of God and eternity, and the consolation that man "cannot be destined for the worms."[98] For Stowe's slaves, religion had been the consolation; for Vincent it was art. He and Theo saw Gauguin as preaching, but in a new pictorial idiom for a new age.

The fantasies of flight from civilization and of returning to nature so central to Gauguin's construction had been tenets of primitivism since the eighteenth century. In the nineteenth, industrialization provoked even more acute nostalgia for the imaginative intuition that was believed to have been lost with the evolution of Western civilization and fostered the hope that it could be rediscovered in children and in cultures considered to be still in their infancy. In France the dream acquired mythic substance with the "discovery" of Tahiti in the 1760s; subsequently appropriated by proponents of colonial expansion, it was ideologically framed by the country's military defeat in the Franco-Prussian War of 1870–71. Attributing this loss to "momentary decadence" and insularity, advocates of expansionism linked colonial acquisition with the promise of national economic and moral reconstitution and rejuvenation. As Gauguin's blithe use of the term "exploit" suggests, he readily adopted this ideology without troubling about its political implications. With the same naïveté that had con-

founded Pissarro, he was unquestioningly enthusiastic about the ease of life in the French colonies.[99]

Gauguin's escapist fantasy would have struck a chord with both van Gogh brothers, who shared a deep-rooted ambivalence about urban life. Theo, since settling in Paris, had repeatedly written to his family in the Netherlands about the alienation he experienced in the turbulent metropolis, where the crowd heightened his acute feelings of loneliness. He longed for the unaffected zest for life and close harmony with nature to be found in the country.[100] Vincent, while acknowledging the intellectual stimulation offered by the city, suspected that urban progress and sophistication were inauthentic and corrupt; in pictures and in people, he valued the naïveté associated with children and "primitive man" (with whom he linked the peasantry) as inherently truthful and honest.[101]

Vincent and Gauguin discovered common ground in their nostalgia for a mythic preindustrial past, and in the seeming similarities in their life experiences that fostered it. Each had come to his artistic vocation relatively late in life and had not yet succeeded in achieving self-sufficiency; each had been wounded by unsympathetic, uncomprehending family members; each construed himself as suffering in the face of the marketplace's conventionality, factionalism, and philistinism; each was perceived as rough in demeanor and character. Gauguin's Martinique adventure, moreover, spectacularly fulfilled Vincent's criteria for creative authenticity: it was nothing less than a dramatization of Vincent's long-held belief that in order to remain true to one's roots and preserve the "fire in one's soul" from extinction, the artist must retain something of the "original character of a Robinson Crusoe or of primitive man."[102]

59

60

More recent paradigms for authenticity reinforced Vincent's old associations. With its "negresses in pink, blue, orange, and yellow cotton clothes under tamarind, coconut, and banana trees, with the sea in the distance," Gauguin's *Négresses* reminded him of Pierre Loti's evocation of tropical scenery in *Le Mariage de Loti* (first published in 1880 as *Rarahu*), a ground-breaking pseudoautobiographical novel set in Tahiti.[103] The book tells the tale of the liaison between the author (see fig. 59), a naval officer on leave in the French protectorate, and a fourteen-year-old native Polynesian girl, Rarahu—the easily if expensively arranged short-term "marriage" referenced in the revised title. Because he wrote about a strange, far-off land, Loti could detail adventures that would otherwise have seemed morally reprehensible, distasteful, or obscene. For most readers—including Vincent and Theo—the dark side of Loti's sexual tourism and its ideological underpinnings were effectively masked by his colorful evocation of Polynesian culture and his "delicacy of feeling." Lauded by critics for these qualities, for its novel form and content, its "freshness," its seemingly artless veracity and believable evocation of Tahiti, the popular *Mariage de Loti* established the reputation of its thirty-year-old author and effectively introduced a new literary genre, one that helped to construct a sugar-coated vision of the colonialist enterprise in the minds of a broad public.[104]

Vincent's association of Gauguin with Loti was based in part on their apparent similarity as sailors and first-person narrators of exotic colonialist romances. Possibly Vincent was aware of another point in common that does not emerge in Gauguin's letters from Martinique but may have in conversation. It seems that Gauguin, while protesting to Mette his virtue in the face of temptation, had entered into a relationship with a native woman of Indian extraction who bore his son the spring following his departure.[105] Discussion of this episode with Vincent would have foregrounded the relationship between artistic and sexual potency, a theme that was to feature prominently in their subsequent collaboration.

Gauguin's initial opinion about his new friend's work is undocumented; his reference some months later to Vincent's "keen eye" is sufficiently opaque to discourage speculation.[106] But Vincent's two sunflower canvases signaled a tribute and provided an imaginative incentive. Though it is not clear who selected the works that were exchanged, the *Sunflowers* speak the emblematic language in which Vincent was fluent. In addition to the symbolism, his offer of two "studies" (*études*) for Gauguin's one canvas—which he clearly considered a "painting" (*tableau*)—constituted an act of deference, tied to the sunflower's traditional meaning.[107]

Picking up on one aspect of this tradition, Vincent and Theo viewed the sunflower as a metaphor for the artist's necessary but potentially perilous dedication to nature. "To my mind," Theo would later observe,

progress is rather like flowers that turn to face the sun. It is impossible to stop them and why? Perhaps it makes them wilt a little sooner! Yet better a small deed…than a long sermon.…All we can do is be useful in our immediate surroundings.[108]

Writing in January 1889, Theo was thinking specifically of Vincent's contribution to realizing the "great movement."[109] A year earlier, however, when his famous sunflower canvases (ch. 3, figs. 55–58; ch. 4, fig 113; and ch. 5, figs. 13, 15) still lay in the future, the Paris sunflower studies seemed an apt homage to the promise that both brothers discerned in Gauguin. When Vincent painted them, he was primarily concerned with pursuing color investigations, as in the floral still lifes that preceded them. In a sense, the act of choosing and offering the studies to Gauguin made Vincent more attentive to the language of the flowers, unleashing the symbolic potential that seems imminent in their writhing forms.

Given Vincent's need to communicate his enthusiasms and beliefs, it is unimaginable that he did not discuss with Gauguin the associations inherent in their exchange of pictures. Highly articulate, and having now devoted the better part of a decade to ruminating about art and the artist's mission, Vincent introduced Gauguin to his unique, richly informed, allusive way of thinking. The dialogue was catalyzing, as is indicated by the contemporaneous emergence in Gauguin's letters of the lineaments of a new mythic persona, to which the sunflower was attached. Botanists, beginning in the sixteenth century, distinguished this member of the Helianthus genus from other species by reference to its country of origin, labeling it variously "Chrysanthemum Perunianum," "solis flos Peruvianus," "Helianthemon Peruvianum," and "Marigolde of Peru." Nineteenth-century French encyclopedias and dictionaries also trace the sunflower to Peru. So current was the connection that a popular illustrator like Jean-Jacques Grandville could personify the sunflower as an Amerindian worshiping the sun in his widely distributed series of fantastic characterizations of flowers (fig. 60). Vincent had doubtless read about the sunflower's Peruvian origin in an enduring favorite, Alphonse Karr's *Voyage autour de mon jardin*.[110] And Gauguin would have been particularly receptive to such associations—of the sunflower, Peru, and the sun that had dominated its flag under Spanish rule—raised as he was amid the still viceregal Spanish culture of Lima.

It was in the light of Vincent's *Sunflowers* that Gauguin first explicitly staked a claim to Peruvian ancestry. In mid-January 1888 he cautioned Mette to remember that he was a man possessed of "two natures . . . the Indian and the tenderhearted"—the savage and the civilized—and that the former was increasingly in ascendance.[111] At this same moment,

59
Photograph of
Pierre Loti, age 22
1872

60
Charles Geoffroy
(French; 1819–1882)
Sunworshiper after
Jean-Jacques
Grandville
(French; 1803–1847)
"Soleil" from
Les Fleurs animées
(Paris, 1846–47)

Steel engraving,
heightened with
watercolor.
Grandville's image
is a popular expression of the scholarly
identification of the
Incas as "Children
of the Sun."

85

In addition to *Young Breton Bathers* [fig. 25], M. Paul Gauguin—whose style, without becoming clearer or lighter, acquires a virile eloquence of line—shows a large Breton landscape that resembles a Martinique landscape which—with its pink copse, thick median tree under which some women doze, ochre road with two black men carrying wicker baskets—recalls the old engraved illustrations of the islands; between the lush greenery, the red clamor of a roof, as in all authentic Gauguin. Barbarous and atrabilious in quality, scant of atmosphere, colored by diagonal stains sleeting from right to left, these proud pictures would sum up the work of M. Paul Gauguin, were not this gritty artist chiefly a potter. He cherishes the hard, ill-omened, coarse-grained clay of stoneware, scorned by others: haggard faces with wide glabellae, snub noses and tiny slits for eyes—two vases; a third: the head of an ancient long-lived ruler, some dispossessed Atahualpa, his mouth rent gulflike; two others of an abnormal, gibbous geometry.

Félix Fénéon, "Vitrines des marchands de tableaux," *La Revue indépendante*, January 1888

61

62a

62b

63

Fénéon published a review of the Boussod et Valadon display, in which he interpreted one of Gauguin's ceramics (fig. 62) as a portrait of the legendary Atahualpa, the last Inca ruler, who was deposed and murdered in 1532 by Spanish conquistador Francisco Pizarro.[112] The identification may have had an ironic undertone, alluding perhaps to Gauguin's war with Pissarro, represented alongside him in the same gallery. The critic's idiosyncratic "grièche artiste" (a "pie-grièche" is a butcherbird, which impales its prey on thorns before devouring it) further connoted the artist's aggressive attitude toward Pissarro and the Neo-Impressionists. Certainly Gauguin's character was at issue for Fénéon, and it colored his reading of the works. He deemed the Brittany and Martinique paintings "barbarous and atrabilious," lacking in atmosphere and (repeating a judgment leveled in 1886) dull in color. But the qualities he found problematic in the paintings—and in the artist—he saw as put to good use in the ceramics. Indeed Fénéon was the first critic to take note of Gauguin's ceramics, and it could be that his invocation of Atahualpa was a response to an interpretation of the pots provided by the artist or his dealer. In any case, over the coming months Gauguin professed his identity with the Peruvian Indian. Given the haute-bourgeois, Spanish colonial environment of his early years in Lima, Gauguin's claim to Peruvian ancestry is implausible if not opportunistic. He realized that it would not be challenged in Europe, where general ignorance of the highly stratified, complex structure of Peruvian society sustained a stereotypical association of the country with its "savage" native peoples (see ch. 1). This identification would emerge as strategically central to the mixed-blood mythos to which he sought to attach his art, and Gauguin's present circumstances fostered its expression in ceramics.

Gauguin fashioned his *Atahualpa* portrait, like another of a Martinique woman (fig. 63) also on view at Boussod et Valadon, during the few weeks that had elapsed since his mid-November return from the Caribbean in a burst of creative energy no doubt sparked by the prospect of the exhibition at Theo's gallery. Vincent's notion of the authentic artist as a kind of Robinson Crusoe or primitive man who needs to be tested in the fire of life to become "confirmed in what…[he is] by nature" may have provided additional impetus, dovetailing with Gauguin's recent positioning of himself as outsider.[113] In this way Vincent helped sow in Gauguin's imagination the seeds of new ideas for establishing and distinguishing his artistic identity.

Expressing this new persona, Gauguin produced ambitious new ceramics that played with the primitive vocabulary he had earlier employed in the pieces fashioned before leaving for the Caribbean (see figs. 38–39). But now he made a stylistic shift from rusticism to an exoticism that drew on a still more distant time and place, fulfilling the expectations of the barbarian character that Fénéon for one would intuit. In the overtly fantastic *Atahualpa* and in other portrait vases, Gauguin subordinated an eclectic variety of sources (see figs. 66–67) to a larger motif so that the vessel *is* the subject and vice versa. The *Atahualpa* pot signaled its "Peruvian" origin through physiognomic exaggerations that Fénéon apparently read as signs of the macrocephalism thought to be characteristic of Peruvian natives.[114] Primarily, however, the piece is comic, informed by a tradition of the grotesque in ceramics seen in English stoneware (see fig. 68). Gauguin thus drew on contemporary popular culture as well as that of faraway lands to fashion his primitivism, an impulse that Seurat shared, but

61
Paul Gauguin
Coming and Going, Martinique
Summer 1887
[not in W]
Oil on canvas
72.6 x 92 cm
Carmen Thyssen-Bornemisza
Collection, Madrid
Cat. 13

62a
Paul Gauguin
Vase ("Atahualpa")
Winter 1887/88
[not in B or G]
Stoneware
H. 23 cm
Private collection

62b
Back view of fig. 62a

63
Paul Gauguin
Martinique woman with kerchief
Winter 1887/88
[B 36, G 52]
Unglazed stoneware, decorated with slip
H. 21.1 cm
Ny Carlsberg
Glyptotek,
Copenhagen

64a
Paul Gauguin
Leda and the Swan
Winter 1887/88
[B 34, G 63]
Unglazed stoneware, decorated with slip
H. 20 cm
Private collection
Cat. 17

64b
Back view of fig. 64a

with very different implications. The openness of both artists to popular culture can arguably be described as democratizing and anti-hierarchical, but for Gauguin this leveling took place in terms of artistic media rather than social class.[115]

Gauguin continued to mobilize the procedures of *bibelotage*—the term Pissarro had used to dismiss his art—in a group of pots that quote (among other sources) the decorative embellishments of Japanese ceramics and Chinese bronzes. The one he referred to as *Cleopatra* (fig. 69) is among the most suggestive examples. It features a reclining nude of Martinique inspiration who wears a kerchieflike headdress, her features perhaps identifying her with the island's population of plantation

workers brought over from the Indian subcontinent.[116] Boldly displaying herself to the viewer, the North African queen is the first in a series of dark-skinned *femmes fatales* that Gauguin would sculpt in clay and wood over the next two years. A number of these, including the *Cleopatra* pot, formally and iconographically embody a blend of the European and the primitive, thereby giving metaphoric expression to the mixed creative lineage that Gauguin claimed.

Cleopatra's immediate European predecessor is Pierre Puvis de Chavannes's celebrated painting *Hope*, specifically the nude version (fig. 70) first publicly exhibited at Puvis's major retrospective, which opened at Durand-Ruel's gallery on 11 November 1887, the moment of

Gauguin's return to Paris. Puvis was France's most famous living artist, a muralist acclaimed by radicals and conservatives alike. The young Parisian vanguard admired his antinaturalistic, "poetic" aesthetic, distinguished by simplified contours and flattened forms: a classicizing vision informed by a "streak of primitivism."[117] Puvis, enthused Fénéon, saw painting from the decorative point of view; and it was as a modernizing Puvis that the critic hailed Seurat in 1886, alluding to the *Grande Jatte*'s simplified, hieratic figures and evocative, almost ritualistic stillness that reminded some critics of Egyptian art.[118]

In *Cleopatra*, Gauguin marked out a different direction for modernizing Puvis, capitalizing on the iconography and special status of

65

66

67

68

69

70

Hope in his oeuvre. Conceived in the aftermath of the Franco-Prussian War, *Hope* reveals Puvis relying heavily on traditional allegorical language to convey the message of renewal and renascent hope: seated in a spring landscape signaling nature's rebirth, the virginal young woman, her unselfconscious nudity symbolic of Truth, holds the olive branch of peace.[119] Appropriating the figure, Gauguin made pointed changes, transforming innocence into experience, virginity into knowing seduction: the breasts are heavier, the pelvis is tilted up and toward the viewer, the budding twig is replaced by the courtesan's fan. The rooting pigs on the pot's other side underscore the theme of earthy physicality. As he would do even more explicitly later in his career, Gauguin here played off Puvis's *Hope* with insolent deference in order to mark his difference, rendering its message ambivalent. In Gauguin's hands the motif could signify hope or the prostitution of hope, a new direction or decadence.

The "pre-civilized" energies that animate *Cleopatra* also emerge (more privately but

more dangerously) in *Leda and the Swan* (fig. 64), the most formally and iconographically complex of Gauguin's portrait vases. Here the artist drew upon classical myth—Zeus's assumption of the form of a swan in order to approach and ravish Leda—and translated it into a fascinating image of the emerging consciousness of desire. Whereas Cleopatra is a knowingly seductive woman, Leda is a young girl with an innocent, quizzical expression. Behind her rises a long-necked swan, a serpentine and phallic presence that she does not overtly acknowledge but seems to intuit. This image of dawning sexuality is complicated by the figure's likeness to Gauguin's young daughter, Aline.[120] Various taboos are unleashed: the specters of rape, bestiality, and incest.

In both *Cleopatra* and *Leda*, Gauguin reconfigured conventional artistic themes—and his own artistic identity—as socially and sexually transgressive. He was now fashioning his life and his art from the same pattern, adopting a strategy not merely of borrowing but of appropriation, transfiguration, and

identification. In the *Cleopatra* pot, he represented Puvis's message but altered its form, suggesting that renewal might come about through the casting of old truths in new forms—forms from outside the Western post-Renaissance tradition. This approach was compatible with the van Gogh brothers' way of thinking, and Gauguin apparently associated the piece with them, requesting that it be sent to Arles immediately upon his arrival there and later making a gift of it to Theo.[121] In form and content, it gave expression to the vanguard mission that Theo summarized in February 1888 when he described Vincent as "one of the advocates for new ideas." And by this he meant something quite specific: "That is to say, there is nothing new under the sun and so it would be better to say for the regeneration of the old ideas which through routine have become diluted and worn out."[122] This statement is pure Carlyle—a metaphor of hope for the future, now adopted as a leitmotif of the van Goghs' relationship with Gauguin.

65
Paul Gauguin
Portrait Vase of Jeanne Schuffenecker
Winter 1887/88
[B 32, G 62]
Unglazed stoneware
H. 19 cm
Private collection
Cat. 15

66
Anonymous
Portrait vase, Mochica
100 B.C.–A.D. 600
H. 18 cm
Musée de l'Homme, Paris

67
Anonymous
Faience jug with the face of a youth in relief
Late 15th century
Earthenware
Musée du Louvre, Paris

68
Martin Brothers
(English; active 1873–1914)
Grotesque figural spoon warmer
1887
Salt-glazed stoneware
H. 16.5 cm
Private collection

69
Paul Gauguin
Cleopatra Pot
Winter 1887/88
[B 17, G 37]
Partly glazed stoneware
H. 13.6 cm
Van Gogh Museum, Amsterdam
(Vincent van Gogh Foundation)
Cat. 16

70
Pierre Puvis de Chavannes
(French; 1824–1898)
Hope
1872
Oil on canvas
70.7 x 80.2 cm
Musée d'Orsay, Paris

Vincent also reacted to Puvis in the retrospective's aftermath. The evaluation of another artist may have offered him and Gauguin an opportunity to carry their nascent dialogue into their art: Puvis's lesson, while current, was finally unsatisfactory to both, if for different reasons. Vincent responded most literally to Puvis's *Hope* by depicting a woman (probably Agostina Segatori) holding a sprig of flowers (1887; Musée d'Orsay, Paris).[123] But a more revealing reflection is the painting that he entitled *Parisian Novels* (*Romans parisiens*) (fig. 71), where the roses refer to Vincent's misremembrance of a detail in Puvis's portrait of a friend (fig. 72). Portraits are rare in Puvis's work, but this example, a striking amalgam of sophistication and simplicity, would remain one of Vincent's most vivid memories of the retrospective, satisfying his ideal in figure painting. While he apparently found Puvis's idealized vision of a classical dream world disconcertingly remote, Vincent welcomed the portrait as evidence of the artist's willingness to forsake (if only momentarily) the Elysian Fields for "the intimacy of our time": it was a "consoling thing" that proved it was possible to see "modern life as something bright, in spite of its inevitable griefs."[124]

Vincent based this assessment not on the artist's style nor on the sitter's identity, but on the work's general subject, "a serene old man… reading a novel with a yellow cover." The book's distinctive yellow binding identifies it as a Naturalist novel and, by extension in Vincent's thought, characterizes the old man as an individual receptive to new ideas.[125] Puvis's reader was the idealizable paternal figure that Vincent's own father had not been— and a reminder of his resolve to emulate the Naturalists and "take action in our own time." When he had first mentioned this aim in the letter to Wil written shortly after his arrival in Paris, he had spoken only of the vague possibility of one day creating works with "youth and freshness in them," of painting "a good portrait."[126] During the winter of 1887–88, he

produced several portraits that attest to this ambition, but *Parisian Novels* is its programmatic statement. An idiosyncratic homage, it attaches Puvis's work to the Naturalist literature that had long been Vincent's touchstone. Although this was an unconventional interpretation of Puvis, Vincent's picture of his set of Parisian novels does participate in contemporary debates about the concept of the "oeuvre," connected to the flourishing genre of artistic biography and to the emerging institution of the retrospective. Vincent held an abiding belief that "one knows such writers as …Zola only when one has a general idea of their works as a whole"; by extension, it was *as a whole* that figure painters (including himself) deserved to be considered.[127] On one level, then, *Parisian Novels* represents Vincent's notion of what Puvis's oeuvre might have been, a potential glimpsed in one atypical portrait. More importantly, it is—like his earlier still life featuring Zola's yellow-jacketed *Joie de vivre* (ch. 1, fig. 3)—a manifesto picture depicting what Vincent hoped his own oeuvre might achieve.

The two works clearly differ in formal terms. With its high-keyed palette, varied brushwork, and blue shadows, the later canvas attests the lessons Vincent had learned from vanguard contemporaries such as Signac (see fig. 73). *Parisian Novels* is a picture of exuberant disarray. The bright yellow, pink, blue, and green jackets play against the tabletop's variegated whites and the wall covering's rich pattern; application with variegated crosshatchings, parallel striations, and stippling enhances the lively chromatics.[128] But the updated formal language expresses his enduring ambition to make painting a gospel on par with that offered by Naturalist literature. None of Vincent's new acquaintances shared this missionary goal, as their responses to the Millet retrospective had suggested. Not until he encountered Gauguin and his work did Vincent truly begin to hope that what he admired in the art of the past might be accomplished in the future.

The fact that Gauguin was averse to Naturalist literature did not prevent Vincent from associating him with the ambition of his still life with books, as the title he assigned it suggests. *Roman parisien* was the subtitle of *Braves Gens* (1886), a novel by Jean Richepin that explores the trials of Parisian artistic life through two performing artists, a musician and a mime, each devoted to the "cult of his art" in the face of an uncaring public.[129] The musician, Yves, is fortunate enough to find a cultured muse and soul mate; he leaves Paris for his native Brittany, where he pursues his art in peace and attains his potential. By contrast Tombre, the mime, remains in the city, where his revolutionary art is misunderstood. He experiences dire poverty, succumbs to despair and alcoholism, and dies.

Vincent had already included the Richepin book, complete with subtitle, in a small still life featuring Naturalist novels painted in the spring, around the time of his letter to Wil.[130] By the end of 1887, the story of Yves and Tombre had assumed new resonance. Gauguin was already making plans to leave Paris for Brittany, having spent a scant three months in the capital. Believing himself "on the verge of being launched" by Theo, he considered it necessary to remove himself for a half year to Pont-Aven, where he would make a "supreme effort for [his] painting." He had settled into the Pension Gloanec by the end of January.[131]

Vincent, despite having talked about leaving for the country since his arrival in Paris, had taken no steps to do so. But the unwholesomeness of urban life and what he termed the disastrous civil wars among vanguard artists had brought him close to Tombre's sorry state; he was, as he would later admit to Gauguin, "quite ill and almost an alcoholic after driving myself on even while my strength was failing—and then withdrawing into myself, not daring to hope."[132] Theo recalled the situation from a different perspective. Having long ago abandoned "what they call *convenances*," Vincent

71
Vincent van Gogh
Parisian Novels
(*Romans parisiens*)
Late 1887
[F 359, JH 1332]
Oil on canvas
73 x 93 cm
Private collection
Cat. 25

72
Pierre Puvis
de Chavannes
*Portrait of
Eugène Benon*
1882
Oil on canvas
60.5 x 54.5 cm
Private collection,
Switzerland

73
Paul Signac
(French; 1863–1935)
*Still Life: Oranges,
Apple, and
Maupassant's
"Au soleil"*
1885
Oil on canvas
32.5 x 46.5 cm
Staatliche Museen,
Preussischer
Kulturbesitz,
Nationalgalerie,
Berlin

A pinkish gray face with green eyes, ash-colored hair, wrinkles on the forehead and around the mouth, stiff, wooden, a very red beard, considerably neglected and sad, but the lips are full, a blue peasant's blouse of coarse linen, and a palette with citron yellow, vermilion, malachite green, cobalt blue, in short all the colors on the palette except the orange beard, but only whole colors. The figure against a grayish white wall.   Vincent to Wil, [22 June 1888]

was not easy to get along with. Their time living together had been extremely difficult, especially in the beginning. "People either love him very dearly, or [are] unable to tolerate him.... Models didn't want to pose for him, he was forbidden to sit and work in the street and because of his volatile disposition this repeatedly led to scenes, which upset him so much that he became completely unapproachable and by the end of it all he'd had more than enough of Paris."[133]

Such is the mood that Vincent sought to express in a self-portrait painted in January or early February 1888 (fig. 74), created in the spirit of reflection as he looked back on two years spent in Paris. The intention to produce a masterpiece is evident in the execution, varied and free but done with great care; the application of color theory; and the signature and date, prominently displayed on the back of the stretcher.[134] It is in fact a pointed and newly confident version of the self-portrait reprising Rembrandt (fig. 7) that had marked his arrival in Paris. The most evident changes are chromatic: Vincent translated the moody chiaroscuro of the earlier canvas into vibrant color, demonstrating that he had evolved from a "harmonist" into a "colorist." Bright, unmixed paint, applied following the theories of complementary colors—green and red in the face, orange and blue in the jacket—dispels the gloom of the earlier work.

Yet for all its brightness, the portrait conveys a sense of unease; the figure is somber and wooden, the features masklike, the eyes dark and impenetrable. It is precisely in this dissonance between the cheerful and the cheerless that Vincent aimed to achieve a "deeper resemblance" than photographic accuracy could provide. However, the full nature of his conception can only be understood through a reference he made when describing the painting from memory to Wil some months later. Resorting to a literary rather than pictorial comparison, he wrote: "You will say that this resembles somewhat...the face of Death—in van Eeden's book."[135]

The book to which he referred—certain that his sister knew it—is Frederik van Eeden's *De kleine Johannes* (*Little Johannes*). A fantastic, quasi-symbolist *bildungsroman*, it describes the title character's spiritual pilgrimage from the innocent paradise of childhood; through youthful infatuation, the pursuit of knowledge; into a period of alienation, doubt, and despair; to paradise regained, a vision of divinity glimpsed not through the Bible but rather in Nature. Indebted to Carlyle's ideas about outworn spiritual forms and crafted for an age crippled by disbelief and disillusion with the advancements of science, *De kleine Johannes*, like *Sartor Resartus*, traces a mythic journey from light into darkness and back again. Vincent's enduring attachment to the story is understandable. Van Eeden's description of Johannes's early years as a solitary child roaming contentedly around the rolling dunes of the Dutch countryside must have triggered vivid memories of his own boyhood. Johannes's yearning for friendship, his subsequent quest for "the Book" of certainties, his rejection of the Bible, and his attendant existential anguish paralleled Vincent's early history; van Eeden's presentation of the metropolis as a dark, miserable, deceptive place also struck a chord. It is in "the great city," at the nadir of his experience, that Johannes meets the figure of Death. With his "bony forehead and deep-set eyes...grave and gloomy, but not cruel, not angry," van Eeden's Death, though "a little unattractive," is not conventionally macabre or frightening, and indeed has iconographic precedents in the Dutch emblematic tradition (fig. 75).[136] Death's

wise presence is the key to the lesson that Johannes learns when he returns to the country: having gone from the joy of innocence to the sorrow of experience, he must achieve a state of grace wherein he reconciles and accepts both as part of life. The book's final image is of a boat on the sea of life, the luminous figure of Nature at one end of the vessel and the dark figure of Death at the other. In his self-portrait Vincent sought to convey the message of life as at once gay and tragic—found in Zola's *Joie de vivre* and now echoed in *De kleine Johannes*—by adopting the aspect of Death, rendered in joyous color. *De kleine Johannes* revalidated his longstanding convictions about how to achieve equilibrium in the face of extremes. His journey to date had in a sense mirrored Johannes's from country to city; he now took the next step.

In February, following Gauguin's departure for Brittany, Vincent abruptly acted on his frequently expressed intention to go south. On 18 February, with Bernard's assistance, he decorated Theo's apartment with Japanese prints and some of his own pictures. The following day, he and Theo visited Seurat's studio for the first time. Several hours later, Vincent boarded a train at the Gare de Lyon bound for Arles.

75

**Ik Schilder Doods gedagtenis /
Om dat haar komst onzeker is.**

74
Vincent van Gogh
*Self-Portrait at
the Easel*
February 1888
[F 522, JH 1356]
Oil on canvas
65 x 50.5 cm

Van Gogh Museum,
Amsterdam
(Vincent van Gogh
Foundation)
Cat. 54

75
Anonymous
Woodcut
"I paint Death's
keepsake because her
arrival is uncertain"
from a 19th-century
broadsheet titled
"Those who have
learned about dying
Need not experience
Death's bitterness"

1
Gauguin and van
Gogh spent the
summer of 1888 in
Brittany and Prov-
ence, respectively

a The port of Pont-
  Aven, c. 1880
b Arles from the
  Trinquetaille
  Quarter, c. 1900/10

When van Gogh and Gauguin left Paris in early 1888, each imagined his destination mythically, in terms conditioned by prevalent contemporary ideas and more importantly by contact with each other in a dialogue that would accelerate with the passing months.

In 1886 Gauguin had been drawn to Brittany by the prospect of living and working inexpensively there; now he sought a mythic locus that would foster his emergent personal and professional identity. After a month in Pont-Aven, Gauguin tried on his new "costume" for Schuffenecker. In a letter Gauguin asked his friend whether he had finished his picture of city roadmenders; the question paved the way for a seemingly extemporaneous, and now often-quoted, observation:

I like Brittany, I find a certain wildness and primitiveness here. When my clogs echo on this granite soil, I hear the dull, muted, powerful tone I seek in painting.[1]

This self-characterization was in fact carefully rehearsed. The oppositional terminology—city versus country, civilized versus primitive—was commonplace, but Gauguin's vocabulary derives from a particular source: Mon Frère Yves (1883), the first of Pierre Loti's three pseudoautobiographical novels dealing with the lives of Breton sailors, so popular that by 1887 it was already in its twentieth printing. Loti's Brittany is a "dark, primitive" place, its hamlets of granite cottages as ancient as its inhabitants, with their "expression[s] of primitive times" (see fig. 2). Evoking this atmosphere aurally, Loti described the repeated sound of "wooden sabots hammering on the hard granite pavé." In the author's relentless characterization of the Breton sailors as naïve, childlike, and simple—culturally backward and anti-urban—the foil is of course Paris. "Parisian,"

as Loti noted, was an insult used in Brittany to signify "no sailor, a weakling, a sick man"; an epithet invoked at the first whiff of the stink of corruption and decadence. The sailors by contrast remained in close touch with their primitive ancestry by virtue of birthplace and occupation: the "hidden savage" at the core of every man, Loti observed, was especially dominant in those who inhabit the primitive world of the sea.[2]

Loti's theme of essential wildness informs the "two natures" letter that Gauguin wrote to Mette in mid-January, just before leaving Paris. Acting on the claim that his tender-hearted self was yielding to the Indian in him, he outlined a plan to work in Brittany for a stretch of seven or eight months in order to become "imbued with the temperament of the local people and their region, an important factor in producing good art." In effect this was a formula for escaping from the strictures of cultural background through an encounter with the "other." The character of Yves is attractive to Loti, who adopts him as his brother, because he is a sort of noble savage. Their relationship replicates the colonialist paradigm: the sophisticated Parisian author imagines himself much simpler owing to contact with Yves; however, when Yves becomes more "complex" as a result of Loti's proximity, he is less compelling.[3]

Gauguin similarly hoped to enter an atavistic state of mind that would counter the scientific rationality of Neo-Impressionism. A conscious act, it required of Gauguin, as of Loti, selective vision in the face of the reality that the "old Brittany of an earlier time [is] almost dead."[4] Works such as Breton Women and Cow (fig. 3) show him attempting to give pictorial expression to the qualities described in his letter to Schuffenecker: the composition is non-hieratic, the palette dull and matte, the expression of the figures mute. Their unre-

sponsive gazes directed toward something unseen by the viewer, they appear transfixed; the scene seems frozen in time, infused with a sinister, mysterious, otherworldly mood.

In being appropriative rather than associative, Gauguin's mode of reading differed from Vincent's. Gauguin's several ironic references later in life to the "effete and blasé" author of Mon Frère Yves, Le Mariage de Loti, and Madame Chrysanthème would seem to mask disquiet about his own use of Loti's books as primers for constructing a site-specific identity, first in Brittany and then in Tahiti.[5] This dismissal was a preemptive move to distance his work from the connections first signaled by Vincent, who immediately saw that Gauguin presented a unity of life and art comparable to Loti's strategic identity. Gauguin's talk of Brittany and his maritime background no doubt prompted Vincent to discuss Loti's Breton novels, just as the Martinique pictures had led to comparison with Le Mariage. In the same vein, Vincent himself would soon seek to enrich his experience of the South through Madame Chrysanthème.

2
Postcard of cabin boys at Saint-Guénole, Brittany
c. 1900/10

3
Paul Gauguin
Breton Women and Cow
(Bretonnes et vau)
1888 [W 252]
Oil on canvas
91 x 72 cm
Ny Carlsberg Glyptothek, Copenhagen

Theo explained his brother's departure for the South of France somewhat prosaically, writing to Wil that Vincent wished to escape the cold, gray Paris winters and to "get sunshine into [his] pictures." But Vincent's decision to follow the sun was symbolic as much as practical, its significance tied up with the sunflower canvases that he had already presented to Gauguin. Claiming subsequently that "Gauguin...owes his superiority to the Midi" —the term "Midi" here embraces a vast geography of warm climates—Vincent found confirmation for widely current ideas about the South's creative potential.[6] Meeting Gauguin helped precipitate a departure that Vincent had entertained, it seems, from the moment he arrived in Paris.

In the late summer of 1886, Vincent had confided to Livens his hope to go to the South of France, "the land of *blue* tones and gay colors," the following spring, if not sooner; this plan related to his interest in developing his sense of color, and he suggested that if Livens "had longings for the same we might combine."[7] It was from a revised perspective that he revived the idea of going south in late 1887. Theo's initial proposal of marriage to Jo Bonger, the sister of his friend Andries Bonger, exacerbated a depression possibly connected to Vincent's break in relations with Agostina Segatori and to his approaching thirty-fifth birthday. He felt the loss of youth and the pressure to decide where his ambitions lay: with personal relationships (a wife and family) or with art alone. He already suspected that he had little chance of achieving the former, but wondered if he had the stamina for the latter. He was disillusioned by the sectarian jealousies dividing the Paris art world, and he mentioned possibly retiring "somewhere down south [to] get away from the sight of so many painters who fill me with disgust as human beings."[8]

But at other moments, Vincent fought against melancholy and bitterness. Jo's initial rejection of Theo's offer allayed fears that his brother would be less able to support his work. From a more optimistic viewpoint, the South was not simply an escape from the present, but a nurturing place where he might recapture "youth and freshness" for himself and his painting. Vincent's desire to infuse his pictures with sunlight was his spiritual gloss on the formal ambitions of vanguard painting, "gay" color the equivalent to the "really good laugh" that leavened Naturalist literature.[9] The mirage of the South satisfied what Guy de Maupassant had suggested was nostalgia for the unknown in *Au soleil* (1884), the book detailing his flight from Paris to North Africa that Vincent's new friend Signac had featured in one of his luminous still-life paintings (ch. 2, fig. 73).

Traditional emblematic associations of the sun with spiritual renewal had been reinforced in Vincent's mind by his recent reading. Frederik van Eeden, in *De kleine Johannes*, imaged the revelation that city-worn Johannes experiences on regaining the Dutch countryside as a "consecration of light." Seeking comparable renewal, Vincent headed to the South in hopes of finding a warmer —more accommodating—North. The Mediterranean climate's restorative potential was both psychic and physical. Theo spoke of the struggle with depression that he and his brother shared as a "combat with mists," using the sun, with its capacity to dissipate fog, as a metaphor for happiness.[10] Part of the South's attraction was quite simply its difference from the North, as Vincent wrote to Wil:

In our native country people are blind as bats and criminally stupid because they do not exert themselves more to go to the Indies or somewhere else where the sun shines. It is not right to know only one thing—one gets stul-

tified by that; one should not rest before one knows the opposite too.[11]

A primary source for Vincent's geography of contrasts was Alphonse Daudet's novels dealing with the temperament of his native Provence. These include the humorous adventure stories featuring the hero Tartarin — *Tartarin de Tarascon* (1872) and *Tartarin sur les Alpes* (1885) (see fig. 5)—as well as *Numa Roumestan* (1881), a satiric tale about a Provençal protagonist who settles in Paris that Vincent had read while still in the Netherlands. Vincent admired Tartarin for his good humor, good intentions, and energy, qualities that served as antidotes against melancholy, the disease fostered in the North.[12]

Drawing on current scientific ideas regarding the physical environment as a psychological determinant, in *Numa Roumestan* Daudet represented North and South as opposites. Paris stands for the North as a whole. Its citizens—spoiled, ambitious, and addicted to fickle fashions—are degenerate and amoral, their coldness a result of the foggy, sorrowful, black night of perpetual winter in which they live. By contrast the South's brilliant sun, intense light, "truly African heat," and exciting mistral winds are so extreme as to have produced a different race of inhabitants, impractical, volatile, nervous. In their tendency to exaggerate everything, Southerners themselves were natural caricatures. Daudet's "effervescing South, mobile and tumultuous like a sea with many currents," was tonic to its inhabitants, the mistral imparting a "flow of health and good spirits" to life's inevitable hardships; this "South of the winds, of the sun, of the mirage, of everything that makes one poetic and widens one's life," was a naturally expansive environment.[13]

Daudet was not the only writer to extol Provence at this time: a visible movement devoted to the revival of Provençal language, literature, and customs had been launched at mid-century by the Félibrige, an association of poets. Although it is unclear precisely how much Vincent knew about the Félibres before going to Arles, the association's most effective chapter (founded in 1879) was based in Paris, where it supported various publishing and proselytizing activities.[14] Parisian consciousness of things Provençal had been raised through a widely publicized "Fête du soleil," held in December 1886 to aid victims of a recent flood of the Rhone (see fig. 4). Mounted in the vast Palais de l'Industrie, the festival was a kind of theme park, featuring windmills and typical habitations, performances of the farandole and other regional dances, and the women of Arles—the Arlésiennes—in their distinctive costumes. A giant electric sun presided over all.

The sun and the sunflower that turns toward it were emblems of Félibrige aspirations and of the South's allure (see fig. 7). The identity between the celestial body and the flower was reinforced linguistically: in French *soleil* means both "sun" and "sunflower." Hoping to encourage a renaissance in painting to parallel that well under way in literature, regional proponents forecast that the sun of the Midi would render "the palette of Southern painters unquestionably more brilliant" than that of their Parisian counterparts.[15]

This meteorology of the spirit struck a particular chord. Embracing the fundamentals of Daudet's vision of the South, Vincent com-pounded its personal relevance by grafting onto it two other constructs. The first involved Vincent's revisionist interpretation of Monticelli's life and work (see fig. 6). He not only revered Monticelli as a colorist equal to Delacroix and responded to his heavily impastoed surfaces, he also believed they shared a personal kinship, even feeling like "his son or his brother." This conviction explains Vincent's preoccupation with Monticelli during his first months in Arles. Clearly associating his own heavy drinking in Paris with stories of Monticelli's excesses and sad end, Vincent became personally invested in proving these tales false. Persistently, he advanced a diagnosis tracing Monticelli's nervous condition to two sources: the strains of working out complex color calculations and the natural exaltation caused by the climate of the South and a life lived in the open air rather than indoors.[16] In Arles Vincent became his own test case. Much as Daudet described the sun as distilling a "terrible kind of natural alcohol," such that inhabitants could get drunk from a few bottles of lemonade, Vincent likewise observed that a small glass of cognac went to his head.[17] This construction of the South explained Monticelli's eccentric behavior. Vincent sought a place that would normalize his personality.

Embracing the fundamentals of Daudet's expansive vision of the South, where Monticelli fit so comfortably, Vincent extended the geography of associations as far as Japan. In his imaginative construal, "Japanese gaiety" and the "good nature of Tartarin" were of a piece—sources of the optimism that was such a crucial ingredient of a consoling art. To see the South was to "understand the Japanese better." The Japanese, like Daudet's Southerners (or Loti's Breton fisherman), had a more childlike temperament and a more intense love of nature than did Parisians. His inclusion of the "simple" Japanese in the broadly understood category of the "primitives" was consonant with the interpretation of Japan then current in French intellectual circles, characterized by a smug sense of cultural and technological superiority on the one hand and a nostalgic longing for a golden age of innocence on the other.[18]

Vincent extrapolated a notion of a Japanese artistic community in counterpoint to his Paris experience. From the exchanges between artists he imagined to be so important to Japanese artists, he deduced a climate of mutual support and harmony; he pictured them "in fact living in a kind of fraternal community, quite unaffectedly, and not in intrigues," "close to nature like simple workmen."[19] But Vincent's fantasy was situated not in Japan but in France, for reasons implicit in his observation that, "if the Japanese are not making any progress in their own country, still it cannot be doubted that their art is being continued in France." This gives expression to the dark side of primitivist interpretation. For Vincent, the Impressionists were the "Japanese of France," achieving for their country what the Japanese once had for their own, by in fact transplanting and revitalizing an art that had become decadent in its native land.[20] France's "civilizing mission" justified expansion into Southeast Asia and the appropriation

LES FÊTES DU SOLEIL AU PALAIS DE L'INDUSTRIE. — LA PROCESSION DE LA TARASQUE. — LA FARANDOLE. — LES LUTTEURS DE M. MARSEILLE. — (DESSIN DE M. GIRARDIN.)

ADOLPHE MONTICELLI — (Dessin de M. Monge)

4
After Auguste
Gerardin
(French; b. 1849)
*Les Fêtes du soleil au
Palais de l'Industrie*
from *Le Monde
illustré,* 1 January
1887, p. 5

5
Tartarin de Tarascon
from Alphonse
Daudet
(French; 1840–1897)
Tartarin sur les Alpes
(Paris, 1885), p. 43
Bibliothèque
Nationale, Paris

6
Jules Monge
(French; 19th
century)
Adolphe Monticelli
from *La Provence* 1,
no. 19 (August 1881)
Bibliothèque
Nationale, Paris

7
Victor Maziès
(French; 1836–1895)
Detail from
Félibrige invitation
1889
Etching
Bibliothèque
Nationale, Paris
Note that the
emblem is based
on Renaissance
prototypes
(see ch. 2, fig. 51).

7

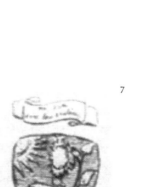

Arles: Past and Present

of cultural artifacts; the enactment of rescue abroad combated decadence at home.[21] This ideology informed Vincent's artistic strategy of viewing southern France as the concrete setting for a Carlylean revitalization of art through the casting of old truths in new light. Refined and transformed, it would emerge as the concept of a "Studio of the South."

And, ultimately, for a Studio of the Tropics. In this thinking, Gauguin factored prominently. His Martinique experience actively fostered the fantasy that the spirit of a vanished golden age of long ago could be recovered in the far away, prompting Vincent to predict, in late March 1888, that "a present-day painter should do something like what one finds in Pierre Loti's book *Le Mariage de Loti,* in which the nature of Otaheite [Tahiti] is described."[22] For now, however, intent on exploiting pictorial opportunities in Arles, Vincent was gripped by a pioneering, entrepreneurial spirit that propelled his thoughts in the direction of Marseilles.

Arles, Theo informed Wil, was to be an "orientation," after which Vincent would probably move on to Marseilles, some fifty-five miles (eighty-nine kilometers) to the southeast. A major port with some four hundred thousand inhabitants and capital of the department of Bouches-du-Rhône, Marseilles held a special attraction for Vincent: the home of Monticelli, it stood for opportunities that had been unavailable in Paris. Most immediately, Vincent imagined that an abundance of works by Monticelli could be acquired inexpensively there in advance of rising market demand. Within hours of arriving in Arles, despite fatigue from his nearly sixteen-hour train journey, Vincent visited an antique dealer in the hope—confirmed in his immediate report to Theo—that he might know where to find a Monticelli.[23] The brothers believed the Marseilles painter's posthumous fate would follow the course of the Generation of 1830: as its practitioners died off, in the 1860s and 1870s, dealers like Durand-Ruel who had stockpiled their work successfully marketed their reputations and profited handsomely from their speculation. The van Goghs also knew that a

similar goal motivated their recent acquaintance Alexander Reid, son of a Glasgow dealer who had come to Paris to study art, work informally at Theo's firm, and acquire paintings for his father's gallery. Reid's interest in Monticelli had already elevated the artist's prices, coincidentally increasing the value of the five pictures Vincent and Theo owned. The prospect of competition stimulated a kind of excited gamesmanship in Vincent, who was after all a former apprentice art dealer; he hoped to gain advantage in the South. Having fallen out with Reid over his lack of interest in contemporary art, he began worrying nonetheless that the Glaswegian might stake a rival claim to the Impressionists. He proposed making a deal: he offered Reid a "free hand with the Marseilles Monticellis" if he would leave the brothers alone in pioneering new markets for Impressionism.[24]

Vincent imagined complex moves, whereby he and Theo would play Reid off against Vincent's old nemesis Herman Gijsbertus Tersteeg and another Dutch dealer, Elbert Jan van Wisselingh. He proposed the creation

25
Vincent van Gogh
A Farmhouse in Provence
(*Un Mas de Provence*)
Mid-June 1888
[F 565, JH 1443]
Oil on canvas
46 x 61 cm

National Gallery of Art, Washington, D.C., Ailsa Mellon Bruce Collection, 1970.17.34
Cat. 56

26
Vincent van Gogh
The Sower
Mid-June 1888
[F 422, JH 1470]
Oil on canvas
64 x 80.5 cm
Kröller-Müller Museum, Otterlo, The Netherlands
Cat. 57

27
Vincent van Gogh
Sketch after Millet's *Sower*
1887
Graphite
In sketchbook no. 2, p. 60
Van Gogh Museum (Vincent van Gogh Foundation)

28
Vincent van Gogh
Sketch of *The Sower* in letter to Bernard
[18 June 1888]
(letter 630/B 7)
Van Gogh Museum, Amsterdam (Vincent van Gogh Foundation)

25

Vincent's *Sower*

At precisely the same moment that Gauguin apprised Theo of his *Breton Girls Dancing*, Vincent announced that he was at work on a new composition, one that, as his extensive comments to his brother and friends reveal, constituted at once a shift in direction and an assertion of artistic identity. It features a lone sower in a field (figs. 26).

Following his plan of producing seasonal cycles of images, Vincent had turned from flowering orchards to a series of drawings and canvases depicting the harvest. The theme had important precedents: the Crau's vast stretches of fields certainly recalled the work of Rembrandt student Philips de Koninck, as well as that of Georges Michel and Jules Dupré. More immediately, the activity and the site evoked landscapes of Cézanne, whose *Harvest* (fig.

emerges in comparison to the earlier work's radically flattened, two-dimensional design. For all the surreal quality of this dance, it is performed on what is, finally, a relatively conventional pictorial stage. It is questionable how long Gauguin himself continued to regard the picture as a satisfactory index of the marriage of personal and professional styles he was seeking to broker. Later that year, in Arles, he observed that his ceramics, although "very savage," were "more the expression of who I am" than was this image.[83] Achieving a comparable stylistic unity in painting remained a struggle.

33) Vincent had seen at the dealer Portier's in Paris. Initiating his own harvest scenes, Vincent recalled the way the Aix-based artist captured the "harsh" aspect of Provence; in his renderings of the subject he sought to achieve an overall harmony of old gold, bronze, and copper—"the very tones of old Cézanne." Some are intimate in conception, showing humble farmhouse compounds, or *mas*, at ground level (see fig. 25); in others Vincent enlarged his ambitions literally, confidently deploying the panoramic scope and deep space of traditional Dutch prototypes and tackling subjects on the bigger scale of the size 30 canvas (92 x 73 cm).[84]

The Sower is both a continuation of this series and a departure from it. In his initial explorations of the harvest theme, Vincent did not amplify the symbolism implied by annual cycles of cultivation and renewal. Indeed he did these landscapes, as it were, against his will, wanting to execute something more ambitious to express what he called his "longing for the infinite, of which the sower, the sheaf are symbols."[85] Setting his sower in a "great field all violet, the sky and the sun very yellow," with ripe wheat in the background, Vincent grappled with the larger background that was the crisis of doubt he had been attempting to keep at bay since the news of Mauve's death. The need to believe in something transcendent inevitably brought with it thoughts of Millet, whose *Sower* (ch. 1, fig. 35)—a canonical image of death and rebirth—was fresh in Vincent's mind from the Barbizon-based artist's 1887 retrospective, where he may have executed the sketch that appears in one of his notebooks (fig. 27). The hint of a likeness between the sketch and Vincent's contemporary self-portraits with beard and hat (see ch. 2, fig. 46) suggests an identification with Millet's powerful figure that he now underscored by describing a "labor-intensive, hard week in the wheat

Here is a sketch of a sower: a large piece of land with clods of plowed earth, for the most part a definite purple.
A field of ripe wheat, in yellow ochre with a little carmine. The sky chrome yellow, almost as bright as the
sun itself, which is chrome yellow 1 with a little white, while the rest of the sky is chrome yellow 1 and 2 mixed.
Thus very yellow.... There are many touches of yellow in the soil, neutral tones produced by mixing purple
with the yellow, but I couldn't care less what the colors are in *reality*.   Vincent to Bernard, [18 June 1888]

26

27

28

fields in the heat of the sun."[86] This conception of the peasant-painter returns to ideas first broached pictorially in his still life of boots (ch. 2, fig. 47), resonant as it is with issues of legacy, continuity, and change. Painting the lone figure of a sower under the blazing sun of Provence, Vincent expressed his symbolic intent to follow in Millet's footsteps and enlarge his path.

The scope of his ambition emerges in the way he framed the enterprise: citing Millet's lack of color, he proposed to Theo that the measure of vanguard ambition—what "after Millet…still remains to be done"—was a "sower, in color and large sized." In other words he aimed to translate Millet's "colorless gray" using a "simultaneous contrast of yellow and violet" that he associated with Delacroix's Apollo ceiling in the Louvre and even more with his *Christ on the Sea of Galilee* (fig. 34), where he felt Delacroix spoke a "symbolic language through color alone."[87] The image of Christ on troubled waters, a parable for the need to have faith, and that of the sower, representing the spreading of its word, had long compelled Vincent, as his early sermon attests.[88] He now conceived his project not only in terms of bridging the harmonist

and colorist traditions, but in compounding the spirituality of Millet's imagery through the symbolic potential of Delacroix's color.

Vincent had wanted to do a sower for "some time, but the things I've wanted for a long time do not always come off." His picture made an affirmative statement in the face of Gauguin's equivocation and Tersteeg's rejection. Although he declared he had no intention of "cramp[ing] anybody's individuality by association"—forestalling what he imagined as Gauguin's reservations—the sower's iconography nonetheless suggests the seminal role that Vincent entertained for himself.[89] It also asserts a tenacious commitment to an idealized vision of the artist, paralleling a less overtly symbolic image of himself on the way to work in the fields of the Crau (fig. 29). With his pose, his hat, and the implements he carries, Vincent's figure echoes the pitchfork-carrying farmworker in Millet's *Departure for the Fields* (fig. 30). But in addition to "father Millet," there is another whom Vincent emulated, for *The Road to Tarascon* occupies a position in a perspective of associations. It recalls a very early drawing, *En Route* (fig. 31), which can be related to the image, evoked in letters, of the Reverend van Gogh traveling at

night with a lantern to comfort the dying with the light of the Word, a scenario associated in turn with Rembrandt's nighttime rendering of the Holy Family's flight into Egypt (fig. 32).[90] The early attempt to follow in his father's footsteps had led to those of Rembrandt and Millet.

The painter as missionary—sower of the word, illuminator of the darkness—had always been central to Vincent's thinking about art. Muted during his time in Paris, when with few exceptions he focused on stylistic concerns, this notion had now resurfaced, reconfirmed by Wagner. The composer saw his art as addressing concerns about the barrenness of traditional religion and the need for spiritual regeneration. He wrote of a future art as a consoling evangel; Benoit called him a preacher.[91] Vincent's *Sower*, as both work of art and model of the artist, expresses similar aims. *The Sower* is nothing less than the image of the art of the future and of its evangel.

Conceived explicitly to be a "masterpiece," *The Sower* was Vincent's most ambitious undertaking since his studies in Paris. With its accumulated significance and longstanding status as a conceptual benchmark, the chal-

29

30

31

32

33

34

Forms of Virility

lenge it posed for him was overdetermined. From the outset it frightened and tormented him with doubt. He began it as a sketch (*esquisse*) but immediately wondered whether he should not "take it seriously and turn it into a tremendous painting [*tableau*]."[92] He put it aside only to pick it up again. Uncharacteristically indecisive, he made numerous changes: he rendered the play of the violet/yellow complementaries more complex by mixing green and yellow into the sky and orange into the fields; recast the original posture of the sower in favor of Millet's; repositioned the figure in the pictorial field; changed the colors of the clothing; and eliminated distracting forms and colors along the horizon line. The picture's worried surface testifies to the struggle, carried out for the most part—and exceptionally—in the quiet of the studio rather than in active battle with the elements.[93]

On 28 June he declared his painting to be completely reworked but the task still incomplete. "Most certainly there is such a *tableau* to make with this magnificent motif, and I hope it will be done one day, either by me or by someone else." The following day word from Theo arrived that distracted him from the struggle. "Your letter brings great news," Vincent replied, "namely that Gauguin agrees to the plan."[94]

Gauguin had evidently sent the letter in which he formally accepted the brothers' offer just days before. He was getting nervous that he had had no reply from Theo to his first response. Though he had not yet abandoned his marketing project, he wanted to hold on to the bird in hand.[95] Again Theo delayed responding, possibly because Vincent, eager to join forces as soon as possible, had complicated matters by suggesting that he could join Gauguin in Pont-Aven, but more likely because Gauguin lacked finances to settle debts and cover travel, and Theo was not in a position to provide them. Perplexed by Theo's silence, Gauguin wrote again on 8 July requesting confirmation.[96]

In the interim Gauguin had begun a new painting, which, as he informed Schuffenecker, was "not at all a Degas.... A struggle [*une lutte*] between two boys by the river, quite in the Japanese style by a ~~French~~ Peruvian savage" (fig. 39).[97] Two weeks later, he informed Vincent of the termination of his "Lutte bretonne," enclosing a sketch (fig. 35) along with a description:

Two boys, one wearing vermilion pants, the other blue ones. Above right, a boy climbing up out of the water—green grass—pure emerald green, shading off into chrome yellow: *unrefined*, as in Japanese *crépons*. Also above, a boiling waterfall in pinkish white, with a rainbow on the edge of the canvas just beside the frame. Below, a white patch, a black hat, and a blue smock.[98]

Gauguin felt certain that Vincent would like his picture, no doubt because in overall con-

ception as well as in certain details, *Young Wrestlers—Brittany* engages in dialogue with *The Sower*. Gauguin's conspicuous inclusion of a "white patch" in the foreground takes a cue from Vincent's original conception of his sower, in which he rendered the figure's trousers white, not in the service of realism but to "help rest the eye and distract it" from the excessive color contrasts dominating the canvas. This use of white came directly from Charles Blanc's *Grammaire des arts du dessin* (1867), an aesthetic treatise familiar to Seurat and the Neo-Impressionists and to Gauguin.[99] Vincent's initial emphatic division of the composition into two zones, of intense yellow and violet, was likewise formally motivated. While his painted border of complementary colors defers to Neo-Impressionism, in a letter to Bernard, Vincent likened *The Sower* to the "wholly primitive manner" seen in old almanacs and successfully captured by Anquetin the previous year in a harvest picture. Announcing the same painting to Russell, he coded such decisions as "abstractions," linking his preoccupation with the "stylish" to the Italian primitives.[100]

Gauguin absorbed Vincent's elaborate exegesis of *The Sower*, declaring himself "wholly in agreement with you about how little exactitude matters in art." Introducing his own picture—which ostensibly features a traditional Breton subject, the wrestling still performed at regional fairs and feast-day celebrations (see fig. 38)—he played it back: "Art is an abstraction; unfortunately we are understood less and less. I would love to reach our goal, meaning my trip to Provence."[101]

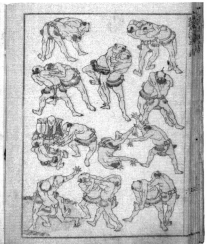

36

37

38

35
Paul Gauguin
Sketch of *Young
Wrestlers—Brittany*
in letter to Vincent
[c. 24/25 July 1888]
(M 1984, letter 158)
Van Gogh Museum,
Amsterdam
(Vincent van Gogh
Foundation)
Cat. 30

36
Katsushika Hokusai
(Japanese;
1760–1849)
Wrestlers from *The
Sketches of Hokusai*
(Nagoya/Edo, 1816),
vol. 3, pp. 6 verso,
7 recto
The Art Institute of
Chicago, Martin
Ryerson Collection,
2577
Cat. 147

37
Pierre Puvis de
Chavannes
(French; 1824–1898)
Pleasant Land
1882
Oil on canvas
25.8 x 47.3 cm
Yale University Art
Gallery, New
Haven,
Connecticut, The
Mary Gertrude
Abbey Fund

38
O. Perrin
(French; 1761–1832)
Breton Games
from *Galerie des
Moeurs: Usages et cos-
tumes des Bretons*
(Paris, 1808)
Bibliothèque
Nationale, Paris

39
Paul Gauguin
*Young Wrestlers—
Brittany (Jeunes
Lutteurs—Bretagne)*
July 1888 [W273]
Oil on canvas
93 x 73 cm
Private collection
Cat. 29

There was validity to Gauguin's claim that his latest work "surpassed what I have done up until now." Comparison of *Young Wrestlers—Brittany* with *Young Breton Bathers* of 1886 (ch. 2, fig. 25) reveals how far from Impressionist models he had moved in the direction of what he now called an abstract, synthetic style. But the contrast also stands with regard to recent pictures like *Breton Girls Dancing*, only weeks old, which underscores the self-consciousness of Gauguin's departure and explains the defensiveness in his claim to Schuffenecker that the work was unlike that of Degas.[102] What makes the *Wrestlers* a breakthrough—a kind of stylistic exorcism that Gauguin had approached in ceramics but had not yet achieved in painting—is the willful incorporation of a primitivism inflected by Vincent's enthusiasm for Japan.

Vincent had already persuaded Bernard and Theo of the practical value of Japanese prints for artists. Gauguin, for his part, had long been aware of Japanese art (a typical album, possibly one of Hokusai's 1815 *manga* series, features in an early still life), but never before had he so overtly appropriated their stylistic characteristics.[103] Possibly consulting a page from the *manga* (see fig. 36) for the figures of the wrestlers, he looked expressly to the compositional principles of Japanese woodcuts for the simplified space in which he set them: a radically tilted shelf of grass emphasized by a

39

40
Émile Wauters
(Belgian; 1846–1933)
*Madness of Hugo van
der Goes* (detail)
1872
Oil on canvas
Musée Royaux des
Beaux-Arts de
Belgique, Brussels

nearly uniform application of color and boldly cropped by the assertive diagonal wedge of foaming water.

Not only did Gauguin dismiss Degas in his description of the picture to Schuffenecker, but he denied his own identity as a "Frenchman," writing instead that a "Peruvian savage" had produced the japonizing vision. Certainly his primitivism had taken a new and innovative form. While Vincent's thinking about *The Sower* may have brought certain formal issues to the fore, the composition itself did not. The small sketches of the painting that Vincent sent to Bernard, Russell, and no doubt Gauguin are not particularly vivid demonstrations of his claim that all of his work had some basis in Japanese art. Vincent's abstraction here is rooted in color rather than design; his spatial construction and figure type remain relatively conventional. Moreover, his interest in the "simplification of color in the Japanese manner," while evident in other current work (see fig. 13), is not immediately legible in *The Sower*.[104] Gauguin made it so in *Young Wrestlers—Brittany*. His insistent contours, broad planes, bold design, and forcible details such as the foremost boy's exaggeratedly large, rigid foot (recalling his sketchbook analysis of Egyptian sculptures in the Louvre)[105] all contribute to an overtly antinaturalistic, multireferential primitivism that goes beyond Vincent's conflation of Japan, Greece, and Naturalist literature. In language that seems responsive to Gauguin, Vincent spoke of "Egyptian calm and great simplicity" and evinced an interest in drawings even more "excessively synthetic" than Japanese prints.[106]

Gauguin's *Young Wrestlers—Brittany*, manifesting stylistic goals different from Vincent's, nonetheless participated in the latter's project of rescuing (and continuing) Japanese art by transplanting it to the South of France. It did so through the conduit of another shared enthusiasm: Puvis, specifically

his *Pleasant Land* (fig. 37), an arcadian vision whose dreamlike calm and order is disrupted only by two small boys wrestling. The work had been included in the artist's 1887 retrospective at Durand-Ruel, and Vincent, once installed in Arles, regarded this picture as evocative of Provence.[107]

Gauguin's quotation of the wrestling motif may also be interpreted in the context of his own plans for working in the Midi. He wrote to Vincent: "It's as if I had need to *struggle* [*un besoin de* lutte], to chip away with hammer blows. After all the research I've just done here, I believe that I can make progress."[108] The French term *lutte*—translatable as struggle, fight, combat, or contest—had long been used to figure the demands of creativity. It had gained particular currency among the Neo-Impressionist vanguard; Seurat designated his major paintings as "toiles de *lutte*" (canvases of *combat*) and as "research canvases, conquests if possible"; Pissarro frequently referred to the group effort in terms of "notre lutte" (our combat) against dissenters like Gauguin.[109] Alluding to this factionalism, Gauguin's picture, like his language, images his own struggle to forge an identity in painting. Playing off Puvis, as he had in the earlier *Cleopatra* pot (ch. 2, fig. 69), in *Young Wrestlers* he essayed a comparable achievement in the medium that permitted him to go toe-to-toe with Seurat, Pissarro, and Signac.

"Lutte contradictoire" (contradictory struggle) was a phrase that Gauguin would use in a letter to Schuffenecker to describe creative stimulus. If in 1886–87 he had begun to harness the hostility he generated among the vanguard into creative energy, the discussions with Vincent in the summer of 1888 helped him give it shape. Quite possibly, Vincent had referred to the productive potential of competition as a reason for Gauguin to come south, given his vivid recollection of the time when he and Rappard were working in tandem at top speed, spurring each other on.[110] The ideal

he had enunciated in 1883 must have seemed pertinent again:

I … find something animating in the thought that one works in one direction, the other in another, yet there is still mutual sympathy. Competition, when it proceeds from jealousy, is quite a different thing from trying one's best to make the work as good as possible, *out of mutual respect*. "Les extrêmes se touchent." I do not see any good in jealousy, but I would despise a friendship which did not call for some exertion on both sides to maintain the level.[111]

The pair of wrestlers, engaged in play that tests and develops their skill and strength, can be seen to illustrate this *wrijving*. The picture's iconography and style also imaged another kind of combat, Vincent's and Gauguin's joint struggle against the incomprehension of their aims. Gauguin framed his discussion of this picture with repeated mention of what he hoped to accomplish after joining Vincent in the Midi, and other signs indicated solidarity as well. *Young Wrestlers*, Gauguin allowed, proved him "completely crazy" to the louts in Pont-Aven. The choice of words would be insignificant were it not for his additional description of his recent works as *toquades* (crazes) and *folies peintes* (crazy paintings), expressions with which Gauguin tacitly placed himself among Vincent's brotherhood of *toqués* (madmen), representative examples of creativity and its demands.[112]

Preoccupied with the relationship between genius and insanity, Vincent had been musing on his own mental state. He informed Theo that when the "storm within gets too loud," he drank a glass too much to "stun" himself, although most of the time he threw himself into his work. From this perspective, painting was a remedial distraction, but Vincent also entertained the contrary proposition that he was "crazy" precisely because of this "blasted painting," and he was not the only one. Had not Jules Dupré seemed "crazy" to Goncourt? And he imagined that younger painters, those committed to the new art, were "still isolated, poor, treated as madmen and as a result of this treatment truly becoming insane."[113] Though he believed in their eventual triumph, he worried about the cost: that Gauguin might share the fate of etcher Charles Méryon, who twenty years earlier had died in a mental institution, suffering from paranoia and religious mania. Vincent, for his own part, looked in the mirror and thought of Hugo van der Goes, the fifteenth-century monk-painter whose madness was the stuff of myth, memorably depicted by Belgian painter Émile Wauters (fig. 40).[114]

Vincent proposed to his various correspondents that all great geniuses are mad, adding that "one must be mad oneself to have boundless faith in them" and concluding: "If this is true, I should prefer my insanity to the sanity of others." His ranks of crazy genius included writers and artists—Balzac, Zola, Delacroix, Rembrandt, Daumier, Millet—and religious visionaries—Moses, Muhammad, Luther, Bunyan, even Christ.[115] He was in good company.

The range of this grouping points to Vincent's reengagement with his old ideas about art as replacement for religion, which he found reiterated in Wagner's credo:

I believe in God, in Mozart and in Beethoven; I also believe in their disciples and apostles...; I believe in the sanctity of the spirit and in artistic truth whole and indivisible...; I believe that this art has a divine source, and that it lives in the heart of all men illuminated by celestial light; I believe that after having tasted the sublime delights of this great art, one is inevitably and forever devoted to it, one is unable to deny it; I believe that everyone, after its intervention, can reach beatitude.[116]

These beliefs had various consequences, as Vincent already knew. Benoit's description of Wagner's all-consuming fruitful struggles to shake off the artistic yoke echoed his own ongoing contemplation of the polarities of the "artistic life" versus the "real life." Writing to Bernard in June, he referred to the painter's labor under *"the back-breaking yoke"* of all-demanding art.[117] Would the sacrifice be worth it? Would he have to resign himself to mediocrity? Could the art of the future be realized in the present? Wagner himself had expressed doubt: "At this moment one cannot create the work of art [of the future], but only prepare its advent...*people totally other than ourselves will be the first to create the genuine work of art.*"

Vincent similarly began to speak with professed contentment of paving the way for future generations.[118] Such statements point to the very essence of Vincent's creative process and provide clues for understanding works like *The Sower*, under way at precisely this time. The painting's meaning is imbricate, made up of overlapping concepts culled from a dense tangle of associative connections. To switch metaphors, Vincent distilled, from the blended experiences of art and life that constituted his reality, a core set of essential notions to which he attempted to give pictorial expression.

Like the sometimes contrapuntal ideas that swarmed in his head and tumbled onto the pages of his correspondence, a resonant aura envelops each of his signature canvases. The aura enveloping *The Sower* embraces—in addition to the murmurings of achievement, ambition, renewal, and spirituality from Millet to Carlyle to Wagner—the following exchange:

You'll come into your own yet, old fellow.... You're bound to. The art of the future is going to be your art. These chaps are where they are now because you've *made* them.
What the hell's the use of having "made" them, if I haven't "made" myself?... You

Not just my pictures but I myself have become especially haggard of late, almost like Hugo van der Goes in the painting by Émile Wauters. Except that, having had all my beard carefully shaved off, I think I'm as much the very placid abbot in that picture as the mad painter so cleverly portrayed in it. And I'm not displeased at falling somewhere between the two, for *one must live*. Vincent to Theo, [25 July 1888]

know as well as I do it was too much for me, and that's just what I can't stomach.

A despairing gesture was enough to indicate his train of thought—his inability to be the genius of his own artistic creed, his frustration at being the forerunner who sows the idea but cannot reap the glory, his despair at seeing himself robbed…before he…had had the strength to produce the masterpiece that would be a landmark of contemporary painting.[119]

The frustrated sower here is Claude Lantier, the neurotic protagonist of Zola's *L'Oeuvre*, whose unrealizable ambition to create from Impressionism an art of transcendent symbolic significance—to produce a true painting (*tableau*) from a lifetime of preparatory studies—leads him to forsake life, love, and family for the "jealous god" of Art and finally precipitates his despair, madness, and suicide.[120] Vincent may have claimed the role of paving the way "for the other painters of the future, who will come work in the South."[121] But he allowed himself a much greater ambition, attended by doubt, that pulsates through his late-June correspondence with Bernard, installed since April in the Breton town of Saint-Briac.

Vincent had developed a special relationship with the twenty-year-old, evident in the contents and tone of blustery camaraderie of his letters to him. Bernard's current preoccupations with art, sex, and religion afforded Vincent the opportunity to debate these subjects with relish. Responding to Bernard's interpretation of John 1:19–21—a passage in which John the Baptist denies being Christ, Elijah, or the prophet, insisting instead that he "only prepares the way"—Vincent analogized that the same would happen today "if you were to ask of impressionism or one of its questing representatives, 'Have you found it yet?' Exactly the same."[122] This was a question that *L'Oeuvre* poses but, in another realm,

Benoit answered. Wagner might have claimed the Baptist's annunciatory role for the art of the future, but history was assigning him another, that of leader calling for the illuminated to "band together like the disciples of a new religion." It was as a Christ figure under a hovering Holy Ghost of Genius that Benoit portrayed Wagner:

This creative spirit, this luminous dove, never ceased hovering over the head of Wagner, the Chosen One; like the star in biblical myths, it guided him, never eclipsed, through the barrenness of life, until reaching the sacred goal sensed at the outset.[123]

Vincent, in the moments of exaltation that painting sometimes afforded him, allowed himself similar visions. Pondering the familiar idea of Christ as artist, he reprised in letters to Bernard his views of the Bible as a source of despair and indignation, in which Christ is the consoling center embedded in its bitter pulp. Allowing that, especially in his own case, the study of Christ aggravated "artistic neurosis," Vincent described him as the greatest of all artists, a molder of the "living flesh" through the "spoken word." In parables like that of the sower, recorded by the evangelists, Christ provided a glimpse of "the art of life—creation, the art of being immortal and alive." Vincent continued, "The patron saint of painters—Luke, physician painter evangelist—who has as symbol, alas, nothing more than an ox, gives us hope."[124] Hope, that is, of what might be accomplished through painting.

In *The Sower* Vincent had attempted to produce a spiritually relevant art, following Millet in depicting the teachings of Christ by forsaking strict realism in the pursuit of symbolic content. However, a greater challenge remained for the artist: "painting the face of Christ in such a way that I can feel him" as he felt him when reading the evangelists. In

his view only two painters in all of history had succeeded in doing this: Rembrandt and Delacroix (see figs. 45, 47). As for his own aspirations, he rather coyly demurred: "I feel only too well that I am an ox [*boeuf*]—being a painter—I who admire the bull [*taureau*], the eagle, and the Man with a veneration that will prevent me from being ambitious."[125] In French slang the phrase he employed—*être le boeuf*—means to work for nothing. More significant, and more complex, is his allusive bestiary, which relies on the traditional attributes of the gospel writers: John's eagle, Matthew's man or angel, Luke's ox (in English) or *taureau* (in French). In representing himself as ox to Luke's bull, Vincent played with the two languages and with the difference between the castrated ox (*boeuf*) and the virile bull (*taureau*).[126] The implication is twofold: it takes balls to depict Christ, and respect for those who have done so ensures humility in ordinary men.

This formulation differs from one that Vincent had offered only the previous week, when he suggested to Bernard that all artists, even Saint Luke, must settle for the existence of the *boeuf* while others enjoy the life of the *taureau*:

Painting and screwing aren't compatible; they weaken the brain. It's damned annoying.

The symbol of Saint Luke, the patron saint of painters, is, as you know, an ox [*boeuf*]. Therefore, one must be patient like an ox if one wants to toil in the artistic field. Still, bulls [*taureaux*] are happy not to have to work at that rotten painting.[127]

Reinstating the *taureau* as the evangelist's attribute made room for the exception, the master of both art and life—and thus opened the door to ambition.

Certainly Vincent was preoccupied by the connection between sexual and creative

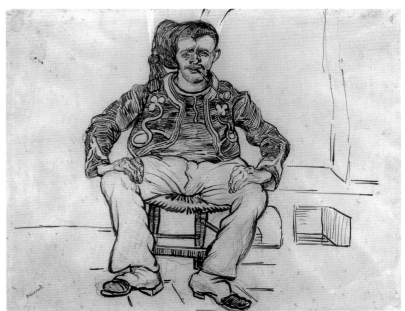

41
Saint Luke and the Ox
17th century
Relief carving
Saint Lucas Guild
entrance, Waag,
Nieuwmarkt,
Amsterdam

42
Émile Bernard
(French; 1868–1941)
Brothel Scene
June 1888
Watercolor
30.8 x 20 cm
Van Gogh Museum,
Amsterdam
(Vincent van Gogh
Foundation)

43
Vincent van Gogh
The Zouave
20 June 1888
[F 423, JH 1486]
Oil on canvas
65 x 54 cm
Van Gogh Museum,
Amsterdam
(Vincent van Gogh
Foundation)

44
Vincent van Gogh
Seated Zouave
June 1888
[F 1443, JH 1485]
Graphite, reed pen
and brown ink,
heightened with
white
52 x 66 cm
Van Gogh Museum,
Amsterdam
(Vincent van Gogh
Foundation)

potency, or rather impotence and its professional equivalent, mediocrity.[128] This preoccupation with virility informs the three studies of a Zouave that he mentioned to Bernard in the *boeuf–taureau* letters of late June. Zouaves were light infantrymen in the French army, quartered at the Caserne Calvin in Arles (see map, fig. 10). Originally recruited from among Algerian tribesmen, by the late nineteenth century the regiment comprised French soldiers, distinguished by exotic uniforms and a reputation to match. Vincent saw the Zouaves as quintessential ladies' men, associating them with the brothels they frequented in Arles's red-light district, sandwiched between rue de la Cavalerie and the Carmelite convent. It was an inquiry following the highly publicized murder of two Zouaves by Italian itinerant laborers outside a *maison de tolérance* that provided Vincent his first "opportunity" to venture inside such an establishment. Having just received a sketch from Bernard of a brothel scene (fig. 42), Vincent proposed one of his Zouave studies in exchange (see fig. 43), setting the stage for a possible future collaboration on a brothel picture.[129]

Vincent met the soldier who sat for these studies through his new friend Paul-Eugène Milliet, a second lieutenant of the Zouaves to whom he was giving drawing lessons. Vincent was somewhat in awe of Milliet's sexual prowess and self-confidence, both of which he demonstrated by spending the evening before a critical test in a brothel.[130] It was the brute sensuality in the unidentified model, whom he described as "a boy with a small face, a bull neck and the eye of a tiger," that appealed to him. To give "vulgar" expression to this characterization, Vincent employed a "savage combination of incongruous tones"—a blood-red cap against a harsh green door—together with the broad planes and bold outlines he associated with Japanese woodcuts (fig. 43).[131] A drawing (fig. 44) makes the point differently and more explicitly. Vincent here positioned his model on a chair so that he directly confronts the viewer, legs spread, and he emphatically delineated the young bull's brazenly displayed virility. In a sense the artist was testing his own prowess. This is the first figure drawing he had executed since arriving in Arles, and despite professed dissatisfaction with the

Zouave group, he was pleased to have done something more important than landscape.[132] What followed, however, was a sequence of events in which he dared to overstep the boundaries he had set for himself (and Bernard) only to beat a hasty retreat.

Following word of Gauguin's agreement, Vincent sent the drawing of the Zouave to Theo, along with a series carried out at the ruins of the medieval abbey of Montmajour. The news had prompted the production of the large pen-and-ink drawings first announced on 8 July; not only did Vincent wish to economize on supplies by working in pen and ink rather than oil, but he also hoped that he could raise funds for Gauguin's journey through their sale.[133] Though he had just professed an interest in doing figures, these are landscapes, magnificent panoramas of the Crau, which he saw in terms of both Japan and seventeenth-century Holland (see maps, ch. 4, fig. 3, and ch. 1, fig. 8), as well as more intimate views of the abbey's lush natural surroundings. Here the reeds, vines, flowers, fruit and olive trees (see fig. 46) reminded him of "Le Paradou," or "Paradise," the garden that serves as the centerpiece of Zola's 1875 novel *La Faute de l'abbé Mouret*.[134]

Symbolic of nature's procreative imperatives, Le Paradou is the site where Abbot Mouret's religious vocation and abstinence are tested. This site thus resonated with Vincent's view of necessary renunciation and with his abiding aim to paint the "drama of sorrow in life," an opposition that he had once framed in terms of garden subjects: "A 'Paradou' is beautiful, but Gethsemane is even more beautiful."[135] This larger aspiration to depict what Saint Luke referred to as the Mount of Olives—where Christ suffered the Agony, praying to be delivered from temptation and to accept the sacrificial will of God, and was betrayed by Judas—motivated Vincent's drawings of the olive trees at Montmajour. In the same letter in which he announced their completion, Vincent informed Theo:

I have scraped off one of the big painted studies, a Garden of Olives with a figure of Christ in blue and orange and an angel in yellow. Red earth, hills green and blue, olive trees with violet and carmine trunks, and green-gray and blue foliage. A citron sky. I scraped it off because I tell myself that I must not do figures of that importance without models.[136]

The matter-of-fact tone and pragmatic explanation belie the enormous ambition at stake.[137] The Gethsemane subject spoke to a spiritual struggle with which Vincent identified, but it also signaled his desire to break free of the debilitating double-bind of the artistic life versus real life. Casting aside his own demurrals, he had dared to paint Christ, the supreme artist, taking on Rembrandt and Delacroix (see figs. 45, 47), after following the latter's example by first observing a real olive grove. Vincent had taken the bull by the horns.

If the news about Gauguin's agreeing to join him had been the spur for this new work, his own issues about creative potency featured prominently as well, as can be inferred from the news he shared with Theo the following day. He introduced it circuitously, by repeating the words that had helped him gather his resolve to paint *The Sower*: "The masterpiece is up to you." Next he invoked a Maupassant character who is disconcerted to discover, at the moment he wishes to marry, that "he could no longer get it up." Then he got to the point: "I begin to resemble him physically." He followed this confession with another maxim—"man becomes ambitious as soon as he becomes impotent"—and, remarkably, concluded that impotence did not bother him, but "I'll be damned if it's going to drive me to ambition." For ambition—more than sex—was the temptation with which Vincent struggled in his own Gethsemane. His current personal, professional, and spiritual doubts exacerbated by the failed canvas, he cast about for a means of steadying himself. It would require, he ventured, an impossibly blind optimism to steady his soul.[138]

47

Somehow Vincent did manage to regain hope, through the initiation of an ambitious figure painting less than two weeks later (fig. 48). Featuring a young Provençal girl seated in a rustic bentwood chair and holding a branch of flowering oleander, *The Mousmé* (like his earlier portrait of Agostina Segatori) alludes to the iconography of Puvis's *Hope* (ch. 2, fig. 70). In the spring, in a letter to Theo, he had referred to the Puvis image when describing his dream that the future might yield an art so lovely and "young" as to be worth the painter's sacrifice of his own youth and of love.[139] Now, in *The Mousmé*, Vincent evoked Hope with an additional layer of reference to Loti's *Madame Chrysanthème*, establishing a conflation of the South, Japan, and Puvis that had everything to do with Gauguin.

A *mousmé*, as Vincent explained to Theo, is "a Japanese girl…twelve to fourteen years old." But there is more to this subject: a *mousmé* is not just any young girl, but a child-woman brokered for short-term "marriages" such as Loti described with the girl known as Madame Chrysanthème. While Vincent was aware of

the terrible toll exacted by "the horrible white man" on the populations of the South Pacific, he was apparently oblivious to the racism, hypocrisy, and cynical, poisonous tone of *Madame Chrysanthème*.[140] Rather, by echoing Loti in referring to "my *mousmé*," he indulged in a fantasy of sexual imperialism consistent with his ambition to be an "exploiter" of the South-as-Japan.

The Mousmé occupied Vincent for the uncharacteristically extended period of a week.[141] Further testimony to its special significance are the two drawings after the picture that he made and sent to Bernard and Gauguin (figs. 49–50). These followed a large group of drawings after recent paintings that Vincent had posted to Bernard in mid-July. In addition to providing an idea of his recent production, Vincent acknowledged his friend's admiration for Cézanne by demonstrating affinity with his Provençal repertoire; he also solicited drawings in exchange that he could use to persuade Theo to take up Bernard's work. A series sent to Russell in July/August, while not executed in the same spirit of aesthetic dia-

logue, was nonetheless freighted from Vincent's point of view, for he hoped that the drawings would generate goodwill and overcome the Australian's reluctance to buy one of Gauguin's Martinique canvases (see ch. 2), thereby providing him the means to come south.[142]

The oleanders that Vincent placed in the *mousmé*'s "sweet little hand" embody a cautious optimism.[143] He associated the flower, native to the Mediterranean region, with another work by Puvis, *Pleasant Land* (fig. 37), which Gauguin referenced in his *Young Wrestlers—Brittany*, and incorporated it into his decorative scheme for the Yellow House, planning to flank the entrance with tubs of oleanders. While Vincent avowed that the oleander spoke to him of love, according to fact and tradition, the plant's beauty belies its poisonousness.[144] Contact of the leaves with sensitive areas of the body can produce sores, and, even more dramatically, inhalation of its perfumes can be fatal. Some French soldiers learned this the hard way when, during the Algerian campaigns, they made

48

49

50

51

52

48
Vincent van Gogh
The Mousmé
c. 23 July 1888
[F 431, JH 1519]
Oil on canvas
74 x 60 cm
National Gallery of
Art, Washington,
D.C., Chester Dale
Collection

49
Vincent van Gogh
Sketch of *The
Mousmé* in letter to
Bernard
[c. 23 July 1888]
(letter 651/B 12)
[F 1504, JH 1520]
The State Pushkin
Museum of Fine
Arts, Moscow

50
Vincent van Gogh
Sketch of *The
Mousmé* in letter to
Gauguin
[c. 23 July 1888]
(F 1722, JH 1521)
Musée d'Orsay, Paris

51
Paul Gauguin
Sketch of Breton
figures in letter to
Schuffenecker
14 August 1888
(M 1984, letter 159)

52
Vincent van Gogh
*Oleanders and Zola's
"Joie de vivre"*
August 1888
[F 593, JH 1566]
Oil on canvas
60.3 x 73.7 cm
The Metropolitan
Museum of Art,
New York, gift of
Mr. and Mrs. John L.
Loeb, 1962
Cat. 60

53
Vincent van Gogh
*Washerwomen at the
Roubine du Roi Canal*
April 1888
[F 1473, JH 1405]
Graphite, quillpen
and reed pen and
brown ink
22.5 x 34.5 cm
Staatliche Graphische
Sammlung, Munich

54
Vincent van Gogh
*Washerwomen at the
Roubine du Roi Canal*
c. 7 July 1888
[F 427, JH 1490]
Oil on canvas
74 x 60 cm
Private collection

55
Vincent van Gogh
Sunflowers
21/26 August 1888
[F 453, JH 1559]
Oil on canvas
72 x 58 cm
Private collection

56
Vincent van Gogh
Sunflowers
21/26 August 1888
[F 459, JH 1560]
Oil on canvas
98 x 69 cm
Destroyed

the mistake of sleeping in huts made of oleander branches.

Yet while it can kill, the oleander can also cure, and these properties account for the flower's biblical associations in the books of Corinthians, in which the Word of Christ presents the choice between death and eternal life.[145] Vincent relied on this complex symbolism for a sumptuous still life, undertaken several weeks after *The Mousmé*, featuring oleanders in a majolica pot set on a table beside two yellow-jacketed novels, one of which is Zola's *Joie de vivre* (fig. 52).[146] The echo of the Nuenen still life (ch. 1, fig. 3) is unmistakable. The pink flowers with their searching, elegant green leaves take the place of the Bible, performing a similar emblematic function.

Perhaps Vincent's retrospective impulse was prompted by news of the illness (and subsequent death on 28 July) of his namesake uncle Cent, which unleashed recollections of Holland, past heartbreak, and the sorrows inherent in the "joie de vivre." But Vincent's recapitulation here of his belief in art's consoling function was part of the larger retrenchment adumbrated in *Parisian Novels* (ch. 2, fig. 71) and now, after months away from the capital and alone with his thoughts, coming into focus. "What I learned in Paris," Vincent informed Theo shortly before beginning the still life, "is *fading away* and … I am going

back to the ideas I had in the country before I knew the impressionists."[147] He was in effect returning to an earlier ideal of a symbolic realism, his aspiration to follow exemplars like Millet now given positive direction and a concrete site. Marshaling the lessons of color, he explored its arbitrary usage as the means to express himself more forcefully, exaggerating reality in order to convey his subjective experience or feeling for it. But while he was comfortable sharing his ideas about "abstract" signification with Gauguin as well as Bernard, he shared them differently, as the tellingly inflected *Mousmé* drawings reveal. In his drawing for Bernard (fig. 49), Vincent respected his friend's antipathy to pointillism by restraining his use of the dot pattern he favored as a graphic equivalent for tone. The drawing for Gauguin (fig. 50) features a dotted background, but the oleander found in the painting (and in Bernard's drawing) is reduced to a constellation of polka dots on the skirt above the hand, possibly in deference to Gauguin's ambivalence about Puvis's use of a comparable symbolic device in *Hope*.[148]

The Mousmé and the portraits that immediately followed—of his new friend Joseph Roulin (ch. 4, fig. 102), postal worker at Arles's railroad station, and of the old peasant Patience Escalier (ch. 4, fig. 122)—reflect his conviction that only by painting the figure could he "cultivate whatever is best and deepest in me." He

linked his portrait of the peasant directly to studies for *The Potato Eaters* and beyond that to representations of the peasantry by Millet and Zola.[149]

Sharing drawings with his friends, he also stated his goal—to raise painting to a "height equivalent to the serene summits which the Greek sculptors, German musicians, the writers of French novels reached." This entailed their combining to execute an idea held in common. *The Mousmé* gave expression to this hope. Finding it impossible to sustain in isolation, Vincent became increasingly invested in Gauguin's arrival.[150] This made for an accelerating emotional roller-coaster ride that lasted from early August to mid-September, as buoyant optimism fed by Gauguin's perceived commitment alternated with despair at reports from him of impediments and delays. Threats to the future served to sharpen Vincent's vision of it; as he articulated its challenges, Gauguin responded in kind.

53

54

55

56

Late July's confidence that Gauguin would soon be joining him evaporated with word that journeying south was still a financial impossibility. Vincent's disappointment, like his anticipation, played out in his work. On 8 August he visited a spot on the Roubine du Roi canal, not far from place Lamartine, where he observed washerwomen working from platforms built along the waterway's embankments; the chimney of the Arles gasworks and the steeple of the Carmelite convent appear in the distance against a setting sun (fig. 53 and map, fig. 10).[151] Here Vincent transformed an initial concept of a workaday scene (fig. 54) into a suggestively cosmic vision, deploying a bird's-eye view and exaggerating and reinforcing the dizzying perspective of the curving embankment with insistently directional brushwork. Disorientingly, illusory deep space is disrupted by areas of color (such as the smokestack) that draw attention to the surface's flatness. Defending the speed with which he painted this and other pictures, Vincent appealed to the rush of inspiration—catching the wave of "feeling…and…emotions so strong that one works without knowing one works, when sometimes the strokes come with a continuity and a coherence like words in a speech or a letter." This rapturous state was addictive: only when he experienced the "exaltation" of absorption in "furiously hard work" did Vincent feel truly alive; company, he believed, would relieve him of the need for this high, freeing him to attempt more "complicated" things.[152]

He had thought relief was in sight, but now he had to confront Gauguin's indefinite postponement. Returning to paint the Roubine du Roi, his disappointment keen, the large figures of the laundresses reminded him of Gauguin's *Négresses* (ch. 2, fig. 58). This reference was a code of sorts for an inevitable comparison between Gauguin's highly mediated approach

in this much-admired picture and his own. Specifically he wondered "what would Gauguin say" about his method of working quickly, which prevented him from being master of his stroke and gave his studies their feverish, "haggard" appearance, however much he tried to attribute it to the rush of inspiration, the time pressures exerted by changing natural effects, or the battle of working in the face of fierce mistral winds. Vincent imagined being advised to use the rapid, on-the-spot studies as starting points for canvases realized in a studio, where he could achieve a "more spiritual touch."[153] The implication of this inner dialogue, as he indicated to Theo, was that he could not do it alone:

I am thinking about Gauguin a lot, and I contend that one way or another, whether it is he who comes here or I who go to him, he and I will like almost the same subjects, and I have no doubt that I could work at Pont-Aven, and on the other hand I am convinced that he will love the country down here. Well, after a year, supposing he gives you one canvas a month, which would make altogether a dozen a year, he will have made a profit on them, not having incurred any debts during that year and having produced without interruption; he will have lost nothing. Whereas the money he will have received from us will be made up largely by economies that will be possible if we set up house in the studio instead of both of us living in cafés. Moreover, provided we keep on good terms and are determined not to quarrel, we shall be in a stronger position as to our reputation.

If we each live alone, it means living like madmen or criminals, in appearance at any rate, and a little bit in reality as well.[154]

But when Vincent proposed to Gauguin that they meet in Pont-Aven, he was disconcerted by the response: tacit acceptance but no concrete plans. Concerned, Vincent decided

57
Vincent van Gogh
Sunflowers
Late August 1888
[F 456, JH 1561]
Oil on canvas
91 x 71 cm
Neue Pinokothek,
Munich

58
Vincent van Gogh
Sunflowers
Late August 1888
[F 454, JH 1562]
Oil on canvas
93 x 73 cm
The National
Gallery, London
Cat. 61

against going to Pont-Aven and attempted to end the stalemate through purposeful action. He sent to Theo—via Milliet—more than thirty recent studies, including *The Sower* and *Washerwomen at the Roubine du Roi Canal*, painted since the first shipment of work, in late May. But while he urged Theo to calculate the budget required to bring Gauguin south, in almost the same breath he worried about the advisability of forcing this outcome because he suspected Gauguin of being more heavily invested in the kind of success attainable only in Paris. With a typical circularity, Vincent opined that Gauguin was sure to be disillusioned, while at the same time allowed that he was sure to triumph. Unwilling to assume responsibility for standing in his way, Vincent once again thought to go north.[155]

Theo, the sounding board for this obsessional debate, responded by promising Vincent the funding that would permit him and Gauguin to get together. Vincent received this letter together with one from Bernard, who had just joined Gauguin and Laval (the latter recently returned from Martinique) in Pont-Aven. Bernard said nothing to indicate that Gauguin intended to join Vincent or wished to have him come to Brittany. Crestfallen, Vincent insisted that with or without Gauguin, he had to escape the "living hell" of being a "perpetual wanderer" and settle in a place where he could work and sleep. What he longed for was a home. He needed money to furnish the Yellow House, for, as he told Theo, he could not continue as he was much longer: "I am falling apart."[156]

To Bernard, Vincent was more restrained, expressing pleasure at his joining Gauguin and describing a new project: a half-dozen pictures of sunflowers to be installed in the studio, "a decoration in which the raw or broken chrome yellows will blaze forth on various backgrounds—blue, from the palest malachite green to royal blue."[157] Like the

still life with oleanders and Zola's *Joie de vivre*, the planned sunflower canvases would encompass both personal and traditional symbolism. Vincent gestured toward the religious sensibility that had already surfaced in Bernard's writings when he likened the effects he envisaged to Gothic stained-glass windows, but he sought a spirituality of both body and soul, in keeping with the proposition that great art "renders infinity tangible and the enjoyment of something beautiful is like the moment of coitus, a moment of infinity." Experiencing art was thus comparable to the exaltation—the loss and transcendence of self—involved in its creation: "Ah! My dear friends, let us crazy ones feel orgasm all the same, through our eyes, no?" And just as the "eye orgasm" ("jouissance de l'oeil") provided by paintings compensated the artist for forsaking "real life," so the sunflowers associated with Gauguin served as a kind of surrogate: "How much I would like to be able to spend these days in Pont-Aven; however, I find consolation in contemplating the sunflowers."[158]

Word from Gauguin that he was prepared to come south "as soon as the opportunity arises" dispelled Vincent's gloom. With an almost gustatory enthusiasm, he threw himself into the sunflower project. It had expanded in his mind from six to twelve canvases that would constitute a "symphony in blue and yellow"—affective, like music, by virtue of their color and "simple technique," comprehensible to anyone with eyes in their head. Racing to complete his canvases before the flowers wilted, Vincent worked feverishly from sunrise to sunset, realizing four of the envisioned twelve. He first produced, in quick succession, two canvases featuring less than a half dozen flowers (figs. 55–56), moving next to a composition of "twelve sunflowers and buds" (there are in fact more) arranged in a yellow earthenware vase against a light blue-green background (fig. 57).[159]

Having completed this exploration of light against light, he painted a contrasting pendant of the same size and featuring the same yellow vase, but "all in yellow," the yellow sunflowers set before a yellow background (fig. 58).[160]

By "simple technique," Vincent meant a manner that was free from the fussy stippling of pointillism. And indeed the procedure in these canvases represents his final disavowal of Neo-Impressionism. He began in customary fashion, establishing the composition with a drawn contour sketch, reinforced it with painted lines, and blocked in the background and primary forms with thin paint layers.[161] Then he picked up speed, sometimes loading the brush with color and in other places using little paint. He did not hesitate to use unmixed color directly from the tube, and often combined pigments incompletely on his palette, so that veins of separate color run through individual strokes.

Vincent devised different systems of brushwork for each element in the picture: the background is a basketweave pattern; the table, a series of loose horizontal strokes; the petals in single flowers and leaves are made up of single marks or small, parallel ones; the centers of these flowers are painted with circular strokes of pure red lake, dotted with a ring of yellow impasto; the petals of full double flowers are short, thick strokes radiating out from more thinly laid in centers. Having held the general shape of most flowers in reserve when applying an initial background layer, he added petal tips over the final ground. Applying new pigment onto still-wet underlying or adjacent areas with a controlled and confident touch, Vincent probably devoted only a single session to each canvas, later reinforcing a few contours and adding his signature.[162]

The sunflower series, first contemplated in a spirit of loneliness, now celebrated Vincent's "hope to live with Gauguin in a studio of our own" while intimating a growing sense of mission. Gauguin, for his part, expressed readiness to participate in his friend's plan, but he was by no means feeling the same blend of personal and ideological longing. To Mette he matter-of-factly stated his plan to spend "six months with a painter who will provide me with food and lodging in exchange for drawings."[163] No doubt Theo's commitment to underwrite his living expenses heightened Gauguin's willingness to go to Arles, but his curiosity had certainly been aroused by Vincent's letters, which contained ideas that Gauguin found useful for mapping his course, just as he unhesitatingly adopted the graphic shorthand of Vincent's *Mousmé* drawing (fig. 50) in sketches after his own recent work (see fig. 51). Bernard acted as an important impetus as well, arriving in Pont-Aven bearing—as Gauguin promptly informed Schuffenecker—"interesting things." Included were not only the "fearless" young man's own recent work but also the drawings and letters Vincent had sent Bernard from Arles.[164]

These letters were of particular significance.[165] While Vincent presumably raised many of the same issues with both Bernard and Gauguin, he was less guarded with his younger friend. The expansive discussions on the issues of art, religion, and sex that feature prominently in his correspondence with Bernard now sparked Gauguin's intense interest, as evidenced by echoes in Gauguin's own letters, beginning with the counsel he offered Schuffenecker immediately after Bernard's arrival:

A piece of advice, do not imitate nature. Art is an abstraction; draw it out from nature while dreaming in front of it and think more about the act of creation than about the result;

it is the only way to ascend to God while imitating our divine master in the process of creation.[166]

Often cited as a programmatic statement of Gauguin's symbolism, this passage derives from the triangulated dialogue between Gauguin, Vincent, and Bernard, and its components can in fact be traced with some specificity. First, as seen above, the notion of "abstraction" (identified with the art of the Japanese and the Italian primitives) had informed the exchange around *The Sower* and *Young Wrestlers—Brittany*.[167] Second, the model of painting-and-dreaming is also a reverberation from the correspondence:

The best pictures are always those one dreams of when one is smoking a pipe in bed, but which never get done.
—Vincent to Bernard, [c. 18 June 1888]

You don't need to knock yourself out over painting, always searching for the absolute. One *dreams* then paints peacefully.
—Gauguin to Schuffenecker, 23 June 1888

This is how Rembrandt painted angels.... He does a self-portrait...in a mirror. He is dreaming and dreaming.... He...dreams on...[and] paints a supernatural angel...from the imagination.
—Vincent to Bernard, [c. 23 July 1888][168]

Finally, Gauguin's reference to God as the supreme artist draws directly upon Vincent's letters to Bernard, with the additional appropriation of the Old Testament figure of Solomon, who has a context in a discussion of leadership in Vincent's letter but is a red herring in Gauguin's:

I don't like Solomon.... Solomon seems to me to have been a hypocritical pagan. I have no respect at all for his kind of architecture, an imitation of other styles, and still less for

his writings: the pagans did better than that.
—Vincent to Bernard, [23 June 1888]

What an artist, this Jesus who carved in humanity itself! And what a damned nuisance, this Solomon!
—Gauguin to Schuffenecker, [12 September 1888][169]

Relying on Vincent's image of Christ as working in living flesh, Gauguin proceeded to write a disquisition that would surely have been better understood by Vincent and Bernard than by his actual correspondent, Schuffenecker:

In the absence of religious painting, what beautiful thoughts one can invoke with form and color. How prosaic are these painters with their trompe-l'oeil view of the material world. We alone drift on the phantom ship with our whimsical imperfection. How much vaster infinity appears to us when faced with something undefined. Musicians are gratified through their ears, but we, with our insatiable and rutting eye, we savor endless pleasures.[170]

Gauguin thus shamelessly lifted and interwove a number of themes from Vincent's letters, some of which were new to him and others of which he used to bolster his own ideas: the sexualized image of the painter's concupiscent eye, the idea of art affording a glimpse of infinity, the symbolic signification of line and color, and the aspiration of painting, via color, to the direct signification of music. Even Wagner makes an appearance: the "phantom ship" is a reference to his *Flying Dutchman*.[171]

Such wholesale appropriation, deplored as opportunistic by Pissarro (see ch. 2), was key to Gauguin's emergent creative strategy. His writing, as here, often reveals sources not yet fully metabolized, but the end product is more than a patchwork of pieces supplied by another. Although a good number of ideas may have been Vincent's, the act of cobbling them together helped Gauguin bring into focus latent ideas of his own, and new meanings emerged as a result.

Inevitably, it is Gauguin's art rather than his writing that attests to the success of this appropriative mode, demonstrated most spectacularly in the painting that has come to be regarded as a breakthrough in the evolution of modern art. He began work on *Vision of the Sermon* (fig. 59) upon Bernard's arrival and completed it, as he announced to Vincent, in the last week of September.[172]

The *Vision*'s originary status has been debated since 1891, when critic Albert Aurier invoked it in crediting Gauguin as the inventor of pictorial symbolism, a style he characterized as privileging the realm of ideas over naturalistic representation. The rival claim was Bernard's, based on a canvas he executed at the same time that he first entitled *Breton Women in the Meadow* (fig. 60). Sometime before 1892 Bernard added the phrase *The Pardon at Pont-Aven*, thus implying that it represents participants in the town's annual religious festival.[173]

Bernard's longstanding fascination with such rustic spectacles was not in and of itself proof of originality, shared as it was by the likes of Dagnan-Bouveret (see ch. 2, fig. 33); rather, *Breton Women* is distinctive for the way he painted it. The work features the hallmarks of the "cloisonnist" style that Bernard and Anquetin had recently pioneered in Paris: strong outlines and flat tints that recall medieval enamels and the tracery of stained-glass windows as well as more recent sources that were also considered primitive, such as Japanese woodcuts and Epinal prints.[174] Gauguin employed similar cloisonnist and compositional tactics in the *Vision*. He laid in a solid background, eliminated the horizon line, radically tilted the ground plane to produce ambiguities of scale, insistently outlined forms with strong contours, and placed decorative emphasis on the Breton coiffes. These stylistic similarities notwithstanding, the *Vision* and *Breton Women* depart from one another in terms of overall impact.

59

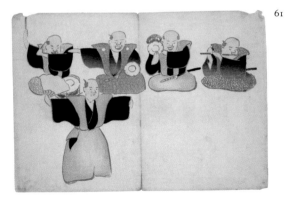

61

59
Paul Gauguin
Vision of the Sermon
(*Vision du sermon*)
Mid-August–mid-
September 1888
[W 245]
Oil on canvas
73 x 92 cm
National Gallery of
Scotland, Edinburgh
Cat. 31

60
Émile Bernard
Breton Women in the
Meadow (*The Pardon*
at Pont-Aven) (*Les*
Bretonnes dans la prairie
[*Bretonnes au pardon*])
August 1888
Oil on canvas
74 x 92 cm
Private collection
Cat. 26

61
Ogata Kōrin
(Japanese; 1658–1716)
Musicians from
The Book of Painting of
Kōrin (Edo, 1802),
vol. 1, pp. 9 verso, 10
recto
The Art Institute of
Chicago, Martin
Ryerson Collection,
31292–95
Cat. 146

63

Examination of the different ways in which the two artists referenced Japanese prints helps to illustrate this point. Gauguin bifurcated his composition with a Hiroshige-like tree trunk that renders the space both deeper and more complicated, while also serving a subtle conceptual role, dividing the women who occupy the left and bottom register from the wrestling figures at upper right and so establishing two zones: that of the figures in prayer and that of their vision. Bernard's composition shares an affiliation with certain Japanese woodcuts (see fig. 61), but the comparison illuminates only the painting's form, not its meaning. In other words, while Bernard addressed an established or conventional subject in a new style, Gauguin attempted both a new subject and a new style. To paint something truly different—the nature of religious experience, as comprehensible for a modern audience—he had to paint differently.

The *Vision* is neither fully reliant upon nor wholly independent of *Breton Women in the Meadow*.[175] Bernard undoubtedly played a catalytic role in Gauguin's painting. Involved in current aesthetic debates and avidly interested in abstract theories regarding the symbolic potential of line and form, he fostered a climate of intellectual inquiry previously lacking in Pont-Aven's artistic community, spurring Gauguin to articulate and give form to his own still vague inclinations.[176] Bernard's daily presence in Gauguin's life introduced a stimulating creative competitiveness that, since arriving in Brittany, Gauguin had found only in Vincent's letters. This is not to say that Bernard's arrival eclipsed the dialogue with Vincent—quite the opposite. Bernard now prompted Gauguin to a more thoughtful engagement with his correspondent.

Indeed the *Vision*'s complex associative structure documents their unfolding dialogue, as does the lengthy description of the completed picture that Gauguin sent, along with a sketch (fig. 62), to Vincent:

I have just painted a religious picture, badly executed, but it interested me to do it and I like it. I wanted to give it to the Church of Pont-Aven. Naturally they don't want it.

A group of Breton women are praying in their pitch-black costumes. The yellow white bonnets very luminous. The two bonnets at the right are like monstrous helmets. An apple tree cuts across the canvas, dark purple with its foliage drawn in clumps like emerald green clouds with patches of green and sun yellow. The ground pure vermilion. At the church it darkens and becomes brownish red.

The angel is dressed in strong ultramarine blue and Jacob in bottle green. The angel's wings pure chrome yellow #1. The angel's hair chrome #2 and the feet flesh orange. I think I have achieved a great rustic and *superstitious* simplicity in the figures. The whole is very severe. The cow under the tree is tiny in comparison with reality, and is rearing up. For me, in this painting, landscape and the struggle [*lutte*] only exist in the imagination of the people in prayer as a result of the sermon, which is why there is a contrast between the real people and the struggle in its disproportionate and imagined landscape.[177]

Gauguin's decision to undertake an overtly religious picture—a seemingly new ambition—must be seen in light of Vincent's earlier failed attempt to realize "Christ with the Angel in Gethsemane." In several details Gauguin's description of his canvas responds to Vincent's of his own, including references to a yellow angel, red ground, and violet tree-trunks, but the connection is more profound. Gauguin devised his innovative presentation of the contrast between reality (the peasants, eyes closed in prayer) and the spiritual experience they imagine (the vermilion landscape, the struggle) in response to the problems Vincent had encountered in his *Gethsemane* and with recourse to solutions Vincent had proposed. Negotiating the problem of invention and credibility in religious pictures, Gauguin in a sense thematized Vincent's evocation of Rembrandt painting angels by dreaming visions so intense that they seemed as real as nature itself.

Gauguin's painting, a response to a dilemma of crucial significance to Vincent, includes details that speak to the issues and the creative competition at stake. Moreover Gauguin implicitly claimed success where Vincent had been forced to admit defeat. His rearing cow—the significance of which has long puzzled interpreters—can be understood as a wry allusion to the debate on the subject of ambition and religious painting that preceded Vincent's failed *Gethsemane*.[178] With obvious horns but no visible udder, the prancing beast, craning its head to witness the epic struggle, shares a kinship with medieval representations of Saint Luke's attribute, the ox, its position in the *Vision*'s artistic field a remarkable echo of mid-eleventh-century illuminated manuscripts acquired by the Bibliothèque Nationale, Paris, in the 1870s (fig. 63). Certainly, in addressing the theme of struggle or wrestling, Gauguin not only reprised his own earlier picture but carried the metaphor of creative struggle directly into the arena of his current discussions with Vincent. In 1888 no one involved in vanguard practice could undertake the theme of Jacob and the angel without feeling the burden of influence exerted by Delacroix's famous realization of the subject in his mural for the Church of Saint-Sulpice (fig. 65). Unveiled in 1861, the picture had a profound impact on the Impressionist generation and remained a touchstone more than twenty-five years later. For this subject, which thus "belonged" to Delacroix, Gauguin employed the yellow-blue combination that Vincent considered the chromatic signature of the Romantic master who alone (since Rembrandt) had risen to the challenge of meaningfully imaging the Bible.[179] Gauguin's *Vision* embodies the challenge both artists faced, that of fulfilling the promise of Impressionism and rivaling the great art of the past.

In *L'Oeuvre*, Zola described Claude Lantier's attempt to "create living flesh," a masterpiece, as "everlastingly struggling with the Real, and being repeatedly conquered, like Jacob fighting with the Angel!"—yet the attempt, however agonizing, was "only way to be God." A desperate cycle of promising starts and near finishes, of scraping clean and starting over, eventually reduces Claude to despair, a madman plagued by feelings of impotence and self-doubt.[180]

L'Oeuvre had special significance to Gauguin (see ch. 2), and he could be confident, from earlier conversations in Paris and recent correspondence, that it was among the books Vincent used as templates for his own experience. The pressure that Claude feels to choose between life and art, his anxiety that he was sowing seeds for a future that he himself will not inherit, echoed in Vincent's letters, as does the fictional character's attendant suspicion that a "hereditary" neurosis will ultimately preclude his success.[181] In their coincident use of the image of the supreme being as artist, Vincent and Gauguin responded not only to each other but also to the shared reference of *L'Oeuvre*.[182]

L'Oeuvre's dramatization of the burden exerted by reputation on creativity also helped Vincent, at precisely this moment, to contrast Gauguin's hopes and chances for success with his own professed horror of it. When Vincent proposed to withstand the "siege of failure" by living "almost like monks… with work our ruling passion," he not only reiterated his own earlier advice to Bernard, but he also echoed Claude Lantier.[183] In the novel, as Claude's desire to produce a masterpiece intensifies in the face of creative impotence, he renounces sex, explaining that "genius must be chaste, its only love must be work."[184] The idea of conserving one's seed in order to channel all one's virility into work was by no means new to the discourse on creativity. Zola participated in a broader discussion on the subject that, addressed by earlier writers, had taken on renewed significance following the French defeat in the Franco-Prussian War. *L'Oeuvre* stands out in this cultural context by featuring the related issues of virility, impotence, and the sexualization of creativity as dominant themes, impressing Vincent enough to inform a remarkable, lengthy letter to Bernard advising abstinence and a monklike existence as the means of making his painting "more spermatic."[185]

Vincent's fears of artistic impotence, like Claude's, were linked to larger existential anxieties only tenuously kept at bay by the fantasy of creating a masterpiece. In *L'Oeuvre* Zola posited that vanguard artists brought to bear on their art a set of aspirations formerly invested in religion; their ambition was nothing less than a bid for immortality, a substitute for belief in God. Claude and other characters talk of art as their religion, a conviction that Sandoz (the author's alter ego) sees as the "stain" of the Romantic legacy, stemming from texts such as Wilhelm Wackenroder's *Outpourings from the Heart of an Art-Loving Monk* (1797) which posit art as a revelation of the divine, its contemplation an act of worship.[186] In the mid-nineteenth century, heirs to Romanticism had to confront the so-called truths of science and deal with the speculative capitalism that increasingly commodified artists and their work. *L'Oeuvre* charts the crisis suffered by the Realist vanguard and their Impressionist successors as life experience challenges youthful ideals and expectations. In one exemplary incident, Claude seeks to console a broken, senior artist whose early masterpiece had been critical to his own development by telling him that he will be remembered "as the father of us all"; the old man makes the unsettling reply: "What does it matter?"[187] Repeatedly Sandoz expresses the doubt—the insidious sense of pointlessness—that begins to haunt the Impressionists as, with age, they inevitably move away from insatiable ambition and the all-consuming labors it demands:

I wonder whether it might not be better to live, and die, unknown? What a cheat for us all if this glory we talk about existed no more than the paradise promised in the Catechism and which even children don't believe in nowadays.

Has it ever struck *you* that posterity may not be the fair, impartial judge we like to think it is? We console ourselves for being spurned and rejected by relying on getting a fair deal from the future, just as the faithful put up with the abomination on this earth because they firmly believe in another life where everyone shall have his deserts. Suppose the artist's paradise turned out to be as non-existent as the Catholic's, and future generations turned out to be just as misguided as the present one and persisted in liking pretty-pretty dabbling better than honest-to-goodness painting!... What a cheat for us all, to have lived like slaves.... Immortality at present depends entirely on the average, middle-class mind.... How could I possibly have the courage to carry on...if I couldn't console myself with the illusion that one day I shall be accepted and understood.[188]

At the beginning of August 1888, Vincent was in the throes of an identical crisis. Haunted by old fears of his nullity and mortality, he worried that in the end his belief in the religion of art would be proved wrong, that he would find out that "not only the Arts but everything else were only dreams, that one was nothing at all oneself." If an ordinary person who believed in the "Christian system" could be confident of eternal life, he asked, why shouldn't an artist with vast ideas—such as a Delacroix—be "any less immortal"? But the thought of posthumous reputation was not enough to allow him to "hold on to this *Moi*." It failed to provide the consolation of simple, traditional, "instinctive" religious belief: "I do not think much of the future life of artists *through their works*. Yes, artists perpetuate themselves by handing on the torch, Delacroix to the Impressionists, etc. But is that all?"[189]

While he attempted to assure himself that he was satisfied to be a pioneer—a link in the chain—Vincent confessed that he suffered from "a terrible need—shall I say the word?—of religion." Tenaciously he clung to his faith in art, stating: "I can well do without God in both my life and also in my painting, but, suffering as I am, I cannot do without something greater than myself, something which is my life—the power to create."[190]

To shore up his beliefs, Vincent began framing his musings in Christological terms. The idea of one generation of painters handing on the torch to the next took on a more consoling aspect when seen as a kind of resurrection, wherein "we see a living man arise immediately in the place of the dead man." Thus Impressionism became the "*resurrection of Delacroix*," even though it did not offer itself as the "final doctrine."[191] The role that Vincent envisaged for himself in this cycle is telling: when he thought of "continuing the same work, living the same life, dying the same death," it was Monticelli he saw himself as resurrecting. He imagined visiting Marseilles with Gauguin, for which occasion he would dress "exactly like Monticelli," in the yellow hat, black jacket, white trousers, and yellow gloves that he remembered from Monticelli's portrait. A similar significance informed the sunflowers he painted "all in yellow" (see fig. 58), their chromatics alluding to the painter who "did the South all in yellow, all in orange, all in sulfur."[192]

By September Vincent's ideas about an art of the future were merging with talk of a "religion of the future," a context in which the South became a true "painter's paradise." In this spirit he began, early in the month, to furnish the Yellow House. His intention to make it an "artist's house," informed in part by an early pilgrimage to the home of Belgian artist Henri Leys (see fig. 64), was symbolically freighted.[193] He now determined that the sunflower canvases would hang in Gauguin's room; like the flower's movements, this decision constituted a form of deference to a higher authority in keeping with his resolve to subordinate his wishes to those of the members of his planned association. Adorning the site of the religion of art, the sunflowers moreover would stand for the mission Vincent saw Gauguin and himself executing, that of preparing richer lives for the painters who would "follow in our footsteps" on the new road they had forged. On the path of pilgrimage,

the house occupied a special position "at the very entrance" to the southern paradise.[194] To furnish it, in addition to two beds for the two upstairs rooms, Vincent purchased a dozen chairs. Hardly necessities, they were symbolic embellishments—the number twelve was associated in his mind with the Pre-Raphaelite Brotherhood, the group of English painters he had invoked when proposing an Impressionist cooperative.[195] He got the facts wrong (the Pre-Raphaelites did not in fact number twelve), but his error reflects his ideal of an association of painters as a loyal discipleship, like Christ's twelve apostles. The same numerical symbolism may help explain why Vincent envisaged painting a dozen sunflower canvases, and why he repeatedly referred to his first large *Sunflowers* as including twelve blossoms, despite there being more.

The Yellow House, in Vincent's thinking, had become the locus for what he now referred to as a "Studio of the South," the very project that Monticelli should have realized. Vincent

and Gauguin would "try to prove to the good people that Monticelli did not die slumped across the café tables…but that the little fellow is still alive. And the thing won't end with us, we shall merely start it off on a fairly solid basis."[196]

In this new schema of death and resurrection, Monticelli became the quintessential artist-martyr, whose final days Vincent imagined as a "regular Gethsemane." The parallel with Christ's Passion fast assumed metaphoric status in the dialogue with Gauguin. In a letter of early September, Gauguin described his current existence—and the artist's life in general—as "a long calvary" on a path filled with "thorns."[197] His imagery possibly alluded to Vincent's recent compositions featuring thistles, traditional emblems of suffering and the Passion, surrounded by swarms of the butterflies that symbolized metamorphosis and rebirth.[198] In these pictures Vincent had given veiled expression to his need for religion and attendant desire to invest his art with what he called a more serious meaning. He dreamed

65

64
Henri de Braekeleer
(Belgian; 1840–1888)
*The Dining Room
in the Residence of
Henri Leys*
1869
Oil on canvas
64 x 94 cm
Royal Museum of Fine
Arts, Antwerp

65
Eugène Delacroix
Jacob Wrestling the Angel
1861
Oil and wax on canvas
714 x 488 cm
Church of Saint-
Sulpice, Chapelle des
Saints-Anges, Paris

once again of painting a sower and other resonantly "poetic subjects."[199]

The two artists' dovetailing language belies profound differences in outlook. The symbolic garb of martyrdom and the Passion was for Vincent insulation against existential despair; for Gauguin a guise and a way of thinking about his position vis-à-vis the rest of the art world, a means to creative invigoration. While Gauguin subscribed to Vincent's notion of "suggestive color," he pointedly rejected the idea that it need be put in the service of "poetic ideas," as the latter had attempted in *The Sower*. To the contrary, Gauguin insisted that *"ALL"* subjects are potentially imbued with deep meaning and, moreover, that "forms and colors brought into harmony are in themselves a poetry" independent of descriptive function.[200] Even more importantly Gauguin did not share Vincent's view of the purpose of pictures. Casting a potential audience in his own image, Vincent spoke of an art of consolation, certain that it would "do some people's hearts good to find poetic subjects again." Though Gauguin had adopted the terms "consolation" and "suffering," his own experience led him to outline different requirements for picture-making: "Without letting myself be caught by the motif, I experience before another's painting a feeling that leads me to a poetic state, depending on the painter's intellectual strength emerging from [the painting]."[201] In other words, for Vincent a painting's subject exerted an emotional appeal, hinting at the poetry hidden within; for Gauguin a painting possessed an intellectual appeal, triggering the poetry hidden in the mysterious recesses of the viewer's own heart.

Yet thanks to their shared vocabulary, fundamental misunderstandings or misalignments remained largely masked by a fantasy of shared purpose. The brothers had issued their invitation to Gauguin in May, but five months would elapse before he ventured south. The delay was critical to the unfolding of the relationship. Had Gauguin been willing and able to join Vincent in the spring, the differences would probably have surfaced immediately, precluding a productive dialogue. As it was, their protracted epistolary getting-to-know-you allowed for fruitful misapprehension. Each gleaned a portrait of the other sketchy enough to allow it to be completed by the projection of their individual needs.

Vincent took the lead in this odd dynamic. He alternated between emotional extremes that, while taxing, fostered creative purpose. Through months of anxious expectancy, his need to believe in the outcome led him to refine, embellish, and focus the ideas involved in his initial invitation to Gauguin. What began as a sketch of a shared life evolved into the concept of a "Studio of the South," an elaborate program of artistic and spiritual renewal to which Vincent gave expression in his letters and—more importantly—in the pictures he began painting to decorate the Yellow House. This decorative cycle functioned not unlike the stained-glass windows to which he had once alluded when describing the *Sunflowers*: as a representation of a symbolic belief system, with its threat of purgatory or hell and promise of heaven, redemption, and salvation. Though shaped by Naturalist literature, the Studio of the South scenario nonetheless offered a credo in counterpoint to the inconclusive and pessimistic message of *L'Oeuvre*. As inventor of the story, Vincent assigned the roles, and the more Gauguin became aware of the nature of the part he was expected to play, the more intrigued he became. Since the collapse of the Impressionist enterprise, he had, in a sense, been looking for the right script, and Vincent's seemed to promise a lead role. As summer became fall, he began to grow into it.

The first week of September found Vincent at an emotional low, overtaken by anxieties that Gauguin would come, hate Arles, and reproach him or that he would not come at all and had never seriously intended to.[202] Vincent rehearsed for Theo the accusation that he wanted to direct at Gauguin:

Look how many months we have had the means to pay the landlords, and yet all the time maintained we couldn't afford to join forces, and meantime wearing ourselves out for the future.

If you had wanted to, why didn't you tell me to come north, I would have done so by now.

It would have cost just a ticket at 100 francs, whereas now, throughout the months this has been dragging on, I have already paid the price of the ticket to my landlord, and you must have done the same to yours, or else you owe him 100 francs. That means a sheer loss of at least 100 francs for nothing at all.[203]

But to avoid a quarrel, in the letter he actually sent to Pont-Aven, he attempted to confine his inquiries to matters of art. Responding around 7 September, Gauguin promised further discussion later, closing with a rallying call to the three of them to remain "united in heart and mind" so that they could inherit their rightful place in the future. But to Vincent's real question, Gauguin offered a disappointing reply: with his debts mounting by the day, his trip south seemed less and less probable.[204]

This news—coinciding with word from Russell definitely declining to buy a Martinique picture—accelerated Vincent's oscillations between anger, ill-maintained indifference, forced optimism, and despair. Reading Gauguin's letter as a "cry of distress," Vincent nonetheless was indignant that Gauguin expected Theo—over and above providing room, board, and spending money in Arles in exchange for pictures—to fund the journey and perhaps even settle accounts in Pont-

Aven without his having to offer the dealer more pictures in exchange. Vincent questioned Gauguin's loyalty, necessarily shared with his wife and children and now further compromised by the reappearance in Pont-Aven of Laval. He accused Gauguin of being a "speculator" and a self-interested "schemer, who seeing himself at the bottom of the social ladder, wants to regain a position by means which will certainly be honest, but at the same time, very politic." But he hesitated to say any of this directly to "so great an artist." The uncertainty left him feeling at sea. While attempting to steel himself for the possibility of remaining alone, he pushed Theo to issue Gauguin an ultimatum—was he coming or not?—hoping that the response to greater forcefulness would be compliance.[205]

Refusing to be thwarted, Vincent pressed ahead. In mid-September he spent his first night, alone, in the Yellow House. This scenario was not what he had imagined, but he insisted that he was happy and would not end up feeling lonesome. Decorating the

house with pictures of "connected and complementary subjects," Vincent struggled to secure its symbolic function as a studio-sanctuary, an antidote to feelings of melancholy and rootlessness that went with the hellish life in cheap hotels that he had endured for the past seven months.[206]

Back in August, when Gauguin first postponed his arrival, Vincent's renewed fears of being forever a wanderer—without native land, family, or destination—had given him the idea of painting the dismal all-night café (*café de nuit*) in Ginoux's establishment, a gaslit, "infernal furnace" where the dispossessed who lacked money for lodgings could find a refuge.[207] It was only in early September, when the prospect of the studio-sanctuary became somewhat brighter, that Vincent undertook, in three all-night sessions, to represent this "place where one can destroy oneself, go mad, or commit crimes" (fig. 66). His thought was to suggest its complex atmosphere—outward Japanese gaiety and Tartarinesque bonhomie masking the inward

hold of the "powers of darkness"—through the juxtaposition of colors with contrasting emotional valences, namely the "blood-red" of the room and the "soft tender" green of the bar.[208] He viewed his expression of "terrible human passions by means of red and green" as an achievement equivalent to *The Potato Eaters* and as a continuation of the investigations initiated in *The Sower*; like these works *The Night Café* relies on exaggeration to convey symbolic meaning. Indeed he felt that *The Night Café* and *The Sower*—expressions of despair and hope—constituted his only attempts at finished paintings since arriving in Arles.[209]

Vincent took refuge in the Yellow House, resolving to continue producing well-thought-out work along these lines and to take more pains with quality and style. He put this into practice in a picture of a sunny corner of the public garden opposite the house on place Lamartine (fig. 69), rendered in thickly applied citron yellow and lime green. The canvas depicts the garden's southeast section, the area

66

close to what Vincent described as the "street of the good little women"—the red-light district around rue du Bout d'Arles, on the other side of the town walls (see map, fig. 19).[210] He set up his easel looking southwest, the pale blue belfry of Saint-Trophîme glimpsed on the horizon at left. A similar view of the garden, painted in July (fig. 67), celebrates a small slice of domesticated nature in the spirit of Alphonse Karr's *Voyage autour de mon jardin* (1845) (see fig. 68), a long-admired meditation on the miracles of the quotidian. While the scene remained the same, Vincent's perspective had changed. He resolutely articulated his aspirations as an agenda to be embodied in the Yellow House: "If what one is doing gives a glimpse into infinity, and if one sees that one's work has its own raison d'être and continues beyond, then one works more serenely." With or without Gauguin, he would bequeath to posterity a studio-sanctuary where a "successor" might live—a vision of the future lent credibility by the fact that there had been predecessors.[211]

Vincent consciously sought to imbue his picture of the garden with allusions to the region's early fourteenth-century renaissance and more specifically to one of its prime movers, the poet Petrarch, who resided near Avignon between 1351 and 1361. Vincent had been much taken by a recent article about Petrarch and his younger friend and protégé Boccaccio, with whom he shared a mission to revive the Virgilian tradition.[212] Their relationship, in the article's idealized terms, was a passionate spiritual and intellectual attachment, transcending sexual love since it was uncompromised by the physical, between two distinct temperaments. Petrarch, a man of many close friendships, was the only true friend of the more solitary Boccaccio, who viewed the older man as his mentor and guide but also exerted a beneficial influence in his own right, persuading Petrarch to put aside his longstanding fear of Dante's influence and

to read the *Divine Comedy*. Both found the contemporary church decadent and admired the purity of the monastic ideal. But above all, their friendship was animated by a shared vision of the poet's lofty position and a belief in the revelatory dimension of poetry. The relationship was intensely close, despite periods of separation. In Padua they spent free evenings after work in Petrarch's little garden; when Petrarch went to Avignon and Boccaccio remained in Italy, they corresponded incessantly, freely exchanging ideas and tolerating differences of opinion.[213] They helped each other to realize their potential as pioneering spirits.

Given Vincent's preoccupations, the attractions of symbolically linking his plans for a southern renaissance with an earlier one fostered through collaborative friendship are obvious. Seeking to evoke this paradigm through the theme of a Provençal garden, he disregarded the fact that Provence is tangential to the Petrarch–Boccaccio story and the garden setting incidental. He felt a sense of communion with Petrarch in experiencing the same Provençal landscape, and he was aware of the tradition, from the medieval period to Zola's Paradou, that invested gardens with symbolic significance.[214] He planted in it his own symbols, beginning with a flowering oleander bush.

Grafting his personal association of the flower with the *mousmé* and her French compatriots, the prostitutes working on the nearby street, onto Boccaccio's reputed fondness for their sisterhood, Vincent believed that he had introduced a "touch of Boccaccio" to his garden.[215] Its larger metaphoric significance was tied up with his intention to transform the Yellow House into an "artist's house," a conception in part inspired by Edmond de Goncourt's *La Maison d'un artiste* (1881), which includes a *jardin de peintre*, a place of refuge in times of broken dreams and failing courage.

Comparable symbolic intent informed this and the other pictures Vincent would refer to as the "*jardin d'un poète.*"[216]

In fact the ideal discipleship to which these pictures allude was in doubt. In addition to the oleander that stood for Boccaccio, Vincent included a note of contrast to the sunny mood, a "weeping tree"—an emblem, along with the cypress, of death and mourning—that introduces the specter of loss.[217] His growing suspicion that Gauguin had postponed coming to Arles not because of finances but rather because he had "another combination in mind" threatened the serenity he hoped to express and to feel.[218] This conjured another garden, one rife with despair and betrayal. Within days of completing *The Poet's Garden*, Vincent reported:

67

68

For the second time I have scraped off a study of Christ with the angel in the Garden of Olives. You see, I can see real olives here, but I cannot or rather I will not paint any more without models; but I have the thing in my head with the colors, a starry night, the figure of Christ in blue, all the strongest blues, and the angel blended citron yellow. And every shade of violet, from a blood-red purple to ashen, in the landscape.[219]

As before, Vincent sidestepped the deeper significance of his endeavor by referring only to the problems inherent in painting figures without models. He began filling in the blanks soon after, first declaring that he would not beseech models to pose because he did not want to behave "like Zola's good painter in *L'Oeuvre*"—a reference to an early episode in the novel when Claude Lantier virtually begs the woman who will become his companion to pose for him. The failed masterpiece with which the book culminates, a realistic urban scene with a female nude personifying the City in the center, baffles and even angers those who see it. Vincent clearly had this in mind when he followed the reference to Claude's model with one to his masterpiece: "Zola does not say in his book how the people who saw nothing supernatural in the painting behaved. But we must not criticize Zola's book." In *L'Oeuvre* Claude's work is criticized by Sandoz for its fusion of realism and "wild, fantastic symbolism." It is offered as evidence of the plight of contemporary artists: attempting to shake off the excessive self-referentiality of Romanticism, they have embraced a realism informed by science; but gradually pessimism causes "old religious fears" to resurface, propelling them toward brain-clouding "mysticism" and the "supernatural." Claude finally succumbs to madness because he forgets that scientifically based "truth and nature are the only possible bases, the essential controlling factors in art."[220]

The parallels between Claude's failed masterpiece and the two failed *Gethsemanes* were obvious to Vincent, but he took issue with two of Zola's guiding premises. He believed that love and religion—albeit not in tradition-

67
Vincent van Gogh
Public Garden with Newly Mowed Lawn and Weeping Tree
5 July 1888
[F 428, JH 1499]
Oil on canvas
60.5 x 73.5 cm
Private collection

68
Tailpiece from Alphonse Karr, *Voyage autour de mon jardin* (Paris, 1851 ed.)

69
Vincent van Gogh
The Poet's Garden (*Le Jardin du poète*)
Mid-September 1888
[F 468, JH 1578]
Oil on canvas
73 x 92.1 cm

The Art Institute of Chicago, Mr. and Mrs. Lewis Larned Coburn Memorial Collection, 1933.433
Cat. 63

al forms—were necessary antidotes to skepticism and the "desperate suffering that makes one despair."[221] And while he explicitly concurred with the dangers of painting from the imagination, he had now done so twice, and failed twice. Essentially Zola's view echoed the famous dictum of Gustave Courbet: "I cannot paint an angel because I have never seen one"; Courbet also advised a student not to paint Christ unless he was a personal acquaintance.[222] Vincent held onto a secret ambition to naturalize the supernatural, as Delacroix and Rembrandt had. Just as he intimated that Claude might have achieved this, he contended that "Rembrandt did not invent anything, and that angel and that strange Christ [see fig. 45] came about because he knew them, felt that they were there." Rembrandt was of course an exceptional seer. In his own quest to intimate a higher reality, Vincent dared to imagine a similar scenario—experiencing a dream so intense that it constituted a reality, there to be painted. He talked of the "terrible lucidity" that he felt while painting, of "losing consciousness of myself" so that "the picture comes to me as in a dream."[223]

Vincent's *Gethsemane* was a dream of artistic martyrdom, embracing Christ, Monticelli, and by extension himself. It is of enormous significance as an experiment on the heels of the garden pictures, which exemplify Vincent's symbolic realism in their mobilizing of personal and established emblems to convey deeper significance. While he meant his picture to be immediately comprehensible, as he explained with regard to the *Sunflowers*, in point of fact were we not privy to his private world through his correspondence, the symbolism of a picture like *The Poet's Garden*, though palpable, would remain illegible. The temptation of the Gethsemane subject was its iconic accessibility, its availability as a ready communicator of the soul's anguish.

How Vincent's dream of a *Gethsemane* related to Gauguin's *Vision* is uncertain. It was only in early October that Vincent informed Bernard that he had mercilessly destroyed this "important canvas."[224] So it seems that Gauguin was unaware of Vincent's most recent attempt at a religious subject when he wrote in the last week of September announcing the completion of his own, *Vision of the Sermon*. Both pictures were nonetheless based on a shared questioning of Realist parameters. Zola's image of Claude wrestling with "the Real," like Jacob with the angel, indeed resonated with Gauguin's notion of "lutte contradictoire" and with Vincent's talk, during his Dutch years, of "wrestling with nature long enough for her to tell me her secret."[225] The secret at issue now was that which Carlyle had charged the artist with uncovering by "wrestling naked with the truth of things"—nothing less than "the great Mystery of Existence." Gauguin suggested something like this in reporting that creating the *Vision* had involved "fighting (in every manner possible)"; now he was resting.[226]

In this same letter, Gauguin also addressed Vincent's suspicion, finally voiced, that Gauguin was planning to found a rival enterprise—"a Studio of the North." Dismissing this notion, Gauguin took Vincent to task for insisting he come to Arles when in fact only money held him back. Had he not already formally pledged himself to the project? He could not consider, as Vincent apparently suggested, skipping out on those who had kindly extended him credit, and he would therefore have to stay in Pont-Aven until he could afford to leave.[227] In the face of Vincent's anxious insistence, Gauguin was calm but firm. If Vincent could not wait and wanted to abandon the plan, he should inform him as soon as possible. He did suggest that Theo lower the prices of his paintings to attract buyers; he was ready to make sacrifices.

Gauguin dealt equally firmly with another matter preoccupying Vincent: the portraits that he wanted for the Yellow House, in the absence of the principals—"the portrait of Bernard by Gauguin and that of G. by B." Vincent made a point of presuming that such portraits already existed, for this would testify to his friends' seriousness of purpose. When he learned from Bernard that this was not the case, Vincent became indignant: "And such fellows call themselves portraitists, living so long together and not making up their minds to pose for each other, and they will separate without having painted each other's portrait!"[228] Gauguin, reading this letter, resented being accused of laziness. *Friends*, he chided, do not get angry with each other. He would do the portrait Vincent wanted, "but not *yet*." What he had in mind was not a copy of the sitter's features, but a deeper resemblance based on his understanding of the subject. For the moment, "I am studying little Bernard, and I haven't captured him yet." He speculated that the idea for the portrait would come to him all at once, and he would probably paint from memory. Certainly the result would be "an abstraction."[229]

Gauguin's letter reassured Vincent, who now felt certain that Gauguin would come to Arles and even speculated to Theo that he would "take root" there. He calculated that Gauguin's participation would increase the importance of "this attempt to paint in the South by 100 percent." Renewed optimism also resurfaced in the just-completed paintings he announced along with this news. One was of a starry sky over the Rhone, painted from a site near the Yellow House; the other was a view of the house itself (figs. 70–71). They were in a sense complementaries.[230]

The starry-night subject was one that Vincent had talked of wanting to do for months. He had ventured it as the background for two idealized portraits of artists. The first, known as

A square size 30 canvas, finally the starry sky painted at night under a gas jet. The sky is greenish blue, the water royal blue, the ground mauve. The town is blue and violet, the gas is yellow and its reflections are russet-gold down to greenish bronze. On the blue-green expanse of sky, the Great Bear sparkles green and pink, its discreet pallor contrasts with the harsh gold of the gas.

Vincent to Theo, [29 September 1888]

70
Vincent van Gogh
The Starry Night over the Rhone (*La Nuit étoilée*)
28 September 1888
[F 474, JH 1592]
Oil on canvas
72.5 x 92 cm
Musée d'Orsay,
Paris, life-interest
gift of M. and Mme

Robert Kahn-
Sriberen
in memory of M.
and Mme Fernand
Moch, 1975, and
entered the collec-
tion in 1995
Cat. 65

The subject is very difficult! But that is just why I want to conquer it. It's terrific, these yellow houses in the sun, against the incomparable freshness of the blue. The whole ground is yellow too.... The house on the left, the one shaded by a tree, is pink with green shutters. That's the restaurant where I go to eat dinner every day.... The night café that I painted is not in the picture; it is to the left of the restaurant.   Vincent to Theo, [29 September 1888]

The Poet, depicts a "fellow artist who dreams great dreams" (ch. 4, fig. 32); apparently Vincent was thinking of Gauguin as a Carlylean hero posed against a backdrop of "infinity."[231] In Gauguin's absence Vincent used young Belgian painter Eugène Boch as a stand-in, setting him against a starry sky intimating the aspirations for the infinite that were Vincent's own. *The Poet* gives expression to his goal of producing consoling art— portraiture that through chromatic "radiance"

hints at the "touch of the eternal" signified in traditional religious painting by the halo.[232] It was precisely this tradition that Vincent had called upon for his other image of the creative artist against a starry sky, his second attempt at depicting Christ in Gethsemane.

The Starry Night over the Rhone speaks to the same longing as *The Poet* and *Gethsemane* —the terrible need for religion that Vincent attempted to satisfy by "going out at night to

paint the stars." It recasts the high drama of the Agony in the Garden into the quiet of an everyday event: two lovers gazing at the firmament.[233] As plentiful as the constellations it seems are the associations hovering over the picture from Vincent's lifetime of reading. Particularly notable luminaries include Walt Whitman, with his vision of the starlit sky as a manifestation of eternity; Thomas Carlyle, who wrote of the stars as the open secret of the universe's mysteries,

71
Vincent van Gogh
The Yellow House
28 September 1888
[F 464, JH 1589]
Oil on canvas
76 x 94 cm
Van Gogh Museum,
Amsterdam
(Vincent van Gogh
Foundation)
Cat. 66

72
Postcard of avenue
de Montmajour,
Arles, postmarked
1906

intimations of a "present God"; and Heinrich Heine, for whom stars suggested answers to "Questions": "What is the meaning of Man? Where has he come from? Where is he going?" In van Eeden's *De kleine Johannes*, the contemplation of natural majesty inspires the protagonist as he wonders to whom he should pray. Witnessing another of nature's great light displays, a sunset over the ocean's infinite vista, Johannes glimpses eternity. "That," he learns, "is the way to pray!"[234]

Like *The Starry Night over the Rhone*, Vincent's portrait of the "house and its surroundings in sulfur-colored sunshine, under a sky of pure cobalt" (fig. 71) is an everyday scene invested with intimations of the extraordinary. Its symbolism is still more personal. With the contrast of saturated blue and vibrant yellow, Vincent situated the picture chromatically in a historical perspective leading from Vermeer to Delacroix. He traced this view into the future through the perspective of avenue de Montmajour, leading past the railway tracks that would bring Gauguin south and beyond—to the "hope" that had begun to "show on the horizon," to the "new era" that Gauguin's arrival would inaugurate.[235] Claude Lantier might have included a large, Puvis-like nude figure to bring the point home. Chromatic

intensity transfigures this street scene, imbuing it with a sense of moment in keeping with Vincent's dream that the house would be the center of the "art of the future," even the church of the "religion of the future," or at least a kind of monastery devoted to its observance. Rules for the community—foreseen by Vincent as including Bernard and Laval—were clear. Gauguin, the first arrival, was to be "head of the studio," keeper of the purse and the "abbot" maintaining order. Theo, having committed himself to Gauguin "body and soul," would serve as the "first dealer-apostle." Vincent, deferring to the man whom Bernard lauded as a "very great master…absolutely superior in character and intellect," would take a secondary position, urging his fellow artists to productivity through his own example.[236]

Vincent had in fact already illustrated himself in this role in a self-portrait painted two weeks earlier (fig. 73), at the moment he asked for portraits of Bernard and Gauguin. Initially he said little about this canvas, remarking to Theo only on its color scheme—his "ashen" face against a malachite background—and mentioning to his sister that he had depicted himself looking "like a Japanese."[237] He deferred discussion of the self-portrait's programmatic intent until early October, after painting the Yellow House and outlining the structure for its community. Gauguin's letter of 1 October, announcing that he and Bernard had accomplished his wish and finished the requested portraits (figs. 74, 76), was inspirational.[238] That both were self-portraits (albeit including abbreviated sketches of one another's images in the backgrounds) would not have been a surprise to Vincent. Bernard had already confessed to finding the task of painting Gauguin impossible; so greatly did he admire Gauguin and so superior did he find his work that he felt afraid in front of him. While dismissive of such nonsense in a reply to Bernard, Vincent admitted to Theo that he could understand, because he was similarly "neurotic."[239] The mastery claimed by Bernard for Gauguin seemed confirmed by

136. — *Arles.* - Gendarmerie et Avenue Montmajour.
Collection J. Poirey.

73

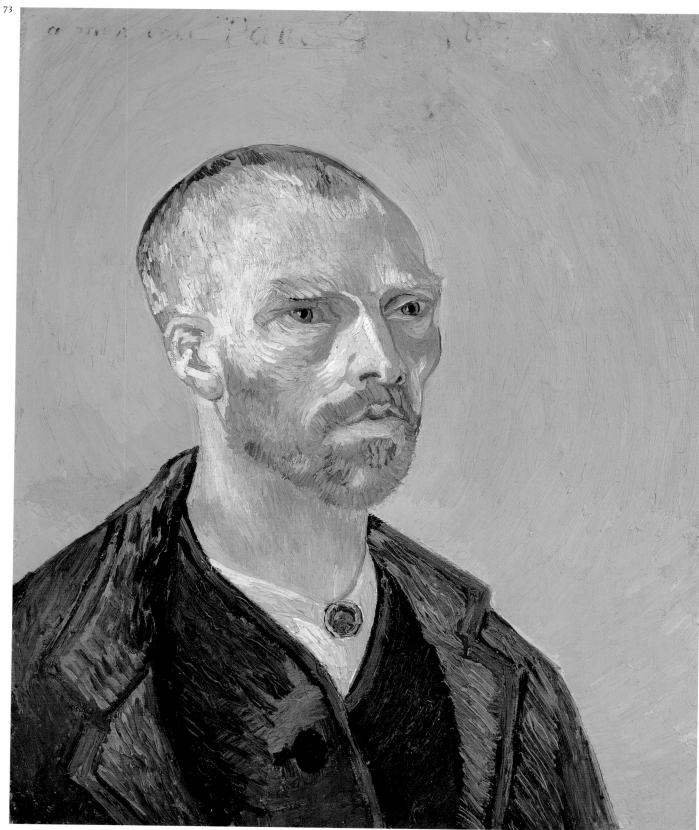

148   Studio of the South

73
Vincent van Gogh
*Self-Portrait Dedicated
to Paul Gauguin
(Bonze)*
c. 16 September 1888
[F 476, JH 1581]
Oil on canvas
61 x 50 cm
Fogg Art Museum,
Harvard University
Art Museums,
bequest from the
Collection of
Maurice Wertheim,
Class of 1906
Cat. 64

74
Paul Gauguin
*Self-Portrait Dedicated
to Vincent van Gogh
(Les Misérables)*
Late September 1888
[W 239]
Oil on canvas
45 x 55 cm
Van Gogh Museum,
Amsterdam
(Vincent van Gogh
Foundation)
Cat. 33

the latter's elaborate explanation, drafted for Vincent, of his self-portrait:

I feel compelled to explain what I intended to do, not because you're not capable of understanding the work on your own, but because I fear it is not successful. It is the face of an outlaw, ill-clad and powerful like Jean Valjean—with an inner nobility and gentleness. The rutting blood inundates the face, and the colors of a furnace-fire enveloping the eyes suggest the volcanic flames that animate the soul of the artist. The line of the eyes and nose, reminiscent of the flowers in a Persian carpet, epitomize the idea of an abstract, symbolic style. The girlish background with its childlike flowers is there to attest to our artistic purity. As for this Jean Valjean, whom society has oppressed, cast out—for all his love and vigor—is he not equally a symbol of the contemporary impressionist painter? In endowing him with my own features I offer an image, a portrait of myself as well as our portrait, to all wretched victims of society who avenge us by doing good.[240]

Reading these compelling words, Vincent was overwhelmed, "moved to the depths of my soul."[241] Gauguin's language and imagery, so close to his own, substantiated the claim that in painting his own image Gauguin had realized, symbolically, a portrait of them both.

Vincent had repeatedly characterized the young vanguard as appearing to the rest of the world to be "madmen or criminals," and he had spoken of the "social isolation" that he and Gauguin faced.[242] When Gauguin assumed these attributes in the persona of Jean Valjean, the outlaw persecuted by society who is the chief protagonist of Victor Hugo's epic *Les Misérables*, he invoked a book that for Vincent had long been a touchstone. His parents had disappointed him in their inability to see beyond Valjean's crime and comprehend Hugo's larger social message; and he had urged van Rappard to read it so that it could function as a shared reference, making it easier for them to communicate. That Gauguin had himself just finished reading the novel suggests a similar dynamic.[243]

Some of Gauguin's resonant imagery echoes his correspondent's. The "furnace fire" around the eyes recalls Vincent's talk of a "furnace of creation" on first learning of Gauguin's willingness to join him, as well as the infernal furnace of the night café; the "rutting blood" suffusing the complexion invokes the much-discussed sexualization of creativity. As Jean Valjean was a thief with a heart of gold, Gauguin's personification has a rough masculine exterior that protects a feminized "artistic virginity," signaled by the flowered wallpaper. Vincent had recently summoned the related cliché of the "virgin heart" with regard to an artist friend, and he had described the effect he intended to achieve in Gauguin's bedroom—the house's prettiest room—as "something like the boudoir of a really artistic woman." Gauguin's symbolic wallpaper—childlike nosegays with large pinkish white blossoms on a yellow background—can further be seen as recalling Puvis's plant symbolism; it also reverses the chromatic effect of the room awaiting him in Arles, with its "white walls hung with large sunflowers."[244] And in comparing his stylized delineation of the face to patterns he saw

75
Vincent van Gogh
Public Garden with a Couple and a Blue Fir Tree
Early October 1888
[F 479, JH 1601]
Oil on canvas
73 x 92 cm
Private collection

75

in Persian carpets, Gauguin engaged with an analogy that Vincent had drawn between his first garden composition and floral carpets of the Renaissance.[245]

The description appeared to put a recognizable face on Vincent's ideals. Gauguin followed it with a reference to Jesus "as artist," and to his and Bernard's plans for going to Arles, adding a postscript verse about painting faces in chrome no. 2—the yellow pigment that Vincent used in the *Sunflowers*—under a "burning sun."[246] This "very, very remarkable letter" led Vincent to believe that he could "count on Gauguin staying with us always." Moreover, he saw the intensity he had brought to bear on his friends as having paid off: Gauguin had "given birth to a picture," he reported to Theo, once again appropriating a metaphor from *L'Oeuvre*.[247] Replying to Gauguin, Vincent explained the dynamic he imagined for their relationship in discussing his pictures of the garden—now referred to for the first time as the "poet's garden"—which he had earmarked for Gauguin's bedroom (see fig. 69):

I have tried to distinguish the basic points of that which constitutes the immutable nature of this country.... I wanted to paint this garden in such a way that one would at once think of the former poet from these parts...Petrarch, and of the new poet—Paul Gauguin.[248]

Seeing himself in the role of the junior, coarser Boccaccio to his friend's older, more established Petrarch, Vincent confided to Gauguin that while months earlier he had been "bereft of hope," he now saw it beckoning. It was invested in Gauguin: "I so much wanted to inform you of my belief that we will succeed in starting something that will endure." This belief was Vincent's true need, although he also discussed the more political and practical

aspects of establishing an artists' cooperative.[249] He had begun to rehearse his role as disciple in the previous month's self-portrait (fig. 73), but not until he received a sign of Gauguin's commitment did he disclose its intended significance:

I've a portrait of myself, all ash gray. The ashen color—which results from the mixture of emerald green with orange lead—on a pale green background, all in harmony with the reddish brown clothing. But exaggerating my own personality as well, I instead looked for the character of a bonze, a simple worshiper of the eternal Buddha. It caused me enough pain.[250]

Responsive to Gauguin, Vincent suggested that his guise evoked the social alienation experienced by "not only myself but an impressionist in general."[251] But his symbolic strategy was different. For while Gauguin's portrait dramatizes a problem—the artist as outcast in contemporary society—Vincent's proposes its programmatic solution.

The persona of a Japanese bonze (a Buddhist monk) harnessed several fantasies: the Wagnerian ideal of proselytizing the art of the future by banding together as "disciples of a new religion"; the belief, which had become a mantra in Vincent's letters to Bernard, that only a monastic life could provide the unity and focus requisite to healthy creativity; and the model of community he attributed to Japanese painters, whose example he implied they emulated in exchanging pictures. The bonze idea, as Gauguin would learn, came from Vincent's reading of *Madame Chrysanthème*, in which Loti described the bonzes' residence—the *bonzerie*—as a "virginal" combination of pure white and wood "the color of fresh butter." Announcing his self-portrait to his sister, Vincent portrayed the house in identical terms: whitewashed

inside, the outside painted "the yellow color of fresh butter."[252] The Yellow House was also a *bonzerie*.

Presenting himself as a "simple worshiper," moreover, Vincent incanted a credo of humble deference in a self-deprecating litany addressed to the "abbot," Gauguin:

I consider my artistic ideas to be extemely pedestrian compared with yours.
I have always felt base animal instincts.
I neglect everything for the external beauty of things, which I cannot convey because I render it so ugly and coarse in my pictures.[253]

Nonetheless, his energy invested what he did with sincerity, "if, however, the subject lends itself to my blunt and clumsy rendering."[254]

In Vincent's calculatedly austere self-portrait, his gauntness is emphasized by the short hair and beard, growing back after having been completely shaved off for the summer. Then he had described himself as looking like a "placid priest"; here, intensity and determination are the overriding affects. His eyes, made purposely "slanting like the Japanese," do not seem to engage the viewer—as is natural when painting from the mirror's returned gaze—but stare past and beyond, as if toward something in the distance.[255] This unblinking focus belies the image's purported simplicity in the same way that ambition complicated Vincent's avowed deference. Vincent shared his competitive impulses with Theo on receiving Gauguin's letter:

I am sufficiently proud to want to impress Gauguin to some extent with my work, so I cannot help wanting to do as much work as possible alone before he comes. His arrival will alter my manner of painting and I will be better for it, I daresay, but all the same I am rather fond of my decorations.[256]

76
Émile Bernard
Self-Portrait Dedicated to Vincent van Gogh
Late September 1888
Oil on canvas
46.5 x 55.5 cm
Van Gogh Museum,
Amsterdam
(Vincent van Gogh
Foundation)
Cat. 27

76

Before sending his portrait to Pont-Aven, Vincent awaited receipt of the package containing those of Gauguin and Bernard. Its arrival the first week of October allowed him to compare his canvas to theirs—especially to Gauguin's. Although reassured to find that his portrait "held its own," he was severely disappointed.[257] For Gauguin's portrait fell seriously short of what he had anticipated from its description. In one regard Vincent's imagination had been remarkably prescient: from Gauguin's reference to Persian carpets, he had deduced that the portrait would readily fit into the Louvre's recently opened gallery containing the Dieulafoy collection of Assyrian art, and he had anticipated that it might owe a debt to that collection's famous ceramic friezes featuring cursively stylized lions (see fig. 80). While Vincent preferred the Greeks and Japanese to the Persians and Egyptians, he did not consider Gauguin wrong to work in the "Persian style."[258] He would get used to it. What disconcerted him when he opened the package was something that he had not anticipated: the picture's pessimism.

After months of intense discussion, Vincent felt familiar with Gauguin's ideas. But, crucially, he had not yet seen the breakthrough paintings in which he gave them expression. Vincent was confident that he would recognize something of himself in what Gauguin had called "our portrait." In fact he could much more readily relate to, and clearly preferred, Bernard's unassuming work (fig. 76). Executed with a Manet-like economy of means, it was "a real painter's portrait" conveying communal purpose with its dedication to Vincent and with the glimpse of a Japanese woodcut at the lower right, below and to the right of the presiding image of Gauguin in Breton outfit.[259] Gauguin's self-portrait, while evidently more ambitious, was deeply disturbing.

While Gauguin's portrait alluded to martyrdom in shared terms, it failed to provide any leavening relief from the "torment" and illness that Vincent read in the "dismal" blue flesh tones. He found "not a shadow of gaiety" in the figure who engages the viewer with a shrewd, knowing look, as if sizing up the opposition he faces. The artist is a prisoner, to be sure, but without a possible escape, without the glimmer of hope such as a star could express. Willfully, Gauguin had created a portrait of melancholy so dark and sad that it broke what for Vincent had become a cardinal rule: that painting offer consolation.[261]

Vincent found the picture upsetting on a personal level as well. Gauguin seemed to have succumbed to the despair against which Vincent constantly defended himself. What he encountered in the image was the specter of another *misérable*, Claude Lantier: "I do not like the horrors of *L'Oeuvre*, except insofar as they show us the path. Our path is not to endure them ourselves nor to make others endure them, but the opposite."[262]

Once again Gauguin had responded to Vincent's ideas, but not as he had intended. A similar situation now arose with Bernard, who responded to the proposed rules for the Yellow House with ideas that Vincent irritably decried as dogmatic and decadent. Bernard had misinterpreted his intent, and Vincent—himself prone to discussing his plans endlessly—essentially told his friend to shut up: "The more one talks about it the less it will happen. If you want to help it onward, you will only have to go on working with Gauguin and me. This is in progress, so don't let's talk about it."[263] Vincent had a

true believer's intolerance for dissenting opinions.

Attempting to put a better face on the situation, Vincent assured himself that Gauguin would paint a very different portrait of himself after six months in Arles: "He will change but must come [now]."[264] Negotiating this profound misunderstanding of Gauguin's aims and intentions with hope of future restoration (and buoyed when Theo managed to sell three hundred francs' worth of Gauguin's ceramics), he worked at an ever more feverish pace on decorations for the house.[265] His whole mind was set on Gauguin coming right away. He met with skepticism Gauguin's claim to be suffering from dysentery and a pulmonary condition, accompanied as it was by plans hatched with Bernard and Laval for making lithographs. Curtly dismissing this project as impractical, Vincent told Gauguin that if he were ill, he should come South at once to recover more quickly, and if he were not ill, he should equally come at once.[266] Mollified by the news that Gauguin had forwarded his trunk and was planning to be in Arles by 20 October, Vincent sent a sketch of a canvas depicting his bedroom (figs. 77–78), describing its flat tints, laid in roughly with thick impasto, and explaining that he had aimed at Seurat-like simplicity expressive of absolute restfulness.[267] However, a certain exaggeration and distortion in fact conveys a quite different effect, one of disturbance. Though this resulted in part from the room's irregular shape (its south wall was on a slant; see ch. 4, fig. 2), Vincent recognized that he was overwrought on the eve of Gauguin's arrival. Evoking a persistent image, he likened himself to Wauters's depiction of Hugo van der Goes (fig. 40), but he believed that he would be spared the fate of "persecution mania" by virtue of his "double nature" of monk and painter: "When in a state of excitement my feelings lead me rather to the contemplation of eternity and eternal life."[268]

He had to watch his nerves. He believed in the South, and he believed himself ready for Gauguin:

I have…pushed what I was working on as far as I could in my great desire to be able to show him something new, and not to be subjected to his influence (for he will certainly influence me, I hope) before I can show him indubitably my own individuality…in the decoration as it is now.[269]

Gauguin was ready too, his preparedness very much the result of the efforts of Vincent and his brother. He was heartened by Theo's sale of his work. Though he could not resist suggesting that Theo look for a *speculative amateur* who might be interested in buying a group of his works inexpensively, he decided to abide by Theo's contrary strategy of raising his prices. Informing Theo he planned to head south by month's end (but leaving open the possibility that his health or the want of an additional hundred francs might interfere), he sent Schuffenecker to the gallery to secure half the amount. With cocky self-assurance,

Gauguin described Theo as "thrilled with me," noting the jealousy of others, like Guillaumin, who sought the dealer's attention. With a sly, worldly-wise shrewdness that recalls the expression captured in his self-portrait, Gauguin observed, "Crazy about me as [Theo] may be, he would not undertake to keep me in the South because of my pretty eyes." Ever on the lookout himself, Gauguin thought he recognized speculative interest. Theo must have picked up on the buzz that had come to Gauguin's ears as well: "Right now there's a very favorable wind blowing *my* way among the *artists*…. He has studied the terrain in a cool Dutch manner and aimed at pushing things as far as possible, exclusively."[270] His raising of Gauguin's prices attested as much.

Though Gauguin cultivated acumen when communicating with the admiring Schuffenecker, the simple fact was that Theo was more the instigator than the beneficiary of the wind filling the sails of Gauguin's reputation. Here Vincent was instrumental. His respectful admiration was more meaningful

to Gauguin than that of the Pont-Aven artists he disdained, and more important to his fortunes than that of Bernard. Seemingly there was mutual regard, for Vincent in turn received from Gauguin "heaps of undeserved compliments," either for the vivid way in which he committed his ideas to paper or for his self-portrait as a bonze, which was the first painting of Vincent's that Gauguin had seen since Paris.[271]

Evidently Gauguin found Vincent's fulsome praise at once heady and suggestive. He even thought that Schuffenecker might use Vincent's letters as testimonials for a prospective buyer. Gauguin of course recognized full well the dangers of idealization. To Theo he allowed that Vincent's intense response to his description of his self-portrait intimidated him precisely because he realized that the actual canvas would inevitably prove inferior to Vincent's imagined version of it. Prescient though this seems on Gauguin's part, it was in fact inadvertent, for he misjudged the grounds of Vincent's "disillusion."[272] His prediction—that Vincent would find the picture

77

78

77
Vincent van Gogh
Sketch of *The Bedroom* in letter to Gauguin
[c. 18 October 1888]
(letter 711/B 22)
Private collection, courtesy Van Gogh Museum, Amsterdam

78
Vincent van Gogh
The Bedroom (La Chambre à coucher)
Mid-October 1888
[F 482, JH 1608]
Oil on canvas
72 x 90 cm
Van Gogh Museum, Amsterdam
(Vincent van Gogh Foundation)
Cat. 68

79
Paul Gauguin
Self-portrait sketch in letter to Schuffenecker
8 October 1888
(M 1984, letter 168)

80
Lion frieze on Susa acropolis from
Marcel Dieulafoy, *L'Acropole de Suse*
(Paris, 1890), pl. III

79

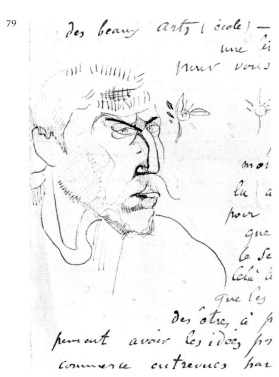

80

insufficiently beautiful or too summarily executed—reveals how unaware he was of the deeper nature of his friend's ambitions.

While the two artists had discussed issues of pictorial symbolism in shared language, each imagined differently the aims it could serve. Vincent's disappointment lay in discovering a symbolic content at odds with the message of consolation that he had read in the Martinique figure pictures. By contrast, Gauguin saw progress. To Schuffenecker he described the self-portrait as "one of my best things," testimony to the active "transformation" his art was undergoing due to his sacrifice of "execution [and] color in favor of style, wanting to impose on myself something different from what is familiar to me."[273] Supplying a pen sketch (fig. 79), Gauguin backed up his claim that the delineation of the nose and eyes constituted a "complete abstraction" linked to Persian art. Particularly telling was his characterization of the flesh tones that struck Vincent as so disturbingly unhealthy:

The color is far from anything in nature: imagine a distant memory of my stoneware twisted by intense heat. All the reds and violets streaked with bursts of flame, as though from a glowing furnace radiating from the eyes, the site of struggles in the painter's thoughts.[274]

Gauguin thus proclaimed that with the self-portrait he had at last assimilated the qualities of his pottery into his painting, and indeed the canvas can be seen to assert the persona initiated in his first ceramic, *The Faun* (ch. 2, fig. 18).

Though he took care to clarify his symbolic intentions to friends, he recognized that the self-portrait would remain incomprehensible— "rebuslike"—to most. But this did not trouble him. Unlike Vincent, he was not seeking to forge a style readily legible to many, but rather an art that would elicit the appreciation of the discerning few; he was willing to forego the accessibility of prose in order to be recognized a poet. Schuffenecker's reference to his "*terrible mysticism*" gratified Gauguin, who declared that he had set out on what he called a symbolic path. However perilous this direction, he must pursue it in order to realize an art true to his fundamental nature. This imperative of self-expression—authenticity—linked Gauguin to Vincent, but Gauguin's version of intense subjectivity was (for the moment) free from his friend's religious anxieties and always imminent despair. Vincent's projection notwithstanding, Gauguin was in fact avowedly optimistic, believing at long last that surely he stood on "firm ground." And Arles loomed large on the road that would lead to his realizing "*first-rate things*."[275] He pragmatically anticipated that his sojourn there would facilitate further progress by relieving him of financial worries, but Gauguin must have recognized Vincent's vital role as sparring partner in the struggles leading to the self-portrait that— painted at his request and meant to impress him (and through him, Theo)[276]—was so evidently a step forward. He informed Schuffenecker that he planned to stay a long time in Arles until the time was right "*to launch*" himself.[277] On Sunday, 21 October, almost six months after Vincent had extended his invitation, Gauguin left Pont-Aven and his friends Laval and Bernard, and set out for Arles.

Collection J. Poirej.

1
Place Lamartine seen
through the porte de la
Cavalerie, Arles, c. 1906

a Café de la Gare
b Restaurant Venissac
c Grocery shop
d The Yellow House

Gauguin left Pont-Aven on Sunday, 21 October. The 685-mile (1,100-kilometer) journey to Arles took many hours and required several train changes (see map, ch. 2, fig. 5). Shortly after 5:00 A.M. on Tuesday, 23 October, Gauguin arrived in Arles and made his way from the station to the all-night café in Ginoux's establishment, where the proprietor recognized him from the self-portrait that Vincent had shown him.[1] A few hours later, he went next door to the Yellow House to join his friend.

Encountering one another anew after ten months of correspondence and negotiation, both artists seem to have been somewhat taken aback. Vincent, his expectations conditioned by Gauguin's *Self-Portrait (Les Misérables)* (ch. 3, fig. 74), was surprised to find his friend in good shape, "even . . . in better health than I am." Gauguin, for his part, informed Theo that he found Vincent a bit agitated.[2] Perhaps this mood had to do with Theo's report that he had just sold Gauguin's *Breton Girls Dancing* (ch. 3, fig. 21) for the generous sum of five hundred francs, a turn of events that immediately upset the balance in a relationship already characterized as an unequal partnership. While Vincent expressed confidence that Gauguin would go on to even greater achievements in Arles, he hoped tentatively that he himself might be similarly successful, in order to reduce the financial burden on Theo. He protested that it was not his fault that his work was not selling at the moment, but he felt "morally crushed and physically drained" by his continued dependence. The arithmetic he now performed in light of Gauguin's windfall was far from encouraging. Projecting a lifetime's expenses at 100,000 francs, Vincent calculated that to cover costs he needed to produce a thousand canvases selling at one hundred francs each (as opposed to the five hundred that Gauguin had just proved himself capable of demanding)—an overwhelming prospect.[3]

Theo, sensing his brother's troubled state of mind, came to his rescue not only with money but with an accounting of their relationship that gave Vincent a more equal footing. It was Theo's job, he insisted, to deal with ignoble commercial matters; Vincent should work without thought of the financial side. The only thing that Theo expected of him was that he continue "as in the past, and create an entourage of artists and friends for us, something which I am absolutely incapable of doing by myself, and which you have been able to do . . . ever since you came to France."[4]

By the time Vincent received Theo's vote of confidence, he was already in a better frame of mind, thanks to a few days in Gauguin's company. To be sure, he remained acutely aware that Gauguin could have afforded to stay put comfortably in Brittany with the money that Theo had just helped him earn; from what Gauguin had said about Pont-Aven, Vincent openly conceded Arles to be inferior in all respects. Obviously ready to defer to Gauguin's opinions, Vincent declared him to be "very, very interesting as a man." Decoded, this observation attributes to Gauguin the self-possession and resourcefulness that Vincent admired in Loti's characters.[5]

Gauguin set out to calm Vincent little by little.[6] Appreciative of a rapt audience, he told colorful tales of his past. After four days of this, Vincent was in the throes of hero-worship:

I knew very well that Gauguin was well traveled, but I did not know that he was a regular mariner, he has experienced every difficulty, that he has been a true rigger on the topmast, a real sailor. This gives me an enormous respect for him and a still more absolute confidence in him as a man. He has, if one must compare him with anything, an affinity with Loti's Icelandic fisherman. . . . What Gauguin tells of the tropics seems marvelous to me. Surely the future of a great renaissance in painting lies there.[7]

Gauguin's mythic identity reconfirmed Vincent's belief that he had found the right partner for his voyage. Eager to embark, he soon reported to Theo that he was feeling better and that, naturally, he and Gauguin had already begun to paint.[8]

For Gauguin, certainly, this was not at all natural. By now it was his standard practice, on visiting a new place, to start with a process of reconnoitering in which drawing featured prominently. Before attempting to paint in Martinique, he executed numerous sketches in an effort to imbue himself with the character of the island. He had used identical language with regard to the land and inhabitants of Brittany when setting goals for his second sojourn there. In Arles he planned to spend a month initiating himself to the nature of the region before undertaking serious work. Years later, writing in Tahiti, Gauguin still protested that he was not one of those artists who could "get off the train, pick up their palette," and dive into painting. But no such preliminary drawings exist to document Gauguin's initial responses to Arles; most likely he made none, for Vincent gave him only a day to settle in before launching them on their first painting campaign. Vincent thus had the advantage of "continuing" what he had been doing, while Gauguin was faced suddenly with "starting something new."[9]

These initial paintings provide the introduction to the history of their time together, just as the pictures they realized during the nine weeks they spent side by side in the Yellow House until the abrupt denouement of 23 December illustrate its subsequent chapters. Yet for various reasons the narrative is often reduced to a short story, an episode within larger histories of modern art. The identification of the corpus of works—three dozen pictures are generally assigned to Vincent for this period, and less than half that number to Gauguin—has proved more difficult than might be expected, as has the establishment

of a secure sequence. Vincent's correspondence, usually such a rich source for documenting his every move, fails us here. With a companion at his side, the flow of letters—averaging one every two days to Theo—became a trickle of only eleven over the two months that Gauguin spent with him; and these are shorter than usual. Certainly the letters that Vincent (and Gauguin) did write to Theo and to other friends and family members point to the issues that the two artists discussed and serve to establish secure dates for certain key paintings. But the identities of works mentioned only in passing have remained uncertain, and the balance—those tentatively linked to Arles by subject, style, or materials—have provoked even more debate. During this period Gauguin and Vincent both painted on canvases cut from the same piece of heavy, coarse jute, so while this support may indicate that a work dates from the time of their partnership, it does not pinpoint its place in the sequence. Moreover, especially in Gauguin's case, the assumption that a picture on a rough-textured support belongs to the Arles period is problematic, insofar as he continued to paint on similarly rough (but different) supports after he left Arles.[10]

Inevitably problems of identification and chronology have impeded an understanding of the unfolding dynamic of the relationship between van Gogh and Gauguin. Nevertheless an remarkably dense array of information can be brought to bear on their collaboration. A new perspective on the dialogue that played out in pictures and in words results from a multipronged evalution of this data. Necessarily our account depends upon the rich body of existing scholarship on both artists, including recent studies illuminating the social and cultural context within which they worked, research addressing the relationship between technique and meaning, and new or revised editions of their letters and writings. To complement this published literature, new technical evidence has been gathered for the specific purpose of illuminating the collaboration. Microscopic study of picture surfaces, x-radiography, infrared reflectography, fiber identification, and chemical/elemental analysis of ground materials have been carried out on as many works putatively assigned to this period as possible (see App.). The results of these investigations, correlated with contemporary letter references, have helped to establish the scope and chronology of the Arles production with greater certainty.

The wealth of primary material generated by the artists themselves is deceptively immediate; at some points surface details obscure broader underlying patterns. A cross-grained reading of Vincent's and Gauguin's writings—not only from the last months of 1888 but including all that came before and after—brings these patterns to light. This contrapuntal procedure is guided by the different habits of mind that emerge so distinctively in the accounts left by each man, shifting intentions and emphases notwithstanding. It assumes that Vincent channeled his powerful need to communicate into conversations with Gauguin, setting forth his idiosyncratic but internally coherent ideology with reference to the myriad visual and textual exemplars that filled his prodigious memory. He was capable of peppering his conversation with verbatim quotations or vivid descriptions of passages and pictures encountered ten or fifteen years earlier; Gauguin's recollection of a "great deal of talking" is surely an understatement.[11] The premise that Vincent shared with Gauguin the dreams and thoughts of a lifetime is substantiated by Gauguin's responsiveness, inferred not only from his pictures but also from echoes in letters and subsequent accounts, notably his several representations of his time with Vincent. Surviving Vincent by thirteen years, Gauguin would write at a continually greater remove from actual events, in service of an evolving agenda. But just as he assem-

bled many later works of art out of elements extracted from photographs, reproductions, and drawings already in his possession by 1888, Gauguin organized his written representations of Vincent around notes, thoughts, and positions developed at the time. The unprecedented overload of information and ideas put forth by Vincent fostered the appropriative strategy that was essential to Gauguin's thinking.

High expectations and intense ambitions shaped their exchange. When Gauguin recalled their first painting expedition—Vincent "continuing" while Gauguin "started something new"—he inadvertently touched on a key to the dynamic. Driving their give-and-take were aims that did not correspond comfortably either to the roles assigned at the beginning or to the new parts played during the ensuing weeks. Vincent, the self-designated junior partner, had already succeeded in fashioning for himself a coherent, all-embracing artistic identity; he hoped Gauguin would share in it and help him actualize his intention to achieve a pioneering, consoling modern art. By contrast Gauguin, who had been assigned the role of mentor and was senior in age and experience, still actively sought the kind of integrated persona that Vincent already commanded.

Each brought a different kind of self-consciousness to the interaction, and physical circumstances heightened the intensity of their exchange. Had they been in Paris, even sharing quarters, they could have found relief from each other's presence in other places and in the company of other artists. But in Arles there was no artists' community and few social distractions. Inclement weather would increasingly force them indoors, confining them to the small spaces and lack of privacy in the Yellow House (see fig. 2). Gauguin could only enter his small, high-ceilinged bedroom through Vincent's adjacent room; both spaces were probably densely hung with Vincent's canvas-

es. Though Vincent had initially thought that the kitchen might double as additional studio space, this was apparently not feasible, perhaps because of the disorderly housekeeping that shocked his more fastidious houseguest.[12] They were always together, therefore, in the 240-square-foot front room on the ground floor—in a sense joined at the easel. For Vincent this proximity fulfilled a longheld fantasy of *gezelligheid* (companionability); for Gauguin, who cultivated independence, the situation was one for which even Vincent's long, passionate letters could not have fully prepared him. These written communications could be picked up and laid down at will, acknowledged or ignored; the experience of working side by side with Vincent in the studio would have been like having a recording of his letters on continuous play: exhilarating perhaps but exhausting surely.

Sunday	Monday	Tuesday	Wednesday	Thursday	Friday	Saturday
		23 Oct ☼	**24** ☼	**25** ⛅	**26** ⛅	**27** ☼ ✉ Theo to Vincent
		✉ Theo to Vincent	✉ Vincent to Theo	✉ Gauguin to Schuffenecker		✉ Gauguin to Theo
28 ☼ ✉ Vincent to Theo (2 letters)						

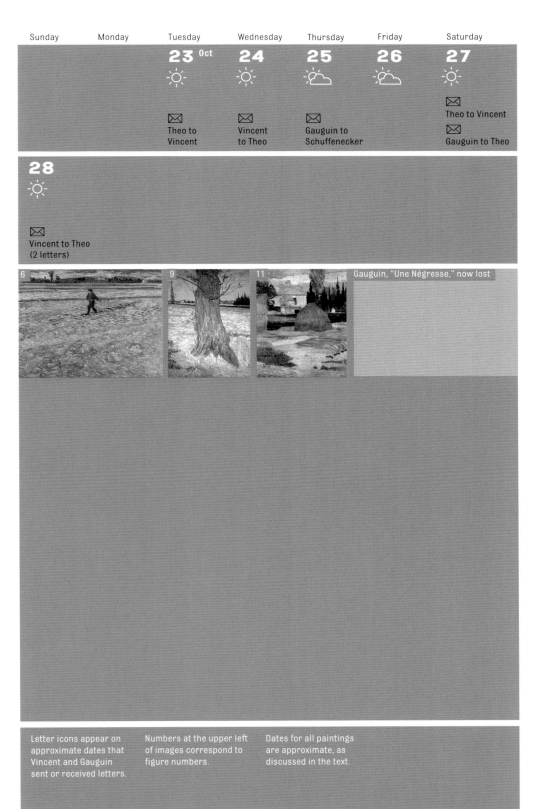

Gauguin, "Une Négresse," now lost

Letter icons appear on approximate dates that Vincent and Gauguin sent or received letters.

Numbers at the upper left of images correspond to figure numbers.

Dates for all paintings are approximate, as discussed in the text.

On their initial excursion, the two artists left the Yellow House and headed out to one of Vincent's favorite areas, the plains of the Crau (see map, fig. 3). By Sunday the twenty-eighth, Vincent sent Theo sketches of his new studies, one of a sower and another of an old tree (fig. 7). At the same time, he mentioned that Gauguin also had two pictures under way: "a negress . . . and a large local landscape."[13] This group of suggestive subjects implies the complex dialogue already in play.

Both of Vincent's paintings give expression to his hopes for the project. Reprising the *Sower* composition of June (ch. 3, fig. 26), with which Gauguin was familiar through letters and drawings, Vincent now made several different choices (fig. 6). The landscape is deeper and site-specific, with the Alpilles and the ruins of the abbey of Montmajour recognizable in the background; the sower is, in Vincent's words, "small and indistinct"; the palette is descriptive, based on nature.[14] Divested of the earlier version's arbitrary chromatics and prominent protagonist, this painting lacks its symbolic intimations and its labored quality. Straightforwardly proclaiming his facility with Impressionist procedure, Vincent executed the painting outdoors, quickly and confidently, allowing the signs of his hand to signal his optimism and ambition. Using a rhythmic, gestural stroke that bears comparison to the graphic shorthand he used in the small pen sketch recording the composition (fig. 7), he suggested furrowed earth with short, cursive marks that do not entirely cover the white ground of the commercially prepared linen canvas. Testifying to Vincent's commitment to *plein-air* painting, to his habit of working very rapidly, and to his determination to control his touch, *The Sower* directly addresses aspects of his practice with which he anticipated Gauguin taking issue. It functioned as an opening salvo, a kind of demonstration piece of Vincent's mastery of his craft.

Oct						
	1	2	3	4	5	6
7	8	9	10	11	12	13
14	15	16	17	18	19	20
21	22	**23**	**24**	**25**	**26**	27
28	29	30	31			

Nov						
				1	2	3
4	5	6	7	8	9	10
11	12	13	14	15	16	17
18	19	20	21	22	23	24
25	26	27	28	29	30	

Dec						
						1
2	3	4	5	6	7	8
9	10	11	12	13	14	15
16	17	18	19	20	21	22
23	24	25	26	27	28	29
30	31					

Yet he had not abandoned overt emblematics, as the other canvas attests. It features an old tree trunk that sprouts new shoots set against a newly plowed field. The bands of yellow and blue paint that bound the field possibly represent the Viguerat canal and its bordering road (see map, fig. 3); farm buildings and the Arles skyline are visible in the distance. Such realistic references notwithstanding, the picture that Vincent called *The Old Yew Tree* (*Le Vieil If*) (fig. 9) had a primarily symbolic impetus. Accessing the yew's longstanding association with death, as well as its remarkable ability to send forth new growth from old wood, Vincent refashioned a traditional emblem of spiritual rebirth (see fig. 8) into an image expressing Carlyle's view that new ideas are the regeneration of old ones. Months before, Vincent had described the desired artistic renaissance as a "green shoot sprung from the roots of the old sawn-off trunk."[15]

More overtly programmatic than *The Sower*, *The Old Yew Tree* is also more complex in execution, with overlapping layers of many mixed tints. In both works the red pigment in the purple paint has faded, muting the intended contrast between violet and yellow. But this contrast was never as strong as in *The Sower* of June, owing to Vincent's use of dispersed brush strokes in *The Sower* and paler tints in *The Old Yew Tree*.[16]

If Vincent presented these canvases as position statements, Gauguin seemingly responded with some symbolic gestures of his own. On his third day in Arles, he wrote asking Schuffenecker to send him the *Cleopatra* pot (ch. 2, fig. 69) and another ceramic. Perhaps he simply wanted to impose a personal element, complementary to his self-portrait, on an environment dominated by Vincent's many decorations. More probably the *Cleopatra* pot seemed pertinent to their early conversations, in which Vincent figured the hope for "new

Ch. 5, Fig. 49

Fig. 6

Ch. 3, Fig. 11

Fig. 9

Abbey of Saint-Pierre
de Montmajour

Mont Majour

Chapel of
Sainte-Croix

Mont de
Cordes

4

5

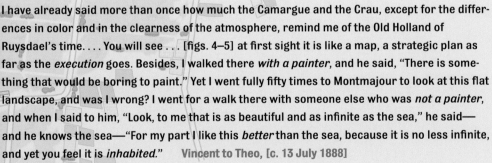

I have already said more than once how much the Camargue and the Crau, except for the differences in color and in the clearness of the atmosphere, remind me of the Old Holland of Ruysdael's time. . . . You will see . . . [figs. 4–5] at first sight it is like a map, a strategic plan as far as the *execution* goes. Besides, I walked there *with a painter*, and he said, "There is something that would be boring to paint." Yet I went fully fifty times to Montmajour to look at this flat landscape, and was I wrong? I went for a walk there with someone else who was *not a painter*, and when I said to him, "Look, to me that is as beautiful and as infinite as the sea," he said— and he knows the sea—"For my part I like this *better* than the sea, because it is no less infinite, and yet you feel it is *inhabited*." **Vincent to Theo, [c. 13 July 1888]**

3
Map of La Crau

4
Vincent van Gogh
*La Crau seen from
Montmajour*
c. 13 July 1888
[F 1420, JH 1501]
Black chalk, pen and
reed pen and brown
and black ink
49 x 61 cm
Van Gogh Museum,
Amsterdam
(Vincent van Gogh
Foundation)

5
Vincent van Gogh
*Landscape near
Montmajour with
Train*
c. 13 July 1888
[F 1424, JH 1502]
Pencil, reed pen and
quill pen and brown
ink
49 x 61 cm
British Museum,
London

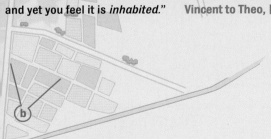

Fig. 43

6
Vincent van Gogh
The Sower
28 October 1888
[F 494, JH 1617]
Oil on canvas
72 x 91 cm
Hahnloser/Jäggli
Stiftung, Villa
Flora, Winterthur,
Switzerland
Cat. 69

7
Vincent van Gogh
Sketch of *The Sower*
and *The Old Yew
Tree*
in letter to Theo
28 October 1888
(letter 719/558b;
JH 1619)
Van Gogh Museum,
Amsterdam
(Vincent van Gogh
Foundation)
Cat. 71

8
"The Willow Tree"
from Jan Luyken,
*De Bykorf des
Gemoeds (The
Heart's Beehive)*
(Amsterdam, 1711).
"With time the
truncated, hollow,
knarled, and with-
ered old willow tree
awakens to a crown
of new shoots,
because virtue
secretly inhabits its
trunk."

9
Vincent van Gogh
*The Old Yew Tree
(Le Vieil If)*
28 October 1888
[F 573, JH 1618]
Oil on canvas
91 x 71 cm
Private collection,
courtesy Christie's
Images New York

6

7

8

9

growth" in their work in terms of Puvis de Chavannes's signature picture (ch. 2, fig. 70) and Gauguin summoned his primitivized quotation of the image in response to his friend's talk of painting in the tropics.[17]

In the context of such discussions, Vincent's report that Gauguin had immediately set to work on "une négresse" begins to make sense. No corresponding picture by Gauguin exists— it was probably soon abandoned and either destroyed or painted over—but the fact that Gauguin set out by reprising a Martinique subject suggests that, like Vincent, he felt

compelled to produce a demonstration piece. Gauguin knew that the van Gogh brothers esteemed him for these paintings and that Vincent's attendant assumptions had been shaken by his *Self-Portrait (Les Misérables)*; his initial effort in Arles can thus be seen as a wry assurance that he was still the "richer Gauguin of the *Négresses*."[18] However, their current talk of a renaissance in the tropics suggests a more subtle intent. Juxtaposing his exotic imagery with Vincent's emblematics, Gauguin responded to his friend's reiterated identification of him as a Loti-like hero. Painted without a model, the figure picture also raised the ques-

tion of the role of memory and imagination in artistic composition. This issue, already broached in their correspondence, would become increasingly urgent with the passing weeks.

The other picture that Gauguin had under way at the same time speaks an entirely different language. Technical analysis confirms the hitherto elusive identity of the "large local landscape" reported by Vincent: it is *Farmhouse in Arles* (fig. 11), a portrayal of a typical Provençal *mas* of the sort found on the Crau, with a stand of the region's characteristic cypresses glimpsed in the right background, as in Vincent's *Old Yew Tree*. X-radiographs reveal that Gauguin painted it on a support with neither precedent nor consequence in his body of work, a piece of pre-primed linen identical to that Vincent used for *The Sower* (see App.).[19]

In addition to supplying Gauguin with the canvas, Vincent had in effect suggested the subject. At the time of the June harvest, he produced two paintings of stacks of wheat in a farmyard (see ch. 3, fig. 25). Gauguin certainly knew the large drawing (fig. 12), which Vincent had sent to Bernard, after the more ambitious of the paintings. This sheet, with its quickly but systematically applied pen strokes, would have given Gauguin little notion of Vincent's canvases, distinguished by wanton impasto, though the landscape studies that accompanied Vincent's relatively restrained *Self-Portrait (Bonze)*, sent to Pont-Aven on 4 October, might have done so.[20] Gauguin was predisposed to equate handwriting or facture with character, and whatever he made of the earlier paintings, he would now have looked at Vincent's frenetic execution with different eyes, correlating the pell-mell brushwork, like the disorderly studio, with Vincent's agitated state. His own *Farmhouse in Arles* proposed calm in response to Vincent's feverishness. Vincent's stacks, atremble on a rising groundline, seem to vibrate in the heat; Gauguin's lone stack sits anchored to the spot, its stability reinforced by the farmyard's rigorous geometry. Following his customary practice, he first sketched the major elements of his composition with brush and blue paint, then developed the surface with short, parallel strokes of paint, using a small brush and a light touch; the consistent vertical orientation of the methodical strokes overcomes the marks' individuality. Adjusting line and tone, Gauguin constantly shifted forms in their spatial planes to separate them or to knit them together. He played with contours, first reinforcing them with blue lines, then hatching over them. He

also played with color, modulating flat planes with intermittent strokes or overlapping layers of varied hues. The picture is deft, delicate, discreet. Situating himself at a remove from Vincent's charged expressive universe, Gauguin was perhaps never closer to Cézanne. And that was the point.

For it was a very different Provençal artist whom Vincent sought to evoke through his expressive application. In recent weeks Monticelli had been very much on Vincent's mind. He imagined that he and Gauguin would soon be resurrecting the Marseilles master (see ch. 3), whose character he glimpsed in the natural exaltation and sweeping rhetorical style of his friend Roulin. Newly aware of the Félibrean call for a southern cultural renaissance, Vincent even thought that he and Gauguin might collaborate on an article for one of the local newspapers exhorting the artists of Marseilles to "continue what their [countryman] Monticelli began." Finally, he had installed his spectacular homage to his hero, *The Green Vineyard* (fig. 10)—its foreground a tangle of juicy, calligraphic brushwork in emulation of Monticelli's hallmark late, heavily impastoed style—in the Yellow House to signal the colorist program he intended them to follow.[21]

Venerating Monticelli so highly, Vincent had to make an effort to accommodate Cézanne— an opposite southern temperament—in his admiration. This effort can be read between the lines of a debate on Cézanne's merits that, beginning in June, had insinuated itself into Vincent's correspondence with Bernard. Knowing that Bernard (and Gauguin) esteemed the Aix master, Vincent had attempted several times to introduce Cézanne into his thinking and discussions. He observed that the Crau landscape near Arles reminded him of an early harvest painting by the artist (ch. 3, fig. 33); he likely knew that Gauguin had once owned this picture, which thus served as

a shared reference among the three artists.[22] The "sketches of Provence" (including the *Stacks of Wheat*; fig. 12) that Vincent sent to Bernard in July further communicated his kinship with Cézanne, or at least his interest in similar subject matter. He acknowledged that his graphic style had nothing in common with Cézanne's, but it was no closer to Monticelli's. Clearly Vincent aimed to show himself evenhanded in his enthusiasm for both Provençal artists when he professed to love the same country as they did, and for the "same reasons, the color and logical composition."[23]

This claimed affinity was a stretch for Vincent, but perhaps he wanted to soften the impact of an earlier, somewhat critical statement about Cézanne:

If you saw my canvases, what would you say of them? You won't find the almost timid, conscientious brush stroke of Cézanne in them. But as I am now painting the same landscape . . . there may well remain certain chromatic affinities. . . . Unintentionally I thought of Cézanne from time to time, at exactly those moments when I realized how clumsy his touch in certain studies is—excuse the word clumsy—seeing that he probably did these studies when the mistral was blowing. As half the time I am faced with the same difficulty, I get an idea of why Cézanne's touch is sometimes so sure, and sometimes so awkward. It's his easel that's reeling.

I have sometimes worked excessively fast. Is it a fault? I can't help it. . . . I went out to do [a picture] at a single sitting . . . expressly while the mistral was raging. Aren't we seeking intensity of thought rather than tranquility of touch?[24]

Worried about the reaction to work painted "quickly, quickly, quickly and in a hurry," Vincent invoked a roster of artists as proof that "quick work doesn't mean less serious work": the Japanese, Monet, Millet, Daumier, Corot,

Daubigny, and of course Monticelli.[25] His professed identification with Cézanne was thus backhanded: while he could empathize with Cézanne's occasional awkwardness, he could not respond to the artist's overriding rationality, to the control he read in his touch.

Vincent placed a premium on the expressive valence of the artist's mark—on its communication of the fearless immediacy attainable only in a state of furious exaltation. Hence his dilemma. Most of the canvases that he executed at one go were *études* (studies), but he aspired to produce *tableaux* (pictures). He had begun to doubt that he would ever manage to paint peaceful, calmly executed pictures.[26] Nonetheless he had imagined that the companionship of the painter of the *Négresses*—an exemplary

tableau—might enable him to advance toward this goal.

Gauguin began *Farmhouse in Arles* (which he left unsigned and possibly unfinished) as a kind of "exercise," but one with a point: he wished to demonstrate a truly Cézannesque approach to a subject specifically associated with the Aix master. Vincent's attempts during the summer to connect his practice to Cézanne's were notional at best. Gauguin, by contrast, in his own reprise of the harvest motif, respectfully adopted Cézanne's manner—not the thick paint of *The Harvest* (a relatively impastoed early example of the kind most likely to appeal to Vincent), but rather the so-called constructive style that Cézanne pioneered in later works, several of which had

once graced Gauguin's collection. In *Farmhouse in Arles*, Gauguin demonstrated the approach that he had pursued in the Brittany canvases now on their way to Theo's gallery (see fig. 76), which were "minimally worked up," perhaps, but "highly thought out" and "intentional"— the very qualities in Cézanne's art that Vincent questioned as timid, conscientious, tranquil.[27]

Yet Gauguin's restraint—the ability not "to get carried away," to bide his time—was among the character traits that earned Vincent's deep respect. It permeates *Farmhouse in Arles*, which was more than an attempt on Gauguin's part to demonstrate calm. Faced with the latter's ardent beliefs about the nature of the art that the Studio of the South would foster, Gauguin needed to stake out his own position. He had

10

10
Vincent van Gogh
The Green Vineyard
c. 3 October 1888
[F 475, JH 1595]
Oil on canvas
72 x 92 cm
Kröller-Müller
Museum, Otterlo,
The Netherlands
Cat. 67

Right now I am tackling a landscape with a blue sky above an immense green, purple, and yellow vineyard, with black and orange vines. Little figures of ladies with red parasols and little figures of grape pickers with their small cart make it even gayer. Gray sand in the foreground. Another size 30 square canvas to decorate the house.   Vincent to Gauguin, [3 October 1888]

11

12

long revered Cézanne as the great "man of the South," discerning an eastern mysticism in his "intense tranquility" and a mysterious ambivalence in his shapes, which coalesce out of separate brush strokes. In the open-endedness of Cézanne's pictures—are the forms descriptive or abstract?—Gauguin glimpsed the possibility of translating thought by non-literary means."[28] This was a notion of symbolism notably different from Vincent's.

These first pictures—Vincent's *Sower* and *Old Yew Tree*, and Gauguin's "négresse" and *Farmhouse in Arles*—suggest that each man departed almost immediately from the role assigned to him in Vincent's model of monk and abbot, Boccaccio and Petrarch. Notwithstanding his admiration for Gauguin, Vincent was determined to assert his individuality in the face of the influence he had both invited

and feared. And Gauguin, for all his desire to fulfill the expectations of the brothers to whom his fortunes seemed tied for the moment, was willing to be exemplary but hesitated to sign on for Vincent's program, now that he recognized its implications. Perhaps more clearly than words, pictures revealed profound differences that they were just beginning to discover.

The two letters that Vincent sent to Theo on 28 October nonetheless brim with optimism. His concerns about money and sales had rapidly receded in the excitement generated by Gauguin's presence and in view of anticipated economies through sharing living expenses and preparing their own paint and canvases. Though Gauguin had not been as forthcoming about Vincent's pictures as the latter might have wished, he had expressed appreciation for the *Sunflowers*, *The Bedroom*, and (surpris-

ingly but perhaps understandably, given his status as newly arrived guest) the just-completed *Sower*. Exuding confidence, Vincent spoke with a sense of adventure about the long-term prospects of the "little studio."[29]

Sunday	Monday	Tuesday	Wednesday	Thursday	Friday	Saturday
	29 Oct ☀	**30** ☀	**31** ☀	**1** Nov 🌧	**2** 🌧	**3** ☁
				✉ Gauguin to Bernard	✉ Vincent to Bernard	Madame Ginoux poses for artists either Saturday or Sunday

The good weather of the first week—mostly clear and warm, with little wind—continued into the second.[30] Taking advantage of this, Vincent and Gauguin stayed outdoors, moving from the Crau to a famous local site, the ancient cemetery known as Les Alyscamps (Elysian Fields), southeast of the old city walls (see map, fig. 19). In the course of about four days, before Thursday's rain interrupted them, Vincent completed three of a total of four views of the site (figs. 20, 24, 27–28), while Gauguin undertook two (figs. 21, 26).

During this time they acted on plans to prepare their own materials, Gauguin purchasing what Vincent described as "twenty meters of very strong canvas"—a rough, coarse jute. The insistent texture of this material, which they used for all but the first of their respective Alyscamps pictures, was only minimally muted by preparation with a thin ground layer. Gauguin may have recognized in the jute its potential to impart to his pictures something of the coarse feel of his ceramics.[31] The jute introduced a challengingly unfamiliar element to their working methods. So did the fact that they addressed the same motif standing side by side. The different approaches taken by Vincent and Gauguin in the Alyscamps give expression to the dialogue in play. If they had begun by asking the question "whose South," through their predecessors Monticelli and Cézanne, they now determined to answer in their own voices.

For Vincent the Alyscamps was new thematic territory. During his months in Arles, he had given a wide berth to the ancient Roman sites that were the town's principal tourist attractions. In the spring he had toyed with the idea of painting the colorful spectacle of the bullfights held regularly from Easter through October in Arles's first-century amphitheater, the largest in France (fig. 15), but he had yet to do so. Writing to Gauguin about the bullfights he attended, Vincent perhaps hoped that the

Oct						
	1	2	3	4	5	6
7	8	9	10	11	12	13
14	15	16	17	18	19	20
21	22	23	24	25	26	27
28	**29**	**30**	**31**			

Nov						
				1	**2**	**3**
4	5	6	7	8	9	10
11	12	13	14	15	16	17
18	19	20	21	22	23	24
25	26	27	28	29	30	

Dec						
						1
2	3	4	5	6	7	8
9	10	11	12	13	14	15
16	17	18	19	20	21	22
23	24	25	26	27	28	29
30	31					

local color and unique subjects offered by Arles would capture his friend's imagination. This apparently worked, for the bullfight was the only subject that Gauguin specifically mentioned when, in July, he noted his ideas for painting in Provence.[32]

The bullfight season had ended by the time Gauguin finally arrived, but the decision to paint in the Alyscamps likewise arose out of expectations built by Vincent. Worried that Gauguin would be disappointed by Arles, Vincent had attempted to link the region's distinguished legacy to its present creative potential: "This part of the country has already seen the cult of Venus—primarily artistic, in Greece—followed by the poets and artists of the Renaissance. Where these things could flourish, impressionism can as well."[33] Vincent had executed the *Poet's Garden* series that decorated Gauguin's bedroom in this spirit, and the town's classical character was certainly a topic of conversation in their first days together.

Gauguin would recall that they spent the day of his arrival "walking about so that I might admire the beauty of Arles and of the Arlésiennes." He later claimed to have been unimpressed, but letters of the time indicate otherwise. Not only did Vincent report that Gauguin was "above all things intrigued by the Arlésiennes," Gauguin himself said as much to Bernard in terms that echo standard touristic descriptions. With their Grecian beauty, elegant hairstyles, and ample shawls, the women of Arles (see fig. 18) reminded him of the figures in procession seen on antique sculpture and vases. This seemed to him proof that his new surroundings offered the resources with which to pioneer what he described as a "beautiful *modern* style."[34]

This interest was hardly original. Virtually all literature on the city paid homage to the local women, who (unlike the men) were seen to retain still-vital hallmarks of Greek and Roman

The young lady is an Arlésienne—the real thing. The curve of the arch, so difficult to render, perfectly executed. The costume reproduced in all its elegant detail. The posture distinguished by that ease and grace so often impressive in the Arlésienne; the face, with delicate lines. Anon., *Le Forum républicain*, 9 September 1888, p. 2

15
C. F. Turchy
(French; 19th century)
Amphitheater
[Roman arena]
from Fernand
Beissier, *Les Étapes
d'un touriste en
France: Le Pays d'Arles*
(Paris, 1889), p. 33

16
Joseph Belon
(French; d. 1927)
Jealous!
1888
Oil on canvas
180 x 200 cm
Museon Arlaten,
Arles

17
After Praxiteles
c. 360 B.C.
Venus of Arles
Marble
H. 1.94 m
Musée du Louvre,
Paris

18
Frédéric Théodore
Lix (French;
1830–1897)
Arlésienne de nos jours
from Fernand
Beissier, *Les Étapes
d'un touriste en
France: Le Pays
d'Arles* (Paris, 1889),
p. 119

ancestry in their classical profiles and noble bearing, qualities for which the distinctive regional costume and the local architecture served as foil. To see them in attendance at the bullfights in the amphitheater, wearing the *mantes* that protected them from the cold mistral, was, guidebook writers promised, to be transported through space and time to witness "Roman virgins" seated on the benches of the Colosseum.[35]

The Arlésienne, paradigmatically presented by Frédéric Mistral in *Mireille*, his 1859 narrative poem in Provençal, became central to the Félibrean construction of the region's essence. Objectified as living statues, these so-called "Athéniennes de la Provence" were identified with the Venus of Arles (fig. 17), an antique sculpture unearthed in the seventeenth century in Arles's Roman theater and eventually installed in the Louvre. The plaster cast retained in Arles symbolized to Mistral the cultural loss that he hoped to recuperate. The Arlésienne was the "Venus of Arles . . . revived"—symbol of noble beauty, chaste love, and ideal motherhood—and the Alyscamps was the site in which she could be presented most potently.[36]

Originally established in pagan times, the Alyscamps remained celebrated into the Middle Ages as a fashionable final resting place for the faithful. During Arles's subsequent decline, local residents and officials pillaged its rich collection of Roman and Early Christian sarcophogi for building materials, gifts, and museum display. Though somewhat dilapidated by the late nineteenth century, the Alyscamps remained one of the town's most vaunted tourist attractions, promoted as an open-air museum.[37] It was central to Arles's nostalgic view of itself, referenced in music performed at local concerts and in works by amateur artists. According to established pictorial convention, the ancient cemetery served as the ideal backdrop for romantic representations

of the Arlésienne, through whom a magnificent past might give rise to an equally glorious future. Vincent, on arriving in mid-February, would have seen an example of such imagery—a picture depicting an Arlésienne awaiting her lover at sunset in the Alyscamps—which a local shopkeeper had put on display just days before.[38] During the summer a more ambitious portrayal of love in the burial grounds became a news item when native son Joseph Belon, back from Paris, undertook an "episode from our local life" as the subject of his next Salon painting. Set at the entrance to the Alyscamps (see map, fig. 19), Belon's canvas (fig. 16) depicts a young man trying to make amends with his jealous girlfriend, dressed in the quintessential Arlésienne costume. Behind them a group dances a traditional farandole around the accurately detailed Saint-Césaire arch abutting the Saint-Accurse chapel. After carefully describing the picture's features and presumed narrative, the reviewer in *Le Forum républicain* concluded that Belon's return to paint sundrenched lands in preference to the City of Light proved the imminence of a southern renaissance in the visual arts.[39]

Vincent inadvertently became part of this story. A reporter for *Le Forum*'s rival weekly, *L'Homme de bronze*, pointed out that Belon was hardly the only painter recording the picturesque sights of Arles: in addition to a Mr. Stein working near the arena and a Mr. Cazil capturing the ruins of the medieval abbey of Montmajour, there was a third, "M. Vincent, an impressionist painter [who] works, we are informed, at night, by gaslight, in one of our squares." The journalist added that the three had been seen together with one or two other artists, sketching the Saint-Accurse chapel. Published on 30 September, the sighting is highly questionable; certainly Vincent described no such excursions in his correspondence.[40] Had the same reporter returned in late October, however, he could have accurately documented the presence of Vincent and

Gauguin, their backs turned to the chapel, each engaged in representing the Alyscamps from closely related but very different perspectives (see map, fig. 19).

Setting up his easel near the northwest entrance to the Allée des Tombeaux, Vincent looked along the converging rows of poplars and stone sarcophagi leading to the twelfth-century church of Saint-Honorat at the allée's end (fig. 20). Photographs (see fig. 22) reveal the liberties that Vincent permitted himself: he shifted the church's tower to the right so that it appears on the central sight line, no longer hidden by the trees at left, and simplified its distinctive octagonal form in the process. Another, more disruptive architectural emphasis in Vincent's painting is the complex of buildings and smokestacks of the railroad workshops located immediately to the northeast, which would have been partially obscured by the row of poplars at Vincent's left and by the embankment directly behind them. Vincent thus acknowledges what most postcard views elide: that the extensive ancient site had been irreparably compromised by modern incursions, reduced to a single walkway flanked with the few sarcophagi that had escaped spoliation. By juxtaposing signs of past greatness and recent progress, he represented his ambivalent feelings about contemporary Arles, which he imagined "infinitely more glorious once, as regards the beauty of the women and their costume. Everything has a blighted, faded quality about it now."[41]

To those unfamiliar with the local topography, Gauguin's picture (fig. 21) might appear to depict a completely different site. His vantage point explains this. Although he set up his easel not very far from Vincent's and faced in the same direction, Gauguin climbed to the path running along the top of the roughly seven-foot embankment that borders the north side of the Allée des Tombeaux.[42] He faced southeast, with the canal on his left and the

19
Site map of Les Alyscamps

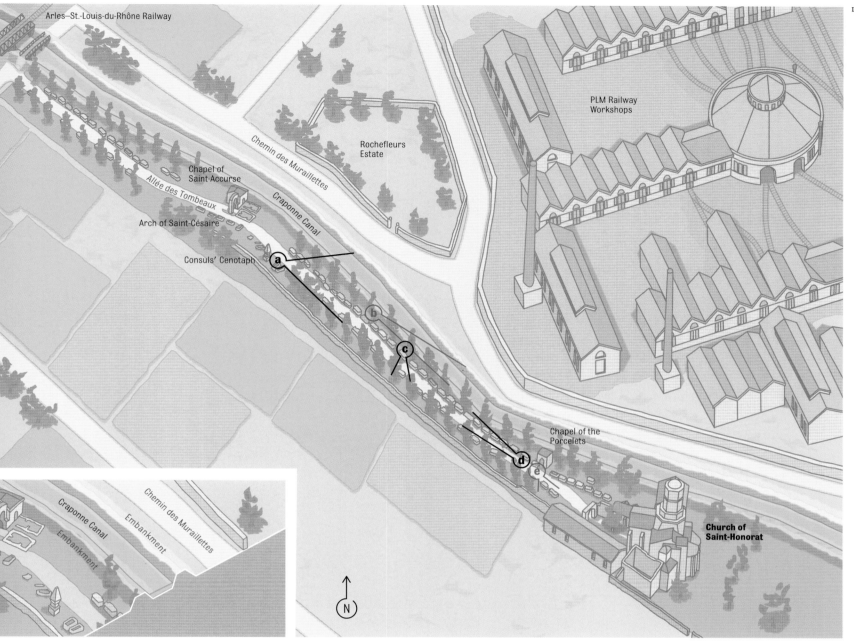

Arles—St.-Louis-du-Rhône Railway

PLM Railway
Workshops

Chemin des Muraillettes

Rochefleurs
Estate

Chapel of
Saint-Accurse

Allée des Tombeaux

Craponne Canal

Arch of Saint-Césaire

Consuls' Cenotaph

Chapel of the
Porcelets

**Church of
Saint-Honorat**

Craponne Canal

Chemin des Muraillettes

Embankment

Embankment

Embankment

N

path before him, so that the poplars at the left in Vincent's painting were to his right, their scale altered by his elevated viewpoint. The promenade below is a mere patch of pink above the bright vermillion bush; Saint-Honorat's octagonal tower rises above the trees directly ahead. Like a professional photographer (see fig. 23), however, Gauguin scrupulously excluded the railroad complex looming to his left, only hinting at its presence with a plume of smoke floating in the sky at the upper left.

The two artists' perspectives varied conceptually as well as topographically; each glimpsed different stylistic opportunities in this site and by extension in the South. "It's strange, Vincent sees plenty of Daumier to do here, but I see highly colored Puvis blended with Japanese."[43] This characterization of Gauguin's, formulated during the Alyscamps campaign, reveals that he responded to Vincent's efforts, begun earlier that month and no doubt continuing in conversation, to shape his friend's vision of the South. As Vincent wrote in early October:

I am only afraid that you will think Brittany more beautiful, indeed, that you will find nothing more beautiful here than Daumier, the locals' faces are often pure Daumier. It shouldn't take you long to discover that antiquity and the Renaissance lie dormant under all this modernity. Well, you are free to revive them.[44]

Daumier, Puvis, and Japan were thus prominent artistic points of reference for Vincent and Gauguin as they plotted out their Alyscamps paintings. But the stakes were not only, or even primarily, formal; nor are they easily defined. Vincent's preoccupation with Daumier was more complex than Gauguin allowed, and his vision of the South did not exclude Puvis—

Fig. 20

Fig. 21

Fig. 27

Fig. 24

Fig. 26

20

quite the opposite. In September he explained to Theo that Provence could be imagined through Puvis's *Pleasant Land* (ch. 3, fig. 37), and he conceded the importance of the country's classical lineage, as symbolized in the Venus of Arles. He did insist, however, on recognizing "the Tartarin and Daumier part of this strange country." In Vincent's personal, associative shorthand, "pure Daumier" signified warmth, wit, sentimental passion, and the ability to discern poetry in the commonplace; the caricaturist's exemplary art forsook literal accuracy for a greater, expressive truth.[68] During his first months in Arles, Vincent was continually reminded of Daumier, whose "worship of sorrow" helped him to process the mixture of opposites—sublimity and ridiculousness, beauty and ugliness, joy and tragedy—that he saw in the South. Unable to think of the neighborhood around place Lamartine in terms of Millet's ennobling vision, he instead characterized it as "absolute Daumier, Zola."[45]

Gauguin arrived at the Yellow House to discover Daumier a reigning household god, his lithographs hung alongside Japanese woodcuts and Vincent's own canvases. In a typical conflation, Vincent readily folded Daumier into his identification with Japan: Daumier, like Hokusai, drew the figure incisively and rapidly, the way Vincent himself did. (In August, "on the spot in the manner of Daumier," he had painted a portrait of Joseph Roulin; fig. 102.) Vincent also saw Daumier in the context of the harmonious relations that he imagined prevailing in the Japanese artistic community, for legend held that Corot had rescued Daumier from dire straits and provided him

21

22

23

20
Vincent van Gogh
*Allée des Tombeaux
(Les Alyscamps)*
c. 29 October 1888
[F 568, JH 1622]
Oil on canvas
89 x 72 cm
Private collection
Cat. 72

21
Paul Gauguin
*Les Alyscamps (The
Three Graces at the
Temple of Venus)*
(*Paysage* or *Les Trois
Grâces au temple du
Vénus*)
c. 29 October 1888
[W 307]
Oil on canvas
92 x 73 cm

Musée d'Orsay,
Paris, bequeathed
by the comtesse
Vitali, in memory
of her brother the
vicomte de Cholet,
1923
Cat. 36

22
Postcard of the
Alyscamps, Allée
des Tombeaux,
Arles, c. 1910/30

23
Dominique Roman
(French; 1824–1911)
Photograph of the
Alyscamps, Arles,
from *Panorama
d'Arles et sa région,
Arles, Montmajour,
Les Baux*
1862/80
Muséon Arlaten,
Arles

with a simple house. This tale of solidarity resonated with Vincent's hopes for his own "artist's house," which he intended should have a Daumier character.[46] Daumier in short became a code word for the methods and purpose of the Studio of the South.

After a week with Vincent, Gauguin must have been fully acquainted with this concept. He countered it with a model that reveals his quite different aspirations. In his lexicon, Puvis (despite his use of traditional symbols) privileged style over content and eschewed narrative to evoke mood through color, line, and composition—like the Japanese. The Puvis/Japan mixture that Gauguin claimed to discern in Arles signaled his conscious effort to pursue "style" above all goals. While Cézanne suggested the possibility of a purely

pictorial language, the antinaturalism and emphasis on design over gesture manifested by Puvis and the Japanese provided a more immediately available model for forging a "modern style" in Arles. Such were the different points of reference that the two artists brought to bear in their Alyscamps canvases.

Vincent, in his initial picture (fig. 20), remained steadfastly true to his central allegiances. To begin with he worked quickly, even more so than he had the previous week on the Crau. His broad brushwork, facilitated by rich, fluid paint and the smooth white ground of a commercially primed linen canvas, conveys an almost manic exuberance. This rough-and-tumble surface, like the signs of modern industry, speaks to the unidealized, "Daumier" part of the mixture inherent to the South, as does

the diminutive couple whom Vincent represented promenading along the Allée des Tombeaux. Designating the "lovers" of his personal iconography as an Arlésienne and a Zouave, Vincent alluded to the debated chastity of the daughters of the Venus of Arles.[47] Their reputation for marmoreal nobility was matched by one for dangerous coquettishness, as displayed in Daudet's celebrated short story "L'Arlésienne," in which a young man's chance meeting with a local woman in Arles leads first to passion and then to death. Whatever the nature of the relationship between the striding male figure in Vincent's painting and the woman in regional costume, the man's distinctive regimental uniform proclaims the transitory nature of the pairing. For the Zouaves, billeted at the nearby Caserne Calvin (see map, ch. 3, fig. 10), were

24
Vincent van Gogh
Les Alyscamps
c. 1 November 1888
[F 569, JH 1623]
Oil on canvas
92 x 73.5 cm
Private collection

25
Postcard of the chapel of the Porcelets and the church of Saint-Honorat, Alyscamps, Arles, c. 1910/30

26
Paul Gauguin
Les Alyscamps
c. 1 November 1888
[W 306]
Oil on jute
72.5 x 91.5 cm
Seiji Togo
Memorial Yasuda
Kasai Museum of
Art, Tokyo
Cat. 37

24

25

27. – ARLES. – Les Alyscamps.
Chapelles des Porcelets et Saint-Honorat.

26

27

These tree trunks are lined like pillars along an avenue where there are rows of old Roman tombs of a blue lilac right and left. And then the soil is covered with a thick carpet of yellow and orange fallen leaves. And they are still falling like flakes of snow.

And in the avenue, little black figures of lovers. The upper part of the picture is a bright green meadow, and no sky, or almost none.   Vincent to Theo, [c. 5 November 1888]

not permanent residents of Arles but merely passing through—like Vincent's friend Milliet, who was en route from French Indochina (Tonkin, northern Vietnam) to North Africa. Locals admired the soldiers, largely accepting their connection with the community's organized prostitution as natural to their age and situation.[48] In the context of Arles's social realities, Vincent's image identifies the Alyscamps as a contemporary lovers' lane, a site for fleeting encounters. Closer in spirit to Zola than Belon, to Daumier than Puvis, this is the Alyscamps not as described in travel guides but as glimpsed in local news items—a trysting ground and a place where desperate young women threw themselves or their unwanted newborns into the Craponne canal.[49]

Gauguin was equally alert to the modern tensions inherent in the Alyscamps, and in particular to the Arlésienne as both idealized object and human subject: "The street girl is as much a lady as any other and looks as virginal as Juno," he reported while at work on his picture. Here he represented a trio of these latter-day Junos on the path bordering the canal, the two at the left wearing the distinctive bodice of the Arlésienne. The evidence of changes that Gauguin made to the right-hand figure suggests that he may have originally intended to represent a man wearing trousers. In any event the mute grouping, devoid of gesture and expression, departs from Vincent's lovers, with their origins in the narrative art of Daumier and writing of Zola. Gauguin's only hint of ironic commentary surfaces in the title he assigned his canvas: "the three graces at the temple of Venus."[50]

In composition and execution as well as in content, Gauguin posited an alternative to the Naturalist bent of Vincent's picture, following a still more complex procedure than he had for *Farmhouse in Arles*. He selected a piece of finely woven cotton, to which he applied a thin chalk ground.[51] After establishing a contour sketch in blue paint, he blocked in broad

28

29

30

31

washes of different colors—an intermediate step that he had skipped in his first Arles landscape—and then worked up the surface with overlapping layers of varied color, using small diagonal strokes that create a shimmering effect. Owing to the ground's absorbency, he could readily rework the surface without muddying the colors. Using a dry, stiff paint and a light touch, Gauguin superimposed a subtle, varied texture throughout, achieving a surface that is neither remarkably smooth nor notably textured.

The canvas, which must have been completed in the studio, can be seen as a considered *tableau* that responds to the impulsiveness of Vincent's *étude*. Gauguin arrived at a solution to a problem that Vincent's hasty brushwork left unresolved: insistent patterning and decorative accents, such as the cloud reflected in the canal's high waters and the red bush at the right, render the foreground pictorially interesting. These elements (together with the apparently invented branches of green leaves at the upper right) also counterbalance the illusion of deep space. With calculating skill, Gauguin deployed perspective in a way that reveals the artificiality of its rules and of devices such as Vincent's perspective frame: the composition's horizontal and vertical divisions are in effect abstract, as is the juxtaposition of hot, intense, advancing colors on the right with cool, receding tones on the left. In *The Three Graces*, Gauguin subordinated narrative and illusionism to style.

Before Gauguin had proceeded very far with his first picture of the Alyscamps, Vincent was ready to begin his second (fig. 24). Working for the first time on a piece from the twenty meters of jute that he and Gauguin primed themselves, Vincent concentrated on familiarizing himself with its properties, producing a variant of his first composition. Gauguin, perhaps equally eager to experiment with the jute, apparently set aside his *Three Graces* and joined his friend to make a second view of his

own (fig. 26). The two stood back to back, Vincent looking down the Allée des Tombeaux, this time in the direction of the Saint-Accurse chapel, while Gauguin faced the entrance portal to Saint-Honorat and the red-roofed structures abutting it to the south (see fig. 25).

The decidedly unconventional painting surface forced both artists to adjust their execution. Gauguin found that the jute fostered his aim to disguise his brushwork; since its rough texture fractured individual strokes, contours, and flat areas, he could work more broadly and directly than usual, without returning to obscure his marks. Perhaps this explains the coruscated color that animates the confined view: autumnal yellows, oranges, and reds playing off the green grass and the cool blues of tree trunks, sarcophagi, and stone wall. Vincent approached the new support with an old compositional idea. The centrally converging perspective both repeats his own just-completed Alyscamps picture and once again pays homage to the Dutch landscape tradition (see ch. 1, fig. 46). The jute may have contributed to the overall effect being one of color rather than of gestural impasto—Vincent characterized the picture as a "study of the whole avenue, entirely yellow"—because individual strokes lose their identity, interrupted by the support's rough texture.[52] Certainly this second picture of the Alyscamps lacks the Naturalist impetus of the first; the site's features are less varied and delineated, the figures less anecdotally grouped.

After this foray Gauguin seemingly returned to the raised spot by the Craponne canal for a final outdoor session on *The Three Graces*. Vincent accompanied him to the site to execute his third Alyscamps canvas, once again looking in a different direction. From the embankment Vincent peered down through the poplar trunks to the promenade below, conceiving closely related compositions that he described to Theo as "two canvases of falling leaves" (figs. 27–28). This letter implies

that the first of the two was the version featuring the two "lovers" walking toward the Saint-Accurse chapel; the other, taking the opposite perspective, portrays an encounter between two more caricatural figures, a quite proper "old fellow" and a woman "as fat and round as a ball." The former's naturalistically lit trees and the latter's schematization and more radical composition bear out this order.[53]

These breakthrough pictures reveal Vincent's readiness to engage directly with the art and practice of his friend. Gauguin customarily mixed *plein-air* with studio work, and he no doubt finished his *Three Graces* in the Yellow House at the end of the week, when rain kept the artists inside. Vincent probably produced the second *Falling Leaves* canvas indoors, having completed the first on site—a notable departure from his usual habit of making only minimal refinements in the studio.[54]

Vincent's overt exploration here of the stylistic principles of Japanese woodcuts is equally new. Never before had he so radically tilted up a broad swath of pictorial space (the horizon disappears altogether in the second canvas), an innovation only partly explained by the artist's elevated viewpoint. The incorporation of other compositional hallmarks of the woodcuts—abbreviated foreground space, insistently oblique perspective, dramatic cropping of forms—reveals the self-conscious pursuit of design that he also underscored in signaling the "pillar-like" tree trunks cut by the frame, imagery that recalls not only Japanese prints but also Puvis's sacred groves.[55]

In the *Falling Leaves* compositions, Vincent demonstrated the Puvis/Japan conflation and his preoccupation with the stylistic principles to which Gauguin had claimed to have sacrificed everything in his *Self-Portrait (Les Misérables)* and *Vision of the Sermon*. The tilted ground plane and violet tree cutting across the *Vision* find their echo in Vincent's *Falling Leaves*. But Vincent responded as well to Bernard's recent production, familiar to him through drawings (see fig. 29) sent in previous months and now through the painting *Breton Women in the Meadow* (ch. 3, fig. 60), brought to Arles by Gauguin. It took on a special status in the Yellow House as a kind of stand-in for the *Vision* (which Gauguin, aware of its importance, had arranged for Bernard to deliver personally to Theo), speaking to recent discussions in Pont-Aven and serving as a kind of teaching example of how a junior artist might follow the precepts that Gauguin espoused.[56]

In his horizontal Alyscamps canvases, Vincent participated in a dialogue with both Pont-Aven pictures by abandoning his customary execution and approach to color. Working with zones of relatively uninflected hues, bounded by heavy outlines, he heightened the chromatic intensity and emphasized the relationships among separate elements rather than the brushwork that describes them. Vincent had for some time reinforced forms with dark blue lines (see fig. 102), but here these contours are more insistent in contrast to the flat color areas they demarcate and rougher and heavier owing to the drag of the brush across the jute surface. This is not to say that the jute impeded Vincent's hand, however; he had learned to compensate by using larger brushes, loading them with paint, and making longer strokes.

Certainly the unaccustomed support invited changes of approach, but it does not, in and of itself, account for these pictures. Vincent took up a question that Gauguin and Bernard had begun to discuss in Pont-Aven and that they now pursued in letters: whether the painter should record shadows in order to "explain" light. Gauguin thought not. Vanguard experiments wanted nothing to do with photographic illusionism; shadows conveying the "trompe l'oeil of the sun" should be suppressed—unless, that is, a composition called for a "necessary form" that the representation of a shadow could fulfill. Japanese artists were aware of this, Gauguin noted, and showed the

way to a purely formal approach to color through their use of harmonies that, while arbitrary, nonetheless manage to evoke "life in the open air and under the unshaded sun."[57] Such ideas inform the decorative patterning of Gauguin's *Three Graces*.

Vincent had already experimented with flat, unshaded tints in *The Bedroom*, but Gauguin's example encouraged him to put the idea into bolder practice and extend it to landscape. Having used shadows to structure the deep space in his first Alyscamps picture (fig. 20), he abandoned its indication altogether in his last. However, while opening himself up to the influence of Gauguin's example, he nonetheless held on to core beliefs. Because he retained his commitment to actual experience, he justified the omission of shadows by reasoning that light acts differently in "these more luminous countries, under the stronger sun."[58] Moreover his second *Falling Leaves* canvas, while attentive to the principles coded as Puvis/Japan, shows clear signs of Daumier, particularly in the caricatural figure of the older gentleman, who seems imbued with the spirit of the artist's character Ratapoil (see fig. 30), much as the lady in red with her parasol and stylized posture recalls the women who populate Japanese woodcuts (see fig. 31). In short, Vincent's new attention to formal issues did not diminish his Naturalist interest in human content. He arranged the tree trunks in both works not simply to parse the surface n a rhythmic pattern, but to frame the figures and to suggest narratives of connection and disconnection.[59] In the case of the lovers, the succession of empty frames around them suggests a movement from a receding past to an expansive future; in the other picture, the sociable individuals in the first frame of the composition are contrasted with the coquettish young woman at the right, who is emphatically bracketed to emphasize her singularity.

As this productive week drew to a close, things seemed to be going well. Writing to

Bernard, Vincent reported his first impressions. In his "qualities as a man," Gauguin clearly fulfilled Vincent's ideal of the painter as a simple laborer who—more natural, loving, and charitable than the decadent Parisian dandies—would foster the kind of communal spirit that he imagined among the Japanese and desired for himself. Moreover Gauguin seemed sufficiently receptive to his touchstone idea of an "association of certain painters" for Vincent to feel his belief in an "great artistic renaissance" reconfirmed. Gauguin, adding a postscript, downplayed Vincent's effusive admiration and remained notably silent on the issue of an association, but he did assure Bernard that he would like the two *Falling Leaves* studies that Vincent had painted on jute and that currently hung in his bedroom.[60] Joining—or possibly replacing—the *Poet's Garden* decorations that Vincent painted in September and early October, the *Falling Leaves* canvases brought the symbolism of deference and creative collaboration associated with the earlier paintings into the present.

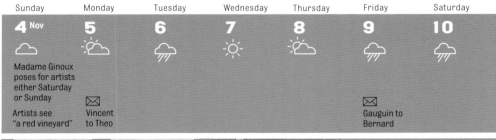

Sunday	Monday	Tuesday	Wednesday	Thursday	Friday	Saturday
4 Nov ☁	**5** ⛅	**6** 🌧	**7** ☀	**8** ⛅	**9** 🌧	**10** 🌧
Madame Ginoux poses for artists either Saturday or Sunday Artists see "a red vineyard"	✉ Vincent to Theo				✉ Gauguin to Bernard	

The two artists were still enjoying a honeymoon period. Their differences appeared intriguing and promising: Vincent reveled in what seemed the realization of a dream; Gauguin drew energy from his friend's intense expectations. The admiration that activated their interaction, while mutual, was disproportionate, and it played out in ways that blurred the personal and professional. Vincent provided an important glimpse into this dynamic when, around 2 November, he made the following observation to Bernard:

Well, here we are without the slightest doubt in the presence of a virgin creature with savage instincts. With Gauguin, blood and sex prevail over ambition.[61]

Written in the knowledge that Gauguin would read it (when adding his postscript to the letter), this characterization, devoid of even a hint of irony, was one in which both parties collaborated. Effectively it reiterated as fact Gauguin's fictional gloss on his *Self-Portrait (Les Misérables)*, doubtless on prominent display in the Yellow House. Much as Gauguin had fashioned the self-portrait in response to Vincent's interests and desires, so now it seems he encouraged—or at least accepted—the embellishment of a virile, macho identity.

From the start Vincent's program for himself and Gauguin included patronage of the brothels in and around rue des Ricolets (see map, ch. 3, fig. 19), and before the end of October, he reported that they had already made several excursions to these establishments and planned to return frequently for purposes of recreation and work. Echoing contemporary beliefs about male sexuality, Vincent justified the scheme in the name of hygiene, convinced that this outlet would keep them free of amatory attachments and foster productivity.[62] Through a somewhat adolescent notion of fraternity, enacted by sharing in and discussing

Oct						
	1	2	3	4	5	6
7	8	9	10	11	12	13
14	15	16	17	18	19	20
21	22	23	24	25	26	27
28	29	30	31			

Nov						
				1	2	3
4	**5**	**6**	**7**	**8**	**9**	**10**
11	12	13	14	15	16	17
18	19	20	21	22	23	24
25	26	27	28	29	30	

Dec						
						1
2	3	4	5	6	7	8
9	10	11	12	13	14	15
16	17	18	19	20	21	22
23	24	25	26	27	28	29
30	31					

32
Vincent van Gogh
The Poet (Eugène Boch)
3 September 1888
[F 462, JH 1574]
Oil on canvas
60 x 45 cm
Musée d'Orsay, Paris

33
Vincent van Gogh
The Lover (Lieutenant Milliet)
c. 25 September 1888
[F 473, JH 1588]
Oil on canvas
60 x 49 cm
Kröller-Müller Museum, Otterlo, The Netherlands

34
Félicien de Myrbach-Rheinfeld
(Austrian; 1853–1940)
Bonzes heading a Funeral Procession from Pierre Loti, *Madame Chrysanthème* (Paris, 1888), p. 126

sexual exploits, Vincent maintained the essential distinction between the artist's life and real life, two mutually exclusive realms of experience.

Vincent had even painted portraits corresponding to the heroes of each domain: *The Poet* (fig. 32), featuring Eugène Boch as Gauguin's surrogate, and *The Lover* (fig. 33), an image of his soldier friend Milliet in uniform. (He hung both portraits above his bed; see ch. 3, figs. 77–78.) Representing the two halves—artistic and sexual—of an ideal of masculine creative prowess, the pendants acknowledged that union of both aspects in a single individual was extremely rare. Vincent maintained that, in order for most "weak, impressionable artists' brains to give their essence to the creation of our pictures," sexual and emotional energies had to be husbanded. After all, he pointed out, Degas's painting owed its virility to the artist's renunciation of a personal life, and Delacroix's greatness was likewise tied to his relative abstinence. But to this well-rehearsed precept, Vincent conceded two spectacular exceptions: Rubens and Courbet. Creative supermen, each had been "a handsome man and a good fucker," as well as a great painter, thanks to the unusual energy and equipoise of mind and body that fell under Vincent's rubric of good health.[63]

Gauguin, it soon appeared, belonged among their ranks. A great artist who displayed remarkable equanimity and suprisingly good health, Gauguin boasted additional achievements "as a man," including success with women.[64] Vincent, whose amorous adventures in Arles had been confined to brothel visits, managed to admire the Zouave Milliet's sexual mastery without envy by using a kind of calculus of creativity: "Milliet is lucky, he has as many Arlésiennes as he wants, but then, he can't paint them, and if he were a painter, he wouldn't have them."[65]

It was a problematic equation. All summer long Vincent had difficulty persuading local women to model for him; in August he had been played for a fool when he attempted to pay a "little Arlésienne" to pose. After an initial sitting, she asked for the balance of what he had promised to pay her in advance, pocketed the money, and disappeared. Gauguin by contrast had no such trouble attracting women to serve as models or muses; though he was married, Vincent noted, he did not act it.[66]

Vincent regretted his lack of the cleverness that ensured his friend's ease with the Arlésiennes.[67] His discovery that the man he had conceived as a "poet" was also a "lover"—a master of life as well as art—accorded Gauguin even greater prowess, challenging his own peace of mind. Yet Vincent, having scripted a southern renaissance led by a masterful "Bel-Ami du Midi" (see ch. 3), fostered this identity by outlining a heroic role that Gauguin could not resist playing. Milliet too had a part in the scenario that Vincent somewhat unwittingly orchestrated.

Since the Zouave was slated to leave Arles in early November for service in Algeria, Vincent lost no time in introducing him to Gauguin. Soliciting Milliet's advice on the matter of Bernard's possible military service in North Africa, Vincent brought up the related topic of the South's creative potential. From this starting point the Studio of the South concept blossomed at once into talk of a parallel project in the tropics, an idea that Gauguin acknowledged was Vincent's.[68] One can imagine it taking shape in Vincent's mind as he listened to Gauguin and Milliet swapping stories about their exploits in France's colonies in the Caribbean, North Africa, and Southeast Asia, calling up Loti's various exotic narratives. Such a dynamic further explains Gauguin's decision to begin his stay in Arles by painting a "négresse" from Martinique—a

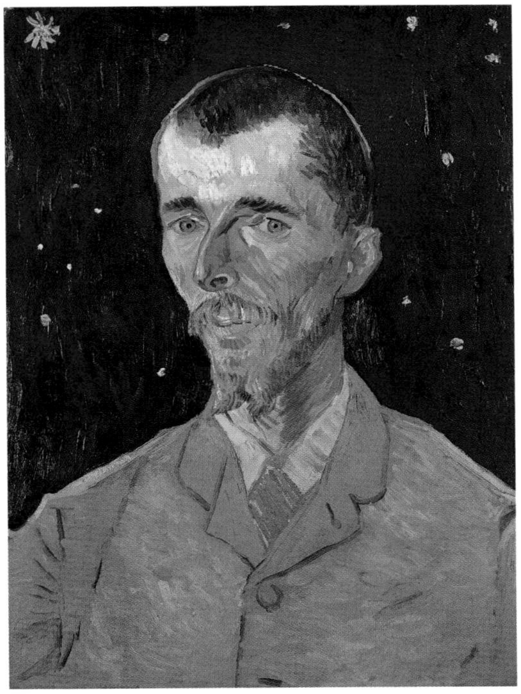
32

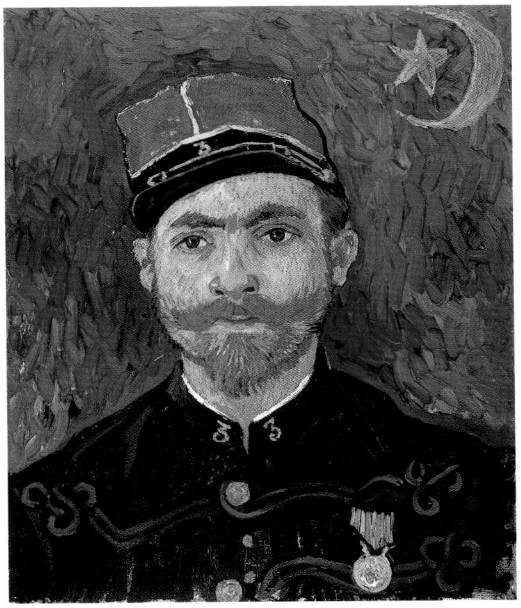
33

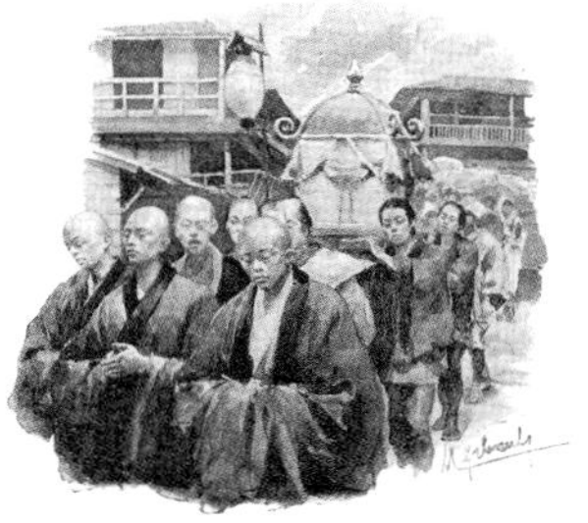
34

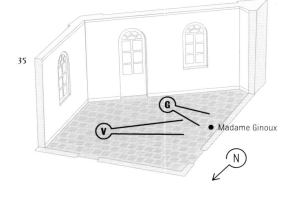

35

● Madame Ginoux

subject suggestive of Loti's Tahitian adventure with Rarahu that provided a symbolic response to Vincent's very different emblem of seminal creativity, *The Sower*, and dovetailed with their discussion of *Madame Chrysanthème*, Loti's Japanese variation of *Le Mariage*.

Gauguin hadn't previously read *Madame Chrysanthème*, but he now acquired Milliet's copy of the illustrated edition in exchange for an unidentified drawing. Vincent had probably read this same volume in June, for he referenced an illustration of a funeral procession of bonzes and *mousmés* (fig. 34) in his *Self-Portrait (Bonze)* (ch. 3, fig. 73).[69] In his identification with Loti's narrative, Vincent had accorded himself a supporting part. Though he stated that he had "had his *mousmé*" (see ch. 3), his use of the possessive did not encompass the role of lover as well as poet, as it did for Loti—and for Gauguin. When Vincent wrote on 28 October that, after less than a week, Gauguin had "already very nearly found his Arlésienne"

(while Vincent consoled himself with his own "modest work" in landscape), he implied that the woman was a trophy, like Rarahu and Madame Chrysanthème, whose conquest conferred access to the culture she represented. This literalized, in Loti fashion, Gauguin's standard requirement to imbibe the character of a foreign locale before attempting to paint it and contributed to the artists' decision to paint in the local lovers' lane, the Alyscamps. It also provides a context for Vincent's excited announcement of around 5 November:

I have an Arlésienne at last, a figure (size 30), slashed on [*sabrée*] in *one* hour, background pale citron, the face gray, the clothes black, black, black, with very harsh Prussian blue. She is leaning on a green table and seated in an armchair of orange wood.[70]

The Arlésienne in question was Marie Ginoux, proprietress of the Café de la Gare on place Lamartine, where Vincent had lived from May to September. Vincent had encountered her

36

35
Studio diagram of
the sitting of
Madame Ginoux

36
Paul Gauguin
Madame Ginoux
(study for *Night
Café*)
c. 4 November 1888
White and colored
chalks and charcoal
on wove paper

56.1 x 49.2 cm
Fine Arts Museums
of San Francisco,
memorial gift from
Dr. T. Edward and
Tullah Hanley,
Bradford,
Pennsylvania
Cat. 38

37
Vincent van Gogh
The Arlésienne
(*Madame Ginoux*)
c. 5 November 1888
[F 489, JH 1625]
Oil on jute
93 x 74 cm
Musée d'Orsay,
Paris, life-interest
gift of Mme R. de
Goldschmidt-
Rothschild,

announced on 25
August 1944, day of
the Liberation of
Paris, and entered
the collection in 1974
Cat. 74

on a daily basis for months, but apparently it took Gauguin to persuade her to act as model, which Vincent would have considered a coup, having resigned himself to being too old and unattractive to induce women to pose for free.[71] It is worth noting that Vincent here used the indefinite article "an" rather than the possessive, whereas earlier he had mentioned "my *mousmé*" and of course Gauguin's Arlésienne. Whether or not Marie Ginoux, forty years old (like Gauguin) and married only two years, was in fact the woman whom Vincent had in mind with that reference, the scenario for the portrait session and the resulting works acknowledge the different relationships among the principals.

Madame Ginoux came to the Yellow House probably during the first weekend of November, dressed in full Arlésienne regalia, possibly her Sunday best. In the front room that served as the studio, she sat for both artists, Gauguin working on a large drawing (fig. 36) in the hour-long session during which Vincent completed his painting (fig. 37). As Vincent noted in May, when he signed the lease, the room was light-filled: a window on the building's east side looked onto avenue de Montmajour, and a fenestrated door and another window faced south, onto place Lamartine.[72] This layout allowed the artists, when painting during the day, to set up their easels at a comfortable distance from one another, with natural light falling on their respective works.

Natural light was not the sole source of illumination in the studio. Anticipating a desire to work after sunset (which occurred at around 5:30 P.M. in November), Vincent had paid to have gaslight installed in the studio and in the kitchen two weeks before Gauguin's arrival. He did not specify the number of gas lamps, but his prediction that he and Gauguin would "paint portraits by gaslight" implies their working together in the same room, the studio.[73] Two light sources would thus have been necessary, to illuminate both

of their easels and a sitter. Experiments carried out in a full-scale model of the studio, assuming the presence of gas lamps on the interior walls, suggest provisional positioning of artists and sitters.

The different vantage points represented in the drawn and painted portraits of Marie Ginoux, together with the different ways that light is represented falling on the sitter in each, argue for only two possible scenarios, the more plausible of which (because least problematic) presumes a daytime session. According to this arrangement (see diagram, fig. 35), Gauguin sat in front of the south window and Vincent positioned himself behind and to the right of Gauguin, taking advantage of the light admitted through the glass panes in the door and the east window. Marie Ginoux sat in the armchair that Vincent had purchased for Gauguin's use (see fig. 71), leaning her right elbow on a table, her back to the west wall.

Her cheek resting on her closed hand, head gently cocked to one side, Marie Ginoux turned toward Gauguin, seated a few feet in front of her. In his drawing, light from the window falls on the right side of her face, on her shoulder, and on the dorsal surface of her hand. She returns his gaze with a frank, confident look that conveys a hint of quizzical assessment, the result of Gauguin's having made her shadowed left eye notably bigger and brighter than her right. The directness of her regard, uncommon in conventional portraiture of the day, suggests that she is not so much sitting to the artist as engaging with him. This is an interaction that Vincent, standing several feet back, observed but did not join. Marie Ginoux's look, as he represented it, excluded him. Attentive to her gaze, he nonetheless awkwardly rendered her right eye as if focused differently from the left. Her body language also shows her attention directed elsewhere: rather than sinking into the chair's embrace, she sits forward, her torso held erect and slightly turned away from

Vincent and toward the other artist in the studio. In place of the Junoesque flavor Gauguin imparted to her physiognomy, Vincent depicted her face as pinched and ashen.[74]

The differences in approach to this subject recall the situation enacted just days before on the path bordering the Craponne canal, when Gauguin chose to represent three women head on while Vincent looked obliquely through the trees to the path below, observing but unobserved. In Vincent's *Falling Leaves*, as well as in *The Arlésienne*, a whiff of voyeuristic reticence seems to bear out the artist's self-characterization as one "content to watch things pass, as a spider waits for flies in its web."[75] Yet while his portrait of Marie Ginoux is in one sense shy, in another it is fiercely assertive.

Vincent could see that Gauguin was working on his drawing of the same subject slowly and carefully, but he deliberately refused to follow this example. The feverish speed at which he painted conveys a message also hinted at in his word choice: *sabrée*, "slashed on," from the verb *sabrer*, "to strike or cut with a sabre," which evokes both the violence and the frantic pace of battle and, colloquially in French, a hasty editorial deletion. To be sure, Vincent had used the word before to signal rapid, aggressive application, but in this context it acquired additional and more specific significance. At a literal level, it may describe the action Vincent felt he had to take to overcome the resistance of the coarse jute. His determination to persist with his quick, gestural strokes constituted an assertion of individuality, a reversal of any compliance with Gauguin hinted at in the two *Falling Leaves* pictures—suggestive of a kind of displaced engagement with the man whose penchant for displays of masculine prowess had led him to bring his fencing equipment with him to Arles.

A curious circularity, typical of their relationship, may help explain the nuances in play here. In a letter to Bernard, which Gauguin surely read, Vincent rather clumsily invoked

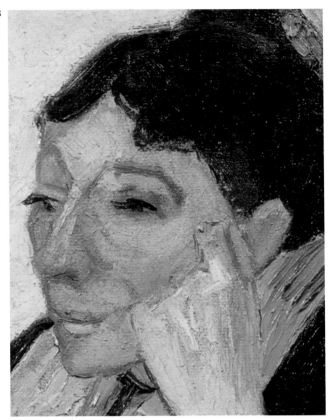

fencing as a metaphor to justify the fury with which he painted as opposed to the composure of a Cézanne: "Is a calm and steady touch always possible? My word—no more, it seems to me, than an assault in a fencing match."[76] Pointed, the figure of speech was inadvertently provocative. He must have been aware that Gauguin, who had studied fencing at school with a celebrated master, had instructed Pont-Aven's harbor master, a fencer of good credentials, in the finer points of the art and had helped him to establish a fencing school. Gauguin believed in the science of arms, valuing a "good head" above a "good hand." Fencing was a game of wits whose strategic imperatives—to study your adversary's habits of mind—had widespread application in life, and he clearly welcomed the opportunity to discuss and demonstrate his point. Bringing his equipment to Arles, he seemingly wished to enact for Vincent's benefit the lesson that it is "the head, always the head"—in sport as in painting.[77] Of course he also relished the opportunity to boast about his skill in quintessentially masculine arts such as fencing and boxing, also practiced by the Breton sailors in Loti's *Mon Frère Yves*; in the context of athletics, the five-foot-four-inch (1.63-meter) painter could think of himself as "tall and long-legged."

Gauguin's devotion to such exercises can be seen in the context of the heightened attention paid to the condition of French masculinity following the nation's defeat by Prussia in 1870–71; it also enhanced his evolving macho persona.[78]

Once Vincent had spoken of himself in terms he now reserved for Gauguin—as a "savage" dominated by strong passions.[79] Now he talked of channeling his virility into his painting. *The Arlésienne* suggests the complexity of this effort. Vincent in effect ceded the subject to Gauguin with a remarkably deft symbolic gesture: plucking one of the pale-pink and red nosegays from the wallpaper of Gauguin's *Self-Portrait (Les Misérables)* and delicately applying it, corsagelike, to Marie Ginoux's bodice.[80] But, never taking well to lessons, he would not cede his manner of working. Starting and finishing his picture in a single sitting, working at a speed not justified in this case by exigencies of weather conditions, Vincent mounted a bravado defense of his creative turf.

Gauguin, in that same hour, began but did not necessarily complete a drawing that was, in any case, preparatory. He first established the

composition with light, tenuous lines of gray chalk, and then worked it up with charcoal and chalks. He delicately sculpted the sitter's face with blended and hatched shading and highlighted the figure with white chalk, setting her against a background of orange diagonal hatching. Finally, he reinforced the figure's contours with dark charcoal lines, which—together with the large format and the degree of finish—suggests that from the beginning Gauguin intended to trace the portrait and insert it into a painting.[81]

Even if Gauguin issued the invitation to Marie Ginoux, the very presence of a sitter in the studio was probably Vincent's idea, for it was he who, following the Alyscamps campaign, reiterated his belief that the "painting of the future" would consist of portraits "comprehensible to the general public."[82] By contrast portraiture had never featured prominently among Gauguin's ambitions. Moreover Vincent was very likely the motivating force behind the picture for which Gauguin's drawing of Marie Ginoux was preparatory. Just before their session with her, he announced that Gauguin had embarked on "a canvas of the same night café I painted [fig. 40] but with figures seen in the brothels." In revisiting

38
Detail of fig. 37

39
Detail of fig. 41

40
Vincent van Gogh
*The Night Café (Le
Café de nuit)*
c. 8 September 1888
[F 463, JH 1575]
Oil on canvas
70 x 89 cm

Yale University Art
Gallery, New
Haven, Connecticut
Cat. 62

41
Paul Gauguin
*Night Café (Un Café
de nuit)*
4–12 November 1888
[W 305]
Oil on jute
72 x 92 cm

The State Pushkin
Museum of Fine
Arts, Moscow
Cat. 39

Vincent's *Night Café*, on view in the Yellow House, Gauguin inserted himself into earlier discussions between Bernard and Vincent about the work and its meaning. Bernard had interpreted Vincent's description of it in light of their talk of painting brothel subjects. Vincent had trouble disabusing him of this idea, finally insisting irritably in early October, "I have already written to you a thousand times that my 'Night Café' isn't a brothel, it is a café"—though he did allow that it was the kind of place where a prostitute might bring her lover.[83]

Gauguin's planned reinterpretation of *The Night Café* seems more in conformity with

Bernard's expectations, showing Ginoux's establishment peopled with figures whom the artists had observed in their excursions to the *maisons de tolérance*. Vincent thought it promised to be "a fine thing."[84] He had reason to be enthusiastic. As he had planned, the brothel visits had resulted in a picture; more satisfying still, Gauguin seemed to have adopted Vincent's vision of Arles, seen through the lens of Daumier and the pages of Zola.

Indeed Gauguin began his *Night Café* (fig. 41) in a studio atmosphere thick with talk of Zola. Vincent was reading *Le Rêve*, the latest novel by the author of *L'Oeuvre* and *La Joie de vivre*. He liked to talk while painting—he found that

he worked with "more animation"—and now, for the first time in his life, he had a captive audience. Gauguin's lack of enthusiasm for Zola, far from silencing Vincent, would have stimulated him to engage in the *wrijving*, aggressive debate, that he held to be the sign of a true, noncomplacent friendship.[85] He no doubt delivered a fervent seminar on everything he had ever thought about Zola and on the higher significance of the Naturalist author's art of consolation.

Vincent was zealous and compelling; Gauguin's interest was evidently aroused, as were his competitive instincts. His *Night Café* in a sense "out-Daumiered" Vincent's. Where Vincent

40

evoked mood—a haunting atmosphere of alienation—Gauguin more literally described the quotidian character of the surroundings. His scene seems lifted from the pages of Zola, Maupassant, and Goncourt, a contribution to a pictorial genre practiced by Degas, Bernard (see ch. 3, fig. 42), and soon by Vincent (fig. 53), among many others. Gauguin, like Degas and Bernard, relied on somewhat caricatural types: the Zouave, the sleeping drunk, and the three homely prostitutes with their fellow in the background; and the *patronne*, seated at a marble-topped table, who dominates the foreground. With subtle adjustments to his drawing, Gauguin transformed Marie Ginoux's expression into a mask of sly, knowing complicity. She presides over the goings-on

behind her, soliciting the viewer's attention and conspiratorially proffering a glass of absinthe, the drink synonymous with dissolute behavior.

Marie Ginoux is not the only recognizable character here. The uniformed figure at the far left bears a generic resemblance to Milliet (who sported a goatee as well as a moustache; see fig. 33), and the bearded figure in profile conversing with the women is Vincent's friend Roulin. Gauguin's *tableau à clef* carried a hint of controversy in the context of late-1880s Arles. Anxieties ran high regarding the illegal prostitution that took place outside the confines of government-licensed brothels. As local chroniclers tirelessly pointed out, the

cafés (known in Provence as *cafetons*) that permitted or even retained prostitutes to ply their trade on their premises, using spirits to fuel commerce, bore responsibility for the current moral "plague." The police joined journalists in declaring a war against *cafetons* that involved the arrest of their proprietors.[86] When Gauguin imported prostitutes from local brothels into his picture, he cast the Ginouxs and their clientele in a dubious light; Madame Ginoux as madam is indeed a characterization that the artist would summon again in a text written almost a decade later (see Coda).

Vincent may subsequently have had to concede that Gauguin's painting, at some level, cast an aspersion on his friend Madame Ginoux and on Arles. A defensive reaction would help explain changes that he made to his own portrait of her following Gauguin's departure: he added a parasol and gloves after the impasto of the table had already completely dried.[87] Attributes of decorous femininity, they bestow on the sitter an aura of propriety that counters the disreputability implied by Gauguin. At the time Gauguin was painting his picture, however, Vincent was evidently pleased by his friend's apparent openness to his ideas.

Gauguin had doubts. He had certainly not foresaken his concern with formal issues, as attested by the boldly outlined and simpified forms, stylized tendrils of blue smoke, and insistent geometry of rectangular shapes and repeated horizontals that collapse the deep space of Vincent's café picture into a series of stacked chromatic zones. But such stylish packaging does not disguise either the picture's Naturalist premise or the forced aspect of its construction. Gauguin elaborated it over a period of roughly a week. Taking particular care with the preliminary stages, after tracing the figure of Marie Ginoux from the drawing and transfering it to the canvas, he made a detailed sketch in dark-blue paint and worked up most of the composition in shades of blue and green.[88] He considered bright yellow for the wall, as initial strokes of color next to Marie Ginoux's face suggest, before deciding upon red, and, improvising, he adopted a very thick horizontal thread as a division in the background. He added the cat, with its traditional iconographic suggestion of female lasciviousness, late in the painting process. His deployment of flat color areas and his juxtaposition of an imposing, essentially monochromatic foreground figure with a more lurid background scene hark back to the bold concept of the *Vision*, but here the composition's impact suffers from the inclusion of many narrative elements within a shallow space.

Gauguin found the result labored, his large figure "much too proper and stiff." Ultimately he recognized that his *Night Café* was indeed more Vincent's kind of picture than his own, volunteering as much to Bernard, to whom he sent a sketch, a description, and this assessment:

I've . . . done a café which Vincent likes very much and I like rather less. Basically it isn't to my taste and the coarse local color doesn't suit me. I like it well enough in paintings by other people, but for myself I'm always apprehensive. It's a matter of education: one cannot remake oneself.[89]

He had tried on Vincent's notion of the South-as-Daumier/Zola and found that it did not fit. But he continued to explore how Vincent's ideas might be adapted to his own purposes. Indeed he turned from his lukewarm judgment of *Night Café* to a proud announcement of the canvas he considered his "best picture of the year."[90] He had painted it after a walk that he and Vincent took in the early evening of Sunday, 4 November, to the vineyards near Montmajour (see map, fig. 3). For both men the event assumed a special significance.

Vincent probably suggested the outing, recalling a solitary excursion he took to the same site in early October, when he produced *The Green Vineyard* (fig. 10), a canvas conceived as a pendant to the first of the *Poet's Garden* group (ch. 3, fig. 69).[91] The pair expressed Vincent's fantasy of a past and future renaissance and his goal of resurrecting Monticelli. Now that his Petrarch had arrived, Vincent wanted to enact the scenario he had imagined so vividly. Walking together like the two Renaissance poets at the end of the day, he and Gauguin saw the sun setting over "a red vineyard, all red like red wine":

In the distance it turned to yellow, and then a green sky with sun, the earth after the rain violet, sparkling yellow here and there where it caught the reflection of the setting sun.[92]

In the same letter, Vincent reported that he was at work on a vineyard picture (fig. 49). Its surface, like that of *The Green Vineyard*, is a rich relief of thickly textured brushwork, strong enough, Vincent believed, to hold its own alongside Monticelli's landscapes.[93]

While the reference to Monticelli shows Vincent holding fast to his established goals, in fact he had made a major concession: he painted *The Red Vineyard*, which incorporates grape gatherers into the landscape, in the studio rather than in front of the motif. Gauguin too had undertaken a canvas featuring "women in a vineyard," and he was painting it "completely *de tête* [from memory]." They could not have done otherwise. Excellent weather had favored 1888's bountiful grape harvest, which employed some six thousand people at its height in mid-September and continued into October. However, by the time of Gauguin's arrival on the twenty-third, the harvest was essentially over; Arles had turned colder, with gleaners replacing harvesters in the vineyards. The grape gatherers, who wore voluminous starched cloth hoods to protect their faces, were absent from the scene that Vincent and Gauguin witnessed on 4 November, as were the gleaners, banned from the vineyards after sundown; Vincent's description makes no mention of laborers of any kind.[94] Had the artists wanted to witness a harvest in progress, they would have had to visit the nearby olive groves, where the harvest was just beginning.

Capturing local color was not the agenda, certainly not for Gauguin. So much did he flout "exactitude" that, as he boasted to Bernard, he represented the Arles vineyard peopled by

43

44

42

45

Breton peasants (fig. 50), even designating the figure standing at left as a woman from Le Pouldu, where her dark, hooded costume—which seems to reference that of the Arles grape gatherers—would have more generic associations with death and mourning.[95] His underlying symbolic intention is implicit in the title he assigned it when sending it to Paris several weeks later: *Grape Harvest* or *Poverty* (*Les Vendanges* or *La Pauvresse*). Gauguin's image does not comment on the lot of the peasant laborer; rather it presents an allegorical central figure, a personification in the tradition most famously exemplified in Albrecht Dürer's *Melancholia I* (fig. 43) and continuing into fashionable art of the late nineteenth century (see fig. 44). In other words the painting is an existential statement rather than a social one. As such, it marks a shift in Gauguin's work in the direction of Vincent's interest in emblematics, manifested in early signature works like *Sorrow* (ch. 1, fig. 42). It was, as Gauguin himself recognized, a milestone and on a road that he and Vincent now traveled together. He made this still more explicit in the suggestive title under which he exhibited it: *Human Miseries* (*Misères humaines*), now its most common designation.[96]

To be sure, Gauguin had laid the groundwork for this effort in Brittany. Late in the summer, he had painted a canvas dedicated to Laval (fig. 45) that includes the glimpse of a child covetously eyeing a display of fruit. She is

45

48

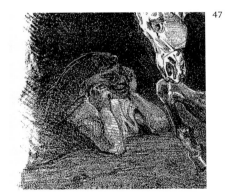

46

47

42
Jean-François Millet
(French; 1814–1875)
The Grape Harvester at Rest
1869/70
Pastel
70.5 x 84 cm
Heliographic reproduction from Alfred Sensier, *La Vie et l'oeuvre de J.-F. Millet* (Paris, 1881), n. pag.

43
Albrecht Dürer
(German; 1471–1528)
Melancholia I
1514
Engraving
24 x 18.7 cm
The Art Institute of Chicago, Clarence Buckingham Collection, 1938.1452

44
James Tissot
(French; 1836–1902)
Melancholia
c. 1868
Photograph
mounted on card
12 x 8.9 cm

From *Galerie Photographie*,
Goupil et Cie
Witt Library,
Courtauld Institute,
London

45
Paul Gauguin
Still Life with Fruit
1888 [W 288]
Oil on canvas
43 x 58 cm
The State Pushkin Museum of Fine Arts, Moscow

46
Pericles Pantazis
(Greek; 1849–1884)
The Little Thief
Oil on canvas
45.5 x 55.2 cm
Private collection

47
Eugène Delacroix
(French; 1798–1863)
Faust and Mephistopheles Galloping through the Night of the Witches' Sabbath (detail)
1828
Lithograph
The Art Institute of Chicago,

the John H. Wrenn Memorial Collection, 1930.1261

48
Jean-Baptiste-Camille Corot
(French; 1796–1875)
The Reaper with a Sickle
1838
Oil on canvas
35.3 x 27 cm
Museum of Fine Arts, Boston, bequest of William A. Coolidge

49
Vincent van Gogh
The Red Vineyard
c. 12 November 1888
[F 495, JH 1626]
Oil on canvas
75 x 93 cm
The State Pushkin
Museum of Fine
Arts, Moscow

50
Paul Gauguin
Human Miseries
(*Grape Harvest* or
Poverty) (*Misères
humaines* [*Les
Vendanges* or *La
Pauvresse*])

4–11 November 1888
[W 304]
Oil on jute
73 x 93 cm
Ordrupgaard,
Copenhagen
Cat. 40

comparable to his figure of Poverty, with her slanting eyes and head-in-hand pose, and also recalls the Delacroix *Faust* lithographs he admired (see fig. 47). The theme has precedents in genre painting; indeed Gauguin's specific source was quite possibly an image of mischievous cupidity by the Brussels-based Greek artist Pericles Pantazis (fig. 46), of whom the critic Joris-Karl Huysmans was reminded when he saw Gauguin's depictions of children in 1882.[97] But by exaggerating the figure's facial features, boldly cropping the forms, and abruptly tilting the space, Gauguin strategically distanced his representation from the Pantazis prototype, blurring the clarity of its narrative. What was straightforward has

become ambiguous—almost willfully provocative—hinting at intentions and meanings that remain stubbornly latent.

In *Human Miseries* Gauguin attempted to push these visual poetics still further while simultaneously experimenting with the prose of his *Night Café*. Vincent's ideas, central to the café image, also emerge in that of the vineyard. The conversations that fed into *Human Miseries* can be inferred from the typically refracted way in which Gauguin played them back in letters to Schuffenecker. Writing in December, Gauguin would cite the picture to illustrate his intent to realize an art that did not "describe" but rather stimulated the viewer to imagine

something beyond (*au-delà*). To evoke emotional states through the language of color and form, he pared down narrative elements so that the picture functions as a "parable rather than a novel in paint." If this made the work incomprehensible to some viewers, so be it; the painter's task was not to explain but to suggest.[98]

The formulation might seem original to Gauguin were it not for his reference in the same context to the spiritual intimations inherent in Corot's landscapes. While Gauguin's admiration of Corot—fostered by Arosa and Pissarro—dated back to the 1870s, this exegesis was new. It echoes several of Vincent's deeply

49

held, carefully formulated concepts: his vision of a symbolic realism, exemplified in the work of Corot, Millet, and Rembrandt; his awe at the sense of transcendence that these artists had intimated vaguely but nonetheless more persuasively than the Reverend van Gogh's explicit sermonizing; and his admiration of the parables as the supreme achievements of the supreme artist, Christ.[99]

Gauguin's *Human Miseries* has a more literal connection to Corot through its affiliation with an early canvas by the Barbizon master (sold at public auction in Paris in January 1887) that features a seated harvester set against a landscape (fig. 48). But while Gauguin's figure bears a certain resemblance to Corot's—particularly in terms of the pose and position close

to the picture plane—the two pictures differ dramatically in mood. In this regard another representation of a vineyard laborer may have come into play: Millet's powerful image of physical exhaustion, *The Grape Harvester at Rest* (fig. 42). If Gauguin, in first contemplating a vineyard composition, did not recall the pastel from either the 1875 Gavet sale of Millet's works, the full-page reproduction in Sensier's 1881 monograph, or the artist's 1887 retrospective exhibition, Vincent surely did. Even had Gauguin never seen the Millet, Vincent could have drawn upon his remarkable memory and descriptive powers to conjure up both the composition (with its high horizon line, centrally placed figure, and pyramidal organization) and Sensier's poignant characterization of the stupified worker, "unable to collect

thoughts other than those pertaining to this vineyard, which demands such a great effort from him."[100] It is possible that Vincent, taking Gauguin to the vineyards that Sunday, envisioned him taking up the same theme. After all, he explicitly regarded the relationship he had helped to forge between Theo and Gauguin as parallel to that between Millet and his impresario Sensier, who suggested compositions to the painter, placed his work, and established his myth.[101]

Gauguin had never before expressed any special reverence for Millet (and never would). Yet his vineyard picture seems to echo Millet's, the way his verbal interpretation of it recalls Sensier's description of mind-numbing fatigue:

Do you notice in the grape harvest a poor disconsolate being; it is not a soul endowed with intelligence, grace, and all the gifts of nature. It's a woman. Both hands under her chin, she thinks of little, but feels the consolation of this earth (nothing but the earth), which the sun inundates in the vineyard with its red triangle. And a woman dressed in black passes by, looking at her like a sister.[102]

This reading bears the undeniable hallmarks of Vincent's influence. Gauguin's reference to the consolation found solely in the natural world reprises the theme of Zola's *Joie de vivre*. In another title for the painting, *Splendors and Miseries* (*Splendeurs et misères*), borrowed from a Balzac novel about courtesans, Gauguin went further in underscoring the oppositional dynamic—sorrowful yet always rejoicing—central to Vincent's thinking about the message that art should convey.[103]

Gauguin's gloss on the woman in black introduces another theme that compelled Vincent: the artist's essential loneliness. At age twenty-one, Vincent had been struck by Romantic author Alfred de Musset's image of Solitude as the poet's constant life companion in "Nuit de décembre," copying the salient lines into one of the albums that can be interpreted as self-portraits (see ch. 1):

Partout où j'ai voulu dormir
Partout où j'ai voulu pleurer
Partout où j'ai touché la terre
Un malheureux vêtu du noir
Auprès de moi venait s'asseoir
Qui me regardait comme un frère.[104]

Vincent's 1875 transcription contains two errors or alterations to the original: his "cry" (*pleurer*) replaces Musset's "die" (*mourir*) in the second line, and "looked at" (*regardait*) takes the place of "resembled" (*ressemblait*) in the last. Now, thirteen years later, he recalled the same verse, making the identical change

in the last line. This is the line that Gauguin paraphrased for his description of the figure in black, substituting "sister" (*soeur*) for "brother" (*frère*) but retaining Vincent's verb. In doing so he identified the figure at the left with Solitude and revealed Vincent's intimate involvement with the picture.[105]

Living and working with Vincent in the Yellow House, Gauguin encountered a lifetime of his deeply felt enthusiasms. Some he already shared, including an admiration for Delacroix, whose presence Gauguin intimated here by characterizing his seated figure as "a poor woman thoroughly bewitched" in a letter to Theo (see fig. 47).[106] Other interests were clearly new. *Human Miseries* suggests that Gauguin listened acutely, selectively, and creatively, and also that he looked closely at what Vincent was doing. In executing this picture, Gauguin modified his customary practice. Though he began as usual, with a dark blue contour sketch, he leaped into more direct painting. Instead of working up individual areas with small hatched strokes, he spread large patches of flat color, thickly troweling the paint with a palette knife. He manipulated the paint surface to an unprecedented degree, accepting the materiality of the paint but working it much as he might a clay surface: wiping, brushing, knifing, pulling it up into peaks, smoothing and retexturing it. The result was a painted surface totally unlike any in his work to date—rich and originally very tactile. His description of his procedure implies a conception based on delineated zones of pure hues, but at a later point the artist scattered touches of varied hues over the areas of color and softened the outlines that he had previously reinforced; in addition his later conservation efforts softened its texture.[107]

Gauguin and Vincent recognized *Human Miseries* as an important achievement. For Gauguin it represented an advance toward a non-literary mode of symbolic expression. Unlike the *Vision*, a complex composition

whose signification requires explanation, *Human Miseries* conveys a desperate, mysterious mood with a simplicity of means. Suggestively juxtaposed rather than narratively connected, the figures evoke the discontinuities of poetry rather than the linear fixity of prose. The realms of dream and reality, partitioned in the *Vision*, are enigmatically blended: does the seated figure imagine her standing companion, like Musset's poet, or is she really there?

Vincent admired the picture for somewhat different reasons. To begin with, the very fact that Gauguin had not spoiled it or left it unfinished—as he had other Arles canvases—was a welcome sign of productivity. Moreover, in both meaning and execution, it manifested the collaborative ideal of which he'd dreamed.

He specifically drew Theo's attention to its surface of "firm impasto," predicting that it would eclipse Gauguin's recent Breton work. Impressive technically, the picture represented a still larger achievement, which elicited Vincent's frank praise: "It is as beautiful as the *Négresses.*"[108]

It is questionable whether Vincent saw his own work profiting to the same degree from their collaboration. Describing his *Red Vineyard* for Theo, he noted the Monticelli-esque qualities—calligraphic, impastoed brushwork—that it shared with its September predecessor, *The Green Vineyard*. But he failed to mention that he had joined Gauguin in working *de tête*, though he had often declared his intention to do so. Tangible evidence points to the differences that this procedure entailed. Working in the studio, unconstrained by changing weather conditions, Vincent became more methodical, as attested by the carefully delineated trees at the upper left and by the figures dotting the landscape. More numerous and more emphatically outlined than was his custom, they appear applied to, rather than integrated with, the natural surroundings. (And indeed Vincent did paint them over the layers that form the landscape.) Just as Gauguin introduced Bretons into his vineyard, Vincent brought figures from the near and far past into his: the woman on the rain-glazed path at the right is an Arlésienne; the horse and cart appear in earlier Arles landscapes; and the bending figures have stepped out of drawings and paintings of Brabant peasants stooping to pull their sustenance from the earth (see fig. 64). The more one studies *The Red Vineyard*, the more one senses Vincent looking at other pictures: at *The Green Vineyard* for the lay of the land and rows of trees; at *Washerwomen at the Roubine du Roi Canal* (ch. 3, fig. 54) for the glistening path that reads almost like a waterway. Working *de tête* here involved the depiction of direct experience at one remove, with reference to earlier pictures painted from life. At an early stage, *The Red Vineyard* was decidedly more violet and yellow, mirroring the chromatics of Gauguin's *Human Miseries*. But while Gauguin added paler tones over a reddish-purple layer, Vincent keyed up the intensity of his field with hot reds, oranges, and yellows, producing an effect of shimmering color rivaling Gauguin's vibrant hues.[109] Something of an assemblage, *The Red Vineyard* is nonetheless visually ravishing.

In the small brothel sketch painted later that week (fig. 53), Vincent followed Gauguin's procedure more closely—and more freely. He resketched and repositioned figures during the painting process, and used an initial rough blue wash to overcome the challenge of the blank canvas and to set the scene's lurid atmosphere. The arrangement of figures recalls, to a certain extent, the background of Gauguin's *Night Café*. Vincent's *Brothel Scene*—its composition partly invented and partly based on Gauguin's example, its execution alternately spontaneous and considered—is something of a hybrid work, a tentative experiment with deliberately limited ambitions. The artist termed it a *pochade*, implying a status even more modest than an *étude* or *esquisse*, and far from the *tableau* of the subject that he still intended to do. In addition to this deprecating assessment, once again Vincent declined to mention that he had painted it in the studio rather than on site, though he did make it clear that it "wouldn't do" to work in this way were Gauguin not with him.[110] Clearly he was both intrigued by and ill at ease with a practice he knew better (after his experiments during the summer) than to attempt on his own.

53

Sunday	Monday	Tuesday	Wednesday	Thursday	Friday	Saturday
11 Nov	**12**	**13**	**14**	**15**	**16**	**17**
		Gauguin to Schuffenecker	Gauguin to Bernard			
	Vincent to Theo	Theo to Gauguin	Gauguin to Theo		Vincent to Theo	Ball at the Folies-Arlésiennes

Around 5 November Vincent had reported to Theo that "our life together is going very well." As he and Gauguin entered their fourth week together, this still held. They were getting their house in order and working out their routines. Gauguin told Bernard that he had taken the budget in hand, holding back further details of the domestic chaos he had encountered upon arrival.[111] Vincent relayed news of his friend's homemaking and culinary talents and his hopes to learn from him. (Gauguin would recall Vincent's one attempt to make soup as a disaster.) Midweek, Gauguin reassured Theo that "the good Vincent and the *grièche* Gauguin live happily together and eat at home, humble food that they cook themselves." He complained only about the terrible rain that prevented them from working out-of-doors and led them both to indulge in what he called "la peinture de chic"—painting without a model.[112]

Working in this way, Gauguin had completed his *Night Café* and realized *Human Miseries*; now, he informed Theo on 14 November, Vincent had produced "a beautiful Dutch garden scene . . . with the family."[113] *A Memory of the Garden (Etten and Nuenen)* (fig. 67) marked a decisive shift in Vincent's working relationship with Gauguin. In undertaking the picture, Vincent had to confront his fears about painting from memory, which he shared with Bernard in early October, after producing a "little canvas" (now lost) in this manner to please his friend that so displeased Vincent himself that he regretted having done it and refused to sign it, "for I never work *de tête*."[114] This claim came with the following statement:

I cannot work without a model. I won't say that I don't turn my back on nature ruthlessly, in order to turn a study into a picture, arranging the colors, enlarging and simplifying; but in the matter of form I am too afraid of departing from the possible and the true.

Oct						
	1	2	3	4	5	6
7	8	9	10	11	12	13
14	15	16	17	18	19	20
21	22	23	24	25	26	27
28	29	30	31			

Nov						
				1	2	3
4	5	6	7	8	9	10
11	**12**	**13**	**14**	**15**	**16**	**17**
18	19	20	21	22	23	24
25	26	27	28	29	30	

Dec						
						1
2	3	4	5	6	7	8
9	10	11	12	13	14	15
16	17	18	19	20	21	22
23	24	25	26	27	28	29
30	31					

I don't mean I won't do it after another ten years of painting studies, but, to tell the honest truth, my attention is so fixed on what is possible and really exists that I hardly have the desire or the courage to strive for the ideal as it might result from my abstract studies. Others may have more lucidity than I do in the matter of abstract studies; . . . indeed you could be in that number, as well as Gauguin . . . and perhaps I myself when I am old. But in the meantime I still feed upon nature. I exaggerate . . . but I do not invent the whole picture.[115]

Vincent had attached this resolution to a report of a much more significant failure, the second *Gethsemane*. In the weeks before Gauguin's arrival, he had twice backed away from representing the supernatural, an effort that he associated with Zola's *L'Oeuvre* narrative; though he had defended Claude Lantier's ill-fated ambition (see ch. 3), his own experience had unnerved him. His renouncement to Bernard, couched in the language of Realism, constituted the retrenchment that had led from the *Gethsemane* to *The Starry Night over the Rhone* (ch. 3, fig. 70).

Vincent reversed his position with *A Memory of the Garden* and the similarly conceived pictures of mid-November in which he more assertively pursued Gauguin's direction. His doing so attests his growing confidence in his friend, whose accomplishments—ranging from cooking and fencing to the "invention" of the Impressionists' white frame—continued to inspire Vincent's awe and reinforced Gauguin's role as the admired senior in their brotherhood.[116] This in turn encouraged Gauguin's posturing, an element of which informs the picture (fig. 55) that he painted while Vincent worked on *A Memory of the Garden*. The composition's elements, identified by Vincent as a "very original nude woman in the hay with some pigs," are difficult to read and interpret.[117] In what seems to be an enclosure (bordered at the canvas's upper edge by a rough stone wall), a woman is seen from behind, stripped to the waist, the pale skin of her bared back and shoulders revealed in sharp contrast to the dark tan of her forearm and hand, normally exposed to the sun. Her left arm is outstretched, her right bent to support her head. The other bold shapes filling the confined space seem to be piles of hay in front of the woman and in the right foreground; to the left the curved back of a pinkish orange pig, identifiable as such by a floppy ear; at the upper right another pig's tail; a red pitchfork in the middle ground; and (possibly) a wooden clog at the right.

The ambiguity of the woman's action—is she seated or standing, kicking her leg to shoo away a pig, sifting or pitching hay, slumping forward in exhaustion?—is not explained by the drawings, made several weeks before in Brittany, upon which Gauguin based the composition (figs. 56–57). The artist may have devised the pose the model assumed in one of the drawings and in the final painting to suggest the activity of winnowing; in her left hand the woman grasps what may be the rim or handle of a winnow, an implement that Millet depicted as an attribute of Ceres, goddess of agriculture and symbol of summer (fig. 59). Possibly the visual clue is in fact a red herring, suggestive but not helpful in a composition that never allows the viewer to arrive at a definitive interpretation. Certainly Gauguin's figure is neither an idealized personification nor a convincing laborer. The image may play on the dual meaning of the French verb *vanner*—to winnow, or to tire out—the expression *être vanné(e)* meaning to be dead beat, exhausted. Overcome by her efforts and by the heat that has led her to remove her bodice, the woman wearily falls forward into a mound of hay. Gauguin here produced the iconographic (and literal) obverse of Millet's triumphantly bare-breasted, pregnant Ceres.

Gauguin would later exhibit the picture under the title *In the Heat (En pleine chaleur)*, suggesting that it treats the trials of physical labor. However, by insistently rhyming the curve of the woman's back with those of the pigs, Gauguin suggested something less than empathetic. In several earlier pictures (see ch. 2, fig. 34; ch. 3, fig. 3), he hinted at a similar comparison between Breton women and the gaggles of geese or herds of pigs and cows they tended, but here he dispelled any doubt of his intent with the title he assigned the work when he sent it to Theo in Paris: *The Pigs (Les Cochons)*.[118] This goes beyond the longstanding and ongoing urban disdain for Breton backwardness that led to an identification of the deeply superstitious peasantry with the animals they husbanded (see ch. 5, fig. 59).

Notable for its misogyny, Gauguin's picture is equally remarkable for the stylistic daring of its shallow pictorial space and abstracted forms. This parallel exaggeration in Gauguin's work of two tendencies, one characterological and the other formal, testifies to the dynamic in play in the Yellow House. If Gauguin fulfilled Vincent's longstanding wish—to find a friend of whom he could say *dat is het*, "that's it"—it was because of his dual prowess. "I am so fond of my friend Gauguin," Vincent would write, "because he has found the means of producing children and pictures at the same time." Now the object of intense admiration and high expectations, Gauguin was encouraged to rise to the occasion, to demonstrate the twin mastery of a Courbet. With *In the Heat* he performed this role in his pictorial daring—Vincent recognized its remarkable "grand style"—and in the sexualized theme implicit in Gauguin's drawings of the Breton model.[119] In one she presents herself (at the artist's instruction) bare-breasted, her uneasiness conveyed by her hand tensely gripping the chairback. In the other, dominance is suggested through the resemblance of the slumping pose to a figure from Delacroix's *Death of Sardanapalus* (fig. 58), one of the concubines put to the sword in the bloody last moments of the beseiged eastern potentate, intent on denying his enemies the spoils of their victory.[120] Gauguin's objectification of woman carries over to the painting, where it is reinforced by the coarse pairing with animals. *In The Heat* thus dovetailed with talk of Arlésiennes and conquest. The language the artist used to discuss it (together with *Human Miseries*) with Theo when shipping a batch of recent work to Paris around 22 November shows him posturing along these lines: "These two . . . canvases are I think virile enough, but a bit coarse, one might say; is it the southern sun that puts us in rut?" Vincent, complicit in this attitude, felt increasingly at ease in the company of a man he had come to consider a great artist

and friend. They were "very happy together," and he was open to Gauguin's example.[121]

Gauguin gave him courage to work without a model as well as the language with which to justify the attempt: "Canvases painted *de tête* are less awkward and have a more artistic look than studies from nature, especially when one works during the mistral."[122] Issues debated in past correspondence and recent practice were at stake here: painting ecstatically and quickly versus reflectively and deliberately; *plein-air* versus studio work; the *étude* versus the *tableau*. If Vincent had hoped that sharing a studio would help him to address these questions, the bad weather that descended on Arles in mid-November afforded the opportunity. He men-

tioned and sketched two paintings—*A Memory of the Garden* and *A Novel Reader* (figs. 67, 60)—but a depiction of spectators at a bullfight (fig. 54) probably preceded them.[123] Vincent had never fulfilled an ambition to depict this local spectacle, no doubt hampered by the impossibility of setting up his easel in the midst of the throngs, and Gauguin, who had expressed interest in doing so himself, arrived after the season's end. Now, in the studio on a gloomy November day, Vincent depicted the colorful, bustling crowd bathed in sunlight, evoking for his friend an Arles experience not to be repeated until the spring.

In *Spectators at the Arena*, Vincent more confidently deployed the loose, indirect technique

54

54
Vincent van Gogh
Spectators at the Arena
December 1888
[F 548, JH 1653]
Oil on canvas
73 x 92 cm

The State Hermitage Museum,
St. Petersburg

55
Paul Gauguin
In the Heat (The Pigs) (Les Cochons [En pleine chaleur])
November 1888
[W 301]
Oil on canvas
73 x 92 cm
Private collection

56
Paul Gauguin
Seated Model, Back View
Charcoal and body color/gouache
26.3 x 40 cm
Van Gogh Museum, Amsterdam
(Vincent van Gogh Foundation)

57
Paul Gauguin
Seated Model, Front View
1888
Charcoal and body color/gouache
26.3 x 40 cm
Private collection

55

56

57

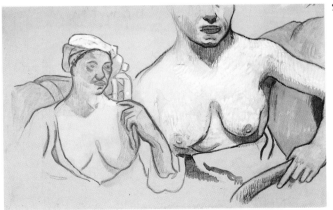

and caricatural style of *Brothel Scene*. He began by blocking in broad, abstract areas of blue, green, and white, without making the initial drawn or painted sketch upon which he typically based his compositions. He worked from the amorphous and general to the more specific, adding brightly colored costumes and embellishing them with parasols, hats, bow ties, and brooches, while allowing the abstract underlayers to play an active role. Foresaking his usual impasto, Vincent wiped off layers and reworked passages; for the arena floor, he applied yellow paint with a palette knife and then retextured it with a brush. Jaunty blue contour lines tie the picture together, tracing an array of generic types peppered with local characters: an Arlésienne resembling Madame Ginoux at center stage; directly to her right, the postal worker Joseph Roulin in profile, with his distinctive beard; and his wife, Augustine, wearing a red shawl and holding their new daughter, Marcelle, born on 31 July.[124]

Conveying a sense of the excitement fostered by the liberating potential of this new technique, the canvas is a masterpiece of sorts—yet Vincent never mentioned it in his letters. Admittedly, he was writing infrequently at this time, but his silence may also indicate that *Spectators at the Arena* meant less to him than the two other memory pictures that followed, which feature fewer but more imposing figures. *A Novel Reader* (fig. 60), a rendition of a staple subject of domestic genre painting,

exhibits something of the quirky graphic stylization seen in *Spectators*, but it is invested with deeper personal significance. As Vincent specified in a letter to Wil, the figure is "holding a yellow book in her hands."[125] That is, she reads one of the yellow-bound Naturalist novels published by Charpentier (see ch. 2), just as Vincent repeatedly advised his sister to do. A personal emblem of the modern artist's potential to realize a new gospel relevant to contemporary life, the yellow book had been the key to Vincent's admiration of Puvis's "consoling" portrait of an old man reading, and he had already included such volumes in several of his own symbolic still lifes (see ch. 1, fig. 3; ch. 2, fig. 71; ch. 3, fig. 52).

With *A Novel Reader*, Vincent effected a translation comparable to that suggested in the 1885 pairing of the yellow book and the Bible. His point of departure was Rembrandt's *Holy Family* (also known as *Reading the Bible*) (fig. 61), which had long been a touchstone: a reproduction of it hung in his Paris bedroom in 1875; seven years later he pinned the sheet to the wall of the studio that he shared with Sien Hoornik in The Hague; other copies were given to Theo and to his sister Anna. The image spoke to him of the joys and almost sacred nature of family life. But while he continued to admire the work for transcending its time and speaking to the present, he had come to feel that it lacked something of the "personal and intimate" qualities required of modern art.[126]

Placing a novel rather than the Bible in the hands of his reader, Vincent not only updated Rembrandt's picture of domesticity, but also intimated his persistent ambivalence about his religious upbringing and about his relations with his family, which had earlier provided the subtext of *Still Life with Bible and Zola's "Joie de vivre"* (ch. 1, fig. 3).

If Vincent was now thinking "more of Rembrandt than might appear from my studies," this was part of a larger reflection on the past. *A Memory of the Garden*, as he described it at different moments in mid-November, evokes the plots of land connected to the parsonages at both Etten and Nuenen, where the van Gogh family lived successively from 1875 until the reverend's death in 1885.[127] During this decade, Vincent lost his job at Goupil's, pursued various paths without success, and committed himself to art. He also became increasingly alienated from his family, and he had hoped to put this period behind him in leaving Holland.

But recently thoughts of home had preoccupied him. Late in September he had received a photograph of his mother that he welcomed as testifying to her apparent good health but found wanting as a likeness, its monochrome offputting. It made him wistful that he had never painted his parents' portraits, as he had intended to do in Nuenen. So in early October he undertook a portrait of his mother based on

58

59

58
Eugène Delacroix
*Death of
Sardanapalus*
(detail)
1827
Oil on canvas
Musée du Louvre,
Paris

59
Jean-François Millet
Ceres (Summer)
1864/65
Oil on canvas
266 x 134 cm
Musée des Beaux-
Arts, Bordeaux

60
Vincent van Gogh
*A Novel Reader (Une
Liseuse de romans)*
c. 16 November 1888
[F 497, JH 1632]
Oil on jute
73 x 92 cm
Sagawa Express Co.,
Ltd., Kyoto, Japan
Cat. 75

61
Rembrandt van Rijn
(Dutch; 1606–1669)
The Holy Family
1638/40
Oil on panel
60 x 77 cm
Rijksmuseum,
Amsterdam

60

61

58
Eugène Delacroix
*Death of
Sardanapalus*
(detail)
1827
Oil on canvas
Musée du Louvre,
Paris

59
Jean-François Millet
Ceres (Summer)
1864/65
Oil on canvas
266 x 134 cm
Musée des Beaux-
Arts, Bordeaux

60
Vincent van Gogh
*A Novel Reader (Une
Liseuse de romans)*
c. 16 November 1888
[F 497, JH 1632]
Oil on jute
73 x 92 cm
Sagawa Express Co.,
Ltd., Kyoto, Japan
Cat. 75

61
Rembrandt van Rijn
(Dutch; 1606–1669)
The Holy Family
1638/40
Oil on panel
60 x 77 cm
Rijksmuseum,
Amsterdam

the photograph (fig. 62), intending to depict her "as I see her in my memory" by means of a "harmony of color."[128] This envisioned harmony corresponds to that of his own *Self-Portrait (Bonze)* (ch. 3, fig. 73), with ashen gray and gray-pink flesh tones pitted against a similar green background; the shared chromatics declare a family affinity, as does Vincent's deployment of thick impasto that carries his imprint in each stroke. It was a kind of recuperative exercise that prompted him also to request a likeness of his father.[129]

The past, but an edited and reshaped past, is the subject of *A Memory of the Garden*. As Vincent elaborated to Wil, he intended the two figures that loom large in the foreground to be suggestive rather than speaking likenesses of her and their mother:

I know this is hardly what one might call a likeness, but for me it renders the poetic character and the style of the garden as I feel them. Similarly, let us suppose that the two ladies out for a walk are you and our mother; let us even suppose that there is not the least, absolutely not the least, vulgar and fatuous resemblance—the deliberate choice of color, the somber violet violently stained by the citron yellow of the dahlias, suggests mother's personality to me. The figure in the Scotch plaid with orange and green checks stands out against the somber green of the cypress, a contrast further exaggerated by the red parasol—this figure gives me an idea of you vaguely like a figure in Dickens's novels.[130]

Though Vincent evoked the prose of Dickens, he insisted that his aim here was to fashion poetry:

I don't know whether you can understand that one may create poetry solely by arranging colors, as one can say consoling things in music.
Similarly the bizarre lines, selected and multiplied, meandering through the picture,

may fail to give the garden a vulgar resemblance, but may present it to our minds as in a dream, depicting its character, and at the same time stranger than it is in reality.[131]

Subjectivity, dream, and consolation are familiar themes from Vincent's earlier discussions, but this outline of a visual poetics based on the language of line, form, and color seems forced. So too his profession of the virtue of "strangeness," which he reiterated in an observation to Theo that things done from the imagination "take on a more mysterious character." Such pronouncements lack the tone of conviction so tangible throughout Vincent's correspondence. In effect they echo Gauguin's vocabulary and concerns, like lessons learned by rote and parrotted back. Indeed Gauguin's so-called Turkish manual of 1885/86 contains a similar admonition: "It is best to paint from memory, then your work will be your own."[132]

A Memory of the Garden is a strangely literal application of this precept—the concept of painting from memory put in the service of a subject that involved a very specific set of personal recollections. Its essentially conflicted origins inflect the work's individual elements and the claims that the artist made about them. While decrying photographic description as vulgar, Vincent in fact only sidestepped the question of models here. There is a detectable resemblance between the older woman and the portrait of his mother, and though the second figure may look nothing like Wil (whom Vincent had not seen in three years), she does bear a strong likeness to Madame Ginoux as seen in *The Arlésienne* (fig. 37). A literal recollection of Nuenen, the stooping "servant" is a straightforward transposition of a Brabant peasant (fig. 64). The exaggerated S-curve of the path faintly echoes stretches of the Nuenen parsonage garden (fig. 66), but this memory was amplified by the view of place Lamartine across the street (see ch. 3, fig. 17). Certainly *A Memory of the Garden*, with its highly styl-

ized linear rhythms marked out by insistent contours, represents a new direction in Vincent's work. But in attempting to empty his representations of resemblance to individual people and places, he simply displaced older memories in favor of more recent ones.

A Memory of the Garden seems a willful demonstration of what Vincent risked when painting *de tête*. He had come to understand that working quickly before a natural motif allowed him to render reality as subjectively experienced and, in a psychic parallel, allowed him to lose self-consciousness through total immersion in his activity. Working from the imagination foreclosed this escape and, in a sense, reversed it. Untethered in the reality of

62

63

the here-and-now, no longer focused by chang-ing weather conditions or a human presence, Vincent's mind could drift. The effort of exe-cuting *A Memory of the Garden* led him deeper into rather than out of himself. Painful recol-lections of the North—the thoughts of acquain-tances and family that overly affected him and that he had expressly tried to forget in Arles—surfaced.[133] If painting quickly, in a rush, afforded ecstatic glimpses of eternity, painting from the imagination led in the opposite direction, to memories of the parsonage gardens he associated with his personal Gethsemane.

Emotional pitfalls were inextricably entwined with creative ones. Painting from (and in) nature not only served to channel Vincent's energies, but it also imposed temporal restric-tions, making the act of painting a race against time. The changing weather or the fading flower ensured a kind of closure: Vincent had to finish the picture before its subject altered. Moreover, as he had realized long before, working in this way distracted him from fun-damental anxieties of authorship:

Just dash something down when you see a blank canvas staring you in the face with a certain imbecility.
    You do not know how paralyzing that star-ing of a blank canvas is; it says to the painter, *You can't do anything.* The canvas stares at you like an idiot, and it hypnotizes some painters, so that they themselves become idiots. Many painters are afraid of the blank canvas, but the blank canvas is afraid of the really pas-sionate painter who is daring—and who has once and for all broken that spell of "you can-not."[134]

This spell that Vincent yearned so constant-ly to break is Carlyle's "everlasting Nay," iterated throughout the artist's life by such figures as his father, other family members, and his former manager at Goupil's, Tersteeg (see ch. 1).

Reliance on the imagination entailed no such motivations, parameters, or protections; without a natural terminus, Vincent could go on—and on and on—never being quite sure whether or not the picture was finished; re-fining, reworking, and generally worrying it to death. Zola chronicled this obsessiveness, uncertainty, and corrosive doubt with painful vividness in *L'Oeuvre.* Vincent had tasted something of this, in varying degrees, with his June *Sower* (ch. 3, fig. 26) and with his *Geth-semanes.* Similar problems beset *A Memory of the Garden.*

In contrast to the loose abandon with which he painted *Spectators at the Arena,* Vincent from the beginning approached *A Memory of the Garden* with more compulsive care; his manner was far from the "simple technique" he advocated when painting the *Sunflowers* (see ch. 3). He followed Gauguin's preparatory methods exactly, establishing a dark-blue sketch and then a highly worked underpainting in pale blues and greens. He then proceeded laboriously to build up thick layers of stiff paint, using short brush strokes of intensely con-trasting colors. The two women's faces are smoother in appearance than their surround-ings; rendered with more fluid paint in somber, gray tones, they seem to float through the surreal landscape setting.

As in other works painted from memory, adjustments and changes were part of the painting's evolution. Microscopic examination reveals that in an earlier state, the painting corresponded more closely to a letter sketch sent to Wil (fig. 65): the older woman's silhou-ette was slimmer and her wrist exposed, the younger woman's shoulder lower and her head and coiffure smaller, the edge of the umbrella rounded, the servant's hips wider, the foreground flowers sparser, the sunflowers simple orbs, the older woman's shawl and the servant's dress modeled without stippling. The changes lie buried in the carefully elabo-

rated surface that, while heavily impastoed, lacks the gestural quality of Vincent's typical brushwork. Developed in layers over time, *Memory*'s thick surface has a somewhat labored, mechanical appearance. The dots of paint—possibly applied directly from the tubes—in fact evoke the time-consuming pointillist proce-dure that Vincent had rejected as insufficient-ly expressive. While the strong, flowing pat-tern of the marks distinguishes them from the rationality of Neo-Impressionist facture, the work nonetheless suggests that Vincent once again saw himself—as in Paris—submitting to a course in a painting style not his own.

Vincent conceived *A Memory of the Garden* as a poem of consolation to hang in his bedroom, along with the symbolic portraits *The Poet* and *The Lover* (figs. 32–33). The sunflowers to the right of the bright yellow dahlias, defined late in the picture's evolution, invoke the hopes tied to the work's realization and to Gauguin's approval of it. This flower, already emblematic of their exchange, had accrued another layer of signifance when Gauguin avowed prefer-ring Vincent's *Sunflowers* to a magisterial still life of the same subject by Monet (fig. 63). Vincent began *A Memory of the Garden* in the first half of November. In early December he reported that he had spoiled it.[135] This failure spoke to the larger failure that occurred in the three intervening weeks.

64

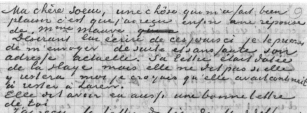

65

66

64
Vincent van Gogh
*Peasant Woman,
Stooping and Gleaning*
July 1885
[F 1279, JH 836]
Black chalk
51.5 x 45 cm
Museum Folkwang,
Essen, Germany

65
Vincent van Gogh
Sketch of *A Memory
of the Garden (Etten
and Nuenen)* in letter
to Wil
[c. 16 November
1888]
(letter 725/W 9, JH
1631)
Van Gogh Museum,
Amsterdam
(Vincent van Gogh
Foundation)
Cat. 76

66
Vincent van Gogh
*The Garden at the
Vicarage at Nuenen*
March 1884
[F 1128, JH 466]
Graphite, pen and
brown ink
40.3 x 54.6 cm
Van Gogh Museum,
Amsterdam
(Vincent van Gogh
Foundation)

67
Vincent van Gogh
*A Memory of the
Garden (Etten and
Nuenen)*
c. 16 November 1888
[F 496, JH 1630]
Oil on canvas
73.5 x 92.5 cm
The State
Hermitage Museum,
St. Petersburg

68
Detail of fig. 67

Sunday	Monday	Tuesday	Wednesday	Thursday	Friday	Saturday
18 Nov ☁	**19** ⛅	**20** ☁	**21** ☀	**22** ☀ Gauguin ships five paintings to Paris ✉ Gauguin to Schuffenecker	**23** ☀ ✉ Vincent to Theo	**24** ☀ Ball at the Folies-Arlésiennes ✉ Gauguin to Schuffenecker
			✉ Gauguin to Bernard			

25 ⛅
✉ Vincent to Theo
✉ Gauguin to Octave Maus

Gauguin "Still Life with Pumpkin," now lost

By around 18 November, signs of trouble had manifested themselves—if not openly acknowledged, at least confided in letters. Later that week Vincent reported to Theo that, since he was beginning to "compose *de tête*," his earlier studies from nature would prove useful documents, helping him recall things he had seen. *A Memory of the Garden* shows him proceeding in precisely this way. "Documents" was a term that Gauguin habitually employed to designate work on paper or canvas resulting from pictorial fact-finding carried out in the field. Such preliminary material served in the off-site, studio-based task of creating the synthetic statement that is the *tableau*. Vincent, who had imagined that he could make similar use of his studies with the encouragement of a companion (see ch. 3), allowed that he benefited from Gauguin's "intelligent company" and from seeing him work. Yet the way he characterized his move in a new direction is revealing: "Gauguin, in spite of himself and in spite of me, has more or less indicated to me that it is time for me to vary my style a little bit."[136] The double "in spite of" and the qualified "more or less" speak volumes about his resistance to Gauguin's suggestions and about the attendant arguments to which he obliquely alluded in the rest of the letter.

Gauguin spoke more directly on this score, at least when confiding to Bernard. Fed up with Arles, he felt out of his element and found both the people and the landscape "slight, mean." And the debates—the *wrijving*—that for Vincent were the hallmark of an active, committed friendship seemed scarcely negotiable:

In general Vincent and I do not see eye to eye, especially as regards painting. He admires Daudet, Daubigny, Ziem, and the great Rousseau, all men I cannot stand. And on the other hand, he detests Ingres, Raphael, Degas, all men I admire; I answer "Sergeant, you're right," so that I can have peace. He likes my

Oct						
	1	2	3	4	5	6
7	8	9	10	11	12	13
14	15	16	17	18	19	20
21	22	23	24	25	26	27
28	29	30	31			

Nov						
				1	2	3
4	5	6	7	8	9	10
11	12	13	14	15	16	17
18	**19**	**20**	**21**	**22**	**23**	**24**
25	26	27	28	29	30	

Dec						
						1
2	3	4	5	6	7	8
9	10	11	12	13	14	15
16	17	18	19	20	21	22
23	24	25	26	27	28	29
30	31					

paintings very much, but when I paint them, he always finds that I have made mistakes here and there. He is a romantic and I am rather inclined to a primitive state. As far as color is concerned, he favors the accidents of impasto as in Monticelli, and I detest messing with brushwork.[137]

Designating Vincent a romantic, Gauguin raised current issues regarding modern practice and threw into serious question whether he and his friend were in fact on the same track. Romanticism was of course the fatal weakness that *L'Oeuvre*'s Sandoz had diagnosed in the Impressionist generation, the characterological root of Claude Lantier's failure. In Neo-Impressionist discourse, it had become an oppositional term: the romantic impressionism of Monet and his followers set against their own scientific practice (see ch. 2). While Gauguin repudiated the movement's analytical pretensions, he shared the Neo-Impressionists' disdain for the obtrusive, gestural mark-making articulated by Fénéon in a June review of Monet's recent work on display at Theo's gallery:

Claude Monet is a spontaneous painter. The word "Impressionist" was created for him and suits him better than anyone else. He is moved suddenly by a sight, but there is nothing contemplative or analytical in him. Thanks to an excessively bravura execution, an improviser's fecundity, and a brilliant vulgarity, his fame grows.[138]

Gauguin's critique of Vincent rested on the same basis. He found substantiation in Vincent's dislike of Raphael, Ingres, and Degas, a trio of painters who—in the traditional aesthetic debate about the relative virtues of line versus color—stood for analysis over spontaneity; controlled contour over excessive, actively brushed color; rationality over emotion; and, according to contemporary formulations proposed by writers such as Charles Blanc, masculinity over femininity.[139]

Gauguin, in his attempt to pioneer a modern, masculine style free of Impressionist gesture, also kept his distance from Neo-Impressionism's impersonal petit point. Trying to forge a different path altogether, Gauguin embraced imagination and mysticism—the pernicious hallmarks of Romanticism repudiated by Sandoz—but evaded its anguished soul searching.[140] In ways that paralleled the Neo-Impressionists' purported scientific approach, he advocated rational process, but heavily bolstered by intuition. In other words he looked forward by looking backward—far back, beyond post-Enlightenment subjectivity to times when the real and the imagined, the visible and the invisible, were bedfellows rather than estranged partners.

Gauguin performed this primitive sensibility in both *In the Heat* and *Human Miseries*, achievements that seemed all the more dramatic when, in mid-November, a picture that Gauguin had painted five months earlier arrived in the studio. Theo had shipped *Breton Girls Dancing* (ch. 3, fig. 21), the sale of which he had announced in late October, so that Gauguin could make minor adjustments, requested by the purchaser, to the area at the left where the outstretched hand nears the canvas's edge. Though Vincent quite liked the earlier picture (now of course seeing it for the first time), he recognized Gauguin's two new works to be "thirty times better"—so innovative was their impastoed yet non-gestural execution that he imagined people would soon be "reproaching Gauguin with no longer being an impressionist."[141]

Vincent countered Gauguin's example, in effect a critique of his own work, in a typically oblique manner. After acknowledging how much he had learned from Gauguin and how ready he was to contemplate change, he gave vent to an outburst: His work would improve, Theo ought to be patient, and they both should

calmly leave our comrades to despise the current [canvases]. Fortunately for me, I know ~~better~~ well enough what I want, and am basically utterly indifferent to the criticism that I work too hurriedly.

In answer to that, I have done some things *even more* hurriedly these last few days.[142]

The unnamed comrades can only be Gauguin, possibly along with anyone else who may have seen the pictures that Vincent sent to Paris in May and August.[143]

Vincent had a history of becoming ornery when faced with opposition. Theo characterized him as one "unable *not* to remark on" what he viewed as wrongheaded, sparing nothing and no one in his outspokenness.[144] But it was another thing to be on the receiving end of criticism. In his all-or-nothing approach to friendship, he demanded shared commitment to intensely held convictions and anticipated no deviation from them. He fiercely resisted teachers, family members, and friends who counseled him to change his behavior or his work (see ch. 1). "I should be acting contrary to my conviction," he had replied when in 1882 Theo proposed that he execute his drawings on a smaller scale. In The Hague he sought, then angrily dismissed, Tersteeg's advice when it ran counter to his thinking. Most dramatically he went into a rage when van Rappard attempted to tell him some "home truths" with regard to *The Potato Eaters*: "I *myself* am the one to tell me some home truths." The issue, always, was authenticity, the need to "paint what I feel and feel what I paint." To criticize his painting was to criticize him; negative opinions were tantamount to physical assault, "as though people were touching my body, . . . so much is my conviction a part of myself."[145]

Whereas Vincent literally defaced a portrait he had drawn of van Rappard (1885; Van Gogh Museum, Amsterdam) and broke with him

69
Vincent van Gogh
Van Gogh's Chair
c. 20 November 1888
[F 498, JH 1635]
Oil on jute
93 x 73.5 cm
The National
Gallery, London
Cat. 77

70
S. Luke Fildes
(English; 1844–1927)
*The Empty Chair,
Gad's Hill—Ninth of
June 1870* from
The Graphic
(Christmas 1870)

71
Vincent van Gogh
Gauguin's Chair
c. 20 November 1888
[F 499, JH 1636]
Oil on jute
90.5 x 72 cm
Van Gogh Museum,
Amsterdam
(Vincent van Gogh
Foundation)
Cat. 78

utterly, now—more sure of himself and more admiring of Gauguin—he demonstrated his resistance to his friend's criticism in a pair of pictures addressing their relationship. One features "*a chair*, wooden and rushbottomed, all yellow on red tiles against a wall (daytime)" (fig. 69); the other, "Gauguin's armchair red and green, night effect, walls and floor red and green also, on the seat two novels and a candle" (fig. 71).[146] These works, which can be seen as displaced portraits, are iconographic opposites (and chromatic complements). The rushbottomed seat, its habitual occupant identified by the prominent signature on the side of an

adjacent wooden box, was one of the twelve chairs that Vincent had acquired in September (see ch. 3). Initially Vincent left the chair and the box empty, later adding the pipe and tobacco to the former and the onions to the latter.[147] With few elements, seen in even, natural light, Vincent achieved an overall "Daumier" effect of simplicity. The yellow and blue color chord harmonizes with that of *The Yellow House* (ch. 3, fig. 71), emblem of all the ambitions associated with the Studio of the South. By contrast, the red and green palette and gaslight illumination employed for Gauguin's chair strike the opposite note, that of Vin-

cent's *Night Café* (fig. 40), a representation of the complex nocturnal realm of the passions.

Both chair portraits are set in the studio, but Vincent composed and executed them differently. He placed his own chair by the door leading from the front room into the kitchen, and took greater pains with shading, detail, and nuances of brushwork. In some areas around the edges of forms, however, he left the jute support exposed; unmasked by the virtually indiscernible barium sulfate ground, the coarse fabric contributes to a rustic effect. By contrast, Vincent painted Gauguin's chair broadly, over the thicker lead white ground with which both artists now began experimenting; the forms appear more synthetic and the space less familiar. Vincent exaggerated the reflection and refraction of gaslight on the uneven red tiles of the floor, which almost takes on the appearance of an exotic carpet; lowered the lamp and bracket for compositional balance; and rendered the whitewashed wall in dark green in order to introduce the complementary contrast central to the picture's signifying intention.[148]

Vincent had acquired the armchair along with the initial dozen and specifically for the guest bedroom, early identified as Gauguin's; its curvaceous lines were in keeping with the room that Vincent aimed to decorate as a "boudoir of a really artistic woman" (see ch. 3). Thus associated with refinement and desire, it was the chair in which Madame Ginoux sat for her portrait session. In effect the thirteenth chair symbolically belonged to the abbot, the head of the studio, and the objects that Vincent set upon it from the outset—a "lighted candle and some modern novels"—vividly emblematize the idealized status accorded its occupant. Vincent had not paired the yellow-jacketed novel (a now-familiar symbol of his artistic ambition) with a candle since his still life of

71

1885 (ch. 1, fig. 3). In that early manifesto image, the candle directly and oppositionally associated with his father is extinguished, alluding to the reverend's recent death and suggesting the inability of his religion to shed light on the experience of modern life. Here the lit candle's symbolic significance as a source of illumination—art providing what his father's church could not—is underscored by its functional irrelevance in a room bathed in gaslight.[149]

These metaphoric portraits have been convincingly linked to Vincent's early enthusiasm for *The Empty Chair* (fig. 70), Luke Fildes's tribute to Dickens, published in *The Graphic* shortly after the author's death in 1870. For Vincent, who acquired a copy of the print in The Hague, this image of the desk where the writer would sit no more concretized his construction of the original *Graphic* illustrators as a brotherhood, its members committed to shared social purpose: when "strong enough to stand on its own feet, the Graphic rented a house" that became a site of an enterprise he considered "holy . . . noble. . . sublime." Even in 1882, when Vincent still cherished dreams of joining ranks with these heroes, he saw the ideal vanishing: "Empty chairs—there are many of them, there will be even more, and sooner or later there will be nothing but empty chairs in place of Herkomer, Luke Fildes, . . . etc." Already their successors in *The Graphic*'s pages had left the "narrow path."[150]

Thus Fildes's print assumed the status of an article of faith; Vincent tried to procure copies for van Rappard and others with whom he sought communion.[151] Six years later, in Arles, the dream of filling new chairs in a new house had not changed, and now everything was literally in a state of readiness. His decision to paint the chairs without sitters thus seems remarkable, especially in light of his earlier chiding of Gauguin and Bernard for not having painted each other's portraits in Pont-Aven. Bernard had confessed his inability to produce

a portrait of Gauguin, whose talent intimidated him; Vincent's picture of *Gauguin's Chair*, its occupant invisible, recalls this dynamic. In their making the pendants asserted the painter's identity; in their iconography they speak to his doubts about his own practice, effectively reiterating his earlier self-deprecating litany contrasting his crude simplicity with Gauguin's refinement (see ch. 3).

These perceived contrasts surfaced in Vincent's response to an invitation, passed on by Theo, to exhibit his work at the headquarters of the vanguard periodical *La Revue indépendante*. In early September he had responded favorably to Theo's idea that he do so, but now he informed his brother that he had changed his mind and was dead set against showing his pictures in what he called a black hole run by scoundrels. He ventured that Gauguin shared his opinion, but made a point of adding that his friend was making no attempt to influence him. Of course Vincent was acutely aware that Gauguin hated the periodical as a mouthpiece of Neo-Impressionism and believed that it was poised to launch a propaganda campaign against "us, the others": Degas, Gauguin himself, Bernard, and so forth.[152] Gauguin relished (and had extensive experience with) this aspect of the artistic struggle. He gleefully shared with friends his rejection of the *Revue indépendante*'s invitation to show his Martinique canvases. Fénéon had called him a "grièche artiste"; he decided to deserve the denomination, insolently turning the *Revue*'s words back on itself. With heavy-handed irony he declared that he must decline since he felt his work insufficient—lacking the requisite luminosity and keenness of observation—to the Neo-Impressionist standard of progressive modernity. Although Vincent hated this kind of factionalism, he joined Gauguin in demonizing the operation and instructed Theo, who had clearly procured the invitation, to reject it.[153]

Following Gauguin's lead alleviated Vincent's own anxieties in this case. He had been skittish about the prospect of an exhibition from the outset. To be sure, he had shown his work publicly before, notably in the Petit Boulevard display that he organized in late 1887, and again in the spring of 1888, when he allowed Theo to send *Parisian Novels* (ch. 2, fig. 71) and two Montmartre landscapes to the fourth Indépendants exhibition. Critical response was sparse, but in a review of the Indépendants, Gustave Kahn had taken exception to the still life: the subject was fine for a "study" but hardly a worthy pretext for a "painting." Hence Vincent's concern in September that Theo make it clear to the exhibition organizers at *La Revue indépendante* that he could only send *études*; it would be a year before he would be ready to show fully developed compositions, or *tableaux*.[154] After two months with Gauguin, reticence had solidified into outright stage fright.

Despite—or rather owing to—having essayed *tableaux* in the studio together with Gauguin, he felt less ready than ever. He panicked at the thought that Theo might show one of his spring orchard pictures to his gallery bosses. As strongly as he dared, given his indebtedness and previous obsession with selling, he urged Theo: "Sell none of it now." He asked his brother to return his *études*—especially the "bad" ones—so he could use them as fodder for more ambitious works. Having sent nothing to Paris since August, he expressed regret that, despite having filled a room with canvases, he still had nothing of his own to include with the shipment of five pictures (*Breton Girls Dancing*, *Les Alyscamps* [*The Three Graces*], *Night Café*, *Human Miseries*, and *In the Heat*) that Gauguin dispatched toward the end of the week. As for showing his work in the capital, Vincent demurred—it would be a year or two before he had the thirty size 30s necessary for an exhibition. In likewise deferred terms, he imagined coming into his own. Lest Theo

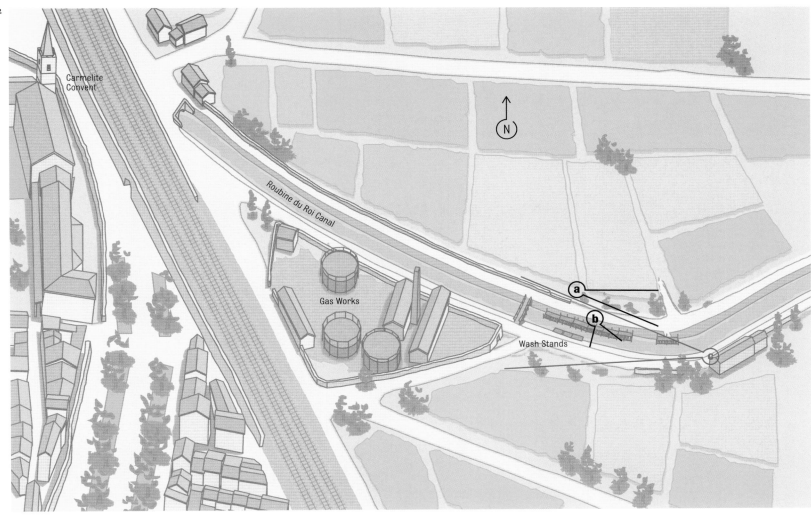

Carmelite Convent

Roubine du Roi Canal

N

Gas Works

Wash Stands

a

b

c

think that Gauguin's praise for the *Sunflowers* had weakened his resolve to paint portraits, Vincent reaffirmed his ambition. All that had changed was his target date: "If at the age of forty I have done a picture of figures like the flowers of which Gauguin spoke, I shall have a position in art equal to that of anyone, no matter who."[155]

The "who" in question was Gauguin, recently turned forty. Vincent, at thirty-five, had five years to redress the night-and-day differences between them. "At the age of forty," he would have produced expressive figure pictures "worth more than a more or less serious success at present." Certainly the success of Gauguin's recent work contributed to Vincent's self-doubt. Gauguin had hit his stride. He now tackled a subject familiar to him from Vincent's drawings (fig. 73): washerwomen at the Roubine du Roi canal (fig. 75).[156] In pointed contrast to Vincent, Gauguin virtually abol-

ished perspective, creating a shallow, claustrophobic space; subsumed brush strokes in pattern; and delineated figures that loom large in proportion to the visual field. Even when compared with other representations and photographs of the site (fig. 74 and map, fig. 72), Gauguin's picture remains somewhat difficult to decipher: we are looking down from the canal's steep embankment at a platform extending out onto the water, its surface obscured at the right by what seems to be a flaming-red bush; the white-and-green foreground patterning can be recognized as laundry laid out on the grass to dry. Emphatically asymmetrical, its volumetric forms flattened into decorative shapes, *Washerwomen* was Gauguin's most daring composition to date. On the one hand, he gave the figures a prominence that indeed recalls the *Négresses*, fulfilling Vincent's expectations; on the other, he significantly advanced and demonstrated his own goal of abstraction.

Meanwhile, earlier in November, Theo had received a shipment of Pont-Aven pictures, which Gauguin had sent to Paris before leaving for Arles. He did not conceal his admiration, declaring that the canvases resonated with the same "strange poetry" as the *Négresses* and, because of their subjects, were even more accessible. Theo's attempts to evoke for family and friends how and why Gauguin's work moved him so profoundly (see quote, fig. 76) reveal his keen sensitivity to the artist's symbolist aims. Drawing an analogy between the language of painting and that of music, Theo described Gauguin's art of suggestion—evoking the responses that nature produces rather than describing nature itself. For Theo, Gauguin surpassed Monet insofar as his art spoke of consolation; he promised to be like Millet, to become the next great artist-preacher (see ch. 2).[157]

Theo was not alone in his admiration. After restretching and framing some of the canvases,

Fig. 82

Fig. 83

Fig. 73

73

74

12 – ARLES – La Toubize

he had exhibited them at Boussod et Valadon. On 13 November he wrote to inform Gauguin that he had sold two, making the artist some six hundred francs richer. He also conferred an even greater accolade. The "great Degas," whose opinion Theo so clearly esteemed, "is such an admirer of your work that he talks about it with everyone" and was planning to buy one of the spring pictures.[158]

Gauguin's spirits soared. He boasted to Bernard that the prospect of Degas purchasing a work was "the greatest flattery"; after all, he had always had "the utmost confidence in Degas's

judgment." Witness to this celebratory mood, Vincent may have expressed reservations—Gauguin had already made note of his "detesting" Degas—but this did not take the wind out of Gauguin's sails. The Impressionist master's interest did much to dispel his memories of past humiliations and to open a prospect onto a sunnier future. He wrote asking Schuffenecker to forward his two Degas etchings (see Coda, fig. 27), and he asked Theo to tell Degas how flattered he was by his praise. He wanted to know the names and addresses of the other buyers, and he began a list of those who owned his work.[159]

The week of 18 November now brought Gauguin still more balm for his ego, an invitation from Octave Maus, founding secretary of the Brussels-based international exhibiting society Les Vingt (The Twenty), to participate in their next show. As Gauguin observed to Schuffenecker, Les Vingt had on two occasions included works by Neo-Impressionists (Seurat and Pissarro in 1887; Signac and Albert Dubois-Pillet in 1888) but had acted as if Gauguin did not exist. Moreover Maus, also coeditor of the influential periodical *L'Art moderne*, was one of the reviewers who in 1886 had misidentified Gauguin as an Impressionist apprentice new-

73
Vincent van Gogh
Washerwoman at the Roubine du Roi Canal
c. 17 July 1888
[F 1444, JH 1507]
Reed pen and ink on wove paper
31.5 x 24 cm

Kröller-Müller Museum, Otterlo, The Netherlands
Cat. 59

74
Postcard of washboards along the Roubine du Roi canal, c. 1895/1925

75
Paul Gauguin
Washerwomen at the Roubine du Roi Canal
Late November 1888
[W 303]
Oil on jute
73 x 92 cm
Museo de Bellas Artes de Bilbao, Spain
Cat. 41

comer (see ch. 2). Relishing his imminent vindication, Gauguin now vowed to mount "a serious exhibition in opposition to the petit point." He wondered whether his disapproving sister, Marie, had gotten wind of his success.[160]

Brimming with optimism, confident and combative, Gauguin flexed his muscles for "the big battle," biding his time until he had the wherewithal to launch his attack on "Signac and Co." Among the pictures he sent to Theo from Arles, he considered *Human Miseries* and *In the Heat* as potent ammunition, and he directed Schuffenecker to go see them. As if to update his friends on the artistic persona behind these achievements, he sent out a recent photograph of his "savage countenance" (fig. 105). With admitted arrogance, he outlined his campaign. For the moment he would follow a regimen: "Hygiene and coitus—these matters settled, and working independently, a man can manage." He advised the despondent Schuffenecker, who had failed even to procure an invitation to show at *La Revue indépendante*: "Calm yourself, eat well, fuck well, ditto for work, and you will die happy."[161] This rough translation of his own prescription might have gratified Vincent were it not for the undeniable fact that Gauguin had long-term plans incompatible with his own.

Vincent stiffly stated to Theo: "I am very glad of Gauguin's success in the matter of continuous sales." But as Gauguin's fortunes waxed, Vincent's confidence waned. Nonetheless he clung to his hopes for the future. Even while he retrenched—deferring assessment of his oeuvre until age forty—he actively formulated a strategy in which Gauguin's good fortune would enable him to settle old scores with his nemesis Tersteeg. His idea, as he explained it to Theo, was to send Jet Mauve a letter filled with sketches and news of Gauguin's recent accomplishments, counting on the fact that the buzz would reach Tersteeg's ears, ultimately validating the Studio of the South enterprise.

Interestingly Vincent did not find it contradictory to state, in this same letter, that if Gauguin "could succeed in founding a tropical studio, it would be magnificent."[162]

Vincent was naturally enthusiastic about a "Studio of the Tropics," for the idea was his, fostered by his imaginative response to Gauguin. Gauguin's descriptions of exotic equatorial regions prompted Vincent to embellish and extend geographically his fantasy of pioneering a great renaissance of painting in the South. To the degree that he entertained an actual location, he had in mind Dutch colonial possessions in the East and West Indies (a rough parallel to Gauguin's focus on French-governed territories). He imagined young Dutch painters like Jacob Meyer de Haan and J. J. Isaacson—both now close to Theo in Paris—founding a "colorist school" in Java; he was sure they would wish to go there immediately if they heard Gauguin's stories. Vincent, deeming himself too old to put to sea, would remain in "the little yellow house," which would serve as "a way station between Africa, the Tropics, and the people of the North."[163] For Vincent a Studio of the Tropics was essentially a metaphor rather than a place:

We haven't arrived at any conclusion yet, nor have we set foot on a new continent.

As for myself—with my premonition of a new world, my firm belief in the possibility of a boundless renaissance in art, my belief that this new art will have the tropics for a home—it seems to me that we ourselves will serve as no more than intermediaries. And that it will be the next generation which will succeed in living in peace.[164]

The fantasy had mythic lineaments: like John the Baptist, Vincent would herald a new artistic testament; like Moses, he would lead the way to a promised land that he himself could not enter.

With talk of a Studio of the Tropics, Vincent attempted to involve Gauguin in his idea of an association of painters bound together by shared ideological and commercial interests; Gauguin's personal history suggested the scenario and seemed to implicate him in its realization. And Vincent's formulation did capture his friend's imagination; from the start Gauguin was clearly as intrigued by Vincent's picture of the future (based on Gauguin's sketches of his own past) as he was by those on his easel. But as a means of recruiting Gauguin to his way of thinking, it backfired.

The two men conceptualized a Studio of the Tropics with overlapping but ultimately different ends. Each listened to the other selectively, selfishly, and to a degree uncomprehendingly. In Vincent's case the *wrijving* that he found so stimulating presumed shared predispositions. Cultural background, personal history, and temperament—his worldview, colored by intense hopes, supporting beliefs, and attendant idealization—conspired to make him deaf to Gauguin's tone and intentions. Gauguin in turn was baffled by what he would describe as the "utter contradiction between [Vincent's] painting and his critical opinions." Despite their differences, Gauguin found Vincent's art compelling, certainly much more so than that of the figures with whom Vincent aligned himself. From a later perspective, it was all too expedient for Gauguin to ascribe Vincent's passion for Monticelli and reservations about Ingres, Degas, and Cézanne to a "disordered brain" and "absence of reasoned logic."[165] Vincent had in fact thought longer and harder about art, arriving at more definite ideas, than had Gauguin.

Gauguin felt the force if not the substance of Vincent's convictions. His inability to perceive the consistency of these beliefs is understandable: they were complex and, after years of mostly solitary reflection, Vincent

76
Paul Gauguin
The Aven River at Pont-Aven
Fall 1888 [W 253]
Oil on canvas
72 x 93 cm
Private collection
Cat. 34

Do you know, there are paintings that are very much like music. There is a Gauguin [fig. 76] at the firm that affects me in the same way as a beautiful symphony. A dead beech, whose leaves have prematurely turned reddish orange, stands in a hilly landscape full of trees in their resplendent foliage. That particular tree is in the center of the picture beside a moss-covered hut, forming, as it were, a magnificent plume; the deep bluish and violet shadows of the full trees stand out against the orange, like two melodies in counterpoint. The orange harmonizes with the rich variety of browns and havannahs in the tilled fields, hard roads cutting through the woods and vanishing in the distance in the hills that rise up to the sky. The blues and violets are echoed in unusual shades of green and fade in parts into the blue of the sky above. A white cloud, a couple of peasant women in pale blue costumes, a verdant meadow in the foreground, add a few eye-catching tones which, like little melodies, relieve the counterpoint of the instruments.

A musician who felt about this painting the way I do would be able to give each color the name of an instrument and make a musical composition of it. There is nothing material in the picture, yet it captures a moment when everything in nature is alive and burgeoning. The strange combination of colors transforms the dead tree into a patch of brightness and where life is most intense one finds the saddest colors of mourning.   Theo to Jo, 27 January 1889

unleashed them in overwhelming torrents. In Arles Gauguin learned to understand Vincent's allusive way of thinking; forced to defend his own positions, he developed them further. Vincent's extension of their mission to faraway lands facilitated the evolution of his savage persona in a direction that distanced him from current Parisian versions of primitivism.

Engaged but somewhat unnerved by the impact of Vincent's personality, Gauguin cannily approached him in the way he suggested facing an erratic fencing opponent: "You must have very irregular and unexpected movements in order to make your adversary believe you are about to do something quite different from what you intend."[166] Thus, when Vincent linked his dream of an "association of certain painters" with fantasies of a renaissance in the tropics, Gauguin assented, but only partially and strictly in the first person:

[Vincent's] idea about the future of a new generation of painters in the tropics seems absolutely correct, and I am still thinking about going back there when I have the resources. Who knows, with a little luck?[167]

Carried away, Vincent avidly discussed plans for Gauguin's return to Martinique, which eventual sales would allow "say in a year."[168] However, the possibility of Gauguin's actually leaving seemed no more real to Vincent than did the prospect of de Haan and Isaacson—neither of whom he had even met—going to Java on his advice.

Vincent's ideas were infectious. By the second week of November, Gauguin had clearly taken them on:

[Theo] Van Gogh hopes to sell all of my paintings. If I am so lucky, I will go to Martinique; I am convinced that now I will paint beautiful things there. And if I get a large sum I will even buy a house there in which to establish a studio where friends could find an easy life for next to nothing.[169]

Gauguin endorsed the plan to return to the tropics on his own terms, which were rooted less in ideology than in the market potential of new subject matter. "I agree a little bit with Vincent," he wrote to Bernard, "the future belongs to painters who depict the tropics, which have not yet been painted, and we need some new motifs for the stupid buying public."[170]

Sales in the short term only fueled the fire. Richer by 1,100 francs since arriving in Arles—more money than he had seen at once since his days at the Bourse—and with the promise of more to come, Gauguin's thoughts immediately turned to leaving. With Theo he outlined his plans in a manner designed to ensure the dealer's continued support. Lest he appear to threaten the Arles arrangement only recently put in place, Gauguin talked of saving enough to leave in one year's time; he characterized his ambition (to paint "nude and clothed *négresses*, etc.") in terms of the van Gogh brothers' admiration; and he further echoed Vincent's vision of the South-as-Daudet when he attributed his desire to do so to the fact that "this infernal southern sun forces you always to concoct schemes." With Schuffenecker he spoke more bluntly, forecasting that next year he would capitalize on the market's need for new motifs and stating his conviction that "the move would secure his future."[171] And it was at this point that he expressed his dissatisfaction with Arles—and Vincent—to Bernard.

As Gauguin's idea of a voyage to the tropics crystallized, Vincent's malaise grew. His airy reference to the chair portraits as "quite amusing" belies the intensity of the emotion invested in them. Even as Vincent painted the chairs, he intuited the possibility of Gauguin's departure: hence his hope, expressed to Theo, that even if Gauguin succeeded in founding a studio in the tropics, the brothers would always remain connected to him through friendship and business. As though to test Gauguin, Vincent fixated on financial aspects, questioning his friend's calculations of the

costs involved. Gauguin reckoned that he had half the two thousand francs he needed to embark on the adventure; but Vincent insisted on a five-thousand franc minimum for the fulfillment of his own version of the scheme, which focused on taking others along to establish "a permanent studio."[172] It was one thing for Gauguin to sanction his mission; it was another for him actually to leave. His dreams threatened, Vincent could not let the matter go. To buy peace, Gauguin feigned acquiescence with the reposte "Sergeant, you're right," echoing a junior policeman in a popular ditty who pays lip service to everything his superior says. Vincent, who predicated friendship on honest communication, must have found this insolent appeasement infuriating.

The chair paintings, while referencing an ideal of joint purpose, speak to Vincent's personal experience. His attempt to negotiate his identity in a relationship with someone he idealized, whose approval he sought, and who proffered instruction that went against the grain revived painful memories: attempting to please his father by undertaking a course of study to which he was temperamentally unsuited, of facing the exams he feared, and of the reverend's brief trip to Amsterdam to help Vincent prepare for them. Vincent had found the momentary companionship heartening, but following his father's departure, had been intensely moved on encountering what—apropos his chair pictures—he would later refer to as the sign of the "absent person":

After I had seen Father off at the station and had watched the train go out of sight, even the smoke of it, I came home to my room and saw Father's chair standing near the little table on which the books and copybooks of the day before were still lying; and though I know that we shall see each other again pretty soon, I was overcome by emotions.[173]

Now, as then, Vincent persevered in a kind of balancing act between compliance and resistance, application and denial. In the same breath as he spoke of Gauguin's leaving, he asked Theo to assess their joint financial situation in a year's time. He expressed curiosity about de Haan's and Isaacson's opinions of Monticelli without mentioning Gauguin's dismissive view of the artist, for he still held to "the pretence of continuing the job that Monticelli started here."[174] The fact that he now embarked on another *Sower* composition seems to substantiate this assertion of individuality, but the sketch that accompanied the letter (fig. 78) tells another story: Vincent was again attempting to incorporate and personalize Gauguin's lessons.

Like *The Red Vineyard*, the new picture translates the experience of an evening walk, during which Vincent had observed a "sickly citron sunset, mysterious and extraordinarily beautiful—Prussian blue cypresses, trees with dead leaves in all sorts of broken tones." And, also like its predecessor, it incorporates elements at odds with the reported scene. Arbitrarily, Vincent united the two motifs with which he had initiated his partnership with Gauguin in late October: the sower (fig. 6) and the old tree sprouting new shoots (fig. 9).[175] While this doubling-up reiterates Vincent's commitment to Monticelli, other aspects of the composition send a message of deference to Gauguin. The emphatic diagonal thrust of the tree trunk recalls not only the Japanese woodcut that Vincent had copied in Paris (see ch. 3, fig. 15) but also Gauguin's *Vision of the Sermon*. And Vincent clearly strove for something of the latter work's overtly symbolic import.

He took an intermediate step on his way to the final conception, apparently executing a version of the motif in the middle of the week of 18 November (fig. 80). Though this work has been variously dated, analysis of the ground layer suggests that Vincent may have cut the canvas from the same piece of preprimed linen that he used for the smaller of the two paintings that immediately followed.[176] An industrial townscape based on that of Arles serves as the background for a sower striding to the right and a plough team moving in the opposite direction, the basic elements in Millet's prototype (ch. 1, fig. 35). Following Gauguin's methods, Vincent developed richer colors and divided the space into broad, schematic planes. However, the emphatic, dark contours and mannerist attenuation of the figure, though striking stylistically, do little to enhance the legibility of the image's symbolic theme of rebirth. With the adjustments that he made in the pair of canvases that followed days later, Vincent made a step in that direction.

The existence of the final *Sower* in two versions—one a size 30 (fig. 77) and the other smaller (fig. 79)—might suggest that the artist proceeded in a more mediated fashion than usual, first making a small oil sketch before embarking on the larger canvas recorded in his letter sketch (fig. 78). He had done this once in April,[177] and Gauguin had certainly followed this practice in the past. However, technical investigation supports the opposite order. It is the large picture, painted on jute, that exhibits features one would expect to see in an initial version: Vincent painted the tree *over* the sky, clouds, and parts of the field, and made changes (obvious in pentiments) to the sower's left leg. By contrast in the smaller version, executed not on jute but on preprimed linen, he knew where he was going right from the start, holding the tree trunk entirely in reserve. The color of the branch crossing the sun further indicates his different approach in the two works. In the large version, he applied the branch in blue over the still-wet paint of the yellow sun, the mixing of these primary colors resulting in a greenish tone toward its tip. In the small version, after an unsuccessful attempt to duplicate this effect, he resorted to adding a green stroke on top of the blue.

Subtle compositional variations likewise suggest that the smaller version is a reprise in which the artist further refined his idea. While the process of reduction resulted in compression of elements and changes of proportion, it is frankly monumental; its space is shallower, the tree broader and bolder, the sower's hand disproportionately emphatic, and his head embedded more fully in the yellow disk of the sun.

More dramatic are the differences that distinguish this pair of canvases from their June and October predecessors. The new composition evidences a dramatic shift away from their veiled emblematics and a bold attempt to embrace both the overt heroism of Millet's prototype and the evident symbolism of Gauguin's *Human Miseries*. Taking his cue from Millet, Vincent placed the figure of the sower close to the picture plane, where it looms, backlit and cast in shadow, a powerful, compact form reduced to its definitive gesture: the forceful hand, outstretched and unclenching, releasing seeds to the fertile ground. In the version painted just days earlier (fig. 80), Vincent experimented with a figure of bright gold against a darker field; here he rendered the laborer in dark tones against a lighter ground. The large tree, the form of its trunk parallel to that of the striding sower, sends out new shoots, living testimony to the natural cycle being enacted. Leaving us in no doubt about the metaphysical significance of the ritual to which we are witness, Vincent positioned the large yellow disk of the sun so that it reads as a natural halo.

The November *Sower* (figs. 77, 79) leaves behind the emblematic tradition's intimation of transcendent meaning in the everyday for a more assertive form of symbolic communication. Vincent was aware of his new picture's importance. "From time to time," he observed to Theo, "there's a canvas which will make a *tableau*, such as the 'Sower' . . . which I think better than the first [June version]."[178] His decision to execute a replica underscores this assessment. Following on the heels of the chair pendants, which emphasize incompatibility or difference, this new treatment of a signature motif speaks to a fascinating ebb and flow of ideas and influence.

77

78

77
Vincent van Gogh
The Sower
c. 25 November 1888
[F 450, JH 1627]
Oil on jute
73.5 x 93 cm
Collection E. G.
Bührle, Zurich

78
Vincent van Gogh
Sketch of *The Sower*
in letter to Theo
[c. 25 November
1888]
(letter 727/558a; JH
1628)
Van Gogh Museum,
Amsterdam
(Vincent van Gogh
Foundation)
Cat. 81

79
Vincent van Gogh
The Sower
c. 25 November 1888
[F 451, JH 1629]
Oil on canvas
32 x 40 cm
Van Gogh Museum,
Amsterdam
(Vincent van Gogh
Foundation)
Cat. 80

79

80
Vincent van Gogh
The Sower
c. 21 November 1888
[F 575a, JH 1596]
Oil on canvas
33 x 40 cm
The Armand
Hammer Collection,
UCLA Hammer
Museum, Los Angeles
Cat. 79

Gauguin apparently matched his friend's openness at this juncture, for Vincent reported that he was at work on a "large still life of an orange-colored pumpkin and apples and linen on a yellow background and foreground." The chromatics of this now-lost work situate it in the context of Vincent's ongoing dialogue with Monticelli's yellow-orange-sulphur vision of the South, his own contribution being the yellow-on-yellow *Sunflowers* hanging in Gauguin's bedroom. Moreover Gauguin's still life expressed his own earlier ideas about contrasting colors, going back to 1885/86, when he considered the following proposition in the so-called Turkish treatise: "It is an ignorant eye that assigns a fixed and unchanging color to each object. Look for harmony, not contrast, for agreement, not clash. . . . Practice painting objects linked up . . . that is, neighboring or put behind a screen . . . of similar colors."[179]

Vincent, having just read *Le Rêve*, contributed a new element to this discussion. Zola's book contains a vivid description of its heroine, Agnès, a gifted embroiderer of church vestments, crafting her masterpiece—a life-sized female saint worked in gold thread on white silk, the hair skillfully realized with ten different, interwoven shades of gold thread covering the red-yellow spectrum. Vincent added Zola's "very very beautiful" word picture to his image bank "precisely because it is, as it were, a question of the color of the different yellows in whole and broken tones," and because chromatic brilliance independently generates a spiritual aura in Agnès's tapestry and in Zola's narrative.[180]

Yellow was the color that Gauguin later proposed as Vincent's chromatic signature. What then was at stake in his own deployment of it at this time? Expressly engaged as he was in taking on Neo-Impressionism, Gauguin seems to have recognized in Vincent's diverse color investigations the polarities around which to organize his own opposition. Vincent had, beginning in Paris with the *Sunflowers* he exchanged with Gauguin (ch. 2, figs. 49–50), experimented with harmonious juxtapositions of contrasting as well as closely allied colors. But instead of acknowledging these parallel explorations, Gauguin later constructed a different, linear scenario, in which he arrived in Arles to find Vincent

in the full current of the Neo-Impressionist school, . . . floundering about a good deal and suffering as a result of it. . . . With all these yellows on violets, all this work in complementary colors . . . he accomplished nothing but the mildest of incomplete and monotonous harmonies. The sound of the trumpet was missing in them.[181]

In this account Gauguin sounds the reveille, awakening Vincent to the expressive potential of close-knit harmonies in yellow. With such selective retrospective claims, Gauguin could grudgingly admit that Vincent helped him to effect the "confirmation of my own original ideas about painting."[182] "Clarification" would have been a more accurate word, supplemented with a measure of appropriation.

Sunday	Monday	Tuesday	Wednesday	Thursday	Friday	Saturday
	26 Nov ☁	**27** ⛅	**28** 🌧	**29** 🌧	**30** ⛅	**1** Dec ☀ ✉ Gauguin to *La Revue Indépendante*
2 ☀ Pianet Ménagerie opens	**3** ☀ ✉ Gauguin to Theo ✉ Vincent to Theo	**4** ☀				

a Van Gogh, *Armand Roulin*
   [F 493, JH 1643]
   Museum Boymans-van Beuningen,
   Rotterdam

b Van Gogh, *Camille Roulin*
   [F 665, JH 1879]
   Museu de Arte de São Paulo, Brazil

For much of November, a mixture of wind and rain had made it only intermittently possible for the two painters to work outdoors. The weather did not improve as they moved into December, when lower temperatures gave the north wind that blew day after day an even more bitter edge. The atmosphere in the studio was overcast by the threats Vincent perceived to his dream of a Studio of the South. While he reported that he and Gauguin worked constantly, he ceased asserting how happy they were together. His suspicions about a rival "Studio of the North" resurfaced; after Gauguin had received the invitation to show with Les Vingt, Vincent conjectured that his friend had begun to consider settling in Brussels. For despite Gauguin's bachelorlike behavior with the Arlésiennes and his confessed incompatibility with Mette, Vincent imagined that he missed his children (whose photographs he carried with him) enough to want to be nearer to them. Hoping to preempt such a move, he ventured that Gauguin could best regain his family's trust by staying in Arles and proving his stability. Vincent tried to realign himself with his own family at the same time, reappointing Theo to the role of brother-in-arms and calling upon him to have faith in their ultimate victory, even though they were not "among the people who are talked about."[183] He meant Gauguin.

In this climate of questioned loyalties, the relationship between Gauguin and Vincent entered a new and differently intense phase. For Vincent the uncertain future prompted thoughts of the past. At this point, it seems, he began sharing with Gauguin the events of his life and the elements around which he had sought to organize it and shape his identity. As a youth he had transcribed formative texts—the German Romantics, Michelet, Renan, and Carlyle—into albums fashioned for friends; he now recalled for Gauguin the same touchstones, along with new ones such as Wagner. As earlier, the impetus of this

Oct						
	1	2	3	4	5	6
7	8	9	10	11	12	13
14	15	16	17	18	19	20
21	22	23	24	25	26	27
28	29	30	31			

Nov						
				1	2	3
4	5	6	7	8	9	10
11	12	13	14	15	16	17
18	19	20	21	22	23	24
25	**26**	**27**	**28**	**29**	**30**	

Dec						
						1
2	**3**	**4**	5	6	7	8
9	10	11	12	13	14	15
16	17	18	19	20	21	22
23	24	25	26	27	28	29
30	31					

self-portraiture was to present his worldview and, certainly in this case, to enlist his companion in it. With reference to these authors and to painter-heroes including Rembrandt and Delacroix, Vincent made his case. Representing his life—before and after turning to art—as an essentially unbroken pursuit of ministry, Vincent articulated his belief in art as religion, in which artists constituted what Carlyle and Wagner termed a perpetual priesthood or discipleship. A proselytizer to the core, Vincent wanted to convert Gauguin to his mission, his passion increasing as his hopes foundered.

As has been aptly observed, Gauguin collapsed life into art by coming to see himself as the "hero of his own history [and] of the painting of his age"; his conception of the artist's role deriving its moral impulse from Carlyle. In this Vincent's contribution was crucial.[184] Having fostered his friend's heroic identity, during their last weeks together Vincent engaged Gauguin in a consideration of the neo-Romantic thinking that he would use to secure it. Fascinated as he was, Gauguin never for a moment thought of changing his plans for imminent departure. Quite the opposite. In the midst of this escalating tension, they continued to paint.

Despite Vincent's confident assessment of *The Sower* (figs. 77, 79) in early December (it is the only memory picture he blessed with his signature during Gauguin's stay), this overtly symbolic painting would have no sequel. A contributing cause was *A Memory of the Garden*, which Vincent reported as "spoiled" in the same breath as he mentioned *The Sower*'s potential. But clearly there were other factors involved in what may be seen as a characteristic retrenchment. Vincent spent the last week of November engaged in doing "something to my liking and something personal": painting portraits of "*a whole family*," the Roulins—the postal worker Joseph Roulin (whom he had portrayed in August; see fig. 102), his wife, their seventeen- and eleven-year-old

sons, and their four-month-old girl. Though these canvases are smaller than usual—all size 15, figure format—Vincent had plans for doing more, "better." Back in his element, he felt himself reassuringly swamped with work that he foresaw would pay dividends "when I'm forty."[185]

Gauguin meanwhile had finished a second picture of washerwomen (fig. 83) and was at work on several landscapes (figs. 82, 87, 118). In preparing these compositions, Gauguin reengaged in his habitual practice of sketching figures and landscape elements that caught his attention for subsequent reference when painting.[186] In the first *Washerwomen*, Gauguin relied on one of these notations (fig. 84) for the distinctive, stylized silhouette of the standing figure's shawl; the same drawing informed the synthetic construction of the kneeling figures in his subsequent engagement with the subject. The latter canvas conveys a sense of place—and of space—more descriptively than the former. The setting is again the Roubine du Roi canal, with the women viewed from the north bank (see map, fig. 72). Whereas in the earlier canvas Gauguin translated Vincent's sense of the vertiginous (see fig. 73) into a resolutely two-dimensional design, here he refrained from subsuming the elements into a pattern; each one—whether animate or inanimate, solid or liquid—manifests similar density and simplicity of contour, as if locked into a preassigned place in a puzzle.[187] Further underscoring the composition's renewed sense of order and deliberation, Gauguin explored the harmonics of closely related shades of blue-gray and olive green in an extensive underlayer that is virtually a monochromatic painting. He carefully brought in contrasting notes of orange, yellow, pink, and red, but allowed cool, calm tonalities to prevail.

Arles Landscape (Path by the Roubine du Roi Canal) (fig. 82) features a closely related site, the landscape as viewed from a point just yards from the canal's north embankment, looking southeast. Gauguin here expanded his palette

to include all colors (even white and near-black), placing the emphasis on high-range tints of yellow, pink, and red, with pale blue and contrasts of deeper green. These colors acquire particular luminosity owing to the artist's choice of a bright lead-white ground, much more reflective than the insubstantial, virtually transparent barium sulfate used until recently (see App.). Here the Roubine du Roi can only be inferred from the horizontal strip of green running behind the diminutive figure in blue; drawings identify the green strip as the canal's southern embankment and the figure as a little girl skipping rope (see fig. 85). Gauguin added the two figures and the dog late in the painting process to what had been a pure landscape with only the white patch of laundry serving as a highly ambiguous narrative device.[188] The dog's long shadow illustrates Gauguin's dictum of "necessary form," for in fact there are two shadows: an abbreviated one reading literally, as if cast by the midday sun; and a longer one that ties the animal's curving shape to the sweep of the pathway. This striking curve along the right side of the composition, like the similar devices in Vincent's *Washerwomen at the Roubine du Roi Canal*, *The Red Vineyard* (fig. 49), and *A Memory of the Garden* (fig. 67), gains dynamism through directional brush strokes. Gauguin nuanced this effect through chromatic balance, applying pink strokes over the yellow road on the right, and adding yellow wash over the pink field on the left.

It may be tempting to argue that Gauguin painted this treatment of *Washerwomen* (fig. 83), as well as *Arles Landscape* (fig. 82), before the *Washerwomen* composition discussed above (fig. 75), but technical evidence suggests otherwise. Apparently he digressed from a predictable modernist stylistic evolution toward even greater abstraction in order to represent a wider, deeper swath of space. In effect he returned to the compositional principles seen in *Les Alyscamps (The Three Graces)* (fig. 21), inflecting them with greater artifice. The space recedes, but not without interruptions from such elements as the large, pale bush set improbably at dead center, poplars bisecting the picture plane, and dog braced against the corner in *Arles Landscape*. Some forms—patches representing laundry, shadow, grass, water—seem to float to the surface while others, like the shrubbery along the edge of the path, are subsumed into large patterns. Poised to rise up and assert the canvases' two-dimensionality, these assertively stylized shapes threaten the landscape space with dis-illusion.

Various specific features of these two paintings, such as the dog in *Arles Landscape* and the cropped heads at the lower left of *Washerwomen*, show Gauguin responding to Bernard's *Breton Women in the Meadow* (ch. 3, fig. 60). Together with Vincent's watercolor copy of the same picture (fig. 81), these quotations point to the issues under discussion. For the terms in which Vincent later described Bernard's composition—"a Sunday afternoon in Brittany," with "elegant modern figures" conceived with the grace of the "ancient Greek or Egyptian art"—imply that he saw the picture as successfully referencing and differentiating itself from Seurat's *Sunday on La Grande Jatte—1884* (ch. 2, fig. 3). Despite his reservations about pointillism's limited expressive capacity, Vincent recognized its inventor's authority. On the eve of Gauguin's arrival in Arles, he had dared to hope that their production might measure up to Seurat's achievement, and even that the latter could be induced to collaborate with them, but he had decided to wait until he knew Gauguin better before sharing the fantasy.[189] Impatient as Gauguin would have been with talk of such a partnership, he was not indifferent to discussion of Seurat's merits and shortcomings, for his resolution to launch a challenge to Neo-Impressionism necessarily entailed addressing the canvas that was virtually the mother of all pointillist pictures. Aspects of his late November landscapes reference the *Grande Jatte*: the placement and attitude of the blue-clad skipping figure in *Arles Landscape* relate her to the running child in Seurat's canvas, and the compositional oddi-

Bernard is ... a young painter—he is certainly not older than twenty—very original. He is trying to do elegant modern figures in the manner of ancient Greek and Egyptian art, graceful in the expressive motions, charming as a result of the daring colors. I saw a picture of his of a Sunday afternoon in Brittany, Breton peasant women, children, peasants, dogs strolling about in a very green meadow; the clothes are black and red, and the women's caps white. But in this crowd there are also two ladies, one dressed in red, the other in bottle green; they make it a very modern thing.

Ask Theo to show you the watercolor that I made after this picture; it is so original that I wanted to have a copy of it.   Vincent to Wil, [10 December 1889]

81
Vincent van Gogh
Breton Women in the Meadow (after Émile Bernard)
December 1888
[F 1422, JH 1654]
Watercolor and graphite on paper
48.5 x 62 cm
Civica Galleria d'Arte Moderna Raccolta Grassi, Milan
Cat. 88

ties described above resonate with devices that Seurat employed in negotiating the deep space of the island setting. Gauguin emphasized the arbitrary, formal thrust of his composition by centrifugally organizing it around the otherwise inconsequential form of the yellow bush that forms its hub.

More overtly dramatic is a vertical composition (fig. 87) featuring tall, sinuous blue trees recalling the row of elegant trunks with which Seurat rhythmically parsed the area behind the *Grande Jatte*'s principal couple. Gauguin added a similarly configured pair—a woman in profile and a man with his features partially obscured by an overlapping form—but the

dramatic implication is quite at odds with the implacable calm of Seurat's masterpiece. There is something vaguely menacing about this interaction that we can only partly witness between the man in a blue worker's shirt and cap, legs planted apart, hands in pockets, head turned, and the object of his gaze, the diminutive, slightly hunched figure of an Arlésienne. Gauguin carried through the aura of threat in the title: "*Vous y passerez, la belle!*" ("*Your Turn Will Come, Pretty One!*").[190]

If Gauguin's *Blue Trees* takes on Seurat at some remove, it engages Vincent up close and directly. The setting suggests the vicinity of Montmajour, with a winding road like the

one leading to the abbey glimpsed at the upper right. Infrared reflectography indicates a faint underlying sketch of a building with a tower silhouetted at the top of the hill, perhaps representing the ruined abbey; vineyards flank the orange path in the foreground. With its yellow sky and blue trees, the work chromatically quotes Vincent's first *Falling Leaves (Les Alyscamps)* composition (fig. 27), then hanging in Gauguin's bedroom. But whereas Vincent deployed a screen of trees to bracket a pair of "lovers," Gauguin used the device to problematize an unclear and seemingly uncomfortable relationship.[191] The insistent, albeit enigmatic narrative incident fits discordantly into the resolutely antinaturalistic setting.

82

83

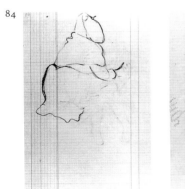
84

85

82
Paul Gauguin
*Arles Landscape
(Path by the Roubine
du Roi Canal)*
Early December 1888
[W 309]
Oil on jute
72.5 x 92 cm
Nationalmuseum,
Stockholm
Cat. 45

83
Paul Gauguin
*Washerwomen at the
Roubine du Roi canal*
Early December 1888
[W 302]
Oil on jute
75.9 x 92.1 cm
The Museum of
Modern Art, New
York, The William
S. Paley Collection
Cat. 44

84
Paul Gauguin
Sketch for
Washerwomen (fig. 83)
Autumn 1888
In Sketchbook from
Arles and Brittany
The Israel Museum
Collection, Jerusalem,
gift of Sam Salz,
New York, to America-
Israel Cultural
Foundation, 1972

85
Paul Gauguin
Sketch of a girl skip-
ping rope with the
Roubine du Roi canal
in the background
1888
Graphite and
watercolor
50 x 36 cm
Dickinson Roundell
Inc., New York

Comparable tensions were at work in the studio. Vincent's Roulin portraits marked a return to naturalist ambitions, accompanied by a reversion to commercially primed canvas. Practical reasons may have guided the switch of materials: the twenty meters of jute that Gauguin had purchased in late October were almost gone; moreover the preprimed canvas could be cut and stretched to size in a matter of minutes, while the jute had to be stretched, primed, and dried in advance. But it is also possible that Vincent was displeased by the coarse effect of his initial attempt to use this support for portraiture, *The Arlésienne (Madame Ginoux)* (fig. 37). He held this genre in such high regard, and so seldom had the opportunity to concentrate on it in this way, that he wanted to use a support more familiar to him—and more tractable—than jute.

Vincent's idea to represent "a whole family" can be linked to his current concerns regarding Gauguin's familial commitment and to his preoccupation with his own choice to sow ideas and pictures rather than progeny. Immediately after the birth of Marcelle Roulin in late July, Vincent had painted two portraits of the proud father (see fig. 102) and expressed the hope that the Roulins would later allow him to paint the baby in its cradle. "A child in

the cradle," he wrote to Theo, "if you watch it at leisure, has the infinite in its eyes." He had made virtually the identical observation six years earlier, when Sien Hoornik brought her newborn son home to the Hague studio. He described then how the sight of the little cradle filled him with emotion and made him feel a part of the natural order, helping him finally to understand the truth of Michelet's saying, "Woman is a religion."[192] He pinned a reproduction of Rembrandt's *Holy Family* (fig. 61) above the cradle that transformed the studio into a real home, and he sketched the motif repeatedly. Vincent's dream that "a *studio with a cradle*" might be a vessel strong enough to weather life's storms had foundered, but in subsequent years the cradle remained a complex personal symbol, entailing loss but also promising reassurance and calm. By the time of Marcelle Roulin's birth, he had regretfully restricted his thoughts of marriage to the realm of art and the pairing of complementary colors.[193] But while art was now exclusively his religion, Vincent remained steadfast in his determination to make a home—not with a wife and children, but with a family of artists.

Vincent had recognized Gauguin as the ideal partner in this enterprise, which since his youth he had cast in terms of a dangerous ocean crossing. "My God, protect me, my

boat is so small and your sea is so great!" This Breton sailors' prayer, committed to an 1875 album and later invoked in times of crisis, had seemingly been answered in the person of Gauguin. Identifying his friend with the men who fished the treacherous seas off Iceland in Loti's *Pêcheur d'Islande* (1886), Vincent fantasized that together they could avoid the type of devastating shipwreck that closes the novel, a metaphor that took on tragic currency at the moment of Gauguin's arrival, when newspapers reported that 165 fishermen had been lost at sea during severe April storms.[194] Gauguin's plans to leave unleashed a tempest against which Vincent would have to fashion his own protection.

Undertaking the Roulin portraits, he wrote, "consoled [him] up to a certain point for not being a doctor."[195] Never had he in fact aspired to be a physician, but he had attempted to minister to body and soul while in the Borinage, an experience he now detailed for Gauguin. His recollection, after years of disavowing this intense religious proselytizing, provides illuminating background to the Roulin series.

Vincent may have begun the group with two depictions of the Roulins' eldest son, Armand (see fig. 88).[196] In both canvases the artist demonstrated a fluent, relaxed application. With thin paint and a masterful touch, he deployed a palette of greens and yellows, which he would continue to use (while allowing himself far greater freedom with impasto and gesture) in the pictures that can be seen as the core of the group, those representing Augustine Roulin alone and with her baby, Marcelle.

Recently Vincent had talked of painting portraits of ordinary people in which color confers the "touch of the eternal" conventionally signified by halos. The first of two images of Augustine Roulin holding her baby (fig. 93) displays lingering traces of traditional iconography, especially as seen in primitive depictions of the Virgin presenting the Christ Child to the priest in the temple or to the viewer; the brilliant yellow background recalls the gold fields used to signify holy space or spirituality in these prototypes (see fig. 90).[197]

Playing white against yellow, complemented by Augustine Roulin's golden hair, Vincent recalled a particular depiction of the Christ Child and the "Holy Virgin, bright yellow, white, and orange" that he had chanced upon two years earlier in Antwerp's church of Sint Andries (fig. 89), a stained-glass window featuring the Virgin in the role of "stella maris," or star of the sea, patron of sailors. Flanked by

86
Paul Gauguin
Winter (Breton Boy Repairing His Sabot)
1888 [W 258]
Oil on canvas
90 x 71 cm
Ny Carlsberg Glyptotek,
Copenhagen

87
Paul Gauguin
Blue Trees ("Vous y passerez, la belle!")
(*Les Arbres bleus*)
Late November 1888
[W 311]
Oil on jute
92 x 73 cm
Ordrupgaard,
Copenhagen
Cat. 42

88
Vincent van Gogh
Armand Roulin
1888 [F 492, JH 1642]
Oil on canvas
66 x 55 cm
Museum Folkwang
Essen, Germany

89
Henri Dobbelaere
(Belgian; d. 1885)
Stella Maris
1866
Stained-glass
window
Sint Andries
Church, Antwerp

90
Gentile da Fabriano
(Italian; c. 1370–1427)
Madonna and Child
Tempera on panel
95.9 x 56.5 cm
National Gallery of
Art, Washington,
D.C., Samuel H.
Kress Collection

91
Vow Made to Notre-Dame de Grâce by Alexandre Gilles and His Crew on the Marquis de Brancas,
7 February 1770
1770

Oil on panel
Notre-Dame de
Grâce, Honfleur,
Calvados
Direction Régional
des Affaires
Culturelles de
Basse-Normandie

a cross and an anchor—symbols of faith and hope—the Virgin and Child are spiritual equivalents of the lighthouse beacon guiding the mariners who battle a storm in an "enormous three-master, quaint and phantasmal."[198] Vincent's language suggests his alignment of the window with comparable talismanic imagery found in popular prints and ex-voto paintings (see fig. 91). A simple image of faith, it had moved him, preoccupied as he was then with family upheaval and questioning his brother's loyalties. Now facing an uncertain future, his thoughts returned to the "divine

Virgin who protects the poor sailors" and who stood for the reassurance and hope that Vincent sought for himself and wished to provide others.[199] He fashioned his two portraits of Augustine Roulin holding Marcelle (figs. 93–94) —a larger composition followed the first in early December—with this joint purpose.

The portrait sessions introduced a new cast of characters, a different atmosphere of sociability, and (at least figuratively) a cradle into the studio. Gauguin, taking breaks from his work on landscape, produced two sketches of Marcelle (fig. 96) that share a tender insight with the numerous drawings he had made of his own children. Discussion of family seemingly prompted Gauguin, later in December, to match his friend in painting a portrait of his own mother (fig. 138) on a scale identical to Vincent's portrait of his mother (fig. 62) and likewise based on a photograph. In his deliberately simplified sketches of the infant, Gauguin encouraged Vincent to privilege style over sentiment. Responsively Vincent went on to execute three related portraits of Marcelle (see

fig. 95) that display, to varying degrees, similarly emphatic contours and synthetic features.[200] But these small canvases were painted only after completion of the initial Roulin series, apparently emerging from the circumstances and discussions surrounding the more ambitious portraits that Vincent and Gauguin each painted of the baby's mother (figs. 97, 100).

Gauguin's picture provides clues revealing the studio set-up (see fig. 99). Madame Roulin sits in the armchair; dark blue squares indicate the glass panels of the door to her left. Behind her, nearly filling the short stretch of wall between the door and the room's southeast corner, hangs *Blue Trees*, recognizable by the yellow road (the artist likely edited out the trees and the couple to minimize distractions in the portrait's background). Gauguin thus seems to have set up his easel near the north wall, where he could make use of the gas lamp. Vincent occupied an area near the southwest corner, served by either a gas lamp on the west wall or by late afternoon sun coming through the south window. From this vantage point, the

92
Maerten van
Heemskerck (Dutch;
1498–1574)
*Saint Luke Painting the
Virgin*
1532
Oil on oak panel
205.5 x 143.5 cm
Frans Halsmuseum,
Haarlem
Vincent was familiar
with this representation, which hung in
Haarlem's town hall
along with the Hals
works he admired.

93
Vincent van Gogh
*Madame Roulin with
Her Baby Marcelle*
Late November 1888
[F 491, JH 1638]
Oil on canvas
63.5 x 51 cm
The Metropolitan
Museum of Art,
New York, Robert
Lehman Collection,
1975

94
Vincent van Gogh
*Madame Roulin with
Her Baby Marcelle*
December 1888
[F490, JH 1637]
Oil on canvas
92.4 x 73.3 cm
Philadelphia
Museum of Art,
bequest of Lisa
Norris Elkins
Cat. 82

95
Vincent van Gogh
Marcelle Roulin
December 1888 [F
441, JH 1641]
Oil on canvas
35.5 x 24.5 cm
Van Gogh Museum,
Amsterdam
(Vincent van Gogh
Foundation)

96
Paul Gauguin
Sketches of Marcelle
Roulin
Autumn 1888
In Sketchbook from
Arles and Brittany
The Israel Museum
Collection,
Jerusalem, gift of
Sam Salz, New
York, to America-
Israel Cultural
Foundation, 1972

east window appears to the left of the sitter, who faced the space between the two artists.

Vincent and Gauguin here courted comparison more directly than they had four weeks earlier, when depicting Marie Ginoux. They engaged the sitter from related points of view and worked on the same scale, in the same medium, and on similar supports. But overall compositional likenesses underscore differences in execution and expressiveness. Characteristically Vincent finished his portrait at one go, while Gauguin required several paint-

ing sessions and possibly more than one sitting. A subsequent evening session might explain the apparently darkened windowpanes and strong shadow cast by the chair in the latter's picture, although it is certainly possible that these elements are so-called necessary forms rather than literally descriptive ones.

Another sitting, moreover, might also explain the different costume worn by the sitter in the two images: in Vincent's a V-shaped neckline, in Gauguin's a high, rounded collar with the hint of a white undergarment (which reap-

pears in Vincent's late December reprise of the subject; fig. 141). Alternatively, since the last-mentioned work obviously relies on Gauguin's for the collar, undergarment, and form of the left sleeve at the wrist, it is possible that Gauguin, working more slowly than Vincent, refined and invented these details as he finished his portrait after the sitting.

Vincent would later remind his friend of the discussions that fed into their portraits: the proposition that art should "offer consolation for the broken-hearted" in the manner of

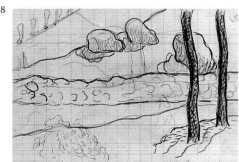

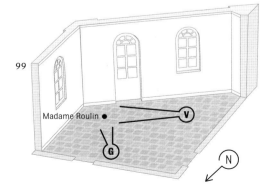

Madame Roulin ●

97
Paul Gauguin
Madame Roulin
Late November 1888
[W 298]
Oil on canvas
50 x 63 cm
The Saint Louis Art
Museum, funds
given by Mrs. Mark
C. Steinberg
Cat. 43

98
Paul Gauguin
Madame Roulin
Landscape sketch
Autumn 1888
In Sketchbook from
Arles and Brittany
The Israel Museum
Collection,
Jerusalem, gift of
Sam Salz, New York,
to America-Israel
Cultural Foundation,
1972

99
Studio diagram of
the sitting of
Madame Roulin

100
Vincent van Gogh
Madame Roulin
1888 [F 503, JH 1646]
Oil on canvas
55 x 65 cm
Oskar Reinhart
Collection,
Winterthur,
Switzerland

Wagner's music, abstractly, through color harmonies.[201] Though these concepts were not new to their discussion, the apparent consensus about them was. Previously Gauguin had not taken on missionary goals, and Vincent had not strayed far from his predominantly literary models.

Vincent apparently secured Gauguin's interest by filtering his core Carlylean beliefs through Wagner, whose writings he had on hand. Gauguin seized on Vincent's copy of Benoit, transcribing several long passages containing ideas that would thereafter feature significantly in his aesthetic position. Given his recent endeavors to forge a personal and professional identity, he was receptive to Benoit's portrait of Wagner as an artist who fiercely asserted his intellectual independence, responded only to "inner necessity," and waged war instead of seeking peace with "the rabble"; he had also compared music with the antimaterialistic, mysterious art that he sought to create.[202] But a new perspective on the artist's mission was at issue when Gauguin transcribed phrases from Wagner's credo:

I believe in God, in Mozart, and in Beethoven; I also believe in their disciples and apostles. . . . I believe in the sanctity of the spirit and in the truth of art. . . . I believe that this art has a divine source.[203]

These are the very lines Vincent had taken deeply to heart when he first read them in May/June. In the midst of such discussions, according to Gauguin's later account, Vincent loaded his brush with his yellowest paint and inscribed on the studio's whitewashed wall:

Je suis Sain d'Esprit / I am sound in mind
Je suis Saint-Esprit / I am the Holy Spirit[204]

Though none of Gauguin's later texts regarding Vincent can be taken as strict documentary reports, there is evidence that this symbolism featured in conversation, even if not in action, in the Yellow House. Echoing Wagner's "sanctity of spirit" ("saintété de l'esprit"), the state-

ment of identity that Gauguin attributed to Vincent and wrote in his own Arles sketchbook (see fig. 104) also implies that they continued the earlier discussion of a brotherhood of artists whose commitment identified them as "crazy" by conventional standards (see ch. 3). Gauguin copied out verbatim Wagner's call to arms: "We will gain the force to accomplish our work with time if we learn to rally like disciples of a new religion, and if we fortify ourselves and our faith with mutual affection." He adopted it as his own, later invoking it on occasion without mention of the composer.[205]

Gauguin's responsiveness to Wagner's theories can be attributed in part to their centrality in emerging Symbolist aesthetics, but the exaggerated terms in which Vincent figured the painter's higher calling evidently fired Gauguin's imagination. In particular he responded to the self-referentiality of Wagner's convictions: "I believe that the disciples of great art will be glorified, and . . . they will return to merge for eternity at the breast of the divine source of all harmony."[206] As would become clear, Gauguin's conversion took the form of mythic thinking and speech rather than actual missionary zeal. Vincent may have found this confusing, for he held more literal apostolic aspirations. He gave expression to these beliefs in his portraits of Augustine and her baby, emulating Saint Luke, patron of painters and limner of the Virgin Mary (see fig. 92), to create a modern Madonna.[207] But it seems that the project of painting Madame Roulin by herself involved fashioning an affective image abstractly or imaginatively, without recourse to traditional iconographic signifiers.

In so doing Vincent carried forward goals for portraiture that he had long framed through the examples of Hals and Rembrandt, both adept at intimating the miraculous in their portrayals of ordinary people.[208] With this in mind, Vincent broached with Gauguin what

he would call "the question of Rembrandt and light": the Dutch painter's performance of "metaphysical magic" through chiaroscuro and his mastery of the unique tonality that Vincent termed "Rembrandt gold." Gauguin agreed with his friend's unconventional identification of the master with color, in addition to chiaroscuro, both essential components in the pictorial music discernible even when distance renders Rembrandt's subject illegible. Moreover Gauguin absorbed Vincent's reverential language, later going one better by designating Rembrandt as "the magician who is essentially a Prophet," a characterization that incorporates another of Carlyle's uppercase synonyms for the artist that features in Vincent's early lexicon.[209]

In their depictions of Augustine Roulin, Vincent and Gauguin, in different ways, faced the challenge of incarnating an archetype. Vincent transformed the studio setting, rendering the whitewashed walls yellow to convey a spiritual as well as solar vitality. The view through the window is a fictional amalgam, combining the stylized serpentine path from *A Memory of the Garden* (fig. 67) with six oversized, improbably placed flower pots containing sprouting bulbs, the larger ones prominently exposed above the soil so that their symbolic significance cannot be overlooked. These homely emblems signal the fertility of the full-bosomed sitter.[210] The paint's materiality and the rough urgency of its application reinforce the sense of earthiness, as do Madame Roulin's lumpy features.

Gauguin by contrast rendered a formal archetype, suggesting the essential within the individual. The figure's emphatic immobility and sense of containment, the geometry of the head, and the impassively masklike visage recall Cézanne's portraits of his wife. This strategy is consistent with his view of portraiture, which can be extrapolated from his approach to Rembrandt: "When I see a portrait

painted by Rembrandt, I scarcely see the facial features that are depicted, whereas I deeply sense the moral portrait of [the painter's] thoughts"; he looked for the lineaments that revealed "the state of the artist's soul."[211] Gauguin's canvas suggests as much. Like Vincent, he represented a picture within his portrait, but instead of opening a window onto the sitter's nature, it evidences the artist's own generative potential.

Vincent had privileged artistic affinities over familial bonds ever since the "calamity and shipwreck" of his attempt to establish a household in The Hague. Thereafter he contented himself with finding glimpses of the eternal in pictures rather than offspring, and he imagined looking back in his last moments on progeny other than a loving family: the pictures he made and might have made. In a remarkably literal manifestation of this notion of procreativity, the series of size 15 Roulin portraits led Vincent to begin literally using pictures to beget pictures, starting with his image of the paterfamilias, Joseph Roulin (fig. 101). It is the only one in the group directly informed by an earlier work, the three-quarter-length August portrait still in the studio (fig. 102), which suggests why it appears to belong to a different stylistic family than the size 15 images of Roulin's elder son, baby daughter, and wife.[212] Whereas in the initial version Vincent had modeled the sitter's face in a sculptural manner, using small directional strokes to feel out the forms, now he laid in flat planes of contrasting colors, composing a sort of mask on the surface rather than an underlying structure. Reprising an earlier picture, Vincent could explore issues of style, undistracted by circumstantial alterations of the motif but nonetheless skirting the dangerous open-endedness involved in composing *de tête*. Even if the artist asked Roulin to pose again—which is debatable—the resulting picture remains a translation of its predecessor, markedly different in conception and shaped in concert with Gauguin. With its areas of uninflected tones, strong outlines, and simplified forms and modeling, this version of the postman's portrait is a notable attempt at pictorial synthesis.

It was a suggestive exercise. Earlier he had watched Gauguin execute his *Night Café* (fig. 41)—first producing a drawing of Marie Ginoux from life and then tracing it onto the canvas. Vincent himself in the past had made occasional use of tracings but not, as Gauguin had done, in order to move from life study to a more synthetic *tableau*. Now he did so, using

the first Roulin pictures to generate the more important portraits he envisioned. Using two different pictures—one of the baby (fig. 93) and another of Augustine by herself (fig. 100)—Vincent fashioned a third, larger and more ambitious, of Augustine Roulin and baby Marcelle together (fig. 94). It was clearly premeditated: he traced their contours from the charcoal underdrawing of their size 15 portraits, anticipating the difficulty of doing so later, after applying thick, slow-to-dry paint layers. With these intermediate tracings, he then transferred Augustine Roulin's head from the horizontal picture and Marcelle's head from the first double portrait (see fig. 103).[213]

His motivations for doing so are arguable. It is possible that he simply wished to block in compositional essentials so that he could save time when the sitters were next in the studio; Augustine Roulin, perhaps with the baby, might well have sat for the portrait's completion. Certainly the picture, though unfinished, bears the hallmarks of immediacy, the rough, frenetic execution arguably attesting the subjects' restlessness. But it is also possible that the tracings functioned like physical memories of the earlier pictures—that they together with the studies emboldened Vincent to carry out portraits from memory. If Vincent indeed asserted his independence with the vigorous brushwork and hybrid use of tracings in the second portrait of Augustine Roulin with Marcelle, he would show himself more respectful of Gauguin's compositional methods and synthetic aims in subsequent portraits of the baby and of her mother (see figs. 95, 141). He produced these, again using tracings, several weeks into December, by which time the calm that Vincent considered important to afford sitters was in short supply, and the give and take between the two artists largely played out.

103

101
Vincent van Gogh
Monsieur Roulin
Early December 1888
[F 434, JH 1547]
Oil on canvas
65 x 47 cm
Kunstmuseum,
Winterthur,
Switzerland

102
Vincent van Gogh
Monsieur Roulin
Early August 1888
[F 432, JH 1522]
Oil on canvas
81.2 x 65.3 cm
Museum of Fine
Arts, Boston, gift of
Robert Treat Paine,
2nd, 1985

103
*Madame Roulin with
Her Baby Marcelle*
(fig. 94)
with overlays to
show tracings
from *Madame Roulin*
(fig. 100) (red) and
*Madame Roulin and
Her Baby Marcelle*
(fig. 93) (blue)

Sunday	Monday	Tuesday	Wednesday	Thursday	Friday	Saturday
			5 Dec ☁	**6** ☁	**7** ⛅	**8** ⛅
				✉ Theo to Wil		✉ Gauguin to Theo
9 ☁	**10** ⛅	**11** ☁ ✉ Schuffenecker to Gauguin ✉ Milliet to Vincent	**12** ☁			

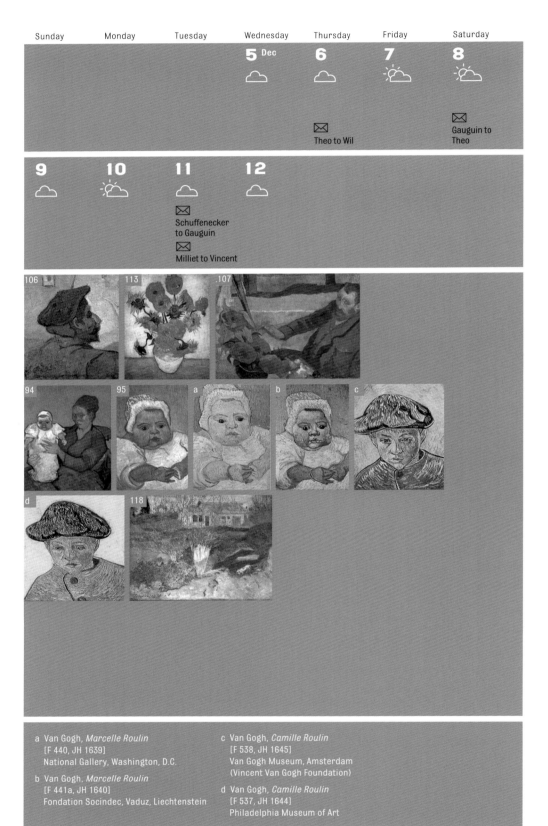

a Van Gogh, *Marcelle Roulin*
[F 440, JH 1639]
National Gallery, Washington, D.C.

b Van Gogh, *Marcelle Roulin*
[F 441a, JH 1640]
Fondation Socindec, Vaduz, Liechtenstein

c Van Gogh, *Camille Roulin*
[F 538, JH 1645]
Van Gogh Museum, Amsterdam
(Vincent Van Gogh Foundation)

d Van Gogh, *Camille Roulin*
[F 537, JH 1644]
Philadelphia Museum of Art

During the first half of December, many days were clear, but high winds and frosty temperatures curtailed outdoor excursions. Inside, by contrast, the atmosphere was heated, as the dialogue between the two men took ever more baroque turns and exaggerated manifestations. The vivid turning point that Gauguin constructed with his 1894 account of Vincent inscribing "Sain d'Esprit/Saint-Esprit" on the studio wall would seem wholly apocryphal in both senses of the word—of doubtful authenticity as well as fabulous—were it not for the fact that Gauguin recorded it (or the idea of it) in his Arles sketchbook (fig. 104) during his last days with Vincent or in their immediate aftermath. The same page also contains an intriguing list, evidently both an index and an aide-mémoire, which points to the heightened mythic inflection of their December discussions:

Incas
Snake
Fly [?] on the dog
Black lion
The murderer in flight
Saül Paul. Ictus
(to) save your honor (money canv[as])
Orla [*sic*] (Maupassant)[214]

Each seemingly enigmatic clue touches on themes already in play over the preceding weeks or even years. "Ictus" refers to the acrostic *Ichthys* for I*esous* Ch*ristos* Th*eou* h*yios* S*oter* (Jesus Christ son of God Savior); *Ikhtus* is also the Greek word for fish, the symbol inscribed by the earliest Christians in Roman catacombs as sign of their belief and fraternity. Gauguin's inclusion of the term in his list—and Vincent's use of both the acrostic and fish symbol in a letter to Gauguin several weeks later—leaves little doubt that Vincent's talk of an association of artists had gone beyond its practical trappings to its religious roots. He had made the same call to van Rappard years earlier, proposing that they join together as "fishermen on

Oct						
	1	2	3	4	5	6
7	8	9	10	11	12	13
14	15	16	17	18	19	20
21	22	23	24	25	26	27
28	29	30	31			

Nov						
				1	2	3
4	5	6	7	8	9	10
11	12	13	14	15	16	17
18	19	20	21	22	23	24
25	26	27	28	29	30	

Dec						
						1
2	3	4	**5**	**6**	**7**	**8**
9	**10**	**11**	**12**	13	14	15
16	17	18	19	20	21	22
23	24	25	26	27	28	29
30	31					

the sea that we call the Ocean of Reality," like the original disciples, whom Christ enjoined to be fishers of men.[215]

Linking the acrostic with "Saül Paul," Gauguin brought the issue of conversion to the forefront. Saul was the tentmaker who used the Latin name Paul after his miraculous vision of Christ on the road to Damascus. The example of the thrice-shipwrecked apostle, whose epistles to the Corinthians include the admonition to be sorrowful yet always rejoicing, had been critical to Vincent in the first stage of his own evangelical career, which had ended in the Borinage. Counting on Gauguin's partnership in the mission's second phase, Vincent identified the former sailor with his New Testament namesake and assigned him a comparable role in the new evangel he imagined.[216]

Vincent's imitation of Christ with the miners in the Borinage had caused his superiors and his family to question the sanity of his sanctity, as Gauguin would underscore in several of his later accounts. The artist's status as social outcast—martyr, like Jesus, or criminal, like Hugo's Jean Valjean—clearly factored into their discussions. But so did a darker construction of madness, as witnessed by another reference found in both Gauguin's list and

Vincent's letter, to Maupassant's short story "Le Horla."

"Le Horla"—Norman dialect for "The Stranger"—is a first-person chronicle of the narrator's decline into paranoia and insanity. Over a period of several months, he gradually loses his grip on reality, becoming convinced that malevolent specters of his hallucinations and nightmares are stalking him. He attempts to rid himself of his demons by means of a violent action that results in the loss of innocent lives; guilt-ridden and terrified, he contemplates suicide at the narrative's conclusion. "Le Horla" may have come to mind when a practitioner of the arts of hypnotism and magnetism (which feature prominently in the story) appeared in Arles in mid-December.[217] But the subject of creativity and madness—of the dangers posed by the imagination unfettered in reality—was already under discussion in the Yellow House, thanks to the shared reference of Zola's *L'Oeuvre* and, more importantly, as a result of their own experiments of the preceding weeks.

Symbolically this theme had become coded with the color yellow. Gauguin intimated as much in his various literary portrayals of Vincent's progress from the Borinage to Arles, a

pilgrimage that included the threat of his incarceration in Gheel, the Belgian town whose name in Dutch translates to "yellow," the color that Vincent considered "fundamental." He directly associated it with the emotional pitch—the "high yellow note"—pursued in recent paintings that had demanded his being "pretty well keyed up" on a regimen of coffee and alcohol.[218] And yellow is a crucial component in the portraits that the two artists painted of each other in December.

In the first days of the month, Vincent, announcing the Roulin series, reported that Gauguin was working on "a portrait of me which I do not count among his useless undertakings."[219] This reticent circumlocution—a positive by way of a double negative—suggests that Gauguin's scrutiny prompted a reaction more complicated than mere modesty. Considering the scolding that Vincent had given Gauguin and Bernard in mid-September, the very fact that the occupants of the Yellow House had not yet painted each other suggests deep-rooted reluctance to do so. When they did attempt such portraits, many issues that could be deflected in conversation came to the surface.

Vincent's limited December correspondence includes no mention of painting Gauguin's

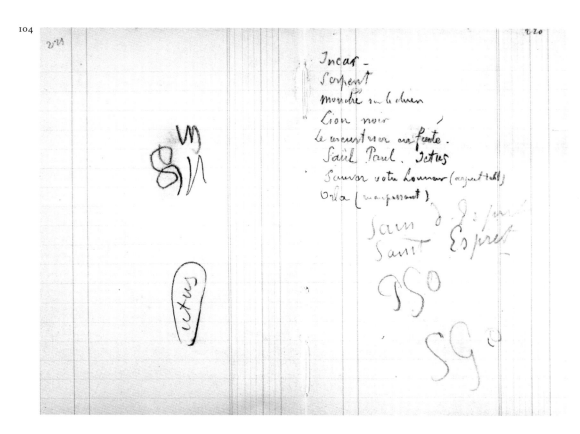

104
Paul Gauguin
Annotated pages
from the Sketchbook
from Arles and
Brittany
Autumn 1888
The Israel Museum
Collection,
Jerusalem, gift of
Sam Salz, New York,
to America-Israel
Cultural Foundation,
1972

105

106

portrait. In fact, nearly a year later, he mentioned that he still hoped to do so one day. This elision makes his strange portrait of Gauguin (fig. 106), evidently set in the studio they shared, all the more intriguing. It is indeniably modest in size and tentative and messy in execution, so much so that its attribution has been questioned.[220] It is, however, clearly autograph. Painted on jute prepared with the same idiosyncratic barium ground with which both artists had experimented in November, it exhibits (notably in the dark green of the coat) the same agitated, chaotic handling found in the second version of Augustine Roulin holding Marcelle (fig. 94) and a similar change in the background color (from pale blue to yellow-green).

Gauguin is seen in partial profile from behind, his right shoulder raised as if to apply brush to the canvas before him, which is predominantly yellow with a rounded orange form glimpsed at the lower right, evidently a reference to the now-lost still life with pumpkin. Vincent might have painted directly from life

(the studio's layout and lighting do not rule this out), but the figure's distinctively angular silhouette is a hallmark of *A Novel Reader* and other pictures executed *de tête*. The likeness is probably something of an amalgam. Details such as the red beret and the painting on the easel seem rooted in observation—Vincent may have surreptitiously sketched a quick underdrawing on the canvas as Gauguin worked—while the awkward rendering of the nose may have resulted from Vincent's referring to the photograph that Gauguin had been distributing to friends (fig. 105) and shifting the head to a less strict profile.[221]

Whatever the circumstances of the portrait's making, one thing is certain. In no other instance did Vincent decline to confront a sitter in this way. Apparently intimidated (like Bernard before him) in the face of Gauguin's talent, Vincent resorted to covert examination, suggesting that he had begun to study his friend with new caution. Other aspects of this charged dynamic can be inferred from Gauguin's portrait of Vincent (fig. 107).

Ostensibly more direct and certainly more ambitious in scale and content than Vincent's portrayal of him, it likewise suggests scrutiny, as well as a surprising degree of premeditation, while allowing several contradictory readings.

Gauguin represented Vincent seated before his easel, in the process of painting five sunflowers in a vase placed on the seat of one of the twelve rush-bottomed chairs. On the wall behind him hangs a landscape of Gauguin's invention, seemingly related to a sketchbook drawing (fig. 98). Hand poised, the artist appears to be contemplating his next gesture on the canvas, studying his subject through half-shut eyes. This expression has been explained with reference to Vincent's habit of squinting when sizing up a motif, but there is nothing in the artist's self-portraits that prepares us for Gauguin's disturbing image of him.[222] The shape and topography of the head appear distorted, the forehead low and sloping, the face and nose flattened, the red-bearded jaw jutting forward, the eyes suggesting a trancelike daze.

105
Photograph of Paul
Gauguin at Pont-
Aven
August 1888

106
Vincent van Gogh
*Paul Gauguin (Man
in a Red Beret)*
c. 1 December 1888
[F 546, not in JH]
Oil on jute
37 x 33 cm
Van Gogh Museum,
Amsterdam
(Vincent van Gogh
Foundation)
Cat. 83

107
Paul Gauguin
*The Painter of
Sunflowers (Le Peintre
de tournesols)*
c. 1 December 1888
[W 296]
Oil on canvas
73 x 92 cm
Van Gogh Museum,
Amsterdam
(Vincent van Gogh
Foundation)
Cat. 46

108
Paul Gauguin
Studies for *The
Painter of Sunflowers*
December 1888
In Sketchbook from
Arles and Brittany
The Israel Museum
Collection,
Jerusalem, gift of
Sam Salz, New
York, to America-
Israel Cultural
Foundation, 1972

109
Paul Gauguin
Compositional
study for *The Painter
of Sunflowers*
December 1888
In Sketchbook from
Arles and Brittany
The Israel Museum
Collection,
Jerusalem, gift of

Sam Salz, New
York, to America-
Israel Cultural
Foundation, 1972

107

108

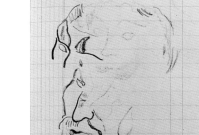

109

The compressed compositional structure generates tension and an aura of menace: the painter seems to have viewed his sitter from above, literally implying superiority. Confined in an exaggeratedly shallow space, Vincent's right shoulder appears squeezed by the advancing yellow of the background canvas, while Gauguin himself and the volumetric still life on the chair seem to crowd him from his left. These countervailing pressures seem strong enough to distort the angle of the body and the shape of the head. The portraitist's act of observation becomes a kind of surveillance, loaded with defensive and aggressive implications.

Gauguin rehearsed the physiognomic distortion in a sketch of Vincent's head and in a compositional study (figs. 108–09).[223] The drawing of the head features a jaw noticeably more underslung than in Vincent's self-portrait as a bonze; the study displays an even more extreme exaggeration, to the point that the painter takes on a distinctly simian appearance. What is at stake here? The sketch and painting sent a message to Vincent at the moment of their making; the canvas also constructed an explanation for Theo, as well as for future viewers, of what was transpiring in the close quarters that had become too small to contain the two men.

Gauguin may have derived the representational idea from Vincent himself, who apparently expressed surprise at Gauguin's intelligence, at odds with the fact that his "forehead was too small, a sign of imbecility."[224] Both artists, along with many of their contemporaries, had a marked interest in reading characterological traits from physical features. Vincent, embarking on a career in art and hoping to hone his skill as a portraitist, had read with fascination a book devoted to the work of Johann Kaspar Lavater and Franz Joseph Gall, founding fathers of physiognomy and phrenology. In the 1880s their ideas about the correlation between an individual's features and character gained new credibility, substantiated by Darwin's theory of evolution, illustrated by means of photography, and applied to the emerging discipline of criminal anthropology. Vincent boasted to van Rappard of his ability to observe "very accurately the physical exteriors of people in order to get at their real mental makeup." The physiognomist's predilection for classification conditioned Vincent's approach to the Roulins, whom he described as "types." But he also understood the term in Carlyle's sense, according to which an artist's body of work was "physiognomical of the whole man."[225]

This reading would have appealed to Gauguin. While Vincent had pored over physiognomic principles, Gauguin had devoured literature on the parallel "science" of graphology, or handwriting analysis. Wishing to decipher character and to understand the creative instincts of artists whom he admired, he practiced with Pissarro's letters and requested from him a sample of Cézanne's penmanship, noting that "mystery, in one's thought, is the sign of a mystic, and . . . the handwriting of mystics is s e p a r a t e d." These were the same terms he used to characterize Cézanne's signature facture. The vocabulary derives directly from contemporary explanations of the graphological system, which posits two basic modes of intellectual apprehension: on the one hand, an analytical, deductive, rational approach to experience, associated with the Occident and manifested in cursive script; on the other, an intuitive, instinctual, and idealist mindset, identified with the "mystical and sensual" Orient and disjoined written characters.[226] Through examination of Cézanne's handwriting, Gauguin seemingly imagined that he could confirm his analysis of the Provençal master's painting style and gain insights into the secret of his genius. Gauguin painted his portrait of Vincent with related motivations. His desire to understand Vincent's achievement was, however, deeply ambivalent.

For all its comic aspects, his drawn study points toward a serious, wideranging consideration of a physiognomics of art, acknowledging artistic affiliations while asserting differences. Caricature—its form and content—was one topic here. Gauguin's Arles notebooks, full of depictions of local types, amply testify to this current interest and a new enthusiasm for Daumier, as does a thumbnail sketch after one of Vincent's Daumier lithographs in a letter to Schuffenecker (figs. 111–12). What attracted him, as he made clear later, was their "purity of line [and] freedom of execution."[227] Like so many of the subjects on which Gauguin subsequently held forth, this evaluation of Daumier emerged from discussions in the Yellow House; making a connection that can only be attributed to Vincent, Gauguin went on to demonstrate bonds of kinship by linking Daumier and Hokusai as members of the same artistic family. Yet his portrait questions whether the same could be said of Vincent and himself.

The issues once again involved the language and aims of art. For Gauguin, what made Hokusai arguably superior to Michelangelo and Raphael was the greater simplicity of his draftsmanship, its freedom from the requirements of illusionistic chiaroscuro: "To draw freely is not to assert something true in nature, but to make pictorial statements that do not disguise thought."[228]

110

Gauguin hammered out his theory of caricature's inherent reductions, exaggerations, and affinities in concert with Vincent, who afforded him the means to consolidate ideas with which he had only toyed up to this point, but could now frame in terms of a larger primitive persona. Line, like form and color, was part of a primordial, prelinguistic system of signs that the artist could manipulate to communicate ideas directly—without recourse to mediated, verbal language or to its visual equivalent, illusionistic realism—to those who possessed the instinctual capacity to understand them. Gauguin intentionally sought to differentiate his conceptualization from theories about the signifying potential of line then current in vanguard circles and manifest in Seurat's art.[229] Privileging mystery and ambiguity, Gauguin rejected the scientific bias of contemporary thinking on the subject, articulating parallel semiological interests with reference to primi-

tive intuition and instinct. In this effort Vincent's associational thinking and extensive mental library served Gauguin well. Availing himself of Carlyle's paradigm identifying the artist-prophet as a kind of latter-day "primitive" man, attuned to Nature's "preternatural" significance, Gauguin posited an intuitive intelligence oppositional to "modern man, who reasons out his emotions," a sensibility who sees the world around him the way he listens to music—directly, without intellectualizing.[230] By December 1888, when Gauguin once again tested his most recent formulations on Schuffenecker, the ideas on the subject that would resurface in his work and writing over the coming decade were largely in place.

Ordering aspects of Vincent's "disordered" thinking to his own ends, Gauguin assigned his partner a very different kind of primitive identity, to which his sketch makes reference. Science—notably Darwin's much-discussed theories—had defined man's connection with nature in provocative evolutionary terms that lent new currency to caricature's staple physiognomic strategy of analogizing physical and characterological aspects between humans and animals. Portraying Vincent as simian painter, Gauguin implied the inferiority of his attitudes, referring not only to Darwin but also to the tradition of *singeries*—monkeys aping human behavior—and to the corresponding pictorial trope in which the monkey-painter represents the lowly, unthinking aspirations of art when practiced as the imitation or mindless copy of nature (see fig. 110).

Fond of expressing home truths in fabular terms, Gauguin engaged with Vincent in casting their differences through a personalized version of La Fontaine's tale of the monkey and the lion. Discussions of Delacroix prompted Vincent to share a favorite simile comparing the Romantic painter at work to a lion devouring his kill, an image of passionate commitment that he extended to the "old lion"

Rembrandt. Gauguin picked up on this not uncommon usage, soon referring to the "redoutable lion" Rembrandt and the "royal tiger" Velázquez.[231]

Whether or not the "black lion" on Gauguin's list also references this dialogue, other sketchbook pages indicate that the arrival in Arles on 2 December of the Pianet Ménagerie played into it. For Vincent this event must have brought to life the opening chapters of *Tartarin de Tarascon*, in which the arrival of a similar menagerie prompts Daudet's protagonist to leave Provence to go lion-hunting in North Africa.[232] Possibly the episode, typical of Tartarin's foolhardy heroics, assumed an edge in light of Gauguin's talk of departure; he would indeed weave a story of lion-hunting into a later fictional account of his liaison with an Arlésienne (see Coda). Clearly the two artists spent some time at the menagerie's display on boulevard des Lices, observing the big cats, a variety of monkeys, and a single elephant (Gauguin devoted a full eight pages of his sketchbook to lions and tigers alone).[233] This singular attachment to a subject, unique in the sketchbooks, suggests how the comic may have been used to discharge the serious. For Vincent—who had already identified Gauguin's *Self-Portrait (Les Misérables)* with the Dieulafoy lions (ch. 3, figs. 74, 80) and who would soon dub his friend the "little Bonaparte tiger of impressionism"—would doubtless have regaled him with a pertinent Delacroix anecdote: the master, out walking with a friend, conceded the necessity of making studies from nature but maintained that "the *ultimate picture* ought to be *made from memory* [*par coeur*]"; when the two parted company, Delacroix, to make his point, startled bystanders by commanding his departing friend in a leonine roar: "Par coeur! Par coeur!" And finally, in his 1882 correspondence with van Rappard, Vincent defended his originality with the proverb "lions don't ape each other."[234]

This is essentially Gauguin's message. Toning down the comic likeness when moving from sketch to painted portrait, he nonetheless touched on the issue of imitation and creation—transcribing from life versus composing from the imagination. He represented the arrangement of sunflowers that Vincent paints in the manner of Vincent's own August *Sunflowers* (ch. 3, figs. 55–58).[235] The two full flower heads (termed doubles) are positioned similarly to those of the yellow-on-yellow version, and the top blossom (disk and rayflowers) in Gauguin's canvas corresponds to the disheveled one at the upper left in Vincent's. Gauguin followed Vincent in heavily reinforcing the rayflowers' contours and also in using dark red lake layers in the center disks (less intense in Gauguin's painting owing to deterioration). Effectively Gauguin's procedure gives the motif studied by the artist the appearance that it took on his canvas, perversely suggesting that Vincent's exercise is one of transcription rather than creation. Gauguin's composition (collapsing flowers, canvas, and brush at a single juncture) even raises the possibility that Vincent actually applies paint to the flowers before him. Finally, Vincent's somewhat dazed expression can imply that his activity is mindless, conducted without heed to his friend's contrasting example as represented by the canvas in the background, an invented construction of bold zones of flat color.

The Painter of Sunflowers illustrates Gauguin's critique of Vincent's working habits and their limitations, along the lines of the larger indictment he would later append to one of his representations of his time with Vincent. Retrospectively Gauguin would contend that while nineteenth-century artists had mastered drawing as a language of direct communication, none—not even Delacroix—had truly understood the expressive potential of color. Gauguin charged the Romantic painter's heirs, even those devoted exclusively to chromatics, with being shackled to verisimilitude

and scientific reasoning, pointing to their incapacity to apprehend "the dreamed landscape." "They looked for things that can be caught by the eye," he claimed, "not those found at the mysterious center of thought." Those he accused of an attachment to the physical so strong that it blinded them to the metaphysical: the Impressionists—and Vincent.[236]

As *The Painter of Sunflowers* intimates, however, Gauguin's feelings about Vincent and his work could not be summarized so definitively or dismissively. Viewed in light of subsequent indictments, Gauguin's portrait comments ambivalently on the painter and on what both artists agreed was a signature creation. The act of transcription is fictional; Vincent could not have been painting real sunflowers in December, for they were not in season. By depicting the still life in a Vincent-like manner, Gauguin hinted that neither he nor Vincent directly observed the motif but rather saw it already transformed by the latter's imagination. In other words, they worked with reference to earlier *Sunflower* canvases, not to actual sunflowers. Certainly there was a basis in fact for this. It was most likely in early December that Vincent reprised the sunflowers on a yellow background, using (as Gauguin did for his portrait) a canvas cut from their remaining jute, primed with a lead white ground (fig. 113).

Seeing this version of the *Sunflowers* as a product of this particular juncture, and in the context of Gauguin's *Painter of Sunflowers*, helps to explain several apparent anomalies. Vincent did not mention it in his correspondence, but he did not reference any pictures after 4 December; he did not sign it, but in fact he signed only two works on jute (figs. 69, 77). It departs stylistically from its August predecessors to a certain extent, but it is consonant with other November/December works, and as in several of the Roulin portraits, Vincent used a tracing of his earlier image to transfer the composition to the new canvas.

Vincent's silence with regard to the second yellow-on-yellow *Sunflowers* and the small portrait of Gauguin points to a particularly fraught moment in their relationship. Several technical aspects of the new *Sunflowers* suggest Vincent's resistance to Gauguin. He laid on pigment very thickly overall, whereas in the August still lifes he had painted many areas thinly; the application here is more direct and the handling rougher (to some extent a result of the coarse jute). Vincent's second versions of compositions typically appear markedly more schematic than their prototypes, but here he aped the original quite closely, simplifying some details but carefully duplicating many nuances of form and brushwork.[237]

Despite profound differences of opinion, the artists' continuing mutual admiration provided the necessary incentive for each to continue engaging with the other. Gauguin remained fascinated, if also maddened, by Vincent's work and ideas, and the *Sunflowers* served as something of a lightning rod for his mixed feelings. Vincent was convinced that Gauguin had a "complete crush" on these canvases. Among the most strikingly phrased of the compliments he paid them was "Ça...c'est... la fleur" ("This...this is the flower")—his implication being that Vincent had not merely represented the flowers, but had succeeded in distilling their very essence, in conveying a kind of metaphysical ideal of Flower.[238] In *The Painter of Sunflowers*, Gauguin implied this by delineating the center of the disk of the uppermost flower in a way that suggests the form of an eye with blue iris; later he would describe Vincent's yellow-on-yellow still lifes as "sunflowers with purple eyes." Possibly an intentional response to the apparently unintentional eyelike shapes found in the sunflowers in Vincent's *Memory of the Garden*, this was a device that Gauguin would embed in *Arlésiennes (Mistral)* (fig. 125) and emphasize in later sunflower still lifes (see Coda, figs. 25–26, 28). The motif appropriates the symbolic language patented by Odilon Redon in charcoal drawings

113
Vincent van Gogh
Sunflowers
c. 1 December 1888
[F 457, JH 1666]
Oil on jute
100 x 76 cm
Seiji Togo Memorial
Yasuda Kasai
Museum of Art,
Tokyo
Cat. 84

and lithographs like *Flower-Cyclops*, which Gauguin owned (see fig. 114), to represent inner vision, the landscape of dreams.[239]

Endowing Vincent with a trancelike, absorbed expression, Gauguin performed something more complex than caricature or ridicule. He and Vincent evidently pondered the creative potential of the state between waking and dreaming. Vincent had earlier summoned Rembrandt's ability to paint angels in this transcendent, hypnagogic state; Gauguin likewise regarded the Dutch master as a magician-prophet, his genius recognizable in even the most humble of his works (see ch. 3). The way Gauguin expressed this idea provides a striking gloss on *The Painter of Sunflowers*: "One must discern [the artist] though hidden behind the flowers he has painted."[240] Of course it was Vincent, not Rembrandt, who painted flowers.

Gauguin's conception of the artist in this statement (and arguably in his portrait) relies on Carlyle's definition of the artist-hero as one who "lives in the inward sphere of things, in the . . . Divine and Eternal which exists always, unseen to most, under the Temporary, Trivial"—a characterization that features among Vincent's formative texts. Gauguin had already, with respect to Cézanne, constructed an ideal of an artist possessing the enlightened, prophetic "Oriental character," the ability to "see God." He had based this conception on graphological texts; Carlyle bolstered this meager intellectual scaffolding. The Scottish philosopher's proposition that the artist is sole heir to primitive man's intuition of the world's divinity became a central component of the heroic role that Gauguin was constructing for himself.[241]

If Gauguin indeed portrayed Vincent in this role—as seer—he also critiqued Vincent's reluctance to subscribe to his own methods. Even the *Sunflowers* that he admired so much seemed

to result from the kind of disorderly thinking Gauguin would castigate. Vincent's "masterpieces of harmony," like those of the Impressionists, struck him as inadvertent in a sense rather than the products of forethought; he could only explain them as natural outpourings, like the "song of the Nightingale."[242]

In summoning this particular analogy, Gauguin once again drew upon Vincent's album persona—Michelet's image of the artist as caged nightingale, sorrowful, conflicted, and subject to attacks of the nerves, to epilepsy (see ch. 1).[243] If Gauguin's nightingale reference is an allusion to Vincent's instability, it is one of his most veiled. He would express himself more explicitly in other accounts. When Gauguin later wrote "Without doubt, that man was crazy [*Fou*]," the statement would come across as strategic, a means of forestalling questions raised by the Dutch artist's biography. The overt intention was to assert his friend's nobility, but the rhetoric manages to plant a seed of doubt about the nature of his achievement. *The Painter of Sunflowers* suggests that Gauguin had already begun thinking along these lines in December 1888.

Vincent's decision to reprise the yellow-on-yellow *Sunflowers* rather than the one set against pale blue-green was doubtless connected with Gauguin's high opinion of it. While he remained close to the model in certain details of form and brushwork, he keyed up the color to a fiercer intensity. The background in the first canvas (ch. 3, fig. 58) is a pale, cream yellow and the round double flowers a deep, smoldering orange; in the second the hot, bright orange-yellow flower heads vibrate against an acid greenish yellow field. Gauguin, notwithstanding his expressed preference, situated the still-life arrangement in *The Painter of Sunflowers* against contrasting zones of blue background and of the dark blue vase; only a hint of yellow-on-yellow appears, at the point where the

uppermost sunflower overlaps the golden band of Gauguin's landscape.[244]

This small detail assumes larger significance in light of Gauguin's subsequent claim to have rescued Vincent from a monotonous fixation on complementary colors, a didactic effort he would recall as follows:

I undertook the task of enlightening him—an easy matter, for I found a rich and fertile soil. Like all original natures that are marked with the stamp of personality, Vincent had no fear of the other man and was not stubborn.

From that day [of my arrival], my van Gogh made astonishing progress: he seemed to divine all that he had in him, and the result was that whole series of sunflowers upon sunflowers in full sunlight.[245]

Gauguin's assertion that Vincent's yellow-on-yellow compositions resulted from his tutelage (see Coda) is patently false, as is his description of Vincent's tractability. Identifying himself as the sun to Vincent's sunflower, the sower of Vincent's fertile ground, Gauguin changed the chronology of events, took credit for Vincent's signature imagery, appropriated his emblematic language, and asserted a suggestively sexualized dominance over him. Written a decade after they parted, Gauguin's grotesque distortion could be attributed to the pressures he felt to defend his reputation—but *The Painter of Sunflowers* reveals that he was already developing this representation in December 1888. The portrait is a first draft of the claims later made in the writing: the composition conveys Gauguin's condescending stance toward "my van Gogh"; his rendering of Vincent's still life as primarily yellow-on-blue implies the transformation for which he would claim responsibility; the rigid, phallic thumb (see fig. 108) poking through the palette intimates sexualized undercurrents both in Vincent's creativity and in Gauguin's identity as inseminating agent. In a sense the portrait—together with

Vincent's December reprise of his August *Sunflowers*—documents Gauguin's claim that Vincent painted "the still life he loved so much" at his instigation and under his supervision.[246]

Why did Gauguin prepare this alibi? Because, to use his own words apropos Vincent, it would seem that Gauguin "had fear of the other man." In Vincent, Gauguin had met his match. There was no precedent in his experience for a relationship of give and take: with Pissarro and the Impressionists, he had assumed a junior position; he had stayed clear of Seurat; and none of the artists with whom he had associated since 1886 (either much younger or less talented than he) could give him a run for his money. There is no doubt that living with Vincent in close quarters for weeks on end was intensely difficult and demanding. But it was also challenging and ultimately rewarding. Gauguin found Vincent's mythic view of the artist's mission compelling and (dangerously) stimulating—more so than he had anticipated. Vincent had been candid about the possibility that Gauguin's presence would have an impact on his work; Gauguin had probably never imagined a conversation of equals. When, in the final weeks of 1888, he did begin to fear Vincent's influence, he was also beginning to fear his person.

Later in December Gauguin offered the picture he titled *The Painter of Sunflowers* to Theo as a gift, observing that from a "geographical point of view" it was not a good likeness, but adding that he had aimed to "convey something of [Vincent's] inner character." Theo concurred; in addition to its being a "great" picture, he considered it "the best portrait that's been made of him in terms of capturing his inner being."[247]

While Theo could accept the portrayal without surprise, Vincent must have found it deeply disturbing, for it held a mirror up to him, showing him the way he was perceived by his friend. Even in its early stages, it signaled a passing comment on the subject's keyed-up emotional state. Gauguin's usual practice at the time was to lay in a figure with muted tints of blue, green, and perhaps orange, but for Vincent's figure, he used remarkably more vibrant hues, giving him a pulsating shock of vermilion hair, a vivid yellow face, green pants, and a yellow-green jacket. The exaggerated effect—amplifying that achieved graphically in the compositional sketch—was subsequently muted by the application of duller, mixed hues.

Vincent would recognize the likeness only insofar as it reflected the particular circumstances in which it was made. Months later he bserved to Theo: "My face has certainly brightened up since then, but it was really me, extremely tired and charged with electricity as I was then." Indeed in late December he characterized his interaction with Gauguin as *"excessively electric."* Gauguin later put a similarly qualified response in Vincent's mouth: "It is certainly I, but it's I gone mad."[248] Whatever Vincent actually said, and whatever the degree of Gauguin's malice aforethought, *The Painter of Sunflowers* overtly renders the brewing tensions that both men would soon have to acknowledge. Their conversations ranged across topics as diverse as Maupassant's "Le Horla," Carlyle, Michelet, Rembrandt, Delacroix, Daumier, Hokusai, the Bible, physiognomy, graphology, evangelism, families, and fables, but the real issue—however thoroughly displaced—was always their own relationship and artistic aims. Among the various conscious and subconscious strategies informing its creation, the portrait given to Theo may have been fashioned by Gauguin as a justification. He was now actively contemplating leaving Arles.

Sunday	Monday	Tuesday	Wednesday	Thursday	Friday	Saturday
				13 Dec ☀️☁️	**14** ☀️☁️ ✉️ Gauguin to Theo	**15** 🌧️ ✉️ Gauguin to Mette
16 🌧️ Artists visit Musée Fabre, Montpellier, 16th or 17th	**17** 🌧️ ✉️ Gauguin to Theo	**18** ☁️	**19** ☁️ ✉️ Gauguin to Theo ✉️ Vincent to Theo	**20** ☁️	**21** 🌧️	**22** 🌧️ ✉️ Gauguin to Shuffenecker
23 🌧️ ✉️ Vincent to Theo						

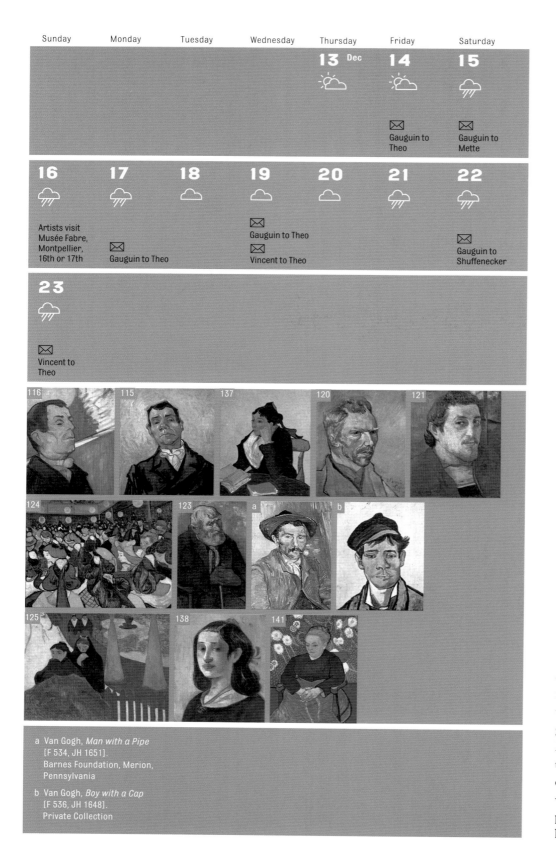

a Van Gogh, *Man with a Pipe*
   [F 534, JH 1651].
   Barnes Foundation, Merion,
   Pennsylvania

b Van Gogh, *Boy with a Cap*
   [F 536, JH 1648].
   Private Collection

The correspondence of both artists decreased in frequency and specificity in December.[249] While this leaves the chronology of the work produced during these final weeks open to conjecture, there can be no doubt that Vincent and Gauguin continued to paint in dialogue with each other.

Possibly in the first half of the month, Joseph-Michel Ginoux—the husband of Marie Ginoux, the "Arlésienne"—came to the Yellow House to pose for both artists (figs. 115–16). The angled ledge in Gauguin's painting suggests one possible scenario, in which Gauguin stationed himself by the east window and the model sat to the left of the window that opened onto place Lamartine, facing Vincent, who set up his canvas to take advantage of the gaslight on the north wall. This configuration would account for the apparent discrepancies in lighting in the two works, but other differences are still more notable. Ginoux looms large in Vincent's portrait, looking down his nose at the artist, his dark, heavy features giving him a somewhat thuggish appearance (fig. 115). Crisp, angular contours define the head, as in Vincent's recent portrait of Joseph Roulin executed on the same scale (fig. 101); an intense yellow-green background surrounds the figure in an aura of vital energy. In Gauguin's smaller portrait (fig. 116), we recognize the same sitter, with his double-breasted jacket, white cravat, distinctive widow's peak, and cursive brows. But Gauguin represented Ginoux from the side, in partial profile, in the act of assessing Vincent through half-shut eyes. The significance of the background configuration remains unclear; it may allude to the yellow lamps hanging in front of the green, orange-bordered balcony in Vincent's *Dance Hall* (fig. 124), executed at around this time and possibly hanging to dry on the studio's south wall, between the door and the window, precisely where Joseph Ginoux sat to pose.[250] But Gauguin's placement of the yellow disk, roughed in above Ginoux's head,

Oct						
	1	2	3	4	5	6
7	8	9	10	11	12	13
14	15	16	17	18	19	20
21	22	23	24	25	26	27
28	29	30	31			

Nov						
				1	2	3
4	5	6	7	8	9	10
11	12	13	14	15	16	17
18	19	20	21	22	23	24
25	26	27	28	29	30	

Dec						
						1
2	3	4	5	6	7	8
9	10	11	12	**13**	**14**	**15**
16	**17**	**18**	**19**	**20**	**21**	**22**
23	24	25	26	27	28	29
30	31					

115
Vincent van Gogh
Monsieur Ginoux
Early December 1888
[F 533, JH 1649]
Oil on canvas
65 x 54.5 cm
Kröller-Müller
Museum, Otterlo,
The Netherlands
Cat. 85

116
Paul Gauguin
Monsieur Ginoux
Early December 1888
[not in W]
Oil on canvas
40 x 31 cm
Van Gogh Museum,
Amsterdam
(Vincent van Gogh
Foundation)
Cat. 47

suggests a play on Vincent's recent *Sower* (figs.
77, 79) and on discussions about portraits
and halos; however, given the subject's rather
dubious characterization, it seems to have
been employed with a hint of irony.

Joseph Ginoux's presence in the studio may
have been connected with Vincent's decision
at around the same time to produce a repetition of the portrait of Ginoux's wife (fig. 137).
Using a tracing of the early November version (fig. 37), Vincent emulated Gauguin's
means and achieved corresponding ends. The
new picture is bolder and more considered
than the first in every respect; the colors are
more intense and the contours crisper, their
rhythms clear and emphatic. It seems to have
been conceived as the *tableau* for which the
first version served as an *étude*. Embracing
Gauguin's synthetism, it goes beyond the portrait of Joseph Roulin (fig. 101) to approach
the decorative effects of the type of chromolith-
ographic posters that currently interested
Seurat.[251] The second portrait of Marie Ginoux
predicts the synthetic structure of Vincent's
subsequent—fourth—depiction of Augustine
Roulin (fig. 141) in that each area of color manifests a distinctive texture: from the thinly
applied, fine directional sculpting of her face
to the loose, expressive brushwork on the
tabletop; from the short, choppy basketweave of the background to the long, supple
strokes of the ribbon. Vincent allowed the
loosely painted preliminary sketch and
exposed ground to serve as the book's pages
and pulled the wooden handle of the brush,
comblike, through wet paint to part her hair.

In refashioning his approach, Vincent made
over his sitter. Here Marie Ginoux is the
Arlésienne of popular imagery. No longer
pinched and wan as in the early November
image, her complexion is more ruddy; her
eyes enlivened with colored shadow; her lips
fuller and more luscious, their bee-stung

115

116

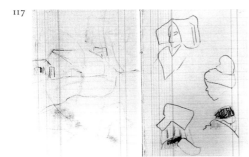

117

shape emphasized with bright red pigment.[252] Forfeiting something of Marie Ginoux's individual presence through the cosmetic enhancement of her features, Vincent instead provided her with attributes—books—that establish her character. Though coquettish, she is nonetheless a reader of novels.

Vincent's glamorizing of the Arlésienne can be related to his desire to reengage Gauguin's interest in the attractions of the South. For Gauguin's enthusiasm was clearly flagging. His portrait of Monsieur Ginoux is half-hearted; its size, unfinished state, and support (a commercially primed canvas supplied by Vincent) suggest that he may have involved himself only at Vincent's instigation. His landscape efforts also reveal increasing disengagement. He may indeed have caught the "sharp flavor" of Arles, but his appetite was gone, and he was thinking of Brittany.[253] *Blue Trees* ("*Vous y passerez, la belle!*") (fig. 87) started out as a remembrance of a Breton scene painted the previous spring (fig. 86), which likewise features a row of blue trees set against a similarly proportioned landscape and yellow sky. In the valley he used the same combination of pale blue scumbles over warm orange washes and sketched a small windswept tree, framed between the blue trunks. Infrared reflectography reveals the earlier picture's

rooftop shapes under the comparable area in the Arles setting; Gauguin superimposed the vineyards of Montmajour, but nonetheless included what seems to be the same little tree just left of center.

Gauguin's nostalgia for the North came to the surface in a landscape that may have been the last in the early December group (fig. 118). He referred to sketches made locally (see fig. 117) and identified Arles by arbitrarily including the Alyscamps' Saint-Césaire arch (see map, fig. 19), but the compositional structure and stylistic vocabulary align it with the Breton landscape that Theo so admired (fig. 76). Refraining from emphatic contours and abstract patterning, Gauguin used small strokes to apply points of vivid, light color, enlivening areas of the foreground with an almost pointillist stippling. The effect is delicate but insubstantial, lacking the synthetic rigor of its November predecessors. Seen alongside the previous weeks' production and in the context of the increasingly charged studio environment, this Arles landscape is less suggestive of a retrenchment or return to earlier ideas than it is of distractedness. The two dogs—red and white—that Gauguin wryly introduced at lower right were more interested in sniffing out new subjects than he was. His thoughts were elsewhere, as Vincent was now painfully aware.

A letter from Schuffenecker that arrived at the Yellow House around 11 December may have ignited a volatile situation. Schuffenecker had, at Gauguin's direction, visited Theo's gallery to see *Human Miseries* and other recent paintings. Their stunning "fecundity and abundance" convinced him that Gauguin would "kill off" all of his contemporaries (save the "colossus," Degas): "But you, you are a giant; you know that [giants] have scaled the heavens. You will pile Ossa on top of Pelion to reach the sky of painting."[254]

Such delirious praise might not have seemed threatening to Vincent had Schuffenecker confined his reference to the mythic Greek giants who scaled Olympus by piling two mountains (Ossa and Pelion) atop one another. But Gauguin's tireless cheerleader continued:

You will not reach [heaven] because it's the Absolute, that is to say God, but you will offer your hand to those who have most nearly approached it. Yes, my dear Gauguin, what awaits you in art is not only success, it is glory beside the likes of a Rembrandt and a Delacroix. And you will have suffered as they did.[255]

It was as if Schuffenecker had eavesdropped on conversations between Vincent and Gauguin, and fashioned his praise of the latter in

117
Paul Gauguin
Sketches for *Arles
Landscape with Two
Dogs* (fig. 117)
Autumn 1888
In Sketchbook from
Arles and Brittany
The Israel Museum
Collection,

Jerusalem, gift of
Sam Salz, New
York, to America-
Israel Cultural
Foundation, 1972

118
Paul Gauguin
*Arles Landscape with
Two Dogs (Paysage
d'Arles avec buissons)*
1888 [W 310]
Oil on canvas
73.6 x 92.3 cm
Courtesy Christie's
Images London

119
Charles Laval
(French; 1862–1894)
*Self-Portrait Dedicated
to Vincent van Gogh*
c. 1 November 1888
Oil on canvas
50 x 60 cm

Van Gogh Museum,
Amsterdam
(Vincent van Gogh
Foundation)
Cat. 53

terms of the aspirations and admirations central to the former. The frame of reference cannot be coincidental; Gauguin must have communicated crucial samplings of a dialogue in which Wagner's credo was effectively amended to propose a holy trinity featuring painters rather than composers: "I believe in God, in Rembrandt, and in Delacroix."

Vincent, faced with the prediction that Gauguin was on the threshold of securing the kind of immortality through art for which he yearned (see ch. 3), must have reacted strongly. This can be inferred from the terse note that Gauguin dispatched to Theo a day or two later.

Dear Monsieur van Gogh,

I would be grateful if you would send me part of the money from the sales of my pictures. All things taken into account, I am obliged to return to Paris; Vincent and I absolutely cannot live side by side without turmoil resulting from our temperamental incompatibility, and he and I need tranquility for our work. He is a man of remarkable intelligence whom I esteem highly and leave regretfully, but I repeat to you it is necessary. I appreciate all your tactful conduct toward me and beg you to forgive my decision.

Cordially yours,
Paul Gauguin[256]

A pair of self-portraits that he and Vincent each produced at around this time (figs. 120–21) speak volumes about the artists' different states of mind. The portraits—ostensibly painted to exchange with Laval (see fig. 119), to whom they were dedicated (Gauguin later reinscribed his to another artist) and who had just sent a self-portrait of his own to Vincent—were created in the fraught context of a more immediate exchange.[257] Vincent's agitation is evident. In contrast to his earlier self-representations, he appears not merely serious and resolved but tense, his features drawn into a scowl of concern and irritation, his green-eyed gaze skittish. The execution seems fierce, the ground revealed between the slashing strokes with which Vincent laid in the background, hair, and a curious lock cutting across his ear.

Gauguin, by contrast, appears the picture of contentment. Gone is the haggard and vaguely sinister expression of *Self-Portrait (Les Misérables)*; the face here is fuller and healthier (as Vincent noted a few weeks later), the expression one of watchful, almost smug self-possession. Gauguin sports a Breton sweater with decorated yoke under his jacket and sits, as does Laval in his self-portrait, beside a window. However, the background scene has nothing to do with Laval's Breton landscape, nor does it suggest the environs of the Yellow House. Rather the predominant purple-blue and pink mountain and mist-laden sky bring to mind the distant views of cloud-wreathed peaks seen in some of Gauguin's Martinique canvases.

The crisis that occasioned Gauguin's urgent missive to Theo passed, at least momentarily; soon after, he instructed Theo to consider it a "bad dream."[258] But the issues that informed both the letter and the self-portraits remained, as Vincent's note to his brother a day or two later makes clear:

119

120
Vincent van Gogh
*Self-Portrait Dedicated
to Charles Laval*
December 1888
[F 501, JH 1634]
Oil on canvas
46 x 38 cm
Courtesy Christie's

121
Paul Gauguin
*Self-Portrait Dedicated
to Charles Laval (later
to Eugène Carrière)*
December 1888
[W 384]
Oil on jute
46.5 x 38.6 cm
National Gallery of
Art, Washington,
D.C., Collection of
Mr. and Mrs. Paul
Mellon
Cat. 48

121

My dear Theo,

Thank you very much for your letter, for the 100-franc note enclosed and also for the money order for 50 francs.

I think that Gauguin was a little disenchanted with the good town of Arles, the little yellow house where we worked, and above all with me.

In fact, there are still serious difficulties to overcome, for me as well as for him, here.

But these difficulties lie more in ourselves than anywhere else.

In short, I think that he'll either simply leave or he'll simply stay.

I've told him to think it over and consider his options before doing anything.

Gauguin is very strong, very creative, but precisely because of that he needs peace.

Will he find it elsewhere if he doesn't find it here?

I await his decision with absolute equanimity.

With a good handshake,
Vincent.[259]

Despite their creative rivalries and jealousies, in Vincent's mind one goal remained preeminent: to keep his dream of a Studio of the South intact. The more Gauguin showed signs of leaving, the more anxious Vincent became, and the more strenuously he importuned his friend to stay. The situation had been played out before, when, in the aftermath of his failed domestic experiment in The Hague, Vincent had sought to enlist Theo as brother-painter (see ch. 1). The many pages that Vincent wrote in his unsuccessful attempt to bring this about allow ready inference of the circumstances that now led Gauguin to risk losing Theo's support by bailing out.

Vincent was capable of incessantly pressing his case, relentlessly marshaling arguments in his favor and turning suspicious and bitter when put off. As he acknowledged remorsefully a month later, he had "involuntarily" caused Gauguin trouble: "Up to the last days I saw one thing only, that he was working with his heart divided between his desire to go to Paris to carry out his plans, and his life in Arles."[260] In the short term, he resolved to back off, to await Gauguin's decision, as he said, with patient resignation—a promise he would find increasingly difficult to keep. But he made an effort, and for a short time a spirit of détente seems to have prevailed in the studio, allowing the artists to continue painting.

Vincent's canvas known as *The Dance Hall* (fig. 124) is an essay in compliance, even more straightforwardly so than the second *Arlésienne*. A multifigural composition painted in

122

123

took a more considered response to Vincent and paid a kind of homage to their work together. He selected a size 30 piece of stretched jute, initially intending to produce yet another landscape suffused with memories of Brittany.[263] Infrared reflectography reveals the beginnings of a vertical composition, blocked in with brush and blue paint (see fig. 128), incorporating some of the animal studies (fig. 129) that he had mined in 1886 for paintings like the *Breton Shepherdess* (see ch. 2, fig. 28). But he changed his mind, turned the canvas on its side, and proceeded with a definitively local subject.

In his Arles sketchbook, Gauguin planned the principal figures, the details of their headdresses (fig. 127), and their grouping, as well as the fountain (fig. 126), bench, and conical shapes of shrubs wrapped against the frost in the park across the street, all of which he could have observed from his bedroom. In his choice of subject and overall composition, Gauguin responded directly to Vincent's *Memory of the Garden* (fig. 67). In both paintings a curving walkway tilts up to the picture plane, a female figure (resembling Madame Ginoux) appears at the left, and a planting occupies the foreground. In this planting, where Vincent incorporated a sunflower, Gauguin (recalling what he had done in *The Painter of Sunflowers*) embedded an eyelike form.[264]

Gauguin imparted a somber, reflective mood and a mysterious sense of occasion through the expressions, gestures, and arrangement of the figures. Madame Ginoux clutches her shawl to her mouth against the cold mistral. This gesture, together with her blank eyes, suggests stifled grief, reinforcing the sense that she leads a solemn cortege. There is a retrospective quality to the picture: it recalls Gauguin's initial enthusiastic comparison of the Arlésiennes to processional figures on Greek urns, and it features two of the three "graces" from his Alyscamps composition of late October (fig. 21). But here a barrier separates the women from the painter, and a funereal aura pervades the brightly colored but chill December landscape. In quoting Vincent, Gauguin too fashioned a memory of the garden. He joined his friend in again celebrating the Arlésienne—but with an elegiac quality.

This spurt of new activity notwithstanding, the artists painted with diminishing ease. "Work," Vincent reported with uncharacteristic understatement, "is not always easy." To relieve the tension, they broke from their normal routine and visited the Musée Fabre in Montpellier, a four-and-a-half-hour train ride from Arles. (This excursion took place on either 16 or 17 December, Sunday and Monday being the only days that the museum was open to the public both morning and afternoon.)[265]

Gauguin proposed the trip, having visited the museum years earlier, when a political mission for the Spanish republicans took him to the area.[266] As he told Vincent, he had been much impressed by Delacroix's pictures—including *Daniel in the Lion's Den*—and by the major Courbets featured in a special gallery (fig. 130) housing the collection assembled by

128  129

Montpellier's native son Alfred Bruyas. As a young man in the early 1850s, Bruyas went to Paris, where he patronized and posed for the still-controversial Delacroix, and then took up the cause of Courbet, the immensely polarizing champion of Realism. Bruyas advanced Courbet's career by purchasing, commissioning, and lending pictures; by recruiting leading critics to publish legitimizing essays on his collection; and by fêting the artist in Montpellier. When Bruyas gave his collection to the city in 1868, he secured his own legend by making a southern public institution one of the premier venues in France for vanguard Realism.

Although Bruyas was a well-known cultural figure, it seems that Vincent was heretofore unaware of him.[267] As Gauguin might have predicted, the discovery made a profound impact. Vincent's letter to Theo immediately following their return to Arles confirms that he was struck as much by the collector as by his collection—precisely the effect that Bruyas had intended to achieve. The deeply narcissistic root of his investment in contemporary art is immediately demonstrated by the thirty-odd portraits of himself that he commissioned from the artists he patronized. Some are serious works of art, notably that by Delacroix (fig. 135) and the four by Courbet (including the latter's celebrated canvas *The Meeting [Bonjour! Monsieur Courbet]*; fig. 131). Most are merely competent and some downright mawkish. In the worst of these (see fig. 132), and in the studio photographs that Bruyas stage-managed with impunity, the collector's self-image emerges most explicitly (see fig. 133):

he saw himself as a Man of Sorrows, a Christ martyred for his lofty beliefs, the possessor of a soul (if not, regrettably, an outward physique) that rendered him more beautiful than mere mortals.

Such melodrama—the sight of a "face so heartbroken and obviously frustrated"—moved Vincent. What appealed to him more than the exaggeratedly anguished representations of the patron, and even more than Courbet's relatively restrained portrayals, were "serene" portraits touched with melancholy by Gustave Ricard and notably by Delacroix. The specific reasons for his preference emerge in his description of the latter portrait for Theo: "A gentleman with a red hair and beard, who bears an amazing resemblance to you and to me, and made me think of that poem by Musset"—a cue for quoting Musset's lines about Solitude looking at him like a brother.[268]

The idea of a brotherhood of redheads was not new. In his attempt four years earlier to recruit Theo to join him as a brother-painter, Vincent had fixed on this common feature. Theo demurred, claiming that physiognomic differences revealed Vincent's superior aptitude for the task, but Vincent, suspecting his father's negative influence, insisted that he and Theo both resembled the Puritans as Carlyle described them, red-headed thinkers as well as men of action who put out to sea on a pioneering religious mission (see ch. 1).[269]

Vincent thought that he had successfully enlisted Gauguin to his brotherhood, but instead

he found himself again facing a future alone. The family likeness to himself and Theo that he perceived in Bruyas allowed him to shore up his identity in a discipleship of like-minded if crazy idealists. He enjoined Theo to acquire a reproduction of Delacroix's *Tasso in the Madhouse* (fig. 134), since he surmised that the painter had given the deranged poet features similar to those of Bruyas. Vincent identified with Bruyas's project to bring modern art to the South, having devoted himself to the same mission. Reassured as he was to discover that another (besides Monticelli) had illuminated this path, Vincent could see that Bruyas had suffered in pursuing his dream. He read defeat in the troubled face and in the gallery itself, which, though filled with fine paintings and intimating "the existence of the *Hope* that Puvis de Chavannes painted," lacked vitality.[270]

In addition to these mixed reactions, Vincent experienced stronger emotions when he and Gauguin began to discuss the pictures. Testing their views in front of actual works of art brought deep-seated disparities to the surface as never before. Vincent's requirement that art have a consoling, missionary purpose colored all of his aesthetic judgments, while Gauguin rejected anything smacking of sentiment. Vincent conceded the magnificence of the Courbets, but avowed that Ricard's and Delacroix's portraits touched him more; if this mention of two such unequal talents in the same breath failed to provoke Gauguin, Vincent's commendation of a portrait by Alexandre Cabanel certainly would have. Vincent could admire the image for conveying what he

imagined to be a truthful idea of Bruyas; for Gauguin this meant little. He was interested only in the painter, and what he saw in Cabanel was fatuousness—his inclusion pointing to an essential weakness in a collection that, despite its great examples, had been assembled without consistent vision. "I hated [Cabanel] during his lifetime," he stated. "I hated him after his death, and I shall hate him till I die myself."[271] In the face of such crimes of judgment, tempers flared on both sides.

"We have been plunged into the magical because, as [Eugène] Fromentin puts it so well, Rembrandt is above all a magician, and Delacroix a man of God, like God's thunder." So observed Vincent opaquely the day after the stormy discussion in the Bruyas Gallery that left him and Gauguin both feeling "as drained as an electric battery after discharge." The point of contention as they stood before the Delacroix portrait of Bruyas was seemingly its affectivity. What apparently bothered Gauguin—enough to mention it in a letter two days later and to include it in a sketch (fig. 126)—was Delacroix's placement of a handkerchief in the sitter's hand.[272] This was a conventional prop, like black clothing to indicate mourning, of the sort that he himself aspired to discard in devising the more suggestive pictorial language seen in paintings like *Human Miseries*. While Vincent responded wholeheartedly to the portrait, it was apparently one of those Delacroixs that provoked in Gauguin "the same feelings that I have after a reading; by contrast if I go to hear a Beethoven quartet, I come out with colored images vibrat-

ing in the depths of my being." Not only did Gauguin thus dare to challenge the suggestive power of one of Vincent's gods, he may have aired a blasphemous idea that he would later commit to paper. In remarking "It pleases me to imagine Delacroix visiting the world thirty years later and undertaking the fight that I've dared to undertake, with his luck and especially his genius, what a renaissance there would be today," he proposed himself as Delacroix's successor and guide.[273]

Inevitably Vincent steered all conversation to the question of the Studio of the South, of an artistic brotherhood, and of Gauguin's thoughts of leaving the order. Even when speaking of Rembrandt, the quintessentially Northern master, Vincent claimed him for the South, footnoting Fromentin. Discussion of the Delacroix portrait of Bruyas fostered a physiognomics of brotherhood and family ties. Vincent cast himself, Theo, and Bruyas—who "resembles us as would a new brother"—as of a single mind. But while gaining one brother, he faced the threat of losing another. To Gauguin, Vincent assigned a different identity, affiliating him with a long-admired work then attributed to Rembrandt, his "strange and superb" portrait in the Louvre's Lacaze gallery of a man holding a walking stick (fig. 136), because he recognized in the sitter's face "a certain family or racial resemblance to Delacroix or to Gauguin." He confided that he had always referred to the picture as "the man coming from afar," or "the wanderer."[274]

In view of this conversation, it is telling that Vincent's many letter references to the Montpellier visit include no mention of the one example in the Bruyas Gallery that dramatizes the relationship between a red-headed southern visionary and an artist-wanderer: Courbet's painting *The Meeting*, known as *Bonjour! Monsieur Courbet*, which commemorates his 1854 visit to Montpellier. In it the patron stands on a roadway, flanked by a servant, his arm outstretched to greet the dominant figure of the painter, who has seemingly just alighted from the receding coach and who moves toward him, walking staff in hand, painting gear on his back. Though Vincent was unaware of Courbet's specific points of reference (which included popular images of the Wandering Jew),[275] his familiarity with emblematics (see ch. 1, fig. 13) would have guaranteed the composition's allegorical resonance. Given the roles he had assigned to himself and Gauguin, this picture of pilgrimage and friendship must have brought to mind the welcome to the South that he had extended to an artist who, as both poet and lover, was larger than life. But Vincent would also have taken in the relationship's subsequent history: Courbet came but did not stay; Bruyas, his dreams never fulfilled, remained a Man of Sorrows. Vincent clung to his hopes for a different outcome, concluding his account of the Montpellier visit with the observation: "As far as founding an artists' colony is concerned, such strange things have been known, and I'll close with what you always say—only time will tell."[276]

130
The Bruyas Gallery
c. 1890/1910
Musée Fabre,
Montpellier

131
Gustave Courbet
(French; 1819–1877)
The Meeting (Bonjour! Monsieur Courbet)
1854
Oil on canvas
129 x 149 cm
Musée Fabre,
Montpellier

132
Antoine Verdier
(French; 1817–1858)
Christ with a Crown of Thorns: Alfred Bruyas
1852
Oil on canvas
55 x 65 cm
Musée Fabre,
Montpellier

133
Alfred Bruyas
1856/58
Lithograph (after photograph)
Musée Fabre,
Montpellier

134
Eugène Delacroix
Tasso in the Madhouse
1839
Oil on canvas
60.5 x 50 cm
Oskar Reinhart
Collection,
Winterthur,
Switzerland

135
Eugène Delacroix
Alfred Bruyas
1853
Oil on canvas
116 x 89 cm
Musée Fabre,
Montpellier

136
Attributed to
Rembrandt van Rijn
*Young Man with
Walking Stick*
1651
Oil on canvas
83 x 66 cm
Musée du Louvre,
Paris

Three or four days later, on Saturday the 22nd, Gauguin confided to Schuffenecker, enjoining him not to breathe a word to Theo:

My situation here is difficult. I owe a lot to [Theo] van Gogh and Vincent, and in spite of some discord, I cannot hold a grudge against a good-hearted person who is sick, who suffers, and who is asking for me. . . . One day I will explain it all to you. In any case, I am staying here, but I remain poised to leave at any moment.[277]

The partnership was unraveling. But Gauguin's long letter, while testifying to the difficulty of the situation, also speaks volumes about all that he had—in his words—consolidated through his exchanges with Vincent. Though Gauguin by no means attributed his assertions, the sharp imprint of Vincent's thinking reveals itself in the glosses on recent paintings that Gauguin now provided and in his theories and accompanying justifications.[278] However, the greater and longer-lasting influence can be seen in what is arguably Gauguin's single most important creation to emerge from the Studio of the South—the verbal self-portrait that he delineated in the same letter:

Vincent sometimes calls me "the man who comes from afar and who will go far." I hope all of those good-hearted people who have loved and understood me will follow me. I just wrote about it to Laval; a better world is coming, where nature will take its course, men will live under the sun knowing how to love.[279]

Gauguin was clothing himself in the persona that Vincent had enabled him to articulate. Cast in language once again provided by Vincent and set under the sun of his mythic South, the artist was pilgrim, leader, prophet of a better world. Gauguin merged this identity with that of Peruvian savage, writing himself into the commonly held identification of the Incas of ancient Peru as "Children of the Sun": "According to legend, the Inca comes directly from the sun, and I will return there. But not everyone comes from the sun."[280]

This enlarged, mythic persona distinguished Gauguin from the Neo-Impressionist vanguard, whose aspirations he likened to those of Icarus, the Greek mythological figure whose desire to ascend to the heavens met disaster when the sun melted the wax wings he had crafted. For himself Gauguin mapped a differ-

ent destination, retooling Wagner's notion of the true disciple's ultimate return to the divine source into a return to the sun, implicitly figuring a Studio of the Tropics. The portrait that he painted of his mother around this time (fig. 138), based on a photograph (fig. 139) and executed on a scrap of used canvas, can thus be seen as responsive to Vincent's identically sized depiction of Anna van Gogh (fig. 62).[281] Initially modeling the facial features, shape of the head and hair, and lace collar quite closely on the photograph, Gauguin proceeded to make the nose wider, the lips fuller, and the jaw more angular. He altered the gaze to engage the viewer more directly, as he did when transposing his drawing of Marie Ginoux to canvas in *Night Café* (figs. 36, 41); and he added a higher collar, brooch, and decorative headdress suggesting the regional costume of Arles. In a most suggestive sequence, he first painted the background red—his signature color—and then changed it to yellow—Vincent's. Gauguin's image provides a contrasting—youthful and exotic—representation of the maternal, bolstering his claim to mythic identity through Aline's Peruvian ancestry. Playing as well off Vincent's *Arlésienne* (fig. 137), it parallels the evocation in Gauguin's written self-portrait of destiny/destination, in a sense reconfiguring the Studio of the South's muse in terms of Gauguin's own lineage. Intimating the regressive dimension of his primitivism, it suggests how the Studio of the Tropics would allow him to recapture the long ago in the far away.

The implications of this effort may have contributed to Vincent's decision to fashion yet another maternal talisman, once again in the form of Augustine Roulin (fig. 141). He relied on a tracing of the larger of his mother-and-baby portraits (fig. 94) for the figure's head and on tracings from the large portrait of her husband (fig. 102) for her hands; the radiating, encrusted yellow and orange strokes in her hair and face relate to the most recent *Sunflowers*. In addition to referring to his own work, close study of Gauguin's *Madame Roulin* (fig. 97)

134

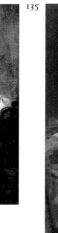

135

resulted in the emphatic geometrizing of the head and its facial planes; the masklike physiognomy; the simplified delineation of blouse, bodice, and bosom; and the rhyming contours of figure and chair. As Gauguin had done in his *Self-Portrait (Les Misérables)*, Vincent evoked the sitter's essence through a backdrop of floral wallpaper, the large dahlia blossoms here suggesting an abundant fecundity and harking back to those in *A Memory of the Garden*, where they are also associated with motherhood. To reinforce this allusion, Vincent placed a loop of rope beneath the sitter's hands (a signifier like the handerchief in Delacroix's portrait of Bruyas), initially indicating it by pulling a dry brush through the wet paint of the skirt's green underlayer. For this detail he mined Rembrandt's picture of domestic spirituality (fig. 61) for a second time. Like the old woman, Madame Roulin uses the rope to rock a cradle, but one that Vincent implicitly placed in the viewer's space. Because this space was also his own, he in a sense fulfilled an earlier idea to decorate his own bedroom with the image of a child in a cradle.[282] The recurrence of the cradle motif at this desperate moment underscores Vincent's intent to fashion an image that would soothe and console him. But latent disturbances erupted before he could complete the painting.

Discussions about artistic identity and divinity grew ever more volatile and exaggerated. Gauguin, as his grandiose verbal and visual self-characterizations attest, could creatively channel the emotions and ideas generated by

these talks. Vincent no longer could. Earlier his mentor Anton Mauve's desertion had choked him with grief at the prospect that "all the happiness he pictured to me will come to naught" (see ch. 1) and now history was repeating itself.[283] As in the past, he ministered to himself by ministering to others, in a displacement of the consoling impulse: he himself was the broken-hearted one for whom he was making his consoling paintings. The sense of religious mission that in recent years he had been able to harness in service of his art once more consumed him, as in the Borinage; the notion of divine purpose was no longer a metaphoric touchstone but a literal cue to behavior, and sanity became unhitched from sanctity.

Affected by the most profound mysticism, reading the Bible, and delivering sermons in all the wrong places to the vilest people, my dear friend came to the point of believing himself to be a Christ, a God.[284]

So wrote Bernard on New Year's Day 1889 to his friend the twenty-three-year-old critic Albert Aurier, relaying Gauguin's account of events that had unfolded in Arles on 22–23 December, contextualized with reference to Vincent's earlier activities in the Belgian mines. But the other, darker side of Vincent's "life as a saint" was the possibility of death as a saint—through betrayal, murder, and martyrdom, the stuff of Gethsemane.

The subject of murder, like that of the Icelandic fishermen, may have been current from the moment of Gauguin's arrival. For it was while he was en route from Brittany to Arles that the newspapers began intense coverage of the shipwreck and of the dramatic denouement of the "Prado Affair," an unsolved murder of 1886 whose celebrity in France would briefly rival contemporary reports from London of crimes committed by the serial killer dubbed Jack the Ripper. In the Prado Affair, a would-be client slashed a streetwalker's throat and made off with her jewels—an occurrence that

attracted little attention until 1888, when a tip prompted the reopening of the case, and a colorful cast of characters surfaced. These included the victim, nicknamed "la Crevette" (the Shrimp), and her alleged murderer's paramour-turned-police informer, known as "la Belle Suédoise" (the Swedish Beauty). None was more vivid than the principal: Prado, a man of many pseudonyms whose flamboyant persona engaged Vincent and Gauguin along with the rest of the readership of *L'Intransigeant* and other French dailies. Prado was handsome, polyglot, and a master of disguise; a thirty-five-year-old career criminal of apparently Spanish descent, he was a world traveler who had lived in Lima; an adventurer who had spied on behalf of a Spanish political faction; and a former runner at the stock exchange.[285] He shamelessly proclaimed himself the illegitimate son of Emperor Napoléon III and a lady of his court and promised his memoirs to an eager public. Charismatic and an inveterate attention-seeker, Prado brilliantly manipulated a press that, mesmerized by this quasifictional figure, actively participated in the creation of the legend they purported to document.

The case assumed special currency for Gauguin and Vincent. Given Gauguin's past exploits and predisposition to role-playing, it is little wonder that he found Prado's creation of fictive identities "extraordinary." Vincent, for his part, had been intrigued by the murder of two Zouaves at a local brothel earlier in the summer (see ch. 3), and he followed such events in dailies like *L'Intransigeant* and *Le Figaro*. Journalists' depictions, beginning in July, of Prado's underworld and its suspicious denizens may have inflected his September depiction of a night café, where one could "go mad or commit crimes" (fig. 40). The discussions that led Gauguin to treat the same theme apparently fed on the fact that Vincent's world and Prado's had intersected. The press drew parallels between Prado's handiwork with the razor and that of his acquaintance the notorious Henri Pranzini, an erstwhile runner in the Paris art

137
Vincent van Gogh
The Arlésienne
(Madame Ginoux)
Early December 1888
[F 488, JH 1624]
Oil on canvas
91.4 x 73.7 cm
The Metropolitan
Museum of Art,
New York, bequest
of Sam A. Lewisohn,
1951
Cat. 86

138
Paul Gauguin
The Artist's Mother
(Aline-Marie Gauguin)
December 1888
[W 385]
Oil on canvas
41 x 33 cm
Staatsgalerie Stuttgart
Cat. 51

139
Photograph of
Aline Gauguin
c. 1840
Private collection

trade who had been convicted of murder and executed in 1887. A ladies' man like Prado, Pranzini had been a boyfriend of Agostina Segatori—or so Vincent informed Gauguin, citing confidences received from the owner of the café Le Tambourin in Paris, where he claimed that both Pranzini and Prado had hatched their plots.[286]

The suggestive similarities between the experience of the killers and artists assumed deeper resonance following Prado's mid-November trial. Protesting innocence and portraying himself as a martyr in this case (he admitted to other murders), Prado was nevertheless found guilty and sentenced to death. This verdict and sentence, clearly compromised by witnesses' self-interest, revived debates about capital punishment. Discussion of this issue now took into account current theories of criminal anthropology that proposed killers as natural born, murder as a social "law," and its analysis as both a fine art and a science. Contemporary publications on this subject include the translation (by one of the Symbolist movement's leading figures) of Thomas de Quincey's *On Murder Considered as One of the Fine Arts* (1827), which appeared in *Le Figaro*'s literary supplement along with reviews of new studies bearing titles such as *Le Manuel du parfait assassin*. Aurier, in a review of the latter drafted while the Prado case was in the headlines (and at the very moment that Gauguin chose to represent himself as Jean Valjean) had underscored current fascination with those he coded "sympathetic killers."[287] And now Jean Valjean's creator, Victor Hugo, again became a reference point for Vincent and Gauguin. Reporting that Prado was reading Hugo's works in prison, the press chronicled the criminal's prolonged appeal for clemency in accounts recalling the novelist's compelling statement

138

139

opposing capital punishment, *Le Dernier Jour d'un condamné* (*The Last Day of a Condemned Man*) (1829), a tale written from the point of view of the condemned.

Years earlier Vincent had been deeply moved by Hugo's fictional account, and he seemingly empathized with the real-life account of Prado's anguished suspense, as narrated in the pages of *L'Intransigeant*. His own uncertainty was likewise becoming unbearable in the days leading up to Christmas 1888. On 22 December, with the outcome of Prado's appeal imminent, *L'Intransigeant* reported that the prisoner, no longer able to maintain his fabled composure, was a nervous wreck, acutely nervous while awake, in his sleep haunted by "Horla"-like nightmares. Distress likewise overwhelmed Vincent's attempts at equanimity as well. His behavior became highly erratic, Gauguin would report: rough and noisy one minute, silent the next.[288] Gauguin was poised to leave, and Vincent knew it. On Sunday the 23rd, perusing *L'Intransigeant*, Vincent's eye fell on a minor news item (fig. 140): the previous evening a nineteen-year-old man returning to his home had been set upon by a knife-wielding assailant, who inflicted a deep cut in his left side. The critically wounded victim was taken to the hospital and, in the account's terse conclusion: "The murderer took flight" ("Le meurtrier a pris la fuite").[289] Vincent tore the paragraph out.

"The murderer in flight" ("Le meurtrier en fuite") is the most provocative ingredient in the indexlike list that Gauguin distilled from his December conversations with Vincent (fig. 104). Within days Gauguin gave his account of what happened that evening to Bernard, who relayed it to Aurier as follows:

The day before my departure, . . . Vincent ran after me (he was going out, it was night), I turned around because for some time he had been acting strangely. But I mistrusted him.

Then he told me: "You are silent, but I will also be silent."

Ever since [it was clear] I had to leave Arles, he was so bizarre that I couldn't take it. He even said to me: "Are you going to leave?" And when I said "Yes," he tore this sentence from a newspaper and put it in my hand: "the murderer took flight."

I spent the night in a hotel, and when I went back all of Arles was in front of our house. Then the police arrested me, because the house was covered in blood. This is what had happened.

Vincent had returned home after my departure, had taken a razor and cut his ear clean through. Then he put a big beret over his head and went to a brothel to take the ear to a wretched girl, telling her: "You will remember me, truly I tell you this." The girl fainted immediately. The police were called and came to the house.

Vincent was hospitalized. His state is worse, he wants to sleep with the patients, chases the nurses, and washes himself in the coal-bucket. That is to say, he continues the biblical mortifications. They had to lock him up in a room.[290]

The local newspaper corroborates the essential facts. Vincent appeared at the brothel at 11:30 P.M., asked for and spoke to a certain Rachel, and then went home to bed. There the police found him the next morning, "giving almost no sign of life."[291] He was taken to the local hospital.

Gauguin, after being questioned by the police, dispatched a telegram to Paris summoning Theo, who took the night train and arrived in Arles on Christmas morning. He learned that Vincent had been exhibiting signs of madness for days. At the hospital he found his brother alternating between clearheadedness and "brooding about philosophy and theology." During the scant day that he spent in Arles, Theo took advantage of a lucid moment to share the news he had passed on to his mother four days earlier: he had again proposed marriage to Jo Bonger, and this time she had accepted. Vincent managed to offer his blessing, but cautioned Theo that marriage should not be regarded as the main object in life.[292]

Gauguin did not go to the hospital, though Vincent apparently asked for him specifically.[293] It appears he took the night train to Paris on 25 December together with Theo. The experiment that was the Studio of the South had come to an end, and its aftermath had just begun.

140

de jours, et ils étaient arrivés à se procurer des sommes assez fortes.
Ils ont été envoyés au Dépôt.

Paris coupe garge. — Un garçon de dix-neuf ans, Albert Kalis, rentrait chez lui, la nuit dernière, rue Vandezanne, lorsqu'il fut assailli tout à coup par un individu qui le frappa au flanc gauche d'un violent coup de couteau.
La victime de cette agression a dû être transportée à l'hôpital de Bicêtre dans un état désespéré.
Le meurtrier a pris la fuite.

141

140
"Faits diverses,"
L'Intransigeant
23 December 1888

141
Vincent van Gogh
*Madame Roulin
Rocking the Cradle*
(*La Berceuse*)
Late December
1888–c. 22 January
1889 [F 508, JH 1671]
Oil on canvas
92.7 x 72.8 cm

Museum of Fine
Arts, Boston,
bequest of John T.
Spaulding
Cat. 89

1
Postcard of La Pointe
Pen'Mane, Grands
Sables bay, Le
Pouldu, c. 1900

2
Aerial view of the
asylum of Saint-
Paul-de-Mausole,
Saint-Rémy, with
the foothills of the
Alpilles in the back-
ground, c. 1940
Van Gogh Museum,
Amsterdam
(Vincent van Gogh
Foundation)

The relationship between Vincent and Gauguin survived the events of December 1888 insofar as their dialogue continued until Vincent's death nineteen months later. But despite intermittent talk (fostered by Vincent) of joining forces once more, they never met again. As had been the case during the months leading up to Gauguin's journey south, they carried on a long-distance conversation through third parties, letters, and (occasionally) works of art, now relying on shared codes devised while together. At the same time, Vincent's long-held conception of the artist's role—founded in Carlyle and latterly Wagner—was attaining cultural currency in the hands of young Symbolist writers and artists. Thus the discussions in Arles, while moving their art in new directions, paved the way for both Vincent and Gauguin to become significant voices in the larger vanguard context. But despite changing circumstances, each continued to act as a crucial absent presence in the other's efforts.

Vincent, for the most part isolated in the South, found himself able to produce canvases that (like those carried out in anticipation of Gauguin's arrival) can be seen as more truly signature, more authentically expressive, than many of the paintings he realized when living with his friend. Gauguin's forceful presence had been problematic, engendering in Vincent a paralyzing mixture of admiration and resistance and provoking oscillating fears of disapproval and undue influence. But with Gauguin out of the picture, Vincent could freely recall and selectively interpret their discussions without the checks of disagreement; he could script for himself the kind of ideal communion he had imagined with historic figures such as Delacroix, Millet, and Monticelli. However misconstrued or distorted, these projected conversations constituted the stimulation on which Vincent thrived. He was now in a position to reflect upon issues of style without pressure to abandon the deep-seated technical and expressive inclinations

at the core of his aesthetic of painting quickly. Even when discordant realities intruded upon this dialogue, Vincent managed to harness the disruptions creatively, honing the missionary zeal with which he practiced his art. Cycles of illness, despair, recovery, and hope would punctuate the remainder of Vincent's life, accompanied by alternations between professional renunciation and ambition, but his commitment to the idea of art as modern gospel only grew stronger in the face of his troubles.

Gauguin remained similarly committed to preaching this message, though for reasons more pragmatic than psychological. The model of the supreme artist never engendered in him the intense belief that for Vincent could result in overidentification; instead it served as a mask that he could don at will. After Arles he needed one. Finding himself in a foment of new ideas, personalities, challenges, and influences, Gauguin made a concerted attempt to fashion a seamless union of life and art that would position him in a leadership role. Current Symbolist intellectual trends, combined with the legacy of his work with Vincent, gave new direction and sanction to his appropriative strategies. But Vincent had provided more than just creative stimulus for Gauguin, because he functioned as an interrogating, propelling artistic conscience. Gauguin's new acquaintances, less demanding intellectually as well as emotionally, failed to check his propensity for self-aggrandizement, which was curbed only occasionally by self-doubt. As in the months preceding his sojourn in Arles, Vincent's periodic proddings would again help Gauguin give shape and expression to ideas arising from new experiences. Memories of the ambitions invested in the Studio of the South and of its downfall haunted the practice of both artists, feeding current preoccupations with martyrdom and betrayal.

"Did Gauguin see it coming?" Wil asked in a distraught January letter to Theo.[1] This was the question that Gauguin recognized would be directed at him as the news of what had happened in Arles spread within the Paris arts community. Knowing that he was perceived (in some quarters at least) as possessing a butcherbird's killer instincts, he was obviously concerned about how others would interpret the events and his share in them. Attempting to justify his actions, he adjusted his account to different audiences and to the situation as it continued to develop.

At first it appeared that Gauguin alone would be able to provide first-hand testimony, for Vincent's recovery seemed highly unlikely. Bernard's letter to Aurier (see ch. 4) implied his friend's imminent death, and Theo prepared himself and the family for the possibility that Vincent would either require lifelong institutionalization or would not survive. Devastated at the prospect of losing his brother, Theo also had to contend with the realization that few were surprised. Even family members (with the exception of Wil) could not disguise their conviction that he had always been insane. His mother said so forthrightly, pointedly noting that "his suffering and ours was a result of it." All of Theo's Paris acquaintances shared this assumption, save the three men who supported him during this trial: Degas, Gauguin, and his future brother-in-law, Andries Bonger.[2]

Gauguin, of course, still needed Theo, particularly as November's forecast of success had proved overly optimistic: Degas had decided against an acquisition, and Theo had not yet made any more sales. Anxious to secure the dealer's continued support, Gauguin assured him of his brother's sanity, while to Bernard he spoke out of the other side of his mouth. Aware of the younger artist's religiosity, Gauguin evidently reprised stories of Vincent's early ministry in the Borinage. Bernard in turn described Vincent's "life of a Saint" replete with the requisite miracle—after a mining explosion, he revived a man whose scars resembled "the traces of a crown of thorns." Swept away by a hagiographic impulse, Bernard confided to Aurier that Vincent's "life of suffering and martyrdom" amply qualified him for sainthood.[3]

Bernard's construction relies on Zola's *L'Oeuvre*, whose failed genius, Claude Lantier, manifests a blend of heroic madness and religious fervor that, as his colleagues recognize, makes his martyrdom inevitable. This was a scenario with which Vincent would be publicly associated following his death.[4] Another character in the novel—Fagerolles, the canny plunderer of others' talent who had succeeded by stealing Claude's ideas—had already provided Pissarro and his circle with a shorthand identification for Gauguin (see ch. 2). In light of recent events, Gauguin took pains to counteract this perception by effectively emulating Fagerolles's true genius for exploiting a new market dynamic, wherein artists hungry for fame and fortune conspired with dealers and critics to court the attention of a fickle public fascinated with celebrity and novelty. Gauguin now worked to devote equal energy to his persona and his art, in the attempt to make them overlap.

This effort involved some editing of Gauguin's own recent biography. An extraordinary letter written sometime in January to an unidentified recipient (possibly a potential buyer) suggests that he had become uncomfortable with the sanctification of Vincent that he himself had apparently helped foster. He informed his correspondent that he had just returned from the South, where he had planned to work for a year with a painter friend; however, the friend had gone raving mad, and for a month Gauguin had lived in fear of a terrible accident. Representing this as the latest in a series of setbacks, Gauguin compared his trials involving money and ignorant art collectors to those of Delacroix. Then, apropos of nothing

at all, he invoked Fromentin on the subject of Rembrandt and the light of North Africa, harking back to Gauguin's Montpellier conversations with Vincent:

Stone crumbles, the word endures. We are far from the time when Christ, this artist who sculpted in living flesh, spoke and persuaded, gently, Today…to tell the so-called truth one must impose it like a storm…. I know what awaits me, and I go calmly from misfortune to misfortune, until the end—but I also know that stone crumbles and that my work will not.[5]

The first and last sentences of this statement reveal its provenance. "Stone crumbles, the word endures" ("Le pierre périra, la parole restera") was, as Gauguin would later observe in his letter of condolence to Theo, one of Vincent's favorite sayings.[6] In summoning it, along with the Jesus-as-artist trope, Gauguin portrayed himself as Christlike, suffering to spread the word, sustained only by the promise of the enduring legacy of his message.

Control of that message became all-important. In Gauguin's initial account to Bernard, Vincent's handing him the newspaper item about the knife assault (see ch. 4) constituted an accusation, implying that Gauguin was responsible for the pain that he felt and then symbolically enacted with his self-mutilation. Vincent's presentation of part of his ear to the prostitute Rachel resonates with sacramental meaning, the artist's gesture and statement echoing Jesus' to his disciples at the Last Supper, in the hours before he proceeded to Gethsemane. There he was betrayed by Judas; as soldiers arrested Jesus, the disciple Simon Peter drew a sword and cut off the ear of the high priest's servant. (In one gospel Jesus then heals the wound with his touch; in another he censures Simon Peter's intervention in preordained events).[7] Thus in this scenario, Gauguin could be implicated as playing Judas to Vincent's Christ.

Gauguin later altered his original narrative so that he became the object of Vincent's aggression. Deleting the detail about the scrap of newspaper, Gauguin instead contended that Vincent had approached him from behind with an open razor; stopped in his tracks by Gauguin's defensive glare, he ran back to the Yellow House, where he turned his violent anger on himself. This version allowed Gauguin to raise—and dismiss—the possibility of guilt on a lesser charge: "Was I negligent…? Should I have disarmed him and tried to calm him? I have often questioned my conscience about this, but I have never found anything to reproach myself with."[8]

Seemingly absolving himself, Gauguin nonetheless remained preoccupied with issues of guilt, innocence, betrayal, justice, and murder, as attested by his continued fascination with the denouement of the "Prado Affair." Prado's appeal to the president for clemency was denied on 27 December. Two days later Gauguin, alerted by a friend in the municipal guard as to the time and place of execution, went, sketchbook in hand, to place de la Roquette, where he joined a motley assembly of invited guests, reporters, curious passersby, and local lowlifes who gathered beginning at 2 A.M. to observe the spectacle (see fig. 3). The artist's recollections of Prado's appearance at sunrise and of jostling in the crowd for a glimpse of the action are consistent with contemporary press reports. Ducking police barricades, Gauguin ran across the square for a better view of the final act. Despite being pushed back repeatedly, he prevailed, glimpsing the fall of the guillotine's blade and watching the executioner lift the severed head out of the box. It was a particularly gruesome sight, for Prado had been improperly positioned, and part of his chin was removed, resulting in a disfigurement that prevented the making of a wax model of the head for display, the immortality conferred on celebrity criminals like Prado's brother in crime, Pranzini (fig. 4).[9] Unlike the

3

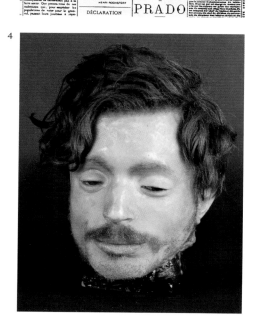

4

other voyeurs in attendance, Gauguin insisted, he had come not to be entertained but to witness a martyrdom. The experience apparently planted the idea of representing himself as a victim of the executioner's blade (fig. 6), but equally critical to the realization of this provocative portrayal was the subsequent news about and from Vincent.

From one day to the next, Vincent recovered. On 2 January he wrote to reassure Theo, and the doctor added a postscript confirming his "over-excitement" to have been only temporary. The following day Roulin corroborated the prognosis, assuring Theo that Vincent was "of quite sound mind" ("très sain d'esprit"). The postal clerk no doubt felt genuine empathy, but he spoke in the private language of the two artists, as if Vincent were conveying a message through him to Gauguin. Indeed one of Vincent's primary concerns was that he had frightened Gauguin, and he asked Theo to tell his friend that he was much on his mind. Attempting to downplay what had happened, Vincent deplored Theo's having been bothered for such a trifle; he reassured his mother and Wil that he had simply been indisposed and that everything was normal.[10] And he took the opportunity of his first outing from the hospital, when Roulin brought him to the Yellow House on 4 January, to write to Gauguin:

Look here—was my brother Theo's journey really necessary, old friend?

Now at least do reassure him completely, and I entreat you . . . to refrain, until after more mature reflection on both our parts, from speaking ill of our poor little yellow house, and to remember me to the painters whom I saw in Paris.[11]

Vincent's attitude toward Gauguin was more ambivalent than he cared to admit. He gave his qualified blessing to Gauguin's projected return to the tropics but hinted at his impracticality. Though pleased by the fact that Gauguin's stay in Arles had had a restful effect on him (attested by the contrasting self-portraits of September and December; ch. 3, fig. 74, and ch. 4, fig. 121), Vincent could barely mask his resentment of a departure that had foreclosed on his plans to minister similarly to other artist friends. Resuming talk of the Dutch market and his old obsession with converting Tersteeg to impressionism, he could not relinquish the Studio of the South.[12]

Gauguin wrote an intentionally mollifying reply about a week later, in which he praised Vincent's June *Sower* and a Paris still life all in yellow, which he had seen at Theo's apartment; told him that he had hung an impression of the *Potato Eaters* lithograph (ch. 1, fig. 48) given to him by Theo alongside Vincent's *Self-Portrait (Bonze)*; and reiterated his esteem for the yellow-on-yellow *Sunflowers* (ch. 3, fig. 58) that he felt exemplified an "essential Vincent style." But his accompanying requests—apparently that Vincent give him the yellow *Sunflowers* and that he forward his fencing gear—fed Vincent's growing sense of grievance.[13]

To Theo, Vincent proposed that Gauguin's attachment to his "toys" signaled their owner's irresponsibility and weak character. Had Gauguin remained more collected when Vincent was wild, Theo could have been spared the expense of an emergency trip south. As always money was an issue, as Vincent contemplated a renegotiation of his arrangement with Theo. Finances had been complicated by Theo's need to settle his account with Gauguin, who evidently spoke to Theo about matters that Vincent had asked him to keep between themselves. Moreover Gauguin seems to have hinted that the brothers had exploited him, and he stipulated that his future dealings with Theo be independent of any connection with Vincent. Hearing of all this from Theo, Vincent did not hide his indignation:

But him, . . . Lord, let him do anything he wants, let him have his independence ?? (whatever that means to him) and his opinions, and let him go his own way as soon as he thinks he knows it better than we do.[14]

He was also deeply hurt. Gauguin had turned a deaf ear to his repeated requests to visit him in the hospital and had cleared out without a word; now he had betrayed his confidence in Paris. Vincent likened his desertion to the definitive incident in Daudet's *Tartarin sur les Alpes* (1885), in which Tartarin and his part-

3
Eugène Rapp
(French; late nine-
teenth century)
The Execution of Prado
from *L'Intransigeant*,
29 December 1898,
front page

4
Maison Tramond
Head of Pranzini
1887
Colored wax, blown
glass, and human
hair
19.2 x 15.5 cm
Musée de la
Préfecture de Police,
Paris

5
Paul Gauguin
*Self-Portrait Jug with
Japanese Print and
Flowers*
May 1889 [W 375]
Oil on canvas
73 x 92 cm
Tehran Museum of
Contemporary Art,
Iran

6
Paul Gauguin
Self-Portrait Jug
c. 1 February 1889
[B 48, G 65]
Glazed stoneware
H. 19.5 cm

Det Danske
Kunstindustri-
museum,
Copenhagen
Cat. 91

5

6

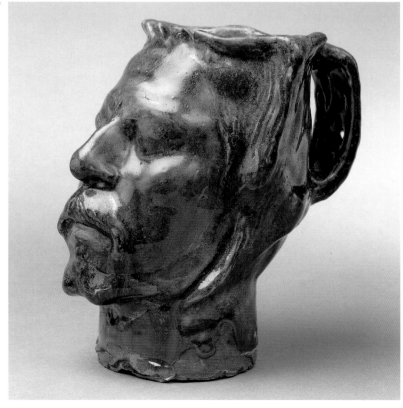

ner, the preposterous braggart Bompard, face a critical moment on a dangerous climb. They have pledged to remain together at all costs, but both men panic, cut the rope binding them to each other, and descend safely by separate routes, each assuming the other lost. Both invent stories that mask their cowardice and mutual betrayal, but the discovery of the piece of rope, cut at both ends, mutely testifies to what actually transpired (see fig. 12). Vincent suggested that Theo remember this episode if he wanted to get the measure of Gauguin, a perfidious but quintessentially Southern spirit.

Vincent described Gauguin as riven by incompatible desires, imputing to his friend grandiose plans for an artists' association and proposing that he might do well to have himself examined by a mental specialist. Gauguin refused to see that the best thing for him would be to forget schemes to go to the North or the tropics and return to Arles. Vincent affirmed that they were fond enough of each other to be able to start again, but he began to speak of "his" rather than "their" Yellow House.[15]

These conflicting feelings inform the pictures that Vincent tackled following his release from the hospital on 7 January. He commenced with still lifes, including one that functions as a self-portrait (fig. 8). Bringing together certain elements from the chair pendants (ch. 4, figs. 69, 71)—the lighted candle, the homely onions—Vincent focused on objects that brought physical and psychological comfort, such as tobacco and pipe, wine, and a letter. Similarly he projected composure in a pair of self-portraits that followed (figs. 7, 9). In both the artist is dressed for the outdoors, in coat and fur hat. As was his custom when practicing this genre, he looked at himself in the mirror, head turned slightly to his right, with the result that his bandaged left ear is prominent. Clearly these are demonstration pieces, designed to prove that he could not be mad if able to work and to counter the damage to his reputation caused by

8

Every day I take the remedy which the incomparable Dickens prescribes against suicide. It consists of a glass of wine, a piece of bread with cheese, and a pipe of tobacco.　Vincent to Wil, [30 April 1889]

9

10
Jan van Eyck
(Flemish; c.
1395–1441)
*Madonna of Canon
van der Paele with
Saints Donatian and
George* (detail)
1434–36
Oil on panel
Groeningemuseum,
Bruges, Belgium

11
Anonymous
*Calvaire de Sainte-
Anne-d'Auray en
Bretagne*, edition
Pellerin, Epinal
Wood engraving
62.2 x 37.5 cm
Musée du Faouët,
Morbihan, Brittany

12
Vignette from
Alphonse Daudet,
Tartarin sur les Alpes
(Paris, 1885), p. 348

12

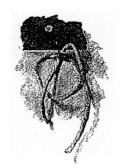

Gauguin's stories. Bundled up, bandaged, and calm, Vincent exudes a stoic acceptance.[16]

In the self-portrait in which he smokes a pipe, Vincent quoted the complementary chromatics of both chair pendants: the bifurcated orange and red background serves here as a complementary foil for the figure's blue hat and green coat. The other example presents a more descriptive setting and makes more pointed references. Vincent situated himself in the same spot where Augustine Roulin had sat when both artists painted her in late November, to the left of the front door (see ch. 4, fig. 99). But in the background, instead of a Gauguin landscape, we see Vincent's own easel and, on the wall, a Japanese print symbolic of the aesthetic, social, and spiritual ideals to which he had dedicated the Yellow House.[17] As Vincent vented to Theo, the house could no longer serve as an artist's refuge since "everyone will be afraid of me"; Gauguin and the group he had duplicitously gathered around him in Pont-Aven while delaying his southward journey were self-interested schemers, blind to the way Vincent had worked and suffered for the community.[18] Albeit an image of martyrdom to a noble cause, the portrait's reserved aspect matches the tone that Vincent strove to maintain when, around 22 January, he confronted Gauguin directly about what had happened.

Vincent acknowledged that his strenuous insistence that Gauguin stay might have contributed to his decision to leave—"unless of course, that departure was planned beforehand?" Not daring to push further, he merely recommended a thorough reading of the Tartarin stories. While he refrained from directing Gauguin's attention to the cut-rope episode, he did charge him with a lapse unforgivable in a sailor: abandoning ship. Gauguin had left Vincent "alone on board my little yellow house" as its captain, whose duty compelled him to be the last to leave. The events of December constituted the shipwreck that Vincent had desperately hoped to avoid. He now informed Gauguin that, during his hallucinatory episodes, his mind had sailed over many seas, encountering Wagner's phantom ship as well as "Le Horla," but he had taken comfort in the tunes that "the woman rocking the cradle sang to rock the sailors to sleep"; in his delirium he sang old nursery rhymes aloud.[19]

Such imagery is intimately connected to the picture of Augustine Roulin holding a cradle rope that Vincent was bringing to conclusion just as their vessel hit the rocks (ch. 4, fig. 141) and that now, in the calm after the storm, he told Gauguin he had just taken up again. What remained to be finished, he noted, were the figure's hands and most likely the final

layers of the skirt, chair, and rope. Assessing the painting for Gauguin in terms of the latter's interest in style, Vincent declared the picture the best "impressionist arrangement of colors" he had yet realized. But the achievement was expressive as well: "I'm sure that if one were to put the canvas as it is in a fishing boat, even one from Iceland, there would be some among the fishermen who would feel they were there, inside the cradle." This imagined scenario, coupled with Vincent's restated aim to make art that offers consolation for the brokenhearted, suggests how the subject of this pictorial "lullaby in colors" had accrued new associations and layers of meaning in the aftermath of the fallout with Gauguin, the news of Theo's engagement, and the reassignment of Roulin to Marseilles.[20]

Vincent from the outset had conceived the work as a "stella maris," evidently inspired by Loti's description of a brightly painted porcelain virgin, mounted midship and flanked by branches of artificial flowers, to which the sailors of simple faith turned for comfort when in rough seas. To underscore his own intention to create a soothing image, he now decided to call his portrait of Augustine Roulin *La Berceuse*, signifying both the woman rocking the cradle and the lullaby that she sings. The title, which he inscribed over the red floor's

10

11

13
Vincent van Gogh
Sunflowers
Late January 1889
[F 455, JH 1668]
Oil on canvas
92 x 72.5 cm
Philadelphia
Museum of Art,
The Mr. and Mrs.
Carroll S. Tyson, Jr.,
Collection, 1963

14
Vincent van Gogh
*Madame Roulin
Rocking the Cradle
(La Berceuse)*
29 January 1889
[F 505, JH 1670]
Oil on canvas
92.7 x 73.8 cm

The Art Institute of
Chicago, Helen
Birch Bartlett
Memorial
Collection, 1926.200
Cat. 112

15
Vincent van Gogh
Sunflowers
Late January 1889
[F 458, JH 1667]
Oil on canvas
95 x 73 cm
Van Gogh Museum,
Amsterdam
(Vincent van Gogh
Foundation)
Cat. 110

thick, already dry paint, recalls Vincent's attachment to this theme, found in Loti and other favorite authors, who drew upon commonplace metaphors of the sea as nurse, its rocking motion and lapping sounds redolent of the comforts of infancy.[21]

Memories of the Zundert parsonage and of his life when he was still his mother's only child had surfaced during Vincent's recent illness. He expressed this regressive impulse in *La Berceuse*, turning not only to Loti's *Pêcheur d'Islande* but also to another literary touchstone, van Eeden's *De kleine Johannes*. Specifically he recalled Johannes's childhood bedroom, adorned with wallpaper featuring a pattern of "huge … flowers in gaudy colors." While this sort of richly colored, elaborately patterned paper might have been beyond the means of people like the Roulins, Vincent's aim was not to describe their domestic surroundings but rather to suggest the figure's symbolic presence; the decorative backdrop alludes to the cloth of honor that early Flemish masters depicted behind the Virgin (see fig. 10).[22]

Vincent deliberately sought to parallel visually van Eeden's writing style, likening the effects of his picture to the inexpensive, unsophisticated color prints marketed to popular audiences (see fig. 11), which communicate their

message directly, like music, and with the "childlike simplicity" he and Theo prized. He imagined his picture causing an audience of sailors (whom he characterized as both children and martyrs) to experience the "old feeling of being rocked." To express the sacred dimension of this consolation, he envisaged flanking *La Berceuse* with flowers, notably the *Sunflowers* Gauguin coveted, in an arrangement recalling Loti's porcelain Virgin and popular religious icons, altarpieces, and stained-glass windows (see figs. 13–16).[23]

Vincent had set to work, once again acting on the long-held conviction that painting could be "the raft that will take us safely to shore after the shipwreck."[24] In crafting his own lifeboat, he now painted pictures that both reference the ill-fated voyage with Gauguin and suggest that he hoped to regain the familiar harbor of the Studio of the South. Gauguin's presumption in angling for the yellow-on-yellow *Sunflowers* annoyed Vincent somewhat, but more importantly it reconfirmed the motif's symbolic function in their relationship and bolstered his sense of identity. He promised Gauguin that he would fulfill his wish by undertaking exact copies of the August pictures, laying claim, like other artists, to a signature subject.[25] Empowered by the feeling of being in a position to please Gauguin, Vincent granted

Theo permission to exhibit the pair of sunflower canvases at Boussod et Valadon, suggesting that they be priced at five hundred francs each, the figure that he assigned to the Monticelli owned by the brothers (ch. 2, fig. 10) and thus a mark of confidence in his own achievement.

Reprising both *Sunflowers* for his friend (figs. 13, 15), Vincent proceeded differently from the December yellow-on-yellow version on jute (ch. 4, fig. 113). In that instance he seemingly attempted to enhance the August prototype by using thicker paint and brighter chromatics while respecting most details of form and brushwork. Now he simplified each shape to a schematic essence. Again returning to trace the first versions, he regularized the patterns of rayflowers, rendering the petal-like forms with greater clarity (see figs. 17–18) so that they align rhythmically with one another and contrast with the double flowers' systematic impasto. Moving one step further from naturalism, he eliminated any sense of realistic lighting and introduced purely artificial colors— cool blue, bright red, and acid green—in the flowers' centers. These re-visions defer to Gauguin's formal ideals, and as if to rekindle his admiration, the January yellow-on-yellow *Sunflowers* is the yellowest of all.

Stylistically as well as thematically linked to Gauguin, the *Berceuse–Sunflowers* grouping memorialized their relationship. Possibly the rope that Vincent placed in Augustine Roulin's hands as a somewhat obscure synecdoche for the absent cradle also constituted a private, Tartarinesque reference to the betrayal that had exacerbated his need for the consoling image (see fig. 12). But it also seems that by working on *La Berceuse*—with Gauguin's *Madame Roulin* (ch. 4, fig. 97), to which it refers, still in the studio—Vincent could imagine their dialogue continuing. How else to explain the burst of activity that followed?

On 23 January Vincent still hoped that Augustine Roulin would feel sufficiently comfortable to come and pose for the hands in the absence of her husband, who had recently been transferred to Marseilles. Five days later the artist reported that he had not only completed the picture, which indeed reveals a second campaign of painting on the hands, but had already realized a second version (fig. 14). On the 30th he wrote to say that he had shown Roulin, back in Arles to visit his family, the two portraits of his wife flanked by the four *Sunflowers* and was at work on a third *Berceuse* (fig. 19). He completed this rendition by 3 February, when he announced a fourth under way (fig. 20).[26]

Though Vincent had on occasion executed second versions of pictures, never before had he repeated himself in this compulsive way.

The stated idea was to create one for Holland, one for the Roulins, and, all importantly, one for Gauguin—Vincent imagined he would want one of the *Berceuse* "edition" that supplemented the *Sunflowers* he so admired. Such productivity, he felt, demonstrated his mental competence. But while he claimed to be calmed by the process of making repetitions, the activity's latent ritual significance proved dangerously stimulating. By late January Vincent returned to December's obsessions, making reference to Monticelli's path, Bruyas's Southern school, artist and dealer apostles, and his conviction that he (and by implication Gauguin) ought to stay in Arles and leave the tropics for others. Claiming that he and Gauguin understood each other at heart, he normalized his own behavior as part of a larger condition suffered by artists and soon to be experienced by everyone; the antidote to this haunting "horla" was the consolation of a Delacroix or a Wagner, figured by Puvis's *Hope*.[27]

The raft had become a speedboat. Vincent himself recognized the signs of the previous month's over-excitement. While he tried (as in the summer) to attribute his agitation to the South, he admitted to moments of feeling "twisted by enthusiasm or madness or prophecy, like a Greek oracle on his tripod." On the one hand, he believed that keeping the Yellow House was critical to his recovery; on the other, he seemed resigned to its foundering and reluctant to play the role of false prophet.

That was on 3 February, the day he announced that he had begun a fourth *Berceuse*. A few days later, Theo received word that Vincent, hearing voices and suffering from paranoid delusions of being poisoned, had been taken back to the hospital.[28]

This second episode altered Vincent's outlook. Within a short time, he returned home on a provisional basis (continuing to sleep at the hospital), but almost immediately neighbors began to circulate a petition to the mayor declaring Vincent a danger to the community, citing his excessive drinking and unwanted attentions to women. Around the 25th, the police, acting on mayoral instruction, readmitted him to the hospital and closed the Yellow House. The Superintendent of Police, in his report of 3 March, concluded that Vincent was mentally deranged and advised his detainment in a special asylum.[29]

Though indignant at being treated as an object of fearful curiosity, Vincent felt chastened. He now foreswore inviting painter friends like de Haan or Koning to Arles, lest they lose their wits as he had. First he blamed Arles and the South (had not Gauguin caught the very same "excessive sensitivity" in the tropics?) and fell back on the rationalization that all painters were crazy. When he resumed work, he executed a fifth *Berceuse* (fig. 21), more naturalistic than its predecessors and seemingly less directly inspired by Gauguin's precepts of design. A brief visit in late March from Paul

Signac, on his way from Paris to the Mediterranean coast, was tonic. Vincent became more accepting of his illness. Recognizing that he had harbored it for a long time, he softened his judgments of those, his parents in particular, who had perceived his symptoms, and he began to experience terrible remorse.[30]

In this light he reassessed the past and faced the future. After weeks of discussion and debate about whether or not he required institutionalization, he agreed to leave the Yellow House and move to another neighborhood. In mid-April he stored his furniture at the Ginoux' and made arrangements to rent an apartment. Ultimately, however, he felt unequal to the challenge of living alone. He talked of joining the French Foreign Legion, so as to cease burdening Theo, who on 17 April married Jo Bonger in Amsterdam. A more practical plan materialized, with Vincent's consent: he would spend a few months in a private asylum housing forty-five patients in Saint-Rémy-de-Provence, a town fifteen miles (twenty-five kilometers) to the northeast of Arles.[31]

In April and early May, before leaving Arles, Vincent realized several impressive paintings, including views of the hospital dormitory and garden.[32] An intimate canvas featuring a patch of grass by a pathway and hovering butterflies (fig. 22) is arguably more personally and professionally revealing. Technically the work is a model of control, the forms built up with long, directional marks that combine like strands of thread into a richly embroidered, multicolored surface pattern. The white ground, which the artist applied himself, shines through between the thick brush strokes, its brightness balanced by passages of black.

With this unassuming subject, Vincent paid homage to Japanese art. The "single blade of grass"—seen in an admired image, a reproduction of which he now hung in his room—exemplified the philosophical wisdom of artists who perceived nature's greatness in its humblest manifestations. *Butterflies and Flowers* speaks to Vincent's renunciation of grandiosity, also voiced in assertions that he sought neither heroism nor martyrdom. This of course referred to his ambitions for the Studio of the South, inspired by the communal spirit he imagined uniting Japanese artists. The butterflies, a leitmotif of van Eeden's, poignantly recall Vincent's positing, just months earlier, his future metamorphosis and afterlife as a "painter-butterfly" (see ch. 3). Hovering among the swarm of white insects, a single butterfly in Gauguin's signature bright red suggests his persistent presence. But Vincent now renounced his project for housing an association of painters.[33]

Claims to the contrary notwithstanding, Vincent remained preoccupied with what his "now shipwrecked studio might have been" as he packed his belongings. Thoughts of Renan's artist-Christ, olive trees, and Gethsemane troubled him, and in one of the last works he made before leaving Arles (fig. 23), Vincent reprised a garden subject—*The Poet's Garden* (ch. 3, fig. 69)—working now with reed pen and brown ink rather than brilliant oils. As he wrote on 3 May, the drawing "turned out very dark and rather melancholy for one of spring."[34] A pictorial obituary of the Studio of the South, the magisterial sheet featuring the weeping tree continues the series of large, independent drawings undertaken in July. More deliberate in handling than these predecessors, the line uncharacteristically spiky, the somber image set the stage for a group of valedictory recastings of earlier themes that Vincent, constantly thinking of Gauguin, would undertake over the following months in the asylum of Saint-Paul-de-Mausole, where he arrived on 8 May.

16
Vincent van Gogh
Sketch of *La Berceuse*
flanked by *Sunflower*
paintings in letter to
Theo
[22 May 1889] (letter
778/592)
Van Gogh Museum,
Amsterdam
(Vincent van Gogh
Foundation)

17
Detail of ch. 3, fig. 58

18
Detail of fig. 15

19
Vincent van Gogh
*Madame Roulin
Rocking the Cradle
(La Berceuse)*
29 January 1889
[F 506, JH 1669]
Oil on canvas
93 x 74 cm
The Metropolitan
Museum of Art,

New York, The
Walter H. and
Leonore Annenberg
Collection, partial
gift of Walter H. and
Leonore Annenberg

20
Vincent van Gogh
*Madame Roulin
Rocking the Cradle
(La Berceuse)*
c. 22 February 1889
[F 507, JH 1672]
Oil on canvas
92 x 72.5 cm
Stedelijk Museum,
Amsterdam
Cat. 113

21
Vincent van Gogh
*Madame Roulin
Rocking the Cradle
(La Berceuse)*
29 March 1889
[F 504, JH 1655]
Oil on canvas
92 x 73 cm
Kröller-Müller
Museum, Otterlo,
The Netherlands

22

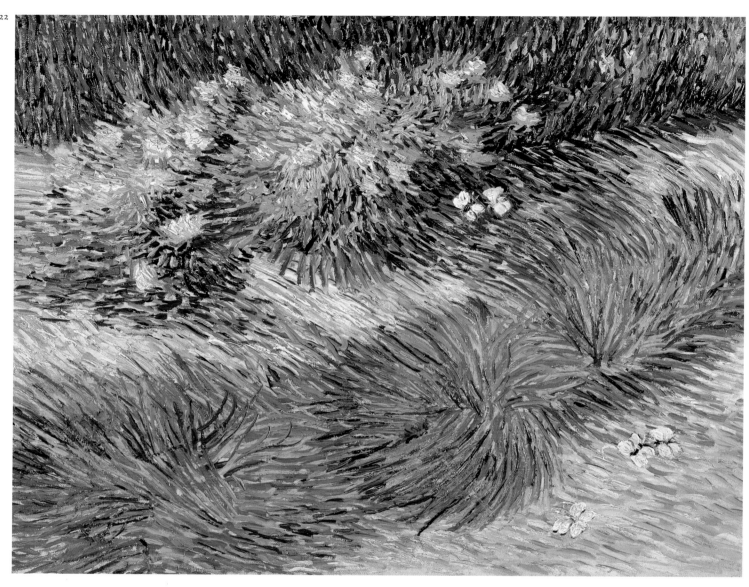

23

22
Vincent van Gogh
Butterflies and Flowers
c. 1 May 1889
[F 460, JH 1676]
Oil on canvas
51 x 61 cm
Private collection
Cat. 114

23
Vincent van Gogh
Weeping Tree
(*L'Arbre pleureur dans l'herbe*)
3 May 1889
Black chalk, reed pen and brown ink on wove paper
49.8 x 61.3 cm

The Art Institute of Chicago, gift of Tiffany and Margaret Day Black, 1945.31
Cat. 115

Gauguin, Spring 1889

About three weeks later, at the end of May, Gauguin moved as well, leaving Paris for Pont-Aven after an eventful five months' uninterrupted stay in the capital.[35] In February twelve of his works had appeared at Les Vingt in Brussels, among them two canvases from Martinique (*Les Négresses* and *Conversation [Tropics]*; ch. 2, fig. 57, and ch. 3, fig. 20); six from Brittany, including *Young Wrestlers—Brittany* (ch. 3, fig. 39) and *Vision of the Sermon* (ch. 3, fig. 59); and three from Arles (*In the Heat*, *Human Miseries*, and *Blue Trees*; ch. 4, figs. 55, 50, 87). Critical response had been mixed. Predictably some commentators took exception to Gauguin's arbitrary palette, notably the blue of the trees in the painting he exhibited as "*Vous y passerez, la belle!*" A more receptive reviewer commended the artist's original application of the principles of Japanese art even in compositions he was unable to decode (possibly a reference to *The Pigs*, here shown under the more decorous title *In the Heat* [*En plein chaleur*]). Octave Maus, the exhibition's organizer, wrote an important assessment for the French Symbolist periodical *La Cravache*. While Maus had detected the influence of Cézanne and Guillaumin in Gauguin's earlier work, he felt that the recent canvases signaled an evolution, a freedom from such dependence. Gauguin now struck him as "one of the most refined colorists I know, and the painter most devoid of any common tricks." Citing Degas's validation, Maus added his own: "I am drawn to the primitiveness of his paintings."[36]

Maus's review positioned Gauguin advantageously for the discussion of past, present, and future trends in art that appeared in the same periodical a couple of weeks later under the title "L'Art symboliste." Applying an evolutionary, medicalized model to the nineteenth century's aesthetic movements, from Romanticism to Naturalism, novelist Paul Adam predicted that in its next phase, art would recover from the emasculating pes-simism that he linked with Naturalism. His language points to key concerns of the moment:

The era to come will be mystical. Mystical and theistic. It will inaugurate the miracle of the man who despises sorrow; who is isolated in imaginative dreams, in habitual hallucinations; who has returned to the primitive, divine essence; and has also become creator, creator of his raptures and of his paradises.[37]

Adam and other members of the emergent Symbolist literary vanguard, with whom Gauguin became acquainted at this time, privileged the spiritual and subjective over the material; became fascinated with syncretism, or the fusion of diverse religious beliefs and practices; and proclaimed the inauguration of an evangelical era. An important new connection was Charles Morice, a twenty-seven-year-old writer whose 1889 survey of literary theory became one of the movement's keystones. Morice would remember first encountering Gauguin at a restaurant favored by young writers; the artist was holding forth to a group that included Jean Moréas, the poet who had published a so-called Symbolist manifesto in the fall of 1886.[38]

Though Gauguin only now came into direct contact with the principal Symbolists, he had already absorbed their ideas sufficiently (and rehearsed them with Vincent) to expound to them confidently. He joined in their condemnation of Naturalism but, in opposition to the classicizing bias of his new audience, proposed what Morice characterized as a doctrine of reasoned primitivism, exemplified by the "cerebral art" of Egypt as an alternative to modern materialism. To be sure, things Egyptian had achieved widespread popularity, its enthusiasts including perpetual bellwether of trends Loti (see fig. 30). Gauguin's pronouncements elicited mixed reactions, as did his overbearing manner and provocative mix of studio speech and sailor's slang. Morice, however, found his formulations compelling insofar as they harmonized with and clarified his own.[39]

Gauguin of course had profited similarly from his discussions with Vincent. Applying ideas developed in Arles, he strove to position himself in Paris's altered vanguard climate. In Gauguin's interaction with Symbolist circles, Vincent acted as a kind of silent partner, just as Gauguin occupied Vincent's thoughts in Provence; both men referred to the recent past in their art and continued to derive energy from the dialogue that played out directly in correspondence and indirectly through Theo.

The dealer's gift of Vincent's *Potato Eaters* lithograph (ch. 1, fig. 46) rekindled Gauguin's interest in producing prints (see ch. 3). Theo, currently involved in publishing a portfolio of fifteen lithographs after paintings and pastels by Degas, convinced Gauguin that he could become better known by doing the same, given the market interest in prints made by painters. Gauguin (joined by Bernard) enthusiastically embraced the project, producing an edition of fifty portfolios of ten subjects based on paintings made in Martinique, Brittany, and Arles. Characteristically, his approach went against the grain of tradition. Rejecting the Bavarian limestone that yielded the suave surface textures prized by lithography's aficionados, Gauguin instead elected to work on zinc plates, commonly used in commercial printing, and exploited their coarser grain: a decision akin to his choice to paint on jute and resulting in comparably rough-textured surfaces. More radical still was the paper on which he printed the edition. Gauguin passed over the white- and cream-toned sheets typically employed for fine-art prints, instead choosing large pieces of arresting canary-yellow paper, the effect of black on a field of bright yellow recalling low-end commercial posters of the 1870s and 1880s.[40]

Paul Gauguin
Leda cover for the
Volpini Suite (*Dessins
lithographiques*)
January–February
1889 [Gu 1, K 1]
Zincograph height-
ened with brush and
water-based colors,
on yellow wove paper
Sheet: 30.4 x 26 cm

The Art Institute of
Chicago, The
William McCallin
McKee Memorial
Collection,
1943.1021a

Paul Gauguin
Dramas of the Sea (*Les
Drames de la mer*)
from the *Volpini Suite*
January–February
1889 [Gu 7, K 2]
Zincograph on yel-
low wove paper
Sheet: 49.8 x 64.9 cm

The Art Institute of
Chicago, The
William McCallin
McKee Memorial
Collection, 1943.1026
Cat. 90

Paul Gauguin
*Dramas of the Sea—
Brittany* (*Les Drames
de la mer—Bretagne*)
from the *Volpini Suite*
January–February
1889 [Gu 8, K 3]
Zincograph on yel-
low wove paper
Sheet: 49.8 x 64.9 cm

The Art Institute of
Chicago, The
William McCallin
McKee Memorial
Collection, 1943.1024
Cat. 90

24

25

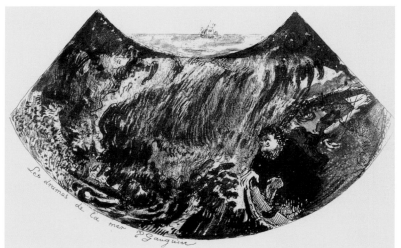

26

The artist carried through the transgressive aura from materials to imagery. For the portfolio cover (fig. 24), he used a composition based on his *Leda and the Swan* ceramic (ch. 2, fig. 64), amplifying its sexual content by adding two goslings, which signify Castor and Pollux, fruit of the coupling between Leda and Zeus; and an apple and serpent that suggest a biblical counterpart to the mythic tale of a fall from grace through lust. The motto of the English Order of the Garter—"homis [*sic*] soit qui mal y pense" ("shamed be he who thinks evil")—curves along the upper right. Elsewhere in this series, Gauguin drew script backward so that it would print in conventional orientation, but this cryptic message appears in reverse. Morally ambiguous and mysterious, the cover image sets the stage for the ten prints inside, which touch on issues of sexuality, good and evil, innocence and guilt.[41]

Vincent is here evoked chromatically by the emphatic yellow field on which Gauguin's designs float, and iconographically by two prints entitled *Dramas of the Sea* (*Les Drames de la mer*). The image of Breton woman on shore praying for the safe return of their men (fig. 26) reiterates the theme of vigil in Loti's *Pêcheur d'Islande*. The second print (fig. 25) (the only one in the series without a painted antecedent) makes more complex allusions. At the top of the oddly shaped composition, a boat sails on calm seas. Below, a storm rages; another vessel lurches on the brink of capsizing, its desperate lone occupant seemingly poised to abandon ship.[42] Gauguin inscribed himself in the drama by conflating his signature with the subject's title. In a sense the zincograph responds to Vincent's figurative assessment of recent events. The pointed contrast between surface calm and troubled depths suggests the basis of the defense that Gauguin was beginning to mount. Over the coming months, Gauguin remained preoccupied with the shared, coded story line of the sea, studying at the Louvre two paintings by Delacroix depicting

boats in troubled waters, *The Barque of Dante* (1822) and *The Shipwreck of Don Juan* (1840). In his own work over the winter and spring, he explored the contrasting associations of the sea with death and regeneration.[43]

In the aftermath of Vincent's early February breakdown, Gauguin made an illuminating statement in the form of a stoneware *Self-Portrait Jug* (fig. 6). Informed, like his earlier portrait vases, by Peruvian, early Italian, and English examples of head-shaped vessels (see ch. 2, figs. 66–68), Gauguin's ceramic builds upon the Jean Valjean characterization in the very medium that he had summoned metaphorically to describe the 1888 canvas (ch. 3, fig. 74). Here he pushed the outlaw-victim identification further: the closed eyes and the blood, streaming from the nose and pooling at the neck, suggest the decapitation inflicted upon Prado and Pranzini—but also the martyrdom of John the Baptist. Gauguin drew on the new currency that Symbolists such as Redon had brought to images of the severed head as a signifier of mystic spirituality and artistic martyrdom (see fig. 27), cultivating a dual identity that Schuffenecker summarized as a "crook...but a holy one." His crime, he hinted in a sketchbook inscription, was originality. But as the jug's lack of ears implies, Vincent's self-mutilation haunted him.[44]

Here Gauguin took on Vincent's recent self-portraits with bandaged ear (which he knew about though apparently had not yet seen), as well as the representations that others were constructing on his behalf. Specifically, Theo perceived a likeness between his brother and a marble head by Rodin of John the Baptist currently on display at Boussod et Valadon (see quote, fig. 28). The association rested on the van Goghs' concept of modern art as a kind of religion, an idea now replete with fresh personal significance and widespread cultural currency.[45] Gauguin's jug responds to Theo's gloss, while drawing on his Wagner-inflected

discussions with Vincent about the role they might play in the art of the future: would they be its prophets, like John the Baptist, or its fulfillment, like Christ? The pattern of blood at the crown of Gauguin's stoneware head suggests a crown of thorns, drawing at once on Vincent's story of the wounded miner in the Borinage and on Verdier's portrait of Bruyas that they saw together in Montpellier (ch. 4, fig. 132), in addition to Vincent's own subsequent sacrificial act.

While in this sense retrospective, the *Self-Portrait Jug* was crafted to image the destiny, fashioned together with Vincent, as the leader of those who loved and understood him. New disciples were to be recruited among the young vanguard artists who shared esoteric, mystical interests. In the fall of 1888, just before leaving Pont-Aven for Arles, Gauguin had (through Bernard) met Paul Sérusier and briefly instructed the twenty-three-year-old in his current theories. Sérusier took the fruit of his lesson—a small, highly abstracted landscape known as *The Talisman* (1888; Musée d'Orsay, Paris)— back with him to the capital, where he told his fellow students at the Académie Julian that he had encountered a "man of genius named Gauguin who revealed to me what real painting is."[46] These young artists of Symbolist bent began to visit the Montmartre branch of Boussod et Valadon, where Theo showed them works by Vincent and Gauguin. When Gauguin returned to Paris at the end of the year, he had sharpened his theories and clothed them in metaphors of religious purpose drawn from Carlyle and Wagner. The gospel that he now expounded resonates in the name that the initiates around Sérusier adopted by spring 1889: "Nabis," the Hebrew word for "prophets." They regarded themselves as an artistic fraternity and, increasingly, as "disciples" of "le nabi Gauguin."[47]

Syncretism dovetailed productively with Gauguin's appropriative strategies and with the associative thinking stimulated by

[Rodin] chose a figure for the precursor of Christ that bears a striking resemblance to Vincent. Even though he had never seen him. The same expression of suffering, that furrowed and contorted brow betraying a life of reflection and ascetism, though Vincent's forehead does slope a little more. The shape of the nose and structure of the head are identical. The mouth is slightly open and its expression suggests that the last sound it uttered was a sigh. Death has left no sign of anguish on that face, nor an aura of eternal peace. Though one sees that the body is lifeless, it has retained an air of tranquility and also an energetic concern with the future.

Theo to Jo, 9–10 February 1889

27
Odilon Redon
(French; 1840–1916)
Head of a Martyr
1877
Charcoal and black
chalk on paper

37 x 26 cm
Kröller-Müller
Museum, Otterlo,
The Netherlands

28
Auguste Rodin
(French; 1840–1917)
*Head of Saint John the
Baptist*
1887
Bronze
H. 19.1 cm
Musée Rodin, Paris
This is a cast of the
marble original.

29
Paul Gauguin
Ictus
1889
Paper collage, water-
color, and oil on
paper
41.6 x 56 cm
Collection Daniel
Malingue

30
Photograph of Pierre
Loti as the Egyptian
deity Osiris
1887

31
Outline drawing of
engraved gem
depicting gnostic
symbol

Vincent, as illustrated by a large watercolor of late January or early February (fig. 29). At one level the image responds to Vincent's letter of 22 January, in which he wrote the word "Ictus" enclosed by the fish symbol, as if to signal his continuing faith in artistic brother-hood. Both pictogram and acrostic feature in Gauguin's watercolor, seemingly written on a wall behind an androgynous youth who is worlds removed from Arles. The seated pose is an amalgam of Egyptian, Greek, and Asian sculptural sources; the conception depends on images conflating Christ and the Egyptian god Horus (see fig. 31), such as that which Gauguin incorporated into a later text on religion.[48]

With its intertwined, enigmatic references to Western and non-Western iconographies, *Ictus* reveals Gauguin's active attempt to fashion a syncretic visual style, fed by an omnivorous diet of art from distant places and past times encountered in museums and noted in a sketch-book. This cross-cultural trawling took him from the Louvre, with its collections of Italian faience ware (see fig. 32 and ch. 2, fig. 67), Egyptian and Assyrian sculpture, and fifteenth-

century Italian painting, to the Museum of Comparative Sculpture in the recently opened Trocadéro complex, which included a plaster cast of the head of Christ from Beauvais Cathedral (fig. 33), to which his *Self-Portrait Jug* has been compared; and from the recently inaugurated Khmer Museum, conceived to showcase sculpture and plaster casts from Angkor Wat and other sites in the new French protectorate of Cambodia, to the Ethnographic Museum, where he saw a Peruvian mummy (fig. 34) whose pose supplanted that of the fore-ground figure in *Human Miseries* as the sym-bol of existential despair.[49]

What fascinated Gauguin in some of these works was the way in which ancient sculp-tors, in rendering human anatomy, privileged formal concerns over verisimilitude; others attracted him by virtue of their direct emotional impact. His *Self-Portrait Jug* spoke to only one aspect of his "outsider" identity: hence his deci-sion to fashion a second stoneware self-portrait (fig. 35) that incorporates various primiti-visms. The new work, which he described as "the head of Gauguin the savage," can be

traced directly to a photograph in his collec-tion of Javanese sculpture and to a terracotta mask from Asia Minor housed in the Louvre (figs. 36–37). The latter object had a particu-lar expressive valence in 1889, having been published by neurologist Dr. Jean-Martin Charcot as an example of an ancient repre-sentation of mental illness.[50] But Gauguin de-flected any potential reference to Vincent's torments by underscoring the piece's identity as a self-portrait, an embodiment of his "pri-mary nature." Its material genesis served figur-atively to amplify its meaning: both the object and the figure it portrays have been "scorched in the ovens of hell"—Gauguin's echo of Vincent's characterization of the independent thinker in the modern age as a Robinson Crusoe–like survivor of the fire of life (see chs. 1, 2). Gauguin also touched on aspects of Vincent's current work: the thumb-sucking gesture ironically suggests a regressive impulse perhaps prompted by Vincent's discussion of *La Berceuse*. The theme of oral gratification car-ries through to the jar's function as a con-tainer for tobacco, the narcotic that Vincent figured as stoking the "furnace of creation."[51]

29

30

31

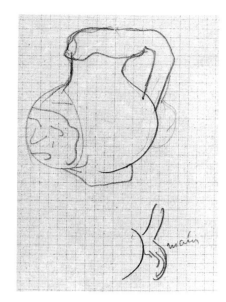

32

Together Gauguin's ceramic self-portraits figure the two natures, tenderhearted and Indian, that he first adumbrated to Mette in 1887, now cast in more ambitious terms. Assuming the guise of Christlike martyr, Gauguin drew upon Carlyle's formulation of the artist-prophet, as well as the Renan-Carlyle-Vincent characterization of Christ as sculptor in living flesh. Deftly incorporating these themes into his art, Gauguin also applied them rhetorically in an article he contributed to Aurier's new periodical *Le Moderniste illustré*, wherein he argued the importance of ceramics:

During the remotest epochs, among the Indians of the Americas, one finds this art constantly favored. God created man with a little bit of mud. With a little bit of mud, one can create metal, precious stones; with a little bit of mud and also a little bit of genius.[52]

"God made *you*, shaped you out of clay": Carlyle cited these words of Muhammad as proof of the prophet's ability to reveal the miraculous foundation of everyday existence. Gauguin, asserting the status in primitive cultures of the medium in which he was currently engaged, laid claim to Muhammad's defining qualities, as outlined by the Scottish philosopher: untutored intellectual acuity, wildness, and the strength to "shape himself into Poet, King, Priest, any kind of Hero."[53]

The various impulses now guiding Gauguin's work in clay come together in the impressive sculpture known as *Black Venus*, which is more probably a grim Salome with the head of John the Baptist in her lap (fig. 39).[54] Giving the Rodin-inspired severed head his own features, Gauguin inscribed himself in a dramatic narrative that he viewed through the lenses of exotic references. The serpentine lotus flower that seems to emerge from the head to rise phallically before the dark figure's loins symbolized generation and fecundity in ancient India and Egypt; the buddhalike pose, as well

as the pendant earrings and the bands decorating the upper arms and torso, derives from another of Gauguin's photographs of ancient Javanese sculpture (fig. 38). Gauguin thus transported the iconography of John the Baptist, Christ's martyred precursor, over time and space, expanding upon the suggestion, expressed in the *Cleopatra* pot (ch. 2, fig. 69), that the art of the future could be nourished in the tropics.

33

Gauguin encountered suggestive models for such geographical displacement at the Paris Universal Exposition, which opened on 6 May, particularly in one of its major attractions, the Colonial Exhibition. A vast state-sponsored effort designed to win the French public over to hitherto controversial policies of expansionism, the display consisted of pavilions housing art, artifacts, and even natives from acquired territories, who lived on the grounds in facsimile environments, a spectacle of Otherness staged for a Parisian audience.

Like many of his contemporaries, Gauguin found the exposition exotic and fascinating. He sketched the rickshaw boys from Tonkin and studied the sculpture included in the Cambodian pavilion, the so-called *pagode* inspired by Angkor Wat, the crown jewel of France's new cultural possessions in Southeast Asia. Next door Gauguin visited the Javanese village, the *kampong*, where he saw a performance by a troupe of dancers from the Dutch colony (fig. 41). Struck by the likeness between their stylized movements and the figurative plaster casts adorning the *pagode* (see fig. 42), Gauguin wrote enthusiastically to Bernard: "My photographs of Cambodian [art] are rediscovered verbatim in the[se] ... dances."[55] The fact that he mistook the Javanese sculpture in his photographs for Cambodian underscores the success of the French campaign to subsume the political implications of colonialism within a broader ideology promising personal renewal.

32
Paul Gauguin
Sketch of faience jug
with the face of a
youth in relief, from
the Album Walter
Sketchbook, p. 55
recto
Graphite
Musée d'Orsay,
Paris, Département
des Arts Graphiques
See ch. 2, fig. 67

33
Head of Christ
15th century
Plaster cast
Church of Saint-
Saveur, Beauvais

34
Peruvian mummy
12th/15th century
Musée de l'Homme,
Paris

35
Paul Gauguin
Self-Portrait Jar
Spring 1889
[B 53, G 66]
Glazed stoneware
H. 28 cm
Musée d'Orsay,
Paris, gift of Jean
Schmidt, 1938
Cat. 92

36
Isidore van
Kinsbergen
(Dutch; 1821–1905)
Detail of *The
Assault of Mara*
from *Oudheden
van Java, De tem-
pel-ruine Boro-
Boedoer*, (Batavia,
1874),
pls. 51–52
Albumen print
Institute Kern,
Leiden, The
Netherlands

37
Terracotta mask
Louvre Campana
Collection
From Jean-Martin
Charcot and Paul
Richer, *Les
Difformes et les
malades dans l'art*
(Paris, 1889), p. 9

35

36

37

38

39

The sections of the Universal Exposition devoted to primitive societies—from the Colonial Exhibition to Buffalo Bill Cody's "Wild West Show"—lent an aura of real possibility to the brochures promoting emigration to the French colonies that were distributed on the exhibition grounds, and to the ideas of renaissance and regeneration central to the Studio of the Tropics concept. The exposition's mix of life and art, past and present, near and far, provided a kind of sanction to Gauguin's syncretist visual tendencies, as his drawing of one of the *pagode*'s plaster reliefs suggests (fig. 40). Brushing the *apsara* (celestial dancer) over a sketch of a fresco by Italian master Sandro Botticelli in the Louvre, Gauguin suggestively equated Cambodian and early Renaissance art, following current assessments that compared the two in terms of quality and purity.

When Gauguin went to Brittany in early June, he seemingly took with him this Cambodian plaster detail, which he claimed to have found on the exhibition grounds, as a kind of talisman of new ideas and approaches. He had begun to entertain the idea of going to Southeast Asia, soon voicing hopes of procuring a cushy position from the Colonial Department in Tonkin.[56] But as indicated by a still life painted before he left Paris (fig. 5), even while he began to contemplate seriously the Studio of the Tropics, the Studio of the South remained very much on his mind. Vincent's most recent pictures had arrived in Paris in May, and one way or another Gauguin was aware of the self-portraits executed shortly after his departure from Arles. Gauguin's canvas addresses both of these directly, adopting from one (fig. 8) the split yellow-and-red background, divided horizontally at the bridge of the nose; and from the other (fig. 7) a Japanese print symbolic of the ideology around which both studio concepts were organized. Inclusion of his *Self-Portrait Jug*, however, proposes his own creative agency.[57]

Vincent in Saint-Rémy, May–Mid-July 1889

In every second letter that Vincent wrote to his brother prior to leaving Arles for Saint-Rémy on 8 May, he asked for news of Gauguin; but despite his intense curiosity about his friend's activities, Vincent had decided not to contact him again until he felt quite normal. He viewed the prospect of his residence in Saint-Paul-de-Mausole as a retreat from the failed campaign launched at the Yellow House a year earlier. Though he was coming to terms with his condition, which the doctors in Saint-Rémy diagnosed as epilepsy, Vincent described himself as in decline, descending the hill instead of climbing it.[58] Work continued to afford him a sense of earning a living as a productive member of society, but he felt his former ambitions and hopes becalmed.

Dark thoughts played beneath the bright surfaces of the canvases that Vincent started painting immediately upon arrival at the twelfth-century monastery (see fig. 2), where he was provided with a studio as well as a bedroom. Difference and isolation form the subtext of *Irises* (fig. 43), the first picture he painted in the garden where he would spend much of his time. Like *Butterflies and Flowers*, *Irises* is a close-up view of a small patch of vegetation—nature in microcosm—but here the artist used the large, size 30 format that he had earlier chosen for his panoramic vistas of the Crau. Despite the expansive size of *Irises*, however, the writhing, overlapping floral forms convey a sense of claustrophobia and confinement that assumes a decidedly symbolic cast owing to the inclusion of a single white iris, rendered with flat, thin paint, standing erect among the crowd of its more animated, highly detailed, and impastoed brethren. Vincent's use of contrasting light and dark colors to establish difference within sameness recalls earlier art-historical examples of Christ's passion, some of which portray a pale, serene Jesus surrounded by swarthy, grimacing torturers. In *Irises* the alone-in-a-crowd theme is legible independent of the biographical facts of the artist's institutionalization and his reluctance to see the friends who continued to occupy his thoughts.[59]

Though disinclined to rejoin the Paris art world, Vincent was not indifferent to news from the capital. On 21 May Theo informed him that Gauguin was working on sculpture and would soon join de Haan in Pont-Aven; in the same letter, he asked Vincent to consider submitting work to the Indépendants exhibition (to open on 3 September) and gave his initial response to the pictures he had just received from Arles. Theo declared the "little sower with the tree, the baby, the starry night, the sunflowers" (ch. 4, figs. 77, 95; ch. 3, figs. 70, 57–58) to be superb, singling out *La Berceuse* and the large portrait of Joseph Roulin (ch. 4, fig. 102) for their vigorous, unconventional beauty. Theo's positive response emboldened Vincent to ask his brother to offer Gauguin (as well as Bernard) a copy of *La Berceuse*.[60]

Theo had spared his brother word of a private exhibition that Gauguin and his friends were

planning for early June and in which they initially conceived Vincent participating. When Vincent saw an article announcing the show, he defensively feigned indifference: "I am inclined to think that a new sect has again been formed, no less fallible than those already existing."[61] In speaking of a new sect, he inevitably recalled his ambitions for the Yellow House, and by a characteristically elaborate sequence of associations, moved on to the subject of an ancient Egyptian dwelling re-created at the Universal Exposition, and thence to a statement about the "eternal tillers of the soil, worshipers of the sun" that reveals his ongoing preoccupation with the recent past:

The Egyptian artists having a *faith*, working by feeling and by instinct, express all these intangible things—kindness, infinite patience, wisdom, serenity—by a few knowing curves and by the marvelous proportions.... When the thing represented and the manner of representing it agree, the thing has style and quality.[62]

What is remarkable about this statement is the evolution it reveals in Vincent's thinking. His references to Egyptian art prior to Gauguin's arrival in Arles had been ambivalent. Indeed the August self-portrait exchange had prompted him to differentiate himself and Gauguin by contrasting his own preference for the art of the Greeks and Japanese over that of the Persians and Egyptians (see ch. 3): Vincent responded to the divinized view of nature he intuited in the former, while Gauguin was attracted to the synoptic stylizations of the latter.

During their two months together, Vincent attempted, with mixed success, to embrace Gauguin's ideas; his letters and paintings reveal uneasy compliance rather than true responsiveness, as if the lessons had been taken in but not wholly taken on. However, this new conviction about Egyptian art suggests that in the months following Gauguin's departure, he had seemingly arrived at a more

genuinely felt reconciliation of their views. Replaying their dialogue as an internal monologue, Vincent could now idealize the Egyptians on his own terms, much as he did the Japanese, but with an emphasis on style that unmistakably echoes Gauguin's interests. Vincent's paintings likewise bear witness to this process.

Theo saw the connection between his brother's remarks about Gauguin's exhibition and his preoccupation with style, and responded accordingly. Having had more time to consider Vincent's recent work, he offered this assessment:

In all of them there is a power of color that you had not previously realized, which is itself a rare quality, but you went further, and if there are those that seek symbolism through the torturing of form, I find it in many of your paintings in the way that they express your view of nature and of living creatures, to which you are so strongly attached.[63]

Theo's reservations about expressive distortion were explicitly connected to the risks he perceived in Vincent's venturing into what he called the mysterious regions of deep feeling. He criticized Gauguin by contrast for pettiness. The exhibition that Gauguin had orchestrated, together with Schuffenecker and Bernard, had opened just days earlier at M. Volpini's Café des Arts, situated in the colonnade under the roof of the Palais des Beaux-Arts, site of the exposition's official art display (which included, alongside hundreds of canvases by academic masters, examples by Degas, Monet, and Pissarro). To Theo's way of thinking, the location implied an attempt to sneak into the Universal Exposition by the back door. But what offended him more—and, he implied, had decided him against lending Vincent's works to the undertaking—was the sickeningly self-important attitude of the organizers, who propagated an exclusionary politics reminiscent of the factionalism that had plagued the Impressionist group.[64]

43
Vincent van Gogh
Irises
10–15 May 1889
Oil on canvas
71 x 93 cm
J. Paul Getty
Museum, Los
Angeles

Theo's criticism eclipsed Vincent's rancor, precipitating a defense of Gauguin and his junior partner, Bernard. Vincent attributed the situation to an understandable need to show their work combined with the vanguard's inherent disunity. Stimulated to demonstrate his ideal of group solidarity, Vincent imaginatively engaged Gauguin (and Bernard) in a dialogue by producing two pictures that he felt sure would be "parallel in feeling" to the work they were currently producing: a landscape with the Alpilles in the distance (fig. 44) and a "new study of a starry sky" (fig. 45).[65]

Both canvases dramatically evidence Vincent's desire to enter into a closer communion with Gauguin, privileging style by means of

emphatic, arbitrary linearity. To be sure, as the proto–Art Nouveau formal rhythms of *Irises* and the curving brush-stroke patterns in other June pictures attest, Vincent had recently been exploring stylistic principles that he categorized as Egyptian. But the urgently dynamic rhythms animating the new works are unprecedented. Vincent painted *Olive Trees in a Mountain Landscape* from nature. But while the undulating forms of the Alpilles have a basis in reality, the wavelike ground line and dominant cloud hovering like a clenched fist in the sky reveal an antinaturalism that marks a departure from the similarly motivated canvases painted together with Gauguin. The work is, as Vincent recognized, more "spontaneous" than the most ambitious of

these Arles exercises, freely deploying Gauguin's ideas about style but through technical means and toward expressive ends that were Vincent's own.

The Starry Night represents an even more explicit and personal response to Gauguin's precepts. Though based on the landscape around Saint-Paul-de-Mausole, with its mountainous setting, tiled rooftops, and prominent spire (see fig. 46), the composition is an invention in which the entire scene—from the ocean-swell forms of the Alpilles in the background to prominent flame-shaped cypresses in the foreground—suggests a hallucinatory dream. It is Vincent's vision of Saint-Rémy, filtered through his recollection of Carlyle's

44
Vincent van Gogh
*Olive Trees in a
Mountain Landscape*
16 June 1889

[F 712, JH 1740]
Oil on canvas
72.5 x 92 cm
The Museum of
Modern Art, New
York, Mrs. John Hay
Whitney Bequest

45
Vincent van Gogh
The Starry Night
17/18 June 1889
[F 612, JH 1731]

Oil on canvas
73.7 x 92.1 cm
The Museum of
Modern Art, New
York, acquired
through the Lillie P.
Bliss Bequest, 1941
Cat. 116

46
Postcard of Saint-
Rémy, c. 1900/10

word-picture of a little church, symbol
of unshakeable faith in the face of a vague,
shoreless universe.[66]

Although the two pictures are not, strictly
speaking, pendants, Vincent saw them as connected. His unconvincing disclaimer that neither represents a return to romantic or religious
ideas points to his intense personal and spiritual investment in them. *Olive Trees*, the third
of fifteen canvases Vincent would devote to
the subject between June and December 1889,
takes advantage of an available motif (the
groves just outside the asylum) to re-engage
with the theme of his failed Gethsemane canvases. Eschewing figurative narrative, Vincent

instead relied on very current symbolic associations linking Christ's Agony in the Garden
with the so-called holy tree.[67] He amplified the
association through the writhing, anguished
contortions of the natural setting. *The Starry
Night* likewise reconsiders a September project, *Starry Night over the Rhone* (ch. 3, fig. 70),
a canvas that Vincent was currently considering as a submission to the forthcoming
Indépendants precisely because he thought
it best not to exhibit anything "too mad." But
here, in revisiting the old idea of painting a
starry night with cypresses, he threw discre-
tion to the winds. The theme of a divinized
nature—"when all sounds cease, God's voice
is heard under the stars"—is no longer latent

but trumpeted in the forceful rhythms of the
unscrolling sky and haloed stars pulsating
responsively with the trees and mountains.[68]
An ecstatic vision of earth and heaven as a
harmonious continuum, the image intimates
a hope transcending the Agony of the Garden.
Vincent concluded his discussion of the pair
with the observation:

Gauguin, Bernard, and I may … not conquer,
but neither shall we be conquered; perhaps
we exist neither for the one thing nor for the
other, but to give consolation or to prepare the
way for a painting that will give even greater
consolation.[69]

44

45

46

The cypresses are always occupying my thoughts, I should like to make something of them like the canvases of the sunflowers, because it astonishes me that they have not yet been done as I see them. It is as beautiful of line and proportion as an Egyptian obelisk. It is a splash of black in a sunny landscape, but it is one of the most interesting black notes, and the most difficult to hit off exactly that I can imagine.   Vincent to Theo, [25 June 1889]

The study is all yellow, extremely thickly painted, but the subject was beautiful and simple. For I see in this reaper...the image of death, in the sense that humanity might be the wheat he is reaping. So it is, if you like, the opposite of the sower which I tried to do before [ch. 3, fig. 26]. But there is no sadness in this death; this one takes place in broad daylight with a sun flooding everything with a light of pure gold.   Vincent to Theo, [5/6 September 1889]

47
Vincent van Gogh
Cypresses
25 June 1889
[F 613, JH 1746]
Oil on canvas
93.3 x 74 cm
The Metropolitan
Museum of Art,
New York, Rogers
Fund, 1949
Cat. 117

48
Vincent van Gogh
The Reaper
June 1889
[F 617, JH 1753]
Oil on canvas
72 x 92 cm
Kröller-Müller
Museum, Otterlo,
The Netherlands

49
Vincent van Gogh
*Arles: View from the
Wheat Fields*
June 1888
[F 545, JH 1477]
Oil on canvas
73 x 54 cm
Musée Rodin, Paris

He had resumed a dialogue that he now largely controlled. "It does one good," he observed when he resumed correspondence with Gauguin, "to talk to the other fellows again even at a distance." Vincent had long profited from his imaginative colloquies with past masters such as Rembrandt, Millet, and Monticelli; now he likewise engaged his contemporaries. Gauguin in the flesh had been overwhelming. At a distance, his presence recalled, he became a more fostering mentor, leaving his erstwhile pupil free to interpret, apply, and connect the lessons as he would. Many times Vincent had told Gauguin that they must not forget that Monticelli and the Barbizon painters had preceded them on this path; now he could say so again without fear of contradiction.[70] At last Vincent could involve Gauguin in resurrecting his Marseilles hero.

The fruit of this displaced exchange, the late June *Cypresses* (fig. 47) attest to the stylistic experimentation that Vincent permitted himself. He consciously prepared and structured these very thickly painted canvases according to the procedures he imagined Monticelli following. Yet the swirling brushwork and

Vincent's comparison of the tree's form to an Egyptian obelisk respond to current conversations. While Vincent had incorporated the "somber … funereal" cypress in earlier canvases for its Provençal typicality, here he emphasized its symbolic association with death. Moreover he explicitly conceived the tree as the "equivalent" and "opposite" of the sunflower, emblem of the hope he had invested in Gauguin and the Studio of the South.[71]

The Reaper (fig. 48), painted at the same time, similarly recasts a hallmark of aspirations for the future—the sower—into its opposite. Here, a metaphoric dark note against a sunny landscape produces an "image of death as the great book of nature," presented in the Bible and in emblematic texts (see ch. 1, fig. 14). Earlier Vincent had spoken of sowing studies in order to reap paintings and, alternatively, of the artist as sower of the harvest that others (dealers, collectors, fellow painters) would reap. Now when Vincent glimpsed a reaper working in the compound's enclosure through the barred window of his room in the monastery, he saw the subject in terms of the end of his attempt to resurrect Delacroix by sowing the seeds of a

renaissance from his Arles *bonzerie*. In *The Reaper*, as in *Cypresses*, Vincent intended the play of dark against light to evoke, as he put it, "death on the point of smiling."[72] The phrase—an echo of the old touchstone "sorrowful yet always rejoicing"—also alluded to a favorite image of accepting the inevitable found at the close of Silvestre's biography of Delacroix: "Thus died—almost smiling—Delacroix, a painter … who had a sun in his head and a thunderstorm in his heart." An ideal that Vincent shared with Bernard, it had also come up in the Montpellier discussion with Gauguin of the Romantic painter.[73]

In addition to memorializing the failed renaissance, *The Reaper* pursues another conversation. Despite its avowed connection with Monticelli's technique, the canvas engages more directly with Gauguin in being a new exercise in yellow. Possibly Vincent recalled a much-admired *Reaper* by Anquetin, which he had paraphrased a year earlier when painting his first major *Sower* (ch. 3, fig. 26) and other harvest scenes (see fig. 49).[74] Zola's *Rêve* was also in his thoughts, as was Theo's enthusiastic description of a picture of an angel by

48

49

Rembrandt (see fig. 62), which he had recently seen at an auction and which he imagined had originally been completely yellow. But a dialogue with Gauguin seems to have been uppermost. Upon completing *The Reaper* around 6 July, Vincent evidently felt sufficiently confident to put ideas to paper, for he broke the silence he had maintained since January to send a letter and a sketch (now lost) to his friend. Possibly at this point he offered his latest investigation of yellow-on-yellow to Gauguin, who would subsequently, and successfully, claim it from Vincent's family.[75]

Right after posting the letter, Vincent began another picture dense with references to past and present, which he entitled *Mountains* (fig. 50). Vincent described it as a view of the mountains at the monastery's doorstep: the Alpilles or, as he dubbed them, "Tartarin's

Alps." At their foot, among olive trees, stands a dark goatherd's hut before which a few sunflowers bloom. The work, based closely on the site, is also an idiosyncratic and oblique response to a book by Swiss author Édouard Rod, sent to Vincent by his sister Wil, that recounts a man's discovery of happiness, after a long search, in bourgeois conventionality. Vincent found the volume's title, *Le Sens de la vie* (*The Meaning of Life*), pretentious and its contents unenlightening; he related to only a few incidental passages describing the simple, harsh existence of mountain peasants, who raised vegetables in small gardens where sunflowers occasionally bloomed. Vincent's claim to have painted *Mountains* under the influence of Rod's book reveals much about the responsive—and highly selective—way in which he experienced influence. In this case he culled a few lines from a text hundreds of

pages long, but something less superficial and literal was in fact at work. For Gauguin is the influence that Vincent imagined and made real in this conscious attempt to invest the exaggerated, emphatic linear rhythms with individual intention and feeling, and in his choice of a palette intended to convey a healthy sadness matching the painter's own, the somber tones virtually overwhelming the gay yellow of the straggling sunflowers.[76]

On completing *Mountains*, Vincent visited Arles to collect paintings left out of the May shipment. Around 16 July, following his return to Saint-Rémy, he embarked on a picture of an entrance to a quarry, employing a similarly restricted palette that he now characterized as Northern.[77] While working on this canvas, he suffered another attack that would keep him from working until early September.

Gauguin had been in Pont-Aven for a month by the time he received Vincent's letter and sketch of *The Reaper*. He had arrived there around 2 June, leaving Schuffenecker to make the final arrangements for the group exhibition in Paris. Gauguin himself never saw the installation of works by the "Impressionist and Synthetist Group" that opened in Volpini's café on 8 June with a somewhat modified cast of characters than had originally been planned. He was represented by a group of twelve pictures that, like the portfolio of zincographs available on request, summarized his work in Brittany, Martinique, and Arles. Gauguin soon learned of Theo's displeasure through Schuffenecker and fired off a defensive letter to the dealer, justifying his actions as self-preservation in the face of the vanguard's lack of solidarity, the senior Impressionists' pursuit of their own interests, and Theo's lackluster support.[78]

Gauguin embellished this representation in a canvas announced to Schuffenecker on the same day (fig. 51): "I have begun a ~~Christ~~ Jesus in the Garden of Olives that will turn out well, I think.... It is a kind of abstracted sadness, and sadness is my line, you know." Gauguin omitted to mention that the work is also a self-portrait. It fully elaborates the recently sketched persona as leader of a discipleship of believers, while introducing the related themes of betrayal and abandonment. In the context of the Volpini show, he spoke of himself as head of an artistic brotherhood, playing the part that Degas had for the Impressionists by laying down the rules of participation; and he condemned Guillaumin's abdication and Pissarro's traitorous defection to official exhibition venues.[79]

Such current motivations notwithstanding, Gauguin drew the primary elements of his depiction of Gethsemane from his Arles experience. He colored his dark hair bright red, a feature that (together with the thin hand clasping the white cloth), evokes Delacroix's portrait of Bruyas (ch. 4, fig. 135). Portraying himself as a member of the van Gogh family of redheads in the context of a subject that Vincent had twice failed to realize, Gauguin scarcely disguised his strategy. He recognized that Vincent's destroyed *Gethsemane* canvases had been self-portraits—at least allusively, through the artist's personal investment in the Gethsemane theme, if not more literally, as Vincent may well have depicted a Christ who bore some resemblance to himself. Gauguin's *Christ in the Garden of Olives* both unmasks and wrests away this identity, appropriating it along with the spiritualized ideal of a discipleship of painters to which it belonged.

The Volpini exhibition increased Gauguin's modest ranks of followers. Aurier championed the show as a bohemian antidote to officially sanctioned art, welcoming the inventive daring of Gauguin, Bernard, and Anquetin, whose essays in simplification demonstrated a "synthetism" of line, form, and color.[80] Early July brought the more considered assessment of a less well disposed reviewer, Félix Fénéon. Contextualizing Gauguin within vanguard developments since the general rejection of Impressionist gesture, Fénéon conceded that he had arrived at a synthetic art by taking a different but analogous route to that of Seurat and his cohorts:

Reality was for him only a pretext for far-reaching creations: he rearranges the materials reality provides, disdains illusionistic effects, even atmospheric ones, accentuates lines, limits their number, makes them hieratic, and in each of the spacious cantons formed by their interlace, an opulent and sultry color sits in bleak glory, without attacking neighboring colors, without yielding its own tone.[81]

While the critic entertained the possibility of Anquetin's influence, he deemed it purely formal, for his work lacked the feeling evident in Gauguin's. And he implied Gauguin's impact on the Breton and Martinique subjects of Bernard and Laval, while making the point that Gauguin's "special spiritual state" precluded emulation. While ambivalent about the work on display at Volpini's, Fénéon implied the emergence of a new vanguard, led by Gauguin, paralleling Neo-Impressionism (whose primary practitioners were conspicuously excluded). Though apparently generating nothing in the way of sales and leaving the organizers with a surfeit of catalogues, the exhibition had in a small but important way been successful.[82]

The Volpini show convinced Sérusier, who had wavered of late, that he ought to have understood "Gauguin the master" better; at the end of June, he left Paris for Brittany to ask his pardon. Bernard was absent; having been forbidden by his father to associate with Gauguin in Pont-Aven, he was in Saint-Briac. But the group did include Laval, as well as de Haan, with whom Gauguin spent much of the summer, first in Pont-Aven, and then, on two different occasions beginning in July, in the more remote village of Le Pouldu, on the Atlantic coast (see map, ch. 2, fig. 5). Gauguin's new Dutch companion, a redhead like Vincent, proved an ideal disciple, quick to learn and possessing the financial resources to subsidize Gauguin's living expenses. Despite both Gauguin's and de Haan's assertions to the contrary, the latter's works remained closely dependent on the former's. Sérusier proved a less tractable disciple; not only did he disagree with Gauguin on theoretical issues, he began to see in his work a lack of *délicatesse*, an "illogical affectation in the drawing ... a search for originality bordering on the fraudulent."[83]

50
Vincent van Gogh
Mountains (Saint-Rémy)
c. 9 July 1889
[F 622, JH 1766]
Oil on canvas
71.8 x 90.8 cm
Solomon R. Guggenheim Museum, New York, Thannhauser Collection, gift of Justin K. Thannhauser, 1978
Cat. 118

It's Christ in the Garden of Olives. A greenish blue twilight sky, trees all leaning together
in a crimsonish mass, purply earth, and the figure of Christ, enveloped in dark ochre clothing and
with bright red hair. Since this painting is not destined to be understood, I shall keep it for
a long time.   Gauguin to Vincent, [late October/early November 1889]

51
Paul Gauguin
*Christ in the Garden of
Olives* (*Christ dans le
jardin des oliviers*)
June 1889 [W 326]
Oil on canvas
73 x 92 cm

Norton Museum of
Art, West Palm
Beach, Florida
Cat. 95

52
Paul Gauguin
La Belle Angèle
1889 [W 315]
Oil on canvas
92 x 72 cm
Musée d'Orsay, Paris

Though Sérusier would soon change his mind again, he had raised pertinent issues. Gauguin was aggressively pushing himself—as he told Bernard in August—"even further in the direction I've already laid out, but to find something more." Deny as he would the pretension to invent something new, he avowed his impatience to reinvent himself, to gain access to "an as yet unknown corner of myself." He could glimpse what he wanted, but felt he had yet to give it expression, describing his recent works to Bernard as maladroit, ignorant experiments. He similarly qualified them as "*preparatory* work for something else" in response to Theo's July request for his latest pictures, but promised to send them off

when he returned to Pont-Aven, which he did at the end of August.[84]

Theo, to his disappointment, found the latest consignment inferior to the Brittany pictures of the previous fall. As he told his brother, the sole canvas he admired as a truly fine Gauguin was *La Belle Angèle* (fig. 52), a painting of a seated Breton woman in local costume, "hands folded … outlines … gray and the background of a beautiful blue lilac with pink and red flowers." Theo praised the work's fresh, countrified qualities, the simplicity he also admired in *La Berceuse*, an example of which Gauguin had accepted as a gift in early July. Gauguin's *Belle Angèle*—despite primitivizing signifiers

such as the Japanese compositional format (noted by Theo) and the inclusion of a ceramic fancifully conflating Indian and Egyptian sources (which Theo failed to mention)—acknowledges *La Berceuse* in various ways: the inscription of the title on the picture; the division of the background into zones, the upper featuring floral wallpaper; the bulky, immobile character of the strongly outlined figure; and the thick, joined hands.[85]

Theo found little else resembling *La Belle Angèle* in Gauguin's extraordinarily heterogeneous group of pictures, which reveal the artist trying to advance on various fronts. Exemplary of an attempt to follow up on works executed with Vincent is a brilliant canvas featuring a peasant couple on a narrow path atop the dizzying cliffs of Le Pouldu (fig. 53). Here Gauguin revisited his first Arles *Washerwomen* (ch. 4, fig. 75), weaving elements of near and far into a more closely worked and chromatically dazzling tapestry, while at the same time constructing a complicated but legible space, with double vistas down to the sea below and straight into the distance ahead. A tour-de-force balance of abstraction and representation, *Flageolet Player on the Cliff, Brittany* is also a complex exercise in linear stylization paralleling Vincent's own "exaggerations," which he compared to the warped lines of old wood—one thinks of *The Starry Night* (fig. 45), which Gauguin had learned about prior to leaving for Le Pouldu in July.[86]

Gauguin pursued another direction in the landscape known as *The Red Cow* (fig. 54), in which areas of color are fewer and less variegated, and linear movement carefully regulated. Related sketchbook drawings attest that Gauguin labored over this picture: deliberation is imprinted on the willful stylization of trees and clouds, and on the division of the composition into bands of clearly defined chromatic zones.[87] The prominent form of the cow—its head cropped and back aligned with

52

53

the gate's top bar—embodies the overall stasis and insistent formalism that locate this work in a creative universe remote from that of Vincent's *Cypresses*. For Gauguin the deployment of style involved subordinating the natural world to principles of pictorial design; Vincent, according primacy to nature, used exaggeration to convey its vitality.

The exchange that Gauguin referred to as their continuing conversation was, in this sense, at cross-purposes, inflected on each side by different circumstances and attendant pressures to create. Vincent, battling with his illness in Saint-Rémy, was spared the competitive atmosphere in which Gauguin worked. De Haan's (and Theo's) close friend J. J. Isaacson gave voice to the almost messianic hopes

being attached to painting when, in his mid-August report from Paris to a Dutch periodical, he asked, "Where is the man who reveals anew our ... earth ... who restores happiness by revealing the divine in matter.... Where is the re-animator who lets us see that?" His answer: Vincent, a "unique pioneer."[88] The newly anointed hero, whomever he turned out to be, had to manifest true originality; signs of discipleship were disqualifying. Pressures to invent brought rivalries to the surface. Isaacson would soon put out the word that Gauguin's recent canvases owed a debt to Bernard, warning de Haan that the older artist would lead him astray; Gauguin took issue with Fénéon's suggestion of his indebtedness to Anquetin; and by September Bernard—pictured by Fénéon as a Gauguin

follower—was in the midst of a personal and professional crisis. Bernard had come to the conclusion that painting had to be "more than a result of synthetized sensations" and that technique, which he believed he woefully lacked, was more important than Gauguin allowed. He believed in Gauguin's path, he wrote, but needed to stray from it, if for no other reason than "perversity."[89]

Now back in Pont-Aven, Gauguin responded quickly, expressing skepticism regarding his friend's newfound belief in technique but agreeing that art should be more than visually harmonious; he avowed his commitment to communicating a message of transcendence in his own work. Perhaps, he concluded, Bernard had seen too much and listened

53
Paul Gauguin
Flageolet Player on the Cliff, Brittany
Summer 1889
[W 361]
Oil on canvas
73 x 92 cm
Indianapolis Museum of Art, Samuel Josefowitz Collection of the School of Pont-Aven, through the generosity of Lilly Endowment Inc., the Josefowitz Family, Mr. and Mrs. James M. Cornelius, Mr. and Mrs. Leonard J. Betley, Lori and Dan Efroymson, and other Friends of the Museum
Cat. 96

54
Paul Gauguin
The Red Cow
Summer 1889
[W 365]
Oil on canvas
92 x 73 cm
Los Angeles County Museum of Art, Mr. and Mrs. George Gard De Sylva Collection
Cat. 97

54

55
Paul Gauguin
Landscape with Two Breton Women
Summer 1889
[not in W]
Oil on canvas
72.4 x 91.4 cm
Museum of Fine Arts, Boston, Gift of Harry and Mildred Remis
Cat. 98

to too many; an artist needs deep beliefs and self-knowledge. For his own part, he strove to become "more and more incomprehensible."[90]

Gauguin's desire to invest his pictorial experiments with spirituality and ambiguity emerges in *Landscape with Two Breton Women* (fig. 55), a highly artificial scene comprising an expanse of demarcated color zones and featuring an elegantly attenuated tree, beside which sit two Breton women. Scrutiny of the more prominent figure reveals her to be eating, but the first and lasting impression is that she is kneeling, head bent, in prayer. This kind of self-conscious search for effect, together with the pronounced linearity, provoked criticism from Sérusier—and ultimately from Theo.

Sincere though Gauguin's expressions of doubt about his recent work may have been, he seemingly achieved a breakthrough of sorts in late August. When he sent off a shipment of pictures to Theo, he added that he had a new canvas, still too wet to include, that he considered more fully realized than the rest. In a letter to Bernard, he outlined future plans to execute a wooden sculpture featuring a monstrous self-portrait, a woman, and a "fox, an Indian symbol of perversity," the last word pointedly echoing Bernard's characterization of his own defection. He concluded by mentioning not one but two paintings with which he was well pleased: apparently the pictures that have come to be known as *Green Christ* (fig. 57) and *Yellow Christ* (fig. 58).[91]

Both canvases represent *calvaires*, the distinctive carved crucifixes erected at public squares, crossroads, and in churchyards throughout Brittany. Authors and illustrators interested in the region's primitive aspects pointed to these objects as evidence of the local population's deep superstitiousness (see fig. 59). Gauguin's *Green Christ* translates onto canvas Loti's characteristic word picture of a coastal *calvaire*, with Christ's black stone arms "stretched out ... like [those of] real men in torture; in the distance the

Channel ... fair and calm ... under the already darkened sky and shade-laden horizon."[92]

Basing his image on the *pietà* group at the foot of the *calvaire* near the church in Nizon, a hamlet within walking distance of Pont-Aven (fig. 56), the artist imaginatively transported it to the shores of Le Pouldu (though he seemingly painted it after returning to Pont-Aven in late August). As he told Theo, he "sought in this painting to make everything exude belief, passive suffering, primitive religious style, and the power of nature with its cry."[93] Elliptical clouds in the leaden sky function as natural haloes for the three holy women supporting the body of Christ, whose right arm, pulled by gravity into a straight vertical, dramatically indicates stiff lifelessness. Informed by the sculptural prototype, Gauguin rendered his figural group in shades of green that bring to mind time's patination of moss and lichen. His use of similar yellow-green for the face of the peasant sitting before the *calvaire* suggests her basic connection to it, as does the parallel incline of her torso and the body of Christ, while (as Gauguin noted) the sheep she tends implies her passivity. In depicting a Christian artifact attached to a specific culture of belief, Gauguin was attempting to craft a broader statement, intimating the continuity of human misery from the past to the present and into the future. For the piece of rope held by the peasant woman references Vincent's *Berceuse*, possibly standing in for a cradle and by extension the next generation, and certainly underscoring the larger artistic ambition that the two men shared.

Though Gauguin did not consider his *calvaire* canvases to be religious pictures per se, their mutually reinforcing iconographic and chromatic strategies do relate to the consoling aims of *La Berceuse*, and likewise convey a broadly spiritual message. In *Green Christ*, as Gauguin would point out to Aurier, he sought to suggest the connection between human suffering and natural forces by harmonizing the gray-

green of the figural group with the dark sky.[94] But he offset the bleakness by introducing contrast, rendering the coastal landscape in the sumptuous palette of pinks, greens, and orange-yellows he had deployed in *Flageolet Player on the Cliff, Brittany* (fig. 53).

A different play of solemnity and brilliance structures *Yellow Christ*. Gauguin based the central motif on a polychrome crucifix in a chapel in Trémalo, near Pont-Aven; behind it he depicted the town nestled among the surrounding hills. But as Gauguin informed sympathetic critics, and through them a wider readership, the chromatic setting was more important than the geographic one, as an initial drawing on canary-yellow paper suggests (fig. 60). Echoing the artist's gloss, Octave Mirbeau described the subject as "a piteous and barbarous Christ ... daubed yellow" in a "completely yellow countryside, agonizing yellow"; Morice saw the yellow Christ "in the yellow heath" as a symbol of sacrifice, of an eternal death that fails to affect life or console the living. This is traditional religion represented by Zola in *La Joie de vivre* and as understood by Vincent, lacking the solace afforded either by nature or by an art that distills and communicates nature. Gauguin's *Yellow Christ* responds to Vincent's *Reaper* in that both works make use of a traditional symbol of mortality (Catholic in the one case and emblematic in the other) and a palette of yellow to intimate the eternal cycle of joy and sorrow, life and death.[95]

56
Calvaire carved in sandstone, Nizon, Brittany, France

57
Paul Gauguin
Green Christ (Breton Calvary)
September 1889
[W 328]
Oil on canvas
92 x 73.5 cm
Musées Royaux des Beaux-Arts de Belgique, Brussels
Cat. 99

58
Paul Gauguin
Yellow Christ (Le Christ jaune)
September 1889
[W 327]
Oil on canvas
92 x 73 cm
Albright-Knox Art Gallery, Buffalo, New York, General Purchase Funds, 1946
Cat. 100

59
Henri Gustave Jossot (French; 1866–1951)
"They'll All Go To Heaven!" ("Ils iront tous au paradis!")
from *L'Ymagier*, no. 3 (April 1895), p. 187

60
Paul Gauguin
Christ
1889
Graphite on yellow paper
24 x 15 cm
Courtesy Christie's Images New York

56

57

By the third week of August, Vincent had recovered sufficiently from his mid-July attack to write Theo a brief note, in which he mentioned having received a kind letter and a Volpini catalogue from Gauguin; he also thanked his brother for sending him the amazing etching after Rembrandt's image of the archangel Raphael (fig. 62) that they had discussed. The print raised the old issue about painting the supernatural, a scenario that Vincent had consistently linked to the idea of Rembrandt painting angels by dreaming before nature (see ch. 3). At another associative level, the *Angel* reminded Vincent of the Dutch master's portrait of the "man with the staff in the Lacaze gallery" (ch. 4, fig. 136), which he identified with Gauguin the painter-wanderer. "If you want to give me great, great pleasure," he told Theo, "then send a copy [of the etching] to Gauguin."[96]

By early September Vincent had resumed painting, but he remained preoccupied with Rembrandt's *Angel*, and by extension the Lacaze "Wanderer" and the "other fellows in Brittany," whom he imagined were busy producing work superior to his own. If he had to do it all over again, he reflected, perhaps he would not have come to the South, which he now saw as the site of Bruyas's lifelong suffering for a lost cause. He began to talk about returning north, to Paris or Brittany, if his health improved. Theo's ambivalence regarding Gauguin's recent canvases, received around 6 September, nurtured such thinking: Gauguin needed reassurance in order to produce better things. "I tell myself," Vincent confided, "that Gauguin and I will perhaps work together again."[97]

As in January, it was with consoling images and self-portraits that Vincent paved the road back into painting in September. He returned to his *Bedroom* (ch. 3, fig. 78), realizing a second version on the same scale as the first but with minor variations (The Art Institute of Chicago). His first self-portrait was a care-fully staged representation of himself as a practicing professional, dressed in a painter's smock (fig. 61). Vincent positioned himself in front of a mirror so that the viewer sees not his left ear—the sign of his illness—but his right. From this vantage point the palette held in his left hand would appear in the mirror as if in his right, on the far side of his body. But determined to emphasize the tools of his trade, Vincent resorted to a fiction: he would have had to hold the palette in his right hand (with which he painted) for it to appear like this in the mirror image that served him as model. A portrait of determination, the picture brilliantly demonstrates that his illness had compromised neither his technical nor his expressive capabilities. Unlike the January examples, distinguished by prominent bandages, only the slightest hint of his trials appears here, in the halo effect created by directional brush strokes in the background.[98]

Vincent connected his current pursuit of portraiture directly to debates with Gauguin on this and related questions during their volatile final weeks together. Though the intensity of their discussions had strained their nerves—and friendship—to the breaking point, Vincent hoped that they could nonetheless secure the main objective: "Some good pictures will come out of it."[99] Under the revivified impression of these memories of the Montpellier Delacroixs, portraits of Bruyas, and conversations they provoked, Vincent painted a *Pietà*, based on a black-and-white reproduction of a Delacroix canvas, and shortly thereafter a copy of the etching of Rembrandt's *Angel* (figs. 62–65). Both exercises touched on the persistent question of the viability of traditionally religious subjects in the modern age: who, apart from these two masters and the evangelists, could affectively paint the face of Christ (see ch. 3)?

Christ's Passion loomed prominently in Vincent's mind in the aftermath of his recent attack, which (like the one he experienced during the last days with Gauguin) had taken what he acknowledged as an absurd religious turn. He now recognized that for many years he had harbored a fear of religion precisely because of its strong attractions, which could blur into identifications. Nonetheless he was stunned to discover that his embrace of a gospel of art rooted in nature—Zola's *Joie de vivre* in place of the Bible (see ch. 1)—had not protected him against the "perverted and frightful ideas about religion" that tormented him during episodes he likened to those a superstitious man might have. Vincent was tempted to attribute his "sickly religious aberrations" to the Catholic atmosphere of the Arles and Saint-Rémy hospitals (both former cloisters); he also suspected the influence of the overly imaginative South, despite the fact that his Borinage experience disproved his claim never to have had similar thoughts in the North. The conflicts ran deep, for while attesting his dread of such exaggeration, Vincent also admitted that during recent periods of intense suffering, thoughts of religion sometimes brought him great consolation.[100]

His reproduction of Delacroix's *Pietà*, inadvertently damaged during his latest episode, comforted him in this way. Vincent deeply admired the way Delacroix had invested the supernatural and historical with the force of present reality; as he saw it, the Romantic master had recognized that the biblical figures had been real people. Vincent now acknowledged that he had cherished a similar ambition, though his concerted effort in this direction, *La Berceuse*, had aroused emotions too strong for him to manage. Had this not been the case, he could have done "portraits of saints and holy women from life which would have seemed to belong to another age, and they would have been drawn from the bourgeoisie of today and yet would have had something in common with the very earliest Christians."[101] Such was the aspiration—together with hopes for a

61
Vincent van Gogh
*Self-Portrait with
Palette*
c. 1 September 1889
[F 626, JH 1770]
Oil on canvas
57 x 43.5 cm
National Gallery of
Art, Washington,
D.C., Collection of
Mr. and Mrs. Paul
Mellon
Cat. 119

brotherhood in faith—that Vincent encoded in the acrostic that he introduced to his and Gauguin's vocabulary.

In the attempt to avoid what he termed religious exaltation, Vincent set himself the task of copying the cherished Delacroix image. Rendering the monochrome in oils, Vincent made Christ's hair a ginger color (as he would the angel's in his rendition of the Rembrandt), almost reflexively projecting an element of self-portraiture possibly abetted by the generic resemblance in the lithograph. Given his current anxieties and earlier ambition to resurrect Delacroix through the Studio of the South, the effort was inevitably symbolic. Restoring the damaged icon, Vincent figuratively revived and recreated it in his own image, further personalizing it in what has been described as a "miraculous palette of deep blues, pinkish browns, and sepulchral greens, many of them suffused with an eerie glow of dull lemon."[102] Drawing analogies to two scenarios of creative collaboration, he likened himself to an instrumentalist interpreting the work of a great composer, and to a painter executing chromatic improvisations on admired masters' pictures, which posed like models.

Translation via color of past into present had been Vincent's ambition in creating *The Sower*

of June 1888 (ch. 3, fig. 26), a revival of Millet in the language of the vanguard. Not surprisingly, then, Vincent undertook a series of interpretations based on black-and-white Millet reproductions immediately following his copies after Delacroix and Rembrandt. Vincent saw that he had chanced upon an activity that afforded him great comfort by giving him the sense of communing with and learning from the masters he revered. In the same breath, he summoned up another collaboration and another teacher, Gauguin, who, though often "genial" enough, had difficulty communicating his true "genius."[103] Vincent now applied himself to the lesson of expressive exaggeration, at a distance from his mentor and in accord with his own priorities.

Copying Delacroix refreshed Vincent's memory of what the master had to offer; in a parallel exercise, he used his recollections of Gauguin's words and pictures to infer lessons without pedagogic intrusion. He merged the two conversations—with Delacroix and Gauguin—in a pair of remarkable pictures, executed in early October, when he resumed painting outside the monastery's confines. In the first Vincent reprised the motif he had been working on (and managed to finish) at the time of his July attack: "an entrance to a quarry." Whereas he had previously adopted

a close-up view, with the quarry entrance largely obscured by foliage, in the October canvas (fig. 67) he emphasized the architectural grandeur of the twin openings, introducing a male figure to provide scale.[104] Its site-specificity notwithstanding, *Entrance to a Quarry* carries religious overtones through the connection to the setting of Delacroix's *Pietà*, which Vincent noted as being at the entrance to a grotto, in accord with traditional representations of Christ's sepulcher (see fig. 66). *Entrance to a Quarry* can be seen as an exercise of the sort Vincent imagined Delacroix carrying out preliminary to painting his *Pietà*, just as he claimed the master had preceded his *Christ in the Garden of Olives* (ch. 3, fig. 47) by studying olive groves.

Vincent carried out the lesson he derived from Delacroix in a manner he conceived as parallel to Gauguin's and Bernard's current practice in Pont-Aven, establishing an interlocking design of large planes of color demarcated by heavy outlines. This required a certain effort, for Vincent avowed to his friends that he felt "an aching void because I am no longer informed at all of what … you and others are doing." In this sense *Entrance to a Quarry* was a dialogue picture, as was another executed at around the same time, *Path through the Ravine* (fig. 68); he described both as "somewhat abstract," in

62

63

The Delacroix is a "Pietà," that is to say the dead Christ with the Mater Dolorosa. The exhausted corpse lies on the ground in the entrance of a cave, the hands held before it on the left side, and the woman is behind it. It is evening after a thunderstorm.... The face of the dead man is in the shadow—but the pale head of the woman stands out clearly against a cloud—a contrast that causes those two heads to seem like one somber-hued flower and one pale flower, arranged in such a way as mutually to intensify their effect.   Vincent to Wil, [19 September 1889]

62
Charles Louis
Courtry
(French; 1846–1897)
after Rembrandt
The Angel Raphael
1889
Etching
19.8 x 18.8 cm
Van Gogh Museum,
Amsterdam
(Vincent van Gogh
Foundation)

63
Vincent van Gogh
*Angel (after
Rembrandt)*
1889
Oil on canvas
54 x 64 cm
Whereabouts
unknown

64
Vincent van Gogh
*Pietà (after Eugène
Delacroix)*
c. 7 September 1889
[F 630, JH 1775]
Oil on canvas
73 x 60.5 cm
Van Gogh Museum,
Amsterdam
(Vincent van Gogh
Foundation)
Cat. 122

65
Celestin Nanteuil
(French; 1813–1873)
after Delacroix
Pietà
Lithograph
21.7 x 16.7 cm
Van Gogh Museum,
Amsterdam
(Vincent van Gogh
Foundation)

66
Andrea Mantegna
(Italian;
1430/31–1506)
*The Resurrection of
Christ*
1456–59
Oil on panel
71 x 94 cm
Musée des Beaux-
Arts, Tours

"Entrance to a Quarry" [has] pale lilac rocks in reddish fields, as in certain Japanese drawings. In the design and in the division of the color into large planes, there is no little similarity to what you are doing at Pont-Aven.   Vincent to Bernard, [c. 8 October 1889]

keeping with the effort to tease out the essence of the Provençal soil. To Bernard (and probably to Gauguin as well) Vincent described the *Ravine* as "two bases of extremely solid rocks, between which flows a rivulet; a third mountain blocking the ravine." While he had painted the work in the spirit of their discussions regarding style, he omitted to mention that he had executed it under quintessentially Vincent circumstances: in the face of the mistral, anchoring his easel with heavy rocks. Possibly he said no more about the subject beyond an allusion to its "fine melancholy," but he would not have had to elaborate further. Gauguin, sufficiently versed in Vincent's emblematic approach to painting nature, would have required no prompts to recognize the symbolic resonance of the two figures negotiating the narrow path bordering the abyss. On seeing the *Ravine* at the Indépendants in March 1890 (see fig. 69), Gauguin immedi-

ately understood the "controlled passion" that Vincent had described to Theo, intuiting that the mountain landscape in fact depicts the spiritual quest in which they had engaged. "Two tiny wanderers seem to climb there, in search of the unknown," Gauguin wrote. "There is a Delacroix-like emotion there, with suggestive color. Here and there red notes as highlights, all with a violet note. It is beautiful and grandiose."[105]

The Crisis of Style

During the six months separating the announcement of *Path through the Ravine* from its exhibition, the dialogue that Vincent and Gauguin had forged in correspondence was disrupted. Theo was the inadvertent instigator, his criticism of what he discerned as similar propensities in their work in fact serving underscore the essential differences that remained.

Early in October Theo had commended some examples from Vincent's most recent shipment of pictures for their expressive drawing. Isaacson, he added, had asked to take certain canvases, including *Mountains* (fig. 50), home for a while, in order to prepare a proposed article about Vincent. But in addressing the question of Vincent's possible return to the North, Theo darkly hinted that his brother might be risking another bout of religious excess should he relocate to Pont-Aven, "for I think Brittany also has something of the

68

69

à votre choix.

Celui dont je parle c'est un
paysage de montagnes. Deux
voyageurs tout petits semblent
monter là à la recherche de
l'inconnu. Il y a là une
émotion à la Delacroix avec une
couleur très sugestive. Par ci
par là des notes rouges comme
des lumières, le tout dans une
note violette. C'est beau et
grandiose.

J'en ai causé
longuement avec
Aurier Bernard
et beaucoup d'autres.

Tous vous font leurs complimenets.
Guillaumin seul hausse les
épaules quand il entend parler
de cela. Je le comprends du reste

67
Vincent van Gogh
Entrance to a Quarry
(*L'Entrée d'une car-
rière*)
c. 5 October 1889
[F 635, JH 1767]
Oil on canvas
52 x 64 cm
Monaco Partners,
L.P.
Cat. 123

68
Vincent van Gogh
*Path through the
Ravine*
October 1889
[F 662, JH 1804]
Oil on canvas
73 x 92 cm
Museum of Fine
Arts, Boston,
bequest of Keith
McLeod

69
Paul Gauguin
Sketch of van Gogh's
*Path through the
Ravine* in letter to
Vincent
[20 March 1890]
(Cooper 1983, GAC
40; M 1991, letter 158)
Van Gogh Museum,
Amsterdam
(Vincent van Gogh
Foundation)

character of a cloister, which is even to be felt in the last Gauguins, I believe." Vincent did not pursue this, but did express his desire that Isaacson postpone his article, as well as his wish to see the most recent work of Gauguin and Bernard and his need to continue to "draw and seek style."[106] The result was works like *Entrance to a Quarry* and *Path through the Ravine*.

At the end of the month, style became a point of contention. Theo had received Gauguin's second batch of recent pictures, which included *Green Christ*, *Yellow Christ*, and possibly *The Red Cow*.[107] Another shipment from Vincent, containing *The Reaper*, *The Starry Night*, and *Cypresses*, arrived at almost the same moment. The cumulative effect of these canvases alarmed Theo, who discerned a shared tendency he considered pernicious. He wrote to Vincent:

I find that you are strongest when doing true things, such as the irises.... I am well aware of what concerns you in the new canvases like the village by moonlight [*The Starry Night*] or the mountains, but I find that the search for style removes the true feeling of things. Gauguin's latest shipment shows the same preoccupations that you have.[108]

This criticism had the effect of reinforcing Vincent's sense of solidarity with his friends. While he conceded that the "great shadowy lines" in his recent work were perhaps not what they ought to have been, he remained determined to practice "drawing which tries to express the interlocking of the masses":

In spite of what you said in your last letter, that the search for style often harms other qualities, the fact is that I feel strongly inclined to seek style, if you like, but by that I mean a more virile, deliberate drawing. I can't help it if that makes me more like Bernard or Gauguin.[109]

Theo directed even harsher criticism at Gauguin, faulting his work for its inclusion of "many more reminiscences of the Japanese, the Egyptians, etc.," a point he underscored by noting, with reference to the artist's figural mannerisms, that he would prefer to see "a Breton woman of the countryside than a Bretonne with the gestures of a Japanese woman." This negative critique—with which, Gauguin learned, Degas concurred—stunned the artist. Given the fact that recent sales had been few and confined to earlier pictures, he considered it a debacle.[110]

Expressing his dismay and seeking to restore his confidence, in a letter to Bernard, Gauguin accused Degas of being too vested in realism to be truly original. To emphasize the distinction between the older Impressionist's priorities and their own, Gauguin referred to reports of the "fine mystical quality" of Bernard's recent work and defended his own aim of expressing his "resigned suffering." In this spirit, he requested Bernard send along the book—doubtless *Peregrinations of a Pariah*—by his grandmother Flora Tristan.[111]

The uproar forced Gauguin to articulate his position, which he outlined in a long letter to Theo. He presented his work in various media as constituting an ensemble:

I seek to express a general state rather than a single thought, and at the same time to give another person the visual experience of an indefinite, never-ending impression. *To suggest* suffering does not mean to specify what sort of suffering; purity in general is what I am seeking to express, not a particular kind of purity. Literature is one thing (and painting another). In consequence, the thought is suggested but not explained.[112]

Suggestion—evocation rather than description—was the hallmark of Symbolist aesthetics.[113] Gauguin cited examples, among them *Green Christ*, with its Breton aura of "superstition and desolation." He dismissed negative responses as the vested interest of the former vanguard, who were challenged by innovations that younger artists carried out with a view to art rather than its market. Degas and the others recognized all too well that he and Bernard had made pioneering strides along a new path during the summer. While he acknowledged overlap between his work and that of Bernard, Gauguin insisted that they were taking different routes to the same goal, a goal that he had pondered for a long time but had only recently formulated. Through his origins, he claimed originality:

You know that I have an Indian, Inca birthright, and everything that I do shows the effects of it. It is the basis of my personality. I seek to counter rotten civilization with something more natural, partaking of savagery.[114]

In closing, Gauguin invoked Vincent; were he nearer at hand, he could guide his brother, now subject to too many opinions, in understanding his new art.

Gauguin's reference to overlap with Bernard had to do with the fact that during the summer the younger artist had also painted the subject of Christ in Gethsemane (fig. 70a), a photograph of which Bernard circulated. Strange as Gauguin found this coincidence, it was equally strange for him to recognize in the composition a likeness of himself, not as Christ but as Judas (see fig. 70b). For whatever reason, Gauguin commended the work, letting the evident accusation pass. Clearly Bernard had heard about Gauguin's *Christ in the Garden of Olives* and had understood its intent and its associations with Vincent. While recasting

70a
Émile Bernard
(French; 1868–1941)
Christ in the Garden of Olives (Gethsemane)
1889
Oil on canvas
Whereabouts
unknown

70b
Detail of fig. 70a

Gauguin in the role of betrayer, he gave his savior red hair and moreover included a yellow angel like the one that Vincent told him he had incorporated in his own failed *Gethsemane* (see ch. 3).[115]

Bernard's picture came under fire in Theo's next letter to Vincent. Heavily influenced by the Italian primitives, Bernard's search for style had resulted in the figures' appearing ridiculous. Theo left his disapproval of its mystical bent to be inferred from his stated preference for "healthy, true things, unsullied by schools or abstract ideas"—the qualities he prized in Vincent's best canvases from nature. Anticipating just such a reaction, Gauguin had withheld from Theo his own *Christ in the Garden of Olives*. But in a letter to Vincent, he provided two sketches (fig. 71): one of a new woodcarving, *Be in Love* (*Soyez amoureuses*), which Theo considered excellently crafted, bizarre in meaning, but beautiful in its combination of lines; the other of the painting, which he presumed would elicit Vincent's sympathy and approval.[116]

Like Vincent, Gauguin imagined that the two of them were working in a kind of dialogue. Vincent's letters encouraged this assumption, as did reports from Paris that the Saint-Rémy

work had become more imaginative; he commended Vincent for remaining mindful of their conversations about *dessin* (embracing the dual sense of drawing and design). Describing his own experiments, he used a common reference against which he clearly still measured himself, *Human Miseries* (ch. 4, fig. 50). This picture, painted alongside Vincent in Arles, still exemplified his attempt to suggest transcendent meaning and create an art of abstract ideas.[117]

While acknowledging the creative achievement of Arles, Gauguin described his current situation with de Haan in Le Pouldu as if in contrast: they lived in a large, rented house overlooking the sea, dined nightly in a nearby inn, and had a ready supply of inexpensive models in the seaweed gatherers who worked the beach. Moreover de Haan was an ideal student, heeding Gauguin's advice and making progress "without losing his individuality." Together they had settled in—and this Gauguin underscored—for "*work and calm*." Gauguin softened the reference to a commodity that had been in short supply in the Yellow House with the concession that he was pursuing their discussion of Rembrandt, studying reproductions (including the *Angel* that Vincent had arranged for him to receive) as part of a con-

certed post-Arles effort to work and reflect. In this context he shared with Vincent the picture embodying his creative labors, one that he had kept to himself, since it was unlikely to be understood. He believed Vincent would like it: "It is Christ in the Garden of Olives."[118]

Possibly Gauguin was being perverse; possibly, despite his understanding of Vincent's aims, he had yet to appreciate fully their ideological basis. In any event he could not have been more wrong about his friend's reaction. Gauguin's *imitatio Christi* infuriated Vincent, who inevitably recognized in it many references to their discussions and his beliefs, encoded and appropriated in Gauguin's image. The negative impact was reinforced when, only days after the arrival of Gauguin's sketch, Vincent received photographs from Bernard of his recent religious pictures, an Annunciation and an Adoration, in addition to the Gethsemane. As his correspondents found when comparing notes, Vincent responded with similar indignation to both of them.[119]

What took Vincent aback was his friends' seemingly casual engagement with a subject he regarded with profound ambivalence: though rife with personal risks and pitfalls, it continued to tempt him against his better

70a

70b

71
Paul Gauguin
Sketches of *Christ in the Garden of Olives* and *Be in Love and You Will Be Happy* (*Soyez amoreuses, vous serez heureuses*) in letter to Vincent [c. 8 November 1889]

(Cooper 1983, GAC 37)
Van Gogh Museum, Amsterdam (Vincent van Gogh Foundation)
Cat. 104

71

judgment. Gauguin's self-presentation as Christ struck Vincent, who had only recently sidled up to a comparable enterprise in his translation of Delacroix's *Pietà*, as a brazen reminder of his own failure to control a similar identification, resulting in his behavior immediately preceding the events of 23 December 1888. Presenting himself in a role to which Vincent aspired but could not handle, Gauguin issued a challenge that his friend took up directly. He judged the works mannered, bogus, and spurious; they fell far short of the deeply moving (and, he assumed, deeply felt) Gethsemane scenes by Delacroix and Corot, images imbued with modernity by virtue of what he read as a direct connection to nature and to contemporary types. "Bernard," Vincent declared scornfully, "has probably never seen an olive tree."[120]

More transparently than before, Vincent represented the dangers of "abstraction" in terms of his personal fears. "Having an epileptic fit" was his self-referential characterization of Bernard's figures, whose attenuation he found "unhealthy." But Vincent's representation of his own approach—"I adore the true, the possible, if I can also attain spiritual ecstasy"—

was deceptively at odds with his actual behavior at certain key moments. His earlier attempts to picture Gethsemane and his recent experience confirmed that his abiding longing for the certainties of religion and his desire to imitate Christ had not been quelled by the gospel of Zola. In a quite literal sense, then, Vincent referred to Gauguin's and Bernard's depictions of *Christ in the Garden of Olives* as a "nightmare." Finally, in order to keep his illness in check, he expressed reluctance to "enter into discussions, sensing danger in those abstractions."[121] Clearly abstraction connoted not only a mode of representation but also a state of mind.

Vincent's response, though provoked by the current situation, nonetheless replayed a familiar pattern. His aesthetics, rooted in his own life experience, had always been intensely personal, forged in response to needs he imagined others sharing and shaped with reference to models he believed they would likewise find comforting. It was, in other words, an aesthetics of equilibrium, conceptualized in terms of health. Vincent reacted poorly to views that tipped this balance, especially when expressed by those in whom he assumed a mutual mindset. Isaacson's recent claims on Vincent's behalf elicited such a response. Reading between the lines, Vincent recognized his countryman as a soulmate, a "grievously suffering human being" who was "happy when he [could] admire"; his writing brought to mind that of Heine, whom Vincent had admired as a youth. But he had subsequently distanced himself from the German Romantic, and felt similarly uneasy about Isaacson: he could empathize with sorrow and anxiety, but such emotions unleavened by a sense of rejoicing or hope produced what seemed to him precisely the aura of sickness that he had devoted himself to dispelling in his own art.[122]

Among the many traits of Gauguin's that Vincent admired were prowess, good health,

and fighting spirit. He reacted to Gauguin's self-portrait as Christ, the ultimate *misérable*, much as he had to his earlier self-portrait as Jean Valjean. This time, however, the transgression was greater. They had spent time together. Vincent believed Gauguin was healthier as a result, and assumed—based on what he intuited in the *Négresses* and *Human Miseries*—that Gauguin shared the credo he had been preaching even before his early still life contrasting the Bible with Zola's *Joie de vivre* (ch. 1, fig. 3). Yet Gauguin did not recognize that the Bible, while admittedly moving, contains a message insufficient to the experience of modern reality and individual emotions such as "joy, ennui, suffering, anger, or a smile." (As an aside, Vincent asked Bernard if he had seen *The Reaper*, his image of an almost smiling death.) Bernard's and especially Gauguin's misguided "biblical compositions" were failures, and not just for the authors. They provoked in Vincent what he described as a "painful feeling of collapse instead of progress."[123]

"Now let's talk," Gauguin replied in an early December letter that, like the new work announced in it, addressed Vincent's criticisms. Somewhat defensively, Gauguin assured his friend that only *Christ in the Garden of Olives* could be considered a religious picture, and even so he had done it as a kind of imaginative exercise to sharpen his subsequent engagement with nature. In most of his recent paintings, he stressed, his primary goal had been to invest his Breton subjects with "the wildness that I see there and that is in me as well." He contrasted the South with Brittany, where the peasantry still existed as if in the Middle Ages and remained oblivious to the progress celebrated at the Universal Exposition. Their coarse speech, their every gesture, even the design of their clothing (see fig. 72), bore the imprint of Catholic ritual and symbol. To convey the superstitious religiosity that he perceived in Brittany, Gauguin had to devise strategies that departed from Vincent's "Southern verve." With Theo's criticism fresh in his mind, he told Vincent that in fact the Bretons did have "almost asiatic" faces.[124]

Vincent's challenge provoked not only this clarification on paper but also a demonstration on canvas. Gauguin told him that he was working on a size 50 canvas, much bigger than those he had employed in Arles. Apparently he had attempted a larger format several weeks earlier, when he tackled an autumn landscape depicting cowherds with their animals on a path flanked by a row of willows (fig. 73). The composition's complexity belies its pastoral theme; competing pictorial claims render the shallow space tense. In the lower half, the disposition of figures on the narrow trail establishes a winding recession into space; the treetops and sky in the upper half constitute a resolutely two-dimensional pattern. But the picture began even more ambitiously than it ended. Though it is now a size 30 canvas, Gauguin started out by priming, stretching, and painting on a grander scale, cropping his

picture at the top and left at a late stage to suppress a more expansive sky and thus to limit the suggestion of deep space. The new size 50 picture, *Seaweed Gatherers* (fig. 74), was of a very different order, its subject—the harvesting of kelp for fertilizer—not merely serving as a pretext for stylistic investigation but addressing existential issues.[125]

Seaweed Gathers is nothing so much as a Breton *Human Miseries* (ch. 4, fig. 50). It also draws upon the suggestion of ritualized procession explored in *Arlésiennes (Mistral)* (ch. 4, fig. 125), rendered with the expressive mannerisms that Gauguin now felt pressed to justify. Vincent, with his direct criticisms, had reintroduced an element of *wrijving* that disrupted Gauguin's Breton calm and spurred him on. *Seaweed Gatherers* is a major achievement, a return to the principles of benchmark Arles canvases. But Gauguin also sought to defend it as a step forward. Challenging Vincent's opposition of the "natural" and the "mannered," he argued that cultural, racial, and temperamental differences define ways of seeing, so that what seems natural to one may appear mannered to another. True, artists of the current generation might lack the genius of the Old Masters, but their vision remained valid:

In art truth is what a person feels in the state of mind he happens to be in. Those who wish to or are able to can dream. Let those who wish to or are able to abandon themselves to their dreams. And dreams always come from the reality of nature. A savage will never see in his dreams a man dressed like a Parisian—etc.[126]

This statement of purposeful, subjective difference carried implications that informed a recent undertaking, which Gauguin outlined for Vincent: to decorate the dining room of the Buvette de la Plage, the Le Pouldu inn run by Marie Henry (see fig. 77). The much-studied results of the effort (in which de Haan and others participated) are by no means strictly

programmatic or easily interpreted, but at one level at least, the project can be seen as Gauguin's response—both playful and in deadly earnest—to the Yellow House and the ideology of the Studio of the South, as well as to current debates about style.[127]

The scheme included two portraits by Gauguin, one of himself and one of de Haan, that are rife with pointed allusions to the shared past with Vincent. In his *Self-Portrait* (fig. 75), the split field of the background summons up recent self-representations (see figs. 5, 9) employing the chromatic identities—saturated red and brilliant yellow—they had adopted. Gauguin's compositional arrangement suggests that his neck is accommodated by a cutaway in the yellow expanse; he fortified this subtle evocation of the executioner's block with a more legible symbol of martyrdom: a halo or nimbus, which plays upon Vincent's ambitions for a spiritualized modern portraiture. But once again Gauguin conflated sinner with saint, raising the specter of the biblical Fall by including a serpent and apples. Possibly, as has been proposed recently, his grasping of the reptile reiterates the Saul/Paul discussion in Arles (see ch. 4): after surviving a shipwreck, Saint Paul suffered a snakebite that caused locals to assume him a murderer until he flung the snake into the fire, thus proving himself to be under divine protection.[128]

Other references to Vincent appear in the portrait of de Haan (fig. 76), whose attributes—lighted lamp, books with legible titles—Gauguin borrowed from Vincent's imagery and even his library. One of the volumes seen here is Carlyle's *Sartor Resartus*, which helped shape Vincent's conception of the artist-hero. Gauguin paired it with *Paradise Lost*, the Milton classic that Carlyle's protagonist Teufelsdröckh references to support the contention that only through productive action can we realize our full potential. But *Paradise*

Lost, however great a masterpiece, treats what Carlyle identified as the antiquated Mythus of the Christian Religion; *Sartor Resartus* calls for a creator who will recast the old truths in a new mythic guise pertinent to the present.[129] In Gauguin's painting, Carlyle's text partially eclipses that of Milton, obscuring "Paradise" so that only the word "Lost" (*Perdu*) can be seen. This compositional ploy intimates the greater relevance of Carlyle's gospel and recalls Vincent's juxtaposition of the Bible with Zola's *Joie de vivre*.

These references have an ironic edge; in a seemingly similar spirit, de Haan showed a penchant that summer for humming the march from Bizet's *L'Arlésienne*, and Gauguin took to performing Schumann's *berceuse*. These tongue-in-cheek references to Gauguin's time with Vincent point to the genuine significance that the ideas formulated in Arles assumed for the artists gathered at Marie Henry's inn. They now included Sérusier, who had repented his previous apostasy and left Pont-Aven to join Gauguin in Le Pouldu on 30 September. Preoccupied with a dream of a

confraternity of like-minded painters, Sérusier embraced Gauguin's leadership and set out to practice and formalize the principles espoused by the older artist. He instantly transmitted to Paris the substance of a text he reported inscribing on the dining-room wall. "Our *Credo*," as Sérusier called it, proved to be nothing other than Wagner's profession of faith in an elect discipleship devoted to great art, which had featured so prominently in the previous December's conversations in the Yellow House; the very act of writing on the wall recalls the "sain d'esprit/saint-esprit" episode.[130]

They are like boxes rising by steps at regular distanced intervals, in blue clothes and black coifs despite the biting cold. The seaweed they are gathering to fertilize their land is ochre, with tawny highlights. The sand is *pink*, not yellow, probably because it is wet, and the sea is a dark color. I see this scene every day and it is like a gust of wind, a sudden awareness of the struggle for life, of sadness, and of our obedience to the harsh laws of nature. It is this awareness that I have tried to put on canvas, not haphazardly, but methodically, perhaps by exaggerating the rigidity of some of the women's poses and the darkness of some of the colors, etc. All this may be *mannered* to some extent, but is there anything in painting we can really call natural?　Gauguin to Vincent, [c. 8–10 December 1889]

72
Paul Gauguin
Sketches of Breton
costume and face in
letter to Vincent
[c. 8–10 December
1889] (Cooper 1983,
GAC 36)
Van Gogh Museum,
Amsterdam
(Vincent van Gogh
Foundation)
Cat. 103

73
Paul Gauguin
*Breton Landscape with
Willows*
Fall 1889 [W 357]
Oil on canvas
92 x 74.5 cm
Nasjonalgalleriet,
Oslo
Cat. 101

74
Paul Gauguin
*Seaweed Gatherers II
(Ramasseuses de varech
II)*
October/December
1889 [W 349]
Oil on canvas
87 x 123.1 cm
Museum Folkwang
Essen, Germany
Cat. 102

If the credo was Wagner's, the means came from Carlyle's thesis of the new gospel as the truth of the old reclothed. Gauguin applied this idea somewhat literally in the picture he described to Vincent as a Breton peasant girl spinning on the seashore accompanied by her dog and her cow (fig. 80). He failed to mention the presence of a sword-wielding angel in a cloud of yellow, which suggests that this is an image of Joan of Arc. According to legend, the martyred fifteenth-century liberator of France was a thirteen-year-old shepherdess when the archangel Michael appeared to her in a vision and announced her mission. Four hundred years later, the Maid of Orléans (where Gauguin spent eight years of his child-hood) was a potent patriotic symbol, the sub-ject of books, articles, the visual arts, and even a temporary museum erected at the periphery of the Universal Exposition. Gauguin's depic-tion, carried out in a modified fresco technique of painting on plaster, seems to take aim at the high naturalism of officially sanctioned art, exemplified by the mural devoted to Joan's vision just unveiled in the Panthéon, Paris (see fig. 78).[131] The features of Gauguin's res-olutely antinaturalistic Joan do not signify "France"; instead she is the quintessential "asiatic" Breton deplored by Theo. The figure's large feet (seen in profile) derive from the *devatas* or dieties that decorated the *pagode* (see fig. 84); the position of the right arm recalls another *devata* sculpture in the Khmer Museum (fig. 79), with a spindle here replac-ing the Southeast Asian deity's lotus, which in turn was incorporated throughout the overall decorative scheme of the painting as a unifying symbolic motif.[132]

In adopting such overtly Asian manner-isms, Gauguin did more than thumb his nose at Theo's criticisms. Emboldened by the dealer's rejection, he took an unabashedly experimental approach in painting that he had also adopted in recent ceramics and

75

76

75
Paul Gauguin
Self-Portrait
1889 [W 323]
Oil on wood
79.2 x 51.3 cm
National Gallery of
Art, Washington,
D.C., Chester Dale
Collection

76
Paul Gauguin
Meyer de Haan
1889 [W 317]
Oil on wood
80 x 52 cm
Private collection

77
Reconstruction of
the dining room at
the Buvette de la
Plage, Le Pouldu
(inn of Marie
Henry)
Courtesy of the
Association des amis
de la Maison Marie
Henry, Le Pouldu

77

small-scale gouaches, willfully viewing one primitive culture through the stylistic lens of another. While Theo apparently found this piggybacking ridiculously forced, Gauguin was earnestly attempting to become the "seeking, thinking artist" he felt he was meant to be. The overlay of Saint Joan on a Breton peasant evokes the theme of sacrifice in the service of revitalizing a weakened France; at another level the conflated primitivisms express Gauguin's ambition to combat the corrupt culture of the West by rejuvenating his vision abroad.[133]

Since August he had been trying to actualize fantasies stimulated by the Colonial Exhibition, pushing Theo to speak to contacts who might help him land a remunerative, undemanding job (such as the post of vice-resident) in Tonkin (northern Vietnam). By November prospects looked gloomy—the failure of earlier work to sell compounded by his dealer's negative response to the new—and as debts mounted, emigration began to seem his only reasonable option. Despite the personal experience that should have taught him better, Gauguin, ever the naïve optimist, unquestioningly absorbed French colonialist propaganda, echoing its regenerative ideology in letters to Bernard (written at the moment he began work on the inn decorations) and enumerating the psychic, professional, and

financial benefits he expected to reap in Tonkin before returning home triumphant.[134]

"Stone crumbles, the word endures," he intoned to Bernard—alerting us once again to Vincent's presence. Gauguin's retailoring of the expansionist paradigm to suit an artistic program depended on the Studio of the Tropics concept, just as his identity as a seeker was rooted in ideas and imagery that Vincent had shared with him. This complex absorption is intimated (if not openly acknowledged) in the final decorations Gauguin produced at the inn. *Bonjour, Monsieur Gauguin* (fig. 85) overtly references Courbet's Montpellier masterpiece (ch. 4, fig. 131), while more subtly invoking the discussions for which that canvas was a lightning rod. Gauguin here subverted some of the principal features of Courbet's prototype: no patron welcomes the artist, and the bleak autumnal landscape under a menacing sky seems likewise inhospitable. Dressed in brown coat and black beret, with walking staff in hand and accompanied by his dog, Gauguin appears in the guise of the Lacaze "Wanderer," Vincent's "man from afar who will go far," an identity he further elaborated with elements from Vincent's compendium of pilgrimage emblems.

The closed gate before which the artist-seeker stands recalls a similar image in Bunyan's *Pilgrim's Progress* (ch. 1, fig. 11). At the story's outset, the hero Christian, having forsaken the City of Destruction, is directed to the gate by Evangelist; he reaches it, after overcoming the Slough of Despond and the arguments of Mr. Worldly Wiseman, who personifies negative social conformity. To pass through it and continue on his journey, he must answer the gatekeeper, who asks: "Who was there? and whence he came? and what he would have?" In Bunyan's narrative the grave gatekeeper is Good-will. In Gauguin's painting, the role is played by an enigmatic, dark-clad

Breton woman, who regards the wanderer mutely and at a remove. A symbolic presence, she apparently derives, like the figure of Solitude in *Human Miseries*, from a classic image-text conflation from Vincent's youth that he had shared with Gauguin. In the 1870s an encounter depicted in a painting by George Boughton (ch. 1, fig. 21) had reminded Vincent of Bunyan's classic book, prompting him to imagine Boughton's characters quoting a poem by Christina Rossetti, misremembered as a conversation between a departing pilgrim and a woman in black. Adding another layer of association, Vincent identified this figure in black with the Pauline dictum "Sorrowful yet always rejoicing," a message central to an art of consolation. All of this—like a code that only two viewers could decipher—inheres in Gauguin's pairing of a pilgrim and a woman dressed in a dark cloak.[135]

Gauguin distilled the message differently in another decoration, one evidently conceived as a kind of symbolic shingle advertising the wanderer's mythic ambition (fig. 82). Before a backdrop of gigantic sunflowers stands a dark-skinned female nude. Her posture relates to that of the spinning peasant (see fig. 80), but a more immediate predecessor is a clay figurine (fig. 83) that Gauguin had fashioned in response to the hieratic Cambodian *devatas* with their stylized gestures: the right hand held vertically between the breasts, the left arm raised and curved over the head (see fig. 84). In this abstracted image, painted on the lower panel of one of the dining-room doors, right below *Bonjour, Monsieur Gauguin*, Gauguin recalled his and Vincent's initial exchange—*Sunflowers* for the *Négresses* (see ch. 2)—and conjoined their individual symbols for an art of the future.[136] The dominant reference to Southeast Asian art and, by extension, to the regenerative experience awaiting him in Tonkin, announced Gauguin's claim to leadership of the Studio of the Tropics. A shrine of art dedicated

78
Jules-Eugène
Lenepveu
(French; 1819–1898)
Joan of Arc's Vision
1889
Oil on canvas
460 x 220 cm
Panthéon, Paris

79
Engraving of
Cambodian *devata*
by Smeeton Tilly
from Count de
Croizier, *L'Art khmer*
(Paris, 1875), p. 72

80
Paul Gauguin
Breton Girl Spinning
(*Joan of Arc*)
November 1889
[W 329]
Oil (?) on plaster
116 x 58 cm
Private collection
Cat. 105

78

79

80

81
Paul Gauguin
*Female Nude with
Flower* (known
as *Lust*)
Late 1889/1890
[G 88]
Partly painted
and gilded wood
and metal
H. 70 cm

The J. F.
Willumsens
Museum,
Frederikssund,
Denmark
Cat. 130

82
Paul Gauguin
*Female Nude with
Sunflowers*
(known as
*Caribbean
Woman*)
November 1889
[W 330]
Oil on wood
64 x 54 cm
Private collection
Cat. 107

83
Paul Gauguin
Female Nude
Clay
Whereabouts
unknown

84
Detail of plaster cast
of Cambodian
devatas taken from
Angkor Wat, from
Le Musée indo-chinois
(Paris, 1916), pl. 4

81

82

83

84

85
Paul Gauguin
*Bonjour, Monsieur
Gauguin*
November 1889
[W 321]
Oil on canvas laid
down on wood
75 x 55 cm

The Armand
Hammer
Collection, UCLA
Hammer Museum,
Los Angeles
Cat. 106

86
Vincent van Gogh
*Garden of the
Hospital (Saint-
Paul-de-Mausole,
Saint-Rémy)*
c. 1 November 1889
[F 660, JH 1849]

Oil on canvas
73.5 x 92 cm
Museum Folkwang
Essen, Germany
Cat. 124

Leaving the South

to a Wagnerian credo interpreted with reference to Carlyle, the inn of Marie Henry supplanted the Yellow House, just as the Studio of the Tropics was to transplant the Studio of the South.

Gauguin's *Christ in the Garden of Olives* had the immediate effect of fracturing the sense of solidarity that Vincent had been nurturing. Now taking distance from Gauguin, Vincent recalled his own (and Theo's) equation of abstract style with unhealthy abstract ideas. Expressing regret at having been led astray by a deceptive credo and its false creative promises, Vincent recanted. Specifically he renounced *La Berceuse*—so loaded with Gauguin associations—and resolved to attack things more straightforwardly in future.[137]

Vincent had anticipated this direction in a canvas that he finished just before learning of his friends' Gethsemane scenes. It too depicts a garden, that of the asylum (fig. 86), and was invested with comparable meaning: the obvious emblematic self-reference surfacing in Vincent's foregrounding of a damaged tree trunk, which he analogized to a somber giant brought low. He went on explicitly to propose the picture as evidence for the possibility of expressing "anguish without making direct reference to the actual Gethsemane." To

85

The nearest tree has an enormous trunk that has been struck by lightning and sawn off. However, a branch still juts high up into the air and sends down a rain of dark green needles. This somber giant—with its hurt pride—contrasts, if you were to lend it human characteristics, with the pale smile of a last rose on the fading bush in front of it. Under the big trees, empty stone benches, mournful little box trees; the sky is reflected—yellow—in a puddle after the rain. A ray of sun turns the dark ochre into orange with its last reflection.   Vincent to Bernard, [c. 20 November 1889]

make his case, Vincent returned to his old touchstone Millet, who had intimated the religious in discreet terms, respectful of modern sensibility. Anticipating that Delacroix's overtly biblical subjects might be introduced as a rejoinder, Vincent spoke of the vast preparatory study necessary before one could even think of taking on the master.[138]

In angry response to Gauguin and Bernard, Vincent pursued his own advice, launching a campaign of canvases featuring olive groves in which he moved away from the urgent, cursive rhythms so recently prominent and adopted a more controlled and relatively impersonal stroke. Striving for coarse earthiness as an antidote to the artifice he saw in Gauguin's and Bernard's works, Vincent produced five pictures representing the olive grove in front of the asylum in different light conditions and at different times of day. They constitute a series that invites comparison with Monet's *Stacks of Wheat*, examples of which had just been shown at Georges Petit's. Vincent, probably aware of them through reviews, would invoke the older Impressionist in discussing the infinite possibilities of his chosen motif. And like Monet, Vincent endowed the varied natural effects with considerable expressive resonance: the version including a sun-filled morning sky bursts with an exuberant sense of promise and hope (fig. 87), while the sunset version conveys just as suggestively a poignant, reflective mood (fig. 90).[139]

87

88

89

I have been working in the olive groves, because [Gauguin and Bernard] maddened me with
their *Christs in the Garden*, which lack all trace of observation. Naturally I have no intention what-
soever of doing anything from the Bible—and I have written to Bernard and Gauguin too
that I considered that our duty is thinking, not dreaming.   Vincent to Theo, [c. 21 November 1889]

90

91

These canvases served as studies for the four *tableaux* depicting women picking olives that followed (see fig. 89). In three of these, Vincent included the ladders that the women used to reach the trees' higher branches, a realistic detail that, together with the artist's deployment of the figures, also brings to mind images of Christ's Passion by, among others, Rubens and Rembrandt (see fig. 88). In January Vincent pointedly sent Gauguin a drawing after the version he painted for his mother and sister.

Writing to his mother and Wil on around 20 December, Vincent intimated the theme's connection with his own personal

Gethsemane by observing that it was the anniversary of his first attack. While claiming to feel better, he admitted that he lived in fear of possible recurrence. The theme of disruption and repair informs two canvases (a study and more finished version) that he had executed just days earlier, featuring road menders at work on Saint-Rémy's tree-lined principal boulevard (fig. 91). The subject of men digging up a street revisits the most ambitious of Vincent's multifigural essays from The Hague, but more recent memory provided the composition and its details.[140] The oblique perspective, established by rows of plane trees, echoes the pair of *Falling Leaves* (*Les Alyscamps*) pictures (ch. 4, figs. 27–28) that

Vincent painted at Gauguin's side and under his influence. The row of large rectangular stone blocks recalls the tombs that line Arles's venerable Allée, a visual association that subtly shifts our reading of the workmen's activity from road mending to grave digging in an oscillating suggestion of death and renewal.

A day or two after writing to Wil, Vincent suffered another attack while painting. Its effects did not last long, and by early January he had recovered sufficiently to contemplate resuming work. But he had come to believe that he must return to the North. He asked Theo about institutions in Holland where one could be cared for and allowed to work. Theo mentioned Gheel, in Belgium, without noting its painful associations. Vincent, however, had another option in mind: he wrote to Gauguin inquiring how long he and de Haan planned to remain in Brittany, whether they wanted him to send the furniture he had stored in Arles, and if they would welcome him as well.[141]

Gauguin replied immediately to this letter, which apparently included Vincent's drawing after *Women Picking Olives*. He praised the sketch and congratulated his friend on having his work included in the Les Vingt exhibition, which had just opened (he had participated in the previous year's show).[142] But Gauguin sidestepped Vincent's question about coming to Brittany, instead posing one of his own, wrapped in borrowed metaphors: when would they reap the rewards of hard work and ideas they had sowed? In so saying he made the points that life in Le Pouldu was difficult and that he was concentrating on plans for Tonkin. Having thus put Vincent off, by month's end Gauguin changed his tune. De Haan was suddenly no longer in a position to support him in Le Pouldu, and so Gauguin wrote to say that life together with Vincent was possible, if only under the right conditions. He suggested Antwerp, where the three of them (he, Vincent, and de Haan) might "found a studio in my name"; in time Theo might set up a branch gallery. This blatantly self-interested counter proposal rested on Gauguin's conviction that the only way to succeed in France was by first leaving and then enacting a heroic return, in the colonialist fashion. Antwerp was of course a fallback destination; Vincent must realize that Tonkin was the focus of his energies.[143]

Gauguin's good opinion meant a great deal to Vincent, who seized on his passing approval of *Women Picking Olives* as a testimony to its worth. Owing to another breakdown on 21 January, Vincent was initially unresponsive to Theo's reports of the positive comments attracted by his work at Les Vingt. When he

resumed correspondence at the end of the month, Vincent seemed more preoccupied with the letter he had just received from Gauguin regarding Antwerp than with his own success.[144] Writing to his old friend John Russell, he passed along news of Gauguin's current situation, expressed his great admiration and sense of indebtedness, and explained that the cause for their parting company had been his illness.

In passing, Vincent mentioned a recent article on his work and included a copy of it, Aurier's "Les Isolés: Vincent van Gogh," which appeared in leading French and Belgian periodicals in January. The artist's seeming nonchalance masked the fact that its publication marked a turning point in his critical reputation, identifying him as a bright new star in the vanguard firmament. As his title suggests, Aurier presented Vincent as an isolated genius, his art and life seamlessly connected, both a great painter and a fanatical believer. Aurier's Vincent was a neo-romantic, tormented creator who stood at the brink of the pathological, envisioning a personal realism that, feeding on a naturalist impetus and informed by idealist tendencies, conveyed a sincerity at once childlike and neurotic. The critic wrote of the artist's "nightmarish" cypresses, his "mountains that arch their backs like mammoths," and his obsessive passion for the solar disk and "that other sun, that vegetable-star, the sumptuous sunflower." Vincent's was an art of excess—strong and agitated, powerfully masculine and hysterically feminine; its maker, like the sower he resembled, driven by an idée fixe about the "necessary advent of a man, a messiah, sower of truth," who would regenerate art. To this end, Aurier maintained, Vincent imagined "displacing the center of civilization [and creating] an art of the tropical regions."[145]

Vincent reacted with ambivalence. On the one hand, Aurier had held up a mirror in which

he did not—or did not wish to—see himself. "No need to tell you," he wrote Theo, "that I hope to keep thinking that I don't paint like that." He worried that the critic in effect advised him to depart further from reality, just as he had resolved to move in the opposite direction. On the other hand, the attention clearly gratified him, for he not only mentioned the article to friends, but also considered sending copies to old naysayers such as Reid and Tersteeg. But he fretted, not simply out of modesty, that the praise would go to his head like alcohol and disturb his calm, stirring up old ambitions and leaving him, in the aftermath of the induced grandiosity, feeling sad.[146]

He also felt that Aurier had given him exaggerated credit for ideas that should be attributed to others, notably to Gauguin, who had after all been the first to actually paint in the tropics. Writing to thank Aurier, Vincent tried to set the record straight. He acknowledged his debt to Monticelli and especially to Gauguin, that "stranger" whom he identified as resembling Rembrandt's portrait of a man in the Lacaze gallery (ch. 4, fig. 136). With regard to color and the question of "the future of 'tropical painting,'" Vincent suggested that Aurier should have accorded primacy to Monticelli and Gauguin. He, Vincent, played only a secondary role.[147]

Anxious that Gauguin would read the article and take offense, Vincent hastened to send him a copy of his letter to Aurier. Gauguin's mention of Antwerp and Aurier's of a Studio of the Tropics had conspired to resurrect old dreams and regrets. Once again Vincent voiced disappointment that Gauguin had not stayed in Arles a little longer and indulged in the fantasy that "together we should have worked better than I have all by myself this year. And now we should have a little house of our own to live and work in, and could even put others up." They could even work together again in the South. In this spirit of

92
Paul Gauguin
Madame Ginoux
(study for *Night Café*)
c. 4 November 1888
White and colored
chalks and charcoal
on wove paper
56.1 x 49.2 cm
Fine Arts Museums
of San Francisco,
memorial gift from
Dr. T. Edward and
Tullah Hanley,
Bradford,
Pennsylvania
Cat. 38

93
Vincent van Gogh
*The Arlésienne (after
Paul Gauguin)*
February 1890
[F 540, JH 1892]
Oil on canvas
60 x 50 cm
Galleria Nazionale
d'Arte Moderna e
Contemporanea,
Rome
Cat. 132

94
Vincent van Gogh
*The Arlésienne (after
Paul Gauguin)*
February 1890
[F 543, JH 1895]
Oil on canvas
60 x 54 cm
Private collection
Cat. 133

95
Paul Gauguin
*Portrait of a Woman with
Still Life by Paul Cézanne*
1890 [W 387]
Oil on canvas
65.3 x 54.9 cm
The Art Institute of
Chicago, Joseph
Winterbotham
Collection, 1925.753
Cat. 129

93

92

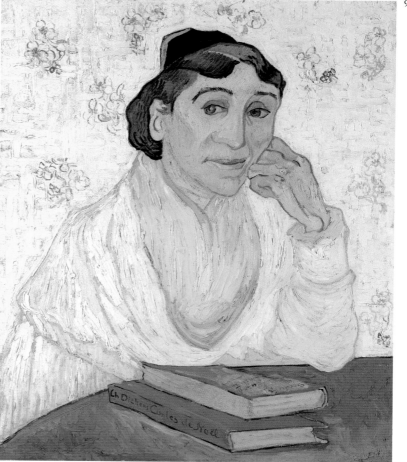

94

resigned retrospection, coupled with an anticipatory longing to remake himself, Vincent carried out a series of pictures based on the drawing of Madame Ginoux that Gauguin had left behind (fig. 92), one of which he now offered to his friend. The fact that the sitter remained sickly after an illness that had begun in December 1888 sharpened the nostalgic reference.[148]

The five new *Arlésiennes*—equaling the number of *Berceuses*—pay homage to the dynamic of their shared past, ritualized in Vincent's execution of canvas after canvas in which he aimed to be "respectfully faithful" to Gauguin's prototype while allowing himself interpretive liberties. He imagined it as a collaborative exercise. Subtle differences in expression and details aside, three of the four extant versions are essentially alike (see fig. 93), featuring Madame Ginoux dressed in black against a pink, striated background, seated at a green table that supports two books with clearly legible titles: *Uncle Tom's Cabin* by Harriet Beecher Stowe and Charles Dickens's *Christmas Stories*. The version painted specifically for Gauguin (fig. 94) is the exception: the dress is pink, the bodice "white that merges into green," and the background pink, floral-patterned wallpaper. This more feminine conception references the symbolism of the floral wallpaper in Gauguin's *Self-Portrait (Les Misérables)* (ch. 3, fig. 74), conveying the sense of his friend's greater refinement that Vincent had also expressed in the appointments for the Yellow House's guest bedroom and in the painting *Gauguin's Chair* (ch. 4, fig. 71). Vincent intended *The Arlésienne* as a symbolic summation of what he believed he and Gauguin had worked for together: a distilled humanist image, in the spirit of Millet, Delacroix, and authors such as those referenced here, expressive of the enlightened, modern consciousness he now referred to as grief nearly smiling.[149] Unchanged over the years, this core belief was

the doctrine of Saint Paul, "sorrowful yet always rejoicing."

On 22 February, while visiting Arles to deliver a copy (now lost) of *The Arlésienne* to Madame Ginoux, Vincent suffered a breakdown that disabled him for two months and ultimately proved decisive. Only two days earlier, he had admitted to his mother that he had been cheered by Aurier's article and by the news that Theo had sold one of the pictures shown in Brussels for four hundred francs. He saw the attack as punishment for success and the cost of the exhilaration of the *Arlésienne* series. In March the pictures that Theo had submitted to the Indépendants exhibition were on view and attracting favorable comments from fellow painters—Monet and Gauguin (who had been in Paris since early February) both proclaimed them the best in show—but Vincent remained unmoved. By 2 May he had recovered enough to admit once and for all that the journey he persistently regarded as a sea voyage was truly coming to an end. He agreed to Theo's proposal that he come north, where he hoped to regain his balance.[150]

The small-scale picture that Vincent produced the next day ostensibly embodies such sentiments (fig. 97). Working from a reproduction of Rembrandt's etching *The Raising of Lazarus* (fig. 96), Vincent focused on the group in the middle ground, editing out the man with raised arms and the looming foreground figure, suggestively portraying himself as the risen Lazarus, and imagining the two Marys as Mesdames Ginoux and Roulin. The large rising sun presiding over the scene has been read as an expression of Vincent's desire to naturalize the biblical, in that the solar disk replaces the divine reviving hand.[151] But in Vincent's close-up, the painter too is a stand-in for Christ, raising his hand, like Rembrandt's figure, before the canvas on which he creates life. Vincent had always seen painting as the means

to revive himself and to resurrect those that came before him. Old identifications died hard.

The contemplated large version of *The Raising of Lazaraus* came to nothing. But Vincent did not want to leave the South before making what he would describe to Gauguin as a "last attempt" (fig. 98). By this he meant a last effort to realize the kind of art they had discussed: painting *de tête*, abstractly, as Gauguin advocated. Why would Vincent venture once again into these dangerous waters? A primary motivation seems to have been Gauguin's expressed interest in making an exchange for the *Path through the Ravine* (fig. 68), a gesture that proved to Vincent that "more and more our taste is becoming the same." Vincent's new picture is an invention, incorporating the quintessentially southern cypress from his June pictures together with the cottage and carriage, motifs from recent drawings that Vincent had identified as memories of the North. The prominence of the night sky, with shining star and crescent moon, recalls *The Starry Night* (fig. 45), as does the style of this likewise exalted vision of reality. In a

95

sketch of the composition for Gauguin (fig. 99), Vincent emphasized the similarity of the two "late wayfarers" marching forward with their walking staffs in synchronized movement. One last time Vincent joined Gauguin imaginatively in a picture that memorializes their southern pilgrimage.[152]

In the final stage of his journey, Vincent left Saint-Rémy for Paris. Arriving there on Sunday, 17 May, he met his sister-in-law and three-and-a-half-month-old nephew and namesake for the first time. During his three days in the capital, he saw neither Gauguin nor any of his recent work because, as he later explained, the city so upset him. A new hope also motivated his precipitous flight from Paris. Late in March Theo had written of someone who might prove helpful, a doctor in nearby Auvers by the name of Gachet, who by coincidence bore a physical resemblance to Vincent. His longings still intact, Vincent had immediately begun hoping for a "lasting friendship," adopting Gachet as "our future friend."[153]

Vincent arrived in Auvers on 20 May. Initially he found Gachet eccentric, evidently suffering more than Vincent himself from a nervous disorder and thus not to be counted upon. But by early June, he reported that he and the doctor had become great friends, united by more than the illness he believed they shared. Gachet, himself an amateur artist and collector, admired both the *Pietà* and the version of the recent *Arlésienne* that Vincent had brought with him. Moreover, Vincent was fascinated to learn that Gachet had not only known Bruyas, but he also shared Vincent's ideas about Montpellier's martyr-patron. Echoing past idealizations, Vincent talked of the doctor as a "perfect friend," regarded him as "another brother," and referred to him as "father Gachet."[154] Clearly Gachet's mental and physical characteristics qualified him as the latest inductee to Vincent's family of redheads. In early June Vincent painted this kindred soul (fig. 100) with a "grief-hardened" expression that relates him to the Montpellier portraits of Bruyas (see ch. 4, figs. 132, 135), deploying the traditional pose of Melancholy

seen in Delacroix's *Tasso in the Madhouse* (ch. 4, fig. 134). If there is an element of self-portraiture here, Vincent also referred to his erstwhile perfect friend Gauguin, insofar as *Doctor Gachet* directly critiques Gauguin's representation of himself, Bruyas-like, as Christ (fig. 51).

Writing to Gauguin in June, Vincent explained that he had endowed his sitter with

the heartbroken expression of our time. *If you like*, something like what you said of your "Christ in the Garden of Olives," not meant to be understood, but anyhow I follow you there, and my brother grasped that nuance at once.[155]

96

97

96
Rembrandt van Rijn
*The Raising of
Lazarus*
1632
Etching
36.5 x 25.7 cm
Van Gogh Museum,
Amsterdam
(Vincent van Gogh
Foundation)

97
Vincent van Gogh
*The Raising of
Lazarus 3 (after
Rembrandt)*
3 May 1890
[F 677, JH 1972]
Oil on thick paper,
mounted on canvas
50 x 65 cm
Van Gogh Museum,
Amsterdam
(Vincent van Gogh
Foundation)
Cat. 134

98
Vincent van Gogh
*A Cypress against a
Starry Sky*
c. 12–15 May 1890
[F 683, JH 1982]
Oil on canvas
92 x 73 cm
Kröller-Müller
Museum, Otterlo,
The Netherlands
Cat. 135

99
Vincent van Gogh
Sketch of *A Cypress
against a Starry Sky*
in letter to Gauguin
[c. 17 June 1890]
(letter 893/643; JH
1983)
Van Gogh Museum,
Amsterdam
(Vincent van Gogh
Foundation)
Cat. 136

Studio of the South

100
Vincent van Gogh
Doctor Gachet
3 June 1890
[JH 2007, F 753]
Oil on canvas
66 x 57 cm
Private collection

Vincent made the above statement—in which a characteristic hint of correction inflects his evident relish of the ongoing dialogue—in response to Gauguin's complimentary assessment of his beautiful, "very curious" *Arlésienne* (fig. 94). Claiming to prefer it to his own drawing, Gauguin commended its immediacy, controlled passion, and the "*equilibrium*" that belied Vincent's state of health. But a patently different equilibrium informs the canvas that can be seen as Gauguin's pictorial response to Vincent's homage (fig. 95). It too is an overt tribute—but to Cézanne. The composition, difficult to place within the artist's 1890 production, features an unidentified female sitter whose pose and frozen demeanor defer to Cézanne's portraits of his wife, seated before a faithfully rendered, slightly enlarged still life by the Aix master that was the prize of Gauguin's collection (ch. 1, fig. 57).[156] As in Arles, Gauguin here made an apparent gesture toward Vincent—painting a woman with dark features and a predominantly pink-and-white costume—while proclaiming profoundly different allegiances. The inclusion of the still life suggestively posits pure pictorial representation in opposition to Vincent's recurrent privileging of literary texts.

The retrospective aura that characterizes Vincent's *Arlésiennes* and Gauguin's *Portrait of a Woman* was, however, fundamentally at odds with the latter's current outlook. By the late spring of 1890, Gauguin was wholly engrossed with the idea of founding the Studio of the Tropics, concocting fundraising strategies, soliciting Theo's promise of support, and persuading Bernard and de Haan to join him. Nothing had come of his efforts vis-à-vis Tonkin, so Gauguin had canvased various opinions and settled on the island of Madagascar, a French territory off the southeast coast of the African continent. Acting as if he had forgotten the idea was Vincent's, Gauguin asked his friend if he recalled their conversations in Arles on the question of founding such a studio. He was now poised,

he announced to Vincent, to carry out the plan—"my dream"—in what promised to be an earthly paradise:

Those who want to go there later will find all that they need to work for little cost. And possibly the Studio of the Tropics will produce the Saint John the Baptist of the art of the future, rebaptized there by a more natural, more primitive, and above all less corrupt life.[157]

In response to this extraordinary statement of appropriation, Vincent merely assented that the future of painting lay in the tropics rather than in Europe, while venturing (without any direct knowledge) that Tonkin had been a more reasonable and desirable destination than Madagascar. But his reservations lay deeper. Though he claimed to be capable of following Gauguin to Madagascar—"for you must go there in twos or threes"—he believed that neither Gauguin nor himself, nor Theo for that matter, was the man to enact that future. He continued to look to the past, attempting to engage Gauguin in the dialogues intimated by the Gachet portrait, *The Arlésienne*, and his last attempt at abstraction; the only future project he discussed was a retrospective print series of "Souvenirs of Provence," along the lines of the Volpini suite, to which he hoped his friend would contribute. Vincent's remaining hopes were connected with Gauguin. He had, he avowed, thought of him daily since leaving the South, and he again broached the question of joining him in Brittany that summer. Imagining their renewed collaboration, Vincent could not resist adding: "We will try to do something purposeful and serious, such as our work would probably have become if we had been able to carry on down there [in the South]."[158]

Gauguin expressed polite pleasure at the prospect of having Vincent with them, but in the same breath, he put him off: Le Pouldu was too remote for someone in Vincent's condition; moreover by September Gauguin him-

self planned to be gone. He was a "condemned man," a "pariah," who must make his way *alone* to the new paradise: "The savage will return to the savage state."[159] This glib accumulation of outsider identities, including reference now to the peregrinations that had earned fame for his maternal grandmother, Flora Tristan, suggests Gauguin's growing ease in the persona that he had strategically tailored since leaving Arles, based on the pattern outlined there. Future promise forms the subtext of a still life featuring one of his own sculptures (which conflates a Martinique woman with the gestures of the Cambodian *devatas*) set on a table beside a vase of roses and against the wall of Marie Henry's inn, with its stylized yellow flowers (fig. 101). Much as Vincent had projected the North on the South, Gauguin was shaping his expectations so extensively that his actual destination was something of a moot point. Hence the effortless shift from Tonkin to Madagascar. Similarly in his art, one primitivizing filter might serve as well as another: Lucas Cranach's representation of the classical goddess Diana (fig. 103) supplanted the Cambodian *devatas* in a tropical fantasy that Gauguin carved out of a block of wood (fig. 102). The recurrence here of the yellow flower with the dark-skinned nude (as in *Female Nude with Sunflowers*; fig. 82) suggests that the sunflower/*négresse* conflation had become symbolic of the journey on which Vincent had not been booked passage. In this context the flower is hardly the symbol of gratitude that Vincent had recently described to his sister and to Aurier. It might be expecting too much to read Gauguin's inclusion of the fox—claimed symbol of perversity—at the base of the freestanding wood sculpture (fig. 81), which combines the same elements to similar ends, as an acknowledgment of his own perfidy. The full-length female figure holds a flower between the fingers of her right hand. A descendant of the sculpted and painted sisterhood created for the inn through which Gauguin gendered his dreams of conquest (figs. 80–83), the freestanding nude

101
Paul Gauguin
Roses and Statuette
Spring/summer 1890
[W 407]
Oil on canvas
73.2 x 54.5 cm
Musée des Beaux-
Arts de Reims,
France
Cat. 128

102
Paul Gauguin
*Reclining Woman
with a Fan in a
Tropical Landscape*
Late 1889/early 1890
[G 74]
Painted oak
35 x 45 cm
Ny Carlsberg
Glyptotek,
Copenhagen
Cat. 108

103
Lucas Cranach
(German; 1472–1553)
Diana Reclining
c. 1537
Oil on panel
48.5 x 74.2 cm
Musée des Beaux-
Arts et
d'Archaeologie,
Besançon

101

103 FONTIS NYMPHA SACRI SOMNVM / NE RVMPE QVIESCO ·

104
Vincent van Gogh
In the Forest (*Sous-
bois*)
c. 24 June 1890
[F 773, JH 2041]
Oil on canvas
50 x 100 cm
Cincinnati Art
Museum, bequest of
Mary E. Johnston,
1967
Cat. 137

105
Vincent van Gogh
Sketch of *In the Forest*
in letter to Theo
[2 July 1890]
(letter 900/646;
JH 2042)
Van Gogh Museum,
Amsterdam
(Vincent van Gogh
Foundation)

106
Vincent van Gogh
Sketch of sailboat
June/July 1890
Graphite on paper
In Sketchbook No. 7,
p. 106
Van Gogh Museum,
Amsterdam
(Vincent van Gogh
Foundation)

takes her place in a symbolic lineage extending from Puvis's painting (ch. 2, fig. 70),
through Gauguin's *Cleopatra* pot (ch. 2, fig. 69),
to Vincent's *Mousmé* (ch. 3, fig. 48). Conceived with Vincent's input, exotically refashioned by Gauguin and erected on a base of
perversity, the carving is a figure of hope.

Vincent was no longer able to craft such a
device for himself. Aurier's article had caused
him to recognize, with some consternation,
that his art was "after all almost a cry of
anguish"; wishing to atone for this, he felt a
desire for self-renewal. His late June exploration of a new panoramic format—double
square, measuring 20 by 40 inches (50 by 100
centimeters)—marked a creative departure.[160]

But an early essay on this expansive scale (fig.
104) remains imbued with the anguish he
wanted to transcend. Choosing a forest as his
setting, Vincent depicted poplars with lilac
trunks, planted in receding rows; at the composition's center, he placed a man and a
woman, the "lovers" that were his personal
symbol of companionship. The ingredients
recall earlier garden pictures, including some
examples of the Poet's Garden, as well as the
horizontal *Falling Leaves* canvases, especially
the one featuring lovers framed by blue tree
trunks (ch. 4, fig. 27). But here Vincent subverted the earlier iconography. There is no
path, and the tree trunks do not create a clear
sense of directional movement, but rather
establish a disorienting maze of multiple per-

spectives, all leading to a dark horizon. These
competing vistas effectively cancel each other
out, engendering the paralysis that seems
to grip the featureless, motionless couple. The
figures appear to be trapped between the trees
that frame them, an effect that Vincent emphasized in the sketch he sent to Theo (fig. 105),
so inert that the vegetation seems to consume
them. The image offers no hint of physical
or imaginative escape.

Vincent read the letter in which Gauguin
discouraged him from thinking of a reunion
in Brittany with a comparable sense of fore-
closure. He told Theo that Gauguin only
thought of Madagascar because he was too
desperate and discouraged to think of any-

104

105

106

where else. And Vincent probably had to face the painful fact that Gauguin had dissembled with his claim to be embarking on his adventure alone. Their mutual acquaintances were well aware that Gauguin had plans to travel with at least one companion, Bernard; Theo certainly knew this by Sunday, 6 July, when Vincent spent the day with him and Jo in Paris, apparently seeing a few friends as well.[161] New causes for anxiety had already arisen by this time. Theo confided that he was having trouble with his employers and was thinking of leaving and setting up on his own. More keenly than ever, Vincent felt that he was a burden on his brother, who now had the added responsibilities of a wife and child. Exacerbating this was Vincent's anxiety to have his future financial relationship with Theo clarified anew, and frustration at his brother's seeming reluctance to do so.[162]

The brief visit to Paris had been more stimulus than Vincent could handle. Back in Auvers his preoccupation with Theo's problems—a storm threatening all of them—was compounded by the sense that his very being was threatened at its roots. He experienced a kind of numbness as a result. While thoughts of Theo's new life prompted familiar regrets about his choice to produce pictures rather than children, Vincent now claimed, "The longing has left me, even though the mental

suffering remains." He painted a number of large canvases featuring vast stretches of wheat under troubled skies that consciously express his sadness and extreme loneliness. A more intimate statement appears in a sketchbook: a single, tense figure sits at the helm of a sailboat on a rolling swell (fig. 106). Given Vincent's history of figuring life as a sea voyage and his persistent longing to recruit a partner, this image of solitary navigation suggests that acceptance came with the cessation of yearning. In mid-July Vincent spoke of being almost too calm— a mood that fostered his depiction of wheatfields as boundless as the sea.[163]

Theo's continuing troubles seemed testimony to the failure to create a protective association of like-minded painters and dealers. On 24 July Vincent wrote his brother to say that the time for such action had passed; personal initiative was of no avail, and he felt reluctant to start over again. Three days later, he shot himself. On Tuesday, 29 July 1890, with Theo at his side, he died of his injuries. The funeral took place the following day, with Bernard among the mourners in attendance. Gauguin, upon learning of Vincent's death, confessed to Bernard that he was not griefstricken, for he had anticipated the suicide and believed Vincent to be better off out of his misery; at least he had had the consolation of Theo's steadfastness and the understanding of a select group of colleagues.[164]

Thirteen years later, in 1903, Gauguin would claim that the last letter he received from Vincent contained his friend's renunciation of the hope to come to Brittany. This seems plausible, especially if Vincent wrote it upon the heels of his upsetting trip to Paris in early July. But Gauguin also claimed—rather less plausibly—that Vincent had announced his intention to commit suicide. Supposedly quoting Vincent, Gauguin wrote in language that sounds ventriloquized:

Dear master (the only time that he spoke that word), after having known you and having caused you distress, it is better to die in a good state of mind than in a degraded one.[165]

Gauguin had complex motivations for retrospectively putting these words in Vincent's mouth. They involved continuing rivalry, to be sure, but also changes in his own fortunes that had fostered empathy with Vincent's isolation and loss of hope.

Crafting the Tahitian Mission

Gauguin outlived Vincent by almost thirteen years, a period during which he was open to many new influences and made great changes in both his life and in his art. The complexity of Gauguin's self-styled mythic quest and the work he produced in Polynesia cannot be contained within a single narrative—his own account least of all.[1] The pains that Gauguin took to write Vincent out of his history effectively call attention to his central presence in it. For Gauguin, Vincent in death became more of a force to be reckoned with than in life, as the period 1890–1903 witnessed the construction of an enduring, heroic image of genius around the Dutch artist, a narrative in which Gauguin, like it or not, was implicated. Certainly Vincent turned out to pose a threat to his reputation different than he had anticipated. And Gauguin's desire to disassociate himself from Vincent can be situated in the historic dynamic whereby "Van Gogh" became a pawn in the ambitious factionalism that pervaded the Paris art scene of the 1890s.[2] But it also points toward Gauguin's own ambition, his lingering sense of indebtedness, and his anxious awareness that the narrative of modern art was still in manuscript form, the final edits yet to be typeset. The construction of the mythic "Van Gogh" relied heavily on the artist's letters, filled with the ideas and passionately held beliefs that had compelled Gauguin. As he literally set out on a journey to fulfill the heroic identity imagined together with Vincent, Gauguin would encounter constant reminders that what he actively continued to seek was being posthumously accorded his friend.

In the months following Vincent's death, Gauguin turned full attention to planning the Studio of the Tropics. In July he had dismissed Bernard's proposal of the South Pacific island of Tahiti as a destination, instead arguing for Madagascar as a nearer, more promising site, offering a richer mix of peoples and religions in addition to women as pliant as those found in Loti's Tahiti. By September, however, Gauguin had changed his mind. Madagascar, as he informed Odilon Redon, was *too* close to civilization, and he had set his sights on Tahiti, where he would nurture the primitive and savage aspects of his art and shift his thoughts from death to eternal life. Conceding his egotism, he proclaimed Wagner's credo as his own: ultimate glory awaited the "disciples of a great art."[3]

Others substantiated Gauguin's admission of vanity. In the weeks following Vincent's funeral, Bernard reported that he was strolling the beaches of Le Pouldu with his disciples like a "self-styled Jesus Christ." Gauguin took issue with the literal truth of this charge— de Haan and Charles Filiger were working elsewhere in Le Pouldu—and proposed a counter-identity: he roamed the beach all right, but as a savage, with long hair à la Buffalo Bill, whittling and shooting arrows.[4] But Bernard had begun to suspect that Gauguin's increased propensity for dress-up involved the ideas of others.

The concept of the Studio of the Tropics seemed to be contested intellectual property at the moment. As Gauguin's plans took shape, they came full circle, fulfilling the idea Vincent imagined shortly after meeting him: that a modern painter would do well to "do something like what one finds in Pierre Loti's book *Le Mariage de Loti*, in which the nature of Otaheite [Tahiti] is described." Yet Gauguin became insistently proprietary, and his force of personality easily won the likes of de Haan, who in a letter of condolence to Theo actually expressed his regret at missing the opportunity

to work with Vincent "on Gauguin's project in a far and foreign land." Sérusier and the Nabis accorded credit to Bernard, along with Gauguin, for conceiving "a colony of aesthetes," where, working in solitude "like the ancient Nabis," they could produce an art that would enlighten the world. And Gauguin more crassly asserted his sole primacy by referring to the project as "La société P. Go et Cº" in letters to Bernard, bidding him to devote all his energy to the scheme's successful realization. He variously characterized the project's motivations; in one letter to Schuffenecker, he described himself as a martyr fleeing a corrupt Europe in order to practice freely his "faith in art"; the next week he spoke as a businessman, anticipating that he would create a demand through his absence and the unavailability of his pictures.[5] That is, he fluently alternated between the idealist language of Vincent (and Wagner) and the more hard-nosed parlance that he had brought to the concept from the moment Vincent presented it to him.

Possibly spurred in part by Aurier's article attributing the Studio of the Tropics to Vincent, Gauguin launched a campaign in late 1890 to shape his profile and gather support for his venture. He was largely successful, to the extent that some of Vincent's partisans felt it necessary, following Gauguin's much-touted departure for the South Pacific in April 1891, to reassert the Dutch painter's authorship of the idea. Bernard was one such voice, defending the independence of his friend's genius in a brief appreciation published in *La Plume*. He not only highlighted Vincent's dream of founding artists' colonies in the Midi and elsewhere, but contended that, though Vincent had studied the paintings of Monticelli, Gauguin, and others, he took after none of them—and was more "personal" than any of them.[6]

Bernard had clearly resigned his membership in "La société P. Go et Cº." He only thinly

2
Paul Gauguin
Loss of Virginity
[W 412]
November
1890/April 1891

Oil on canvas
90 x 130 cm
The Chrysler
Museum of Art,
Norfolk, Virginia,
gift of Walter P.
Chrysler, Jr.
Cat. 131

3
Hans Holbein the
Younger (German;
c. 1497–1543)
*The Dead Christ
in the Tomb*
1521

Tempera on lime-
wood panel
30.5 x 200 cm
Kunstmuseum Basel

disguised his reasons for doing so in a more developed profile of Vincent that he prepared for another periodical at around the same time, in which he contrasted Vincent's selfless efforts on behalf of Gauguin and others with a vanguard "we" consisting of dreadful egoists who made excess the aim of art. Gauguin was the target here, for various reasons. His conduct in the fall of 1890 had appalled Bernard. In September Theo, having tried in vain to interest Durand-Ruel in showing Vincent's paintings, had decided to mount a private exhibition in his new apartment at 8, Cité Pigalle. Bernard was instrumental in preparing the space and installing the works. But at the beginning of October, Theo fell ill, exhibiting signs of dementia that were in fact manifestations of tertiary syphilis. After a month-long hospitalization in Paris, Theo was taken back to the Netherlands, where he died in January 1891. Gauguin responded to this sad event by deploring his own bad luck, and even pondering if something might be gained from this reversal. Moreover, he attempted to dissuade Bernard from promoting Vincent's reputation, arguing that it was strategically disastrous to recall Vincent "and his madness" at the moment of his brother's suffering from the same condition, not only for "friend Vincent," but for themselves, because it was bound to reinforce the perception that "our painting is mad."[7]

Gauguin's concern on this score was not entirely misplaced. Aurier, after all, had construed Vincent's life and work as a seamless whole, hailing his genius while invoking his madness, and this trope dominated critical assessment—for better or worse—following his death. Quite suddenly Vincent's work became more widely visible: first in Theo's private exhibition, held from late September through December 1890; then, beginning in February 1891, at Les Vingt in Brussels; and the following month at the Indépendants in Paris. Some reviewers explicitly compared

Vincent, with his nervous constitution and fanatical worship of art, to *L'Oeuvre*'s Claude Lantier. Frederik van Eeden, whose book *De kleine Johannes* Vincent had so admired, reciprocated in late 1890 with a deeply felt appreciation of the emblematic resonance of the deceased artist's pictures—and he also reinforced Vincent's immediate status as an *isolé* by suggesting that other painters did not regard him as one of their own because, properly speaking, he was not a painter, but rather a saint. However, Vincent's presentation at Les Vingt was not that of an *isolé*: his paintings and drawings were displayed in the same room with Gauguin's sculpture. This installation, together with awareness of their shared history, led critics to pair them. Hostile reviewers called them "unhinged"; apologists hailed them as misunderstood martyr-heroes. In any case they pluralized the status of *isolé*.[8]

As Vincent attracted critical attention over the fall of 1890 and spring of 1891, resentment may have come to inflect Gauguin's original misgivings about being associated with his former friend. At the Indépendants, in which Gauguin did not participate, some saw Vincent and Seurat as the leaders of the two manifestly different tendencies on view there. Though Gauguin was mentioned in conjunction with Vincent as a practitioner of an art of ideas, a good number of the attributes that Gauguin coveted were fast becoming central to the vocabulary used to construct Vincent's posthumous reputation: his role as apostle and prophet; the attributes of sincerity, instinctiveness, and (the ultimate prize) "genius." Gauguin wanted acknowledgment of his own genius to come from more significant quarters than the reliable Schuffenecker.[9] To this end he brazenly enlisted the participation of anyone who might be of assistance.

Among the most reluctant was Pissarro, who in May 1891 would complain about Gauguin's adroitness in "getting himself elected (that is

the word) a man of genius.... There was no way to achieve this ascent, other than by facilitating it himself." Yet Pissarro, along with Bernard, despite the negative opinions they vented in private, did contribute to the ascent in question, as did more wholehearted admirers Charles Morice, de Haan, and others. In various ways they promoted Gauguin's cause in the influential circle including Symbolist poet Stéphane Mallarmé and writer Octave Mirbeau, with the result that he was hailed as the leader of the Symbolist school of painting. Aurier acknowledged this in an essay of March 1891 that considerably enhanced Gauguin's critical reputation; Mirbeau promoted him in the marketplace with two February articles that helped advertise an exhibition of thirty works to be auctioned at the end of the month to raise travel funds for the artist. Mirbeau represented Gauguin as a poet-apostle and a demon, refined and barbarous; a man whose nostalgia for the tropical countries of his mythic origin impelled him to Tahiti. There he would renew himself and recover from the torments resulting from the loss of "a tenderly loved, tenderly admired friend, poor Vincent van Gogh, one of the most magnificent temperaments in painting, one of the most beautiful souls among artists in whom our hope was confided." The hope and admiration were certainly Mirbeau's, as became evident in the article he devoted to Vincent weeks later, in which he mourned the extinction of the artist-apostle's flame of genius.[10] Gauguin played his hand accordingly.

But his strategems were less successful among his old friends. In January Bernard proposed to Schuffenecker and other colleagues that they form a "Society of Unknowns" ("Société des anonymes"), a group united against the cult of personality, pursuit of popularity, intrigues, and "dishonest plagiarism"—opposed, in short, to everything that Gauguin embodied. Learning of this, Gauguin protested a clear conscience, but nonetheless he had to contend with

Schuffenecker's charge of failing to promote anyone but himself. Gauguin's loyal supporter for almost twenty years, Schuffenecker had clearly reached his limit. In early February he wrote to Gauguin that they should part ways: "You are made for domination, I for independence." The friendship would never be fully restored. That same month Bernard, upset because Gauguin's anointment as the premier Symbolist painter excluded recognition of his own contributions, broke with Gauguin on the eve of his auction. Bernard now avowed that he had always detested Gauguin's *Christ in the Garden of Olives* (ch. 5, fig. 51) as nothing more than idolatrous, self-pitying egomania.[11]

In the Symbolist literary camp, by contrast, Mallarmé spoke of Gauguin as possessing a "sympathetic nature ... tormented by the pain of art." Aurier deemed *Christ* a sublime expression of transcendence; Jules Huret pub-

lished an interview with Gauguin in which he uncritically accepted both the artist's identification with his image of Christ and his explanation that the picture was "meant to convey the crushing of an ideal, pain as divine as it as human"; and Mirbeau acquired the canvas for himself.[12]

But outside the charmed confines of this intellectual circle, Gauguin met with more skepticism. Some who reviewed Gauguin's ceramics at Les Vingt saw the artist's self-presentation as a kind of "bohemian *look at me*," dismissing the Breton get-up and long hair as merely a ploy for calling attention to a purportedly "naïve, sincere" art. "Gauguin has invented Gauguinism," quipped another critic, noting the artist's penchant for presenting himself as more primitive than the primitives. This perception also emerged in the reading of Gauguin's ceramics as invoking

"resurrected Hindu, Tibetan, Javanese, and medieval" elements woven together by a "tailor of images."[13] In some instances the negative, ad hominem response followed from the art itself; by an already established tradition, those hostile to vanguard practice extended their denigration to its producers. In other cases, however, it seems clear that Gauguin's aggressive persona colored the evaluation of his achievement.

Vincent's art was likewise viewed as an "affirmation of personality," to use Mirbeau's words. But the search for validation of artistic worth in personal character served Vincent well. His authenticity, sincerity, and integrity stood virtually above question, and his illness effectively removed his motives from suspicion. Not so Gauguin, whose recent antics and schemes had added to his dubious reputation as an opportunist, *grièche* in his dealings with

4
Émile Bernard
(French; 1868–1941)
*Madeleine Bernard
in the Bois d'Amour,
Pont-Aven*
1888
Oil on canvas
138 x 163 cm
Musée d'Orsay, Paris

5
Map of Tahiti and
Hiva Oa, Marquesas
Islands

people and a *pasticheur* in his use of artistic source material (see ch. 2). Soured by the rapid rise of Gauguin's reputation, Félix Fénéon, who had responded favorably to his work in the 1889 Volpini show, now suggested that his progress depended on others, namely Bernard, whom the critic credited with initiating the older artist into a new style, new subject matter, and a new interest (notably lacking heretofore) in reading. Cleverly assimilating these into a knowing primitivism, Gauguin had indeed inverted the initial roles, becoming teacher to Bernard's student. In the work presented at the pre-auction exhibition, Fénéon identified other influences: Monet, Cézanne, and, in the recent Arles pictures, Vincent.[14] Bernard clearly had a hand in this account of Gauguin's appropriative tendencies, and revenge would continue to motivate his efforts in shaping Vincent's posthumous reputation.

Gauguin had associated Bernard, in their correspondence of 1889, with perversity, symbolized in his visual lexicon by the fox (see ch. 5). This symbolism suggests that, on one level, the enigmatic picture known as *Loss of Virginity* (fig. 2) may refer to the interpersonal conflicts and shifting allegiances that animated the months leading up to Gauguin's departure for Tahiti. The supine, immobile nude has been seen to allude to Bernard's chaste 1888 painting of his sister, Madeleine, reclining fully dressed in the woods of Pont-Aven (fig. 4). In view of the fact that Madeleine had rejected Gauguin's advances (compounding the narcissistic injury by preferring the youthful Laval), the association of fox and female may attribute perfidy to both brother and sister. If it is an image of betrayal, the message is complicated by the possibility that the model for the nude was seamstress Juliette Huret, who was pregnant with Gauguin's child when he left for Tahiti. More overt iconographic references overlay the private ones. By featuring a nude holding a flower in a landscape, Gauguin

once again resurrected Puvis's *Hope* (ch. 2, fig. 70). But this is Hope laid flat—prostituted (*horizontale*) or martyred. Boxed in by the band of dark grass that runs the width of the picture, Gauguin's figure specifically recalls Holbein's famous *Dead Christ* (fig. 3). Other references to religious imagery include the overlapping feet, seen in depictions of Christ on the cross, and the cyclamen in her hand, which carries traditional associations with the sorrow of the Virgin Mary.[15]

Perversity, lost innocence, martyrdom, hopelessness: the themes conflated in Gauguin's picture call up discussions with Vincent in which Puvis's *Hope* consistently served as a touchstone. In light of his recent decorations for Marie Henry's inn (see ch. 5), Gauguin's canvas can be seen as the abandonment of the hope associated with the Studio of the South—figured in the cultural terms of the decadent West and here symbolized by the prone, pale body—for a new hope of the artist's invention. As he had hinted even earlier in the *Cleopatra* pot of 1887/88 (ch. 2, fig. 69), he envisaged hope as a dark-skinned woman of exoticist imagining.

Neither Gauguin nor his Symbolist supporters seemed to notice that this sexualized dream of creative rebirth in the tropics had lost much of its freshness in the ten years since Loti published *Le Mariage*. The escapist fantasy was a such a cliché that Daudet satirized it in the last of his Tartarin stories, *Port Tarascon* (1890). In this novel Tartarin, unhappy with the state of affairs in France and his head filled with explorers' accounts and colonialist propaganda, leads his townspeople from Provence to Oceania. Armed with letters of permission from French officials, sixty-year-old Tartarin assumes the position of Governor of the Free and Independent Colony of Port Tarascon, bartering alcohol and tobacco for land with the local king, whose twelve-year-old daughter (having been

4

properly baptized by the Catholic priest) he proceeds to "marry."[16]

Gauguin had never shared Vincent's enthusiasm for Daudet, so it is unlikely that he knew of Tartarin's last adventure—and the failure and death with which it concludes—when he launched himself on a similar narrative. Moreover, in the spring of 1891, Gauguin seemed to be riding a wave of success that fostered a Tartarinesque blindness to reality. The auction of his work, held on 23 February at Hôtel Drouot, netted him almost ten thousand francs. In March, following a brief (and, as it turned out, final) visit to his family in Copenhagen, he wrote to the Minister of Public Education and Fine Arts requesting a government-sponsored artistic mission to Tahiti. Thanks to his influential connections, Gauguin received funding to "study and ultimately paint the customs and the landscapes" of Tahiti.[17] On 23 March Gauguin was feted at a banquet hosted by Mallarmé. On 1 April, aboard the *Océanien*, he set sail from Marseilles.

Gauguin arrived in Papeete, capital of Tahiti, in June 1891 (see map, fig. 5). He docked just days before the death of Tahiti's last native ruler, King Pomare V, an event symbolizing the problem that the artist faced on reaching his destination: his arrival was belated. Although aspects of the king's funeral revealed a potent native culture, the corrupting effects of colonization were everywhere evident. "Tahiti is becoming completely French," Gauguin complained to Mette. "Little by little, all the ancient ways of doing things will disappear. Our missionaries have already imported much hypocrisy and they are sweeping away part of the poetry."[18] He determined to distill such poetry as remained.

He began, according to his custom, with a period of incubation, during which he studied the local landscape and its inhabitants. What distinguished this undertaking from Gauguin's earlier confrontations with Otherness (in Brittany, Martinique, and Arles) was his self-conscious sense of "being on an official artistic mission. The "documents" he avidly assembled—numerous drawings and some painted studies—constituted his research. As he had explained in his application for funding, he intended to make pictures that fixed the country's character and its light, the language echoing that of the government-sponsored "scientific missions" (*missions scientifiques*), fact-finding expeditions touted as the intellectual by-products of colonialist expansion.[19]

A landscape that Gauguin painted in the months following his arrival reveals the documentary impetus of this initial investigation (fig. 6). *The Big Tree (Te raau rahi)* features accurate depictions of hibiscus shrubs; mango, coconut, and banana trees, which yield staple foods; a tropical almond tree, used in local medicine; and a native man husking a coconut, apparently for the nearby figures that can be construed as his family. Though the scene is picturesque, Gauguin clearly paid attention to local nature and practices. A shift in this aim can be seen in a painting he executed in the spring or fall of the next year of a purau tree (as the title he inscribed in misspelt Tahitian attests), a type of hibiscus (fig. 7). Here Gauguin took liberties in imposing his vision, later evocatively likening the pandanus leaves that littered the shore to a "whole oriental vocabulary—letters (it seemed to me) of an unknown, mysterious language." Nature afforded him license for the whiplash stylizations that animate the picture's foreground, the leaves serving as both reference and point of departure for more purely formal experimentation.[20]

While landscape did feature in Gauguin's official Tahitian project, another goal was to invent a revisionist exoticism for the representation of the native population and their culture. This required a greater leap from *étude* to *tableau*. He adopted the strategy of rooting his imagination in the reality of Tahiti, intending to depict subjects who would proclaim their authenticity as true "Maories" and not models from the studios of Paris. To this end, he deliberately sought to reverse the Western practice, pervasive from guidebook illustrations to high art, whereby the natives of foreign lands were made attractive to Europeans through the imposition of classical standards of beauty—essentially converting them into Minervas and Pallas Athenas. Gauguin's letters and paintings attest that it was the "country's female type" he sought to liberate

5

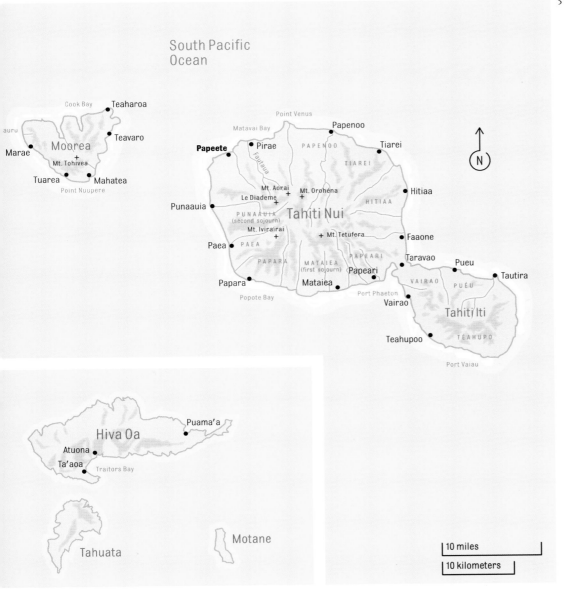

from these representational constraints. As previously in Arles and as mirrored in the pages of Loti's *Mariage*, he engaged in sexualized fieldwork. Soon after arriving on the island, he formed a relationship with a local woman, which he broke off because she was "half white [and] glossy from contact with all these Europeans," and thus would not enable him to fulfill "the goal I had set myself." Gauguin's subsequent companion, thirteen-year-old Tehamana, whom he called Tehura in his recollections, better met his needs. Of Polynesian origin, less experienced, and more "impenetrable" to Gauguin's understanding, she became, through their arranged "marriage," the muse he required, in effect playing Rarahu to his Loti. He announced her pregnancy to a friend in the fall of 1892 as his contribution to the local culture (Tahitians adored children and raised them communally) and a sign of prowess ("I am sowing my seed everywhere"). He signaled this potency to Mette at the same time by boasting of his productivity in painting some forty-four pictures in eleven months.[21]

A "stepping stone to other, better work": thus Gauguin described the "study [*étude*] of a native woman" that he painted soon after his arrival (fig. 8). He sent the work to Paris in the spring of 1892 as a sample of the oeuvre he intended to withhold until he could arrange an exhibition devoted to it. His modest description notwithstanding, he evidently felt confident that he had captured the unconventional beauty and mysteriousness of the Tahitian female type, expressing his hope that the picture's "novelty" would attract attention in the market. Still more ambitiously he felt it would establish him as being in "possession of the Oceanic character," the undisputed first to literally pioneer an art of a sort that no one in France had seen before. "You know," he pointedly joked to new confidant, painter Georges-Daniel de Monfreid, "she is mine, not Bernard's"—implying with the feminine pronoun both the art and the woman.[22]

In calling *Woman with Flower* an *étude*, Gauguin may have acknowledged the apparent straightforwardness of his presentation of the handsome subject, who wears the shapeless "Mother Hubbard" dress imposed on native women by missionaries. Thus acknowledging the pervasiveness of European influence, Gauguin nonetheless intimated, by means of the fanciful background, that its reach did not extend to the inner world behind the woman's impassive countenance. Above a band of red, a plane of yellow serves as foil for a pattern of flowers that seem to spring to life, as if detaching themselves and dropping into her hand; the blossoms in her hair threaten to become part of the backdrop, the hair ribbon also taking on a life of its own as it snakes through the field of yellow.

Personal symbolic resonances proliferate: the background is an inverted rendition of that seen in the self-portrait he painted for Marie Henry's inn; its flowers echo those in his earlier *Self-Portrait (Les Misérables)*; the dark ribbon playing against a yellow ground quotes his portrait of his mother (ch. 5, fig. 75; ch. 3, fig.

74; ch. 4, fig. 138). These sources in turn would seem to implicate Vincent. Gauguin's "Tahitienne" recalls their discussions of the Arlésienne and, more specifically, Vincent's embodiment of the South-as-Japan fantasy, likewise imbued with reference to Loti: *The Mousmé* holding a stalk of oleanders (ch. 3, fig. 48), an early symbol of hope for the Studio of the South.

The drawing of *The Mousmé* that Vincent had sent to Gauguin in 1888 (fig. 23) was apparently among the "small circle of comrades"—the collection of photographs, prints, and drawings—that accompanied Gauguin on his journey. And this might not have been the only drawing by Vincent to provide Gauguin with a lens through which to represent the Tahitians. An obvious kinship, in terms of both approach to the subject and graphic stylization, links Vincent's pen-and-ink sketch after his portrait of Patience Escalier (fig. 9) and Gauguin's 1891 drawing of a Tahitian woman with a black headdress (fig. 10).[23]

Gauguin turned to such sources to assist him in dealing with a challenge that faced him back in Paris, suggested by Schuffenecker's

response on seeing *Woman with Flower*: "But this isn't Symbolism, is it?" Informing this reaction—in addition to what Gauguin perceived as Schuffenecker's stupidity and Bernard's duplicity—was the disappointing absence of the mythic cues of cultural difference.[24] Gauguin, who had himself expected to find a rich panoply of such signs, had experienced a similar disappointment. As he moved about the island, he saw precious little evidence, in terms of artifacts and beliefs, of Tahiti's precolonial past. He would seize upon what objects he could find, together with books and his pictorial comrades, in his effort to re-create lost art, architecture, and cultural practices and to clothe the paucity of what the missionaries had so effectively stripped away. In this process of mythic invention, Vincent's role may have been overshadowed by a host of other formal references, ranging from Java to Egypt to ancient Greece, but the guiding spirit of Gauguin's undertaking remained the hope transplanted from Arles.

Throughout his first Tahitian sojourn, Gauguin was plagued by physical and financial problems, hardships that led him to contemplate returning to France after only nine months on the island. The fecklessness

8

9

10

11

of those on whom he now depended, and the failure of Boussod et Valadon to promote him effectively, frequently reminded him of the stalwart support Theo had shown him. But while reiterating that Theo's death had been his own personal disaster, he continued to believe in a promising future. "To hope," he lectured Mette, "is basically to live. I must live in order to do my work, to the last, and I can only do it by forcing my illusions to the utmost, by creating for myself a dream of hope."[25]

This is the subtext of the painting Gauguin sketched for Sérusier (figs. 11–12) in a March 1892 letter. In it he hinted that lack of money would soon force his return, but the gloss he provided on his current paintings (an example of which [fig. 8] Sérusier might soon see in Paris) shows him as always attempting to guide his friend's appreciation of it. The work was, he exclamed, "quite ugly, quite crazy. Dear Lord, why have you made me like this? I am cursed. What a religion is the ancient Oceanian reli-

gion. What a marvel! My brain is worn out, and everything that this suggests to me is frightening." His lighthearted rhetoric disguised the reality of his situation, as does the canvas he evoked, in which a brilliantly colored landscape and a large tiki of Gauguin's invention serve as backdrop for a nude, seated on a vibrant pareo manufactured in England. The inscribed title identifies her as Vairaumati, a figure drawn from ancient Polynesian mythology. According to texts Gauguin read, Vairaumati was a beautiful mortal who married the creator god, became a goddess, and spawned the Arioi, a secret religious society whose cultural practices Gauguin saw as the vital force that had animated Tahiti's distant glory days. Neither the exotic accessories nor the profile positioning and lighted hand-rolled cigarette she holds disguise Vairaumati's affiliation with Puvis's talismanic *Hope*. By depicting the legendary beauty with a cigarette, the attribute of a Parisian tart, Gauguin possibly meant to reference the prostitution rife within the latter-day Arioi society, while

12

13

14

suggestively recasting the theme of prostituted hope from *Loss of Virginity*. In a variant composition, *The Seed of the Arioi* (fig. 13), Gauguin translated the Puvis prototype more directly, replacing a sprouting seedling in the hand of the dark-skinned nude and creating a brilliant, lush background that contrasts vividly with the bleak setting of *Hope*.[26]

Through such overt appropriation, Gauguin made a claim for the pictorial regeneration central to the Studio of the Tropics concept. Moreover, by transforming his model, he attested his cultural immersion. The pidgin Tahitian titles he inscribed on this and other pictures were part of the same legitimizing strategy, intended to imply that he was painting a living tradition. (Gauguin would attribute his knowledge of Maori legend, dependent on books by European authors, to his *vahine*, Tehamana.) The self-consciousness of this intention emerges with the comparison of these two works and another painted at the beginning of his stay, a spectacular hybrid representing a haloed Tahitian Mary and Christ

Child receiving the local greeting, "Io Orana," from a yellow angel and attendants. After applying himself to the task of imbibing ancient Polynesian cosmology, he could dispense with most of the trappings of Christian iconography. But as a portrait of Tehamana that he painted during his last months on the island (fig. 14) testifies, mythic Tahiti was necessarily a fragile construction. Entitled *Tehamana Has Many Parents (Merahi metua no Tehamana)*, the work presents a frontal view of his young companion, wearing a missionary dress and set against a background suggestive of her roots. Gauguin spoke only rudimentary Tahitian, and he invented Tehamana's connection to her ancestry. The yellow glyphs and the Hindu-inspired idol, copied from other sources and cobbled together, have no coherent meaning in this context—nor would it signify for Gauguin's anticipated audience, except in evocative terms.[27] While evocative of the complexities of Tahitian history and identity, *Tehamana Has Many Parents* also testifies to the authenticity of Gaguin's own lived experience in a way that inevitably recalls Loti's Rarahu.

Gauguin's dependency on extra-Tahitian sources would only become an issue in the face of purported ethnographic accuracy; for the most part, he could not be challenged. Gauguin's compositions representing Tahitian cultural practices are to a considerable extent gorgeous inventions, escapist projections onto a culturally impoverished but naturally luxurious Tahiti, a process aligned with Vincent's choice to see Japan and Holland in Provence. By March 1893 Gauguin had, by his count, completed some sixty-six pictures (figures, nudes, and landscapes), in addition to a number of "ultrasavage" sculptures. While insisting to his wife that he was going native, in June Gauguin at last received government underwriting for passage back to France, always the final destination of the Studio of the Tropics.[28]

Gauguin counted on a triumphant return: not only had he built up a sense of achievement and confidence in his South Seas strategy, he had received encouraging indications from Paris. An April 1892 article by Aurier on Symbolism, unequivocally identifying Gauguin as the movement's prime initiator, fostered the artist's sense of omnipotence. While Gauguin conceded that younger adherents of Symbolism were "not without talent," he maintained that they owed everything to him: "It is I who formed them. Nothing of what they do derives from them: it comes from me." Additionally he had received word from Theo's replacement at Boussod et Valadon, Maurice Joyant, that the critical tide had turned in favor of the artists associated with him. Though Sérusier for one remained loyal enough to refer to his absent, former teacher as "the doyen of the Nabis," this did not shield Gauguin, now preoccupied with his age, from wondering if his acolytes would have stifled him had he not turned decisively in another direction by going to Tahiti. This had literally and aesthetically given him some distance from the younger artists, who still propagated his Breton vision. "It will take them some time yet to follow me down this road," he pronounced with satisfaction.[29]

Gauguin's exaggerated sense of strategic imperative arose in part from his awareness of grudges borne against him by the likes of Schuffenecker, but he knew that he had a more serious opponent in the "young serpent" Bernard, whose rancorous accusations of intellectual theft continued to surface in the vanguard press. Bernard most effectively cast aspersions on Gauguin through his apparently selfless promotion of Vincent's posthumous reputation. In April 1892 he organized an exhibition of Vincent's work at Le Barc de Boutteville's commercial gallery, a stronghold of Symbolism, which led even a doubter like acerbic young critic Camille Mauclair to declare Vincent a "great yet incomplete artist," a meteoric presence who disappeared too soon, like Monticelli and Seurat.[30] A year later Bernard engineered a coup with even more lasting implications when he got the influential *Mercure de France* to publish an extensive series of selections from Vincent's correspondence.

These extracts from the letters appeared steadily over the course of 1893, then intermittently until 1897. Illustrated with examples of facsimile manuscript and with full-page reproductions of sketches and independent drawings, they provided unprecedented, intimate access to Vincent's life, artistic aims, and relationships. Given the restricted visibility of his paintings, the bulk of which were now in the Netherlands with Theo's widow, the perpetuation of the artist's memory through his writing ensured that his life became better known than his art. And as editor, Bernard helped shape Vincent's reputation—and his own—through his selections and commentary. In his preface to the first group, comprising letters written to him, Bernard claimed that Vincent's texts, together with his paintings, proved that he had possessed a sublime vision and had lacked "all egoism and ambition." The saintly construction implies its opposite, namely Gauguin, conspicuously absent from Bernard's gloss if not from Vincent's correspondence. Letters to Theo were published beginning with the fifth installment, printed in August and coinciding with Gauguin's return to France. Bernard here drew attention to the brothers' devotion to the cause of impressionism and support of artists such as Degas, Monet, Pissarro, Renoir, and Seurat. Again Gauguin's name (not always spelled out in the *Mercure* transcriptions, but often coded "G") appeared only from Vincent's pen, as the object of his selfless admiration and solicitude, and not from Bernard's.[31]

Gauguin did not allow the cold reception he received at Boussod et Valadon (Theo's

successor having already quit) to dim his plans to take Paris by storm. In short order he made arrangements, with Degas's help, for a November exhibition at Durand-Ruel's gallery, and by October he was at work on a "book on Tahiti" intended to facilitate the understanding of his paintings. In his efforts to prove that the trip to the tropics had not been "craziness," he displayed a ruthless selfishness that now finally caused Mette to give up on him. The previous spring, with Gauguin still in Tahiti, she had helped arrange for a number of Gauguin's recent paintings to be shown in a Copenhagen group exhibition featuring contemporary French art. Gratified by her artist friends' admiration of Gauguin's achievement, Mette echoed them in writing to Schuffenecker, with whom she remained in contact. As it turned out, Gauguin's work had shared a room with pictures by Vincent, loaned by Theo's widow, Jo, who found it fitting and touching that the two friends were thus reunited.[32] It was a delicacy of feeling Gauguin now displayed in cultivating the support of the literary and artistic vanguard.

He may have recognized that he would do well to temper the larger-than-life persona (see fig. 15) he was performing. This may explain his display in October–November, at Le Barc de Boutteville, of his copy of Manet's *Olympia*. Painted just before leaving for Tahiti, the work can be interpreted as an act of deference, an acknowledgment of creative debts. The same venue had just mounted an exhibition called "Portraits of the Next Century" ("Portraits du prochain siècle"), including self-portraits by both Gauguin and Vincent. Quite possibly the Vincent example was the one owned by Gauguin, *Self-Portrait (Bonze)* (ch. 3, fig. 73; the Gauguin has not been identified). Clearly Gauguin lent himself to a related enterprise, organized by the periodical *Essais d'art libre*, which the same month announced plans to publish a series

of "synthetic" written portraits, fifteen to twenty lines long, devoted to contemporary luminaries in the arts and sciences. An initial list of subjects included Mallarmé, Verlaine, Anquetin, Bernard, and Gauguin, whose profile would be authored by writer Jean Dolent. When the announcement reappeared in the next issue, the roster of those to be portrayed had expanded to include Puvis, Manet, Monet, Renoir, as well as Vincent van Gogh—his literary portraitist none other than Paul Gauguin.[33]

As the single painter-author in the projected roster, Gauguin may have anticipated an opportunity to burnish his reputation in the Mallarmé circle (and to prepare the way for reception of the larger literary effort of this moment, his Tahitian account). An equally potent motivation may have been the opportunity to assert control over the perception of his relationship with Vincent. Had the assignment been given to Bernard (who, having written poetry, might seem the more likely candidate), the resulting portrait certainly would have resembled those he had already sketched in his introductions to the correspondence published in the *Mercure*, with Gauguin serving as negative foil to Vincent's virtue. And Bernard was not the only one of Gauguin's detractors to exploit this contrast. In reviewing the exhibition of portrait paintings, Mauclair paired Gauguin's and Vincent's self-representations. Professing his admiration of Gauguin's work and his eagerness to see the "négresses" he had painted in Oceania, Mauclair nonetheless deemed his self-portrait ridiculous, dismissing the artist's persona together with his art. "I will easily forget his face," he wrote, going on to declare that he could not say the same of the self-portrait by Vincent, a personal testimonial, like his other pictures, in which his noble personality shone through—recognizable, even had it not been signed, as truly original.[34] The unflattering juxtaposition suggests how difficult it was for Gauguin to escape the issue of character and originality.

As it turned out, *Essais d'art libre* never did print the written portraits, which would have offered a quite different pairing, one more effectively controlled by Gauguin. Dolent, in describing Gauguin, would seemingly have foregrounded the reverence for Vincent that he included in a later, published profile: "When Gauguin says 'Vincent,' his voice is gentle."[35] And Gauguin, depicting Vincent, opened his narrative thus: "At a dealer's, a still life for five francs: pink shrimps . . . on pink paper; and Zola's yellow book." (*La Joie de vivre*).[36]

Here Gauguin evoked Paris in December 1886, when Vincent was virtually unknown. The still life is apparently a conflation of two compositions: an apparently lost study of shrimps and *Still Life with Bible and Zola's "Joie de vivre"* (ch. 1, fig 3). Their author, whose lineaments Gauguin sketched with quick strokes that in effect re-present Vincent's self-portraits, first appears to him like a cowherd, with his old coat and rabbit-fur hat (see ch. 5, figs. 7, 9);

closer inspection reveals blue eyes of childlike innocence set in a sunburned face, a face with the smile of a martyr. Gauguin's Vincent is a painter of mountain torrents, flowers, gardens: canvases realized "passionately, glimpsed in a flash of reason—tinted chrome—executed too hurriedly, one might say." The feverish sense of urgency stems from the intuition of his early death.[37]

With a concision that presumes the intended audience's acquaintance with his subject, Gauguin evoked the brief career of the painter-martyr, concluding with an evocative dream sequence:

I still see him, Him. . . ; he is in the plains, he strides along. I do not know if he is holding a palette in his hand, but his gesture is that of a sower. On the glowing horizon, the huge sun, rapidly losing its shape, brushes against the glittering line: it shoots its golden arrows through the fields and finally, like a ghost ship [*vaisseau fantôme*], sinks into the colossal element. Then it is night—the sower disappears: I no longer see Vincent.

With its allusions to the sower, the sun, and Wagner, this passage references their time together in Arles, casting Gauguin in the role of elegist rather than participant or agent.

Gauguin had probably not yet drafted this text when the November installment of Vincent's correspondence appeared in the *Mercure*, letters to Theo that conclude with a long paragraph in which Vincent, concerned about Gauguin's financial straits, attempted to enlist Theo's support in bringing him to the South. This glimpse of the relationship between Gauguin and the van Gogh brothers provided a kind of backdrop to the exhibition of forty-one Tahitian pictures that opened at Durand-Ruel's gallery on 10 November. The stakes were high, the outcome mixed. Financially it was an outright disaster. Only eleven paintings

had been purchased by the time the show closed on the 25th, which meant that Gauguin would not recoup part of the recent windfall from his uncle Zizi he had had to put up to cover the costs of the show. Critically it fared better, receiving considerable attention, though not all of it as laudatory as Gauguin reported to Mette.[38]

In fact the general response like the reviews ranged from enthusiastic to indignant and dismissive, according to a more reliable observer, Pissarro. Men of letters were largely impressed, collectors perplexed, and painters divided. Pissarro himself was deeply ambivalent, and not won over by Gauguin's theoretical posturings about selflessly leading the way for young artists to similarly renew themselves through contact with primitive cultures. Pissarro concluded that his erstwhile protegé, though not without talent, "always poaches on others' territory; now he is pillaging the natives of Oceania."[39]

The incensed reactions of Pissarro and others point toward the risks entailed in simultaneously creating art and a persona to match. Even when successful, this rendered the work dangerously dependent on its creator; with his theatrical appearance and propensity to spin theoretical justifications, Gauguin could stand in the way of a deeper appreciation of his art by casting a shadow of "quasi-celebrity" that may have demonstrated strength of character to some, but appeared to others as mere "puffism." Hence the mixed response to Charles Morice's preface to the exhibition catalogue. Morice, consistently loyal to Gauguin, preemptively defended the painter's authenticity, claiming that he had undertaken the Tahitian voyage not simply to renew himself with new subject matter, but for ideological and personal motivations relating to his Inca background. Gauguin's Tahitian vision, according to Morice, departed from the "perfumed confections of Pierre Loti," instead revealing

Tahiti as it was before contact with "our terrible sailors."[40]

Some commentators, uncritically citing the preface, hailed a wonderful adventurer whose exploits recalled those of the "European conquerers of yesteryear"; others commended his ethnographic accuracy. Mirbeau echoed Morice in distancing Gauguin's work from the taint of speculation and the "suspect scents" of *Le Mariage de Loti*. However, some saw no such distinction, and the Gauguin-Loti identification could be seen in two very different lights. From a literalist, politically conservative point of view, Gauguin's portrayal of the "land of little Rarahu" was wholly acceptable. By contrast the anarchist press condemned artist and novelist equally for their selfish pursuit of pleasure and complicity in colonialist repression.[41]

Crucially, many detractors honed in on the pretention rather than the politics, the character as much as the creativity, taking issue with the strategic preface, the ridiculous titles, the grandiloquent exegeses. This type of controversy swirled around Gauguin over the next year and a half; the pages of the *Mercure* provide an instructive case study. In December Morice threw himself back into the fray, reiterating his defense of Gauguin's genius and describing the sincere, valiant artist's sadness upon returning to encounter a solidly united opposition, including liars and thieves who had in his absence exploited and claimed his discoveries while turning opinion against him. In 1892, while still in Tahiti, Gauguin had lost a supporter when Aurier died. The *Mercure* replaced him with Mauclair, who detested the Tahitian work, lumping it dismissively with the Orientalism that had been popular for decades and calling it "colonial art," all the while going out of his way to insist that the artist was "honest" nonetheless, and so hinting at the issue of appropriation.[42]

Gauguin attempted his own defense in an essay in which, invoking Wagner, he sought to represent the true genius as an explorer rather than a prophet, the victim of that contemporary "plague": plagiarism coupled with mediocrity. The artist's new champions, notably poet Julien Leclerq, answered Mauclair more directly and in more revealing terms. In an issue of the *Mercure* containing another of Mauclair's sly attacks, Leclerq justified Gauguin's appropriation and re-creation as part of the artistic process. He also claimed that Gauguin, far from indulging in cheap Orientalism, was immortalizing a culture on the brink of extinction. Finally, referring to Vincent's correspondence being published at this very moment, he invoked the artist who had responded so strongly to Gauguin's Martinique paintings that he evaluated subsequent work with the wish that his friend would become again "the richer Gauguin of the *négresses*" (see chs. 2 and 3). Quoting this "precious" testimony from an unimpeachable source, Leclerq imagined what Vincent would have written about the Tahitian pictures were he alive: "'Ah! The rich Gauguin of the *négresses*, how quickly he has returned!'"[43]

Leclerq thus overtly used a connection that Gauguin had shown himself newly anxious to proclaim (and control) in the immediate aftermath of his Durand-Ruel exhibition. In his second literary portrait of Vincent, published in the January 1894 issue of *Essais d'art libre* under the title "Natures mortes" (the evocation of death lost in the English translation "Still Lifes"), Gauguin began by describing a painting of yellow sunflowers against a yellow background in a yellow pot on a yellow table, signed Vincent, that hung "in my yellow room" with yellow curtains. In fact this room was, as insiders would have recognized, the studio that Gauguin had rented on rue Vercingétorix. He had painted the walls chrome yellow and adorned them with Tahitian pictures in frames repainted to match (they had been white for the exhibition) and with paintings by Cézanne and Vincent.[44] Having established Vincent's attachment to yellow as well as his own adoption of it, Gauguin turned to their time together in Arles. There, "both of us crazy," they had waged "continuous battle"—for color: Vincent obsessed with yellow, Gauguin with a contrasting red. Gauguin devoted the remainder of "Natures mortes" not to Vincent's pictures but to his imitation of Christ: his attempts to follow in his reverend father's footsteps, the incident involving the mine catastrophe in the Borinage, subsequent threats of institutionalization, and finally the Arles episode in which he inscribed "Je suis sain d'Esprit / Je suis Saint-Esprit" with intense yellow paint on the walls of their studio. Ostensibly, Gauguin's insistent repetition of the word "crazy" in conjunction with Vincent was intended to suggest a laudatory if abnormal selflessness. However, the effect is suspiciously close to Mauclair's use of the word "honest" with regard to Gauguin. Certainly Gauguin represented his former friend in terms of his acts, which demonstrated his lifelong commitment to the role of preacher-consoler and showed him to be a man who, as van Eeden had suggested, was not so much a painter as a saint. This Vincent could sanction but not threaten. Gauguin enveloped himself in his chromatic aura.[45]

"Better than any other until now, Gauguin seems to have understood the role of the evocative setting." So observed a reviewer who described the Tahitian work as a dream of an edenic, free existence—transcending rather than merely reproducing the tropical reality that provided its framework.[46] Gauguin valued this appraisal and applied the understanding to his life in Paris. On the stage of the "burning yellow atelier," Gauguin presented himself as an exotic bohemian, in his choice both of dress and of company: outfitted in astrakhan hat and *gilet*, he went about with a pet monkey and a thirteen-year-old substitute for Tehamana, a Ceylonese girl nicknamed Annah la Javanaise. He received four awestruck students whom he briefly instructed in his role of professor of the so-called Fiji Academy. At the rue Vercingétorix studio, he also hosted weekly gatherings of painters, writers, and musicians at which he would give readings from the evolving manuscript devoted to his Tahitian experience. Gauguin's "book," a report of his spiritual and artistic rejuvenation through contact with the primitive Other as embodied in Tehamana/Tehura, describes a foray outside the boundaries of Western civilization that, while cut short by the call of duties back home, leaves the protagonist more in touch with his primitive self, at once younger and wiser. Structurally indebted to Loti, albeit more complexly nuanced, it can be seen as a Symbolist *Mariage de Gauguin*. Gauguin's title, *Noa Noa*, Tahitian for "perfume," suggests his persistent belief that he could effectively translate Loti's "suspect scents" into an authentic idiom, despite the criticism he had received on that score. To complement the text, he made drawings and woodcuts that were to be part of an eventual publication co-authored with Morice. In a parallel endeavor, Gauguin executed a painting entitled *Day of the God (Mahana no atua)* (fig. 16). This literally brilliant fabrication, pieced together of elements from books on the South Pacific, photographs, and his own current graphic work, exceeds anything he had attempted in Tahiti in terms of mythic ambi-

tion. Monumental in effect though not large in scale, it functions as a sort of compendium of Polynesian cosmology, recalling the murals of Puvis de Chavannes.[47]

This ambition proved difficult to sustain. Gauguin spent April through November 1894 in Brittany, where a fractured ankle curtailed his painting and forced him to channel his energy into experimental prints. The canvases he did produce suggest his difficulty in re-engaging with Breton subject matter. Quite possibly he felt impeded both by the example of his own past and by the current practice of the so-called School of Pont-Aven. Gauguin drew criticism for exerting undue dominance over these followers, whose work indeed manifested the stylistic mannerisms that had become evident in his own Breton work by the time of his initial departure for the South Pacific. Gauguin did make a notable effort to re-present Brittany in a painting of a figure wearing a Tahitian missionary dress, set against the Pont-Aven landscape (fig. 17). Her devotional gesture is informed by Borobudur photographs and by early Flemish religious painting, which Gauguin saw on a trip to Belgium with Leclerq. However, another ingredient may also have contributed to the image. The satu-

rated yellow of the girl's dress and the wing-like shapes flanking her (clearly evident in the paint surface), gray-blue with markings like peacock feathers, may reference the black-and-white reproduction of Rembrandt's "yellow" angel that Vincent had arranged for Gauguin to receive from Theo (ch. 5, fig. 62).[48]

The projection of Tahiti on Brittany suggests that Gauguin's mind was elsewhere by late summer 1894, and indeed he began to concoct plans to return to the South Seas with two new painter friends from the Pont-Aven group.[49] Gauguin went back to Paris to begin gathering resources for a second voyage in November, and the following month, he opened his studio for an exhibition. This was the occasion of Leclerq's positing Vincent's likely admiration of Gauguin's Tahitian work.

The theme of hope reappeared in Gauguin's work in two quite different but equally opaque expressions at this moment. One is a now-lost monotype depicting a dark-haired, petulant nude against a tropical background (fig. 18); she fails to proffer the viewer a sign of renewal in the form of a flower, but her rounded abdomen raises the possibility that she is pregnant. The other is a drawing that accom-

16

17

panied a poem by Morice in praise of Puvis (fig. 20), published in the *Mercure* a few weeks after a January banquet honoring the painter's seventieth birthday that both Gauguin and Morice attended. The poet's florid homage extols Puvis's ability to reveal the divine and eternal in the real. Though Gauguin's drawing directly references Puvis's iconic *Hope*, its message is more ambivalent. Here Hope does not gaze out, directly and clear-eyed, at the viewer, but rather averts her eyes, turning away not only from the sprig held in her outstretched hand, but also from the shapes beyond—the legs and feet of the crucified Christ.

The image was a position statement. Placed at the foot of the cross, Hope stands in for a penitent Magdalen, suggesting a return to the themes of *Loss of Virginity* (fig. 2) and its attendant critique of Western culture. Hope's literal aversion to the Passion finds a parallel in Gauguin's current dialogue with playwright August Strindberg, whom the artist had asked

to provide a preface for the catalogue of the 18 February 1895 auction he was planning. Strindberg declined, but Gauguin in fact printed the letter in which he explained his reasons for doing so as a prefatory essay. Professing incomprehension of Gauguin's troubling vision, Strindberg had, as he wrote, gone to the museum to study a more familiar creation, Puvis's *Poor Fisherman* (fig. 19)—only to find himself put off by its aura of resigned suffering. He went on to set up a contrast that takes to extremes the polarities that Vincent raised in pairing the Bible and Zola's *Joie de vivre* (ch. 1, fig. 3). By rejecting the passive God of Western convention in favor of the savage gods of the freedom-seeking artist, Strindberg effectively offered a roundabout vindication of Gauguin and his mission.[50]

Things in Paris had not turned out as Gauguin had anticipated, and his departure—once again undertaken alone, and once again for Tahiti—was embittered. He confronted his

detractors by declaring, in one interview, that critics misunderstood him precisely because he had not followed others: "I would rather be a *misérable* than a plagiarist." Morice represented him not so much as leaving as going into exile, "without hope of return," his decision prompted by disgust with the putrid atmosphere of the West. Alerting his interviewer to his forthcoming book, Gauguin anticipated finding consolation in the free land that he identified with the fragrant: *Noa Noa*.[51]

19

18

20
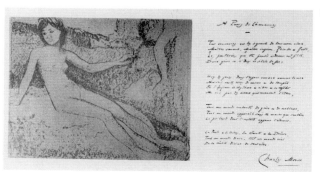

21

Gauguin arrived back in Papeete in September 1895 to find areas of the capital outfitted with electric lights. Dismayed to find this would-be Eden disappearing so fast, he announced plans to escape European contamination by moving to the Marquesas, the remote group of islands situated some 750 miles (1,208 kilometers) to the northeast of Tahiti (see map, fig. 5). But six years would pass before he did so.

From the inauspicious beginning, things only got worse. Gauguin struggled with continuing financial difficulties and increasingly severe health problems. He moved to Punaauia, a village fifteen miles (24 kilometers) south of Papeete, where he installed himself with his most recent teenaged companion. By 1896 he described himself as without hope, a lifelong *misérable*, going crazy, condemned to martyrdom, contemplating suicide. While such characterizations continued earlier self-dramatizations, a more deeply felt despair began to color his outlook and his art. He expressed his increasing pessimism in a painting of a Tahitian fisherman and his family on the seashore at Punaauia, with the island of Moorea and setting sun in the background (fig. 21). Executed in a lush palette of violet blues and pinks, the canvas is sumptuous but melancholy, striking a note in keeping with the designation that Gauguin inscribed on a variant version: "*Le Pauvre Pêcheur*" (*The Poor Fisherman*). Echoing the exchange with Strindberg, the picture transposes Puvis's theme of resignation and suffering to Tahiti. With its palpably rich surface and sense of torpor and loss, this is a *Human Miseries* set in a tropical paradise.[52]

The mood is darker still in a self-portrait that Gauguin painted following his July 1896 stay in Papeete's hospital (fig. 22). Wearing a tunic-like costume that could be a hospital shirt, the artist presents himself squarely to the viewer, a warily reproachful expression on his face. The forms flanking him in the enclosed, gloomy space are only barely discernible: at the right what appear to be two Polynesian sculpted

22
Paul Gauguin
*Self-Portrait near
Golgotha*
1896 [W 534]
Oil on canvas
76 x 64 cm
Museu de Arte de
São Paulo, Brazil

23
Vincent van Gogh
Sketch of *The
Mousmé*
c. 23 July 1888 [F 1722,
JH 1521], given to
and inscribed by
Paul Gauguin

Pen and ink on paper
15 x 13 cm
Musée d'Orsay,
Paris

24
Paul Gauguin
*Where Do We Come
From? What Are We?
Where Are We
Going?* (*D'Où venons-
nous, que sommes-
nous, où allons-nous*)
1897 [W 561]

Oil on canvas
139 x 375 cm
Tompkins
Collection, courtesy
Museum of Fine
Arts, Boston

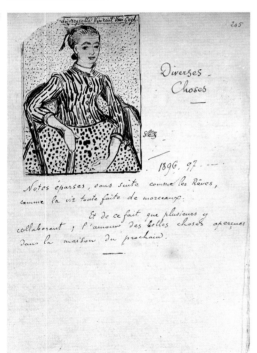

heads, and at the left the foot of the cross. The inscription—"Near Golgotha P. Gauguin – 96"—proclaims the theme. Harking back to his self-portrait as Christ in the Garden of Olives, Gauguin here posited a more personal and complex identification, one specific to his current circumstances. He stands between the savage gods and the God of resignation, the oppositional pairing invoked by Strindberg. The expression is very un-Christlike, more defiant than resigned. This was the posture Gauguin adopted in life, fending off guilt by becoming angry when accused of criminally taking flight of his family. If he was a criminal, so be it: such was the price of great art.[53]

The atmosphere of death Gauguin evoked in his self-portrait became a still more tangible reality in the months that followed. In the spring of 1897, a "brutal" letter from Mette informed him that their daughter, Aline, had died of pneumonia. Shortly thereafter his correspondence with his wife came to an end. As Gauguin's deteriorating health (including a series of heart attacks) made it increasingly difficult for him to paint, he channeled his energies into writing. In the bound volume that already contained his illustrated "Noa Noa" manuscript, he appended another set of writings that he described as "scattered notes, discontinuous like Dreams; like life made up of bits and pieces" and entitled "Diverses Choses" ("Miscellaneous Things"). "Diverses Choses" is indeed a mixed bag, comprising for the most part views and theoretical positions on art and artists, an earlier text on religion, scattered citations from Wagner, the so-called Turkish treatise, press clippings, and a miscellany of anecdotes and literary essays. The title page he devised for it (fig. 23) invokes Vincent as a kind of presiding spirit, for it features his drawing after *The Mousmé*, with Gauguin's inscription "du regretté Vincent van Gogh" ("by the lamented Vincent van Gogh"). And Gauguin's description of the heterogeneous contents of "Diverses Choses"

summons Vincent's dreams for the Yellow House: "And from the fact that several collaborate there, the love of beautiful things glimpsed in the house that is to come [*la maison du prochain*]."[54]

As despair and death displaced the optimism and fantasy of rebirth inherent to the Studio of the Tropics, Gauguin's thoughts turned to Vincent and their time together in Arles. Memories and imagination equally served as the basis for a bizarre, rambling story in "Diverses Choses" that Gauguin crafted to demonstrate the hypocrisy evidenced in both sexual and Salon conventions. The tale's first-person narrator is a preacher's son who settles in Arles following military service in North Africa. The *patronne* of a large brothel offers the young bull the hand of her convent-raised daughter, the virginal Augustine, and the management of the family business; he accepts. Exiled from society by day but hosting it by night, the couple prospers. Augustine is enthroned at the counter of the red salon like a beautiful, black-haired Madonna, faithful to her duties and to her husband, whom the locals address as Monsieur Louis (a louis being the brothel's going rate). At one point the protagonist goes to Paris, where he meets the painter Manet—a very handsome "male" type—who, intrigued by M. Louis and his tales of African lion hunts, wants to paint his portrait.

Gauguin's *Night Café* (ch. 4, fig. 41), featuring Marie Ginoux in the role of *patronne*, might serve as an illustration for this story, while the woman's name and Madonna association suggest links to Vincent's portraits of Augustine Roulin (see ch. 4, figs. 93–94). The tale resonates with the artists' conversations about life, art, sex, and literature. Elsewhere in "Diverses Choses," Gauguin explicitly cited Daudet's *Tartarin de Tarascon*, which includes a lion-hunting episode, as having formed Vincent's vision of "an extraordinary South to be expressed in bursts of flames" of chrome yellow.[55]

This statement appears in the context of Gauguin's account of his trip to Arles, where he would join Vincent, following his "numerous solicitations," and serve as head of the Studio of the South. Though more prosaic than his Paris efforts on the same theme, Gauguin's "Diverses Choses" essay similarly privileges Vincent's evangelism, portraying him as a preacher who revolted against his father, preached in the mines, worked miracles, narrowly escaped institutionalization, and left the church. Only an initial reference hints at the period of weeks during which the two artists "fervently" worked together. Thus Gauguin depicted Vincent not so much as an author of works of his own, but as subject; the sole act of painting described is Gauguin's own. His portrait, *The Painter of Sunflowers* (ch. 4, fig. 107), is here characterized as an image of a kind, humble, Christlike figure, an interpretation that Gauguin bolstered by paraphrasing Dolent's lines about the reverence with which Gauguin uttered Vincent's name.[56]

In this representation of the Arles period, in short, Gauguin once again recognized Vincent's saintliness (and asserted his own awareness of it) while avoiding mention of his contribution to modern painting, an emphasis he repeated in the other narrative involving Vincent in "Diverses Choses."

Presented under the title "Les Crevettes roses" ("The Pink Shrimps"), it closely follows the text drafted in Paris for *Essais d'art libre*, but with some interesting departures. The story begins in Paris in the winter of 1886, with the poor artist trudging through the snow, hoping to interest a dealer in buying his still life of shrimps. Gauguin has removed the Naturalist novel from the still life, but not its message: Vincent gives the five-franc pittance that he receives for his painting to a destitute prostitute, inspired by a book—a modern gospel—that he had read. The scene shifts to the winter of 1894, and the sales room of an auction house. There the same still life sells for one hundred times the amount paid to the artist. Gauguin leaves the temple of commerce, pondering Vincent's noble gesture and the injustices suffered by the dedicated artist at the hands of contemporary society.[57]

News from Paris fed the strains of identification and rivalry that inform these representations. Scarcely had Gauguin left France when the *Mercure* published an open letter to Mauclair from Bernard in which the latter revisited the issues of originality and plagiarism, recounting how Vincent—the first artist to appreciate Bernard's own pictorial innovations—had put him in contact with Gauguin who subsequently applied the advances to realize his *Vision of the Sermon* (ch. 3, fig. 59). Through the *Mercure* Gauguin kept abreast of news in the French capital, where the controversy continued in his absence, reignited by the

appearance of his pictures at various exhibitions. The increased visibility of Cézanne, whose works had hitherto been little seen, introduced a critical new element to debates about vanguard leadership and primacy. In January 1896 Mauclair, praising the Cézannes on display at Ambroise Vollard's gallery, observed that Gauguin's art, despite its philosophical window dressing, came entirely from the Provençal master. Gauguin attempted in vain to persuade the *Mercure*'s editor to fire the critic.[58]

One year later a new voice in the same periodical added injury to insult. André Fontainas complicated Mauclair's equation by comparing Vincent's works on view at Vollard's with those shown there by Gauguin, and evaluating both vis-à-vis Cézanne. His conclusion: Vincent's considerable role—alongside Cézanne's—in the most recent movements in French painting had yet to be fully appreciated. Vincent's influence, he continued, "seems as important as that of Paul Gauguin, and less contradictory" (insofar as less self-conscious). The belated publication of the last installment of Vincent's correspondence, in August 1897, perpetuated the issue by happenstance. The group of letters includes the one in which Vincent connected Puvis's *Hope* to the hopes he placed in his partnership with Gauguin, and mentioned Bernard's belief in Gauguin's absolute superiority. Rather than editing this out, Bernard added a footnote—a "perfidious annotation," according to Gauguin—explain-

24

25
Paul Gauguin
Sunflowers on an Armchair
1901 [W 603]
Oil on canvas
73 x 92.3 cm

The State
Hermitage
Museum,
St. Petersburg
Cat. 144

26
Paul Gauguin
Sunflowers and Mangoes
1901 [W 606]
Oil on canvas
93 x 73 cm
Private collection

ing that this primacy had been proposed and accepted solely by Vincent, who in elevating Gauguin to the position of leader had started all the trouble.[59]

Gauguin apparently finished "Diverses Choses" later in 1897. In December of that year, he embarked on the most ambitious picture of his career, rivaling that of Seurat's *Grande Jatte* (ch. 2, fig. 3) in scale and exceeding it in terms of thematic reach. The artist proclaimed the work's philosophical underpinnings in the title he inscribed at the upper left, over a zone of chrome yellow that he likened to a wall: *Where Do We Come From? What Are We? Where Are We Going?* (*D'Où venons-nous, que sommes-nous, où allons-nous*) (fig. 24). This is nothing less than the series of great existential questions asked by such as Heine, Carlyle, Vincent, and now Gauguin. Visually, the composition is a universe removed from Vincent, but the influence of Arles echoes in Gauguin's characterization of it as an evangel, a parable, like *Human Miseries* (ch. 4, fig. 50). In some ways a continuation on a heroic scale of *Day of the God*, the Polynesian *summa theologica* composed in Paris, the mood here is darker and more brooding. Gauguin considered *Where Do We Come From?* a kind of testament he wished to make before dying, and even claimed to have unsuccessfully attempted suicide upon signing it.[60]

He would create more testaments before his death in 1903, some prompted by his frustration with island politics, others by the politics of the Paris art world. Dispatched to France in late 1898, his masterpiece was exhibited with eight other paintings at Vollard's gallery; the dealer, working through Monfreid, purchased the whole group, but at a low price, which angered the artist. Nor was Gauguin pleased by Fontainas's review in the *Mercure*, in which the critic damned him with faint praise. Admitting at the outset that he had never liked Gauguin's work, Fontainas went on to commend the artist for leaving and breaking

free of the affected simplicity of the Pont-Aven style and ceasing to pursue glory among the literary set. Nonetheless he found the Tahitian work problematic, faulting *Where Do We Come From?* for the opacity of its allegory; it had failed—where Puvis succeeded—to communicate the meaning of the painter's dream to the viewer, save through the title. As for its artistic merits, Fontainas ventured only that Gauguin had "invented his *dessin*, perhaps, close though it is to that of van Gogh or even of Cézanne." This rankled terribly. "I come out of 'Cézanne, van Gogh, Bernard'!—what an adroit *pasticheur* am I!" Gauguin complained with heavy irony to Monfreid. Gauguin responded to Fontainas, managing to offend him in the course of defending himself; then he wrote again to argue that his work functioned like biblical parables, at once literal and mysterious. Some could not see this, he explained, which is just what he had told his friend Puvis when *The Poor Fisherman* met with incomprehension. Gauguin thus enlisted his well-known contemporary as a fellow traveler, even in some sense the beneficiary of his wisdom, while privately accusing him of achieving legibility through recourse to commonplace symbols.[61]

Apparently, however, *Hope* remained a personal talisman, associated as it was with Vincent and the Studio of the South. The nostalgia that accompanied Gauguin's growing despondency informed his request that Monfreid send him seeds for his garden, including a variety of sunflowers; their blossoming, he wrote, afforded him a bit of pleasure in the absence of hope. (Vincent had expressed a similar sentiment in his last weeks.) Reminding Gauguin of France, the flowers also provided motifs for a number of still lifes undertaken in 1899, it seems at Vollard's behest.[62] But in 1901—after a year in which he apparently abandoned painting altogether in favor of writing and drawing—Gauguin returned to the genre with motives of his own, painting four striking pictures of sunflowers, as remarkable for their allusive retrospection as for their sheer

beauty. Two of these feature sunflowers in a plaited basked set on a cloth-draped armchair (see fig. 25), a composition looking back to his early career, notably the 1880 picture *To Make a Bouquet* (ch. 1, fig. 53). In the early canvas, a door reveals a glimpse of the family garden; here a window frames the face of a passing young Tahitian, acknowledgment of the changes twenty years had brought in the artist's personal circumstances. His family is absent, but Vincent is insistently present, the arrangement on the chair recalling the similar set-up in Gauguin's *Painter of Sunflowers*. The flower eye (see ch. 4, fig. 114) suggested there now takes on distinct lineaments, detaching itself from the bouquet to hover like a dull bronze sun in a dark sky, or like a monstrance elevating the Host in Catholic sacrament. The form also recalls Aurier's discussion of Gauguin as possessor of the "inner eye" of the mystic or visionary.[63]

If this still life functions, through its multiple references, as a kind of double portrait, another canvas in the group intimates Gauguin's role in transplanting the Studio of the South to the South Seas (fig. 26). In it the flowers symbolic of their exchange and ambitions are contained in a Maori vessel of carved wood. But the tropical studio has not entirely subsumed its predecessor; at the right a single flower head, its form like an eye staring blindly upward, lies in a Nagayo-ware dish, whose Japanese origin evokes Vincent's fantasy of the Yellow House as *bonzerie*.[64] And the Arles collaboration emerges even more literally in the most iconographically elaborate of the sunflower canvases (fig. 28). Two images appear on the wall behind the flowers and above the contrasting shapes of the Maori and Japanese vessels. The lower one is Gauguin's Degas etching of a brothel interior with a nude bending toward a dressing table (fig. 27). Alluding perhaps to the role of brothel visits in the Arles confraternity, Degas's nude here plays off that seen in the image above it: Puvis's *Hope*. Through this juxtaposition Gauguin suggested innocence compromised; by representing the

25

26

figure with her gaze completely averted from the viewer—failing to favor the artist with her regard—he transformed her into an emblem of his own pessimism.

This personal symbolism carries through to the floral arrangement. The positioning of the two flower heads on the table at the lower right recalls one of the two sunflower canvases (ch. 2, fig. 49) that Vincent gave to Gauguin in exchange for the *Négresses*. But Vincent's paintings were not among the pictorial companions that Gauguin took back to the tropical island. Having left these two canvases behind in Paris with other works of value, he had within months of his arrival asked Schuffenecker to arrange for their sale. Ironically it would be years before he learned what had happened to them or received any benefit from his sacrifice.[65] Suffused with melancholy, *Sunflowers with Puvis de Chavannes's "Hope"* eulogizes two men for whom hope had proved false.

Painted on the eve of a last quest to attain the rejuvenation promised by the Studio of the Tropics fantasy—the journey to the Marquesan island of Hiva Oa, finally undertaken in September 1901—the sunflower series privately recognizes Vincent's role in ways that Gauguin would never acknowledge publicly. He would come closest to doing so in a manuscript that he sent from Atuona, on the island of Hiva Oa (see map, fig. 5), to Fontainas in September 1901, hoping that the *Mercure* would publish it. As its title indicates, "Racontars de rapin" ("A Dauber's Gossip") is an insider's perspective on the art world, affording its author the chance to shape the recent past, acknowledge debts, and settle old scores. Critics are a particular target; Gauguin took them to task for their continual investigation of stylistic "paternity," which had fostered the current mania among painters for fetishizing their originality when in fact none is born of a piece, but is instead a link in a chain.

Confessing himself troubled by "all the fathers that have been attributed to me," Gauguin acknowledged Pissarro as one of his masters and conceded Cézanne special status as sui generis. The apparent modesty scarcely hid an ambition to wrest the history of modern art, still in the process of being written, away from the combined forces of officialdom, the press, and the market. To this end Gauguin concluded his "Racontars" with a list of the "most important" artists, beginning with the post-Romantic generation, proceeding to the Impressionists and Neo-Impressionists, and finally presenting an unnamed group that ranged from Anquetin to van Gogh.[66]

While Gauguin excluded Bernard from these ranks, he showed himself able to recognize those different from, as well as unequal to, himself (Seurat and Signac; Anquetin and Sérusier). But clearly Vincent posed a problem, one that spilled over to the letter to Fontainas that accompanied the manuscript. Returning tenaciously to the critic's 1897 observation that his work owed a debt to Vincent, Gauguin marshaled as exculpatory evidence Vincent's published letter to Theo of summer 1888, in which he anticipated the force of Gauguin's influence prior to his arrival in Arles; and his 1889 letter to Aurier proclaiming his debt to Gauguin. And he also bid Fontainas look carefully at the paintings that Vincent had painted before and after—*avant et après*—Gauguin's stay in Arles.[67]

Then came the betrayal. Unable to resist guiding Fontainas's interpretation, Gauguin went on to explain how he had rescued Vincent from the influence of Neo-Impressionist color theory. Under Gauguin's aegis, the yellow/violet complementaries disappeared and Vincent, "following my advice and my instruction, … proceeded wholly differently. He painted yellow sunflowers on a yellow ground, etc." Of course, Gauguin confided to Fontainas,

he said all this "*completely between ourselves, to let you know I wish to take nothing away from van Gogh.*" He had broken his usual silence on the subject of his noble friend only to set the record straight; he did not seek glory for himself.

But ultimately he did, and anxiety that he might fail led to further betrayal. The myth of Vincent—fed by the life, the letters, the works, and their representation and interpretation—was coalescing before his eyes. Gauguin did not need the critical press to remind him of this; he received confirmation even from an important new collector of his own work, Gustave Fayet. In this collection Gauguin's paintings joined those of Cézanne, Degas, and Renoir, but the patron linked him most readily with Vincent, whose *Spectators at the Arena* (ch. 4, fig. 54) he also owned. Fayet wrote to Gauguin of his admiration for the Vincent who emerged from the published correspondence and of his interest in the references to Gauguin found there.[68] Gauguin could only feel ambivalence: it was gratifying to enter the ranks of those he had long admired, less so to be classed with a man whom he wished to regard as a former pupil.

When Gauguin received the news, in February, that the *Mercure* had rejected his

"Racontars," he said it was all to the good. He had just completed a longer manuscript covering the spectrum of his existence—early memories and intellectual formation, his art and that of others, his loves and hates. Determined to have it published, he again asked Fontainas to use his influence. Entitled *Avant et après* (see fig. 1), it includes the episode that Gauguin had previously restricted to a confidential cover letter: the before-and-after story of his time with Vincent in Arles, embellished with some remarks about the madness of the final days. Elsewhere in the memoir, the title's chronological bookends find another echo, again with regard to Vincent. "Avant" signals the third incarnation of the story of the shrimp still life; "après" marks the account of its rise in the market when it is too late to do the artist any good.[69] This "before and after" embraces the full temporal extent of their relationship and succinctly predicts the fate that Gauguin would share with Vincent.

Vincent had assisted Gauguin in discerning the mythic lineaments by which, since 1888, he had charted his course. But Gauguin, advancing his aims ruthlessly, had sacrificed family and friends. In exile he confronted the price he had paid for a success that seemed perpetually deferred. Homesick and ill on Hiva Oa in 1902, he confessed to his friend Monfreid that he was contemplating a return to France. Monfreid counseled him against this. In Gauguin's absence legend was accumulating around him and around the pictures that seemed to arrive in Paris out of a mysterious void. "Enjoying the immunity of the great departed," Gauguin had already "passed into *the history of art*"—like the unmentioned Vincent. Still Gauguin hoped to escape this sentence, entertaining a scheme in early 1903 of slipping into France—only friends need know—and moving on to disappear in Spain. But he stayed put in the Marquesas and died on 8 May 1903. When news of his death reached France three and a half months later, Morice immediately went to work solidifying the myth. In an October homage in the *Mercure*, he invoked the emblematic wanderer of *Bonjour, Monsieur Gauguin* (ch. 5, fig. 85) and quoted Gauguin's most recent—and self-justifying—

text detailing his time with Vincent in Arles, thus fulfilling his friend's wish to set the record straight. Morice leavened the negative effect of this account by including the "touching" story about the fate of Vincent's five-franc still life. But the time for such defensive strategizing was quickly passing. In a written tribute Morice orchestrated in November, Signac hailed the man whom he and his Neo-Impressionist colleagues had once dismissed as a coarse sailor, proclaiming Gauguin a modern Odysseus whose voyage had benefited the world.[70]

As the evolutionary history of modern art would be written in the early twentieth century, the issues of influence and transmission would loom large. But Gauguin's professions of primacy vis-à-vis Vincent proved unnecessary. The weeding process entailed in the creation of modernism's master discourse resulted in a narrowing of the field and a removal of competing claims that finally allowed the cohabitation of two mythic personas, both so self-evidently original and independent that even their time together was largely consigned to the margins of their respective biographies. Each had effectively shaped his own mythic narrative: Vincent in the corpus of letters, begun well before meeting Gauguin; Gauguin through rewriting the scenario they had invented together. In a very real sense, each fulfilled these narratives with reference to the other and to the Studio of the South—an enduring, but ultimately elusive, motivating force.

28

APPENDIX

TRACING AN INTERACTION: SUPPORTING EVIDENCE, EXPERIMENTAL GROUNDS

BY KRISTIN HOERMANN LISTER, CORNELIA PERES, AND INGE FIEDLER

Gauguin's influence on Vincent, Vincent's effect on Gauguin; the confluence or counterpoint of their individual ideas and practices; their joint experimentation with new materials and techniques; their opposing positions and diverging paths—these are some of the issues that can be clarified and better understood through technical examination of the two artists' work. Each step in the painting process—initial choice of support and ground, underdrawing, application of paint layers, and later compositional changes—contributes to the work's final appearance, and each suggests the artist's particular concerns. For this study we gathered a variety of quantitative information about individual works of art, including canvas thread counts and ground samples, which supplemented visual examination. The character of the brushwork, glimpses of underlayers, and experiments to determine drying time of grounds and paint layers revealed other aspects of the works' making, such as number of sittings or speed of execution. As we learned more about each painting, patterns in each artist's use of materials and techniques emerged, together with relationships among works. At this point we compared these patterns to the hypotheses formulated by the curatorial team based on letter references and other primary and secondary material (including mappings of sites and weather during *plein air* sessions). The goal was to arrive at a probable sequence of paintings produced while Vincent and Gauguin were together in Arles—an unfolding dialogue between the two artists, played out upon their canvases. Our findings turned out to be, in most cases, mutually corroborative. Many of the insights gained by delving beneath the paint surface have been incorporated into chapter 4's chronicle of the Arles period. Here we present the analytical data and technical arguments, with a focus on supports and grounds, that were used in conjunction with curatorial research to establish a chronology for the period in Arles.

Over the past three years, Cornelia Peres, formerly head of conservation at the Van Gogh Museum, Amsterdam, and Kristin Hoermann Lister, conservator at The Art Institute of Chicago, examined twenty-nine of thirty-six paintings by Vincent and sixteen of twenty-one by Gauguin, including nearly all of the pictures in public collections that the artists painted during their nine-week sojourn together in Arles.[1] We also examined important pictures from the preceding months and following year, including Vincent's series paintings of *Sunflowers*, *La Berceuse*, and *The Arlésienne*. The research has involved unprecedented cooperation from institutions around the world, which allowed us to examine the paintings under the microscope in their conservation studios, provided x-radiographs that were assembled for comparative study, and in many cases provided canvas fiber and ground samples for analysis (Table 2). In order to obtain consistent analytical results, most samples were brought to The Art Institute of Chicago, where microscopist Inge Fiedler coordinated the analysis. We are recording information resulting from this extensive study on a computer database that can be updated, revised, and searched by subject to reveal different patterns. Much of the research is still in progress and will be presented in future publications, particularly in the forthcoming *Van Gogh Museum Journal* of 2002.[2] The technical data and analysis should not be regarded simply as material facts and forensic proof, but as elements of a continuing process of discovery and interpretation, raising new questions while answering others.

Supports

Gauguin joined Vincent in Arles on 23 October 1888 and less than two weeks later, Vincent reported: "Gauguin has bought a chest of drawers for the house, and various utensils, and also 20 meters of very strong canvas."[3] Fiber analysis has identified this canvas as jute, and comparison of thread counts and weave patterns as revealed in x-radiographs has indicated that the two artists shared the material equally, using it for their paintings almost exclusively from the time of its purchase until it was depleted in December (Table 1; fig. 3). Both artists' stock of canvas was low before they bought the jute. Gauguin had probably brought only a small piece of unprimed cotton with him from Brittany, and one day prior to his friend's arrival, Vincent had written to Theo asking him to send ten meters of canvas as soon as possible. But two days later, Vincent wrote back to say, "We shall probably give Tasset [his usual supplier of paint and canvas] a miss altogether, because we are going—to a large extent—to make use of cheaper paints, Gauguin as well as I. As for the canvas, we shall prepare it ourselves for the same reason."[4]

The choice of jute as a painting support was highly unorthodox, though the Impressionists had experimented with somewhat coarser canvas weaves.[5] Gauguin was open to experimenting with more unusual supports, having already abandoned the pre-primed linen favored by most artists of the day for cheaper cotton that he primed himself. He would have been familiar with jute (and aware of its low cost) from his brief stint as a tarpaulin salesman in

Denmark a few years earlier, for the material had many common uses, ranging from sacking to carpet backing to tarpaulins. Vincent had himself expressed an interest in coarse canvas earlier that year: "Tasset's absorbent canvas would suit me much better if the canvas itself were three times as rough."[6] Though Vincent and Gauguin seemingly chose the jute for its affordability—and a mistaken regard for its long-term strength—they undoubtedly felt that its crude texture might serve their primitivist inclinations (see fig. 1).[7] Certainly they intended to paint serious pictures on it: all of their works on jute are a standard size 30 (figure) format, 92 x 73 cm, save a few smaller portraits, seemingly painted on the remnants.[8] Paintings of this large size are more than experimental studies; they are considered *tableaux* for exhibition or decorative ensembles, embarked upon with the shared ambition and high expectations that characterized the artists' relationship in its early stage.

In their first days together, before purchasing the jute, Vincent and Gauguin began their artistic dialogue in Arles using supports they had on hand. Pressed by Vincent into beginning a new painting on the second day after his arrival, Gauguin might not have had the materials or the time to prime his own cotton.[9] Thus he borrowed a piece of pre-primed linen from Vincent for his first picture, *Farmhouse in Arles* (W 308). While this work has not previously been dated to this early period in Arles, the canvas' thread count and weave characteristics find an exact match in Vincent's *Sower* (F 494, JH 1617), which

indicates that the two were cut from the same piece of fabric, while Vincent's reference to Gauguin's "large local landscape" in a letter of 28 October including a sketch of his *Sower* suggests that the works were painted at the same time (Table 1).[10] We know that in those first few days Gauguin also began another painting, which Vincent referred to as a "Négresse," but the work is now lost.[11] By the next week, when they went to paint at Arles's famous Roman burial ground, Gauguin had had the opportunity to prime his own cotton canvas. The thread count, weave, and fibrous surface appearance of *Les Alyscamps (The Three Graces at the Temple of Venus)* (W 307) match that of his *Self-Portrait (Les Misérables)* (W 239), painted the previous month, suggesting that Gauguin brought this particular piece of cotton with him from Brittany. Vincent painted his first Alyscamps picture, *The Allée des Tombeaux (Les Alyscamps)* (F 568, JH 1622), on his usual commercially primed linen. Then both artists took up the newly purchased jute.

Scholars have published various lists of the pictures that were most likely painted on this jute, often assigning differing thread counts to the canvases.[12] Comparison of x-radiographs has now determined a group of identical canvases, consistently measuring 5.2 (warp) x 6.5 (weft) threads per centimeter (threads/cm), all undoubtedly cut from the same larger piece of jute fabric (Table 1; fig. 3).[13] Determination of the jute's characteristics enabled the resolution of several basic questions having to do with the extent of the Arles oeuvre. A

TABLE 1: CANVAS THREAD COUNTS AND SIZES[1]

JUTE

Painting (van Gogh)	Size	Painting (Gauguin)	Size
Thread count: 5.2 x 6.5 per cm (Range: 5–5.5 x 6–7; number of counts: 100; average +/- variance: 5.22 +/- 0.02 x 6.45 +/- 0.04)			
Les Alyscamps [F 569, JH 1623] (no thread count)	30[2]	Les Alyscamps [W 306][3]	30
Falling Leaves (Les Alyscamps) [F 487, JH 1621] (no thread count)	30	Human Miseries [W 304]	30 (includes 2cm added strip on left edge)
Falling Leaves (Les Alyscamps) [F 486, JH 1620]	30	In the Heat (The Pigs) [W 318] (no thread count)	30
The Arlésienne (Madame Ginoux [F 489, JH 1625]	30	Night Café [W 305]	30
The Red Vineyard [F 495, JH 1625] (no thread count)	30	Still Life with Pumpkin [W 312; lost][4]	?
Spectators at the Arena [F 548, JH 1653]	30	Washerwomen at the Roubine du Roi Canal [W 303]	30
A Novel Reader [F 497, JH 1632] (no thread count)	30	Washerwomen at the Roubine du Roi Canal [W 302]	30
Memory of the Garden (Etten and Neunen) [F 496, JH 1630]	30	Arles Landscape (Path by the Roubine du Roi Canal) [W 309]	30
The Sower [F 450, JH 1627]	30	Arles Landscape with Two Dogs [W 310][5]	30
Van Gogh's Chair [F 498, JH 1635]	30	Blue Trees ("Vous y passerez, la belle!") [W 311]	30
Gauguin's Chair [F 499, JH 1636]	30	The Painter of Sunflowers [W 296]	30
Sunflowers [F 457, JH 1666]	30 (later extended; 4-cm strip added on the top edge)	Arlésiennes (Mistral) [W 300]	30
Paul Gauguin (Man in a Red Beret) [F 546]	6	Old Man with a Cane [W 318]	not a standard size 70 x 46cm
		Self-Portrait Dedicated to Charles Laval (Later to Eugène Carrière) [W 384]	6
		Self-Portrait [W 297][6]	8

COTTON

Painting (van Gogh)	Size	Painting (Gauguin)	Size
Thread count: 25 x 24 per cm[7] (Range: 24.5–26 x 22.5–25)			
		Les Alyscamps [W 307]	30
		The Artist's Mother (Aline-Marie Gauguin) [W 385]	(6 presently; size has been reduced)[8]
Thread count: 19 x 19 per cm (Range: 18.5–19.5 x 19–20)			
		Madame Roulin [W 298]	15

PRE-PRIMED LINEN

Painting (van Gogh)	Size	Painting (Gauguin)	Size
Thread count: 16 x 16 per cm (Range: 15.5–16.5)			
The Sower [F 494, JH 1617] 30	30	Farmhouse in Arles [W 308]	30
Thread count: 15x12 per cm (Range: 14.5–15.5 x 11.5–13.5; number of counts: 35; average +/- variance: 15.04 +/- 0.07 x 12.5 +/- 0.2)			
Monsieur Ginoux [F 533, JH 1649]	15	Monsieur Ginoux [no W]	6
Armand Roulin [F 493, JH 1643]	15		
Madame Roulin [F 503, JH 1646]	15		
Madame Roulin with Her Baby Marcelle[9] [F 491, JH 1638]	15		
Madame Roulin with Her Baby Marcelle [F 490, JH 1636]	30		
Marcelle Roulin [F 441, JH 1641]	5		
The Dance Hall [F 547, JH 1652]	25		
Thread count: 11.5 x 18 per cm (Range: 11.5–12.5 x 16.5–19.5; number of counts: 55; average +/- variance: 11.64 +/- 0.07 x 18.0 +/- 0.2)			
Brothel Scene [F 478, JH 1599]	6		
The Sower [F 575a, JH 1597]	6		
The Sower [F 451, JH 1629]	6		
Monsieur Roulin [F 434, JH 1647]	15		
Armand Roulin [F 492, JH 1642]	15		
Camille Roulin [F 538, JH 1645]	6		
Camille Roulin [F 537, JH 1644]	6[10]		
Madame Roulin Rocking the Cradle (La Berceuse) [F 508, JH 1671]	30		
Thread count: 12 x 12 per cm (Range: 12–12.5 x 11–12)			
Marcelle Roulin [F 440, JH 1639]	5		
The Arlésienne (Madame Ginoux) [F 488, JH 1624]	30		
Man with a Pipe [F 534, JH 1651]	15? (size has been reduced)[11]		
Linen or cotton, Thread count: 18 x 25 per cm (Range: 17.5–19 x 24–26)			
Camille Roulin [F 665, JH 1879]	15		

1 Unless otherwise stated, thread counts were measured on x-radiographs by Eva Schuchardt. Threads were counted over a 2 cm distance, then divided in half. At least five different areas on each canvas were measured. For each group, a statistical average was taken of all counts to determine the thread count designation. The *range* indicates the spread for all individual counts. The *variance* reflects the scatter of measurements about the average value, 68% of the measurements falling within the quoted uncertainty. For larger groups of canvases, thread count designations were based on this standard method of statistical analysis. For smaller groups statistical analysis is not meaningful so the most frequent counts were used as the thread count designation.

2 Sizes correspond to stretcher sizes available from color merchants (with slight variations by year and merchant). The standard size formats used here are taken from the *Bourgeois aîné* (Trade Catalogue) of 1888, illustrated in David Bomford et al., *Art In the Making: Impressionism*, exh. cat., National Gallery, London (1990), p. 46. Sizes of paintings may vary by a few centimeters, usually as changed by later re-stretching or cutting. Size 30 figure format is 92 x 73 cm, size 25 figure format is 81 x 65 cm, size 15 figure format is 65 x 54 cm, size 8 figure format is 46 x 38 cm, size 6 figure format is 41 x 33 cm, size 5 landscape is 35 x 24 cm, size 5 figure format is 35 x 27 cm.

3 Thread count provided by Sjraar van Heugten.

4 This painting is only known from description in Vincent to Theo, [c. 25 Nov. 1888], 727/558a. It is not known if it was painted on jute, although it is likely, since that was his primary support at that time. The size is also not known. Although Gauguin's still lifes are generally smaller, *Still Life with Japanese Print* (W 375), painted soon after Arles, is a size 30.

5 Thread count measured on back of canvas.

6 Thread count provided by Walter Rossacher.

7 The same thread count is found in several canvases painted by Gauguin in September, the month before he came to Arles, including *Self-Portrait (Les Misérables)* [W 239].

8 The top, bottom, and right sides were folded over the stretcher and cut after painted, so the original size of the portrait is not known.

9 Thread count provided by Charlotte Hale.

10 The bottom edge was extended in an early restoration. The original size 6 format has been restored recently by covering the extension with the frame.

11 The bottom and right edges were folded over the stretcher and cut after painting, so the original size is not known.

number of the pictures under consideration (Gauguin's *Old Man with a Cane* [W 318], *Self-Portrait Dedicated to Laval* [W 384], and *Self-Portrait* [W 297]) had not been firmly dated to this period, and the attribution of two of the works (Vincent's *Portrait of Gauguin* [F 546] and *Sunflowers* [F 457, JH 1666]) had been questioned.[14] All of these works on jute can now be securely placed in Arles.

After characterizing the jute, we considered the alignment of individual works on the larger piece of fabric. Warp and weft directions were determined by evidence of the selvage (the outer warp threads, around which the weft threads turn back into the weave). In most cases, tacking margins were cut during the lining process—an unfortunate practice. They remain intact in several examples: selvages were found on four paintings by Gauguin, *Washerwomen* (W 303), *Arlésiennes (Mistral)* (W 300), *Landscape with Farm* (W 310), and *The Painter of Sunflowers* (W 296).[15] Manufacturers of jute fabric used distinctive warp threads, often dyed, at the selvage; in this jute the selvage is comprised of four uncolored cotton warp threads, a characteristic that has yet to be tied to a particular maker or geographical area.[16] Though the fabric's exact width cannot yet be ascertained, it was likely between 110 and 150 cm. If it were narrower, selvages would appear on both short edges of the size 30 canvases, and if wider, the artists, ever mindful of cost, would surely have cut more pieces in the perpendicular direction, with less waste.[17] With a width in this range, the paintings can be placed to account for exactly twenty meters of fabric as specified by Vincent (fig. 3).

Before proceeding with a discussion of grounds, a final word on the artists' use of jute is in order. Gauguin's subsequent employment of the support has in the past posed problems with the identification of his works from the Arles period. When he arrived in the South Pacific, eighteen months after leaving Arles,

Gauguin once again began painting on jute, and when he returned to France between his Tahitian sojourns (from August 1893 to June 1894) he painted a number of pictures on a jute fabric very similar to that he had used in Arles, but with a slightly looser weave.[18] After he returned to Polynesia for good in 1895, it became his preferred support.[19] None of the jute that he used in Tahiti appears to match the Arles jute, although this has not been checked comprehensively. Vincent did not use jute again after Gauguin's departure from Arles.

TABLE 2: SUPPORT AND GROUND ANALYSIS

Painting	Support[1]	Inorganic (pigments)[2]	Organic (medium)	Comments
Chalk grounds				
Gauguin, *Self-Portrait Dedicated to Vincent van Gogh (Les Misérables)* [W 239]	Cotton[3]	Calcium carbonate (plus minor to trace amounts of sodium, silicon, sulfur and iron)[4]	Protein with some starch[5]	
Gauguin, *Les Alyscamps* [W 307]	Cotton	Calcium carbonate (plus minor amounts of sulfur and silicon)[4]	Protein with some starch[5]	
Van Gogh, *Falling Leaves (Les Alyscamps)* [F 486, JH 1620]	Jute	Calcium carbonate (plus trace amounts of aluminum and silcon)[6]	Protein, possibly some oil[5]	
Barium grounds				
Gauguin, *Human Miseries (Grape Harvest* or *Poverty)* [W 304]	Jute	Barium sulfate (plus minor amounts of silicon and calcium)[4]	Unidentified medium (plus beeswax and trace of conifer resin)[5, 7]	The presence of beeswax interfered with the attempt to identify the binding medium.[5] Conifer resin and beeswax probably from the wax lining.[7] Chalk on reverse, assumed to be old lining adhesive, was subsequently removed.[8]
Gauguin, *Washerwomen at the Roubine du Roi Canal* [W 303]	Jute	Barium sulfate (plus minor to trace amounts of silicon and calcium)[4]	Protein and starch[9]	
Gauguin, *Old Man with a Cane* [W 318]	Jute	Traces of barium sulfate particles in an organic binder[10]	Insufficient sample; possible protein was found[5]	Low percent of inorganic pigment to binder
Gauguin, *Madame Roulin* [W 298]	Cotton	Barium sulfate and calcium carbonate mixture? (The following elements were detected: major amounts of barium, calcium, and sulfur; minor to trace amounts of sodium, aluminum, silicon, chlorine, potassium, and iron in an organic binder.)[4]	Animal glue and starch[9]	Low percent of inorganic pigment to binder
Van Gogh, *Spectators at the Arena* [F 548, JH 1653]	Jute[11]	Barium sulfate (plus trace of calcium)[12]	Animal glue and oil[13]	
Van Gogh, *Memory of the Garden (Etten and Neunen)* [F 496, JH 1630]	Jute[11]	Barium sulfate (plus minor to trace amounts of silicon, calcium, and potassium)[4, 14]	Animal glue and oil[13]	
Van Gogh, *Van Gogh's Chair* [F 498, JH 1635]	Jute	Barium sulfate (plus chlorine, and minor to trace amounts of calcium and silicon)[4, 14]	Linseed oil (with traces of animal glue)[15, 16]	Glue possibly associated with consolidation treatment at cracks.
Van Gogh, *Paul Gauguin (Man in a Red Beret)* [F 546]	Jute	Barium sulfate (plus chlorine and minor to trace amounts of aluminum, silicon, potassium, and calcium)[4, 10]	Protein (plus trace of oil and conifer resin)[5, 7]	Oil and conifer resin possibly from the lining adhesive, which contains lead white, oil, and conifer resin.[5, 7]
Lead and lead/zinc grounds				
Gauguin, *Washerwomen at the Roubine du Roi Canal* [W 302]	Jute	Lead white (plus possible trace of silicon)[4]	Drying oil and possibly some wax[5, 7]	There is a chalk layer on reverse; SEM/EDX analysis indicated calcium (plus sulfur and traces of magnesium, aluminum, silicon, and iron).[4] Painting has an aqueous lining. Wax possibly from original wax coating.[17]
Gauguin, *Blue Trees ("Vous y passerez, la belle!")* [W 311]	Jute	Lead white (plus possible trace of silicon)[4]	Drying oil[5]	There is a chalk layer on reverse; SEM/EDX analysis indicated calcium plus trace of sulfur.[4] Chalk, mixed with a protein medium, was also found on canvas front of one sample.[4, 5]
Gauguin, *The Painter of Sunflowers* [W 296]	Jute[18]	Lead white (plus possible trace of silicon)[4, 18]	Walnut oil with small percent of non-drying oil (castor oil)[18]	
Gauguin, *Arles Landscape (Path by the Roubine du Roi Canal)* [W 309]	Jute	Lead white (plus possible trace of silicon)[4]	Drying oil[5]	
Gauguin, *Arlésiennes (Mistral)* [W 300]	Jute	1 Top layer consists of two separate layers: (a) lead white and zinc white on top, and (b) lead white, plus trace of zinc white underneath. 2 Bottom layer consists of calcium carbonate (plus minor to trace amounts of magnesium, aluminum, silicon, sulfur, and iron)[10]	1 Drying oil[5] 2 Protein and wax[5]	Wax probably from wax emulsion cleaning.[19]
Gauguin, *Self-Portrait Dedicated to Charles Laval (Later to Eugène Carrière)* [W 384]	Jute	Lead white (plus minor amount of silicon)[4]	Drying oil[5]	There is a chalk layer on the reverse of canvas; SEM/EDX indicated calcium (plus sulfur, silicon, and minor to trace amounts of magnesium, aluminum, and potassium).[4]
Van Gogh, *Gauguin's Chair* [F 499, JH 1636]	Jute	1 Top layer consists of a mixture of almost equal amounts of zinc white and lead white. 2 Bottom layer contains lead white plus a few percent magnesium.[4, 10]	Drying oil[5]	Painting is wax lined. Starch, possibly a size layer, was found in addition to oil in one sample.[5]
No ground				
Gauguin, *The Artist's Mother (Aline-Marie Gauguin)* [W 385]	Cotton	No apparent ground	Protein[5]	Protein is probably a size layer.[5]

Painting	Support[1]	Inorganic (pigments)[2]	Organic (medium)	Comments
Van Gogh, *Brothel Scene* [F 478, JH 1599]	Linen	Possibly two layers of lead white: top layer contains coarser lead white particles; the bottom layer also contains trace of silicon.[10]	Not analyzed	Top layer of lead white was present on 1 of 2 samples analyzed.[10]
Van Gogh, *The Sower* [F 575a, JH 1596]	Linen	Single layer of lead white (plus barium sulfate and possibly some silicon)[10]	Linseed oil[7]	
Van Gogh, *The Sower* [F 451, JH 1629]	Linen	Single layer of lead white (plus barium sulfate and possible trace of silicon)[6]	Drying oil, conifer resin and beeswax[7]	Protein, probably a size layer, detected in small spot.[5] Conifer resin and beeswax probably from the wax lining.

1 Fibers identified using polarized light microscopy and microchemical tests by Inge Fiedler and Eva Schuchardt, The Art Institute of Chicago, unless otherwise indicated.

2 Inorganic compound identifications are based on SEM/EDX (Scanning Electron Microscopy/ Energy Dispersive X-Ray Spectrometry) elemental analysis coupled usually with FTIR (Fourier Transform Infrared Microspectroscopy) spectra. Minor or trace elements detected by SEM/EDX are noted in paentheses, without being assigned to specific compounds.

3 Fibers analyzed by Dorothy Catling, former-ly of the Forensic Laboratory, Metropolitan Police Force, London, facilitated by Ashok Roy, National Gallery, London.

4 SEM/EDX analysis conducted by Michael Bayard and Inge Fiedler. Use of instrument courtesy of McCrone Research Institute, Chicago.

5 FTIR analysis conducted by Michelle Derrick and Richard Newman, Museum of Fine Arts, Boston.

6 SEM/EDX analysis by Muriel Geldof and Karin Groen, Instituut Collectie Nederland, in collaboration with Kees Mensch, Shell Research and Technology Centre, Amsterdam (SRTCA).

7 GC/MS (Gas Chromatography/Mass spectrometry) analysis conducted by Richard Newman, Museum of Fine Arts, Boston. GC/MS procedure: samples were heated for one to two hours in 10–20 microliters of a transesterification

reagent, Alltech 'Meth Prep 2' (0.2N [m-tri-fluoromethylphenyl] trimethylammonium hydroxide in methanol) mixed 1:1 by volume with benzene).

8 Conservation report, personal communi-cation, Henrik Bjerre, Statens Museum for Kunst, Copenhagen.

9 FTIR analysis conducted by Mary Miller, MVA, Inc., Atlanta.

10 SEM/EDX analysis of paint cross sections conducted by Tim Vander Wood, MVA, Inc., Atlanta.

11 Fiber identification provided by Helen Mikolaychuk, The State Hermitage Museum, St. Petersburg.

12 XRF (X-Ray Fluorescence) analysis courtesy of Alexander Kossolapov, The State Hermitage Museum, St. Petersburg.

13 Binding medium analysis conducted by Liudmila Gavrilenko, The State Hermitage Museum, St. Petersburg.

14 EDX analysis courtesy Ashok Roy.

15 GC/MS analysis courtesy of Raymond White, National Gallery, London.

16 FTIR analysis courtesy of Raymond White.

17 Conservation treatment report, The Museum of Modern Art, New York.

18 See Vojtěch Jirat-Wasiutyński and H. Travers Newton in Peres et al. 1991, pp. 90–102, 103–111.

19 Conservation Treatment report, The Art Institute of Chicago Conservation Department.

Grounds for the Jute

After cutting the jute and tacking it onto stretchers or strainers, the artists prepared a ground—combining one or more binding media with a pigment or filler—and applied it to the canvas surface with a brush or knife.[20] The grounds were unevenly applied—gener-ally thin but with a slight build-up at the periphery, and often do not extend to the edges of the canvas. It is not known how many canvases the artists would have primed at one time. Presumably they had a number of size 30 stretchers at their disposal and would have stretched and primed canvases in batches, so that they could minimize preparation time and, later, could have several works in progress simultaneously. As the rough texture and loose weave of the jute presented unfamiliar chal-lenges, the artists experimented with various options for grounds. Ground analysis suggests that Vincent and Gauguin first tried chalk as a filler, then barium sulfate, and then lead white and lead/zinc white mixtures (Table 2).[21] This

sequence provides new evidence for a par-ticular chronological ordering of the paintings (see fig. 3).

Chalk/Glue

Chalk/glue grounds are found on both of the samples available for paintings from the Alyscamps campaign, Gauguin's *Three Graces* (W 307) on cotton and Vincent's *Falling Leaves* (F 486, JH 1620) on jute. Though a lead white/oil ground was then more commonly used, Gauguin preferred the absorbency of chalk/glue priming.[22] He wrote to Georges-Daniel de Monfreid in 1899: "For the last twelve years, as you know, I've been painting on absorbent canvas and I have had to my own taste the desired color effects and color stability."[23] Such grounds absorbed oil out of the paint layer, which facilitated Gauguin's technique of thinly layering colors, as the brushstrokes dried quickly and he could apply successive layers without muddying them. Moreover the

colors would darken less with age, and the hues—although less deeply saturated—would be bright, the values close, and the surface more matte. Earlier in 1888 Gauguin charac-terized this effect in auditory terms: "I like Brittany. I find a certain wildness and primi-tiveness here. When my clogs echo on this granite soil I hear the dull, muted, powerful tone I seek in my painting."[24] Painting on an absorbent ground could quite literally be com-pared to walking on sound-absorbing soil; the coarseness of the jute would add an even more powerful, primitive aspect.

Vincent too had recently expressed a desire for more absorbent grounds; a month after arriving in Arles he had "bought some coarse canvas here, and had it prepared for matte effects," having depleted his stock of commer-cially primed, absorbent canvas. Vincent did not "care overmuch for oil," and knew that an absorbent ground would help him achieve "fresher colors which would perhaps darken less," but in larger terms it served his rustic aesthetic and preference for a less polished effect; as he wrote to Theo, "We do not object to the canvas having a rough look."[25]

Barium Sulfate

Very soon after beginning to paint on jute in early November both artists abandoned the chalk/glue priming in favor of a highly idiosyncratic barium sulfate ground. Unknown in the works of any other artists, its use is apparently restricted to this group of paintings on jute by Vincent and Gauguin. What prompted this unusual choice? The artists clearly wished to exploit, rather than mask, the jute's rough texture, and thinly applied barium sulfate allowed the support to assert itself while creating enough of an isolating layer to prevent the oil paint from soaking into the highly absorbent jute fibers.[26] This type of ground has a porous, translucent beige appearance; indeed it is almost invisible, and canvases prepared with it often look unprimed.[27] The seemingly raw jute would thus have asserted a crude visual presence, providing an underlying earthy tonality that may have colored the artists' approach as they painted on it. For Gauguin the jute recalled the brown stoneware ceramics he had made in the winter of 1886–87 using a coarser-bodied clay.[28] Certainly both Gauguin and Vincent adopted broader, simpler handling in many of their works on jute. Without a white ground, Gauguin's thin overlapping veils of color were not effective, and he applied the paint more thickly (as in *Human Miseries*) and opaquely (as in *Night Café*) on these jute works than in his other paintings. Vincent usually did use thick impasto, but on jute it lost its crisp, gestural form and took on a rougher edge. He worked with broad, flat planes in *Falling Leaves* (F 486, JH 1620) and *Spectators in the Arena*, virtually abandoning his impasto in the latter. Analysis has confirmed barium sulfate grounds on four jute paintings by Vincent and three by Gauguin (who also used it on one cotton canvas) (Table 2); because the ground's distinctive appearance allows identification through visual examination, we can surmise that Vincent used it on at least three other works that he completed, painting more quickly than Gauguin, during the time they experimented with the ground (see fig. 3).

In preparing supports with barium sulfate, Gauguin used a mixture of glue and starch, as he had with his chalk grounds, while Vincent used mixtures of glue and oil (Table 2). Preliminary re-creations of these grounds have indicated that both the starch and oil made the glue grounds easier to brush out thinly. An oil/glue mixture took only slightly longer to dry than the starch/glue, and remained flexible for a longer period. Barium sulfate tends to become transparent in oil, although too much oil in the medium darkens the jute fibers.[29] Many factors may have influenced the artists' choices of media, including ease of application, drying time, appearance, absorbency, strength, flexibility, and aging characteristics. Further research is needed to correlate the actual appearance and components of the paintings themselves with the results of test re-creations of similar grounds. It is particularly important to consider not only what Vincent and Gauguin may have understood from contemporary sources to be the relative merits of these components and mixtures, but also the actual working properties they encountered.[30]

Lead White

The barium sulfate grounds may have proved unsatisfactory in some way, for analysis has revealed that sometime in the week of 19 November, both artists began painting on canvases prepared with lead white in oil instead. They must have decided to change grounds earlier still, since a lead white ground requires about one week to dry. Gauguin executed at least four paintings on this lead white ground.

Then for *Arlésiennes (Mistral)* (W 300), one of his last works on jute, he used a mixture of lead white and zinc white, even slower to dry; Vincent also employed a mixture of both whites for one of his final paintings on jute, *Gauguin's Chair* (F 499, JH 1636).[31] A transition from the virtually transparent barium sulfate to the opaque white grounds serves as another potential dating indicator, suggesting, for instance, that Gauguin produced the experimental and abstract *Washerwomen* (W 303) with a barium sulfate ground, before executing the more spatially resolved and restrained version of the same subject (W 302), which has a lead white ground. It also suggests that Vincent painted his own comparatively naturalistic chair (on barium sulfate) before the more synthetic picture of Gauguin's (on lead white). Indeed Vincent's mention of the chair pendants in a letter from around 23 November can even serve as a tentative moment for the switch to lead white.[32]

Both artists may have decided they preferred reflective white grounds for enhanced color effects, although the chalk ground they used at first in late October could have also provided this.[33] However, this was apparently not the immediate reason for Gauguin's shift to white lead grounds, for he did not take advantage of it in his second *Washerwomen* (W 302; his first lead white ground), in which heavily worked-up blue and green underlayers largely obfuscate the ground's luminosity. However, in the two later Arles landscapes on lead white grounds (W 309, W 310) he exploited reflective effects by using his former technique of applying myriad colors in overlapping strokes. Vincent may have chosen the lead white ground because he found the jute treated with barium sulfate to be simply too absorbent, preventing him from achieving the saturated colors and strong tonal contrast that he preferred. His thicker paint layers were also more vulnerable to flaking if too much oil was wicked out by an absorbent ground and canvas.[34]

TABLE 3: CANVAS SHIPMENTS MENTIONED IN LETTERS

Date/letter	Receipt of canvas	Requests canvas	Out of canvas
[c. 12 September 1888] (684/535)		"I'll need another 5 meters of ordinary canvas at 2.50 francs, but of course when Tasset is figuring the weight of the parcel, he should send a meter more or a meter less so as not to double the postage."	
[c. 17 September 1888] (687/539)			"My paints, my canvas and my purse are all completely exhausted today."
[c. 26 September 1888] (691/541a)	"Thank you . . . for the consignment of canvas and colors from Tasset's . . . "	"What does Père Tanguy say of the gross-grained paints now? I think I must warn him at once that I still want 5 or even 10 meters of canvas."	
[c. 27 September 1888] (692/541)		"It is very urgent for me to have . . . 5 meters of canvas, too."	
[c. 29 September 1888] (695/543)		"Tanguy's parcel has arrived [apparently only containing paint] . . . I now hope to be able to do something for the next exhibition during the autumn. What is most urgent now is 5 or even 10 meters of canvas."	
[3 October 1888] (698/544)			"I haven't any more canvas left."
[8 October 1888] (703/546)		"I must also buy some canvas and prepare it myself, as Tasset's has not yet come. Would you ask him as soon as possible if he has sent it off, 10 meters or at least 5 of ordinary canvas at 2.50 francs."	
[8–9 October 1888] (704/547)		"*Tasset has not sent any canvas.* It is very, very urgent, do please order 10 or any rate 5 meters from him at once. It is very urgent, because already I have bought some canvas here."	
[c. 9 October 1888] (705/548)	"I received notice of the arrival of Tasset's canvas. Great!"		
[c. 22 October 1888] (715/551)		"As soon as you can, at once even if it's possible, I need 10 more meters of canvas at 2.50 francs."	
[24 October 1888] (717/557)		"We shall probably give Tasset a miss altogether, because we are going . . . to make use of cheaper paints. . . . As for the canvas, we shall prepare it ourselves for the same reason."	
27 October 1888 (718/T3) Theo to Vincent		"Tasset will send you the paints and the canvas shortly."	
[c. 5 November 1888] (722/559)	"Gauguin has bought . . . 20 meters of very strong canvas [jute]."		
[c. 16 November 1888] (724/562)	"Tasset's package arrived the day before yesterday, and we were very pleased with it."		
[c. 13 April 1889] (762/584)		"I have been obliged to ask Tasset for 10 meters of canvas and some tubes."	

For both artists, it seems probable that the change to lead white was partially motivated by a concern for the stability of the glue grounds.[35] Lead white in oil was historically advocated for priming canvases because it provides a stronger, more flexible and cohesive layer than glue grounds, which tend to become brittle or friable and more likely to flake when the support is not held rigid or is exposed to moisture. Vincent usually removed his completed pictures from their stretchers or strainers and, once the paint was nominally dry, stacked them. Imprints from the overlying canvas onto the still-soft impasto beneath frequently resulted from this practice. He then shipped groups of pictures to Theo in Paris, who had them mounted onto new stretchers. When Gauguin sent five paintings to Theo around 22 November, he removed them from their stretchers and rolled them for shipment. The jute was difficult to stretch evenly, and Gauguin gave Theo special instructions for doing so:

The way to do it is to stretch them as much as possible and dampen them overall, and not key out the stretcher until later when the canvases are dry and limp. That way they take the form of the stretcher well. You probably know all that better than I. . . . As I am sending them freshly painted, I am anxious to know if they have arrived in good shape.[36]

Shipping the unrestrained canvases, restretching them, and applying moisture could well have caused flaking of ground and paint.

Gauguin learned from Schuffenecker, in a letter of 11 December, that his *Human Miseries* already showed signs of a serious flaking problem when Theo exhibited it in Paris.[37] Gauguin surmised that it was "caused by the preparation," namely the barium sulfate ground, and he later confirmed this in a letter to Vincent from Paris.[38] But even before this, concern for stability probably persuaded the artists to abandon the glue ground in favor of oil-based priming.

It is interesting to note that chalk grounds turn up once again in Gauguin's later jute paintings—on the reverse of several canvases with lead white grounds on the front (Table 2).[39] When this type of layer was previously noticed in isolated instances, it was presumed to have

been added by a later restorer during the lining process rather than by Gauguin himself. Of the paintings with chalk on the reverse, however, one is unlined, one has a wax lining, and several others have aqueous linings, making it improbable that the chalk layer was connected with the lining process.[40] More likely, the chalk ground is further evidence of the intensive experimental process in which both artists were engaged at this time. There are several possible explanations for Gauguin's application of the chalk layer. Perhaps he became dissatisfied with the chalk/glue ground in late October/early November, setting aside canvases primed with it and then retrieving them about a month later to turn them over and re-prime them with new lead white grounds. Perhaps in Arles he had turned

over a chalk-primed canvas simply to make use of the other side, and found that it served a purpose in providing added stability, for he seems to have proceeded on this assumption in later instances.[41] For *Arlésiennes (Mistral)*, Gauguin actually added a second lead/zinc-white ground directly *over* the earlier chalk ground, largely obscuring the jute's texture.

The combination of lead white on the front and chalk on the reverse may serve as a useful indicator for establishing the sequence of Gauguin's works from this period.[42] Two of his self-portraits (W 384, W 297) have frequently been dated to after the Arles period.[43] Both works, however, are executed on the jute purchased in Arles, and *Self-Portrait Dedicated to Charles Laval* (W 384) has a lead

GAUGUIN

 W 306  W 305 **B**  W 304 **B**  W 301 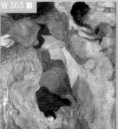 W 303 **B** 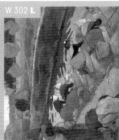 W 302 **L** *Still Life with Pumpkin W 312; lost*

VAN GOGH

 F 569  F 487  F 486 **C**  F 489 **B**  F 495 **B**  F 548 **B**  F 497

Thread count and orientation
White background: confirmed jute fiber, thread count and orientation
Yellow background: jute fiber, thread count and orientation not confirmed

Size
Existing tacking margins were generally 2 cm or less, so size 30 canvases (92 x 73 cm) with tacking margins are measured at 96 x 77 cm on the diagram, except those with wider tacking margins and smaller canvases as listed:

W 318: 74 x 51 cm
W 309 with wider tacking margins: 83 x 96 cm
W 384: 44 x 36 cm
W 297: 50 x 41
F 450, JH 1627 with wider tacking margins: 79 x 96 cm
F 546: 41 x 36 cm

Ground
White letter: confirmed ground analysis
Black letter: ground estimated by appearance

C   chalk
B   barium sulfate
L   lead white
LZ lead white/zinc white

white ground on the front and chalk on the reverse, suggesting it should be dated to December 1888.[44] The other self-portrait (W 297) has a layer on the reverse that may tie it to the December canvases, but since a painting datable to 1889 is depicted within it, Gauguin probably completed it after leaving Arles. Perhaps Gauguin had already cut, stretched, primed, or even begun this picture in Arles and then finished it later.

At the end of November, spurred on by Vincent, the two artists turned their attention to portraits. A few months after arriving in Arles, Vincent had written that he believed the most enduring aspect of his oeuvre would be portraiture: "The best thing to do would be to make portraits, all kinds of portraits of women and children."[45] Outside of sporadic sittings using some friends and locals from Arles as models, however, Vincent had not had the opportunity to fully explore the genre he so admired. In November he embarked on a more extensive campaign in which Gauguin, to a lesser extent, participated. The jute, as noted above, led the artists to modify their handling; correspondingly it may have influenced their choice of subjects. Considerations of subject in turn affected the choice of support.

Some jute still remained, but Vincent's mid-November shipment of pre-primed linen offered an alternative (see Table 3; fig. 2).

Gauguin executed six portraits—modest in scale—at this time, two on cotton, one on pre-primed linen, and three on the remaining jute. He saved his last five large pieces of jute (with the exception of that used for his *Painter of Sunflowers*) for the landscapes he was painting concurrently. Gauguin executed his unfinished portrait of *Monsieur Ginoux* (Van Gogh Museum) on a piece of pre-primed linen he obtained from Vincent, as he had done for *Farmhouse in Arles* at the beginning of his stay. A comparison of thread counts and weave characteristics reveals it to be the same canvas Vincent used for his own portrait of the

3
Diagram of 20-meter
length of jute

same subject (F 533, JH 1649) (Table 1). Perhaps Ginoux's sitting for the artists was impromptu, and Gauguin had insufficient time to prime a piece of jute or cotton; perhaps its unfinished state indicates that the pre-primed support (or the sitter) did not engage him. He painted his other male portraits (*Old Man with a Cane* [W 318], *The Painter of Sunflowers* [W 296], and *Self-Portrait Dedicated to Charles Laval* [W 384]) on the coarse jute, while executing his two portraits of women (*Madame Roulin* [W 298] and *The Artist's Mother* [W 385]) on cotton with a much finer weave. This male/female dichotomy reflects in exaggerated form the long-standing tradition that women should be portrayed in a more refined manner.[46] Apparently Gauguin had run out of the small supply of cotton he had initially brought from Brittany and used for his *Three Graces* (W 307). The cotton used for *Madame Roulin* is of a different weave, but the portrait of Gauguin's mother is painted on a canvas, cut out of an earlier composition, with a thread count matching that of the *Three Graces*. Though the earlier work is completely covered, its blue and green paint layers are visible at the edge where Gauguin cut through them. He commonly worked up his compositions in blue and green underlayers before applying final colors, so their presence here may indicate that the underlying work remained unfinished. Conceivably it is part of the now-lost "Négresse" that Vincent reported to Theo during the first weeks.[47]

Vincent threw himself much more wholeheartedly into portraiture than did Gauguin. At the end of November, he began a series of paintings on pre-primed linen depicting members of the Roulin family. There were technical reasons why he might have preferred this support for portraiture. In rendering a sitter, Vincent's usual technique was to sculpt a face with distinct, directional brushstrokes, but the coarse texture of the jute tended to disrupt individual strokes. He had learned this when executing his first version of *The Arlésienne (Madame Ginoux)* on jute; the effect was decidedly coarse, although this was in part due to the speed with which it was painted—"slashed on in an hour."[48] When a few weeks later he had the opportunity to paint multiple portraits of the Roulins, Vincent apparently wished to proceed differently. Pre-primed linen allows for a higher degree of definition than jute; moreover it was also more practical for the intensive campaign he had in mind because it could be cut and stretched to size in a matter of minutes, while the jute had to be primed and dried in advance.[49] The idiosyncratic jute was more distracting to paint upon and less acceptable to sitters (who often received a version as compensation). The notable exception is Vincent's *Portrait of Gauguin*, painted on a remnant of jute, perhaps because Vincent felt the material had become emblematic of his friend, who had initially purchased it.[50]

As with works on jute, technical evidence can be brought to bear in establishing a more definite sequence for Vincent's paintings on pre-primed linen from the Arles period. A brief overview of our approach is presented here, though further study is still required.[51] After Vincent failed to find inexpensive paints and canvas to his liking in Arles, he relied on his brother to place orders for painting materials with his suppliers in Paris, Tasset et L'Hôte and "Père" Tanguy, who then sent them on to Arles (Table 3).[52] The correspondence between Vincent and Theo therefore serves to document Vincent's use of materials, though he also supplemented his supplies with local purchases that he occasionally mentioned in his letters. Vincent generally requested a five- or ten-meter piece of pre-primed linen canvas,

sometimes specifying the quality and whether it should come from Tasset or Tanguy. Knowing the orders he placed and the pictures he painted, it becomes possible to determine which individual pictures were cut from each larger piece. For this purpose, the pictures were first grouped by thread count (Table 1), but thread counts are relatively consistent for each supplier and are sometimes identical across different orders. The size and ground layers, by contrast, exhibit slight differences in layering, particle size, and trace elements, allowing for more precise groupings.[53] It was beyond the scope of this study consistently to obtain ground samples of Vincent's commercially primed canvases for comparison with those he used before and after Gauguin's stay, but recent research conducted by Ella Hendriks, conservator at the Van Gogh Museum, in collaboration with the Netherlands Institute of Cultural Heritage, has established that comparative ground analysis can be an important tool for distinguishing between these shipments and thus for dating the works.[54] Examination and comparison of x-radiographs reveal further evidence of manufacturers' priming procedure—such as the cusping that resulted when the fabric (often 2 x 10 meters) was stretched onto the priming frame, as well as the application marks left by the knife used to spread the ground across the canvas—which can be used to link one painting with another.[55] Finally, by determining the warp and weft direction of the canvas, matching irregularities in the weave and ground application, and noting which paintings exhibit primary cusping on their edges, a group of paintings can be roughly aligned and fit onto the larger piece of canvas in a manner similar to that demonstrated for the twenty-meter piece of jute.

While this process may seem to reduce the works of art to mathematical equations and minute bits of data, in fact the resulting ordering of the paintings brings new connections to light, uncovering choices the artist made and circumstances that influenced his choices. Until beginning the portraits of the Roulins, Vincent's commitment to the jute was so complete that he ventured to paint only three small (size 6; 41 x 33 cm) studies on pre-primed canvas (*Brothel Scene* [F 478, JH 1599] and two *Sowers* [F 451, JH 1629; and F 575a, JH 1596]), though he apparently still had larger pieces of it remaining from his last shipment, of 9 October. All three small pictures are painted on the 11.5 x 18 threads/cm canvas most commonly provided by Tasset.[56] Only the *Sower* from the Van Gogh Museum (JH 1629) is generally considered to have been painted in November, based on a letter reference (with a sketch) of around 25 November that mentions the larger version of the composition.[57] The two others, *Brothel Scene* and *The Sower* (JH 1596), have been dated to early October, before Gauguin's arrival, but ground analysis strongly suggests that the latter was cut from the same piece of canvas as the Van Gogh Museum *Sower*.[58] Analysis of *Brothel Scene*'s ground is inconclusive, but the canvas is small enough to have been a leftover scrap from a still earlier order. Moreover, it closely resembles the early November *Spectators at the Arena* (on jute) in terms of its very atypical technique, suggesting a short-lived foray into painting *de tête* (from memory), inspired by Gauguin, that Vincent tried on both supports, perhaps first as an experiment on the small pieces of pre-primed canvas.

The order in which Vincent painted the late November/early December portraits has never been deciphered, but certain groupings are suggested by similarities in canvas type and painting technique, in conjunction with an early December letter reference, which mentions sitters and canvas size: "I have made

portraits of a *whole family*, that of the postman whose head I had done previously—the man, his wife, the baby, the little boy, and the son of sixteen. . . . Size 15 canvases."[59] Six size 15 portraits are therefore considered to comprise this first group: two versions of *Armand Roulin* (F 493, JH 1643; F 492, JH 1642), *Joseph Roulin* (F 434; JH 1647), *Camille Roulin* (F 665, JH 1879), *Madame Roulin* (F 503, JH 1646), and *Madame Roulin with Her Baby Marcelle* (F 491, JH 1638).[60] Comparison of thread counts reveals that Vincent used three different types of canvas for this group (though not necessarily successively). The two portraits on 11.5 x 18 threads/cm canvas—*Joseph Roulin* and one of the portraits of Armand (F 492, JH 1642)— probably represent the last pieces of canvas remaining from the 9 October shipment. They were cut from adjacent pieces of canvas; a diagonal band of thicker ground left by the priming knife as well as a double-thread weave defect match up when x-radiographs of the works are placed edge to edge.[61] The portrait of Camille (F 665, JH 1879) is painted on a canvas of 18 x 25 threads/cm, which is anomalous to the period and provides no clue as yet for dating.[62] The unusually broad handling (the facial planes constructed with flat abstract patches of ruddy color, sharp highlights, and green shadows) conforms to that used for the portrait of Joseph Roulin from this group and in the larger, size 30 *Madame Roulin and Her Baby Marcelle* (F 490, JH 1637) painted soon thereafter. This schematic technique probably evolved from Vincent's recent work *de tête*, and reflects a search for a more synthetic method of painting, another stylistic experiment particular to this moment. The three remaining size 15 portraits—of Armand (F 493, JH 1643), Madame Roulin (F 503, JH 1646), and Madame Roulin and baby Marcelle (F 491, JH 1638)— are all painted on a different canvas, of 15 x 12 threads/cm, which may belong to the ship-

ment that arrived in mid-November, probably the ten meters of 2.50-franc canvas Vincent requested the day before Gauguin's arrival (see Tables 1 and 3).[63] Vincent went on to use it for the size 30 paintings *Madame Roulin with Her Baby Marcelle* (F 490, JH 1637) and *The Dance Hall* (F 547, JH 1652), and both artists used it for their portraits of Joseph-Michel Ginoux (no W number; and F 533, JH 1649).

These eight pictures on 15 x 12 threads/cm canvas account for only a 2.25-meter length of two-meter-wide fabric, only a quarter of the ten meters Vincent asked for in October, yet Vincent did not use this canvas again for some time. Theo may have reduced the order after Vincent informed him that he would be preparing his own canvas.[64] If this is the case, and the Roulin project depleted Vincent's supply of 15 x 12 threads/cm canvas, it would explain why a small group of paintings from this period (*Marcelle Roulin* [F 440, JH 1639], *The Arlésienne* [F 488, JH 1624], and *Man with a Pipe* [F 534, JH 1651]) are painted on a different, 12 x 12 threads/cm canvas, a type known to be available locally.[65]

Vincent's *La Berceuse* (F 508, JH 1671), painted on a size 30, 11.5 x 18 threads/cm canvas, likely coincided with a new shipment of canvas, as a number of pictures that followed in January 1889 are also on the same support. However, there is no mention of a December shipment in the letters; indeed, after mid-November 1888, Vincent neither requested nor acknowledged receipt of canvas until mid-April 1889.[66] X-radiographs of several December and January pictures reveal that two versions of *La Berceuse* (JH 1671, Museum of Fine Arts, Boston; and JH 1670, The Art Institute of Chicago) have priming marks that match those of two January pictures, *Still Life with Drawing Board and Onions* (F 604, JH 1656) and *Sunflowers* (F 458, JH 1667). A distinctive 14–18-cm band of thicker ground along one edge of all four canvases indicates that they were all cut from one side of the same large piece of primed fabric. While the order of the five versions of *La Berceuse* is open to conjecture, this provides further evidence that these two are among the first, perhaps preceded by the two size 6 versions of *Camille Roulin* (F 538, JH 1645; and F 537, JH 1644), also painted on the 11.5 x 18 threads/cm canvas. These two synthetically stylized portraits seem to be precursors to the *Berceuse*, with similar radiant yellow faces sculpted of small encrusted strokes. The brushwork of the first (JH 1645) searches out the form, while in the second (JH 1644) it is played back more deliberately and rhythmically, indicating that this is the order in which Vincent painted them.

Areas for Further Research

The thread counts of the Roulin portraits only begin to tell the story of their interrelationships. As is suggested in chapter 4, Gauguin encouraged Vincent to compose a picture from the imagination rather than transcribing an actual site or model. To this end, Vincent employed a system of tracing that is more fully described in the forthcoming *Van Gogh Museum Journal* of 2002. Such case studies constitute narratives of production within the larger narrative of the Arles oeuvre. The "big picture," constructed from the pieces of data, was our first priority, as outlined here: to identify and place in sequence the works Vincent and Gauguin produced in dialogue with one another, encountering new materials and subjects side by side. Ongoing interpretation of the data already collected; further technical examination and ground analysis of these and other works by the artists; and investigation of specific areas such as their use of tracings and the variations in the composition of their paints will continue to shed even more light on the question of their mutual influence.

Acknowledgment

The authors wish to thank Ella Hendriks, Van Gogh Museum, Amsterdam, for sharing her own research into many of these issues, and for her advice during the writing of this appendix.

Methodology

The following general aspects of each painting were systematically examined (among many others specific to each object and conditions of examination): format (changes in size since painted); canvas (characteristics including tacking edges); ground (characteristics including method of application); underdrawing (Vincent almost invariably used a contour sketch, while Gauguin's are not readily apparent); underlying painted sketch (found in Vincent's paintings in dark blue and various other colors, and invariably in dark blue in Gauguin's); underpainting or initial lay-in (Vincent sometimes blocked in thin, flat underlayers in some areas, while Gauguin usually worked up primary forms with blue and green tones before applying final colors); paint quality (consistency, inclusions, gloss, fading and discoloration, color contrast, modulations, and mixing); brushwork (brush size, application patterns and gestures, modeling, layering, surface texture, impasto, palette-knife work, imprints, contour work, expressive character, speed); build-up order and number of sessions (which areas were still wet when adjacent or subsequent layers were painted, and the order in which different areas were painted); changes by the artist (at any stage of the drawing and painting process); signature and inscriptions (including significant inscriptions or labels on reverse); changes in appearance (due to aging, damage, or conservation treatment); technical and stylistic interchange between Vincent and Gauguin (sharing of materials, techniques, motifs, and approach). In addition to the microscope, optical aids included an Inframetrics infrared vidicon camera, which allows layers below the paint surface to be seen. Vincent's paint layers were generally too thick to allow lower layers to be viewed; Gauguin's thinner paint layers were more easily penetrated. This revealed that during the painting process, Gauguin made many changes and adjustments as he developed his compositions. X-radiographs were used to study canvas, brushwork, build-up, compositional adjustments, and paint quality.

1 The intention to undertake such an extensive technical research project was spurred on by the 1998 symposium at the National Gallery, London (organized jointly with the Van Gogh Museum), which addressed the recently questioned authenticity of a number of paintings by van Gogh (mainly his *Sunflowers*). The symposium spotlighted the important role that a comprehensive body of technical information covering an artist's oeuvre, materials, and working methods can play in resolving questions of attribution, dating, and an artist's perceived development. We examined the following works from this nine-week period. By Vincent: *Marcelle Roulin* (F 441, JH 1641), *Paul Gauguin (Man in a Red Beret)* (F 546), *Camille Roulin* (F 538, JH 1645), *Gauguin's Chair* (F 499, JH 1636), *The Sower* (F 451, JH 1629), *Madame Roulin Rocking the Cradle (La Berceuse)* (F 508, JH 1671), *Van Gogh's Chair* (F 498, JH 1635), *The Sower* (F 575a, JH 1597), *Brothel Scene* (F 478, JH 1599), *Man with a Pipe* (F 534, JH 1651), *Les Alyscamps* (F 486, JH 1620), *The Arlésienne* (F 489, JH 1625), *Camille Roulin* (F 434, JH 1644), *Memory of the Garden (Etten and Neunen)* (F 496, JH 1630), *Spectators at the Arena* (F 548, JH 1653), *Marcelle Roulin* (F 440, JH 1639), *The Sower* (F 494, JH 1617), *Madame Roulin* (F 503, JH 1646), *The Sower* (F 450, JH 1627), and *Monsieur Roulin* (F 434, JH 1647); by Gauguin: *Monsieur Ginoux* (no W), *The Painter of Sunflowers* (W 296), *Washerwomen* (W 303), *Arlésiennes (Mistral)* (W 300), *Farmhouse in Arles* (W 308), *Blue Trees* (W 311), *Human Miseries* (W 304), *Old Man with a Cane* (W 318), *Madame Roulin* (W 298), *Arles Landscape* (W 309), *Washerwomen* (W 302), *The Artist's Mother* (W 385), *Les Alyscamps* (W 307), and *Self-Portrait Dedicated to Charles Laval* (W 384).

Other works were examined on the gallery wall. By Vincent: *The Red Vineyard* (F 495, JH 1625), *Madame Roulin with Her Baby Marcelle* (F 491, JH 1638), *The Arlésienne* (F 488, JH 1624), *Monsieur Ginoux* (F 533, JH 1649), *The Dance Hall* (F 547, JH 1652), *Armand Roulin* (F 493, JH 1643; and F 492, JH 1642), *The Allée des Tombeaux (Les Alyscamps)* (F 568, JH 1622), and *The Old Yew Tree* (F 573, JH 1618); by Gauguin: *Night Café* (W 305), and *Arles Landscape* (W 310).

The following paintings from this period were not examined. By Vincent: *Les Alyscamps* (F 569, 1623), *A Novel Reader* (F 497, JH 1632), *Self-Portrait* (F 501, JH 1634), *Marcelle Roulin* (F 441a, JH 1640), *Camille Roulin* (F 665, JH 1879), *Boy with Cap* (F 536, JH 1648), and *Sunflowers* (F

457, JH 1666); by Gauguin: *In the Heat (The Pigs)* (W 301), *Les Alyscamps* (W 306), *Self-Portrait* (W 297), *Still Life with Pumpkin* (W 312; lost), and *Négresse* (lost).

2 This volume will cover topics including Vincent's use of tracing and his *Sunflower* and *Berceuse* series.

3 Vincent to Theo, [c. 5 Nov. 1888], 722/559.

4 For Vincent's request for canvas, see letter to Theo, [c. 22 Oct. 1888], 715/551 (see Table 3). "We shall probably give": Vincent to Theo, [24 Oct. 1888], 717/557.

5 See Anthea Callen, *The Art of Impressionism: Painting Technique and the Making of Modernity* (New Haven/London, 2000), pp. 31–32.

6 Vincent to Theo, [15 May 1888], 612/488. Earlier in Paris, Vincent had painted his *Portrait of a Man with a Skullcap* (1886 [F 289, JH 1203]; Van Gogh Museum, Amsterdam) on a canvas with a pronounced coarse texture, actually a twill weave, where four threads pass through each shed to create a coarse texture. Thank you to Ella Hendriks for examining the weave.

7 For Gauguin's perception of the jute as cheap, see letter to Theo, [22 Nov. 1888], M 1984, letter 183; as durable, see letter to Bernard, [c. 2 Nov. 1888], M 1984, letter 177. For discussion of Gauguin's choice of jute and grounds, see H. Travers Newton in Peres et al. 1991, pp. 106–07; and Carol Christensen, "The Painting Materials and Technique of Paul Gauguin," in *Studies in the History of Art: Conservation Research 41* (Washington, D.C., 1993), p. 65. For a discussion of relatively rapid degradation of jute, see Cornelia Peres in Peres et al. 1991, pp. 112–23.

8 The almost exclusive use of size 30 canvases, while painting on jute, was unusual for both artists. Smaller sizes predominated for both, although they had each used still larger canvases earlier in their careers. Vincent began using size 30 canvases more consistently in anticipation of Gauguin's arrival, while Gauguin had begun to use this format more frequently in 1886. Both artists continued to use size 30 after their joint enterprise more than any other single size. Immediately after Gauguin's departure, however, Vincent returned to smaller canvases, while Gauguin continued to produce primarily size 30 works. As his career progressed, he painted on larger canvases. Vincent did not do so until Auvers, when he turned to a large double-square format (50 x 100 cm), using it as frequently as the size 30.

9 Although Gauguin occasionally painted on unprimed canvas before coming to Arles, some of his paintings that appear unprimed and are published as such may actually have thin grounds. One such case is *Self-Portrait (Les Misérables)* (W 239), which

recent analysis reveals to have a thin chalk ground.

10 This linen does not have the same thread count (16 x 16 threads/cm) as the canvas Vincent normally ordered; it was probably purchased in Arles. On 8 October Vincent informed Theo that he was out of canvas and had bought two canvases locally (704/547), but the next day he wrote that he had received an order from Tasset (705/548). Thus he probably did not use the two local canvases at that time; perhaps he now shared them with Gauguin to paint *The Sower* and *Farmhouse in Arles*. A ground sample from *The Sower*, which might provide more conclusive data, was not available for analysis. The sketch of *The Sower* is in Vincent to Theo, [28 Oct. 1888], 719/558b.

11 Vincent to Theo, [28 Oct. 1888], 719/558b. This letter gives no indication of the support material used.

12 See Newton in Peres et al. 1991, pp. 106, 110 n. 15; Dorn 1999, p. 53 n. 52; Bailey 1996, p. 54 n. 11; and a forthcoming article by Antonio De Robertis, "I Girasoli Contesi."

13 Counts were taken over 2 cm (then divided in half) in at least five spots on each canvas. Statistical analysis of 100 measurements, all of which lie between 5–5.5 threads/cm and 6–6.5 threads/cm, reveals them to be very tightly bunched with an average +/- variance of 5.22 +/- 0.02 and 6.45 +/- 0.04. (The term variance signifies that 68% of the measurements fall within the quoted uncertainty.) Thank you to C. J. Lister, Argonne National Laboratory, for providing statistical analysis.

14 The attributions to Vincent are supported, most recently, in Dorn 1999; and Bailey 1996.

15 Some tacking margins could not be examined because they were covered with paper tape. We would have more definitive proof that the jute paintings were cut from one piece of fabric if the same pattern of thick threads was found to run though a group of pictures. Although these thicker threads are not apparent on x-radiographs, they are often visible in raking light. The present exhibition will provide the opportunity to make such comparisons.

16 Private communication between Dorothy Catling, presently at the Dept. of Biological Sciences, University of Durham, England, and John McKenna, Verdant Works Museum, Dundee Industrial Heritage, Ltd., Dundee, Scotland.

17 The exact width of the fabric is of interest because it determines more exactly how many paintings could be cut from this particular piece and can be theoretically assigned to this period.

18 Thank you to Ella Hendriks for bringing *Paris in Snow* to our attention and for providing its thread count. Thanks also

to Mary Serbera for providing an x-radiograph of *Portrait of Upaupa Scheklund*. Both works, dating to 1984, are painted on jute with slightly lower thread counts than the Arles jute; the tighter weave of the Arles jute can be clearly seen by comparing x-radiographs of Arles works with that of the portrait.

19 See Gauguin to Monfreid, [Jan. 1900], Joly-Segalen 1950, letter 60. For Gauguin's canvases, see Christensen (note 7), pp. 64–70.

20 A pattern of parallel ridges can sometimes be discerned, and in several paintings the jute fibers were pulled up through the rough ground surface, suggesting that a brush rather than a knife was used.

21 Though it is possible that the artists switched back and forth between different grounds, the chronology of certain paintings—confirmed by letter references and suggested by stylistic development—supports a sequential progression through these different grounds, with overlaps of a couple of days. For example Vincent's *Sower* (F 450, JH 1627; probably on a barium ground) is mentioned in letters two days after *Gauguin's Chair* (on lead white/zinc ground); see Vincent to Theo, [c. 25 Nov. 1888], 727/558a. Since the latter was completed very quickly, perhaps *The Sower* had been initiated first, but finished later. It is also possible that some canvases with chalk grounds were prepared at the beginning of their time together and set aside until December (when they were re-primed with lead white).

22 Callen has pointed out that absorbent grounds were preferred by Impressionists, but there is no body of analysis supporting the theory that these were usually chalk in glue. They may often have been lead white-in-oil grounds with lower proportions of medium or admixtures of chalk to increase absorbency. For discussions of absorbent grounds, see Callen (note 5), p. 52; Christensen (note 7), pp. 70–73; Vojtěch Jirat-Wasiutyński and H. Travers Newton, "Absorbent Grounds and the Matt Aesthetic in Post-Impressionist Painting," in *Contributions to the Dublin Congress. Painting Techniques: History, Materials, and Studio Practice*, ed. by Ashok Roy and Perry Smith (London, 1998), pp. 235–39; and Newton in Peres et al. 1991, p. 107.

23 Gauguin to Monfreid, [Sept. 1899], Joly-Segalen 1950, letter 58.

24 Gauguin to Schuffenecker, [late Feb./early Mar. 1888], M 1984, letter 141 (excerpt); dated to c. 20 Feb. in M 1989, p. 61 (in full).

25 "Bought some coarse canvas": Vincent to Theo, [9 Mar. 1888], 585/467. "Care overmuch": Vincent to Theo, [26 Aug. 1888], 672/527. Vincent hoped to attain fresher col-

ors through less finely brayed, less oil-rich paints, but the same effect is fostered by an absorbent ground.

26 This stained effect is indeed often seen at the edges of the jute pictures, where the paint extends beyond the ground and is absorbed into the unprimed jute canvas. Over time the oil absorbed into the canvas fibers also hastens deterioration and darkening of the fibers. A size layer (usually diluted animal glue) normally serves to isolate the canvas. Experiments done for this study to recreate similar looking barium sulfate grounds suggest that the proportion of barium sulfate to medium was relatively low. The barium sulfate decreased the gloss and saturation of the binding medium and provided just enough bulk to the layer so that it could be brushed onto the top of canvas threads without soaking in completely, filling the interstices of the weave slightly. Its function fell somewhere between that of a size and a ground layer, mitigating the absorbency and coarse texture of the jute, but only minimally.

27 Barium sulfate is inexpensive, easily ground and dispersed, and absorbs little oil. The oil absorption for natural barium sulfate ranges from 6–14; chalk is variable, with an oil absorption range from 13–22; the range for lead white is 7–13; and for zinc white 12–20 (Colour Index, vol. 2 [Bradford, England/Research Triangle Park, North Carolina, 1957], pp. 2806–07). It has been commonly used since 1820 as an extender, especially in lead white grounds. It is also commonly used as a filler in oil paints because it becomes transparent in an oil medium. In watercolors and glue-based media, on the other hand, it is more opaque and has been used as a white pigment, sometimes referred to as "permanent white." Barium sulfate was available in two forms, the mineral barite and the precipitated form called blanc fixe, both introduced commercially in the 1810s. Blanc fixe is whiter and more opaque than barite, which can vary in shade depending on trace elements. Based on the coarse particle size and beige color, the natural form of barium sulfate was most likely used by the two artists. For more information on barium sulfate, see R. D. Harley, Artists' Pigments c. 1600–1835, 2d ed. (London, 1982), pp. 174–76; R. J. Gettens and G. L. Stout, Paintings Material, a Short Encyclopedia (New York, 1966), p. 96; and R. L. Feller, "Barium Sulfate—Natural and Synthetic," Artists' Pigments, a Handbook of Their History and Characteristics, vol. 1 (Washington, D.C., 1986), pp. 47–64. Vincent made no request in his letters to Theo for either chalk or barium sulfate, and these were most likely obtained locally.

28 See Gray 1980, p. 29; and Bodelsen 1964, p. 46. Vincent made several references in earlier and later letters equating painting to working the earth; see letter to Theo, [c. 20–22 Oct. 1889], 813/612; and 449/402, 502/405, 509/410.

29 For this study, ground mixtures were re-created based on the results of different ground analyses and then applied to stretched jute fabric using brush and palette knife.

30 For artist manuals, see Callen (note 5), p. 222 n. 7. As she has noted, many of the effects discussed in these manuals and repeated by later authors are theoretical concerns passed on from one author to the next, and do not reflect the actual working properties experienced by artists.

31 While a thin lead white ground takes about a week to sufficiently dry for use, a glue-based ground can be painted on after a few hours (depending on weather conditions), although its surface remains soft. These drying times were determined through test re-creations (see note 29). The lead white/oil grounds were most likely used straight from a tube. They apparently mixed the lead white and zinc white paints themselves, however, since the proportions vary in different areas and layers. Although zinc white is a purer white, absorbs less oil, and is less prone to yellowing with age, it is notoriously slow to dry, is more difficult to brush out, and creates a more brittle film. During the nineteenth century there was an ongoing debate over the relative merits of each and it had been proposed that a mixture combined the advantages of both. Perhaps Vincent and Gauguin mixed the two as an experiment, or perhaps their supply of lead white was running low. On 22 October, Vincent had requested from Theo twenty large tubes of zinc white and ten of lead white, before knowing they would be using the lead white for grounds (715/551).

32 Vincent to Theo, [c. 23 Nov. 1888], 726/563. This should not be taken as a certain date for the transition, as two days later Vincent mentioned he was working on a Sower (probably on a barium sulfate ground); see above, note 22. Vincent had only two large pieces of jute left when they switched to lead white grounds, which he used for Gauguin's Chair and possibly for Sunflowers (F 457, JH 1666; its ground has not been tested). While the latter, Vincent's presumed final painting on jute, has been variously dated, it appears likely that it was painted in early December. A thorough examination of the painting with x-ray and ground analysis might provide further information for establishing its position in the chronology.

33 After Arles Gauguin returned to absorbent glue-based chalk grounds. Although only a few analytical results for Gauguin's 1889 grounds were available, these were primarily chalk: Flageolet Player on the Cliff, Brittany (W 361), Breton Landscape with Willows (W 357), Haymaking (W 352). Female Nude with Sunflowers (W 330), painted on a pine panel, has a lead white ground. For Gauguin's continued preference for chalk grounds see Christensen (note 7), pp. 70–73.

34 On Vincent's preference, see Cornelia Peres in Peres et al. 1991, p. 41. Adhesion problems are often found in Vincent's thicker impasto. Underneath the outer skin the paint is often found to be crumbly and dry, as if there is too little medium to bind the pigment properly.

35 See Jirat-Wasiutyński/Newton 2000, p. 120; and idem, "Paul Gauguin's Paintings of Late 1888: Reconstructing the Artist's Aims from Technical and Documentary Evidence," in Appearance, Opinion, Change: Evaluating the Look of Painting, ed. by Victoria Todd (London, 1991), pp. 26–31.

36 For Gauguin's November shipment and his stretching instructions, see letter to Theo, [c. 22 Nov. 1888], M 1984, letter 183. Vincent usually shipped his paintings to Theo in flat parcels, although he occasionally mentioned sending them in rolls.

37 The paint layer of Human Miseries was unusually thick for Gauguin, and hence more vulnerable to flaking. When he returned to thinner paint layers and normal canvases after Arles, he may have been comfortable once again painting on chalk/glue grounds. Vincent, who used still thicker layers, had not yet shipped any of his jute pictures to Theo and did not do so until the following May. Though Gauguin's pictures appeared to have arrived in Paris safely (see Gauguin to Theo, [c. 4–7 Dec. 1888], M 1984, letter 187), a few days later Schuffenecker wrote to Theo about the flaking problem (see 11 Dec. 1888, M 1984, letter CI). See also Bodelsen 1964, p. 221 n. 144; Jirat-Wasiutyński/Newton, p. 239 n. 12; and Christensen (note 7), p. 72.

38 Gauguin to Theo, [3rd week Dec. 1888], M 1984, letter 192. When Gauguin finally saw the pictures in January, he wrote to Vincent, "The whole Vintage [Human Miseries] has flaked because of the white which has separated" (Cooper 1983, GAC 34; M 1991, letter 98). By "white" he probably meant the ground layer, although the appearance of the barium sulfate ground is more beige than white. He then continued the letter with a description of his method of re-adhering the lifting paint.

39 Because most of the paintings examined for this study had already been lined, these grounds on the reverse were only discovered fortuitously; if noted in previous condition reports, they were often thought to be a component of the lining adhesive, though when examined for this study, the chalk could be distinguished as a separate layer between the original canvas and lining adhesive. It could not be determined whether the chalk layer was applied before or after the pictures were painted.

40 Washerwomen (W 302) and Self-Portrait Dedicated to Laval (W 384) had aqueous linings, while Paris in Snow (W 529) was first lined with wax. Human Miseries had a chalk layer—possibly applied when a narrow painted strip was added to the left side—which was removed when an aqueous lining was replaced with a wax lining. Chalk also turned up on the back of a fiber sample from Blue Trees, but it is not known if this was an errant bit of chalk or if the entire reverse was previously coated. Self-Portrait (W 297), reported to have a partial coating on the reverse, is apparently unlined. On the paintings we examined, the chalk layers were not applied to the reverse while the paintings were on stretchers because the chalk can be seen to extend to the canvas edges, which were subsequently cut when lined. The chalk layer was either added to the reverse after the painting was removed from the stretcher (for shipping or to reuse the stretcher), or it was applied as the initial ground, after which the canvas was removed from the stretcher, turned over and re-stretched, before the lead ground was applied to the new face. Analysis identified identical trace elements in the chalk layers on the front of Arlésiennes (Mistral) (W 300) and the reverse of Washerwomen (W 302). The composition of the chalk layer on the reverse of Self-Portrait Dedicated to Charles Laval (W384) is also very similar. This suggests that as for Arlésiennes, the other chalk layers were the initial grounds applied by Gauguin.

41 Alternatively, he might have applied chalk to the reverse of canvases with lead white grounds on the front for a specific purpose after completing the work and removing it from its stretcher. He seems to have done this in a later painting on jute, Paris in Snow (1894), which has a white layer, presumed to be chalk, on the reverse that was applied after the picture had been painted and removed from its stretcher. Paris in Snow has no ground on the front of the canvas, so Gauguin may have added a stiff layer on the reverse to help stabilize the picture. Thank you to Ella Hendriks for examining Paris in Snow.

42 Perhaps for Vincent's works as well: Vincent's first Berceuse (on pre-primed linen) (F 508, JH 1671)—begun in December, soon after Gauguin's examples—has a layer presumed to be chalk

on its reverse, suggesting that Vincent may also have made a similar experiment to promote greater stability. Thank you to Frank Zuccari for bringing the layer on the reverse to our attention. Although the layer was not analyzed, it had been observed to be very soft, unlike white lead in oil, when it was thinned in preparation for relining.

43 Most recently Bogomila Welsh-Ovcharov has suggested a date of 1889–90 for W 384 (Hartford 2001, pp. 32, 158 nn. 86, 88) and a date of 1893–94 for W 297 was suggested in Graz, Austria, Landesmuseum Joanneum, *Paul Gauguin: von der Bretagne nach Tahiti. Ein Aufbruch zur Moderne*, exh. cat. (2000), no. 3. Ronald Pickvance, however, has given the more likely dates of late 1888 for W 384 and early 1889 for W 297 (Pickvance 1998, cat. 43, p. 371).

44 Thank you to Walter Rossacher, Landesmuseum Joanneum, Graz, Austria, who counted the threads and noted the layer on the reverse while the picture was on loan to the 2000 exhibition there. The compositions of the ground and the layer on the reverse are not known.

45 Vincent to Theo, [4 May 1888], 606/482.

46 See for example Callen (note 5), p. 84. His use of a finer support was perhaps in response to Vincent's return to more ordinary pre-primed linen for his portraits.

47 The portrait of Gauguin's mother is so heavily painted that it was not possible to evaluate whether there was a ground layer. A sample from the edge indicated only a protein size layer without inorganic material, which might make it an anomaly within the Arles pictures, although *Madame Roulin* (W 298) and *Old Man with a Cane* (W 318), also have a very low percentage of inorganic material in their protein-based ground layers.

48 Vincent to Theo, [c. 5 Nov. 1888], 722/559.

49 In August, after receiving a higher grade of canvas (5.50 francs per meter compared to his usual 2.50 francs) from Tasset, he wrote Theo: "If I do a portrait, or indeed anything that I am anxious to make lasting, he [Tasset] may be sure that I'll use it" (658/517), indicating that portraiture held pride of place in his oeuvre and deserved a higher-quality support.

50 Until recently, *Portrait of Gauguin* was not consistently attributed to Vincent, but the identification of a barium sulfate ground on the 5.2 x 6.5 threads/cm canvas, when combined with stylistic evidence, places the picture firmly within his oeuvre. Other aspects of the picture, such as the character of the brushwork and the scene depicted, in close technical comparison with other paintings of this period, also confirm Vincent's hand (see ch. 4).

51 Continuing studies undertaken by the Van Gogh Museum in collaboration with the Netherland Institute for Cultural Heritage and Shell Research and Technology Centre, Amsterdam (SRTCA), involve systematic investigation of the build-up and composition of the ground layers found in paintings by van Gogh from each period of his production. The results will be published in a new series of collection catalogues. Currently works from the Antwerp and Paris periods are under investigation.

52 See Cornelia Peres in Peres et al. 1991, p. 27.

53 Canvas bolts would have been ordered from the same manufacturer, usually in the Low Countries, often then cut and primed by the French color merchant, usually in ten- or twenty-meter lengths; see Callen (note 5), p. 59. Vincent's different orders might be on fabric cut from the same large bolt, or on canvas from the same manufacturer, woven on the same loom with the same type of thread. Therefore, the thread counts are likely to be the same. But since the ground material would have been mixed up fresh each time a group of ten- or twenty-meter lengths of canvas was primed, its composition and application is likely to differ from shipment to shipment.

54 See Ella Hendriks and Louis van Tilborgh, "Van Gogh's *Garden of the Asylum*: Genuine or Fake?" *Burlington Magazine* 143, no. 1176 (Mar. 2001), pp. 151–52. The composition of the glue sizing, the type and ratio of white pigments (including lead white, zinc white, barium sulfate, and chalk), particle size, the number of layers, and the trace quantities of colored pigment can be compared in different samples.

55 See ibid., p. 150. For a general discussion of nineteenth-century canvases, see David Bomford et al., *Art in the Making: Impressionism*, exh. cat., National Gallery, London (1990), pp. 44–50; and Callen (note 5), pp. 30–47. For van Gogh's canvases in particular, see Elisabeth Ravaud, "The Use of X-Radiography to Study Paintings by Cézanne and Van Gogh in the Gachet Collection," in *Cézanne to Van Gogh: The Collection of Doctor Gachet*, exh. cat. by Anne Distel and Susan Alyson Stein, The Metropolitan Museum of Art, New York (1999), pp. 68–70. This stretching prior to priming causes deformations in the canvas around the edges, referred to as primary cusping or scalloping. The cusping and the knife marks from the ground application are visible on the x-radiographs. Secondary cusping occurs when the artist re-stretches each individual canvas, but these are usually less pronounced deformations and occur at smaller intervals. After commercial priming the canvas was cut from the priming frame, usually leaving the selvage edges behind, so the selvages cannot be used to determine the outer edges of the fabric, as could be done for the jute. However, the primary cusping of the outer edges can be used for a similar purpose. Also, as Ella Hendriks has pointed out, the warp direction can often be distinguished on the x-radiograph because the threads are aligned at more regular intervals (private communication). Therefore repeated thread counts of the weft threads will vary slightly while counts of the warp threads will be more consistent. Statistical analysis of the Arles canvas groups bears out this distinction between warp and weft. For the jute, where the warp direction is known from the selvage, the variance from the warp's average count of 5.22 was +/- 0.02, while the variance from the 6.45 weft average was +/- 0.04, which means that the warp threads were twice as regularly spaced as the weft. A similar comparison held true for the 15 x 12 and 11.5 x 18 threads/cm canvases. By this reasoning, in the former, the warp threads are those spaced at 15/cm and in the latter, the warp threads are those spaced at 11.5/cm because both measurements are almost three times more consistent than the weft spacing (variances of 15.04 +/- 0.07 compared to 12.5 +/- 0.2; and 11.64 +/- 0.07 compared to 18.0 +/- 0.2).

56 This canvas is the same type referred to as 12 x 17 threads/cm in Hendriks/van Tilborgh (note 54) and as 12 x 18 threads/cm in *Cézanne to Van Gogh* (note 55). The numbers may vary depending on the method used to find the average and the particular piece of canvas, but could also possibly reflect the inclusion of some 15 x 12 threads/cm canvases along with the 11.5 x 18 threads/cm group. The statistical analysis used to determine the thread count designations for this study are described in Table 1, note 1. See also above, note 55.

57 Vincent to Theo, [c. 25 Nov. 1888], 727/558a.

58 In order for ground analysis to provide more conclusive evidence other examples from each possible shipment must be analyzed for comparison. Ground samples can easily be taken from the edge of a canvas where they will not disrupt the paint layer, but it is important that they include the complete layer and be mounted as cross-sections.

59 Vincent to Theo, [c. 4 Dec. 1888], 728/560.

60 While Vincent does not specifically mention *two* portraits of Armand in his letter, the two versions of the subject (JH 1642, 1643), though on disparate canvas types, were probably painted at the same time. Both faces, set against green backgrounds, are carefully modeled with small strokes and virtually no impasto, exceptions to Vincent's usual thickly applied paint and a reflection of Gauguin's influence on his technique. Other paintings at this time that show Gauguin's influence, particularly *Dance Hall*, *Spectators at the Arena,* and *Brothel Scene*, also exhibit less impasto than Vincent customarily used.

61 X-radiographs of paintings on pre-primed canvas from the 9 October shipment were not included in this study but some might also exhibit the diagonal band of thick ground. Further ground analysis should distinguish between the various shipments of 11.5 x 18 threads/cm canvas.

62 This painting was not examined, though the Museu de Arte de São Paulo, Brazil, kindly allowed an x-radiograph to be made for this study.

63 The 15 x 12 threads/cm canvas was apparently provided by Tasset. Vincent used it again in Auvers and Saint-Rémy, and for a version of *La Berceuse* (F 507, JH 1672) presumably painted later in Arles.

64 Vincent did receive orders that were not of a standard size on occasion (see Hendriks/van Tilborgh [note 54], p. 150 n. 49) and he did specify that Tasset should vary the amount by a yard more or less to minimize shipping costs.

65 Thread counts in the 12 x 12 threads/cm range are found in several other paintings from Arles, but x-radiographs were not available for comparison. Another work previously dated to this period, *Portrait of a One-Eyed Man* (F 532, JH 1650), was probably painted at a later time, as its unprimed canvas of 18 x 18 threads/cm appears identical to one Vincent used in Saint-Rémy for *Olive Trees* (F 709, JH 1760). Thank you to Ella Hendriks for comparing the x-radiographs.

66 On 13 April Vincent wrote to Theo that he had ordered ten meters of canvas (762/584). Since Theo was in Holland for his marriage at that time, Vincent probably ordered canvas directly from Tasset but informed Theo so he could pay for it. Our thanks to Leo Jansen, Editor of the Van Gogh Letters Project, for providing this explanation.

NOTES

All citations of letters include the correspondents' names, date (in square brackets if not inscribed on the letter by the writer), source, and reference number. Full citations for abbreviated sources appear in the Selected Bibliography. For van Gogh's letters, the numbers established in the first complete English and French editions (1958 and 1960) are used, in anticipation of the revised edition under way at the Van Gogh Museum, which will provide new numbers. These are preceded by the numbers currently used in the Dutch edition of the letters from 1990. For Gauguin's letters, the numbers established in Merlhès's edition (1984) are used, updated if appropriate from the same author's subsequent publications (1989 and 1991). Letters published in other contexts (such as Theo van Gogh's correspondence collected in *Brief Happiness*) and other writings (such as Gauguin's memoir *Avant et après*) are identified with abbreviated bibliographic citations and the page number and/or numbering system used in that source. Unpublished material is cited with permission of and in accord with the reference system used by the holders.

In instances where we propose redating a letter, reasons are briefly given in the appropriate note. In general, for van Gogh's letters, the chronology established in the Dutch edition of 1990 is followed, in conjunction with Pickvance 1984; and for Gauguin's, that in Merlhès 1984. Subsequent research has already resulted in certain changes and will continue to do so; when possible, we have taken the most recent information into account and identify it accordingly.

Whenever possible, the effort was made to read primary documentation in the original languages: Dutch, French, and occasionally English. Thanks are due to Victor Merlhès, researcher for the Centre National de la Recherche Scientifique, France, for sharing his firsthand knowledge of Gauguin's writings and to Leo Jansen of the Van Gogh Museum for checking our citations against van Gogh's original manuscripts. We subsequently relied upon a number of readily accessible English translations: notably Thomson 1993, Washington 1988, van Gogh 1958, and van Gogh 1996. In consultation with linguists Leo Jansen and Silva Tokatlian, we have made a number of refinements to previously published translations and moreover are presenting many passages in English for the first time.

Citations for bold-faced quotations: p. 2 Vincent to Wil, [c. 22 June 1888], 633/W 4; p. 3: Gauguin, Avant et après, p. 203.

1 Roskill 1970a; see also Roskill 1979.
2 See Druick/Zegers 1991.
3 See van Uitert 1977, 1978–79, 1980, 1981–82; Pollock 1980a, 1980b, 1988, 1992; and Silverman 1992, 1994, 1995; Naomi Margolis Maurer's comparative study, *The Pursuit of Spiritual Wisdom: The Thought and Art of Vincent van Gogh and Paul Gauguin* (Maurer 1998), also deserves mention in this context. This seems to be a particularly fruitful moment for van Gogh–Gauguin studies. *Van Gogh and Gauguin: Electric Arguments and Utopian Dreams*, by Bradley Collins, Jr., is forthcoming; Debora Silverman's important *Van Gogh and Gauguin: The Search for Sacred Art* (Silverman 2000) appeared just as this manuscript was nearing completion. Though we were therefore unable to incorporate her findings integrally into our text, we do draw attention (in notes) to particular areas of overlap, and we have benefited from Silverman's previously published work on the artists. *The Search for Sacred Art*—rigorously researched, incisively argued, and illustrated with a wealth of comparative imagery—offers many areas of discussion not presented here and promises to open new avenues of investigation.
4 See "Letters" in the Selected Bibliography. Our research is greatly indebted to recent scholarship on both artists' correspondence. In 1984 Ronald Pickvance addressed the chronology of van Gogh's letters from Arles (Pickvance 1984, App. I, pp. 260–63), suggesting significant date changes; the 1990 Dutch edition of van Gogh's letters substantially updates the standard 1958 and 1960 English and French editions, and includes new letters and previously omitted passages; and Jan Hulsker has published corrections to the dating and translation of many letters from the entire range of the correspondence (Hulker 1993). Currently the Van Gogh Museum, Amsterdam, and the Constantijn Huygens Institute for Text Editions and Intellectual History, The Hague, are conducting a thorough reevaluation and translation of the van Gogh correspondence; see Hans Luijten, "'As it came into my pen': A New Edition of the Correspondence of Vincent van Gogh," *Van Gogh Museum Journal* (1996), pp. 89–102; and Leo Jansen, "The Van Gogh Letters Project: New Findings and Old," *Van Gogh Museum Journal* (1997–98), pp. 58–67. Victor Merlhès, researcher for the Centre National de la Recherche Scientifique, France, and expert on Gauguin's correspondence, in examining the complex epistolary relationship between the van Gogh brothers and Gauguin, has posited the existence and extrapolated the content of the now-lost letters that constitute approximately half of the full corpus of correspondence (Merlhès 1991 and 1996). He has also published numerous other primary documents relating to Gauguin's life and work (M 1984, M 1989, M 1991, and M 1995).
5 Van Uitert 1977; Pollock 1992, p. 16.
6 The various resonances of this decision—Vincent's identification with his hero Rembrandt, his intention to establish a market identity, his desire to distance himself from his family and concomitantly to align himself with the "common man"—are discussed in the following chapters.

CHAPTER 1: ORIGINS

Citations for bold-faced quotations: p. 12: Vincent to Theo, [c. 21–28 Mar, 1883], 334/276; *p. 14: Vincent to Theo, [23 Jan. 1889], 744/573; p. 17: Vincent to Theo, 8 Apr. 1877, 11/91.*

1 On *vanitas* still lifes featuring books, see Sam Segal, "Natures mortes aux livres," in *Sébastien Stoskopf*, exh. cat., Musée de l'Oeuvre Nôtre-Dame, Strasbourg (1997) pp. 86–93. The sources consulted for emblemata include C. B. Huet, "Letterkunde—Kronijk en Kritiek," *De Gids* 27, no. 4 (1863), pp. 99–128; Hendrik Smilde, "Cats onder de menschen," in *Jacob Cats in Dordrecht* (Groningen/Batavia, 1938), pp. 278–305; P. Minderaa, *Aandacht voor Cats bij zijn 300-ste Sterfdag* (Zwolle, 1962); B. A. van Es, *Zedenkundig vermaan voor jong en oud* (Culemborg, 1977); N. F. Noordam, "Cats als volksopvoeder," in *Geschiedenis van opvoeding en onderwijs* by Bernard Kruithof et al. (Nijmegen, 1982), pp. 307–17; Marie van Dijk, "Spel- en speelkultuur in de negentiende eeuw," *Volkskundig bulletin* 9 (1983), pp. 73–78; A. S. Q. Visser et al., *Emblem Books in Leiden* (Leiden, 1999); Michael Bath, "English Emblem Books Post-1700," in *Speaking Pictures: English Emblem Books and Renaissance Culture* (London/New York, 1994), pp. 255–81; and K. J. Höltgen, "The Victorian Emblematic Revival," in *Aspects of the Emblem* (Kassel, 1986), pp. 141–96.

2 Émile Zola, *Joie de vivre*, trans. as *Zest for Life* by Jean Stewart, preface by August Wilson (London, 1955; repr. 1968). On this painting, see Joan Greer, "'Een man van smerten ende versocht in Krankheyt': Het christologische beeld van de kunstenaar in van Goghs stilleven met open bijbel," *Jong Holland* 13, no. 3 (1997), pp. 30–42. See Hope B. Werness, "Some Observations on van Gogh and the *Vanitas* Tradition," *Studies in Iconography* 6 (1980), pp. 123–36; Roskill 1979, p. 157; Amsterdam 1990, cat. 10, pp. 54–55; Maurer 1998, pp. 51–53; Sund 1992, pp. 109–13; Pollock 1980b, vol. 1, pp. 222–28; Jean Seznec, "Literary Inspiration in van Gogh," *Magazine of Art* 48, no. 8 (1950), pp. 282–88; and Carl Nordenfalk, "Van Gogh and Literature," *Journal of the Warburg and Courtauld Institutes* 10 (1947), pp. 132–47.

3 Zola, *Joie de vivre*, p. 174.

4 For these and other observations about this painting, see Pickvance 1998, cat. 18, p. 263. For Gauguin in Copenhagen, see M 1984, letters 56–79 and the accompanying notes.

5 Johannes Paulus Stricker, "Het Geloof in Jesus Christus de Eenige Weg tot Zaligheid" (Belief in Jesus Christ, the Only Way to Salvation), in *Christelijk Album* (Amsterdam, 1858), p. 196; cited in Kathleen Powers Erickson, *At Eternity's Gate: The Spiritual Vision of Vincent van Gogh* (Grand Rapids, Mich., 1998), p. 29. On the Groningen doctrines, see ibid. (where the van Goghs are misidentified as Calvinists); Tsukasa Kōdera, "Van Gogh and the Dutch Theological Culture of the Nineteenth Century," in *Vincent van Gogh International Symposium: Tokyo, October 17–19, 1985* (Tokyo, 1988), pp. 141–70; Silverman 1994; and Cliff Edwards, *Van Gogh and God: A Creative Spiritual Quest* (Chicago, 1989), pp. 41, 193 n. 7.

6 On the cultural context of the *dominocratie*, and its implications for Vincent's formation, see the excellent account and analysis in Silverman 1994; and for the *bijschriftenpoëzie*, see Kōdera 1990, pp. 14–26. Three examples cited in Kōdera 1990 are: J. J. L. Ten Kate, *Nieuwe belooning, Kindergedichtjes* (Amsterdam, 1850); Eliza Laurillard, *Kunst-juweeltjes voor de salon-tafel met bijschriften van E. Laurillard*, 2 vols. (Haarlem, 1871); idem, *Klimop, gedachten en beelden des geloofs, proza et poëzy* (Amsterdam, 1871).

7 On typology as practiced in the nineteenth century, with particular application to the visual arts, see George P. Landow, *Victorian Types, Victorian Shadows: Biblical Typology in Victorian Literature, Art, and Thought* (Boston, 1980). On the reading of emblems in this period, see B. F. Scholz, "Jacob Cats' *Silenus Alcibiadis* in 1618 and 1862: Changes in Word-Image Relations from the Seventeenth to the Nineteenth Century," *Word and Image* 4, no. 1 (Jan.–Mar. 1988), pp. 67–80. Scholz notes (p. 69) that emblematic interpretations were viewed as fixed and universal.

8 For the van der Maaten image in the reverend's study, see Vincent to Theo, 29 June 1875, 36/29; for his use of it in a sermon, see Vincent to Theo, 27 Aug. 1877, 127/107 (paragraph omitted from English editions).

9 Following the 1648 Treaty of Munster, which formalized the Republic of the United Provinces' independence from Spain and from the southern provinces remaining under Spain's control, Catholicism was only tolerated in the north by a government closely allied to the Dutch Reformed Church. Freedom of worship came only in the wake of the French Revolution, when France declared war on and subsequently occupied the United Provinces, which, based on the French model, became the Batavian Republic in 1795. Twenty years later the Congress of Vienna created a United Kingdom of the Netherlands, a geopolitical reunification under an autocratic Calvinist monarch of the historically Catholic Spanish-Austrian southern provinces with those of the Protestant north. The southern provinces' unilateral declaration of independence (creating Belgium) met with military resistance from the Dutch (1831–33). New national borders were only ratified in 1839, approximating those that had defined the Dutch Republic during its seventeenth-century golden age.

10 The society—the Maatschappij tot bevordering van Welstand, voornamelijk onder Landlieden—was established in 1822 and headquartered in Breda. Theodorus's father, the Reverend Vincent van Gogh, had served as its bookkeeper for forty years. See Frank Kools, *Als een boer van Zundert: Vincent van Gogh en zijn geboorte plaats* (Zutphen, 1990).

11 "Exile": Vincent to Theo, [early Sept. 1876], 90/82a-l. Vincent and his brother understood his illness to be epilepsy, as Dr. Peyron would later diagnose (see Peyron to Theo, 26 May 1889, Hulsker 1971, letter VIII). Since his death, the source of Vincent's illness has been the subject of a great deal of speculation. For an analysis, see Pollock 1990a, pp. 69ff. For a summary of diagnoses, see Elmyra van Dooren, "Van Gogh: Illness and Creativity," in *The Mythology of Vincent van Gogh*, ed. by Tsukasa Kōdera and Yvette Rosenberg (Tokyo/Amsterdam, 1993), pp. 325–45. It is as difficult to attribute Vincent's leaving school to financial reasons as it is to scholastic or disciplinary ones. See Anne Stiles Wylie, "Vincent's Childhood and Adolescence," *Vincent: Bulletin of the Rijksmuseum Vincent van Gogh* 4, no. 2 (1975), pp. 13–15.

12 Father to Theo, Jan. 1873, VGM FR, inv. b2596 V/1982; Vincent to Theo, 28 Jan. 1873, 4/4; Vincent to Theo, 17 Mar. 1873, 5/5; Mother to Theo, 31 May 1873, VGM FR, inv. b2630 V/1982; Vincent to Theo, 20 July 1873, 11/10; Vincent to the van Stockum-Haanebeek family, 7 Aug. 1873, 12/10a; Vincent to Theo, 30 Apr. 1874, 22/16; Mother to Theo, 28 Oct. 1874, VGM FR, inv. b2729 V/1982, cited in Hulsker 1990, p. 22; Father to Theo, 28 Oct. 1874, VGM FR, inv. b2728 V/1982; Anna to Theo, 25 Apr. 1875, cited in Hulsker 1990, pp. 23–24; Vincent to Theo, 8 May 1875, 33/26. For more van Gogh family correspondence, see Jan Hulsker, "The Elusive van Gogh, and What His Parents Really Thought of Him," *Simiolus* 19, no. 4 (1989), pp. 243–55.

13 Vincent to Theo, 12 Nov. 1881, 181/157. He extended the metaphor: "The passions are the little ship's sails.... And he who gives way entirely to his feelings in his twentieth year catches too much wind and his boat takes in too much water." See Hulsker 1990 for a fuller account of Vincent's life at this time. The conventional understanding is that Vincent fell in love with his landlady's daughter, Eugenie Loyer. For a more recent interpretation of the facts, see Elly Cassee, "In Love: Vincent van Gogh's First True Love," *Van Gogh Museum Journal* (1996), pp. 109–17.

14 Thoré's text appeared in two volumes, *Les Musées de la Hollande, Amsterdam, et La Haye* (Paris, 1858); and *Les Musées de la Hollande, Musée van der Hoop à Amsterdam, et Musée de Rotterdam* (Paris, 1860). See Frances Suymann Jowell, "Thoré-Bürger and the Art of the Past" (Ph.D. diss., Harvard University, 1971), p. 180, for the significance of his pseudonym. Vincent first mentioned reading *Les Musées de la Hollande* in a letter to Theo, 19 Nov. 1873, 15/12. On Vincent's interpretation, see Pollock 1980b, vol. 1, pp. 30ff and ch. 5. Thoré's call for the creation of a national museum to better display the glories of the Dutch School was answered by the opening of the Rijksmuseum in 1885. "Abstractly": Thoré 1858, p. 204.

15 "Mystic ideas"; "the great revelator": Thoré 1858, p. 323; Thoré 1960, p. 4 (note 14).

16 "Revelation and a gospel": Vincent to Theo, 31 July 1874, 27/20.

17 Copied for Willem and Caroline van Stockum-Haanebeek, Oct. 1873, 14/11a (appears in full in Dutch edition of 1990); also copied in an album for the wife of the minister he worked for in England beginning July 1876; Pabst 1988, pp. 60–61, 65, 69. Vincent wrote the passage in French.

18 Johannes Paulus Stricker, *Jezus van Nazareth volgens de Historie Geschetst* (Amsterdam, 1868), p. 140; cited in Erickson (note 5), pp. 30–31.

19 See van Gogh, Albums 1 and 2; facs. in Pabst 1988, pp. 9–37. Vincent read Renan's *Jésus* (1864), a version of his *Vie de Jésus* from which the more controversial passages were eliminated.

20 For Carlyle, see Album 2, pp. 21–23; facs. in Pabst 1988, p. 25. For Renan, see Album 2, p. 29; facs. in Pabst 1988, p. 27. Vincent was introduced to Carlyle through Hippolyte Taine, *L'Idéalisme anglais: Étude sur Carlyle* (Paris, 1864).

21 "Lost the soul out of him": Carlyle, *Past and Present* (London, 1843), p. 123; copied by Vincent into Album 2, p. 21; facs. in Pabst 1988, p. 25. See also Taine (note 20), p. 172.

22 Alfred de Musset, "La Nuit de décembre," *Musset: Poésies complètes*, ed. by Maurice Allem (Paris, 1957), pp. 310–15; trans. in *The Complete Writings of Alfred de Musset* (New York, 1905), p. 343. Vincent copied the poem into Album 1, p. 20; facs. in Pabst 1988, p. 24. See also ch. 4, note 104.

23 "What is the meaning of Man" comes from Heine's *Buch der Lieder* (Hamburg/Paris, 1837), Zweiter Cyklus ("Die Nordsee"), no. 7 ("Fragen"); trans. by Hal Draper, *The Complete Poems of Heinrich Heine: A Modern English Version* (Cambridge, Mass./Boston, 1982),

p. 155. Vincent copied passages into Albums 2 and 3 (see Pabst 1988). Taine (note 20), p. 108, gave the related Carlyle passage (from *Sartor Resartus*, p. 17; and *On Heroes*, p. 9) in English—"But whence?—O Heaven, whither?"—as well as a French equivalent: "D'où venons nous? O Dieu, où allons-nous?" For Vincent's conception of homeland (*patrie*) at this time, see letters 18/13a, 33/26, and 55/43. "Battle": Theo to Jo, 26 July 1887, *Brief Happiness*, letter 1. Variations of "sorrowful but always rejoicing" occur in over sixteen letters from Vincent spanning the period 1875–78, as well as in his sermon.

24 On mental or physical illness, see Theo to Vincent, 7 Sept. 1875, 45/36a.

25 Vincent copied the text of his sermon in English for Theo in letter 96; quotes in following paragraph are from this source. For Vincent in England, see Bailey 1992; on the sermon and *Pilgrim's Progress*, see Silverman 1992.

26 Vincent's description of this painting has long perplexed scholars; he named neither the artist nor the title, and his recollection of the scene contains several departures from the actual painting. Ronald Pickvance (*The English Influences on Vincent van Gogh*, exh. cat., University Art Gallery, Nottingham [1974], p. 19) and Hope B. Werness ("Vincent van Gogh and a Lost Painting by G. H. Boughton," *Gazette des beaux-arts*, ser. 6, 106 [Sept. 1985], pp. 71–75) have convincingly argued that Vincent was referring to George Boughton's *God Speed! Pilgrims Setting out for Canterbury, Time of Chaucer*, exhibited at the Royal Academy in 1874. It is clear from letter references (88/74, 99/82) that Vincent linked the painting to Bunyan's *Pilgrim's Progress*. For more on Vincent and this painting, see Bailey 1992, pp. 63–67; Ronald de Leeuw, "George Henry Boughton and the 'Beautiful Picture' in van Gogh's 1876 Sermon," *Van Gogh Museum Journal* (1999), pp. 49–61; and Silverman 1992, p. 102. For the currency of the emblem of the storm at sea, see fig. 18 from a sixteenth-century emblem book (Georgette de Montenay, *Emblemes ou devises chrestiennes* [Lyons, 1571]); repub. (without ills.) as *Hondered Christelijke Zinnebeelden naar Georgette de Montenay door Anna Roemers Visscher. Uitgegeven door A. D. Schinkel* (The Hague, 1854), p. 11.

27 The gospels relate that Christ, moments before Judas betrayed him into the hands of his crucifiers, thrice called to God, "Abba, Father all things are possible to thee; remove this cup from me, yet not what I will, but what thou wilt" (Mark 14:36). In Vincent's letter to Theo of early September 1876 (90/82a), he echoed this passage, invoking "Abba, Father" three times. "Oh Jerusalem":

Vincent to Theo, [7/8 Feb. 1877], 102/85; see Matt. 23:37–39 and Luke 13:34–35. For Vincent's attachment to the Gethsemane theme in painting, see Soth 1986.

28 Lies to Theo, 4 Feb. 1877, VGM FR, inv. b2503 V/1982.

29 "Heavy depression": Vincent to Theo, [7 Mar. 1877], 106/92. "Preacher ... and sower": 22 Mar. 1877, 109/89 (Vincent reiterated the latter metaphor on 22 Apr. 1877, 112/93 among many other instances).

30 Vincent recalled his studies in Amsterdam in letters to Theo; see [c. 15 Aug. 1879], 153/132. Letters of the period outline his activities and thoughts: 121/101a, 125/105, 130/110. On his uncles and father as preacher-artists, see 19 May 1877, 114/95. "Dat is het": Vincent first used this phrase in his letter to Theo, [Jan. 1874], 17/13. "I need it": [7/8 Feb. 1877], 102/85.

31 For Vincent on *A Young Citizen*, see letters to Theo of 21 Oct. 1877, 131/111; 19 Nov. 1877, 133/113; and 22 July 1878, 144/123. "Knows no *joy*": Father to Theo, 2 Mar. 1878, cited in Jan Hulsker, "1878, a Decisive Year in the Lives of Theo and Vincent," *Vincent: Bulletin of the Rijksmuseum Vincent van Gogh* 3, no. 3 (1974), pp. 16–17.

32 Vincent to Theo, 9 Dec. 1877, 136/116.

33 "Cheer you": Vincent to Theo, 22 July 1878, 144/123; 3 Apr. 1878, 142/121.

34 For Vincent's plans to work in the Borinage for three years, see Vincent to Theo, 15 Nov. 1878, 147/126. See also Musée des Beaux-Arts de Mons, *Van Gogh en Belgique*, exh. cat. (1980); and Jan Hulsker, "The Borinage Episode: The Misrepresentation of van Gogh and the Creation of a New Myth," in *The Mythology of Vincent van Gogh*, ed. by Tsukasa Kōdera and Yvette Rosenberg (Tokyo/Amsterdam, 1993), pp. 309–23. On Geel, see ibid., pp. 314–15. In the nineteenth century, the name of the town was spelled "Gheel"; the "h" was dropped in the twentieth. The current spelling for "yellow" in Dutch is "geel." Earlier, the two spellings were interchangeable (see for example Karel van Mander's famous *Den grondt der edel vry schilder-const* [Amsterdam, 1618]). The site was widely renowned, for the shrine of Saint Dympna, patron of the insane, had been a thirteenth-century pilgrimage destination. Karl Baedecker, *Belgium and Holland: Handbook for Travellers* (Leipzig, 1881), pp. 150–51, described the "colony of lunatics." See also *Geel: Psychiatric Family Care*, pamphlet published by the Ministry of the Flemish Community (n.d.). The authors are grateful to Wilfried Bogaerts and Willy Andries of the archives of the Public Psychiatric Hospital, Geel, for information on the hospital.

35 Vincent to Theo, July 1880, 154/133. For a detailed and insightful analysis of the struc-

ture and concerns of this extremely important letter, see Pollock 1980b, vol. 2, App. 3, pp. 624–37. Quotations in the following paragraphs are from this letter. On Vincent's desire to become an artist, see also Hulsker, "The Borinage Episode" (note 34), pp. 314ff.

36 On Hugo, see also Vincent to Theo, [c. 12–18 Dec. 1882], 295/253. "Molting season": July 1880, 154/133.

37 Carlyle, *Sartor Resartus*, pp. 123, 42, 129. On *Sartor* see Kerry McSweeney and Peter Sabor, intro. to 1987 ed., pp. vii–xxxvi, esp. p. xxiii; John D. Rosenberg, *Carlyle and the Burden of History* (Cambridge, Mass., 1985), p. 12; and Herbert L. Sussmann, *Fact into Figure: Typology in Carlyle, Ruskin, and the Pre-Raphaelite Brotherhood* (Columbus, Ohio, 1979), esp. intro. and chs. 1 and 4.

38 Carlyle, *On Heroes*, p. 147.

39 "Know what thou canst": Carlyle, *Sartor Resartus*, p. 126. All quotes from Vincent are from his letter to Theo of July 1880, 154/133.

40 Gauguin, *Avant et après*, p. 153.

41 See Marks-Vandenbroucke 1956, pp. 9–62; M 1984, pp. 320–23; and Isabelle Cahn in Washington 1988, pp. 2–3.

42 On Clovis Gauguin's plans for life in Lima, see Gauguin, *Avant et après*, pp. 108–10.

43 On this incident and for a brief history of Tristan, see Marks-Vandenbroucke 1956, pp. 9–23. See also Dominique Desanti, *A Woman in Revolt: A Biography of Flora Tristan*, trans. by Elizabeth Zelvin (New York, 1976).

44 On Don Pio and avarice, see Flora Tristan, *Peregrinations of a Pariah*, trans. and ed. by Jean Hawkes (Boston, 1986), p. 138. The sources on Peru consulted for this chapter include Clements R. Markham, *A History of Peru* (Chicago, 1892); Jose Rufino Echenique, *Memorias para la Historia del Peru (1808–1878)* (Lima, 1952); Ruben Vargas Ugarte, S. J., *Historia General del Peru*, vol. 9, *La República (1844–1879)* (Lima, 1971); Orin Starn et al., eds., *The Peru Reader: History, Culture, Politics* (Durham/London, 1995); Sweetman 1996, pp. 6–28.

45 Gauguin, *Avant et après*, p. 111.

46 Clements R. Markham, *Cuzco: A Journey to the Ancient Capital of Peru; and Lima: A Vist to the Capital and Provinces of Modern Peru* (London, 1856), p. 386. For descriptions of nineteenth-century Lima, see Carlos Milla Batres, ed., *Imágen del Perú en el siglo XIX: Léonce Angrand* (Lima, 1972); J. J. von Tschudi, *Travels in Peru* (New York, 1854); Ernest Grandidier, *Voyage dans l'Amérique du Sud, Pérou et Bolivie* (Paris, 1861); Manuel A. Fuentes, *Lima, or Sketches of the Capital of Peru* (London, 1899); E. George Squier, *Peru, Incidents of Travel and Exploration in the Land of the Incas* (New York, 1877); Hildegardo Cordova Aguilar, "La ciudad de Lima: Su evolución y desarrollo metropli-

tano," *Revista Geográfica* 110 (July–Dec. 1989), pp. 231–65; Douglas Keith McElroy, *The History of Photography in Peru in the Nineteenth Century, 1839–1976* (Albuquerque, 1977); Juan Manuel Ugarte Elespuru, *Lima y lo Limeño* (Lima, 1966); Paul Gootenberg, "Population and Ethnicity in early Republican Peru: Some Revisions," *Latin American Research Review* 26, no. 3 (1991), pp. 109–57. Gauguin described his mother wearing this distinctive dress while living in Lima: "How graceful and pretty my mother was when she put on her Lima costume, the silk mantilla covering her face and allowing a glimpse of only one eye": Gauguin, *Avant et après*, p. 113.

47 Gauguin, *Avant et après*, pp. 111–12.

48 Manuel Fuentes, *Lima* (London, 1866), pp. iv–vi; see also Deborah Poole, *Vision, Race, Modernity* (Princeton, N.J., 1997).

49 "Pure spanish blood": Tristan, *Peregrinations*, quoted in Marks-Vandenbroucke 1956, p. 27. For Gauguin's assertion of his grandmother's and mother's noble background, see *Avant et après*, pp. 108, 111. The inventory of Aline's possessions included in her will exhaustively lists the contents of her house in Saint-Cloud and is signed and dated 16 June 1868 by Gustave Arosa. See departmental archives, town hall, Hauts-de-Seine, "12 juillet 1867, Inventaire après décès de Madame Gauguin, 30 août clôture, 16 juin 1868, Inventaire supplétif."

50 On Gauguin's Spanish accent, see *Avant et après*, p. 183. Guillaume Gauguin died on 9 April 1855.

51 "Theological study": ibid., p. 124. For a consideration of the impact on Gauguin of the three-year period at the Petit Séminaire, see Marks-Vandenbroucke 1956, p. 30; Amishai-Maisels 1985, pp. 11–12; Sweetman 1996, pp. 30–32; and especially Silverman 1995. Silverman's suggestion here of the importance of "Gauguin's receptivity to subjectivist, idealist and antirational definitions of reality and self-expression" (pp. 105–06) is a central thesis of her recent book (Silverman 2000). Our view of the Gauguin–van Gogh dynamic, while not discounting the potential influence of Gauguin's stay at the school, calls into question its formative primacy. Gauguin cannot be considered the typical product of the school, since his stay there was comparatively brief (he entered three years later and left four years earlier than most); see Émile Huet, *Histoire du Petit Séminaire de la Chapelle-Saint-Mesmin* (Orléans, 1913), pp. 285ff. Whether Gauguin, like philosopher Ernest Renan (1823–1892) a quarter of a century earlier, or his nearer contemporary Gabriel Monod (1844–1912) (see Silverman 2000, p. 435 n. 8) shared a close connection with the school's compelling founder and then archbishop of

Orléans remains open to question. Dupanloup is not listed as a regular instructor during Gauguin's time there (ibid., p. 193). Indubitably, however, Dupanloup's vision informed the precepts of the education that Gauguin received, however indifferent a student he might have been. Silverman amply demonstrates that Gauguin's education at the Petit Séminaire was one of the definitive experiences of his youth, along with his years in Lima; both served him while he sought, during the period he was close to Vincent, to articulate his intellectual positions.

52 Gauguin, *Avant et après*, p. 183. This can be gleaned from Gauguin's contention that he learned there "a little of the spirit of Escobar—which helped him in the struggle." See Pierre Larousse, *Grande Dictionnaire universel du XIXe siècle*, 1870 ed., s.v. "Antonio Escobar y Mendoza," for the common connotation of the name "Escobar" as one who adjusts his conscience in accord with his passions and interests.

53 "This word 'trade' in my mother's mind meant something shameful": Gauguin, *Avant et après*, p. 183. On the association of seamstresses and dressmakers with prostitution, see Anthea Callen, *The Spectacular Body: Science, Method, and Meaning in the Work of Degas* (New Haven, Conn., 1995), pp. 5, 59. For Aline's admonition to Gauguin, see her will (note 49). On Arosa, see M 1984, pp. 319ff.; and Marks-Vandenbroucke 1956.

54 On Gauguin's inheritance, see Washington 1988, p. 4. On Gauguin in the Arosa circle, see Marks-Vandenbroucke 1956; and M 1984, pp. 319–20 n. 2.

55 On this period, see Merete Bodelsen, "The Dating of Gauguin's Early Paintings," *Burlington Magazine* 107, no. 747 (June 1965), pp. 306–13; M 1984, pp. 329–31 n. 20; and Charles Stuckey in Washington 1988, pp. 11–16. See also Bodelsen 1970 for Gauguin as a collector. Recommended by Arosa, Gauguin worked for stockbroker Paul Bertin from 1872 until late 1876 or early 1877; by 1879 he was employed by banker André Bourdon, and in 1880 by the Thomereau agency (see Washington 1988, pp. 4–6).

56 Vincent to Theo, 1 Nov. 1880, 159/138; and 2 Apr. 1881, 163/142.

57 Vincent described the Kee Vos episode in detail in letters to Theo of Nov. 1881. Five months later, in a letter of mid-May 1882, Vincent detailed the incident further and included the account of holding his hand in the flame (227/193).

58 "Father Michelet": Vincent to Theo, [18 Nov. 1881], 184/159; [19 Nov. 1881], 185/160. "Father Millet": 23 Nov. 1881, 187/161. "Essentially I am *not*": [7/8 Dec. 1883], 413/345a. He had used the signature "Vincent" from summer 1881. Later he used his first

name because the French could not pronounce "van Gogh"; see Hartrick 1939, p. 40; and van Uitert 1981–82, pp. 228–29 nn. 25–26.

59 "If I can only continue": Vincent to Theo, 7 Sept. 1880, 156/135. "Nervous constitution": [18 July 1882], 248/216. "Express himself": [25 Feb. 1882], 206/177. "Make [his] living": 15 Oct. 1880, 158/137. On his autodidacticism at this time, see Pollock 1980b, vol. 1, p. 34, and ch. 1, pt. 4, "A Copybook Apprenticeship," pp. 51–61; see also Silverman 1994, pp. 150ff. "You must wait": Vincent to Theo, [c. 11 Mar. 1882], 209/180.

60 Such metaphors are found in letters to Theo including [18 Sept. 1882], 266/232; and [30 Mar./1 Apr. 1883], 335/227. See Sund 1988b; and Louis van Tilborgh, "The Sower," in *Van Gogh and Millet*, trans. by Martin Cleaver, exh. cat., Rijksmuseum Vincent van Gogh, Amsterdam (1988), pp. 156–59, and passim.

61 On Vincent's sense of lineage, see 2 Apr. 1881, 163/142. "Evangelical tone": 24 Sept. 1880, 157/136. "Apostolic"; "acted Gospel"; "sowing in the seedfield": Carlyle, *Sartor Resartus*, pp. 141, 140, 132, 151. "Seed": Vincent to van Rappard, [c. 21 Mar. 1883], 333/R 32. On the sower and reaper in Vincent's symbolic pictorial vocabulary, see Sund 1988b.

62 "Sublime": Vincent to Theo, 24 Sept. 1880, 157/136. On Millet's art as consolatory, see Vincent to Theo, [5 Nov. 1882], 282/242; and [14 May 1882], 227/193: "whenever I feel depressed I look at *The Diggers* by Millet." "Duty": [26–27 Nov. 1882], 490/248. On Hugo, specifically *Les Misérables*, see Vincent to Theo, [30 Mar.–1 Apr. 1883], 335/277. "Awful Reality": Carlyle, *On Heroes*, p. 135.

63 "Sea that we call": Vincent to van Rappard, 23 Nov. 1881, 188/R 6. For Vincent's use of a carpenter's pencil, see letter to Theo, [1 May 1882], 221/195. On Jesus as a carpenter, see [27 July 1883], 371/306. In late October/early November 1883, Vincent remarked to Theo, "When one is thirty, one is just beginning," citing other painters' biographies as evidence (404/339). On van Rappard, see Hans Lutz, "Anthon van Rappard, klem tussen traditie en moderniteit," *Kerende Tijden* 190 (1997), p. 40; and J. Brouwer et al., *Anthon van Rappard* (Amsterdam, 1974) (reviewed by Griselda Pollock, *Burlington Magazine* 117, no. 872 [Nov. 1975], pp. 743–44). Theo already knew van Rappard, having met him in Paris.

64 "Books and reality and art": Vincent to Theo, [11 Feb. 1883], 314/266. "Pale face": [c. 25–29 Jan. 1882], 307/262. On Vincent's relationship to Sien and his construction of gender and domesticity, see Zemel 1997, ch. 1. Vincent's apprehension of Sien foreshadows what Pollock (1998, p. 97) refers to as Vincent's "profoundly displaced and imaginary relations to people" during the period

1888–89 that would, we argue, be part and parcel of his relationship with Gauguin.

65 "Good sermon": Vincent to Theo, [c. 11 Mar. 1882], 209/180. "Nonentity": Vincent to Theo, [21 July 1882], 250/218. The drawing is signed and annotated: "Comment se fait-il qu'il y ait sur la terre une femme seule—délaissée / Michelet" ("How can there be on earth a woman alone, abandoned / Michelet"). On *Sorrow*, see Greer (note 2); Amsterdam 1990, pp. 64ff.; and Zemel 1997, pp. 26–30. For Vincent's lithograph after *Sorrow*, see Sjraar van Heugten and Fieke Pabst, *The Graphic Work of Vincent van Gogh: Cahier Vincent 6* (Amsterdam, 1995), cat. 2, pp. 38–43.

66 "English style": Vincent to Theo, [c. 10 Apr. 1882], 215/186. On Zola in this context, specifically his novel *L'Assommoir*, which attributes a woman's fall to her environment, see 244/212, 382/317, 339/280. On penetration of life and art, see letter to van Rappard, [4 Feb. 1883], 309/R 20. On Vincent and *The Graphic*, see Ronald Pickvance, *The English Influences on Vincent van Gogh*, exh. cat., University Art Gallery, Nottingham (1974); and Bailey 1992. Linda Nochlin has linked the pose of the figure of *Sorrow* with the iconography of the "fallen woman" in "Lost and *Found*: Once More the Fallen Woman," *Art Bulletin* 60, no. 1 (Mar. 1978), pp. 139–53.

67 For Vincent testing others' "real feeling about art," and for real vs. conventional, see Vincent to Theo, [11 Feb. 1883], 314/266. "Respecting a whore": [Oct. 1884], 467/378. For the renewed threat of Gheel, see [14 May 1882], 226/198; and [2/3 June 1882], 234/201. "Friendship": Vincent to van Rappard, [c. 22–29 Oct. 1882], 275/R 28; see also 314/266, 358/295. "Cabin"; "*dat is het*": Vincent to Theo, [Jan. 1876], 66/52.

68 "Firm *faith*": Vincent to Theo, [11 Mar. 1883], 329/274. On his love of drawing: [c. 12–16 Jan. 1882], 199/170; on venturing into new media: [3 Sept. 1882], 261/228; pilot making headway: [12/13 May 1882], 225/197; painful memories: [22 June 1882], 239/208; launching boat in The Hague: [5/6 Aug. 1882], 255/223; comfortable barge: [5 Aug. 1882], 254/222; love as a sailor does ship: [c. 3 Mar. 1883], 325/271; harbor or refuge: [2 Apr. 1883], 336/278.

69 "Life means painting": Vincent to van Rappard, [c. 8 May 1883], 343/R 34; van Rappard and *The Graphic*: [2/3 Dec. 1882], 292/250; and [c. 9 Feb. 1883], 313/R 25. For van Rappard's recollections, see Lutz (note 63), p. 40.

70 For Vincent's differences with Tersteeg and Mauve at this point, see letters to Theo of March–May 1882, esp. 211/182, 213/184, 219/190, 221/195; and to van Rappard, 231/R 8.

71 For Tersteeg as "the everlasting no": Vincent to Theo, [c. 2 July 1883], 360/297. For Vincent

imagining harmony among painters, see 298/256 and 354/292. For intrigues, see 231/R 8, 253/221, 278/R 16, 298/256, and 309/R 20. On the "homeland of painters" concept, see Pollock 1980b, vol. 1, pp. 36–42.

72 Robinson Crusoe: Vincent to van Rappard, [18/19 Sept. 1882], 267/R 13.

73 "Healthy melancholy": Vincent to Theo, [c. 15 Sept. 1883], 389/324. "Miles and miles": [c. 3 Oct. 1883], 395/330.

74 "Sinking ship": Vincent to Theo, [29 Oct. 1883], 402/337. On Vincent and the reality and fiction of Drenthe, see Pollock 1998, pp. 82–84, 101.

75 On brothers-painters, see Vincent to Theo, [29 Oct./15 Nov. 1883], 404/339. "Reddish hair"; "self-engrossed": [29 Oct./15 Nov. 1883], 403/338. "Family life"; "obey"; "merge": [28 Oct. 1883], 401/336. "Feeling, thinking": [c. 17 Dec. 1883], 416/347.

76 "Implacable": Vincent to Theo, [6/7 Dec. 1883], 412/345. Break decisively: [21 Dec. 1883], 417/348. "Tangled threads": [3 June 1883], 350/223.

77 On the symbolic significance of the weaver in Vincent's work, see Silverman 1994 and 2000, where weaving is presented as a metaphor for Vincent's entire career. For additional considerations of the weaver series, see Linda Nochlin, "Van Gogh, Renouard, and the Weaver's Crisis in Lyon: The Status of a Social Issue in the Art of the Late Nineteenth Century," in *Art, the Ape of Nature: Studies in Honor of H. W. Jansen*, ed. by M. Barasche and L. F. Sandler (New York, 1980), pp. 660–88; Pollock 1980b, vol. 1, ch. 4; Zemel 1985; and Zemel 1997, ch. 2.

78 For Carlyle quotations, see *Sartor Resartus*, pp. 164, 179. For Delacroix and Blanc, see for example Vincent to Theo, [June 1884], 452/370, 454/372.

79 Vincent to van Rappard, [late Mar. 1884], 440/R 43.

80 For Vincent's devotion to and Theo's dislike of Leon Lhermitte, a follower of Millet, see [21 Mar. 1884], 441/362; and [early Apr. 1884], 444/363a. Carlyle discusses following a leader in *On Heroes*, pp. 154–55. For Vincent on Manet, see his letter to Theo, [24 Jan. 1884], 429/355. See note 88.

81 Vincent to Theo, [Oct. 1884], 467/378; emphasis in original. On Vincent's reading of *Au bonheur des dames*, see Sund 1992, pp. 85–88.

82 For an example of Mouret as coded reference, see Vincent to Theo, [2nd half Sept. 1884], 464/379. "Abstract": Zola, *Joie de vivre*, p. 44. "All is vanity": Vincent to Theo, [c. 14–18 Mar. 1882], 211/182; the reference is to Solomon's lament in the book of Ecclesiastes (1:2). In a similar vein, in this same letter Vincent spoke of doing battle with the haunting "nightmare" of "Nada," a specter he associated with Goya's art.

82 The image's main elements, pipe and flowers,

deserve further explanation. Vincent wrote to Theo about one of his run-ins with their father: "He comes out with … 'You will be the death of me' while he sits there smoking his pipe": Vincent to Theo, [7/8 Jan. 1882], 198/169. The plant's botanical name is *Lunaria annua*; French names for it include "médaille de Judas," "Monnaie du pape," and "oublie." In English it is referred to as "honesty" or "pennyflower." It appears in an earlier still life (November 1884 [F 76, JH 542]; Van Gogh Museum, Amsterdam). Vincent painted his *Basket of Apples* (September 1885 [F 99, JH 930]; Van Gogh Museum, Amsterdam) over his second still life depicting a vase of honesty; see van Tilborgh/Vellekoop 1999, cat. 33, pp. 176–77, 180. For a similar interpretation, see Greer (note 2), pp. 34–35.

84 "To be myself": Vincent to Theo, [c. 13–17 Apr. 1888], 497/410. "La joie (?)": [c. 11 Apr. 1885], 495/399. Tailoring it to himself, Vincent misremembered Mouret's conversation with Vallagnosc, which occurs on pp. 58–62 of *The Ladies' Paradise*, trans. from the 50th French ed. (London, 1887).

85 On this picture, see van Tilborgh/Vellekoop 1999, cat. 7, pp. 66–71.

86 "At home": Vincent to Theo, [c. 13 Apr. 1885], 496/400. "Us civilized people": [c. 30 Apr. 1885], 501/404. See Pollock 1980b, vol. 1, pp. 259–89; idem, "Van Gogh and the Poor Slaves: Images of Rural Labour as Modern Art," *Art History* 11, no. 3 (Sept. 1988), pp. 408–32; Amsterdam 1990, cat. 7, pp. 48–49; and van Tilborgh/Vellekoop 1999, cat. 26 , pp. 136–45, and the sources cited therein.

87 Vincent to van Rappard, [2nd half Aug. 1885], 529/R 57.

88 "Truer… truth"; "incorrectnesses"; "as they feel them": Vincent to Theo, [July 1885], 522/418. "All reality": [4 Oct. 1885], 536/425. Vincent could accept Zola's much-repeated definition of art ("nature seen through temperament") put forth in his volume of art criticism, *Mes Haines* (1866), but only if the revelatory mission of painting was factored in. He faulted Zola, whom he considered to have achieved this in his novels, for failing to recognize this in painting and for omitting discussion of Millet but admiring Manet, whom Vincent found more clever than profound; see [19 Aug. 1882], 259/226; [c. 2 July 1883], 361/R 38; and [c. 11 July 1883], 363/299.

89 "I shall become darker": Vincent to Theo, [end Oct. 1884], 469/383. On Vincent's "mental image bank" consisting of largely black-and-white examples, see Pollock 1980b, vol. 1, p. 38. For Vincent's assessment of "harmonists" and "colorists," see Vincent to Theo, [late Oct. 1885], 539/428.

90 Vincent to Theo, [early June 1885], 510/411.

On this picture, see van Tilborgh/Vellekoop 1999, cat. 28, pp. 152–59.

91 "A *faith*": Vincent to Theo, [5 Apr. 1885], 493/398. "Expresses something"; "Romance and romanticism are of our time, and painters must have imagination and sentiment. Fortunately realism and naturalism are not free from it. Zola creates, but does not hold up a *mirror* to things, he creates *wonderfully*, but he *creates*, *poetizes*, that is why it is so beautiful": [end Oct. 1885], 540/429. Vincent's still life typifies what Pollock (1998, p. 108) refers to as van Gogh's "idiosyncratic connotational system." See also Roskill 1979, pp. 157ff.

92 Vincent to Theo, [c. 15–20 Nov. 1885], 545/434.

93 Gauguin and Pissarro possibly met at an art-supply shop run by Madame Latouche; see M 1984, pp. 324ff.; Jirat-Wasiutyński/Newton 2000, p. 34; and Pickvance 1998, p. 37. See also letters to Pissarro of 1879–80, M 1984, letters 6–12. On the Gauguin-Pissarro relationship, see Washington 1988, cat. 2, pp. 19–20, Pickvance 1998, cat. 3, p. 258. On the 1879 exhibition, see Ronald Pickvance in San Francisco 1984, pp. 243–71. The invitation to join the exhibition was clearly offered at the last minute; Gauguin's letter of acceptance to Pissarro is dated 3 Apr. 1879; M 1984, letter 6, and p. 331 n. 22. For the Pissarros that Gauguin lent to the exhibition, see ibid, p. 333 n. 27; and San Francisco 1984, pp. 269–70. As a painter-patron, Gauguin was preceded by Henri Rouart, successful engineer, amateur painter, and friend of Degas's who lent works, time, financial support, and his own paintings (which were largely ignored by critics) to the Impressionist shows beginning with the first, in 1874.

94 On Gauguin's work in Pontoise, see Gauguin to Pissarro, 26 Sept. 1879, M 1984, letter 11, and p. 334 n. 30. For comparison of works by Pissarro and Gauguin at this moment, see Washington 1988, cat. 2, pp. 19–20; Pickvance 1998, cat. 3, p. 258; and Jirat-Wasiutyński/ Newton 2000, p. 42. The latter provides an illuminating discussion of Gauguin's technical language and structure with respect to his mentor.

95 For the reception of Gauguin at the fifth exhibition, see San Francisco 1984, pp. 304–05; and M 1984, pp. 338–39 n. 36. For Monet, see Émile Taboureux, "Claude Monet," *La Vie moderne* (12 June 1880), pp. 380–82.

96 Richard R. Brettell has analyzed the still life as a portrait of Gauguin's marriage as interpreted through a fable by Jean de La Fontaine in *Monet to Moore: The Millennium Gift of Sara Lee Corporation* (New Haven/London, 1999), cat. 12, pp. 48–51. For more on the rootwood tankard, see Pickvance 1998, cat. 18, p. 263.

97 In *Avant et après* (p. 183) Gauguin claimed to have whittled in his youth in Orléans: "A little later I was whittling one day with a knife, carving dagger-handles without the dagger, all sorts of little fancies incomprehensible to grown people. A good old woman who was a friend of ours exclaimed in admiration, 'He's going to be a great sculptor.'"

98 For Degas's influence on Gauguin's sculpture, see Theodore Reff, *Degas: The Artist's Mind* (New York, 1974), pp. 262–64; and Washington 1988, cat. 6, pp. 25–26. The object relates to a Degas drawing, *Project for Portraits in a Frieze*, shown in 1881, and to the better-known Degas sculptures *Little Schoolgirl* and *Little Fourteen-Year-Old Dancer*. For Pissarro's interest in the primitives, see his letters to Lucien from the latter half of 1883, esp. B-H, vol. 1, letters 164, 167, 171, 180, 190, 197–98, 202–03.

99 "Elegant figures": Henri Trianon, *Le Constitutionnel*, 24 Apr. 1881; repr. in Berson 1996, vol. 1, p. 368. "Gothically modern": Joris-Karl Huysmans, "L'Exposition des indépendants en 1881," in *L'Art moderne* (Paris, 1883); repr. in ibid., vol. 1, p. 352.

100 On movements and "isms," see Jensen 1994, pp. 40–41, 90–106; on the 1881 exhibition, see Fronia E. Wissman in San Francisco 1984, pp. 337–52; Gauguin to Pissarro, [11/12 May 1883], M 1984, letter 36, and pp. 342–44 n. 46.

101 See letters from Gauguin to Pissarro of December 1881 and January 1882, M 1984, letters 20–22.

102 Monet was willing to shed Caillebotte if Pissarro would dismiss one of his adherents, implying Gauguin; Renoir too talked dismissively of the "Pissarro-Gauguin combination." See Joel Isaacson in San Francisco 1984, pp. 373–76. On Durand-Ruel's purchases, see Bodelsen 1970, p. 593.

103 See Jensen 1994, pp. 40–41, 63–67, 90–106; Martha Ward, "Impressionist Installations and Private Exhibitions," *Art Bulletin* 73, no. 4 (Dec. 1991), pp. 599–622; and Pollock 1992.

104 For Gauguin on Cézanne, see letter to Pissarro, [25/29 July 1883], M 1984, letter 38. For the Cézannes Gauguin owned, see Merete Bodelsen, "Gauguin's Cézannes," *Burlington Magazine* 104, no. 710 (May 1962), pp. 204–11. For Gauguin's inattention to his job, see letters to Pissarro from late September/early October 1883, M 1984, letters 40–41.

105 For group dynamics, see letters to Pissarro from late July/early August 1882, M 1984, letters 26–27. For Gauguin's recognition of his stake in the Impressionist exhibitions, see letter to Pissarro, [Jan./Feb. 1883], M 1984, letter 32.

106 See letters of fall 1883 from Gauguin to Pissarro, M 1984, letters 40–42; and from Pissarro to Lucien and to Eugène Murer, B-H, vol. 1, letters 185–86, 188. "Notes synthé-

tiques" were first published as "Notes synthétiques de Paul Gauguin," *Vers et prose* (1910), pp. 51–55; facs. in Cogniat/Rewald 1962. See Rewald's introduction to the text, pp. 37–53; and Vojtěch Jirat-Wasiutyński, *Paul Gauguin in the Context of Symbolism* (New York/London, 1978), pp. 16–30.

107 Gauguin to Pissarro, [end July 1884], M 1984, letter 50. For other works featuring the tankard, see the contemporary *Sleeping Child* (depicting Clovis (1884 [W 81]; private collection), double portrait of Clovis and Aline (1884 [W 82]; private collection), and the somewhat later one of Clovis and Pola (1885 [W 135]; private collection). On this painting, see Washington 1988, cat. 13, pp. 36–37. For the tankard, see note 96.

108 Gauguin to Schuffenecker, [late Nov./early Dec. 1884] and 14 Jan. 1885, M 1984, letters 57, 65. Gauguin met Schuffenecker when the latter joined the firm of Bertin in 1872 (see note 54).

109 On Durand-Ruel's Société de Saint-Luc, see Gauguin to Pissarro, [late Dec. 1884/ early Jan. 1885], M 1984, letter 61. "Republican philosophy": Gauguin to Pissarro, 30 Jan. 1885, M 1984, letter 68.

110 Gauguin to Schuffenecker, 25 May 1885, M 1984, letter 78; to Pissarro, [end May 1885], letter 79.

111 The painting seems to depict the attic of the apartment at 51 Nørregade, where the family moved in April; see Washington 1988, p. 8.

112 "Salvation": Gauguin to Pissarro, [May 1885], M 1984, letter 79. Pickvance has identified the blond child against the window in *Still Life in an Interior* (fig. 4) as Clovis, and posits a correlation between Clovis and the Norwegian tankard; Pickvance 1998, cat. 18, p. 263.

Citations for bold-faced quotations: p. 79: Vincent to Theo, 3 Apr. 1878, 142/121; p. 80: Gauguin to Schuffenecker, [early July 1887], M 1984, letter 129; Vincent to Wil, [31 July 1888], 657/W 5; p. 86: Fénéon trans. in Halperin 1988, p. 214; p. 92: Vincent to Wil, [22 June 1888], 633/W 4.

1 On Gauguin in Dieppe, see Sweetman 1996, pp. 122ff.; and Pickvance 1998, cat. 20–21, pp. 263–64.

2 Gauguin to Pissarro, [13 Aug. 1883], M 1984, letter 39. On Gauguin and Spanish politics, see M 1984, pp. 388–89 n. 119; and Sweetman 1996, pp. 103–08, 124–25.

3 Gauguin to Mette, 29 Dec. 1885, M 1984, letter 92.

4 Degas, cited in Ward 1986, p. 423. The following discussion of the 1886 exhibition draws heavily on Ward's account; and the account of the art market and the evolving dealer-gallery system is indebted to Jensen 1994. See also Nicholas Green, "Dealing in Temperaments: Economic Transformation of the Artistic Field during the Second Half of the Nineteenth Century," *Art History* 10, no. 1 (Mar. 1987), pp. 59–78.

5 For Pissarro and Seurat in this context, see Ward 1986. For Ward's description of the *Grande Jatte* as a "manifesto picture" and a "focal point for the formation of a new critical avant-garde," see pp. 427–28.

6 Félix Fénéon, "Les Impressionnistes," *La Vogue* (13–20 June 1886), pp. 261–75; repr. in Halperin 1970, vol. 1, pp. 29–38. See also Ward 1986, p. 428.

7 Fénéon first used the term "néo-impressionnisme" in print in his article "L'Impressionnisme aux Tuileries," *L'Art moderne de Bruxelles* (19 Sept. 1886); repr. in Halperin 1970, vol. 1, pp. 53–58. *L'Oeuvre* was first published in book form in 1886.

8 Zola, *L'Oeuvre*, pp. 419–20.

9 See Robert J. Niess, *Zola, Cézanne, and Manet: A Study of "L'Oeuvre"* (Ann Arbor, Mich., 1968).

10 "Moderniste impressionniste": Bernard to his parents, 3 June 1886, Harscoët-Maire 1997, p. 121. For *L'Oeuvre*, see letter to his parents of 11 July 1886, ibid., p. 133. "The modern"; "steeped": Bernard to his parents, 2 July 1886, ibid., p. 130.

11 Theo to Wil, 25 Apr. 1887, VGM FR, inv. b911 V/1962; trans. in Hulsker 1974, p. 12.

12 Gauguin to Mette, [c. 22–29 June 1886], M 1984, letter 101. Mette's serialized translation of *L'Oeuvre*—"Mestervaerket, Pariserroman af Emile Zola"—ran as a "cut-out feuilleton" in *Politiken* from mid-May to mid-August 1886; subsequently the entire book was offered as a bonus to subscribers.

13 See the reviews by Jean Ajalbert, Henry Fèvre, Marcel Fouquier, and Octave Maus excerpted in Berson 1996, vol. 1, pp. 456–57.

14 Fénéon, "Les Impressionnistes" (note 6); repr. in Halperin 1970, vol. 1, p. 33; discussed in Ward 1986, pp. 436–38.

15 Pissarro to Lucien, 8 May 1886, B-H, vol. 2, letter 334.

16 The manuscript is reproduced (with an accompanying explanation of extant and presumed versions) in Herbert 1991, App. P; Jirat-Wasiutyński/Newton 2000, p. 62, dispute the Persian attribution, claiming: "It may well have been made up from various sources by Gauguin himself as a hoax and a commentary on a number of contemporary artistic doctrines."

17 "Mysterious *écriture*": Gauguin to Schuffenecker, 14 Jan. 1885, M 1984, letter 65. "Petit point": [14 Aug. 1888], M 1984, letter 159; see also M 1984, letters 178, 184; and M 1995, pp. 39–40. This 1889 work in question is *Pointillist Still Life* (1889 [W 376]; private collection, United States). The authors agree with Ronald Pickvance (conversation September 1998) that a still life with horse's head listed in the catalogue raisonné of Gauguin's work as W 183 was in fact painted by Schuffenecker, whose contemporary experiments in the Neo-Impressionist style feature a comparable palette and handling. See also Jirat-Wasiutyński/Newton 2000, p. 224 n. 11.

18 Vincent to Theo, [c. 28 Jan. 1886], 558/447. For an overview of Vincent's life in Antwerp, see Hulsker 1990, pp. 209–21.

19 Vincent to Theo, [14 Feb. 1886], 564/453. See also Vincent to Theo, [mid-Feb. 1886], 563/452.

20 Letter to Theo announcing his arrival in Paris: [c. 1 Mar. 1886], 570/459. For more in-depth information on van Gogh's artistic production in Paris, see Rewald 1956, ch. 1; Bogomila Welsh-Ovcharov, *Vincent van Gogh: His Paris Period, 1886–1888* (Utrecht/The Hague, 1976); Welsh-Ovcharov 1988; and George T. M. Shackelford, "Van Gogh in Paris: Between the Past and the Future," in Detroit 2000, pp. 87–125. Vincent habitually wore clothes handed down to him by Theo and his father; see Vincent to Theo, [20 Aug. 1882], 260/227; and [20–21 Aug. 1883], 380/315. Although his Paris self-portraits show him in a variety of smarter attire, when working he donned the blue shirt of a zinc-worker, as recalled by Signac and Gustave Coquiot in *Vincent van Gogh* (Paris, 1923), p. 140. On Vincent's self-portraits as a staging of his professional identity, see Zemel 1997, ch. 4.

21 "Mistakes"; "in prison": Vincent to Theo, [early Feb. 1886], 559/448. "To produce": [first half Feb. 1886], 561/450. Vincent's improved appearance: Theo to Mother, [June/July 1886], VGM FR, inv. b942 V/1962; trans. in Hulsker 1974, p. 8.

22 Vincent to Theo, [2nd half Oct. 1885], 539/428.

23 "Slovenly, ugly": Vincent to Wil, [c. 22 June 1888], 633/W 4. All comments to Livens are from a letter, written in English, of [Aug./Oct. 1886], 572/459a. This letter is erroneously dated [Aug./Oct. 1887] in the 1958 English edition of the letters; it is probably a typographical error, however, since it appears between letters dated 1886.

24 Theo to Mother, [June/July 1886], VGM FR, inv. b942 V/1962; trans. in Hulsker 1974, p. 8. For the van Gogh brothers' discussions of Cormon, see letters 466/381, 559/448, and 560/449. See also Hartrick 1939, pp. 47–48. For Vincent's experience at Cormon's and a description of his social orbit, see Welsh-Ovcharov 1988, pp. 16–20.

25 Vincent to Livens, [Aug./Oct. 1886], 572/459a; emphasis in original.

26 On *Bowl with Zinnias and Other Flowers*, see Amsterdam 1990, cat. 14, pp. 60–61. For Theo's purchases of Monticellis, see Amsterdam 1999, p. 157.

27 Theo to Mother, [June/July 1886], VGM FR, inv. b942 V/1962; trans. in Hulsker 1974, p. 8. On this painting, see Welsh-Ovcharov 1988, cat. 6, pp. 50–51.

28 Vincent illustrated his perspective frame in a letter to Theo, [5 Aug. 1882], 254/222. For more information on his early use of the frame, see Pickvance 1984, pp. 54–55; and Sjraar van Heugten, *Vincent van Gogh: Drawings*, vol. 1, The Early Years, 1880–1883 (Amsterdam, 1996), pp. 17–25. Debora Silverman has explored the perspective frame's symbolic import in Silverman 1992, pp. 94–115; Silverman 1994; and Silverman 2000, pp. 62–67, 141, and 403–05. Vincent abandoned this device in May 1888. "There are colors": Vincent to Wil, [c. 22 June 1888] 633/W 4. See also Welsh-Ovcharov 1988, cat. 20, p. 78, and cat. 33, p. 104.

29 See Welsh-Ovcharov 1988, pp. 21–22.

30 Signac to Pissarro and Pissarro to Signac, [late July/early Aug. 1886], B-H, vol. 2, no. 349 n. 1.

31 "Badly brought up": Gauguin to Signac, [first half July 1886], M 1984, letter 103. See also Seurat to Signac, [16–17 June 1886], M 1984, letter XXVII. "Tactlessness": Seurat (quoting Pissarro) to Signac, 19 June 1886, M 1984, letter XXVIII. On this incident, see Herbert 1991, pp. 403–04; Jirat-Wasiutyński/Newton 2000, pp. 61–62; and M 1984, p. 429 n. 199.

32 The sketchbook image echoes an object that Gauguin included in the background of an 1882 pastel portrait of Aubé ([W 66]; Musée du Petit Palais, Paris); see Washington 1988, cat. 10, pp. 32–33. Bracquemond showed prints at the Impressionist exhibitions of 1874, 1879, and 1880. On Bracquemond and Chaplet, see M 1984, pp. 426–28 n. 196; on Aubé, see ibid., pp. 428–29 n. 197. On Chaplet, see Jean d'Albis, *Ernest Chaplet, 1835–1909* (Paris, 1976), pp. 94–95; and Washington 1988, cat. 10, pp. 32–33.

33 Fauns (alone or in groups) were among the preferred subjects of decorative sculptors of the eighteenth century, of whom Clodion (Claude Michel; French, 1738–1814) is the prime representative. Fifteenth-century Nordic imagery situated the "savage man" in the entourage of satyrs Dionysus, Silenus, and Pan; see Paris, Musée du Louvre, *Clodion, 1738–1814*, exh. cat. by Anne L. Poulet (1992), p. 142 passim. Among the best-known examples (through reproductions) in Gauguin's time were a Roman copy of Praxitiles' *Satyr* (370 B.C.; Museo Nazionale Romano) and the more overtly caprine *Dancing Faun* (c. 312 B.C.; Museo Archeologico Nazionale, Naples), which was excavated at Pompeii in 1830.

34 For a discussion of the symbolism of the centaur, see The Art Institute of Chicago, *Odilon Redon: Prince of Dreams*, exh. cat. by Douglas W. Druick et al. (1994), p. 45; and Douglas W. Druick, "Moreau's Symbolist Ideal," in *Gustave Moreau: Between Epic and Dream*, exh. cat. by Geneviève Lacambre et al., The Art Institute of Chicago (1999), pp. 37–38.

35 Gauguin to Mette, [Jan. 1886], M 1984, letter 94. On Brandes and *Politiken*, see *Politikens Historie Set Indefra, 1884–1984: En scrapbog samlet og keommenteret af Bo Bramsen*, vol. 1, 1884–89 (Copenhagen, 1983). On Brandes and Gauguin, see Bodelsen 1970, pp. 601ff.; and M 1984, pp. 425–26 n. 194.

36 Gauguin to Mette, [c. 22–29 June 1886], M 1984, letter 101. Gauguin had just read the poem published in *La Vogue* (7–14 June 1886), pp. 220–21. See Gauguin to Bracquemond, 24 June 1886, M 1984, letter 100, for the firing of *The Faun*.

37 Bodelsen 1964, p. 14, examines the association of the "PGO" signature with Gauguin's ceramics. See *1811 Dictionary of the Vulgar Tongue: A Dictionary of Buckish Slang, University Wit, and Pickpocket Eloquence*, intro. by Robert Cromie (Northfield, Ill., 1971), s.v. "pego." This association was first observed by Wayne Andersen, *Gauguin's Paradise Lost* (New York, 1971), pp. 186, 255. See also the reference to Gauguin's dog, "Pegau," in Guillaume Le Bronnec, "La Vie de Gauguin aux îles Marquises," *Bulletin de la Société des Études Océaniennes*, ser. 5, 9 (Mar. 1954), p. 210. Dogs are frequently inserted into Gauguin's paintings.

38 "Make art": Gauguin to Bracquemond, [c. 8–12 July 1886], M 1984, letter 105. See also Gauguin to Mette, [c. 1–15 June 1886], M 1984, letter 99. In August 1885 Gauguin had mentioned his intention to go to Brittany the

following summer; Gauguin to Mette, 19 Aug. 1885, M 1984, letter 83.

39 For an introduction to Pont-Aven, see M 1984, pp. 432–36 n. 203. For a more complete history of Gauguin's production in the province, see Denise Delouche, *Gauguin et la Bretagne* (Rennes, 1996). See also idem, *Peintres de la Bretagne: Découverte d'un province* (Paris, 1977). Fred Orton and Griselda Pollock were the first to examine critically Gauguin's primitivizing approach to Pont-Aven; see Orton/Pollock 1980, pp. 314–44. See also Catherine Bertho, "L'Invention de la Bretagne: Genèse sociale d'un stéréotype," *Actes de la recherche en sciences sociales* 35 (1980), pp. 45–62. Nina Lübbren elaborated the notion of "place-myth" in "Rural Artists' Colonies in Nineteenth-Century Europe" (Ph.D. diss., University of Leeds, 1996), ch. 2.

40 Bernard's walking tour of Brittany lasted from May to July 1886; his itinerary apparently did not include Pont-Aven. For his interest in regional religious festivals, see his letters to his family in Harscoët-Maire 1997, pp. 113ff. "Some boys bathing": Hartrick 1939, p. 32. See also Jirat-Wasiutyński/Newton 2000, pp. 63–64, for fellow artist Henri Delavallée's recollections of Gauguin's *plein-air* and studio practices

41 For Pissarro's strategy of deliberate awkwardness, see Ward 1996, p. 53. "Cachet": Pissarro to Lucien, 30 July 1886, quoted in Herbert 1991, p. 179 n. 14. This letter is reproduced in B-H, vol. 2, letter 348, although it is noted in Herbert 1991 that relevant portions of it were inadvertently omitted from that publication.

42 See Jirat-Wasiutyński/Newton 2000, pp. 63ff.

43 See Hartrick 1939, p. 31; and Gauguin to Mette, [15 Aug. 1886], M 1984, letter 111. "Strongest painter": Gauguin to Mette, [late July 1886], M 1984, letter 110.

44 "Romantic Impressionists": Pissarro to Lucien, [3 Nov.? 1886], B-H, vol. 2, letter 360. "The Impressionists are passé": 3 Dec. 1886, B-H, vol. 2, letter 361. Gauguin's creative harnessing of hostility is discussed by Françoise Cachin in Washington 1988, p. xxiii.

45 See Washington 1988, cat. 24, pp. 69–70. On the impact of Gauguin's work in ceramics on his development of a synthetist style, see Merete Bodelsen, "The Missing Link in Gauguin's Cloisonism," *Gazette des beaux-arts*, ser. 6, 53 (May–June 1959), pp. 329–44. "Ceramic sculpture": Gauguin to Mette, [c. 25 July 1886] and [mid-Sept. 1886], M 1984, letters 107, 112.

46 See Braun 1986.

47 The sketchbook page is published in Gray 1980, fig. 18, p. 27. The Degas motif is found in *Vase Decorated with the Half-length Figure of a Woman* (winter 1886/87 [B 7, G 12]; Kunstindustrimuseet, Copenhagen); the

48 Gauguin to Bracquemond, M 1984, letter 114. *Le Nouveau Petit Robert*, 1996 ed., s.v. "colombin," given as a synonym for *étron*, or "turd."

49 "Fifty-five"; "small products": Gauguin to Bracquemond, [late Nov. 1886], M 1984, letter 116. "Artistic": Gauguin to Mette, 26 Dec. 1886, M 1984, letter 115. On the Union Centrale's exhibition, see Gauguin to Mette, 26 Dec. 1886, M 1984, letter 115. The exhibition took place between 13 August and 4 December 1887 at the Palais de l'Industrie; see M 1984, p. 443 n. 212.

50 On the Salon de la Nationale, see Debora Silverman, *Art Nouveau in Fin-de-Siècle France* (Berkeley, Calif., 1989), p. 208. Pissarro to Lucien, [17 Sept. 1886], B-H, vol. 2, letter 353.

51 See Berson 1996, vol. 2, p. 180.

52 See Gauguin to Mette, 6 Dec. 1887, M 1984, letter 137.

53 Pissarro to Lucien, 23 Jan. 1887, B-H, vol. 2, letter 387.

54 This was the charge Pissarro leveled at Charles Toché (French; 1851–1916), a painter of stylized, decorative images based on his travels, who was successfully launched at Petit's in January 1887 and hailed by Albert Wolff (in *Le Figaro*, 14 Jan. 1887, pp. 1–2) for his "sincere vision"; see Pissarro to Lucien, 23 Jan. 1887, B-H, vol. 2, letter 387. This discussion of Pissarro's primitivism is informed by Ward 1996, pp. 19ff., 33ff.

55 Pissarro to Lucien, 23 Jan. 1887, B-H, vol. 2, letter 387.

56 On Gauguin in Martinique, see Karen Kristine Rechnitzer Pope, *Gauguin and Martinique* (Ph.D. diss., University of Texas, Austin, 1981; Ann Arbor, Mich., 1984). For a technical analysis of Gauguin's Martinique paintings, see Jirat-Wasiutyński/Newton 2000, pp. 76–84.

57 Welsh-Ovcharov 1988, cat. 30, p. 98. Seurat began to experiment with painted frames in 1887; see Herbert 1991, pp. 204–06, App. A; Ward 1996, pp. 118–22; and Inge Fiedler, "A Technical Evaluation of the *Grande Jatte*," *The Art Institute of Chicago Museum Studies* 14, no. 2 (1989), pp. 173–79. For a general discussion of artists' frames, see Isabelle Cahn, *Cadres de peintres*, exh. cat., Musée d'Orsay, Paris (1989); and Amsterdam, Van Gogh Museum, *In Perfect Harmony: Picture and Frame, 1850–1920*, exh. cat. by Evan Mendgen et al. (1995).

58 Theo to Lies, 15 May 1887, VGM FR, inv. b912 V/1982; trans. in Hulsker 1974, p. 12. For Vincent's experimentation with and rejection of the rational surfaces of Neo-Impressionism, see Ward 1996; and Welsh-Ovcharov 1988, cat. 30, p. 98.

59 "*Faith* in color": Vincent to Livens, [Aug./Oct. 1886], 572/459a. Vincent to Bernard, [summer 1887], 578/B 1; and Mannheim 1990, p. 108. For Bernard's (and Anquetin's) hostility to Signac's new work, see Pissarro to Lucien, [13 Mar. 1887], B-H, vol. 2, letter 403.

60 "Regular course in impressionism": Vincent to Theo, 27 Aug. 1888, 673/528. Vincent to Wil, [c. 27 Aug. 1888], 674/W 8. The comparison between Vincent's work and Monticelli's portrait is made in Welsh-Ovcharov 1988, cat. 39, p. 116. On the Paris self-portraits, see also Shackelford (note 20).

61 "Guide and counselor": Vincent to Theo, [c. 13 Apr. 1885], 496/400. "Hardly any color": 3 May 1889, 771/590. See ch. 1, note 89.

62 Paul Signac, *D'Eugène Delacroix au néo-impressionnisme*, intro. by Françoise Cachin (1889; repr. Paris, 1964). On Seurat's drawing technique, see Herbert 1991, p. 54.

63 Pissarro to Lucien, 16 May 1887, B-H, vol. 2, letter 424. On the issue of Millet being collected in "the circles most opposed to the developments in modern art" and on his declining reputation, see Griselda Pollock, *Millet* (London, 1977), p. 6.

64 On *A Pair of Boots*, see Amsterdam 1990, cat. 19, p. 70. See Vincent to Theo, [c. 13 Apr. 1885], 496/400; and Vincent to Wil, [summer/fall 1887], 576/W 1.

65 For Vincent and Japanese prints, see M. E. Tralbaut, "Van Gogh's Japanisme," *Mededelingen van de Dienst voor Schone Kunsten van de Gemeente 's Gravenhage* 9, nos. 1–2 (1954), pp. 6–40; Fred Orton, "Vincent's Interest in Japanese Prints: Vincent van Gogh in Paris, 1886–87," *Vincent: Bulletin of the Rijksmuseum Vincent van Gogh* 1, no. 3 (1971), pp. 2–12; Amsterdam, Van Gogh Museum, *Japanese Prints Collected by Vincent van Gogh*, exh. cat. (1978); Akiko Mabuchi, "Van Gogh and Japan," in *Vincent van Gogh*, exh. cat., National Museum of Western Art, Tokyo (1985), pp. 154–79; Kōdera 1990, ch. 4; and Kōdera 1991.

66 Theo conveyed Vincent's wish to retrieve the prints in a letter to his mother of 22 Mar. 1887, VGM FR, inv. b909 V/1962; trans. in Hulsker 1974, p. 12.

67 "Gave myself up": Vincent to Wil, [summer or fall 1887], 576/W 1. "Most poignantly tragic": [30 Mar. 1888], 593/W 3.

68 "Because I go about": Vincent to Theo, [c. 13 Apr. 1885], 496/400. Vincent here paraphrased Millet, as quoted in Alfred Sensier, *La Vie et l'oeuvre de J.-F. Millet* (Paris, 1881), p. 217. See Louis van Tilborgh, "Van Gogh, Disciple of Millet," in *Van Gogh and Millet*, trans. by Martin Cleaver, exh. cat., Rijksmuseum Vincent van Gogh, Amsterdam (1988), pp. 30–67. For Vincent's dislike of models posing in their Sunday best, in which "neither knees, elbows, shoulder blades, nor any other part of the

body have left their characteristic dents or bumps," see Vincent to Theo, [early Aug. 1881], 169/148.

69 See Carlyle, *Sartor Resartus*, pp. 181, 183; *On Heroes*, pp. 154–55.

70 Pissarro to Lucien, [26 May 1887] and [28 May 1887], BH, vol. 2, letters 428, 430; Lucien to Pissarro, 2 June 1887, in Ann Thorold, ed., *The Letters of Lucien to Camille Pissarro, 1883–1903* (Cambridge/New York, 1993), pp. 94–95. The shoemaker's shop was located at 13, rue Lepic; the van Goghs lived at 54.

71 On the comparison between the shoe and sunflower still lifes, see Pickvance 1984, pp. 35–36. On the nascent symbolism of the Paris *Sunflowers*, see Amsterdam 1990, cat. 18, p. 65; and Welsh-Ovcharov 1988, cat. 58, pp. 154–55.

72 Joost van den Vondel, "Inwyjinge der Schilderkunste, Op Sint Lukas Feest, 1654," in *De Werken van Vondel*, vol. 5, 1645–1656 (Amsterdam, 1931), p. 820. For Vondel and Saint Luke's Feast, see Dedalo Carasso, ed., *Helden van het Vaderland: Onze geschiedenis in 19de-eeuwse taferelen verbeeld* (Amsterdam, 1991), pp. 27–28.

73 "Sunflowers," *Harper's Weekly* (13 May 1882), p. 301.

74 In 1882 Wilde discussed the significance of the sunflower in a lecture he gave in New York on the English renaissance of art. For "evangel," see *Ye Soul Agonies in Ye Life of Oscar Wilde* (New York, 1882), pp. 3, 9. "Also symbolize": Vincent to Aurier, [10/11 Feb. 1890], 854/626a.

75 Vincent to Theo, [early July 1884], 454/372.

76 On the Petit Boulevard exhibition, see Welsh-Ovcharov 1988, pp. 33, 155; Pickvance 1984, p. 36; and Saint Louis Art Museum, *Vincent van Gogh and the Painters of the Petit Boulevard*, exh. cat. (2001).

77 Roland Dorn in Mannheim 1990, pp. 381–83; on communal effort, see Mannheim 1990, p. 33.

78 For Pissarro's low esteem of Schuffenecker's talent, see Pissarro to Lucien, [8 May 1886], B-H, vol. 2, letter 334. Signac dismissed Schuffenecker as "Gauguin II": Pissarro to Signac, [Apr. 1887?], cited in B-H, vol. 2, letter 415 n. 1.

79 On Chaplet, see Gauguin to Schuffenecker, 25 Aug. 1887, M 1984, letter 131; Gauguin to Mette, 24 Nov. 1887, M 1984, letter 136. On Theo as a dealer, see Rewald 1973. See also Richard Thomson, "Theo van Gogh: An Honest Broker," in Amsterdam 1999, pp. 61–148. "Center of the impressionists": Gauguin to Mette, 6 Dec. 1887, M 1984, letter 137.

80 On the initial meeting of Gauguin and the van Gogh brothers, see M 1984, pp. 470–71 n. 236; and M 1989, p. 55. Merlhès speculates that Gauguin, accompanied by Guillaumin or Schuffenecker, met Theo and possibly

Vincent at Boussod et Valadon.

81 At this point Theo was not purchasing works outright for the firm but rather taking them on consignment, paying Gauguin after a sale was made; the dealer made no outright purchases of Gauguin's art for the firm until April 1890. See Richard Thomson in Amsterdam 1999, p. 139. On Theo's purchase of works by Gauguin, see M 1984, pp. 471–72 n. 236; and Amsterdam 1999, p. 168. A receipt made out to Theo and dated 4 Jan. 1888 is reproduced as Cooper 1983, GAC 1. Theo described the work's installation in the sitting room in Theo to Wil, 6 Dec. 1888, VGM FR, inv. b916 V/1962. In the months that followed, Theo included Gauguin in a number of Boussod et Valadon displays: exhibition of the work of Pissarro, Gauguin, Guillaumin (Dec. 1887); pastels by Degas and work by Gauguin (Jan. 1888); work by Gauguin, Schuffenecker, and Federico Zandomeneghi (Apr. 1888); work by Gauguin (Nov. 1888); recent work by Pissarro and a sculpture and ceramics by Gauguin (Feb. 1890); see Amsterdam 1999, pp. 131, 187–88.

82 Huyghe 1952, p. 222. Months later Vincent referred to their exchange in letters 644/510 and 740/571.

83 "High poetry": Vincent to Bernard, [c. 20 May 1888], 614/B 5. Among his sisters, Theo wrote about art most frequently to Wil; after he and Jo Bonger became engaged in December 1888, the affianced couple exchanged frequent letters (published as Brief Happiness) during the months before their marriage on 18 April 1889. "That is art": Theo to Jo, 1 Feb. 1889, Brief Happiness, letter 35.

84 Theo to Jo, 1 Feb. 1889, Brief Happiness, letter 35.

85 In 1885 Theo reported to his mother that a Paris acquaintance to whom he had shown Vincent's work said that Vincent "would exceed Millet"; Theo to Mother, [c. 1 June 1885], VGM FR, inv. b939 V/1962; trans. in Hulsker 1974, p. 5.

86 For Theo on Degas, see Theo to Wil, 6 Dec. 1888, VGM FR, inv. b916 V/1982; Theo to Jo, 24 Jan. 1889, Brief Happiness, letter 26; Theo to Wil, 27 Nov. 1889, VGM FR, inv. b926 V/1962; and Theo to Jo, 1 Feb. 1889, Brief Happiness, letter 35. For Vincent on Degas, see Gauguin to Bernard, [2nd half Nov. 1888], M 1984, letter 182; and Richard Kendall, "'I kept on thinking about Degas [...]': Vincent van Gogh and the 'little lawyer,'" Van Gogh Museum Journal (1999), pp. 30–41. For Vincent on Seurat, see Vincent to Theo, [c. 27 Aug. 1888], 673/528.

87 "Cast a ray of light": Theo to Jo, 10 Feb. 1889, Brief Happiness, letter 41. "Figure painting": Vincent to Theo, [4 May 1888], 606/482.

88 Theo to Wil, 6 Dec. 1888, VGM FR, inv. b916 V/1962.

89 "Sentiments": Theo to Jo, 10 Feb. 1889, Brief Happiness, letter 41."Our inner life": 22 Jan. 1889, Brief Happiness, letter 23.

90 Theo to Wil, 6 Dec. 1888, VGM FR, inv. b916 V/1962.

91 "One day": Theo to Jo, 23 Jan. 1889, Brief Happiness, letter 24. "New movement": 16 Mar. 1889, Brief Happiness, letter 72.

92 For the issue of the importance of an artist's life in assessing his work as it relates to Neo-Impressionism, see Ward 1996, pp. 17–18. On the Barbizon painters treated monographically, see Christopher Parsons and Neil McWilliam, "'Le Paysan de Paris': Alfred Sensier and the Myth of Rural France," Oxford Art Journal 6, no. 2 (1983), pp. 38–58; Nicholas Green, The Spectacle of Nature: Landscape and Bourgeois Culture in Nineteenth-Century France (Manchester/New York, 1990); and Jensen 1994, pp. 110–11, 119–20. "In the main": Theo to Wil, 6 Dec. 1888, VGM FR, inv. b916 V/1962.

93 "True poets": Vincent to Bernard, [c. 20 May 1888], 614/B 5. See Jensen 1994, pp. 151–54.

94 "An adventurer": Vincent to Livens, [Aug./Oct. 1886], 572/495a. "A wanderer": Vincent to Theo, [6 Aug. 1888], 660/518. Vincent read Carlyle's Sartor Resartus in English. When discussing the book (directly or indirectly) in letters to Theo, he translated Carlyle's "wanderer" as "voyageur," as would the book's first French translator, Edmond Barthélemy, in 1895–97, when it was serialized in Le Mercure de France.

95 "Boring": Gauguin to Mette, [mid-Mar. 1887], M 1984, letter 121. "Reinvigorate": [late Mar. 1887], M 1984, letter 122. "Easy": Gauguin to Schuffenecker, [c. 12 May 1887], M 1984, letter 125. "Like savages": Gauguin to Mette, [c. 1 May 1887], M 1984, letter 124.

96 "Negro cabin": Gauguin to Schuffenecker, [early July 1887], M 1984, letter 129. "The natives": Laval to Ferdinand Loyen du Puigaudeau, [June 1887], M 1984, letter XXXV. "Martyrdom": Gauguin to Antoine Favre, 25 Aug. 1887, M 1984, letter 132. See also Gauguin to Mette, 20 June 1887, M 1984, letter 12; Gauguin to Schuffenecker, 25 Aug. 1887, M 1984, letter 131.

97 "Life and reality": Vincent to Theo, [c. 24 Jan. 1885], 483/393.

98 Vincent to Theo, 26–27 Nov. 1882, 290/248. Pabst/van Uitert 1987, p. 81, notes that Vincent referred to Stowe's Uncle Tom's Cabin by three titles in letters: the Dutch (De Negerhut), in June 1879, 151/130; the English, on [26/27 Nov. 1882], 290/248; and the French, on [29 Mar. 1889], 757/582; [30 Apr. 1889], 768/W 11; and [c. 22 Jan. 1889], Cooper 1983, VG/PG. In French, he used the following slightly different designations: La Case de l'oncle Tom, L'Oncle Tom, and La

Cabane de l'oncle Tom. When Gauguin referred to the "case à négre" that he inhabited in Martinique, Vincent most likely instantly made the association to this much-admired book.

99 Gauguin to Mette, 20 June 1887, M 1984, letter 127. For more on expansionism and colonial acquisition, particularly as expressed via the Universal Exposition of 1889, see Druick/Zegers 1991, p. 17. See also Albert Guérard, France: A Modern History (Ann Arbor, Mich., 1969).

100 Theo to Lies, 19 Apr. 1887, VGM FR, inv. b910 V/1982; trans. in Hulsker 1990, p. 242.

101 For Vincent's use of these terms, see for example letters to Theo, 3 Apr. 1878, 142/121; [c. 3–5 Dec. 1882], 293/251; 28 Oct. 1883, 401/336; and to van Rappard, [late Mar. 1884], 440/R 43.

102 Vincent to Theo, 3 Apr. 1878, 142/121.

103 "Negresses in pink": Vincent to Wil, [31 July 1888], 657/W 5.

104 See Theo to Mrs. van Stockum-Haanebeck, 10 July 1887, van Gogh 1958, letter T 1a. On the reception of Rarahu, see Nicolas Serban, Pierre Loti, sa vie et son oeuvre (Paris, 1924), pp. 247–52.

105 See Maiotte Dauphite, Paul Gauguin a rencontré l'Inde, en 1887, à la Martinique (Carbet, Martinique, 1995).

106 Gauguin to Theo, 22 May 1888, M 1984, letter 146.

107 On [c. 21 Apr. 1888], 602/478, Vincent described making a two-for-one exchange. In a letter to Wil, [31 July 1888], 657/W 5, Vincent called Gauguin's picture a tableau (only referring to his own étude in the singular). In January 1889, after the end of their collaboration in Arles, he called Gauguin's work a petit toile ([17 Jan. 1889], 740/571). Aside from two passing references in Vincent's letters to Theo ([15 July 1888], 644/510; [17 Jan. 1889], 740/571), there is very little documentary evidence about the exchange of works. Merlhès has suggested that Gauguin chose Vincent's sunflower pictures and allowed Vincent to select among his work in exchange (M 1991, p. 12). It seems that Vincent generally offered whatever paintings he had on hand for his trades, though he occasionally allowed the other artist to make the selection, as he did with Russell, in June 1888 (see Vincent to Russell, [c. 17 June], 629/501a).

108 Theo to Jo, 23 Jan. 1889, Brief Happiness, letter 24.

109 Ibid.

110 Alphonse Karr, Voyage autour de mon jardin (1845; Paris, 1851 ed.). Vincent insisted Theo buy the book on 10 Aug. 1874, 28/21. He referred to Karr again in 1882 ([26–27 Nov. 1882], 290/248) and 1889 (25 June 1889, 785/596). See Pierre Larousse, Grande

Dictionnaire universel du XIXe siècle, 1873 ed., s.v. "Hélianthe." For other nineteenth-century sources on the sunflower, see Debra N. Mancoff, Sunflowers (Chicago, 2001).

111 "Two natures": Gauguin to Mette, [c. 22 Jan.–6 Feb. 1888], M 1984, letter 139; dated to c. 22 Jan. 1888 in M 1989, p. 61. Gauguin claimed to Mette that the ascendancy of his savage over his civilized self was brought on by her indifference.

112 Félix Fénéon, "Vitrines des marchands de tableaux," La Revue indépendante (Jan. 1888); repr. in Halperin 1970, vol. 1, pp. 90–91.

113 Gauguin incised many of his pots with numbers indicating their position in the sequence of his ceramic production. Bodelsen 1967, p. 218, identified the beginning of Gauguin's post-Martinique ceramic work as the pot bearing the incised number 56 (Fonsmark 1996, cat. 8). The pot in the shape of the head of a Martinique woman (B 31, G 49; Fonsmark 1996, cat. 9), overtly dependent on his Caribbean stay, is incised with the number 64. The Atahualpa pot is closely linked in form, decoration, and color to a pot that bears the number 61 (now Musée du Petit Palais, Paris, known to neither Gray nor Bodelsen; see Dominique Morel, "Trois céramiques de Gauguin au Musée du Petit Palais," Revue du Louvre 48, no. 3 [June 1998], pp. 70–74, [ill.]). "Primitive man": Vincent to Theo, 3 Apr. 1878, 142/121. When Vincent made this statement, it was with a distinct religious inflection; in the letter he continues, "through God's mercy." The conviction would carry through in a more secular sense throughout his life.

114 On this aspect of the popular perception of the Peruvian "savage," see Douglas Druick and Peter Zegers, "Scientific Realism, 1873–1881," in Degas, exh. cat., The Metropolitan Museum of Art, New York (1988), pp. 197–211. For examples of Peruvian types that influenced Gauguin's ceramics, see Braun 1986, pp. 37–38. See also the grotesque head that decorated the façade of the Echenique residence in Lima, where Gauguin lived as a child (ch. 1, fig. 30).

115 For a discussion of Seurat's "neo-primitivism," see Herbert 1991, pp. 174–75. While incorporating popular imagery, Seurat upheld the traditional prioritization of oil painting in the hierarchy of media.

116 A sketch relating to this pot appears in the sketchbook Gauguin used in Rouen and Brittany (Cogniat/Rewald 1962, p. 73), leading Bodelsen to date the pot to the winter of 1886/87 (B 17). The facts that Gauguin had this sketchbook with him in Brittany and in Arles in 1888, that the version of Puvis's Hope to which the pot apparently refers was first publicly exhibited at the Durand-Ruel

1887 retrospective, and that the figure type is informed by the Martinique experience, support a redating to the winter of 1887–88. Gray based his dating of this work (G 37) to the winter of 1886/87 on the related sketch on p. 25 of the so-called Album Briant, a sketchbook in the Musée du Louvre, Paris (RF 30273). However, the same sketchbook contains drawings related to *Les Négresses (Among the Mangoes [Tropics])* as well as to ceramics post-dating his return from Martinique (e.g. *Martinique woman with kerchief* [fig. 63], and *Portrait Vase of Jeanne Schuffenecker* [fig. 65]).

117 For contemporary views of Puvis as "poetic" and "primitive," see Louise d'Argencourt et al., *Puvis de Chavannes, 1824–1898*, exh. cat., National Gallery of Canada, Ottawa (1977), pp. 112, 153. See also Herbert 1991, pp. 6, 139, 174; Richard J. Wattenmaker, *Puvis de Chavannes and the Modern Tradition*, exh. cat., Art Gallery of Ontario, Toronto (1975), p. 21; Robert Herbert, "Seurat and Puvis de Chavannes," *Yale University Art Gallery Bulletin* 25, no. 2 (Oct. 1959), p. 23; and Robert Rosenblum, *Nineteenth-Century Art* (New York, 1984), p. 270. The Puvis retrospective ran from 11 November to 11 December 1888. Included as well was the larger, more famous, clothed version of *Hope* (1872; Walters Art Gallery, Baltimore), first exhibited at the Salon of 1872.

118 "Comme d'un Puvis modernisant": Fénéon on Puvis in 1883, cited in d'Argencourt et al. (note 117), p. 154. For Fénéon on Seurat and Puvis, see Fénéon (note 6). For Egyptian resonances in Seurat, see Mirbeau, "Exposition de peinture (1, rue Laffitte)," *La France* (21 May 1886), pp. 1–2, repr. in Berson 1996, vol. 1, pp. 465–66; "Half-a-Dozen Enthusiasts," *The Bat* (25 May 1886), pp. 185–86, repr. in Berson 1996, vol. 1, pp. 435–36; Maurice Hermel, "L'Exposition de peinture de la rue Laffitte," *La France libre* (28 May 1886), pp. 1–2, repr. Berson 1996, vol. 1, pp. 456–57.

119 For the symbolism of the olive branch, see d'Argencourt et al. (note 117), pp. 112–13; for that of the green oak leaf, or the oak twig of valor and civic triumph, see Aimée Brown Price, *Puvis de Chavannes: A Study of the Easel Paintings and a Catalogue of the Painted Works* (Ph.D. diss., Yale University, 1972; Ann Arbor, Mich., 1977), p. 409. For a discussion of *Hope*, see idem, *Pierre Puvis de Chavannes*, exh. cat., Van Gogh Museum, Amsterdam (1994), cat. 146, pp. 237–38.

120 For photographs of Aline Gauguin, see Washington 1988, fig. 50, p. 50, and fig. 91, p. 381.

121 Gauguin to Schuffenecker, 25 Oct. 1888, M 1984, letter 174 (excerpt); M 1989, pp. 124–25 (in full).

122 Theo to Wil, [24–26 Feb. 1888], VGM FR, inv.

123 For a discussion of the various datings and identifications of this work, usually titled *L'Italienne*, see Roland Dorn in Detroit 2000, p. 253 n. 35; and Dorn 1990, p. 248.

124 On the relationship between Vincent's work and the Puvis canvas, see Amsterdam 1990, cat. 29, p. 88. "Elysian Fields": Vincent to Bernard, [c. 4 Aug. 1888], 659/B 14. "Modern life": Vincent to Theo, [c. 15 Dec. 1889], 830/617.

125 "A serene old man": Vincent to Bernard, [c. 4 Aug. 1888], 659/B 14. On Charpentier novels, see Douglas Druick and Michel Hoog, *Fantin-Latour*, exh. cat., National Gallery of Canada, Ottawa (1983), cat. 42, p. 141.

126 "Youth and freshness": Vincent to Wil, [summer/fall 1887], 576/W 1.

127 See Vincent to Wil, [30 Mar. 1888], 593/W 3. "One knows": Vincent to van Rappard, [c. 21 May 1883], 347/R 35. See also Vincent to Theo, [c. 4–8 Aug. 1883], 374/309. On the book still lifes in this context, see van Uitert 1981–82, pp. 223ff.

128 See Vincent's description of the picture in his letter to Theo, [17 Oct. 1888], 712/555.

129 See Vincent to Theo, [10 Mar. 1888], 586/468; and Amsterdam 1990, cat. 29, p. 88. On the novel, see Sund 1992, pp. 142–43.

130 See *Three Novels* (spring 1887 [F 335, JH 1226]; Van Gogh Museum, Amsterdam), which includes depictions of Zola's *Au bon-heur des dames* (1883) and Edmond de Goncourt's *Fille Élisa* (1877). See Sund 1992, p. 145.

131 "On the verge": Gauguin to Mette, [c. 1–7 Jan. 1888], M 1984, letter 138. See also M 1984, p. 471 n. 239.

132 "Disastrous civil wars": Vincent to Bernard, [c. 17 July 1888], 647/B 11. "Quite ill": Vincent to Gauguin, [3 Oct. 1888], 699/544a.

133 Theo to Jo, 14 Feb. 1889, *Brief Happiness*, letter 46.

134 See Amsterdam 1990, cat. 34, p. 98. Numerous dates have been assigned to this work; Amsterdam 1990 dates it to January 1888; Welsh-Ovcharov 1988 gives a date of mid-February, right after opening of Louvre show of portraits by Old Masters (cat. 68, p. 174); Shackelford states that the work "must have been substantially complete" when show opened (Detroit 2000, p. 121); Zemel 1997 asserted that it was completed "almost immediately after" the Petit Boulevard exhibition (p. 154).

135 Vincent to Wil, [c. 22 June 1888], 633/W 4.

136 Van Eeden, *De kleine Johannes*, pp. 146, 149.

Citations for bold-faced quotations: p. 115: Vincent to Bernard, [18 June 1888], 630/B 7; p. 121: Vincent to Theo, [25 July 1888], 652/514; pp. 145–46: Vincent to Theo, [29 Sept. 1888], 695/543.

1 Gauguin to Schuffenecker, [late Feb./early Mar. 1888], M 1984, letter 141 (excerpt); dated to 20 Feb. in M 1989, pp. 61–63 (in full).

2 Loti, *Mon Frère Yves*, pp. 63, 85, 109, 158, 161–62. The connection between Gauguin's text and Loti's novel was first pointed out by Amishai-Maisels 1985, pp. 16–17.

3 Loti, *Mon Frère Yves*, p. 203. "Imbued": Gauguin to Mette, [c. 22 Jan.–6 Feb. 1888], M 1984, letter 139; dated to c. 22 Jan. in M 1989, p. 61 n.1.

4 Loti, *Mon Frère Yves*, p. 296.

5 Gauguin, *Avant et après*, p. 47.

6 "Get sunshine": Theo to Wil, [24–26 Feb. 1888], VGM FR, inv. b914 V/1962; trans. in Hulsker 1974, p. 13. "Gauguin ... superiority": Vincent to Bernard, [c. 18 Sept. 1888], 688/B 16. On the uses of the French term "Midi," which can include North Africa, see Guy de Maupassant, *Au soleil*, 5th ed. (Paris, 1884), pp. 74–75.

7 Vincent to Livens, [Aug./Oct. 1886], 572/459a. Already in the spring of 1887, Theo had reported to the family that had not gone "to the country as he first intended": Theo to his mother, 28 Feb. 1887, VGM FR, inv. b906 V/1962; trans. in Hulsker 1974, p. 9.

8 Vincent to Theo, [summer 1887], 575/462. For the "sectarian" nature and "narrow-mindedness" of vanguard painters and groups, see Vincent to Bernard, [fall 1887], 578/B 1. Cf. ch. 1, note 71.

9 Vincent to Wil, [summer/fall 1887], 576/W 1.

10 Van Eeden, *De kleine Johannes*, p. 216. Vincent's reading of this book at this time is confirmed by his letter to the painter Arnold Hendrik Koning, [c. 23 Jan. 1889], 745/571a, in which he referred to having given Koning the book, an event that must have taken place during the time they were both in Paris, that is, from September 1887 until February 1888; see Han van Crimpen, "Introduction," *Brief Happiness*, p. 54 n. 57. "Combat with mists": Theo to Lies, 13 Oct. 1885, VGM FR, inv. b903 V/1962.

11 Vincent to Wil, [c. 22 June 1888], 633/W 4.

12 See Vincent to Wil, [summer/fall 1887], 576/W 1; and Vincent to Theo, [3 Sept. 1888], 677/531, where he links Tartarin and Candide. On Vincent's identification with Tartarin, see Sund 1992, p. 172. Vincent referred to *Tartarin de Tarascon* within days of his arrival in Arles ([c. 25 Feb. 1888], 580/464). He mentioned "just reading" *Tartarin sur les Alpes* in March (585/467). He had read *Numa Roumestan* by 1883 or

1884; see Sund 1992, p. 84.

13 See Alphonse Daudet, *Numa Roumestan*, trans. by Charles de Kay (Boston, 1900). For Daudet's conception of the North, see pp. 170, 186, 286, 322, 367, 369; for the South, see pp. 7, 30, 43, 76, 196, 200, 395. See also Thérèse Roqueplo, "Le Thème du Soleil dans 'Numa Roumestan,'" *La Revue des sciences humaines*, n.s., facs. 125 (Jan.–Mar. 1967), pp. 101–16.

14 Vincent mentioned having read an article about the "Filibres" in a letter to Theo, [14 Oct. 1888], 709/553; possibly a three-part article in the 26 Aug. and 2 and 9 Sept. 1888 issues of *Le Forum républicain* or an article by Paul Mariéton, "En Provence: Sensations d'un Félibre," *L'Homme de bronze*, 14 Oct. 1888, p. 1; cited in Dorn 1990, p. 279.

15 For the Félibrean use of the sunflower, see Ködera 1990, figs. 37–41, pp. 32–33. For the sunflower's various associations in French, see Émile Littré, *Dictionnaire de la langue française*, 1991 ed., s.v. "tournesol": "Plante à grande fleur radiée, dite aussi soleil"; s.v. "soleil": "Soleil, ou tournesol, ou grand soleil des jardins, noms vulgaires de l'*helianthus annuus*." The association is similar in Provençal, where *vira-soleu* (sunflower) is composed of the words for "to turn" (*virar*) and "sun" (*soleu*). "The palette of Southern painters": "Choses d'art," *Le Forum républicain*, 4 Nov. 1888, p. 2.

16 "His son": Vincent to Wil, [c. 27 Aug. 1888], 674/W 8. Other statements about Monticelli and the South come from Vincent to Theo, [c. 21 Apr. 1888], 602/478; [c. 3 May 1888], 605/481; [29 June 1888], 638/507; [10 Oct. 1888], 707/550. For Vincent's reverence for Monticelli, see Aaron Sheon, "Monticelli and van Gogh," *Apollo* 85, no. 64 (June 1967), pp. 444–48; and Sheon 1978, pp. 81–90.

17 See Daudet, *Numa Roumestan* (note 13), p. 320; Vincent to Theo, [9 Apr. 1888], 596/474.

18 "Japanese gaiety"; "good nature": Vincent to Theo, [9 Sept. 1888], 680/524. "Understand the Japanese": [4 Oct. 1888], 702/B 19. "Simple": [c. 5 June 1888], 623/500. See also Vincent to Theo, [24 Sept. 1888], 690/542; [18 Mar. 1888], 590/B 2; Vincent to Bernard, [c. 23 July 1888], 651/B 12. On the subject of Vincent and Japan, see Ködera 1991; and Elisa Evett, "The Late Nineteenth-Century European Critical Response to Japanese Art: Primitivist Leanings," *Art History* 6, no. 1 (Mar. 1983), pp. 83–106. For Vincent's mediated vision of the South as a mythical construct—the projections onto the South (of Japan, Holland, etc.), the expectations as shaped by art and literature, and the desire to recapture an imaginary past that was key to his project—see Pollock 1998, who characterizes the journey south as much in time as in space. See also ch. 1, note 64.

19 "In fact living": Vincent to Bernard, [3 Oct. 1888], 700/B 18. "Close to nature": Vincent to Theo, [c. 22 Sept. 1888], 689/540. According to Kōdera 1990 (p. 60), "the exchange of works was not characteristic of Japanese painters.... It seems probable that he was again projecting his own ideal onto Japanese painters."

20 "If the Japanese": Vincent to Bernard, [18 Mar. 1888], 590/B 2. See Vincent to Theo, [7 May 1888], 607/483; [15 July 1888], 644/510; and [15 July 1888], 646/511.

21 See Druick/Zegers 1991, pp. 123ff.

22 Vincent to Wil, [30 Mar. 1888], 593/W 3.

23 "Orientation": Theo to Wil, [24–26 Feb. 1888], VGM FR, inv. b914 V/1962; trans. in Hulsker 1974, p. 13. Vincent to Theo, [21 Feb. 1888], 579/463.

24 On Reid, the van Gogh brothers, and Monticelli, see Sheon, "Monticelli" (note 16); Sheon 1978, p. 82; and Frances Fowle, "Vincent's Scottish Twin: The Glasgow Art Dealer Alexander Reid," Van Gogh Museum Journal (2000), pp. 94–96. By stockpiling the work of Rousseau (following his death in 1867) and Millet, Durand-Ruel had created a virtual monopoly that allowed him to control the market; see Jensen 1994, pp. 49ff. "Free hand": Vincent to Theo, [c. 25 Feb. 1888], 580/464; see also [26–28 Feb. 1888], 581/465.

25 On playing Reid against Tersteeg and van Wisselingh, see Vincent to Theo, [26–28 Feb. 1888], 581/465; and [10 Mar. 1888], 586/468.

26 When friends told him there was nothing much going on in Marseilles, he decided to wait till his nerves were steadier before satisfying his curiosity, not wanting, as he said, to "get worked up": Vincent to Theo, [c. 4 May 1888], 606/482; see also [5 July 1888], 639/508. "As for visiting Aix": Vincent to Bernard, [9 Apr. 1888], 597/B 3.

27 Ten letters to Theo and to Bernard refer to the latter's military service in North Africa; in the first three, Vincent says he will visit Bernard there ([9 Apr. 1888], 596/474; [9 Apr. 1888], 597/B 3; [c. 5 June 1888], 623/500); the remaining seven exhort him to go there. See also Bernard's letter to his parents, 26 Apr. 1888, Harscoët-Maire 1997, pp. 162–63.

28 For Mistral, see Arles 1999, p. 72, which cites his 1884 essay. Vincent to Theo, [5 July 1888], 639/508. "Refuge"; "heightened emotions": J. Autran, "Preface," La Vie rurale, vol. 2 of Oeuvres complètes (Paris, 1875), p. 45. Vincent quoted from this volume in Album 1, pp. 1–16; facs. in Pabst 1988, pp. 9–12. For Carlyle, see The French Revolution, ed. by K. J. Fielding and David Sorensen (Oxford, 1989), vol. 2, ch. 3, pp. 20–27.

29 See Fernand Beissier, Les Étapes d'un touriste en France: Le Pays d'Arles, 2d ed. (Paris, 1889), pp. 2ff.

30 John Murray, A Handbook for Travellers in France (London, 1890), part 2, p. 156. "Appearing to doze off": Beissier (note 29), p. 2.

31 See Murray (note 30): for the canals, pp. 84ff.; for the railways, pp. 93ff.; for the Paris-Lyon-Méditerranée line, pp. 134ff.; for agriculture, pp. 95ff.

32 Beissier (note 29), pp. 3–4. "Choses d'Art," Le Forum républicain, 9 Sept. 1888, p. 2. Pickvance 1984, p. 12, makes this point.

33 See "Arles—Questions Félibréennes—L'École d'Arles," L'Homme de bronze, 23 Sept. 1888; "Carnet d'un fantaisiste," Le Forum républicain, 30 Sept. 1888, p. 2. For a rebuttal, see "L'École Félibréenne d'Arles," Le Forum républicain, 21 Oct. 1888.

34 "Peered out": Vincent to Gauguin, [17 Oct. 1888], 711/B 22. "As beautiful": Vincent to Bernard, [18 Mar. 1888], 590/B 2; see also Vincent to Theo, [c. 14 Mar. 1888], 587/469.

35 Vincent to Theo, [18 Mar. 1888], 589/470.

36 "Pretence to local color"; "passionate"; "glorious": Vincent to Russell, [c. 21 Apr. 1888], 600/477a. "He explains the artist's liberty": Vincent to Theo, [18 Mar. 1888], 589/470.

37 Guy de Maupassant, "Le Roman," preface to Pierre et Jean (Paris, 1899). The preface had been published in the Supplément littéraire du Figaro (7 Jan. 1888).

38 See for example Orchard in Blossom (1888 [F 553, JH 1387]; National Gallery of Scotland, Edinburgh). The point is made in Pickvance 1984, cat. 8, p. 47. While Vincent initially drew the skyline of Arles in his first snowscape (fig. 11), in a second, unfinished, snowscape, Landscape with Snow (1888 [F 290, JH 1360]; Solomon R. Guggenheim Museum, New York), he did feature the mountains in the distance.

39 Vincent to Wil, [30 Mar. 1888], 593/W 3. On Provence as a screen for Vincent's vision of Holland, see Pollock 1998.

40 See London, Royal Academy of Arts, The Hague School: Dutch Masters of the Nineteenth Century, exh. cat. by Ronald de Leeuw et al. (1983), cat. 53, p. 207, where the point is made of Vincent's debt (throughout his career) to Hague School models.

41 "Today's palette": Vincent to Wil, [30 Mar. 1888], 593/W 3. See also Amsterdam 1990, cat. 35, pp. 100–02.

42 Vincent to Theo, [c. 2 Apr. 1888], 594/473. On Vincent's interest in painting orchards, see Pickvance 1984, pp. 45–53; and Amsterdam 1990, cat. 37–43, pp. 104–17.

43 "I should very much like to do this series of nine canvases. You see, we may consider this year's nine canvases as the first idea for a definitive decoration a great deal bigger (this present one consists of size 25 and 12 canvases), which would be carried out along just the same lines at the same time next year": Vincent to Theo, [c. 13 Apr. 1888], 599/477.

44 See van Eeden, De kleine Johannes, pp. 70–71; and Vincent to Wil, [c. 28 Feb. 1888], 582/W 2. The metaphors involving cockchafers, salad worms, and metamorphosis that Vincent invokes here come directly from van Eeden; see pp. 45–51, 71–75.

45 "Penetrate to the core of life": see for example Carlyle, On Heroes, p. 135. Vincent to Wil, [c. 28 Feb. 1888], 582/W 2. See van Eeden, De kleine Johannes, pp. 71–75.

46 "Better and different"; "painter butterfly": Vincent to Bernard, [23 June 1888], 635/B 8. "What I am the larva of": [24 June 1888], 636/B 9.

47 "Color": Vincent to Theo, [2nd half Nov. 1884], 472/386. This point is made in Amsterdam 1990, cat. 35–36, pp. 100–01.

48 "As if we were dead": Vincent to Theo, [c. 9 Mar. 1888], 585/467. "Break the ice in Holland": [9 Apr. 1888], 596/474. See also Vincent to Theo, [26–28 Feb. 1888], 581/465; [18 Mar. 1888], 589/470; [c. 11 Apr. 1888], 598/476; [24 Mar. 1888], 591/471; [30 Mar. 1888], 592/472; [c. 2 Apr. 1888], 594/473; and Vincent to Wil, [c. 28 Feb. 1888], 582/W 2.

49 Vincent to Theo, [c. 2 Apr. 1888], 594/473.

50 See Pickvance 1984, p. 42.

51 Ibid.

52 Vincent to Theo, [1 Sept. 1888], 676/530. On the Hôtel-Restaurant Carrel, see [c. 24 Apr. 1888], 603/479.

53 Vincent's plans for his house and studio can be found in his letters to Theo throughout the summer and fall of 1888. For his first conception, see his letter to Theo, [1 May 1888], 604/480. For an overview and analysis, see van Uitert 1978–79.

54 Ginoux had acquired the property earlier that year. See the "Avis d'acquisition" in L'Homme de bronze, 1 Jan. 1888, p. 3.

55 "Real painter's studio": Vincent to Theo, [5/6 Aug. 1882], 255/223. "Petticoat crisis": [1 May 1888], 604/480. Vincent couched his plans in military terms throughout this letter (and elsewhere): "campaign"; "wasting one's powder"; "expedition." "Painters join hands": [11 Mar. 1883], 329/274; see also [c. 3 May 1888], 605/481.

56 Vincent to Theo, [1 May 1888], 604/480.

57 "Quite a number": Vincent to Bernard, [18 Mar. 1888], 590/B 2. "If any painter": Vincent to van Rappard, [2nd half June 1885], 513/R 52. "Taking a house alone": Vincent to Theo, [c. 17 Nov. 1883], 408/341. "I could quite well share": Vincent to Theo, [1 May 1888], 604/480. In this letter he continued: "Perhaps I could come to some arrangement with McKnight," suggesting that he was still considering alternatives should Gauguin decline. For the Yellow House as Vincent's

utopian alternative to the Parisian art market, see Zemel 1997, pp. 194ff.

58 "A permanent studio": Vincent to Theo, [c. 10 May 1888], 609/485. "So I am beginning": [10 May 1888], 610/486. "Loneliness, worries": [c. 20 May 1888], 613/489. See also Vincent to Theo, [c. 7 May 1888] (two letters), 607/483, 608/484. For Vincent's shipment of paintings to Theo, see Hulsker 1993, p. 59.

59 Vincent to Bernard, [c. 20 May 1888], 614/B 5.

60 Vincent to Theo, [28 May 1888], 617/492.

61 Vincent to Theo, [28 May 1888], 618/493. On Vincent's view of the artist's work as his pulpit, see Sund 1988b, p. 663.

62 Draft of a letter from Vincent to Gauguin, [28 May 1888], 619/494a.

63 Vincent to Theo, [29 May 1888], 620/495. In this same letter, Vincent mentioned a now-lost letter to Gauguin and discussed his plan for a union: "I have written to Gauguin, and said only that I was sorry we were working so far from one another, and that it was a pity that serveral painters did not combine for one campaign."

64 Vincent to Theo, [c. 5 June 1888], 623/500. See also [c. 4 June 1888], 622/499.

65 "Risking": Vincent to van Rappard, 21 Nov. 1881, 186/R 5. "We are now sailing": Vincent to Bernard, [c. 17 July 1888], 647/B 11.

66 See Benoit 1887, pp. 163–65, 4, 8. Vincent announced he was reading the book in a letter to Theo, [c. 5 June 1888], 624/494.

67 For all quotes, see Vincent to Theo, [c. 4 May 1888], 606/482. Vincent used the Wagner-inflected phrase "new art" ("l'art nouveau") for the first time in this letter. "Eternal fight"; "merciless war": Benoit 1887, pp. 12, 28. Vincent conjoins Bel-Ami with Au bonheur des dames in his letter to Theo of [c. 27 Aug. 1888], 673/528: "Au bonheur des dames and Bel-Ami are no less true, however. They are different ways of looking at things." On Bel-Ami, see Sund 1992, pp. 176–77.

68 Benoit 1887, pp. 134, 167.

69 "Personal [and] original": Vincent to Theo, [c. 27 Aug. 1888], 673/528; he specifically mentioned Seurat, Signac, and Anquetin. "Exploiters"; "more and more individual": [12/13 June 1888], 627/497.

70 Gauguin to Vincent, [c. 29 Feb. 1888], M 1984, letter 142. Vincent referred to the letter on [c. 9 Mar. 1888], 585/467. See also Gauguin to Schuffenecker, [late Feb./early Mar. 1888], M 1984, letter 141 (excerpt); dated to 20 Feb. 1888 in M 1989, pp. 61–63 (in full).

71 Gauguin to Vincent, [c. 14–16 Mar. 1888], M 1984, letter 143.

72 See Gauguin to Schuffenecker, 26 Mar. 1888, M 1984, letter 144. See also M 1984, letter 145; dated there to 27 Apr. 1888 based on the postmark of the envelope thought to have originally enclosed it. It now appears

that this envelope corresponds to a lost letter, and that letter 145 should actually be dated to the beginning of April. For the Signac reference, see M 1984, p. 479 n. 248.

73 For Vincent's reference to this painting, see his letter to Russell, [c. 17 June 1888], 629/501a. Félix Fénéon, "Aux vitrines dans la rue," *La Revue indépendante* (May 1888); repr. in Halperin 1970, vol. 1, p. 111. *Soilé* is a word used in the Middle Ages to indicate grain mixed with rye; see Halperin 1988, p. 215. The installation at Boussod et Valadon also included a statuette by Rodin, a Neo-Impressionist still life by Schuffenecker, and a Zandomeneghi nude.

74 Gauguin to Schuffenecker, [27 Apr. 1888], M 1984, letter 145 (excerpt); dated to early April in M 1989, pp. 64–66 (in full). For the attempt to sell Gauguin's painting, see Gauguin to Theo, [c. 5–8 June 1888], M 1984, letter 149. For Vincent's efforts to persuade Russell to buy the work, see [17 June 1888], 629/501a; and Pickvance 1984, p. 253.

75 For Gauguin's distress, see Gauguin to Theo, 22 May 1888, M 1984, letter 146. For Cézanne, see Gauguin to Schuffenecker, [early June 1888], M 1984, letter 147. For the fifty francs and invitation, see lost letter from Theo to Gauguin, [early June 1888], M 1984, letter XL; M 1984, pp. 283–84 n. 255.

76 For Gauguin's birthday, see Gauguin to Schuffenecker, [early June 1888], M 1984, letter 147; and Gauguin to Mette, [c. 10–30 June 1888], M 1984, letter 154. "Art and business": Gauguin to Theo, [c. 5–8 June 1888], M 1984, letter 149.

77 Vincent to Theo, 12 June 1888, 626/496.

78 Gauguin to Schuffenecker, [c. 15–18 June 1888], M 1984, letter 152; dated to 2nd week of June in M 1989, p. 68. On 4 June Theo opened an exhibition of ten of Monet's recent Antibes pictures. For the Monet prices, see Gauguin to Schuffenecker, [early June 1888], M 1984, letter 147; and ch. 4, note 3.

79 "Touching": Gauguin to Theo, [c. 5–8 June 1888], M 1984, letter 149. "While working": Gauguin to Schuffenecker, [15/18 June 1888], M 1984, letter 152; dated to 2nd week of June in M 1989, p. 68 n. 1.

80 Vincent to Theo, [12 June 1888], 626/496; [c. 15 June 1888], 628/498; Vincent to Bernard, [c. 18 June 1888], 630/B 7.

81 For Gauguin's Breton landscapes, see for example *Breton Women and Cow* (fig. 2) and *Hilly Landscape with Two Figures* (1888 [W 256]; The National Museum of Western Art, Tokyo), in Washington 1988, cat. 42, p. 92. Gauguin included a sketch of the figures from the latter picture in his letter to Schuffenecker of [27 Apr. 1888], M 1984, letter 145 (excerpt); dated to early April in M 1989, pp. 64–66 (in full). "Breton gavotte":

82 See Washington 1988, cat. 44, pp. 94–96.

83 Gauguin to Bernard, [2nd half Nov. 1888], M 1984, letter 182. Gauguin was discussing a pastel based on the painting.

84 "Old Cézanne": Vincent to Theo, [12/13 June 1888], 627/497; see also 626/496. For a discussion of the harvest series, see Pickvance 1984, pp. 93–101; and Amsterdam 1990, cat. 46–48, pp. 122–27.

85 Vincent to Bernard, [c. 18 June 1888], 630/B 7.

86 "Great field": Vincent to Russell, [c. 17 July 1888], 629/501a. "Labor-intensive": Vincent to Theo, [21 June 1888], 631/501. For Vincent's sketch after *The Sower*, see van der Wolk 1987, sketchbook 2, pp. 87, 136, 283–84.

87 "After Millet": Vincent to Theo, [21 June 1888], 631/501. "Colorless *gray*"; "simultaneous contrast"; "symbolic language": [28 June 1888], 637/503. See also Vincent to Bernard, [c. 18 June 1888], 630/B 7; and [23 June 1888], 635/B 8.

88 In his sermon of 1876, Vincent evoked life's troubled waters with a reference to the storm in Psalm 107 and to Christ walking on the sea in Mark 6:17–21. He also spoke of God as a sower who "give[s] His blessing in the seed of His word that has been sown in our hearts"; see Vincent's sermon as in ch. 1, note 25. See also Sund 1988b, pp. 666ff.; and Silverman 1995, pp. 104ff.

89 Vincent to Theo, [21 June 1888], 631/501.

90 On this drawing, see Sjraar van Heugten, *Vincent van Gogh: Drawings*, vol. 1, The Early Years, 1880–1883 (Amsterdam, 1996), cat. 13, pp. 72–74. The drawing accompanied a letter of [Jan. 1881], 161/140; see Vincent to Theo, 18 Sept. 1877, 130/110, for the description of his father and association with Rembrandt (see ch. 1, note 31). For Vincent's copies after reproductions of Millet, especially after Alfred Sensier's monograph *La Vie et l'oeuvre de J.-F. Millet* (Paris, 1881), see van der Wolk 1987, pp. 282–83. On the sower as Vincent's "alter ego," see Sund 1988b, p. 668. On critics' identification of Vincent with the sower, see van Uitert 1981–82, pp. 136–37.

91 Benoit 1887, pp. 63–64, 167, 226.

92 "Masterpiece": Vincent to Theo, [28 June 1888], 637/503. "Take it seriously": [21 June 1888], 631/501. Vincent's ambition to produce a masterpiece is noted in Amsterdam 1990, cat. 49, p. 128.

93 For Vincent's work in the studio, see Pickvance 1984, p. 103. For his various changes to the work, see Amsterdam 1990, cat. 49, pp. 128–29. For the symbolic import of *The Sower*'s surface, see Silverman 1995, p. 106; and Silverman 2000, pp. 81–82.

94 "Most certainly": Vincent to Theo, [28 June 1888], 637/503. "Your letter": [29 June 1888], 638/507.

95 For Gauguin's acceptance, see lost letter, Gauguin to Vincent, [c. 25–27 June 1888], M 1984, letter 155. This is also referred to in Gauguin to Theo, [c. 25–27 Sept. 1888], M 1984, letter 165, and pp. 488–89 nn. 261–62. See also Gauguin to Schuffenecker, 23 June 1888, M 1984, letter 153.

96 See Vincent to Theo, [29 June 1888], 638/507; and Gauguin to Theo, [7/8 July 1888], M 1984, letter 157.

97 Gauguin to Schuffenecker, 8 July 1888, M 1984, letter 156.

98 Gauguin to Vincent, [24/25 July 1888], M 1984, letter 158.

99 Vincent to Bernard, [c. 18 June 1888], 630/B 7. For *The Sower* and Blanc, see Amsterdam 1990, cat. 49, pp. 128–29. For the broad influence of Blanc's *Grammaire*, see Misook Song, *Art Theories of Charles Blanc, 1813–1882* (Ann Arbor, Mich., 1984), ch. 3.

100 "Abstractions"; "stylish": Vincent to Russell, [c. 17 June 1888], 629/501a. "Wholly primitive": Vincent to Bernard, [c. 18 June 1888], 630/B 7.

101 Gauguin to Vincent, [24/25 July 1888], M 1984, letter 158. Denise Delouche, "Gauguin et le thème de la lutte," in *Gauguin: Actes du colloque Gauguin, Musée d'Orsay, 11–13 janvier 1989* (Paris, 1991), pp. 157–71.

102 Gauguin to Vincent, [24/25 July 1888], M 1984, letter 158. The legacy of Degas, evident in *Young Breton Bathers*, lingers still in another canvas depicting the same subject (summer 1888 [W 275]; Hamburger Kunsthalle), which immediately preceded *Young Wrestlers—Brittany*. See Pickvance 1998, cat. 33–34, pp. 266–67; and Washington 1988, cat. 47–48, pp. 98–100.

103 For Vincent on Japanese prints, see Vincent to Theo, [15 July 1888], 644/510; and ch. 2, note 65. For Gauguin's still life, see *Vase and Cachepot* (1882 [W 78]; Ny Carlsberg Glyptotek, Copenhagen). Later, in his manuscript "Diverses Choses," Gauguin would glue in pages from, among others, the *Denshin Kaishu-Hokusai Manga*, p. 239.

104 Vincent to Bernard, [c. 6–11 June 1888], 625/B 6. 172. For Vincent's claim that his works have some basis in Japanese art, see Vincent to Theo, [15 July 1888], 644/510.

105 See the *Album Walter*, sketchbook dating to 1888–93, Musée du Louvre, Paris, pp. 42 verso, 56 verso. See also Druick/Zegers 1995, figs. 13a–b, pp. 13–14.

106 "Egyptian calm": Vincent to Bernard, [c. 18 June 1888], 630/B 7. "Excessively synthetic": Vincent to Theo, [15 July 1888], 646/511.

107 On Puvis's *Pleasant Land* as Provençal, see Vincent to Theo, [c. 17 Sept. 1888], 687/539. On rescuing Japanese art, see Vincent to

Theo, [15 July 1888], 644/510.

108 Gauguin to Vincent, [24/25 July 1888], M 1984, letter 158.

109 For Seurat, "toiles *de lutte*," see Herbert 1991, p. 5. "Our combat" ("notre lutte"): see Pissarro to Signac, [end July/early Aug. 1886], B-H, vol. 2, letter 349; Pissarro to Lucien, 17 Sept. 1886, B-H, vol. 2, letter 353.

110 "Contradictory combat" ("lutte contradictoire"): Gauguin to Schuffenecker, 14 Aug. 1888, M 1984, letter 159. "Top speed": Vincent to Theo, [c. 3 Mar. 1883], 325/271.

111 Vincent to Theo, [c. 21 Mar. 1883], 332/275. The phrase "creative competition" comes from van Uitert 1977, esp. pp. 150–51. Van Uitert also discusses Vincent's need for *wrijving* in this article (pp. 150–51 n. 13).

112 Gauguin to Vincent, [24/25 July 1888], M 1984, letter 158. For Vincent and the construction linking the artist and madness, see Pollock 1980a, pp. 69ff.

113 "Storm within"; "blasted painting": Vincent to Theo, [c. 22 July 1888], 650/513. "Still isolated": [c. 5 June 1888], 624/494.

114 Vincent to Theo, [c. 25 July 1888], 652/514.

115 Vincent to Bernard, [c. 25 July 1888], 653/B 13. See also Vincent to Theo, [28 May 1888], 617/492; [6 Aug. 1888], 660/518.

116 Wagner in Benoit 1887, p. 68.

117 "Artistic life"; "real life": Vincent to Theo, [c. 20 May 1888], 613/489. "Back-breaking yoke": Vincent to Bernard, [23 June 1888], 635/B 8. On Wagner, see Benoit 1887, pp. 5, 7.

118 On Vincent paving the way, see for example letters to Theo, [c. 4 May 1888], 606/482; and to Wil, [c. 22 June 1888], 633/W 4. "At this moment": Wagner in Benoit 1887, p. 43.

119 Zola, *L'Oeuvre*, p. 345.

120 Ibid., p. 405.

121 Vincent to Theo, [8 Aug. 1888], 661/519.

122 "If you were to ask": Vincent to Bernard, [23 June 1888], 635/B 8. Bernard claimed Brittany's atmosphere moved him from atheism to religion; see London, Royal Academy of Arts, *Post-Impressionism: Cross-Currents in European Painting, 1880–1905*, exh. cat. (1979), p. 41. Though Vincent protested he had always refrained from advising Bernard to read the Bible (see [23 June 1888], 635/B 8), what Bernard knew of his past and the tone of his recent correspondence may well have been influential.

123 Benoit 1887, pp. 5–6, 29.

124 Vincent to Bernard, [23 June 1888], 635/B 8.

125 "I feel": Vincent to Bernard, [24 June 1888], 636/B 9. "Painting the face of Christ": [23 June 1888], 635/B 8.

126 For the symbolism of Saint Luke, the ox, and the bull, see Herbert Thurston and Donald Attwater, eds., *Butler's Lives of the Saints*, vol. 4 (Westminster, Md., 1981). Vincent had always admired, as he told Theo in 1883, Gustave Doré's saying, "I have the patience

of an ox [*un boeuf*]": 28 Oct. 1883, 401/336.

127 Vincent to Bernard, [c. 18 June 1888], 630/B 7

128 He worried that "just as a man loses his balls over the course of his life," so too one might eventually see one's "capacity for artistic creation fade": Vincent to Theo, [1 Sept. 1888], 676/530. For the equation between sexual and creative energies, see Zemel 1997, ch. 3, esp. pp. 98–100.

129 On the exchange with Bernard, see Vincent to Bernard, [24 June 1888], 636/B 9. On the murder, see Vincent to Theo, [c. 14 Mar. 1888], 587/469; *Le Forum républicain* and *L'Homme de bronze* of 18 Mar. 1888; and *L'Intransigeant* of 16 Mar. 1888. For Vincent's gendered construction of the Zouaves, see Zemel 1997, pp. 94–98.

130 On Millet's sexual confidence, see Vincent to Theo, [c. 13 Aug. 1888], 664/522. On the drawing lessons, see Pickvance 1984, cat. 100, p. 172.

131 Vincent to Theo, [21 June 1888], 631/501; and Vincent to Wil, [31 July 1888], 657/W 5.

132 Vincent to Theo, [23 June 1888], 634/502. See also Pickvance 1984, cat. 52–53, p. 106.

133 Vincent to Theo, [8 July 1888], 641/505; [c. 9 July 1888], 642/506. For Vincent's hopes that Theo might interest fellow dealer Georges Thomas in buying his pen-and-ink drawings, see his letter to Theo, [c. 13 July 1888], 643/509. See also Pickvance 1984, pp. 109ff.

134 Vincent to Theo, [c. 9 July 1888], 642/506.

135 Vincent to Theo, [c. 4 Sept. 1883], 384/319.

136 Vincent to Theo, [8 July 1888], 641/505. Pickvance has identified *Rocks with Trees, Montmajour* (1888 [JH 1503]; Van Gogh Museum, Amsterdam) and *Olive Trees, Montmajour* (fig. 46) as the "two new big" drawings referred to in this letter; see Pickvance 1984, cat. 54–55, p. 111.

137 See Vincent to Theo, [7/8 Sept. 1889], 802/605. On the significance of the 1888 *Gethsemane* attempts, see Soth 1986; and Pollock 1998, pp. 103–10. For another interpretation, see van Uitert 1980, p. 83.

138 For the maxim "the masterpiece is up to you," see Vincent to Theo, [28 June 1888], 637/508. All other quotations: [c. 9 July 1888], 642/506.

139 Vincent to Theo, [c. 20 May 1888], 613/489.

140 "Horrible white man": Vincent to Bernard, [c. 20 May 1888], 614/B 5. Vincent discusses in this letter a book he had read "about the Marquesas Islands," possibly Max Radiguet's illustrated *Les Derniers Sauvages* (1860; repr. 1882) or Herman Melville's *Typee* (1846); see Eisenman 1997, p. 42 and n. 11. "A *mousmé*": Vincent to Theo, [c. 25 July 1888], 652/514. See also Sund 1992, p. 171.

141 Vincent to Theo, [c. 25 July 1888], 652/514.

142 On the drawings for Bernard, Gauguin, and

Russell, see Mark Roskill, "Van Gogh's Exchanges of Work with Émile Bernard in 1888," *Oud Holland* 86, nos. 2–3 (1971), pp. 142–79; Charles M. Millard, "A Chronology for Van Gogh's Drawings of 1888," *Master Drawings* 12, no. 2 (summer 1974), pp. 156–65; Jan Hulsker, "The Intriguing Drawings of Arles," *Vincent: Bulletin of the Rijksmuseum Vincent van Gogh* 3, no. 4 (1974), pp. 24–32; and Pickvance 1984, pp. 124ff.

143 Vincent to Bernard, [c. 23 July 1888], 651/B 12.

144 See Vincent to Theo, [c. 17 Sept. 1888], 687/539; and [c. 25–28 Apr. 1889], 766/587. On *Pleasant Land*, see Aimée Brown Price, *Pierre Puvis de Chavannes*, exh. cat., Van Gogh Museum, Amsterdam (1994), p. 167; and above, note 107. On oleander, see Pierre Larousse, *Grande Dictionnaire universel du XIXe siècle*, 1873 ed., s.v. "laurier-rose."

145 Arthur Henkel and Albrecht Schöne, *Emblemata: Handbuch zur Sinnbildkunst des XVI. und XVII. Jahrhunderts* (Stuttgart, [1967]), pp. 341–42, note the connection with 1 Cor 1:18 and 2 Cor 2:16.

146 See Pickvance 1984, cat. 93, pp. 162–63.

147 "What I learned in Paris": Vincent to Theo, [11 Aug. 1888], 663/520. "Joie de vivre": [c. 19 July 1888], 648/512.

148 For this observation, see Pickvance 1984, p. 125. For Vincent's arbitrary use of color, see letters to Bernard, [c. 4 Aug. 1888], 659/B 14; and to Theo, [11 Aug. 1888], 663/520. For Gauguin's opinion of Puvis's flower symbolism, see Gauguin to Morice, July 1901, Malingue 1949, letter 174.

149 For Vincent's references to the peasants depicted in his *Potato Eaters* (ch. 1, fig. 47) and in the work of Zola and Millet, see Vincent to Theo, [c. 25 July 1888], 653/B 13; [8 Aug. 1888], 660/519; [11 Aug. 1888], 663/520; and Vincent to Bernard, [c. 18 Aug. 1888], 669/B 15. "Whatever is best": Vincent to Theo, [c. 3 Aug. 1888], 658/517.

150 "Height equivalent": Vincent to Bernard, [c. 6–11 June 1888], 625/B 6. For Vincent's fraught anticipation of Gauguin's arrival, see Vincent to Wil, [31 July 1888], 657/W 5; and van Uitert 1978–79.

151 On this picture and related drawings, see Pickvance 1984, cat. 22, pp. 63–64; cat. 50, pp. 104–05. For Gauguin's financial problems, see Vincent to Theo, [c. 3 Aug. 1888], 658/517: "I have had a letter from Gauguin, in which he talks about painting and complains of not having enough money to come here." On [c. 4 Aug. 1888], 659/B 14, Vincent told Bernard that Gauguin would join him as soon as he or the van Gogh brothers could find the money.

152 Vincent to Theo, [c. 7 July 1888], 640/504. Pickvance has dated this letter to 16 June

(see Pickvance 1984, pp. 260–63, for his chronology of letters).

153 Vincent to Theo, [6 Aug. 1888], 660/518; [8 Aug. 1888], 661/519.

154 Vincent to Theo, [9 Aug. 1888], 662/521.

155 Vincent to Theo, [c. 14 Aug. 1888], 665/524.

156 "Living hell": Vincent to Theo, [c. 13 Aug. 1888], 664/522. "Perpetual wanderer": [8 Sept. 1888], 679/533. "Falling apart": [c. 18 Aug. 1888], 668/523. For a permanent home as a precondition for working, see [c. 13 Aug. 1888], 664/522; [c. 18 Aug. 1888], 668/523; and [4 Sept. 1888], 678/532.

157 Vincent to Bernard, [c. 18 Aug. 1888], 669/B 15. Vincent's ambition fed on his memory of the decoration featuring large sunflowers he had admired in the window of Duval's restaurant next door to Theo's boulevard Montmartre gallery; see Vincent to Theo, [c. 21 Aug. 1888], 670/526, and ch. 2, fig. 1.

158 "Renders infinity tangible": Vincent to Bernard, [c. 23 July 1888], 651/B 12. "Ah! My dear friends"; "how much I would like": [c. 18 Aug. 1888], 669/B 15.

159 Vincent to Theo, [c. 21 Aug. 1888], 670/526. In an exhaustive article dealing with Vincent's various *Sunflowers* (Dorn 1999), Roland Dorn has argued that Vincent indeed began with an image of twelve flowers and later added a thirteenth: the one nestled immediately to the right of the green-and-brown seed head. Microscopic examination of the paint surface and technical analysis of the x-radiographs, however, strongly suggest that this form was part of the original composition. First, there is no evidence of another layer of paint beneath it. Second, some of the strokes making up the flowers adjacent to the "thirteenth" overlap it, and were thus applied after it had been painted. Third, close examination of the x-radiographs and of the morphology of the brushwork reveals that there are possibly two yellow blossoms at lower left rather than one—thus bringing the total to fourteen.

160 "Light against light": Vincent to Theo, [c. 21 Aug. 1888], 670/526. "All in yellow": Vincent to Wil, [c. 27 Aug. 1888], 674/W 8. See also Vincent to Wil, [c. 21 Aug. 1888], 671/W 6; to Theo, [c. 27 Aug. 1888], 673/528. On the sunflower series and its larger purpose as "decoration," see Dorn 1988, pp. 376ff.

161 The contour sketch is probably charcoal; where visible, the painted sketch reinforcing these contours is green in the first version but orange for the yellow-on-yellow *Sunflowers*.

162 He would later simplify this method when executing copies of these and other signature paintings, resulting in progressive schematization (see chs. 4 and 5).

163 "Hope to live": Vincent to Theo, [c. 21 Aug. 1888], 670/526. "Six months": Gauguin to

Mette, [2nd half Aug. 1888], M 1984, letter 161.

164 On this meeting, see Vincent to Theo, [c. 21 Aug. 1888], 670/526. "Interesting things": Gauguin to Schuffenecker, 14 Aug. 1888, M 1984, letter 159. On Vincent's *Mousmé* drawing for Gauguin and its influence, see Merlhès 1996, p. 101.

165 Several authors rightly identify the important role of van Gogh's letters to Bernard as sources of inspiration for Gauguin in the summer of 1886. See for example Amishai-Maisels 1985, pp. 18–37, esp. pp. 21–23 and nn. 34–36; M 1984, pp. 498–499 n. 272; and M 1989, pp. 87ff.

166 Gauguin to Schuffenecker, 14 Aug. 1888, M 1984, letter 159.

167 Vincent to Bernard, [c. 4 Aug. 1888], 659/B 14. For the echoes in the correspondence and its significance on the development of both artists during the summer of 1888, see Merlhès 1996, p. 101.

168 "The best pictures": Vincent to Bernard, [c. 18 June 1888], 630/B 7. Vincent had sent a (now-lost) letter to Gauguin just days before ([c. 14–16 June 1888], M 1984, letter XLV). "You don't need": Gauguin to Schuffenecker, 23 June 1888, M 1984, letter 153. "This is how Rembrandt": Vincent to Bernard, [c. 23 July 1888], 651/B 12.

169 "I don't like Solomon": Vincent to Bernard, [23 June 1888], 635/B 8. "What an artist": Gauguin to Schuffenecker, M 1984, [3rd week Aug. 1888], letter 162; dated to 12 Sept. in M 1989, pp. 87–89.

170 Gauguin to Schuffenecker, M 1984, [3rd week Aug. 1888], letter 162; dated to 12 Sept. in M 1989, pp. 87–89.

171 On art and music, see for example Vincent to Theo, [c. 27 Aug. 1888], 673/528.

172 Gauguin first exhibited this painting as *La Vision du sermon* (*The Vision of the Sermon*) in 1889, but it is listed in the catalogue of his February 1891 sale as *La Vision après le sermon* (*The Vision after the Sermon*). This discrepancy, as Merlhès has suggested, could be a simple error or perhaps Gauguin's attempt to make the painting more accessible to the public; see M 1989, p. 98 n. 2. See also Silverman 2000, pp. 99, 447 n. 31. On the date of its completion, see Gauguin to Vincent, [c. 25–27 Sept. 1888], M 1984, letter 165. See also Washington 1988, cat. 50, pp. 102–05; Merlhès 1996, pp. 105ff.; Silverman 1995, pp. 104ff.; and Silverman 2000, pp. 99ff., 447 n. 31. While Silverman interprets the *Vision* with reference to Gauguin's educational formation at the Petit Séminaire, we see the work's gestation more as a response to the dialogue with Bernard and Vincent and in terms of the latter's catalytic role. See Amishai-Maisels 1985, pp. 25ff., for Gauguin's offer of the picture to a local

church.

173 Many scholars have addressed the justifications for either Bernard or Gauguin as originator of the cloisonnist technique. For a discussion and brief bibliography of the debate, see Roskill 1970b, pp. 109, 290–92. Subsequent contributions to the literature include Mary Anne Stevens, "Innovation and Consolidation in French Painting," in London, Royal Academy of Arts, *Post-Impressionism: Cross-Currents in European Painting, 1880–1905*, exh. cat. (1979), pp. 19–25, 41–42; Welsh-Ovcharov 1981, pp. 17–61 and cat. 104; Vojtěch Jirat-Wasiutyński, "Paul Gauguin's Paintings, 1886–91: Cloisonism, Synthetism, Symbolism," *RACAR: Revue d'art canadienne. Canadian Art Review* 9, nos. 1–2 (1982), pp. 35–46; Amishai-Maisels 1985, ch. 1, esp. pp. 17–32; Washington 1988, cat. 50; and Vojtěch Jirat-Wasiutyński in Mannheim 1990, pp. 48–51. The Pardon at Pont-Aven took place on Sunday, 16 September 1888. For Bernard's fascination with rustic subjects, see letter to his parents, June 1887, Harscoët-Maire 1997, p. 146. For Aurier's definition of Symbolism, see "Le Symbolisme en peinture: Paul Gauguin," *Mercure de France* 2 (Mar. 1891), pp. 155–64; trans. in Prather/Stuckey 1987, pp. 150–56.

174 Édouard Dujardin, in an article about Louis Anquetin, first gave currency to the term "cloisonnisme"; see "Aux XX et aux Indépendants. Le Cloisonnisme," *La Revue indépendante* 6 (Mar. 1888), pp. 487–92.

175 Other sources include Degas's early theater pictures, in which looming spectators in the foreground contrast with diminutive performers in the distance (see Roskill 1970b, p. 105) and Manet's bullfight pictures (see New York, The Metropolitan Museum of Art, *Manet, 1832–1883*, exh. cat. [1983], esp. cat. 33, pp. 110–14). "Foreign" sources from the Near and Far East provided ideas about pictorial space and syntax. For Persian influences on Gauguin, see Fereshteh Daftari, *The Influence of Persian Art on Gauguin, Matisse, and Kandinsky* (New York/London, 1991), ch. 1.

176 Rewald 1956, p. 196.

177 Gauguin to Vincent, [c. 25–27 Sept. 1888], M 1984, letter 165.

178 For interpretations of the cow, see Roskill 1970b, pp. 104–05; Mathew Herban III, "The Origin of Paul Gauguin's *Vision after the Sermon: Jacob Wrestling with the Angel* (1888)," *Art Bulletin* 59, no. 3 (Sept. 1977), pp. 417–18; Vojtěch Jirat-Wasiutyński, Letter to the Editor, *Art Bulletin* 60, no. 2 (June 1978), pp. 397–98; Silverman 1995, p. 110; and Silverman 2000, p. 105.

179 Vincent mentioned Delacroix's use of yellow and blue in various letters, to Theo, includ-

ing [c. 11 Apr. 1888], 598/476; [28 June 1888], 637/503; [c. 26 Sept. 1888], 691/541a.

180 See Zola, *L'Oeuvre*, pp. 282–83.

181 Zola, *L'Oeuvre*, p. 52. Vincent referred to his own "neurosis" as a "fatal inheritance" in his letter to Theo, [3 May 1888], 605/481.

182 "Create living flesh": Vincent to Bernard, [23 June 1888], 635/B 8. "Only way to be God": Zola, *L'Oeuvre*, p. 86. In a letter to Schuffenecker from that summer (14 Aug. 1888, M 1984, letter 159), Gauguin exhorts him to "pay more attention to the act of creation than to the result. That's the only way of advancing toward God, by imitating our divine master and creating."

183 Vincent to Theo, [c. 14 Aug. 1888], 665/524. Vincent wrote to Gauguin at precisely this time (see M 1984, letter LXI; M 1991, letter 37). For Vincent's earlier advice to Bernard, see [23 June 1888], 635/B 8; [c. 4 Aug. 1888], 659/B 14.

184 See Zola, *L'Oeuvre*, pp. 280, 399, 405, 406.

185 "Spermatic": Vincent to Bernard, [c. 4 Aug. 1888], 659/B 14. On channeling seed into creativity, see Sund 1992, pp. 139, 293 n. 3. See also Tamar Garb, *Bodies of Modernity: Figure and Flesh in Fin-de-Siècle France* (New York, 1998), pp. 33–34.

186 Zola, *L'Oeuvre*, p. 419; Wilhelm H. Wackenroder, *Herzensergiessungen eines kunstliebenden Klosterbruders* (Berlin, 1797). Notable artists' groups conceived along these lines in the nineteenth century include the German Nazarenes (1818–1840s) and the French Confrérie de Saint Jean L'Évangéliste (1839–40).

187 Zola, *L'Oeuvre*, p. 301.

188 Ibid., pp. 301–02, 373–74.

189 Vincent to Theo, [6 Aug. 1888], 660/518.

190 "Terrible need": Vincent to Theo, [c. 29 Sept. 1888], 695/543. "I can well do": [3 Sept. 1888], 677/531.

191 "We see a living man": Vincent to Wil, [c. 27 Aug. 1888], 674/W 8. "Resurrection": Vincent to Theo, [c. 17 Sept. 1888], 687/539. Many of these sentiments reflect Tolstoy's belief (as described in Vincent to Theo, [24 Sept. 1888], 690/542) that man dies completely, but living humanity endures forever. The source of Vincent's information on Tolstoy was an article in *La Revue des deux-mondes*, 15 Sept. 1888; see M 1984, p. 500 n. 276.

192 Vincent to Wil, [c. 27 Aug. 1888], 674/W 8.

193 Vincent to Theo, [c. 29 Sept. 1888], 695/543. In this and in other letters to Theo ([c. 16 Sept. 1888], 685/537; [c. 22 Sept. 1888], 689/540; [28 Oct. 1888], 720/558), Vincent articulated his intent to create an "artist's house," practical and uncluttered. He had a longstanding curiosity about the way admired artists lived and worked; he had made a pilgrimage in March 1880 to see Jules Breton's home and studio in

Courrières (Vincent to Theo, 24 Sept. 1880, 157/136); see also Hulsker 1990, p. 84.

194 "Follow": Vincent to Theo, [26 Aug. 1888], 672/527. "At the very entrance": [c. 17 Sept. 1888], 686/538–538a.

195 Vincent to Theo, [9 Sept. 1888], 680/534; [c. 15 June 1888], 628/498. On the Yellow House as *Gemeinschaftsideal* (ideal community) and the connection between the Pre-Raphaelites and the twelve chairs, see Kōdera 1990, p. 60.

196 Vincent to Theo, [24 Sept. 1888], 690/542. See also Vincent to Wil, [c. 27 Aug. 1888], 674/W 8.

197 "Regular Gethsemane": Vincent to Wil, [c. 27 Aug. 1888], 674/W 8. "Long calvary": Gauguin to Vincent, [c. 7–9 Sept. 1888], M 1984, letter 163.

198 Vincent referred to two of these paintings, *Two Thistles* (1888 [F 447a, JH 1551]; location unknown) and *Thistles* (1888 [F 447, JH 1550]; private collection), in letters to Theo ([c. 13 Aug. 1888], 664/522; [c. 21 Aug. 1888], 670/526) and to Bernard ([c. 18 Aug. 1888], 669/B 15). See the drawing *Thistles along the Road* (1888 [JH 1552]; Van Gogh Museum, Amsterdam).

199 "More serious": Vincent to Theo, [c. 12 Sept. 1888], 684/535. "Poetic subjects": [4 Oct. 1888], 701/545—the phrase is used a propos *The Starry Night over the Rhone* (fig. 70), *The Green Vineyard* (ch. 4, fig. 10), and *The Poet's Garden* (fig. 69).

200 Gauguin to Vincent, [c. 7–9 Sept. 1888], M 1984, letter 163.

201 "Do some people's hearts good": Vincent to Theo, [4 Oct. 1888], 701/545. "Without letting myself": Gauguin to Vincent, [c. 7–9 Sept. 1888], M 1984, letter 163.

202 See Vincent to Theo, [1 Sept. 1888], 676/530; [3 Sept. 1888], 677/531; [4 Sept. 1888], 678/532.

203 Vincent to Theo, [4 Sept. 1888], 678/532.

204 See Vincent to Theo, [8 Sept. 1888], 679/533; and Gauguin's response to Vincent, [c. 7–9 Sept. 1888], M 1984, letter 163.

205 "Cry of distress": Vincent to Theo, [c. 11 Sept. 1888], 683/536. "Speculator"; "schemer": [c. 17 Sept. 1888], 686/538–538a. "So great an artist": [c. 17 Sept. 1888], 687/539. "At sea": [c. 12 Sept. 1888], 684/535.

206 "Connected and complementary": Vincent to Theo, [c. 16 Sept. 1888], 685/537. "Studio-sanctuary": [c. 18 Aug. 1888], 668/523. "Hellish": [c. 13 Aug. 1888], 664/522; see also Vincent to Theo, [c. 17 Sept. 1888], 686/538–538a; [8 Sept. 1888], 679/533.

207 "Wanderer": Vincent to Theo, [6 Aug. 1888], 660/518. "Infernal furnace": [8 Sept. 1888], 679/533; [9 Sept. 1888], 680/534.

208 Vincent to Theo, [9 Sept. 1888], 680/534. Vincent's mention of "the powers of darkness in a tavern" is most likely a reference

to novels by two authors he admired greatly, Tolstoy and Zola. Both Tolstoy's *The Powers of Darkness* and Zola's *L'Assommoir* address the destructive effects of alcohol and describe, as Vincent said, places "where one can destroy oneself." See Jean Seznec, "Literary Inspiration in Van Gogh," *Magazine of Art* 43, no. 8 (1950), p. 286; Kōdera 1990, p. 46; Amsterdam 1990, cat. 58, pp. 148–49; and Ronald Pickvance, "Van Gogh's *Night Café*: Synthesis at Work," in *Vincent van Gogh International Symposium: Tokyo, October 17–19, 1985* (Tokyo, 1988), pp. 343–60.

209 "Terrible human passions"; "investigations": Vincent to Theo, [8 Sept. 1888], 679/533. "Only attempts": [9 Sept. 1888], 680/534.

210 "Street of the good little women": Vincent to Theo, [c. 17 Sept. 1888], 687/539. "Well thought-out": [c. 17 Sept. 1888], 686/538–538a.

211 Vincent to Theo, [c. 17 Sept. 1888], 686/538–538a. The connection between this painting and Karr's book, *Voyage autour de mon jardin* (1845; Paris, 1851 ed.), is made in van Uitert 1978–79, p. 195 n. 57. See ch. 2, note 110.

212 See Vincent to Theo, [c. 17 Sept. 1888], 687/539; and Van Uitert 1978–79, pp. 192–94. The article in question was Henry Cochin, "Boccacce d'après ses oeuvres et les témoignages contemporains," *La Revue des deux-mondes* (15 July 1888), pp. 373–413.

213 Carlyle, however, in *The French Revolution*, ed. by K. J. Fielding and David Sorensen (Oxford, 1989), vol. 2, p. 20, imaged Petrarch alone in a garden in Avignon: "twanging and singing by the Fountain of Vaucluse hard by, surely in a most melancholy manner."

214 See A. Bartlett Giamatti, *The Earthly Paradise and the Renaissance Epic* (New York, 1989), pp. 126–27.

215 Vincent to Theo, [c. 17 Sept. 1888], 687/539. On Boccaccio's sensuality, see Cochin (note 212).

216 "Artist's house": Vincent to Theo, [c. 16 Sept. 1888], 685/537. "Jardin d'un poète": Vincent to Gauguin, [3 Oct. 1888], 699/544a. See also Edmond de Goncourt, *La Maison d'un artiste* (Paris, 1881; 1898 ed.), pp. 372ff; van Uitert 1978–79, pp. 182–83, establishes Vincent's familiarity with the book. Goncourt's book is noted in Maurice de Fleury, "La Maison d'un moderniste," Part I, *Le Figaro littéraire* (15 Sept. 1888), pp. 146–47, an article to which Vincent referred in a letter to Theo, [c. 16 Sept. 1888], 685/537. Though the Goncourts may have been Vincent's inspiration for the *maison d'un artiste*, he was dismayed by the fact that great wealth had purchased their haven: "It's a poor way of doing things to wait till one is very rich, and that is what I do not like about the de Goncourts . . . they ended by buying their home and their tran-

quility for 100,000 francs": Vincent to Theo, [c. 18 Aug. 1888], 668/523. See also Dorn 1990, p. 233. On the "poet's garden" series, see Jan Hulsker, "The Poet's Garden," *Vincent: Bulletin of the Rijksmuseum Vincent van Gogh* 3, no. 1 (1974), pp. 22–32; van Uitert 1978–79, pp. 192–96; Ron Johnson, "Vincent van Gogh and the Vernacular: The Poet's Garden," *Arts Magazine* 53, no. 6 (Feb. 1979), pp. 98–104; John House, "In Detail: Van Gogh's Poet's Garden, Arles," *Portfolio* (Sept.–Oct. 1980), pp. 28–33; Pickvance 1984, cat. 104–09, pp. 178–84; Dorn 1988, pp. 378–89; and Amsterdam 1990, cat. 61–63, pp. 156–61.

217 See for example Karr (note 211), pp. 185ff. "Weeping tree": Vincent to Theo, [c. 16 Sept. 1888], 685/537.

218 Vincent to Theo, [c. 27 Sept. 1888], 692/541.

219 Vincent to Theo, [c. 22 Sept. 1888], 689/540.

220 Vincent to Theo, [c. 29 Sept. 1888], 695/543. For Sandoz's critique of Claude's failed masterpiece, see Zola, *L'Oeuvre*, pp. 407, 419–22.

221 Vincent to Theo, [c. 29 Sept. 1888], 695/543. Vincent ascribes this view to Tolstoy.

222 For Courbet, see Linda Nochlin, *Realism* (Harmondsworth, England, 1971), p. 83.

223 "Rembrandt did not invent": Vincent to Bernard, [c. 23 July 1888], 651/B 12. "Terrible lucidity": Vincent to Theo, [c. 29 Sept. 1888], 695/543.

224 Vincent to Bernard, [4 Oct. 1888], 702/B 19.

225 Vincent to Theo, [c. 24 Jan. 1885], 483/393. "Wrest[ling] directly": [c. 17 Dec. 1883], 416/347.

226 Gauguin to Vincent, [c. 25–27 Sept. 1888], M 1984, letter 165. See Carlyle, *On Heroes*, pp. 1, 165.

227 For Vincent's suggestion that Gauguin skip out on his creditors, see Vincent to Theo, [c. 17 Sept. 1888], 686/538–538a: "If someday he decamps from Pont-Aven with Laval or Maurin without paying his debts, I think in his case he would still be justified, like any other creature at bay." "Studio of the North": Gauguin to Vincent, [c. 25–27 Sept. 1888], M 1984, letter 165.

228 "The portrait": Vincent to Theo, [c. 12 Sept. 1888], 684/535. "Such fellows": Vincent to Bernard, [c. 18 Sept. 1888], 688/B 16.

229 Gauguin to Vincent, [c. 25–27 Sept. 1888], M 1984, letter 165.

230 Vincent to Theo, [c. 29 Sept. 1888], 695/543. Vincent enclosed two sketches in this letter, one of *The Starry Night over the Rhone* (JH 1593) and a rough one of *The Yellow House* (JH 1590). Dorn 1990, pp. 92–93, 389, pairs the two paintings as pendants in the unified decorative scheme for the Yellow House.

231 Vincent to Theo, [11 Aug. 1888], 663/520. For the connection of the conception with Gauguin and Carlyle, see van Uitert 1978–79, pp. 188–90; and Amsterdam 1990, cat. 56, pp.

142–43. For Vincent's previous mention of the subject, see Vincent to Theo, [9 Apr. 1888], 596/474; [c. 22 Sept. 1888], 689/540; to Bernard, [9 Apr. 1888], 597/B 3; [c. 18 June 1888], 630/B 7; and to Wil, [9 and 16 Sept. 1888], 681/W 7.

232 Vincent to Theo, [3 Sept. 1888], 677/531.

233 Vincent to Theo, [c. 29 Sept. 1888], 695/543.

234 Carlyle, *Sartor Resartus*, pp. 198, 200; Carlyle, *On Heroes*, p. 69; Heine, *Buch der Lieder* (Hamburg/Paris, 1837), Zweiter Cyklus ("Die Nordsee"), no. 7 ("Fragen"); trans. by Hal Draper, *The Complete Poems of Heinrich Heine: A Modern English Version* (Cambridge, Mass./Boston, 1982), p. 155; and van Eeden, *De kleine Johannes*, pp. 73–75. See Albert Boime, "Vincent van Gogh's *Starry Night*: A History of Matter and a Matter of History," *Arts Magazine* 59 (Dec. 1984), pp. 86–103.

235 "House and its surroundings": Vincent to Theo, [c. 29 Sept. 1888], 695/543. "Hope"; "horizon"; "new era": [3 Oct. 1888], 698/544; see also [c. 17 Sept. 1888], 687/539. On this picture, see Amsterdam 1990, cat. 60, pp. 152–54.

236 Vincent to Theo, [3 Oct. 1888], 698/544; [c. 29 Sept. 1888], 695/543.

237 "Ashen": Vincent to Theo, [c. 22 Sept. 1888], 689/540. "Like a Japanese": Vincent to Wil, [9 and 16 Sept 1888], 681/W 7. On this self-portrait, see Pickvance 1984, cat. 99, p. 171; Merlhès 1996, pp. 107ff.; and Vojtěch Jirat-Wasiuyński et al., *Vincent van Gogh's "Self-Portrait Dedicated to Paul Gauguin" an Historical and Technical Study* (Cambridge, Mass., 1984).

238 Gauguin to Vincent, [1 Oct. 1888], M 1984, letter 166.

239 On Bernard's admiration for Gauguin, see Vincent to Bernard, [c. 18 Sept. 1888], 688/B 16. "Neurotic": Vincent to Theo, [c. 17 Sept. 1888], 687/539.

240 Gauguin to Vincent, [1 Oct. 1888], M 1984, letter 166.

241 Vincent to Theo, [3 Oct. 1888], 698/544.

242 "Madmen": Vincent to Theo, [9 Aug. 1888], 662/521. "Social isolation": Vincent to Theo, [c. 14 Aug. 1888], 665/524.

243 For Vincent on *Les Misérables*, see Vincent to Theo, [30 Mar.–1 Apr. 1883], 335/227; and to van Rappard, [c. 25 May 1883], 348/R 36. For his parents' negative response to *Les Misérables*, see their letter to Theo, 5 July 1880; trans. in Hulsker 1990, pp. 85–86: "He sent us a book by Victor Hugo, but that man takes the side of the criminals and doesn't call bad what really is bad.... Even with the best of intentions that cannot be accepted." Hulsker says the book by Hugo is "probably" *Les Misérables*, but the authors suggest it could be *Dernier Jour*. See Sund 1992, pp. 40–41, for the suggestion that this is the

book to which Vincent referred in a letter to Theo, [July 1880], 154/133. For the influence of *Les Misérables* on Gauguin, see M 1989, pp. 85–86, 92ff.; and Merlhès 1996, pp. 103ff.

244 "Furnace of creation": Vincent to Theo, [29 June 1888], 638/507. "Virgin heart": [c. 15 June 1888], 628/498. Vincent used the latter phrase in reference to the Danish artist Christian Mourier-Petersen (called Swedish in Vincent's letter). "Something like"; "white walls": [9 Sept. 1888], 680/534.

245 See Vincent to Bernard, [15 July 1888], 645/B 10, in which Vincent referred to the garden composition *Newly Mowed Lawn with Weeping Tree* (1888 [F 1450, JH 1509]; private collection, New York).

246 Gauguin to Vincent, [1 Oct. 1888], M 1984, letter 166. For Vincent's use of chrome yellow in his *Sunflowers*, see Vincent to Bernard, [c. 18 Aug. 1888], 669/B 15.

247 Vincent to Theo, [3 Oct. 1888], 698/544. See Zola, *L'Oeuvre*, p. 304.

248 Vincent to Gauguin, [3 Oct. 1888], 699/544a.

249 Ibid. In this letter Vincent discussed safeguarding the "means of production" (paints, canvases) and securing their "true share" of any profits.

250 Ibid.

251 Vincent to Theo, [4 Oct. 1888], 701/545.

252 "Virginal"; "color of fresh butter": Pierre Loti, *Madame Chrysanthème* (Paris, 1888), p. 220. "Yellow color": Vincent to Wil, [9 and 16 Sept. 1888], 681/W 7. For the monastery as model community and the idea of exchange as common among Japanese artists, see ch. 2, note. 19.

253 Vincent to Gauguin, [3 Oct. 1888], 699/544a.

254 Ibid.

255 "Placid priest": Vincent to Theo, [c. 25 July 1888], 652/514. "Slanting": [4 Oct. 1888], 701/545.

256 Vincent to Theo, [3 Oct. 1888], 698/544.

257 Vincent to Theo, [4 Oct. 1888], 701/545.

258 For this gallery, see "Au Louvre: La Salle Dieulafoy," *L'Intransigeant*, 8 June 1888, p. 2, which cites among the most beautiful things of collection "the murals from the palace of Darieus, in red brick, enameled, with their lions and archers." For Vincent's comments on Gauguin's "Persian style," see Vincent to Theo, [3 Oct. 1888], 698/544.

259 Vincent to Theo, [4 Oct. 1888], 701/545. In his inscription to Vincent on the canvas, Bernard used the archaic form of the word *copain* (friend or mate), *compaing* (which he misspelled "copaing"). This older form carries the sense of *compagnon* and its greater guild sense of brotherhood. The print at the lower right (with a sail just visible) seems to be in the manner of Hiroshige, though it cannot be identified with certainty.

260 Vincent to Theo, [4 Oct. 1888], 701/545; authors' emphasis.

261 "Torment"; "dismal"; "not a shadow": Vincent to Theo, [4 Oct. 1888], 701/545. For the melancholy aspect of Gauguin's painting, see [8–9 Oct. 1888], 704/547. For the artist as prisoner, see [3 Sept. 1888], 677/531. See also an earlier letter to Theo addressing this theme, [July 1880], 154/133: "Do you know what makes the prison disappear? Every deep, genuine affection. Being friends, being brothers, loving, that is what opens the prison, with supreme power, by some magic force.... Moreover, the prison is sometimes called prejudice, misunderstanding, fatal ignorance of one thing or another, suspicion, false modesty."

262 Vincent to Theo, [8 Oct. 1888], 703/546. This opinion, expressed to Theo, was quite possibly repeated to Gauguin himself. For Vincent's perception of Gauguin's despair, see Vincent to Theo, [24 Sept. 1888], 690/542.

263 Vincent to Bernard, [3 Oct. 1888], 700/B 18.

264 Vincent to Theo, [8–9 Oct. 1888], 704/547.

265 It is unclear whether Theo purchased the ceramics at this time for the gallery to sell, or if he had the pieces on consignment. Through a lost letter from Theo to Gauguin, [c. 4–6 Oct. 1888], M 1984, letter LXXVI, Gauguin apparently learned of the sale, and in Gauguin to Theo, [7/8 Oct. 1888], M 1984, letter 167, Gauguin acknowledged the sale: "The 300 francs will turn everything around, and I will leave for Arles around the end of the month." Rewald stated only that Theo "took over 300 frs worth of his potteries"; Rewald 1973, p. 31. Amsterdam 1999, p. 131, states that Theo, believing that he would be able to sell them, bought 300 francs' worth of Gauguin's ceramics in October 1888.

266 Vincent to Theo, [10 Oct. 1888], 706/549; quoting his (now-lost) letter to Gauguin, see M 1984, letter LXXX.

267 Vincent to Gauguin, [17 Oct. 1888], 711/B 22.

268 Vincent to Theo, [c. 21 Oct. 1888], 714/556.

269 Ibid.

270 *Speculative*": Gauguin to Theo, [7/8 Oct. 1888], M 1984, letter 167. "Thrilled"; "crazy about me": Gauguin to Schuffenecker, 16 Oct. 1888, M 1984, letter 172.

271 "Heaps of undeserved compliments": Vincent to Theo, [10 Oct. 1888], 706/549. Vincent sent off his portrait at the same time as he received those by Gauguin and Bernard, as he reported in a letter to Bernard, [4 Oct. 1888], 702/B 19. For a listing of the probable contents of the shipment, see ch. 4, note 20.

272 Gauguin to Theo, [7/8 Oct. 1888], M 1984, letter 167. For Vincent's letters as testimonials, see Gauguin to Schuffenecker, 8 Oct. 1888, M 1984, letter 168.

273 Gauguin to Schuffenecker, 8 Oct. 1888, M 1984, letter 168.

274 Ibid.

CHAPTER 4: ARLES

275 For all quotes, see Gauguin to Schuffenecker, 16 Oct. 1888, M 1984, letter 172.

276 See Françoise Cachin in Washington 1988, pp. xx–xxiii.

277 Gauguin to Schuffenecker, 8 Oct. 1888, M 1984, letter 168.

Citations for bold-faced quotations: p. 163: Vincent to Theo, [c. 13 July 1888], 643/509; p. 167: Vincent to Gauguin, [3 Oct. 1888], 699/554a; p. 178: Vincent to Theo, [c. 5 Nov. 1888], 722/559.

1 For Gauguin's itinerary, see M 1984, p. 510 n. 294. Gauguin, *Avant et après*, p. 24.

2 "Better health": Vincent to Theo, [24 Oct. 1888], 717/557. "Agitated": Gauguin to Theo, [27 Oct. 1888], M 1984, letter 175.

3 For Gauguin's sale, see Theo to Vincent, 23 Oct. 1888, 716/T 2. "Morally crushed": [24 Oct. 1888], 717/557. As a point of comparison, Theo had recently sold one of Monet's Antibes paintings for 3,000 francs in June; see Rewald 1973, p. 23. See Gauguin to Schuffenecker, [early June 1888], M 1984, letter 147, in which Gauguin pointed out, "it's not too much to ask 400 francs for a Gauguin in comparison to 3,000 francs for a Monet."

4 Theo to Vincent, 27 Oct. 1888, 718/T 3.

5 On the juxtaposition between Pont-Aven and Arles, see Vincent to Theo, [28 Oct. 1888], 720/558; and [28 Oct. 1888], 719/558b. "Very, very interesting": [24 Oct. 1888], 717/557. Vincent had made a similar comparison between the Danish painter Christian Mourier-Petersen and Loti, expressing his admiration for his friend's self-possession and resourcefulness, which he associated with the characters "you find in Pierre Loti's books": Vincent to Theo, [26 May 1888], 615/490.

6 Gauguin to Theo, [27 Oct. 1888], M 1984, letter 175.

7 Vincent to Theo, [28 Oct. 1888], 719/558b.

8 Ibid.

9 "Character": Gauguin to Schuffenecker, [early July 1888], M 1984, letter 129 (excerpt); dated to 14 July in M 1989, pp. 39–42 (in full). On Brittany, see Gauguin to Mette, [c. 22 Jan.–6 Feb. 1888], M 1984, letter 139; dated to c. 22 Jan. in M 1989, p. 61. "To initiate": Gauguin to Theo, [27 Oct. 1888], M 1984, letter 175. "Get off the train"; "continuing"; "starting something": Gauguin, *Avant et après*, pp. 24, 28, 31.

10 Thread counts for all of Gauguin's post-Arles works on rough canvas are not available, but the thread count of the Arles jute seems to be unique (see App.).

11 Gauguin, *Avant et après*, p. 28.

12 Part of Vincent's decorative scheme for the Yellow House included "at least six very large canvases" for Gauguin's bedroom ([c. 9–16 Sept. 188] 681/W 7). These included the two sunflower paintings from August as well as the series of four *Poet's Garden* paintings. Soon after his arrival, Gauguin reported in a postscript to Vincent's letter to Bernard ([c. 2 Nov. 1888] 721/B 19a) that two of Vincent's *Alyscamps* paintings were hang-ing in his room. If all eight of the intended canvases were indeed installed in Gauguin's tiny bedroom (roughly 29 square feet; 8.8 square meters), they must have been double-hung—the height of the wall, roughly 10 1/2 feet (3.18 meters), would allow for that. See Jan Hulsker, "The Poet's Garden," *Vincent: Bulletin of the Rijksmuseum Vincent van Gogh* 3, no. 4 (1974), pp. 24–32; Pickvance 1984, cat. 104–09, pp. 178–84; and Dorn 1990, pp. 117–23, 229 n. 221, 378–85, 394–95, 401–03. On Vincent's bad house-keeping, see *Avant et après*, p. 31. One instance of Vincent's working in the kitchen area is a drawing, *Seated Zouave* (fig. 44), which appears to have been done in the kitchen, as a stove is visible behind the figure.

13 Vincent to Theo, [28 Oct. 1888], 719/558b.

14 Ibid.

15 Vincent to Theo, [c. 25 July 1888], 652/514. On the yew's funereal associations, see Pierre Larousse, *Grande Dictionnaire universel du XIXe siècle*, 1873 ed., s.v. "If"; and Jeremy Harte, "How Old is that Old Yew?" *At the Edge* 4 (Dec. 1996), pp. 1–9.

16 In both paintings, Vincent changed the color of the trees at the horizon from green and blue to orange, either to suggest the changing season or to heighten color intensity.

17 On the *Cleopatra* pot, see Gauguin to Schuffenecker, 25 Oct. 1888, M 1984, letter 174 (excerpt); M 1989, p. 124 (in full). Vincent to Theo, [c. 20 May 1888], 613/489.

18 Wildenstein's connection of this picture with the pastel *La Négresse* (1888 [W 299]; Van Gogh Museum, Amsterdam) is unconvincing. There is nothing to suggest that Gauguin worked in pastel while in Arles. Moreover, *La Négresse*, by virtue of its medium, handling, and relationship to other works by Gauguin, must be dated to 1889/90. "Richer Gauguin": Vincent to Theo, [c. 4–7 Oct. 1888], 701/545. On the dating of this letter, see Jan Hulsker, "De nooit verzonden brieven van Vincent van Gogh. De paradox van de publicatie," *Jong Holland* 14, no. 4 (1998), pp. 42–52 (English summary on p. 64).

19 Both canvases have identical thread counts (16 x 16 threads per centimeter) and weave density. Some of the canvases that Vincent used in Arles have this thread count, but they are not the majority. A survey of works painted by Gauguin immediately before and after Arles for which thread counts were available uncovered no canvases matching this thread count. During the Arles period, however, Gauguin painted almost exclusively on jute and sometimes on cotton, which he primed himself, with two exceptions: he used pre-primed linen, given to him by Vincent, for this *Farmhouse in Arles* (at the beginning of his stay) and for *Monsieur* Ginoux (at the end); see App.

20 In a letter to Bernard, [3 Oct. 1888], 700/B 18, Vincent proposed a number of works he would send to Brittany in exchange for works by Bernard and other artists in Pont-Aven: *Self-Portrait (Bonze)* (ch. 3, fig 73), *Quay with Men Unloading Sand Barges* (F 449, JH 1558), *Garden behind a House* (F 578, JH 1538), *Thistles* (F 447, JH 1550), *A Pair of Shoes* (F 461, JH 1569), and an unidentified landscape painted "during the fury of an evil-minded mistral." See Mark W. Roskill, "Van Gogh's Exchanges of Work with Émile Bernard in 1888," *Oud Holland* 86, no. 2–3 (1971), pp. 142–79.

21 Vincent, for instance, described his work *The Tarascon Diligence* (1888 [F 478a, JH 1605]; The Henry and Rose Pearlman Foundation, Inc., New York) as "painted à la Monticelli with spots of thickly laid on paint": Vincent to Theo, [13 Oct. 1888], 708/552. On Roulin, see [10 Oct. 1888], 707/550. On the southern cultural renaissance, see [17 Oct. 1888], 712/555; and [14 Oct. 1888], 709/553. On *The Green Vineyard*'s connection to Monticelli, see Amsterdam 1990, cat. 65, p. 164.

22 Vincent to Theo, [12/13 June 1888], 627/497. Just prior to making this observation, Vincent had received a letter from Gauguin mentioning the pictures he had been forced to sell. See lost letter (M 1984, letter 148) referred to in letter to Theo, [12 June 1888], 626/496. It is unclear if Cézanne's *Harvest* was part of this collection. Gauguin is included in the painting's provenance in John Rewald et al., *The Paintings of Paul Cézanne: A Catalogue Raisonné* (New York, 1996), vol. 1, no. 31; and Bodelsen 1970, cat. 5, stated that Gauguin "may have owned" it. In M 1984, pp. 386–87 n. 115, however, it is suggested that he did not. Regardless, Gauguin used the Cézanne as the point of departure for a fan-shaped composition featuring a stack of wheat (1884 [W 116]; private collection, Copenhagen). He also incised the Cézanne motif into a ceramic vase; see Merete Bodelsen, "Gauguin's Cézannes," *Burlington Magazine* 104, no. 710 (May 1962), figs. 44–47, p. 211.

23 Vincent to Bernard, [c. 17 July 1888], 647/B 11.

24 Vincent to Bernard, [24 June 1888], 636/B 9. The picture Vincent was working on was *Sunset: Wheat Fields near Arles* (1888 [F 465, JH 1473]; Kunstmuseum Winterthur, Switzerland). For a recent examination of the performance and meanings of gesture in nineteenth-century painting, see Richard R. Brettell, *Impression: Painting Quickly in France, 1860–1890*, exh. cat., Sterling and Francine Clark Art Institute, Williamstown, Mass. (2000), esp. Coda.

25 "Quickly, quickly": Vincent to Bernard, [24 June 1888], 636/B 9. "Quick work": Vincent to Theo, [23 June 1888], 634/502. For Vincent's comments on painting quickly, see, for example, 623/500, 638/507, 640/504, 648/512, 667/525, 670/526, 684/535, 685/537, and 693/B 17.

26 Vincent to Theo, [c. 19 July 1888], 648/512.

27 Gauguin to Theo, [27 Oct. 1888], M 1984, letter 175.

28 "Carried away": Vincent to Theo, [28 Oct. 1888], 720/558. "Man of the South"; "intense"; "translat[ing]": Gauguin to Schuffenecker, 14 Jan. 1885, M 1984, letter 65.

29 Vincent to Theo, [28 Oct. 1888], 720/558.

30 Information about the weather in Arles during fall of 1888 has been gleaned from the Bulletin annuel de la Commission météorologique du département des Bouches-du-Rhône of that year, published in M 1989, App. I, pp. 260–61, and kindly supplied by the author of that work. We have also relied on weather reports published in the two Arles weekly newspapers, L'Homme de bronze and Le Forum républicain.

31 Vincent to Theo, [c. 5 Nov. 1888], 722/559.

32 On Vincent's interest in bullfighting, see letters to Theo, [9 Apr. 1888], 596/474; [3 Sept. 1888], 677/531; to Bernard, [9 Apr. 1888], 597/B 3; and to Koning, [29 May 1888], 621/498a. For Gauguin on bullfighting, see letter to Vincent, [24/25 July 1888], M 1984, letter 158.

33 Vincent to Gauguin, [3 Oct. 1888], 699/544a.

34 "Walking about": Gauguin, Avant et après, p. 18. "Above all things": Vincent to Theo, [28 Oct. 1888], 719/558b. "Beautiful modern style": Gauguin to Bernard, [end Oct. 1888], M 1984, letter 176. Merlhès places this letter at the end of October or early November, suggesting a date of c. 4 November. Given that Gauguin makes no mention of the Alyscamps paintings to which he refers in his postscript to Bernard ([c. 2 Nov. 1888], 721/B 19a), we place this letter at the end of October.

35 Fernand Beissier, Les Étapes d'un touriste en France: Le Pays d'Arles, 2d ed. (Paris, 1889), pp. 114ff. For a typical guidebook account, see John Murray, A Handbook for Travellers in France (London, 1890), part 2, pp. 156–61. Mistral advised those who wanted to see Arlésiennes to go "to the Arles Arena for the bullfights or to the Lices, on the promenade." Mistral cited in Pierre Pasquini, "'La vraie' Mireille," in Arles 1999, p. 72. Gustave Flaubert also extolled "the women of Arles! ... with their skirts ... their comportement ... their robust and svelte stature, they resemble the antique Muse": cited in ibid., p. 30. This publication informs the following discussion.

36 Shortly after its discovery, the Venus d'Arles had been given to Louis XIV to curry favor. For the Arlésienne as the rebirth of the Venus of Arles, see Pierre Serna, "Émile Fassin et les femmes de son moulin ... ," in Arles 1999, pp. 28–36.

37 On the Alyscamps, see Murray (note 35) pp. 157–59; Beissier (note 35), pp. 73–81; and Pierre Larousse, Grande Dictionnaire universel du XIXe siècle, 1873 ed., s.v. "Alyscamps (Les)."

38 See the "Nos Concerts" column in L'Homme de bronze of 10 June, 30 Sept., and 7 Oct. 1888, noting works including "Un Soir de mai aux Alyscamps," played at place de la République. Works reported in the "Chronique artistique" of the two week-lies—Le Forum républicain and L'Homme de bronze—since Vincent's arrival in Arles include a portrait of an Arlésienne, studies of the ruins of Montmajour by two different artists, and three works dealing with the Alyscamps. The painting on display by Armand Ronin was described as a "page locale pleine de charme," in "Chronique Artistique," L'Homme de bronze, 12 Feb. 1888, pp. 1–2. For Joseph Félon, who, beginning in the 1850s, helped establish this genre in paintings and lithographs, see Arles 1999, cat. 60, pp. 112–13. See also Arles, Muséon Arlaten, Dominique Roman (1824–1911): Objectif Provence, exh. cat. (1997), cat. 138.

39 "Choses d'art," Le Forum républicain, 9 Sept. 1888, p. 2.

40 "Chronique artistique et musicale," L'Homme de bronze, 30 Sept. 1888, p. 2; cited in Dorn 1990, p. 387. This somewhat incredulous reference must be to Vincent's very recent stint painting a café terrace on place du Forum at night by gaslight. Vincent refers to the circumstances of painting this work, Café Terrace on Place du Forum, Arles, at Night (1888 [F 1519, JH 1580]; Dallas Museum of Art), in his letter to Eugène Boch, [2 Oct. 1888], 696/553b.

41 An exception to the idealized vision of Les Alyscamps, a postcard where a smokestack can be seen through the trees, is illustrated in Pickvance 1984, fig. 58, p. 200. Railroads had also truncated the site by this time. Prosper Mérimée, among many others, commented on the dilapidation of the Alyscamps; see Arles, Musée Réattu, Charles Nègre Photographe: 1820–1880, exh. cat. (1980), cat. 73, p. 173. See also Beissier (note 35), pp. 78–79; and "Chronique locale," L'Homme de bronze, 30 Sept. 1888, p. 3. "Infinitely more glorious": Vincent to Theo, [24 Sept. 1888], 690/542. See also Vincent to Theo, [c. 4 May 1888], 606/482: "It's a filthy town, this"; "They [the Arlésiennes] are in their decadence."

42 On Vincent's Alyscamps pictures, see Pickvance 1984, cat. 115–17, pp. 198–200.

43 Gauguin to Bernard, [end Oct. 1888], M 1984, letter 176.

44 Vincent to Gauguin, [3 Oct. 1888], 699/544a.

45 "The Tartarin and Daumier part": Vincent to Theo, [c. 17 Sept. 1888], 687/539. "Absolute Daumier": [c. 17 Sept. 1888], 686/538; see also [13 Oct. 1888], 708/552. For Vincent's early admiration of Daumier, see 297/255, 298/256, 310/264, 312/165, 314/266, 356/R 37, 358/265, and 522/418.

46 See Vincent to Theo, [11 Aug. 1888], 663/520. "On the spot": [15 Aug. 1888], 667/525. "Maison d'artiste": [9 Sept. 1888], 680/534. On Daumier and Japanese community, see also: [29 June 1888], 638/507; [15 Aug. 1888], 667/525; [24 Sept. 1888], 690/542; [3 Oct. 1888], 698/544. On the subject of Daumier and the maison d'artiste, see Dorn 1990, pp. 230–31 n. 26.

47 The issued was raised in the article on the Félibres that Vincent mentioned in a letter, [14 Oct. 1888], 709/553. See ch. 3, note 14.

48 Arles's two dépots de zouaves as well as its battailon de chasseurs were composed of troops in transit. See Félix Deretz, "Deux Zouaves assassinés," L'Homme de bronze, 18 Mar. 1888, pp. 1–3. For the reputation of the Zouaves, see Zemel 1997, pp. 94–98.

49 See for example the suicide of the eighteen-year-old girl reported in Le Forum républicain, 8 July 1888, p. 2, and the discovery of the drowned newborn discussed in L'Homme de bronze, 30 Sept. 1888, p. 3.

50 "The girl": Gauguin to Bernard, [end Oct. 1888], M 1984, letter 176. Gauguin seems to have altered what was originally a (presumably male) figure in trousers to depict a woman wearing a white fichu before settling on the less legible, but definitely female, costume seen in the final painting. "Les trois grâces au temple de Venus": Gauguin to Theo, [c. 22 Nov. 1888], M 1984, letter 183. In an inventory Gauguin sent to Boussod et Valadon in 1890, he referred to this picture as "Paysage d'Arles avec trois Arlésiennes"; see Rewald 1973, p. 49.

51 Gauguin began using thin chalk grounds early in his career and increasingly after 1886; see Carol Christensen, "The Painting Materials and Technique of Paul Gauguin," in Studies in the History of Art: Conservation Research 41 (Washington, D.C., 1993), p. 71; and Jirat-Wasiutyński/Newton 2000, p. 75.

52 Vincent to Bernard, [c. 2 Nov. 1888], 721/B 19a.

53 Vincent to Theo, [c. 5 Nov. 1888], 722/559. For discussions of where the two canvases were painted, see Pickvance 1984, cat. 116–17, pp. 199–200; and Dorn 1990, pp. 405–06. Given the circumstances and the similarity of the two pictures, a scenario involving both

plein-air and studio work seems likely. There are precedents for this practice; see, for example, the two versions of Orchard Surrounded by Cypresses (F 554, JH 1388; F 513, JH 1389).

54 On Vincent's touching up his canvases in the studio to give them "a certain unity," see Vincent to Theo, [c. 13 Apr. 1888], 599/477; and [7/8 Sept. 1889], 802/605.

55 Vincent to Theo, [c. 5 Nov. 1888], 722/559.

56 Vincent greatly admired the Bernard picture, apparently preferring it to the Vision (which he never mentioned in his letters). He did not consider Bernard's work a religious picture; Pickvance 1984, p. 213.

57 Gauguin to Bernard, [end Oct. 1888], M 1984, letter 176.

58 Vincent to Theo, [c. 5 Nov. 1888], 722/559.

59 The connection of the figure of the old man with Daumier's character Ratapoil is made by Pickvance 1984, cat. 117, p. 200. The pictures have also been connected to the metaphor of the pilgrim's progress; see Amsterdam 1990, cat. 72–73, p. 177.

60 Vincent to Bernard, [c. 2 Nov. 1888], 721/B 19a.

61 Ibid.

62 Vincent to Theo, [28 Oct. 1888], 720/588. See also his letter to Bernard, [c. 2 Nov. 1888], 721/B 19a; and the draft of a letter from Vincent to Gauguin, [28 May 1888], 619/494a, in which he outlined his plan of "living like a monk who goes to the brothel once a fortnight." For Vincent's conception of the artist-monk, see Zemel 1997, p. 100.

63 Vincent to Bernard, [c. 4 Aug. 1888], 659/B 14.

64 On Gauguin's success with women, see Vincent to Theo, [c. 14 Mar. 1888], 587/469.

65 Vincent to Theo, [24 Sept. 1888], 690/542.

66 "Little Arlésienne": Vincent to Theo, [c. 29 Aug. 1888], 675/529. "He is married, but he doesn't look it very much": [c. 4 Dec. 1888], 728/560.

67 Vincent to Theo, [c. 4 Dec. 1888], 728/560.

68 Gauguin to Bernard, postscript in Vincent to Bernard, [c. 2 Nov. 1888], 721/B 19a.

69 This drawing was reported in Vincent to Theo, [c. 12 Nov. 1888], 723/561. Kōdera 1990, p. 56, first pointed out the connection between the illustration of the bonzes and mousmés and Vincent's Self-Portrait.

70 Vincent to Theo, [c. 5 Nov. 1888], 722/559.

71 For details on Marie Ginoux (née Marie Julien; 1848–1911) and her husband, Joseph-Michel Ginoux (1835–1906), see Dorn 1990, pp. 407–08. Vincent to Bernard, [4 Oct. 1888], 702/B 19.

72 Roland Dorn's proposals for the disposition of the decorations in the rooms of the Yellow House (Dorn 1990, pls. XXII, XXII) are based on Léon Ramser's 1922 plan of the building (repr. in ibid., pls. XVIII, XIX). His proposals

do not show the east-facing windows in either the studio or Gauguin's bedroom that are visible in Vincent's painting (ch. 3, fig. 71), watercolor (F 1413, JH 1591; Van Gogh Museum, Amsterdam), and letter sketch (F 1453, JH 1590; location unknown) of the Yellow House's exterior. Our study presumes the existence of these windows.

73 On 10 October (706/549), Vincent wrote to Theo that he expected the gas to be installed at any moment; he planned, in fact, "to begin a new [painting] this evening, *when the gas is lit.*" Andreas Blühm has recently suggested that the furrows visible in the street in Vincent's depiction of the Yellow House are evidence of this municipal project; see Blühm and Louise Lippencott, *Light!: The Industrial Age, 1750–1900: Art and Science, Technology and Society*, exh. cat, Van Gogh Museum, Amsterdam (2001), p. 202. The gaslight simulations carried out at the exhibition demonstrated the greenish yellow tinge of this type of illumination. "Paint portraits": [28 Oct. 1888], 719/558b.

74 It is possible that the face may have lost some pink nuances. Vincent produced gray here (and in *Memory of the Garden*) by mixing red and green paints; the latter now predominates.

75 Vincent to Theo, [24 Sept. 1888], 690/542.

76 For Vincent's earlier description of his work as "slashed on," see letter to van Rappard, [c. 31 Oct. 1882], 278/R 16. Vincent also employed the verb *sabrer* in letters to Theo, [c. 25 July 1888], 652/514; and to Wil, [c. 10 Dec. 1889], 829/W 16. In his first missive to Vincent after the latter's December breakdown, Gauguin asked him to send the fencing equipment he had left behind in Arles ([c. 9–14 Jan. 1889], van Gogh 1990, letter 739; Cooper 1983, GAC 34). A few days later, in an uncharacteristically bitter letter to Theo, Vincent mocked Gauguin's pretensions and added that he would "hasten to send [Gauguin] his toys by parcel post. Hoping that he will never use more serious weapons" ([17 Jan. 1889], 740/571). "Calm and steady": Vincent to Bernard, [24 June 1888], 636/B 9.

77 See Ronald Pickvance, *Gauguin and the School of Pont-Aven*, exh. cat., San Diego Museum of Art (1994), cat. 87, p. 121. Gauguin's discussion of fencing goes on for pages in *Avant et après*, pp. 210–17.

78 Gauguin, *Avant et après*, pp. 217–18; and Loti, *Mon Frère Yves*, p. 98. On French masculinity, see Tamar Garb, *Bodies of Modernity: Figure and Flesh in Fin-de-Siècle France* (New York, 1998), pp. 34–35, 55ff.

79 See, for instance, Vincent to Theo, [c. 17 Dec. 1883], 416/347: "I also thought of Michelet's saying (who had it from a zoologist), 'Le mâle est très sauvage.' And because at this

time of my life I know myself to have strong passions and believe that I should have them, I grant that I may well be 'très sauvage' myself."

80 The authors are indebted to Cornelia Peres for making this observation. The flower was painted over dry layer of white, which dries more quickly.

81 Our thanks to Kristin Lister, Robert Flynn Johnson, Karin Breuer, and Debbie Evans for this information.

82 Vincent to Bernard, [c. 2 Nov. 1888], 721/B 19a.

83 "A canvas of the same": ibid. "I have already written you": Vincent to Bernard, [4 Oct. 1888], 702/B 19. Although *type* can refer to a man in general, in nineteenth-century argot, it had the specific connotation of the lover of a prostitute: see Georges Delesalle, *Dictionnaire Argot-Français & Français-Argot* (1896; repr., Paris, 1998), s.v. "type."

84 Vincent to Bernard, [c. 2 Nov. 1888], 721/B 19a.

85 Vincent reported reading *Le Rêve* on [c. 2 Nov. 1888], 721/B 19a. See Sund 1992, pp. 166–67. See Vincent to Theo, [mid-Nov. 1884], 473/387. On painting alongside others, he observed, "I work with more animation when I have some conversation." Gauguin considered Zola "not much of a painter," characterizing his gloomy Naturalism as a predilection for "bituminous tones": Gauguin, "Diverses Choses," p. 264.

86 See *Le Forum républicain*, 1 Jan. 1888, 4 Mar. 1888, and 21 Apr. 1889. And *L'Homme du bronze*, 5 Aug. 1888 and 10 Feb. 1889.

87 The blue gloves resemble those in a January 1889 still life ([F 502, JH 1664]; Collection Mr. and Mrs. Paul Mellon, Upperville, Va.), so perhaps Vincent added the gloves to *The Arlésienne* around that time.

88 Although Gauguin had not spent much time on this *ébauche*-like step in some of the preceding pictures (like *Les Alyscamps* [fig. 26], and *Farmhouse in Arles* [fig. 11]), this type of underpainting was part of his standard practice in many pictures, including *Self-Portrait (Les Misérables)* (ch. 3, fig. 74).

89 Gauguin to Bernard, [2nd week Nov. 1888], M 1984, letter 179.

90 Ibid.

91 For the October visit, see Vincent to Eugène Boch, [2 Oct. 1888], 696/553b; and Vincent to Theo, [3 Oct. 1888], 698/544.

92 Vincent to Theo, [c. 5 Nov. 1888], 722/559.

93 Ibid. On Monticelli, see Vincent to Theo, [c. 12 Nov. 1888], 723/561.

94 "Women in a vineyard": Vincent to Theo, [c. 5 Nov. 1888], 722/559. For information on the 1888 grape harvest in Arles, see *L'Homme de bronze* and *Le Forum républicain* of 16 Sept., 30 Sept., and 7 Oct. 1888. See also *L'Homme de bronze*, 21 Oct. 1888, which notes that it

had been unseasonably cold.

95 For the suggestion regarding mourning costume, see Dorra 1978, p. 12. For the title, see Gauguin to Theo, [c. 22 Nov. 1888], M 1984, letter 183.

96 Gauguin exhibited the work as *Misères humaines* at Les Vingt in Brussels in 1889; see *Les XX, Bruxelles. Catalogue des dix expositions annuelles* (Brussels, 1981), p. 184. He also showed it under that title at the Volpini exhibition in June 1889; see *Catalogue de l'Exposition de peintures du groupe impressionniste et sythétiste*, cat. 43. For the connection to Dürer, see for example Amishai-Maisels 1985, pp. 147–48; to Vincent's *Sorrow*, see Gösta Svenaeus, "Gauguin and van Gogh," *Vincent: Bulletin of the Rijksmuseum Vincent van Gogh* 4, no. 4 (1976), p. 31.

97 Joris-Karl Huysmans, "Appendice (1882)," in *L'Art moderne* (Paris, 1883), p. 288. At the time Gauguin wrote Pissarro that he was unfamiliar with Pantazis' work; see Gauguin to Pissarro, [11 or 12 May 1883], M 1984, letter 36. Pantazis lived and exhibited in Brussels, and appeared in the first Les Vingt exhibition in 1884; see M 1984, p. 380 n. 104. The success of Gauguin's interpretation of the theme is such that some have read the picture, independently of any possible textual or visual sources, as symbolizing "suppressed gluttony"; see Pickvance 1984, cat. 188, p. 206.

98 Gauguin to Schuffenecker, [c. 20 Dec. 1888], M 1984, letter 193 (excerpt); dated to 22 Dec. in M 1989, pp. 238–43 (in full).

99 For Gauguin's admiration of Corot, see letter to Pissarro, [May/June 1882], M 1984, letter 23, and p. 320 n. 2.

100 On Corot's *Reaper with Sickle*, see New York, The Metropolitan Museum of Art, *Corot*, exh. cat. by Gary Tinterow et al. (1996), cat. 70, p. 172. "Visage": Burty as quoted in Alfred Sensier, *La Vie et l'oeuvre de J.-F. Millet* (Paris, 1881), p. 356.

101 See Vincent to Theo, [4 Oct. 1888], 701/545: "you are as fortunate, or at least fortunate in the same way, as Sensier if you have Gauguin."

102 Gauguin to Schuffenecker, [c. 20 Dec. 1888], M 1984, letter 193 (excerpt); dated to 22 Dec. in M 1989, pp. 238–43 (in full). In 1902 Gauguin included Millet in a list of the most important French painters following Delacroix and Ingres; see discussion in Victor Merlhès, *Racontars de rapin* (Tahiti, 1994), index.

103 *Splendeurs et misères des courtisanes* was one of the novels that Balzac included in his *Comédie humaine*. Gauguin listed the picture by this title in his sketchbook from Arles and Brittany (Huyghe 1952, p. 223). Bodelsen 1964, p. 193, noted that "consola-

tion of the earth" echoes Vincent's language. Henri Dorra made the connection between "poor disconsolate being" and the line from Michelet that Vincent inscribed on *Sorrow* (ch. 1, fig. 42); see Dorra 1978, pp. 12–17.

104 "In every land where I would sleep, / In every land where I would weep, / In every land where I would die, / There sat, nor would he make reply, / My ill-starred brother, clad in gloom. / As though arisen from the tomb": Alfred de Musset, *The Complete Writings of Alfred de Musset* (New York, 1905), p. 343. See also ch. 1, note 22.

105 Vincent also quoted Musset in his letter to Theo, [17/18 Dec. 1888], 730/564. The connection has been pointed out by Dorra 1978, p. 15; and Amishai-Maisels 1985, pp. 148, 170 n. 78.

106 Gauguin to Theo, [14 Nov. 1888], M 1894, letter 181.

107 Gauguin described *Human Miseries* at the time of its execution as painted "simplement sur la grosse toile dans la pâte avec des divisions de couleur": letter to Schuffenecker, [last week Nov. 1888], M 1984, letter 184; dated to 22 Nov. in M 1989, p. 181). See Jirat-Wasiutyński/Newton 2000, p. 123. The paint surface of the picture, sent to Paris late November 1888, had immediately begun flaking. To remedy this, Gauguin, on his return to Paris, followed a procedure he described as follows: "you stick newspapers on to your canvas with *flour paste*. Once they've dried, you place your canvas on a smooth board and press down *hard* on it with very hot flat-irons. All the flaws in your paint will remain, but they will be smoothed over and you will have a *very beautiful* surface": Gauguin to Vincent, [c. 9 Jan. 1889], van Gogh 1990, letter 739; Cooper 1983, GAC 34.

108 For Gauguin's productivity, see Vincent to Theo, [c. 6 Nov. 1888], 722/559. "Firm impasto": [c. 23 Nov. 1888], 726/563. "It is as beautiful": [c. 12 Nov. 1888], 723/561.

109 Originally the painting would have been more vibrant still, as the violets in the foreground have faded over time.

110 Vincent to Theo, [c. 12 Nov. 1888], 723/561. For the problems dating this painted brothel sketch, see note 114.

111 "Our life together": Vincent to Theo, [c. 5 Nov. 1888], 722/559. Gauguin to Bernard, [c. 9–12 Nov. 1888], M 1984, letter 178.

112 On Gauguin's culinary skills, see Vincent to Theo, [c. 12 Nov. 1888], 723/561: "He knows how to cook *perfectly.*" On Vincent's soup, see Gauguin, *Avant et après*, pp. 31–32. "The good Vincent": Gauguin to Theo, [14 Nov. 1888], M 1984, letter 181. Gauguin was responding to a letter from Theo (13 Nov. 1888, M 1984, letter XCIII) in which Theo had expressed his pleasure that the two were

getting along well.

113 Gauguin to Theo, [14 Nov. 1888], M 1984, letter 181.

114 Vincent to Bernard, [4 Oct. 1888], 702/B 19. The identity of this small painting is unclear. Roskill has posited that Vincent painted two brothel images: the *petit toile* mentioned here to Bernard, which was subsequently lost, and a second version, *Brothel Scene* (fig. 53)—the *pochade de bordel* mentioned to Theo in letter 723/561; see Roskill 1970b, pp. 126–27; and Roskill 1970a, pp. 58–59, 70–71. Hulsker (see JH 1599, p. 364) however, has asserted that Vincent was speaking of the Barnes Foundation picture in the letter to Bernard, and therefore dates the work to c. 9 October. We presume this first (lost) painting depicted an encounter between a prostitute and her pimp, and was meant to be an exchange of sorts for the brothel drawings Bernard had sent with his self-portrait. We, too, date *Brothel Scene* to November due to technical and stylistic reasons that link it to *A Novel Reader* (fig. 60) and *Spectators at the Arena* (fig. 54), painted at that time.

115 Vincent to Bernard, [4 Oct. 1888], 702/B 19.

116 Vincent to Theo, [c. 12 Nov. 1888], 723/561. Isabelle Cahn noted that the Impressionists had been using the white frame since the 1870s and that Pissarro's use of this device attracted particular notice at the third group exhibition in 1877. Thereafter, it was closely associated with the new or "young" school of painting. See Isabelle Cahn, *Cadres de peintres*, exh. cat., Musée d'Orsay, Paris (1989), pp. 65–68.

117 Vincent to Theo, [c. 16 Nov. 1888], 724/562.

118 Gauguin exhibited twelve paintings at Les Vingt in 1889, under the following titles: *Aux mangos (Tropiques)*, *Conversation (Tropiques)*, *Paysage breton*, *Breton et veau*, *Berger et bergère*, *Lutteurs en herbe*, *Vision du sermon*, *En plein chaleur*, *Misères humaines*, *Au presbytère*, *Les Mas*, and *«Vous y passerez, la belle!»*; Huyghe 1952, p. 73. "Les cochons": see Gauguin to Theo, [c. 22 Nov. 1888], M 1984, letter 183; and Huyghe 1952, p. 72. For an earlier essay linking the female nude and the pig, see *Two Girls Bathing* (1887 [W 215]; Museo Nacional de Bellas Artes, Buenos Aires). Jirat-Wasiutyński/Newton 2000, p. 69, pointed out that in addition to perpetuating the nostalgic view of rural women, *Four Breton Women* (1886 [W 201]; Neue Pinakothek, Munich] makes an implicit link between the women and the animals they tend, and noted that in traditional Breton society, women had been "treated as beasts of burden."

119 "Dat is het": see ch. 1, notes 30, 67. "I am so fond": Vincent to Wil, [20 Jan. 1890], 843/W 19. "Grand style": Vincent to Theo, [c. 16 Nov.

120 The relationship has been pointed out in Roskill 1970b, p. 144.

121 "These two canvases": Gauguin to Theo, [c. 22 Nov. 1888], M 1984, letter 183. "Great artist and friend": Vincent to Theo, [c. 16 Nov. 1888], 724/562. "Very happy together": Vincent to Wil, [c. 16 Nov. 1888], 725/W 9. For the identification of rural women with animals and for insight into what Vincent brought to discussions of phallic mastery, see Griselda Pollock, *Differencing the Canon: Feminist Desire and the Writing of Art's Histories* (London/New York, 1999), ch. 3, esp. pp. 50–57.

122 "Courage": Vincent to Wil, [c. 16 Nov. 1888], 725/W 9. "Canvases painted *de tête*": Vincent to Theo, [c. 12 Nov. 1888], 723/561.

123 Vincent to Wil, [c. 16 Nov. 1888], 725/W 9. All three works are on jute cut to a size 30 format.

124 See Pickvance 1984, cat. 139, p. 231; Pickvance 2000, cat. 71, p. 305.

125 Vincent to Wil, [c. 16 Nov. 1888], 725/W 9.

126 For the print in Vincent's bedroom, see Vincent to Theo, 6 July 1875, 37/30; in his studio with Sien, [6 July 1882], 245/213; as copies given to Theo and Anna, 13 Aug. 1875, 40/33 and 6 Oct. 1875, 53/41. "Personal and intimate": [21 July 1882], 250/218. For additional references to Rembrandt's painting, see letters 42/35, 47/37a, and 147/126. For Vincent and Rembrandt's *Holy Family*, see also Arikawa 1981, pp. 55–56 n. 49.

127 "More of Rembrandt": Vincent to Theo, [c. 25 Nov. 1888], 727/558a. He identified the garden as Etten in his letters to Theo and Wil of [c. 16 Nov. 1888], 724/562, 725/W 9; and as Nuenen in letter to Theo, [c. 4 Dec. 1888], 728/560.

128 See Vincent to Theo, [c. 22 Sept. 1888], 689/540. "How I would have like to have painted portraits of our own family." "As I see her": [8 Oct. 1888], 703/546.

129 The importance of this color scheme can be surmised from Vincent's frequent references to it in his letters. He reported that it took "a terrific amount of trouble to get the combination of ashen and gray-pink tones": Vincent to Theo, [c. 22 Sept. 1888], 689/540. See also Vincent to Theo, [c. 16 Sept. 1888], 685/537; [c. 17 Sept. 1888], 687/539; Vincent to Gauguin, [3 Oct.1888], 699/544a; and Vincent to Theo, [4 Oct. 1888], 701/545: "The head is modeled in light colors painted in a thick impasto." The original gray-pink (grays created by mixtures of red and green) now has a more yellowish-green appearance due to the fading of red components. For Vincent's request for his father's likeness, see his letter to Theo, [8 Oct. 1888], 703/546.

130 Vincent to Wil, [c. 16 Nov. 1888], 725/W 9.

131 Ibid.

132 "Take on": Vincent to Theo, [c. 16 Nov. 1888], 724/562. For the "Turkish treatise," see ch. 2, note 16.

133 See Vincent to Theo, [c. 2 Apr. 1888], 594/473.

134 Vincent to Theo, [Oct. 1884], 467/378.

135 For Gauguin preferring Vincent's sunflowers to Monet's, see Vincent to Theo, [c. 23 Nov. 1888], 726/563. For *Memory of the Garden*, see, [c. 4 Dec. 1888], 728/560.

136 "Compose *de tête*"; "intelligent company"; "Gauguin, in spite": Vincent to Theo, [c. 23 Nov. 1888], 726/563. "Documents": Gauguin to Pissarro, [May/June 1882], M 1984, letter 23.

137 "Slight, shabby"; "in general": Gauguin to Bernard, [2nd half Nov. 1888], M 1984, letter 182. This translation is informed by that of H. Travers Newton in Peres et al. 1991, p. 107.

138 Félix Fénéon, "Calendrier de juin [1888]," *La Revue indépendante* (July 1888); repr. in Halperin 1970, vol. 1, p. 113.

139 See Anthea Callen, *The Spectacular Body: Science, Method, and Meaning in the Work of Degas* (New Haven/London, 1995). For color as feminine, see pp. 111–16.

140 Zola, *L'Oeuvre*, pp. 419–20.

141 On the sale and adjustments to *Breton Girls Dancing*, see Theo to Gauguin, 13 Nov. 1888, M 1984, letter XCIII; and Gauguin to Theo, [14 Nov. 1888], M 1984, letter 181. "Thirty times better"; "Reproaching": Vincent to Theo, [c. 23 Nov. 1888], 726/563.

142 Vincent to Theo, [c. 23 Nov. 1888], 726/563.

143 For a different interpretation of this remark, see Pickvance 1984, p. 235.

144 Theo to Jo, 14 Feb. 1889, *Brief Happiness*, letter 46. Theo went on to note: "He cannot be detached in his dealings with people. It is *either* one thing *or* the other."

145 "I should be acting": Vincent to Theo, [2/3 Dec. 1882], 292/250. "I myself": Vincent to van Rappard, [2nd half June 1885], 515/R 53. "As though people": [2nd half Aug. 1885], 529/R 57.

146 Vincent to Theo, [c. 23 Nov. 1888], 726/563. On these pictures, see Pickvance 1984, cat. 141, p. 235; Dorn 1990, pp. 425–28; Amsterdam 1987, p. 236; Amsterdam 1990, cat. 76–77, pp. 184–85. For a psychoanalytic interpretation, see H. Blum, "Les Chaises de Van Gogh," *Revue française de psychanalyse* 12 (1958), pp. 83–93.

147 The red-lake component of the red and purple paints used in *Gauguin's Chair* has faded, so that the shadows now appear blue. Vincent added his signature at a later point, when the underlying paint of the box was dry but still soft, most likely before Gauguin departed. His initial description of the work mentions no still-life elements on the chair. In January he mentioned that he was working "again … on my own empty chair with a

pipe and tobacco pouch": Vincent to Theo, [17 Jan. 1889], 740/571. Around this time he painted a still life featuring pipe and tobacco (ch. 5, fig. 8), and he added the objects to *Van Gogh's Chair* over a dry layer of paint.

148 Many scholars have referred to a patterned carpet in *Gauguin's Chair*, but no evidence suggests that Vincent purchased a carpet or rug for Gauguin's room—or for the studio, where he painted the picture. The seeming pattern was thus most likely informed by the play of light on the red tiles.

149 "Lighted candle": Vincent to Aurier, [10 or 11 Feb. 1890], 854/626a. The candle and books were part of Vincent's initial design, included in the underdrawing. For an aspect of the books' symbolism, see Vincent to Theo, [c. 21–28 Mar. 1883], 334/276: "Love is something eternal…. There is the same difference in a person before and after he is in love as there is in an unlighted lamp and one that is burning. The lamp was there and it was a good lamp, but now it is shedding light too, and that is its real function."

150 Martin Bailey made the connection between this image and Vincent's paintings of empty chairs; see Bailey 1992, p. 92. "Empty chairs": Vincent to Theo, [c. 11 Dec. 1882], 294/252.

151 For his attempts to procure copies for van Rappard and another fellow artist, H. J. van der Weele, see [c. 27 Feb. 1883], 323/R 29; [c. 3 Mar. 1883], 325/271; and [c. 5 Mar. 1883], 327/R 30.

152 For Vincent on the *Revue indépendante* exhibition, see letters to Theo, [9 Sept. 1888], 680/534; [c. 12 Nov. 1888], 723/561. "Us, the others": Gauguin to Bernard, [c. 9–12 Nov. 1888], M 1984, letter 178. Gauguin attributed his inside information to Theo, but it is unlikely that the dealer had in fact dismissed Seurat and Signac as tradesmen specializing in "petits points" or reported a plot afoot. See also M 1984, p. 512 n. 299; and Gauguin to Schuffenecker, [last week Nov. 1888], M 1984, letter 184; dated to 22 Nov. in M 1989, p. 181.

153 For Gauguin's rejection of the *Revue indépendante* invitation, see Gauguin to Schuffenecker, [first half Dec. 1888], M 1984, letter 188 (excerpt); dated to 24 Nov. in M 1989, pp. 182–85 (in full). For Vincent's rejection, see his letter to Theo, [c. 12 Nov. 1888], 723/561.

154 Gustave Kahn, "Peinture: Exposition des Indépendants," *La Revue indépendante* (18 Apr. 1888), p. 88; cited in Amsterdam 1990, cat. 29, p. 88. Vincent to Theo, [9 Sept. 1888], 680/534.

155 "Sell none of it"; "at the age of forty": Vincent to Theo, [c. 23 Nov. 1888], 726/563. For Gauguin's shipment of pictures, see Gauguin to Theo, [c. 22 Nov. 1888], M 1984, letter 183.

Gauguin catalogues raisonnés

[B] Bodelsen 1964
Bodelsen, Merete. *Gauguin's Ceramics: A Study in the Development of His Art*. London, 1964.

Field 1973
Field, Richard S. *Paul Gauguin: Monotypes*. Exh. cat. Philadelphia Museum of Art, 1973.

[G] Gray 1980
Gray, Christopher. *Sculpture and Ceramics of Paul Gauguin*. Rev. ed. New York, 1980.

[Gu] Guérin 1927
Guérin, Marcel. *L'Oeuvre gravé de Gauguin*. Paris, 1927.

K
Kornfeld, Eberhard, Harold Joachim, and Elizabeth Morgan. *Paul Gauguin: Catalogue Raisonné of His Prints*. Bern, 1988.

W
Wildenstein, Georges. *Gauguin*. Edited by Raymond Cogniat and Daniel Wildenstein. Vol. 1, catalogue. Paris, 1964.

Van Gogh catalogues raisonnés

F
Faille, J.-B. de la. *L'Oeuvre de Vincent van Gogh: Catalogue raisonné*. Four vols. Paris/Brussels, 1928. Revised edition: *The Works of Vincent van Gogh: His Paintings and Drawings*. New York, 1970.

[JH] Hulsker 1996
Hulsker, Jan. *The New Complete van Gogh: Paintings, Drawings, Sketches*. Amsterdam/Philadelphia, 1996.

Secondary sources and exhibition catalogues

Amishai-Maisels 1985
Amishai-Maisels, Ziva. *Gauguin's Religious Themes*. New York/London, 1985.

Amsterdam 1987
Uitert, Evert van, and Michael Hoyle, eds. *The Rijksmuseum Vincent Van Gogh*. Amsterdam, 1987.

Amsterdam 1990
Amsterdam, Rijksmuseum Vincent van Gogh. *Vincent van Gogh: Paintings*. Exh. cat. by Evert van Uitert, Louis van Tilborgh, and Sjraar van Heugten, 1990.

Amsterdam 1999
Amsterdam, Van Gogh Museum. *Theo van Gogh, 1857–1891: Art Dealer, Collector, and Brother of Vincent*. Exh. cat. by Chris Stolwijk and Richard Thomson, with a contribution by Sjraar van Heugten, 1999.

Arikawa 1981
Arikawa, Haruo. "'La Berceuse': An Interpretation of Vincent van Gogh's Portraits." *Annual Bulletin of the National Museum of Western Art, Tokyo* 15 (1981), pp. 31–75.

Arles 1999
Arles, Muséon Arlaten, *Arlésienne: Le Mythe*. Exh. cat. by Pascale Picard-Cajan, 1999.

Bacou 1960
Bacou, Roseline. *Lettres de Gauguin, Gide, Huysmans, Jammes, Mallarmé, Verhaeren . . . à Odilon Redon*. Paris, 1960.

Bailey 1992
Bailey, Martin. *Van Gogh in England: Portrait of the Artist as a Young Man*. Exh. cat. Barbican Art Gallery, London, 1992.

Bailey 1996
Bailey, Martin. "Van Gogh's Portrait of Gauguin." *Apollo* 144, no. 413 (July 1996), pp. 51–54.

Benoit 1887
Benoit, Camille. *Richard Wagner, musiciens, poètes et philosophes, aperçus et jugements précédés de lettres inédites en France et traduits de l'allemande pour la première fois*. Paris, 1887.

Berson 1996
Berson, Ruth, ed. *The New Painting: Impressionism, 1874–1886: Documentation*. Vol. 1, reviews. San Francisco, 1996.

B-H
Bailly-Herzberg, Janine. *Correspondance de Camille Pissarro*. Five vols. Paris, 1980 (vol. 1), 1986 (vol. 2), 1988 (vol. 3), 1989 (vol. 4), 1991 (vol. 5).

Bodelsen 1967
Bodelsen, Merete. "Gauguin Studies." *Burlington Magazine* 109, no. 769 (Apr. 1967), pp. 217–27.

Bodelsen 1970
Bodelsen, Merete. "Gauguin, the Collector." *Burlington Magazine* 112, no. 810 (Sept. 1970), pp. 597–601.

Braun 1986
Braun, Barbara. "Paul Gauguin's Indian Identity: How Ancient Peruvian Pottery Inspired His Art." *Art History* 9, no. 1 (Mar. 1986), pp. 36–54.

Carlyle, *On Heroes*
Carlyle, Thomas. *On Heroes, Hero-Worship, and the Heroic in History*. Berkeley/Los Angeles, 1993. (First published 1841.)

Carlyle, *Sartor Resartus*
Carlyle, Thomas. *Sartor Resartus*. Edited and with an introduction and notes by Kerry McSweeney and Peter Sabor. Oxford/New York, 1987. (First published 1836.)

Detroit 2000
Detroit Institute of Arts. *Van Gogh Face to Face: The Portraits*. Exh. cat. with essays by Roland Dorn, George S. Keyes, Joseph J. Rishel with Katherine Sachs, George T. M. Shackelford, Lauren Soth, and Judy Sund; and a chronology by Katherine Sachs, 2000.

Dorra 1978
Dorra, Henri. "Gauguin's Dramatic Arles Themes." *Art Journal* 30, no. 1 (fall 1978), pp. 12–17.

Dorn 1988
Dorn, Roland. "Vincent van Gogh's Concept of 'Decoration.'" In *Vincent van Gogh International Symposium: Tokyo, October 17–19, 1985*. Tokyo, 1988, pp. 375–84.

Dorn 1990
Dorn, Roland. *Décoration: Vincent van Goghs Werkreihe für das Gelbe Haus in Arles*. Hildesheim/Zurich/New York, 1990.

Dorn 1999
Dorn, Roland. "Van Gogh's *Sunflowers* Series: The Fifth Toile de 30." *Van Gogh Museum Journal* (1999), pp. 42–61.

Druick/Zegers 1991
Druick, Douglas W., and Peter Zegers. "Le Kampong et la pagode: Gauguin à l'exposition universelle de 1889." In *Gauguin: Actes du colloque Gauguin, Musée d'Orsay, 11–13 janvier 1989*. Paris, 1991, pp. 101–42.

Druick/Zegers 1995
Druick, Douglas W., and Peter Zegers. *Paul Gauguin: Pages from the Pacific*. Exh. cat. Auckland City Art Gallery, New Zealand, 1995.

Van Eeden, *De kleine Johannes*
Eeden, Frederik van. *Little Johannes*. Translated by Clara Bell. London, 1895. Originally published in Dutch as *De kleine Johannes* (The Hague, 1887).

Eisenman 1997
Eisenman, Stephen. *Gauguin's Skirt*. New York, 1997.

Field 1977
Field, Richard S. *Paul Gauguin: The Paintings of the First Trip to Tahiti*. New York/London, 1977.

Fonsmark 1996
Fonsmark, Anne-Birgitte. *Gauguin Ceramics: Ny Carlsberg Gyptotek*. Translated by Dan A. Marmorstein. Copenhagen, 1996.

Halperin 1970
Halperin, Joan U. *Félix Fénéon: Oeuvres plus que complètes*. Two vols. Geneva, 1970.

Halperin 1988
Halperin, Joan U. *Félix Fénéon: Aesthete and Anarchist in Fin-de-Siècle Paris*. New Haven/London, 1988.

Harscoët-Maire 1997
Harscoët-Maire, Laure. "Lettres d'Émile Bernard (1886–88): De Cancale à Saint-Briac." *Le Pays de Dinan* 17 (1997), pp. 113–82.

Hartford 2001
Hartford, Wadsworth Atheneum Museum of Art. *Gauguin's Nirvana: Painters at Le Pouldu, 1889–90*. Exh. cat. edited by Eric M. Zafran, 2001.

Hartrick 1939
Hartrick, Archibald S. *A Painter's Pilgrimage through Fifty Years*. Cambridge, 1939.

Herbert 1991
Herbert, Robert. *Georges Seurat, 1859–1891*. Exh. cat. The Metropolitan Museum of Art, New York, 1991.

Hulsker 1971
Hulsker, Jan. "Vincent's Stay in the Hospitals at Arles and St.-Rémy: Unpublished Letters from the Reverend Mr. Salles and Doctor Peyron to Theo van Gogh." *Vincent: Bulletin of the Rijksmuseum Vincent van Gogh* 1, no. 2 (1971), pp. 21–39.

Hulsker 1974
Hulsker, Jan. "What Theo Really Thought of Vincent." *Vincent: Bulletin of the Rijksmuseum Vincent van Gogh* 3, no. 2 (1974), pp. 2–28.

Hulsker 1990
Hulsker, Jan. *Vincent and Theo van Gogh: A Dual Biography*. Ann Arbor, Mich., 1990.

Hulsker 1992
Hulsker, Jan. "Van Gogh, Roulin and the Two Arlésiennes." Parts 1 and 2. *Burlington Magazine* 134, no. 1074 (Sept. 1992), pp. 570–77; no. 1076 (Nov. 1992), pp. 707–15.

Hulsker 1993
Hulsker, Jan. *Vincent van Gogh: A Guide to His Work and Letters*. Amsterdam, 1993.

Jensen 1994
Jensen, Robert. *Marketing Modernism in Fin-de-Siècle Europe*. Princeton, N.J., 1994.

Jirat-Wasiutyński/Newton 2000
Jirat-Wasiutyński, Vojtěch, and H. Travers Newton, Jr. *Technique and Meaning in the Paintings of Paul Gauguin*. Cambridge/New York, 2000.

Kōdera 1990
Kōdera, Tsukasa. *Vincent van Gogh: Christianity versus Nature*. Amsterdam/Philadelphia, 1990.

Kōdera 1991
Kōdera, Tsukasa. "Van Gogh's Utopian Japonisme." In *Catalogue of the Van Gogh Museum's Collection of Japanese Prints*. Amsterdam, 1991.

12
Gauguin
Martinique (At the Pond's Edge)
Martinique, summer 1887 [W 222]
Oil on canvas
54 x 56 cm
Van Gogh Museum, Amsterdam
(Vincent van Gogh Foundation),
S220 V/1962
Ch. 2, fig. 58

13
Gauguin
Coming and Going, Martinique
Martinique, summer 1887
[not in W]
Oil on canvas
72.6 x 92 cm
Carmen Thyssen-Bornemisza
Collection, Madrid
Ch. 2, fig. 61

14
Gauguin
Conversation (Tropics)
(Conversation [Tropiques])
Martinique, summer 1887 [W 227]
Oil on canvas
61.5 x 76 cm
Private collection
Chicago only
Ch. 3, fig. 20

15
Gauguin
Portrait Vase of Jeanne
Schuffenecker
Paris, winter 1887/88 [B 32, G 62]
Unglazed stoneware
H. 19 cm
Private collection
Ch. 2, fig. 65

16
Gauguin
Cleopatra Pot
Paris, winter 1887/88 [B 17, G 37]
Partly glazed stoneware
H. 13.6 cm
Van Gogh Museum, Amsterdam
(Vincent van Gogh Foundation),
V37 V/1978
Ch. 2, fig. 69

17
Gauguin
Leda and the Swan
Paris, winter 1887/88 [B 34, G 63]
Unglazed stoneware, decorated
with slip
H. 20 cm
Private collection
Ch. 2, fig. 64

18
Van Gogh
Fishing in Spring, the Pont de
Clichy (Asnières)
Paris, spring 1887 [F 354, JH 1270]
Oil on canvas
49 x 58 cm
The Art Institute of Chicago, gift of
Charles Deering McCormick,
Brooks McCormick, and Roger
McCormick, 1965.1169
Ch. 2, fig. 44

19
Van Gogh
Self-Portrait
Paris, spring 1887 [F 345, JH 1249]
Oil on artist's board, mounted on
cradled wood panel
41 x 32.5 cm
The Art Institute of Chicago, Joseph
Winterbotham Collection, 1954.326
Ch. 2, fig. 45

20
Van Gogh
Self-Portrait with Straw Hat
Paris, summer 1887
[F 526, JH 1309]
Oil on canvas, mounted on wood
panel
34.9 x 26.7 cm
The Detroit Institute of Arts, City of
Detroit Purchase, 22.13
Chicago only
Ch. 2, fig. 46

21
Van Gogh
A Pair of Boots (Les Souliers)
Paris, summer 1887
[F 333, JH 1236]
Oil on canvas
33 x 40.9 cm
The Baltimore Museum of Art, The
Cone Collection, formed by Dr.
Claribel Cone and Miss Etta Cone of
Baltimore, Maryland, 1950.302
Ch. 2, fig. 47

22
Van Gogh
Flowering Plum Tree (after
Hiroshige)
Paris, summer 1887
[F 371, JH 1296]
Oil on canvas
55 x 46 cm
Van Gogh Museum, Amsterdam
(Vincent van Gogh Foundation),
S114 V/1962
Amsterdam only
Ch. 3, fig. 16

23
Van Gogh
Two Sunflowers
Paris, summer 1887
[F 375, JH 1329]
Oil on canvas
43.2 x 61 cm
The Metropolitan Museum of Art,
New York, Rogers Fund, 1949, 49.41
Ch. 2, fig. 49

24 *
Van Gogh
Two Sunflowers
Paris, summer 1887
[F 376, JH 1331]
Oil on canvas
50 x 60 cm
Kunstmuseum, Bern, Switzerland,
gift of Professor Dr. Hans R.
Hahnloser, 2140
Ch. 2, fig. 50

25
Van Gogh
Parisian Novels (Romans
parisiens)
Paris, late 1887 [F 359, JH 1332]
Oil on canvas
73 x 93 cm
Private collection
Chicago only
Ch. 2, fig. 71

1888

26
Émile Bernard (French; 1868–1941)
Breton Women in the Meadow (The
Pardon at Pont-Aven) (Les
Bretonnes dans la prairie
[Bretonnes au pardon])
Pont-Aven, August 1888
Oil on canvas
74 x 92 cm
Private collection
Ch. 3, fig. 60

27
Bernard
Self-Portrait Dedicated to Vincent
van Gogh
Pont-Aven, late September 1888
Oil on canvas
46.5 x 55.5 cm
Van Gogh Museum, Amsterdam
(Vincent van Gogh Foundation),
S206 V/1962
Ch. 3, fig. 76

28
Gauguin
Breton Girls Dancing (La Ronde des
petites Bretonnes)
Pont-Aven, June 1888 [W 251]
Oil on canvas
73 x 92.7 cm
National Gallery of Art, Washington,
D.C., Collection of Mr. and Mrs. Paul
Mellon, 1983.1.19
Ch. 3, fig. 21

29
Gauguin
Young Wrestlers—Brittany
(Jeunes Lutteurs—Bretagne)
Pont-Aven, July 1888 [W 273]
Oil on canvas
93 x 73 cm
Private collection
Ch. 3, fig. 39

30
Gauguin
Sketch of *Young Wrestlers—*
Brittany in letter to Vincent
Pont-Aven, [c. 24/25 July 1888]
(M 1984, letter 158)
Pen and ink on paper
21 x 13.6 cm
Van Gogh Museum, Amsterdam
(Vincent van Gogh Foundation),
B844 V/1962
Ch. 3, fig. 35

31
Gauguin
Vision of the Sermon (Vision du
sermon)
Pont-Aven, mid-August–mid-
September 1888 [W 245]
Oil on canvas
73 x 92 cm
National Gallery of Scotland,
Edinburgh, NG1643
Ch. 3, fig. 59

32
Gauguin
Sketch of *Vision of the Sermon* in
letter to Vincent
Pont-Aven, [c. 25–27 September
1888] (M 1984, letter 165)
Pen and ink on paper
11.7 x 15.5 cm
Van Gogh Museum, Amsterdam
(Vincent van Gogh Foundation),
B847 V/1962
Ch. 3, fig. 62

33
Gauguin
Self-Portrait Dedicated to Vincent
van Gogh (Les Misérables)
Pont-Aven, late September 1888
[W 239]
Oil on canvas
45 x 55 cm
Van Gogh Museum, Amsterdam
(Vincent van Gogh Foundation),
S224 V/1962
Ch. 3, fig. 74; front cover (detail)

34
Gauguin
The Aven River at Pont-Aven
Pont-Aven, fall 1888 [W 253]
Oil on canvas
72 x 93 cm
Private collection
Chicago only
Ch. 4, fig. 76

35
Gauguin
Farmhouse in Arles (Mas d'Arles)
Arles, c. 28 October 1888 [W 308]
Oil on canvas
91 x 72 cm
Indianapolis Museum of Art, gift in
memory of William Ray Adams,
44.10
Ch. 4, fig. 11; ch. 4, fig. 14 (detail)

36
Gauguin
Les Alyscamps (The Three Graces
at the Temple of Venus) (Paysage
or *Les Trois Grâces au temple du*
Vénus)
Arles, c. 29 October 1888 [W 307]
Oil on canvas
92 x 73 cm
Musée d'Orsay, Paris, bequeathed
by the comtesse Vitali, in memory
of her brother the vicomte de
Cholet, 1923, R.F. 1938-47
Ch. 4, fig. 21

37
Gauguin
Les Alyscamps
Arles, c. 1 November 1888 [W 306]
Oil on jute
72.5 x 91.5 cm
Seiji Togo Memorial Yasuda Kasai
Museum of Art, Tokyo, L0-179
Ch. 4, fig. 26

38
Gauguin
Madame Ginoux (study for *Night*
Café)
Arles, c. 4 November 1888
White and colored chalks and char-
coal on wove paper
56.1 x 49.2 cm
Fine Arts Museums of San
Francisco, memorial gift from Dr. T.
Edward and Tullah Hanley,
Bradford, Pennsylvania, 69.30.78
Ch. 4, fig. 36; ch. 5, fig. 92

39
Gauguin
Night Café (Un Café de nuit)
Arles, 4–12 November 1888 [W 305]
Oil on jute
72 x 92 cm
The State Pushkin Museum of Fine
Arts, Moscow, 3367
Ch. 4, fig. 41; ch. 4, fig. 39 (detail);
App., fig. 1 (detail)

40
Gauguin
Human Miseries (Grape Harvest or Poverty) (Misères humaines [Les Vendanges or La Pauvresse])
Arles, 4–11 November 1888 [W 304]
Oil on jute
73 x 93 cm
Ordrupgaard, Copenhagen, 223 WH
Ch. 4, fig. 50; ch. 4, fig. 52 (detail)

41
Gauguin
Washerwomen at the Roubine du Roi Canal
Arles, late November 1888 [W 303]
Oil on jute
73 x 92 cm
Museo de Bellas Artes de Bilbao, Spain, 82/18
Ch. 4, fig. 75

42
Gauguin
Blue Trees ("Vous y passerez, la belle!") (Les Arbres bleus)
Arles, late November 1888 [W 311]
Oil on jute
92 x 73 cm
Ordrupgaard, Copenhagen, 254 WH
Ch. 4, fig. 87

43
Gauguin
Madame Roulin
Arles, late November 1888 [W 298]
Oil on canvas
50 x 63 cm
The Saint Louis Art Museum, funds given by Mrs. Mark C. Steinberg, 5:1959
Ch. 4, fig. 97

44
Gauguin
Washerwomen at the Roubine du Roi Canal
Arles, early December 1888 [W 302]
Oil on jute
75.9 x 92.1 cm
The Museum of Modern Art, New York, The William S. Paley Collection, SPC 15.90
Ch. 4, fig. 83

45
Gauguin
Arles Landscape (Path by the Roubine du Roi Canal)
Arles, early December 1888 [W 309]
Oil on jute
72.5 x 92 cm
Nationalmuseum, Stockholm, NM 1735
Ch. 4, fig. 82

46
Gauguin
The Painter of Sunflowers (Le Peintre de tournesols)
Arles, c. 1 December 1888 [W 296]
Oil on jute
73 x 92 cm
Van Gogh Museum, Amsterdam (Vincent van Gogh Foundation), S225 V/1962
Amsterdam only
Ch. 4, fig. 107

47
Gauguin
Monsieur Ginoux
Arles, early December 1888
[not in W]
Oil on canvas
40 x 31 cm
Van Gogh Museum, Amsterdam (Vincent van Gogh Foundation), S256 V/1962
Ch. 4, fig. 116

48
Gauguin
Self-Portrait Dedicated to Charles Laval (later to Eugène Carrière)
Arles, December 1888 [W 384]
Oil on jute
46.5 x 38.6 cm
National Gallery of Art, Washington, D.C., Collection of Mr. and Mrs. Paul Mellon, 1985.64.20
Ch. 4, fig. 121

49
Gauguin
Old Man with a Cane
Arles, December 1888 [W 318]
Oil on jute
70 x 45 cm
Petit Palais—Musée des Beaux-Arts de la Ville de Paris, PPP 623
Ch. 4, fig. 123

50
Gauguin
Arlésiennes (Mistral)
Arles, mid-December 1888 [W 300]
Oil on jute
73 x 92 cm
The Art Institute of Chicago, Mr. and Mrs. Lewis Larned Coburn Memorial Collection, 1934.391
Ch. 4, fig. 125

51
Gauguin
The Artist's Mother (Aline-Marie Gauguin)
Arles, December 1888 [W 385]
Oil on canvas
41 x 33 cm
Staatsgalerie Stuttgart, 2554
Ch. 4, fig. 138

52
Gauguin
Sketchbook from Arles and Brittany
1888–1901
Graphite and charcoal on lined ledger paper
218 pages; each 17 x 10.5 cm
The Israel Museum Collection, Jerusalem, gift of Sam Salz, New York, to America-Israel Cultural Foundation, 1972
Ch. 4, figs. 84, 96, 98, 104, 108, 109, 117, 126, 127

53
Charles Laval (French; 1862–1894)
Self-Portrait Dedicated to Vincent van Gogh
Pont-Aven, c. 1 November 1888
Oil on canvas
50 x 60 cm
Van Gogh Museum, Amsterdam (Vincent van Gogh Foundation), S24 V/1962
Amsterdam only
Ch. 4, fig. 119

54
Van Gogh
Self-Portrait at the Easel
Paris, February 1888
[F 522, JH 1356]
Oil on canvas
65 x 50.5 cm
Van Gogh Museum, Amsterdam (Vincent van Gogh Foundation), S22 V/1962
Ch. 2, fig. 74

55
Van Gogh
Pear Tree in Blossom
Arles, April 1888 [F 405, JH 1394]
Oil on canvas
73 x 46 cm
Van Gogh Museum, Amsterdam (Vincent van Gogh Foundation), S39 V/1962
Ch. 3, fig. 16

56
Van Gogh
A Farmhouse in Provence (Un Mas de Provence)
Arles, mid-June 1888
[F 565, JH 1443]
Oil on canvas
46 x 61 cm
National Gallery of Art, Washington, D.C., Ailsa Mellon Bruce Collection, 1970.17.34
Ch. 3, fig. 25

57
Van Gogh
The Sower
Arles, mid-June 1888
[F 422, JH 1470]
Oil on canvas
64 x 80.5 cm
Kröller-Müller Museum, Otterlo, The Netherlands, 303-18
Ch. 3, fig. 26

58
Van Gogh
Stacks of Wheat near a Farmhouse
Arles, c. 17 July 1888
[F 1426, JH 1514]
Pencil, quill pen and reed pen, and brown ink on wove paper
24 x 31.5 cm
Szépmüvészeti Múzeum, Budapest, 1935–2792
Ch. 4, fig. 12

59
Van Gogh
Washerwomen at the Roubine du Roi Canal
Arles, c. 17 July 1888
[F 1444, JH 1507]
Reed pen and ink on wove paper
31.5 x 24 cm
Kröller-Müller Museum, Otterlo, The Netherlands, 306-20
Ch. 4, fig. 73

60
Van Gogh
Oleanders and Zola's "Joie de vivre"
Arles, August 1888 [F 593, JH 1566]
Oil on canvas
60.3 x 73.7 cm
The Metropolitan Museum of Art, New York, gift of Mr. and Mrs. John L. Loeb, 1962, 62.24
Chicago only
Ch. 3, fig. 52

61
Van Gogh
Sunflowers
Arles, late August 1888
[F 454, JH 1562]
Oil on canvas
93 x 73 cm
The National Gallery, London, NG3863
Amsterdam only
Ch. 3, fig. 58; ch. 5, fig. 17 (detail)

62 *
Van Gogh
The Night Café (Le Café de nuit)
Arles, c. 8 September 1888
[F 463, JH 1575]
Oil on canvas
70 x 89 cm
Yale University Art Gallery, New Haven, Connecticut, bequest of Stephen Carlton Clark
Ch. 4, fig. 40

63
Van Gogh
The Poet's Garden (Le Jardin du poète)
Arles, mid-September 1888
[F 468, JH 1578]
Oil on canvas
73 x 92.1 cm
The Art Institute of Chicago, Mr. and Mrs. Lewis Larned Coburn Memorial Collection, 1933.433
Ch. 3, fig. 69

64
Van Gogh
Self-Portrait Dedicated to Paul Gauguin (Bonze)
Arles, c. 16 September 1888
[F 476, JH 1581]
Oil on canvas
61 x 50 cm
Fogg Art Museum, Harvard University Art Museums, bequest from the Collection of Maurice Wertheim, Class of 1906, 1951.65
Ch. 3, fig. 73; front cover (detail)

65
Van Gogh
The Starry Night over the Rhone (La Nuit étoilée)
Arles, 28 September 1888
[F 474, JH 1592]
Oil on canvas
72.5 x 92 cm
Musée d'Orsay, Paris, life-interest gift of M. and Mme Robert Kahn-Sriberen in memory of M. and Mme Fernand Moch, 1975, entered the collection in 1995, R.F. 1975-19
Chicago only
Ch. 3, fig. 70

66
Van Gogh
The Yellow House
Arles, 28 September 1888
[F 464, JH 1589]
Oil on canvas
76 x 94 cm
Van Gogh Museum, Amsterdam (Vincent van Gogh Foundation), S32 V/1962
Ch. 3, fig. 71; p. xiii; (detail); back cover (detail)

67
Van Gogh
The Green Vineyard
Arles, c. 3 October 1888
[F 475, JH 1595]
Oil on canvas
72 x 92 cm
Kröller-Müller Museum, Otterlo, The Netherlands, 300
Ch. 4, fig. 10

68
Van Gogh
The Bedroom (La Chambre à coucher)
Arles, mid-October 1888
[F 482, JH 1608]
Oil on canvas
72 x 90 cm
Van Gogh Museum, Amsterdam
(Vincent van Gogh Foundation), S47
V/1962
Amsterdam only
Ch. 3, fig. 78

69
Van Gogh
The Sower
Arles, 28 October 1888
[F 494, JH 1617]
Oil on canvas
72 x 91 cm
Hahnloser/Jäggli Stiftung, Villa
Flora, Winterthur, Switzerland
Amsterdam only
Ch. 4, fig. 6; ch. 4, fig. 13 (detail)

70 *
Van Gogh
The Old Yew Tree (Le Vieil If)
Arles, 28 October 1888
[F 573, JH 1618]
Oil on canvas
91 x 71 cm
Private collection
Ch. 4, fig. 9

71
Van Gogh
Sketches of *The Sower* and *The Old Yew Tree* in letter to Theo
Arles, 28 October 1888 (letter 719/558b; JH 1619)
Pen and ink on paper
folded sheet: 21.1 x 26.7 cm
Van Gogh Museum, Amsterdam
(Vincent van Gogh Foundation),
B605 V/1968
Ch. 4, fig. 7

72
Van Gogh
Allée des Tombeaux (Les Alyscamps)
Arles, c. 29 October 1888
[F 568, JH 1622]
Oil on canvas
89 x 72 cm
Private collection
Ch. 4, fig. 20

73
Van Gogh
Falling Leaves (Les Alyscamps)
Arles, c. 1 November 1888
[F 487, JH 1621]
Oil on jute
72 x 91 cm
Private collection
Ch. 4, fig. 27

74
Van Gogh
The Arlésienne (Madame Ginoux)
Arles, c. 5 November 1888
[F 489, JH 1625]
Oil on jute
93 x 74 cm
Musée d'Orsay, Paris, life-interest
gift of Mme R. de Goldschmidt-
Rothschild, announced on 25
August 1944, day of the Liberation
of Paris, and entered the collection
in 1974, R.F. 1952-6
Ch. 4, fig. 37; ch. 4, fig. 38 (detail)

75
Van Gogh
A Novel Reader (Une Liseuse de romans)
Arles, c. 16 November 1888
[F 497, JH 1632]
Oil on jute
73 x 92 cm
Sagawa Express Co., Ltd., Kyoto,
Japan
Ch. 4, fig. 60

76
Van Gogh
Sketches of *A Memory of the Garden (Etten and Nuenen)* and *A Novel Reader* in letter to Wil
Arles, [c. 16 November 1888] (letter 725/W 9; JH 1631, 1633)
Pen and ink on paper
folded sheet: 21.1 x 26.9 cm
Van Gogh Museum, Amsterdam
(Vincent van Gogh Foundation),
B709 V/1962
Ch. 4, fig. 65

77
Van Gogh
Van Gogh's Chair
Arles, c. 20 November 1888
[F 498, JH 1635]
Oil on jute
93 x 73.5 cm
The National Gallery, London,
NG3862
Ch. 4, fig. 69

78
Van Gogh
Gauguin's Chair
Arles, c. 20 November 1888
[F 499, JH 1636]
Oil on jute
90.5 x 72 cm
Van Gogh Museum, Amsterdam
(Vincent van Gogh Foundation),
S48 V/1962
Ch. 4, fig. 71

79
Van Gogh
The Sower
Arles, c. 21 November 1888
[F 575a, JH 1596]
Oil on canvas
33 x 40 cm
The Armand Hammer Collection,
UCLA Hammer Museum, Los
Angeles, AH.91.42
Ch. 4, fig. 80

80
Van Gogh
The Sower
Arles, c. 25 November 1888
[F 451, JH 1629]
Oil on canvas
32 x 40 cm
Van Gogh Museum, Amsterdam
(Vincent van Gogh Foundation),
S29 V/1962
Ch. 4, fig. 79

81
Van Gogh
Sketch of *The Sower* in letter to
Theo
Arles, [c. 25 November 1888] (letter
727/558a; JH 1628)
Pen and ink on paper
folded sheet: 21.1 x 27 cm
Van Gogh Museum, Amsterdam
(Vincent van Gogh Foundation),
B605 V/1968
Ch. 4, fig. 78

82
Van Gogh
Madame Roulin with Her Baby Marcelle
Arles, December 1888
[F 490, JH 1637]
Oil on canvas
92.4 x 73.3 cm
Philadelphia Museum of Art,
bequest of Lisa Norris Elkins, 1950,
1950-92-22
Ch. 4, fig. 94

83
Van Gogh
Paul Gauguin (Man in a Red Beret)
Arles, c. 1 December 1888
[F 546, not in JH]
Oil on jute
37 x 33 cm
Van Gogh Museum, Amsterdam
(Vincent van Gogh Foundation),
S257 V/1962
Ch. 4, fig. 106

84
Van Gogh
Sunflowers
Arles, c. 1 December 1888
[F 457, JH 1666]
Oil on jute
100 x 76 cm
Seiji Togo Memorial Yasuda Kasai
Museum of Art, Tokyo, LO-175
Ch. 4, fig. 113

85
Van Gogh
Monsieur Ginoux
Arles, early December 1888
[F 533, JH 1649]
Oil on canvas
65 x 54.5 cm
Kröller-Müller Museum, Otterlo,
The Netherlands, 267-12
Ch. 4, fig. 115

86
Van Gogh
The Arlésienne (Madame Ginoux)
Arles, early December 1888
[F 488, JH 1624]
Oil on canvas
91.4 x 73.7 cm
The Metropolitan Museum of Art,
New York, bequest of Sam A.
Lewisohn, 1951, 51.112.3
Ch. 4, fig. 137; App., fig. 2 (detail)

87
Van Gogh
The Dance Hall
Arles, mid-December 1888
[F 547, JH 1652]
Oil on canvas
65 x 81 cm
Musée d'Orsay, Paris, life-interest
gift of M. and Mme André Meyer,
1950, entered the collection in
1975, R.F. 1950-9
Ch. 4, fig. 124

88
Van Gogh
Breton Women in the Meadow (after Émile Bernard)
Arles, December 1888
[F 1422, JH 1654]
Watercolor and graphite on paper
48.5 x 62 cm
Civica Galleria d'Arte Moderna
Raccolta Grassi, Milan, R.G. 139
Ch. 4, fig. 81

89
Van Gogh
Madame Roulin Rocking the Cradle (La Berceuse)
Arles, late December 1888–c. 22
January 1889 [F 508, JH 1671]
Oil on canvas
92.7 x 72.8 cm
Museum of Fine Arts, Boston,
bequest of John T. Spaulding,
48.548
Ch. 4, fig. 141

1889

90
Gauguin
Volpini Suite (Dessins lithographiques)
Paris, January–February 1889
Ten zincographs plus cover on yellow wove paper
approx. 50 x 65 cm (each sheet
varies)
The Art Institute of Chicago, William
McCallin McKee Memorial
Endowment, 1943.1021-30 and
1943.1021a
Shown:
Dramas of the Sea: A Descent into the Maelstrom (Les Drames de la mer: Une Descente dans le maelstrom) [Gu 8, K 3], 1943.1024
Ch. 5, fig. 25
Dramas of the Sea, Brittany (Les Drames de la mer, Bretagne) [Gu 7, K 2], 1943.1026
Ch. 5, fig. 26

91
Gauguin
Self-Portrait Jug
Paris, c. 1 February 1889 [B 48, G 65]
Glazed stoneware
H. 19.5 cm
Det Danske Kunstindustrimuseum,
Copenhagen, 962
Ch. 5, fig. 6

92
Gauguin
Self-Portrait Jar
Paris, spring 1889 [B 53, G 66]
Glazed stoneware
H. 28 cm
Musée d'Orsay, Paris, gift of Jean
Schmit, 1938, OA.9050
Ch. 5, fig. 35

93
Gauguin
Salome (known as *Black Venus*)
Paris, spring/summer 1889
[B 49, G 91]
Glazed stoneware
H. 50 cm
Nassau County Division of
Museums at Sands Point Preserve,
Port Washington, New York,
72.50.779
Chicago only
Ch. 5, fig. 39

94 *
Gauguin
Self-Portrait Jug with Japanese Print and Flowers
Paris, May 1889 [W 375]
Oil on canvas
73 x 92 cm
Tehran Museum of Contemporary
Art, Iran
Ch. 5, fig. 5

95
Gauguin
Christ in the Garden of Olives
(*Christ dans le jardin des oliviers*)
Pont-Aven, June 1889 [W 326]
Oil on canvas
73 x 92 cm
Norton Museum of Art, West Palm
Beach, Florida, 46.5
Ch. 5, fig. 51

96
Gauguin
*Flageolet Player on the Cliff,
Brittany*
Le Pouldu, summer 1889 [W 361]
Oil on canvas
73 x 92 cm
Indianapolis Museum of Art,
Samuel Josefowitz Collection of the
School of Pont-Aven, through the
generosity of Lilly Endowment Inc.,
the Josefowitz Family, Mr. and Mrs.
James M. Cornelius, Mr. and Mrs.
Leonard J. Betley, Lori and Dan
Efroymson, and other Friends of
the Museum, 1998.168
Chicago only
Ch. 5, fig. 53

97
Gauguin
The Red Cow
Le Pouldu, summer 1889 [W 365]
Oil on canvas
92 x 73 cm
Los Angeles County Museum of Art,
Mr. and Mrs. George Gard De Sylva
Collection, M.48.17.2
Ch. 5, fig. 54

98
Gauguin
Landscape with Two Breton Women
Pont-Aven, summer 1889 [not in W]
Oil on canvas
72.4 x 91.4 cm
Museum of Fine Arts, Boston,
gift of Harry and Mildred Remis
1976.42
Ch. 5, fig. 55

99
Gauguin
Green Christ (Breton Calvary)
Pont-Aven, September 1889 [W 328]
Oil on canvas
92 x 73.5 cm
Musées Royaux des Beaux-Arts de
Belgique, Brussels, 4416
Ch. 5, fig. 57

100
Gauguin
Yellow Christ (*Le Christ jaune*)
Pont-Aven or Le Pouldu, September
1889 [W 327]
Oil on canvas
92 x 73 cm
Albright-Knox Art Gallery, Buffalo,
New York, General Purchase Funds,
1946, 46:4
Ch. 5, fig. 58

101
Gauguin
Breton Landscape with Willows
Le Pouldu, fall 1889 [W 357]
Oil on canvas
92 x 74.5 cm
Nasjonalgalleriet, Oslo, NG.M.
01006
Ch. 5, fig. 73

102
Gauguin
Seaweed Gatherers II
(*Ramasseuses de varech II*)
Le Pouldu, October/December 1889
[W 349]
Oil on canvas
87 x 123.1 cm
Museum Folkwang Essen, Germany,
G51
Ch. 5, fig. 74

103
Gauguin
Sketches of Breton costume and
face in letter to Vincent
Le Pouldu, [c. 8–10 December
1889] (Cooper 1983, GAC 36)
Pen and ink on paper
folded sheet: 22.8 x 17.7 cm
Van Gogh Museum, Amsterdam
(Vincent van Gogh Foundation),
B869 V/1962
Ch. 5, fig. 72

104
Gauguin
Sketches of *Christ in the Garden of
Olives* and *Be in Love and You Will
Be Happy (Soyez amoreuses, vous
serez heureuses)* in letter to
Vincent
Pont-Aven, [c. 8 November 1889]
(Cooper 1983, GAC 37)
Pen and ink and watercolor on
paper
26.9 x 20.9 cm
Van Gogh Museum, Amsterdam
(Vincent van Gogh Foundation),
B866 V/1962
Ch. 5, fig. 71

105
Gauguin
Breton Girl Spinning (Joan of Arc)
Le Pouldu, November 1889 [W 329]
Oil (?) on plaster
116 x 58 cm
Private collection
Ch. 5, fig. 80

106
Gauguin
Bonjour, Monsieur Gauguin
Le Pouldu, November 1889 [W 321]
Oil on canvas laid down on wood
75 x 55 cm
The Armand Hammer Collection,
UCLA Hammer Museum, Los
Angeles, AH.90.31
Ch. 5, fig. 85

107
Gauguin
Female Nude with Sunflowers
(known as *Caribbean Woman*)
Le Pouldu, November 1889 [W 330]
Oil on wood panel
64 x 54 cm
Private collection
Ch. 5, fig. 82

108
Gauguin
*Reclining Woman with a Fan in a
Tropical Landscape*
Le Pouldu, late 1889–early 1890
[G 74]
Painted oak
35 x 45 cm
Ny Carlsberg Glyptotek,
Copenhagen, MIN 1909
Ch. 5, fig. 102

109 *
Van Gogh
Self-Portrait with Bandaged Ear
Arles, early January 1889
[F 529, JH 1658]
Oil on canvas
64 x 50 cm
Private collection
Ch. 5, fig. 9

110
Van Gogh
Sunflowers
Arles, late January 1889
[F 458, JH 1667]
Oil on canvas
95 x 73 cm
Van Gogh Museum, Amsterdam
(Vincent van Gogh Foundation),
S31 V/1962
Ch. 5, fig. 15; ch. 5, fig. 18 (detail); p.
iii (detail)

111 *
Van Gogh
Sunflowers
Arles, late January 1889
[F 455, JH 1668]
Oil on canvas
92 x 72.5 cm
Philadelphia Museum of Art, The
Mr. and Mrs. Carroll S. Tyson, Jr.,
Collection, 1963, 1963-116-19
Ch. 5, fig. 13

112
Van Gogh
*Madame Roulin Rocking the Cradle
(La Berceuse)*
Arles, 29 January 1889
[F 506, JH 1670]
Oil on canvas
92.7 x 73.8 cm
The Art Institute of Chicago, Helen
Birch Bartlett Memorial Collection,
1926.200
Ch. 5, fig. 14

113
Van Gogh
*Madame Roulin Rocking the Cradle
(La Berceuse)*
Arles, c. 22 February 1889
[F 507, JH 1672]
Oil on canvas
92 x 72.5 cm
Stedelijk Museum, Amsterdam,
A965
Ch. 5, fig. 20

114
Van Gogh
Butterflies and Flowers
Arles, c. 1 May 1889
[F 460, JH 1676]
Oil on canvas
51 x 61 cm
Private collection
Ch. 5, fig. 22

115
Van Gogh
*Weeping Tree (L'Arbre pleureur
dans l'herbe)*
Arles, 3 May 1889 [F 1468, JH 1498]
Black chalk, reed pen and brown
ink on wove paper
49.8 x 61.3 cm
The Art Institute of Chicago, gift of
Tiffany and Margaret Day Blake,
1945.31
Ch. 5, fig. 23

116
Van Gogh
The Starry Night
Saint-Rémy, 17/18 June 1889
[F 612, JH 1731]
Oil on canvas
73.7 x 92.1 cm
The Museum of Modern Art, New
York, acquired through the Lillie P.
Bliss Bequest, 1941, 472.41
Chicago only
Ch. 5, fig. 45

117
Van Gogh
Cypresses
Saint-Rémy, 25 June 1889
[F 613, JH 1746]
Oil on canvas
93.3 x 74 cm
The Metropolitan Museum of Art,
New York, Rogers Fund, 1949, 49.30
Ch. 5, fig. 47

118
Van Gogh
Mountains (Saint-Rémy)
Saint-Rémy, c. 9 July 1889
[F 622, JH 1766]
Oil on canvas
71.8 x 90.8 cm
Solomon R. Guggenheim Museum,
New York, Thannhauser Collection,
gift of Justin K. Thannhauser, 1978,
78.2514 T24
Chicago only
Ch. 5, fig. 50

119
Van Gogh
Self-Portrait with Palette
Saint-Rémy, c. 1 September 1889
[F 626, JH 1770]
Oil on canvas
57 x 43.5 cm
National Gallery of Art, Washington,
D.C., Collection of Mr. and Mrs. Paul
Mellon, 1988.74.5
Chicago only
Ch. 5, fig. 61

120
Van Gogh
*The Bedroom (La Chambre à
coucher)*
Saint-Rémy, c. 5 September 1889
[F 484, JH 1771]
Oil on canvas
73.6 x 92.3 cm
The Art Institute of Chicago, Helen
Birch Bartlett Memorial Collection,
1926.417
Chicago only

121
Van Gogh
The Reaper
Saint-Rémy, early September 1889
[F 618, JH 1773]
Oil on canvas
73 x 92 cm
Van Gogh Museum, Amsterdam
(Vincent van Gogh Foundation),
S49 V/1962

122
Van Gogh
Pietà (after Eugène Delacroix)
Saint-Rémy, c. 7 September 1889
[F 630, JH 1775]
Oil on canvas
73 x 60.5 cm
Van Gogh Museum, Amsterdam
(Vincent van Gogh Foundation),
S168 V/1962
Ch. 5, fig. 64

123
Van Gogh
Entrance to a Quarry (*L'Entrée
d'une carrière*)
Saint-Rémy, c. 5 October 1889
[F 635, JH 1767]
Oil on canvas
52 x 64 cm
Monaco Partners, L.P.
Ch. 5, fig. 67

124
Van Gogh
Garden of the Hospital (*Saint-Paul-
de-Mausole, Saint-Rémy*)
Saint-Rémy, c. 1 November 1889
[F 660, JH 1849]
Oil on canvas
73.5 x 92 cm
Museum Folkwang Essen, Germany,
G64
Chicago only
Ch. 5, fig. 86

125
Van Gogh
Olive Grove
Saint-Rémy, November 1889
[F 710, JH 1856]
Oil on canvas
74 x 93 cm
The Minneapolis Institute of Arts,
The William Hood Dunwoody Fund,
51.7
Chicago only
Ch. 5, fig. 87

126
Van Gogh
Olive Grove
Saint-Rémy, November 1889
[F 586, JH 1854]
Oil on canvas
74 x 93 cm
Göteborg Museum of Art, Sweden,
GKM 590
Ch. 5, fig. 90

127
Van Gogh
Large Plane Trees (*The Road
Menders*) (*Les Grandes Plantanes*)
Saint-Rémy, December 1889
[F 658, JH 1861]
Oil on canvas
73.7 x 92.8 cm
The Phillips Collection, Washington,
D.C., 0799
Ch. 5, fig. 91

128
Gauguin
Roses and Statuette
Le Pouldu, spring/summer 1890
[W 407]
Oil on canvas
73.2 x 54.5 cm
Musée des Beaux-Arts de Reims,
France, 943.1.1
Ch. 5, fig. 101

129
Gauguin
*Portrait of a Woman with Still Life
by Paul Cézanne*
Paris or Brittany, 1890 [W 387]
Oil on canvas
65.3 x 54.9 cm
The Art Institute of Chicago, Joseph
Winterbotham Collection, 1925.753
Ch. 5, fig. 95

130
Gauguin
Female Nude with Flower (known
as *Lust*)
Le Pouldu, late 1889/Paris, 1890
[G 88]
Partly painted and gilded wood and
metal
H. 70 cm
J. F. Willumsens Museum,
Frederikssund, Denmark, Gamle
Samling 14
Ch. 5, fig. 81

131
Gauguin
Loss of Virginity
Paris, November 1890/April 1891
[W 412]
Oil on canvas
90 x 130 cm
The Chrysler Museum of Art,
Norfolk, Virginia, gift of Walter P.
Chrysler, Jr., 71.510
Coda, fig. 2

132
Van Gogh
The Arlésienne (*after Paul
Gauguin*)
Saint-Rémy, February 1890
[F 540, JH 1892]
Oil on canvas
60 x 50 cm
Galleria Nazionale d'Arte
Moderna e Contemporanea, Rome,
5164
Ch. 5, fig. 93

133
Van Gogh
The Arlésienne (*after Paul
Gauguin*)
Saint-Rémy, February 1890
[F 543, JH 1895]
Oil on canvas
60 x 54 cm
Private collection
Ch. 5, fig. 94

134
Van Gogh
The Raising of Lazarus (*after
Rembrandt*)
Saint-Rémy, 3 May 1890
[F 677, JH 1972]
Oil on thick paper, mounted on
canvas
50 x 65 cm
Van Gogh Museum, Amsterdam
(Vincent van Gogh Foundation),
S169 V/1962
Ch. 5, fig. 97

135
Van Gogh
A Cypress against a Starry Sky
Saint-Rémy, c. 12–15 May 1890
[F 683, JH 1982]
Oil on canvas
92 x 73 cm
Kröller-Müller Museum, Otterlo,
The Netherlands, 312–12
Ch. 5, fig. 98

136
Van Gogh
Sketch of *A Cypress against a
Starry Sky* in letter to Gauguin
Saint-Rémy, [c. 17 June 1890]
(letter 893/643; JH 1983)
Pen and ink on paper
folded sheet: 21.8 x 34 cm
Van Gogh Museum, Amsterdam
(Vincent van Gogh Foundation),
B691 V/1962
Ch. 5, fig. 99

137
Van Gogh
In the Forest (*Sous-bois*)
Auvers, c. 24 June 1890
[F 773, JH 2041]
Oil on canvas
50 x 100 cm
Cincinnati Art Museum, bequest of
Mary E. Johnston, 1967.1430
Ch. 5, fig. 104

138
Gauguin
Her Name Is Vairaumati (*Son Nom
est Vairaumati*)
Mataiea, 1892 [W 450]
Oil on canvas
91 x 68 cm
The State Pushkin Museum of Fine
Arts, Moscow, 3266
Coda, fig. 12

139
Gauguin
The Seed of the Arioi (*Te aa no
areois*)
Mataiea, 1892 [W 451]
Oil on burlap
92.1 x 72.1 cm
The Museum of Modern Art, New
York, The William S. Paley
Collection, SPC 14.90
Coda, fig. 13

140
Gauguin
The Hibiscus Tree (*Te burao*)
Mataiea, 1892 [W 486]
Oil on canvas
68 x 90.7 cm
The Art Institute of Chicago,
Joseph Winterbotham
Collection, 1923.308
Coda, fig. 7

141
Gauguin
*Tehamana Has Many
Parents* (*Merahi metua no
Tehamana*)
(*The Ancestors of Tehamana
[Les Aïeux de Tehamana]*)
Mataiea, 1893 [W 497]
Oil on canvas
76.3 x 54.3 cm
The Art Institute of Chicago,
gift of Mr. and Mrs. Charles
Deering McCormick, 1980.613
Coda, fig. 14

142
Gauguin
Day of the God (*Mahana no atua*)
Paris, 1894 [W 513]
Oil on canvas
68.3 x 91.5 cm
The Art Institute of Chicago,
Helen Birch Bartlett Memorial
Collection, 1926.198
Coda, fig. 16

143
Gauguin
Dugout Canoe (*Te Vaa*) (*The Poor
Fisherman [Le Pauvre Pêcheur]*)
Punaauia, 1896 [W 544]
Oil on canvas
96 x 130 cm
The State Hermitage Museum, St.
Petersburg, 9122
Coda, fig. 21

144
Gauguin
Sunflowers on an Armchair
Punaauia, 1901 [W 603]
Oil on canvas
73 x 92.3 cm
The State Hermitage Museum, St.
Petersburg, 6516
Coda, fig. 25; p. ii (detail)

145 *
Gauguin
*Sunflowers with Puvis de
Chavannes's "Hope"*
Punaauia, 1901 [W 604]
Oil on canvas
65 x 77 cm
Private collection
Coda, fig. 28

146
Ogata Kōrin (Japanese; 1658–1716)
Musicians, from *The Book of
Painting of Kōrin* (Edo, 1802), vol. 1,
pp. 9 verso and 10 recto
Woodblock-printed album; 2 vols.
Each page 27.2 x 19.1 cm
The Art Institute of Chicago, Martin
Ryerson Collection, 31292-95
Chicago only
Ch. 3, fig. 61

147
Katsushika Hokusai (Japanese;
1760–1849)
Wrestlers, from *The Sketches of
Hokusai* (Nagoya/Edo, 1816), vol. 3,
pp. 6 verso and 7 recto
Woodblock-printed book; 14 vols.
Each page 23 x 15.9 cm
The Art Institute of Chicago, Martin
Ryerson Collection, 2577
Chicago only
Ch. 3, fig. 36

148*
Hokusai
People in a Shower, from *The Form
of Painting of Hokusai*
(Edo/Osaka/Nagoya, 1819), p. 18
verso
Woodblock-printed book
each page: 25.8 x 18.1 cm
The Art Institute of Chicago, Martin
Ryerson Collection, 1103
Ch. 4, fig. 31

149
Utagawa Hiroshige (Japanese;
1797–1858)
Plum Garden at Kameido, from the
series *One Hundred Famous Views
of Edo*
1857
Woodblock print
36 x 24.1 cm
The Art Institute of Chicago,
Clarence Buckingham Collection,
1925.3752
Chicago only

LENDERS TO THE EXHIBITION

Names of public institutions and private collectors are followed by catalogue numbers.

Public Institutions

Belgium
Musées Royaux des Beaux-Arts de Belgique, Brussels: 99

Canada
National Gallery of Canada, Ottawa: 9

Denmark
Det Danske Kunstindustrimuseum, Copenhagen: 91
J. F. Willumsens Museum, Fredrikssund: 130
Ny Carlsberg Glyptotek, Copenhagen: 108
Ordrupgaard, Copenhagen: 40, 42

France
Musée des Beaux-Arts de Reims: 128
Musée d'Orsay, Paris: 36, 65, 74, 87, 92
Musée du Petit Palais, Paris: 49

Germany
Museum Folkwang Essen: 102, 124
Staatsgalerie Stuttgart: 51

Great Britain
Laing Art Gallery, Newcastle upon Tyne: 5
The National Gallery, London: 61, 77
National Gallery of Scotland, Edinburgh: 31

Hungary
Szépmüvészeti Múzeum, Budapest: 58

Israel
The Israel Museum, Jerusalem: 52

Italy
Civica Galleria d'Arte Moderna, Milan: 88
Galleria Nazionale d'Arte Moderna e Contemporanea, Rome: 132

Japan
Hiroshima Museum of Art: 4
Seiji Togo Memorial Yasuda Kasai Museum of Art, Tokyo: 37, 84

The Netherlands
Kröller-Müller Museum, Otterlo: 57, 59, 67, 85, 135
Stedelijk Museum, Amsterdam: 113
Van Gogh Museum, Amsterdam: 3, 8, 11, 12, 16, 22, 27, 30, 32, 33, 46, 47, 53–55, 66, 68, 71, 76, 78, 80, 81, 83, 103, 104, 110, 121, 122, 134, 136

Norway
Nasjonalgalleriet, Oslo: 101

Russia
The State Hermitage Museum, St. Petersburg: 143, 144
The State Pushkin Museum of Fine Arts, Moscow: 39, 138

Spain
Museo de Bellas Artes de Bilbao: 41

Sweden
Göteborg Museum of Art: 126
Nationalmuseum, Stockholm: 45

Switzerland

Hahnloser/Jäggli Stiftung, Villa Flora, Winterthur, Switzerland: 69

United States
Albright-Knox Art Gallery, Buffalo, New York: 100
The Art Institute of Chicago: 1, 6, 10, 18, 19, 50, 63, 90, 112, 115, 120, 129, 140–42, 146–47, 149
The Baltimore Museum of Art: 21
The Chrysler Museum of Art, Norfolk, Virginia: 131
Cincinnati Art Museum: 137
The Detroit Institute of Arts: 20
Fine Arts Museums of San Francisco: 38
Fogg Art Museum, Harvard University Art Museums, Cambridge, Massachusetts: 64
Indianapolis Museum of Art: 7, 35, 96
Kimbell Art Museum, Fort Worth, Texas: 2
Los Angeles County Museum of Art: 97
The Metropolitan Museum of Art, New York: 23, 60, 86, 117
The Minneapolis Institute of Arts: 125
Museum of Fine Arts, Boston: 89, 98
The Museum of Modern Art, New York: 44, 116, 139
Nassau County Division of Museums at Sands Point Preserve, Port Washington, New York: 93

National Gallery of Art, Washington, D.C.: 28, 48, 56, 119
Norton Museum of Art, West Palm Beach, Florida: 95
Philadelphia Museum of Art: 82
The Phillips Collection, Washington, D.C.: 127
The Saint Louis Art Museum: 43
Solomon R. Guggenheim Museum, New York: 118
UCLA Hammer Museum, Los Angeles: 79, 106

Private Collections

Monaco Partners, L.P.: 123
Sagawa Express Co., Ltd., Kyoto: 75
Carmen Thyssen-Bornemisza Collection, Madrid, Spain: 13
Anonymous lenders: 14, 15, 17, 25, 26, 29, 34, 72, 73, 105, 107, 114, 133

INDEX

Numbers in italic type refer to pages with illustrations. All chapters have been indexed; the Appendix and Notes have not.

A

Aesthetic Movement, 77
Adam, Paul, 274
Allée des Tombeaux. *See* Les Alyscamps
Alpilles, 285, 290
Les Alyscamps, 170–73, *175*, 176, *177*, 178, 180–81, 320
Amsterdam, the Netherlands, 20, 39. *See also* maps
Angkor Wat, Cambodia, 279, 280, *283*
Angrand, Léonce, *House on Calle de Gallos, 26*
Anquetin, Louis, 57, 78, 109, 291; *Harvest,* 117, 289
Antwerp, Belgium, 40, 56, 321
Apocalypse of Saint-Sever, 136
apsara, 283, 283
Arioi, 340–41
Arlésienne, 98, *171*, 171–72, 176, 178, 183–84, 186, 246, 253, 339
Arles, Provence, France, 1–3, *94–95*, 100–02, *101–03*, *147*, *156–57*, *171*, 178, *212*. *See also* maps
Arosa, Gustave, 29
L'Art moderne, 213
Atahualpa, 87
Atelier Libre, Paris, 57
Aubé, Jean-Paul, 29, 61, 68; *Vase, 61*
Aurier, Albert, 134, 259, 265, 291, 334–35; "Les Isolés: Vincent van Gogh," 321, 323, 341, 344
Autran, Joseph, 17, 100
Auvers-sur-Oise, France, 324

B

Balzac, Honoré de, 194
Le Barc de Boutteville gallery, 341–42
Beauvais Cathedral, 279, *280*
Beecher Stowe, Harriet. *See* Stowe, Harriet Beecher
Beethoven, Ludwig van, 110–11
Bel-Ami. *See* Maupassant, Guy de, *Bel-Ami*
Bell, Alfred, "Vocavi et renuistis," *79*
Belon, Joseph, *Jealous!, 171,* 172
Bemmel, P. H. van, photograph of van Gogh's *Sower, 39*
Benoit, Camille, 110, 121–22, 231. *See also* Wagner, Richard
Bernard, Émile, 55, 57, 64, 72, 78, 126, 188, 291, 294, 297, 327, 331; 327, 331; friendship and break with Gauguin, 132, 333–36, 341–42, 349–50; friendship with van Gogh, 122, 133; and Japanese art, 74, 136, 153; prospect of coming to Arles, 108, 113, 153; publication of van Gogh's correspondence, 342, 349; and van Gogh's posthumous reputation, 257, 264–65, 333–34

Breton Women in the Meadow (The Pardon at Pont-Aven) [cat. 26], 134, *135*, 136, 181, 223
Brothel Scene, 123, 124
Christ in the Garden of Olives (Gethsemane), 306–08, *307*
Madeleine Bernard in the Bois d'Amour, Pont-Aven, 336, *336*
Self-Portrait Dedicated to Vincent van Gogh [cat. 27], *147, 152,* 153
Tree-Lined Lane in Brittany with Figures, 179, 181
Bernard, Madeleine, 336
bijschriftenpoëzie (poetic commentary), 11
Bizet, Georges, *L'Arlésienne,* 310
Blanc, Charles, 34, 45; *Grammaire des arts du dessin, 57,* 117
Boccaccio, Giovanni, 142, 151
Boch, Eugène, 146, 183
Boggs, Frank, 57
Bolívar, Simón, 25
Bonger, Andries, 97, 264
Bonger, Johanna. *See* Gogh-Bonger, Johanna (Jo) van
bonze, 151, *183.* See also van Gogh, Vincent van, *Self-Portrait Dedicated to Paul Gauguin (Bonze)*
Borinage, Belgium, 21, 227, 264, 277
Borobudur (central Java), 280, *281, 282,* 345
Botticelli, Sandro, 283
Boughton, George, *God Speed!,* 19, *19,* 313
Bouillot, Jules, 29
Boussod, Valadon et Cie, *51,* 57, 81, 108, 277, 341–42
Bouveret. *See* Dagnan-Bouveret, Pascal-Adolphe-Jean
Bracquemond, Félix, 61, 69, 70
Braekeleer, Henri de, *The Dining Room in the Residence of Henri Leys, 138*
Brandes, Edvard, 63, *63*
Breitner, George, 57
Breton, Jules, *Festival of Saint John, 112,* 113; *The Reapers,* 113, *113*
Breton, Jules and Émile, 34
Brittany, France, 64–65, 96, 297, 306, 309, 345; regional costume, 64, 65, *66,* 309; *See also* Pont-Aven, Brittany; and Le Pouldu, Brittany
Brongniart, Alexandre, *Traité des arts céramiques,* 46
Bruyas, Alfred, 254–55, *255,* 272, 324
bullfights, 170–71, *171,* 198
Bunyan, John, 11; *Pilgrim's Progress, 12,* 19, 83, 313

Bürger, Willem. *See* Thoré, Théophile
Buvette de la Plage, Le Pouldu, Brittany. *See* Henry, Marie, Inn of

C

Cabanel, Alexandre, 254–55
Café des Arts. *See* Volpini show
Caillebotte, Gustave, 43
calvaires, 297, *298*
caricature, 41, 238
Carlyle, Thomas, 18, 20–22, 75, 82–83, 89, 146–47, 222, 242, 280, 285; *The French Revolution,* 100; *On Heroes and Hero-Worship,* 22, 34; *Sartor Resartus,* 22, 33, 34, 75, 309–10;
Carriès, Jean, *The Sleeping Faun,* 62, *62*
Castilla, Ramón, 25, 28
Cats, Jacob, *Alle de Wercken (Complete Works),* 12, *12*
Cézanne, Paul, 3, 9, 44–45, 55, 100, 114, 166–67, 169, 238, 327, 349, 352; *The Harvest,* 114, *117,* 166–67; *Still Life with Bowl, Glass, Knife, Apples, and Grapes, 45,* 69, 111
Chaplet, Ernest, 61, 68–69, 81
Charcot, Jean-Martin, 279; *Les Difformes et les malades dans l'art, 281*
Chavannes, Pierre Puvis de. *See* Puvis de Chavannes, Pierre
Chazal, André, 25
Christ, as artist, 133, 193, 265, 273, 280; Passion, 284, 300
cloisonnism, 134
Colonial Exhibition. *See* Universal Exposition, Paris, 1889
colonialism, 84–85, 98–99, 111, 126, 280, 313, 336, 344; effects of in Tahiti, 337, 339
Copenhagen, Denmark, 9–10, 41, 47
Cormon, Fernand, 57
Corot, Jean-Baptiste-Camille, 29, 174, 192–93; *The Reaper with a Sickle, 191,* 193
Courbet, Gustave, 144, 183, 254; *The Meeting (Bonjour! Monsieur Courbet),* 254–55, *254,* 313
Courtry, Charles-Jean-Louis, *The Angel Raphael,* 300, *302,* 307
Cranach, Lucas, *Diana Reclining,* 327, *329*
La Cravache parisienne, 275

D

Dagnan-Bouveret, Pascal-Adolphe-Jean, 65; *Breton Women,* 65, *67; Breton Women at a Pardon,* 65, *67,* 134
Daubigny, Charles-François, 34
Daudet, Alphonse, 75, 97–98, 238

"L'Arlésienne," 176
Numa Roumestan, 97
Port Tarascon, 336
Tartarin de Tarascon, 98, 239
Tartarin sur les Alpes, 97, *98,* 266, 268, *270*
Daudet, Henri, *Le Vieux Montmartre,* 60
Daumier, Honoré, 39, 173–74, 176, 181; *Ratapoil, 179,* 181; *The Thrill of the Chase, 239*
Decker, Coenraad, *View of Haarlem from the Dunes,* 10
Degas, Edgar, 3, 40–41, 43–44, 52, 69, 70, 82, 117, 183, 213, 264, 306
  Behind the Scenes, 71
  Brothel Scene, 350, *352*
  Little Fourteen-Year-Old Dancer, 43
  Three Women at the Races, 67
Delacroix, Eugène, 29, 34, 39, 45, 69, 116, 183, 239, 255, 272, 289, 304, 317
  Alfred Bruyas, 254–55, *256, 257,* 291
  Apollo ceiling, 57, 116
  The Barque of Dante, 277
  Christ in the Garden of Olives (The Agony in the Garden), 125, 302
  Christ on the Sea of Galilee, 116, *117*
  Daniel in the Lion's Den, 253
  Death of Sardanapalus, 200
  Faust and Mephistopheles Galloping through the Night of the Witches' Sabbath, 191, 192
  Faust and Mephistopheles in the Harz Mountains, 62, *63*
  Jacob Wrestling the Angel, 72, 137, *139*
  Pietà, 300, 302, *303*
  The Shipwreck of Don Juan, 277
  Tasso in the Madhouse, 254, *256,* 324
Delaroche, Paul (after), *Christ in the Garden of Gethsemane, 18,* 20
devatas, 283, 312–13, *314, 315*
Diaz, Narcisse, 58
Dickens, Charles, 21, 202; *A Tale of Two Cities,* 20; *Christmas Stories,* 323; *Little Dorrit,* 34
Dieppe, France, 52
Dieulafoy collection, Louvre, Paris, 153, *155*
Dobbelaere, Henri, *Stella Maris, 227,* 227–28
Dolent, Jean, 342–43, 349
Drenthe, The Netherlands, 33–34
Drexel, Jeremias, *De sonnebloeme (The Heliotropum),* 79
Dupanloup, Félix-Antoine-Philibert, 28–29
Dupré, Jules, 34, 114, 121
Durand-Ruel, Paul, 43–44, 52, 88, 343
Dürer, Albrecht, *Melancholia I,* 191, *191*
Dutch Reformed Church, 11–12

E

Ecce Homo, 19, 32
Echenique, José Rufino, 25, 28
Eeden, Frederik van, 334; *De kleine Johannes,* 93, 97, 104, 147, 271
Eliot, George, *Silas Marner,* 34
emblematic tradition, 11–12, *12, 13, 18,* 19, 93, 162, *164,* 289
Essais d'art libre, 342–44
Ethnographic Museum, Paris, 279
étude. See "tableau vs. étude"
ex-voto, 227
Eyck, Jan van, *Madonna of Canon van der Paele, 270*

F

Fabriano, Gentile da, *Madonna and Child,* 227
Fagerolles. *See* Zola, Émile, *L'Oeuvre*
faience ware, 88, 279, *280*
Fayet, Gustave, 352
Félibrige, 98, 100–01, 166; emblem, 98, *99*
Fénéon, Félix, 54–55, 87–88, 111, 291, 294, 336
Fildes, S. Luke, 32; *The Empty Chair, Gad's Hill—Ninth of June 1870, 208,* 210
Filiger, Charles, 333
Fontainas, André, 349–50, 352–53
Franco-Prussian War, 84, 88, 137, 187
French Indochina. *See* Southeast Asia
Fromentin, Eugène, 255

G

Gachet, Paul, 324
Gall, Franz Joseph, 238
Gauguin, Aline (daughter), 29, 89, 348
Gauguin, Aline Marie (née Chazal; mother), 24–25, 27–29, *259*
Gauguin, Clovis (father), 24–25
Gauguin, Clovis (son), 47, 52
Gauguin, Emil (son), 29, 41
Gauguin, Guillaume (paternal grandfather), 28
Gauguin, Isidore (Zizi; paternal uncle), 28, 343
Gauguin, Mette Sophie (née Gad; wife), 10, 29, 41, 43, *44,* 45, 47, 49, 55, 62, 342, 348
Gauguin, Paul, *44, 236;* appropriative strategies, 70, 133–34, 335–36, 343; and Egyptian art, 120, 274; and folk arts, 43, 68; and graphology, 166, 238; identification with Christ, 140, 277, 280, 291, 333, 348; identification with Pierre Loti, 96, 183–84, 227, 341, 343–45; and Japanese art, 117, 119–20, 136, 173, 176, 181, 238; mixed blood/claim to Indian lineage, 28, 85, 87, 256, 306; and Neo-Impressionism, 55, 61, 68, 96, 207, 210, 214, 223–24; painting method, 166–67, 169, 178, 180, 187; and portraiture, 187, 232; and primitivism, 69–70, 87, 96, 120, 239, 256, 274, 279, 313, 336; pursuit of style, 176, 293; seen as sailor, 61, 69, 109, 111, 158; signs himself "P Go," 63; and Symbolism, 275, 277, 279, 334–35, 339, 341–42
  Works—Ceramics, 61, 68–69, 87–88, 280
  Atahualpa. See "Vase ('Atahualpa')"
  Cleopatra Pot [cat. 16; B 17, G 37], 88–89, *89,* 162, 280, 330, 336
  The Faun [cat. 6; not in B or G], 61–63, *62,* 68, 155
  Female Nude, 316
  Leda and the Swan [cat. 17; B 34, G 63], *87,* 89, 277
  Lidded vase with Breton girl and sheep [B 1, G 27], 69
  Martinique woman with kerchief [B 36, G 52], *86,* 87
  Portrait Vase of Jeanne Schuffenecker [cat. 15; B 32, G 62], *88*
  Salome (known as *Black Venus*) [cat. 93; B 49, G 91], 280, *282*
  Self-Portrait Jar [cat. 92; B 53, G 66], 279, *281*
  Self-Portrait Jug [cat. 91; B 48, G 65], *267,* 277, 279, *283*
  Vase ("Atahualpa") [not in B or G], *86,* 87
  Vase decorated with Breton scenes [B 9, G 45], 68
  Vase with four handles decorated with Breton peasant figures [B 26, G 21], 68
  Works—Paintings
  Les Alyscamps [cat. 37; W 306], *177,* 180
  Les Alyscamps (The Three Graces at the Temple of Venus) (Paysage or *Les Trois Grâces au temple du Vénus)* [cat. 36; W 307], 172–73, *175,* 178, 180–81, 222
  Arlésiennes (Mistral) [cat. 50; W 300], 240, 251, *252,* 253, *253,* 309
  Arles Landscape (Path by the Roubine du Roi Canal) [cat. 45; W 309], 222–24, *224*
  Arles Lanscape with Two Dogs (Paysage d'Arles avec buissons) [W 310], 246, *246*
  The Aven River at Pont-Aven [cat. 34; W 253], *215*
  Apple Trees, Hermitage, Pontoise [W 33], *41*
  The Artist's Mother (Aline-Marie Gauguin) [cat. 51; W 385], 228, 256, *259,* 339
  La Belle Angèle [W 315], 293, *293*
  The Big Tree (Te raau rahi) [W 439], 337, *338*
  Blue Trees ("Vous y passerez, la belle!") [cat. 42; W 311], 224, *226, 228,* 246, 274
  Bonjour, Monsieur Gauguin [cat. 106; W 321], 313, *316,* 353
  Breton Girls Dancing (La Ronde des petites Bretonnes) [cat. 28; W 251], *112,* 113–14, 119, 158, 207
  Breton Girl Spinning (Joan of Arc) [cat. 105; W 329], 312–13, *314*
  Breton Landscape with Willows [cat. 101; W 357], 309, *310*
  Breton Shepherdess [cat. 5; W 203], 64, *66,* 253
  Breton Women and Cow (Bretonnes et vau) [W 252], 96, *96*
  Breton Women Chatting (Bretonnes causant) [W 201], 64–65, *67,* 113–14
  Christ in the Garden of Olives (Christ dans le jardin des oliviers) [cat. 95; W 326], 291, 292, 307–09, 324, 335
  Coming and Going, Martinique [cat. 13; not in W], 82, *86*
  Conversation (Tropics) (Conversation [Tropiques]) [cat. 14; W 227], *110,* 111, 274
  Day of the God (Mahana no atua) [cat. 142; W 513], 345, *345,* 350
  Dugout Canoe (Te vaa) (The Poor Fisherman [Le Pauvre Pêcheur]) [cat. 143; W 544], 347, *347*
  Farmhouse in Arles (Mas d'Arles) [cat. 35; W 308], 165–67, *168, 169*
  Female Nude with Sunflowers (known as *Caribbean Woman*) [cat. 107; W 330], 313, *315,* 327
  Flageolet Player on the Cliff, Brittany [cat. 96; W 361], 293, *294,* 297
  Grape Harvest. See "Human Miseries"
  Green Christ (Breton Calvary) [cat. 99; W 328], 297, *298,* 306
  Her Name Is Vairaumati (Son Nom est Vairaumati) [cat. 138; W 450], *340,* 340–41
  The Hibiscus Tree (Te burao) [cat. 140; W 486], 337, *338*
  Human Miseries (Grape Harvest or *Poverty) (Misères humaines [Les Vendanges* or *La Pauvresse])* [cat. 40; W 304], 190–95, *193, 194,* 217, 246, 274, 279, 307, 309, 313, 350
  In the Heat (The Pigs) (Les Cochons [En pleine chaleur]) [W 301], 197–98, *199,* 274
  Io Orana Maria, 341
  Landscape with Two Breton Women [cat. 98; not in W], *296,* 297
  Loss of Virginity [cat. 131; W 412], *335,* 336, 346
  Madame Roulin [cat. 43; W 298], 228–29, *230,* 232, 256–57
  Martinique (At the Pond's Edge) [cat. 12; W 222], *81,* 82
  Meyer de Haan [W 317], 309, *312*
  Monsieur Ginoux [cat. 47; not in W], 244–46, *245*
  Les Négresses (Among the Mangoes [Tropics]) (Aux mangos [Tropiques]) [cat. 11; W 224], *80,* 82, 84, 129, 165, 194, 211, 274
  Night Café [cat. 39; W 305], *187,* 188–90, *189,* 195, 233, 348
  Old Man with a Cane [cat. 49; W 318], *250,* 251
  Olympia (after Manet) [W 413], 342
  The Painter of Sunflowers (Le Peintre de tournesols) [cat. 46; W 296], 235–36, *237,* 238–40, 242–43, 349–50
  The Poor Fisherman. See "Dugout Canoi (Te vaa) (The Poor Fisherman [Le Pauvre Pêcheur])"
  Portrait of a Woman with a Still-Life by Paul Cézanne [cat. 129; W 387], *323,* 327
  The Red Cow [cat. 97; W 365], 293–94, *295*
  Resting Cows [W 160], *52*
  Roses and Statuette [cat. 128;

Gauguin (cont.)
W 407], 327, *328*
*Seaweed Gatherers II
(Ramasseuses de varech II)*
(cat. 102; W 349], 309, *311*
*The Seed of the Arioi (Te aa no
areois)* [cat. 139; W 451], *340,*
341
Self-Portrait [W 25], *28,* 29, 49
Self-Portrait [W 323], 309, *312,*
339
Self-Portrait at the Easel [cat.
2; W 138], *48,* 49
*Self-Portrait Dedicated to
Charles Laval (later to
Eugène Carrière)* [cat. 48; W
384], 247, *249*
*Self-Portrait Dedicated to
Vincent van Gogh (Les
Misérables)* [cat. 33; W 239],
147, *149,* 150–51, 153–55,
162, 182, 187, 247, 257, 277,
323, 339
*Self-Portrait Jug with
Japanese Print and Flowers*
[W 375], *267,* 283
Self-Portrat near Golgotha [W
534], 347–48, *348*
Sleeping Child [W 81], *46,* 47
Still Life in an Interior [W 176],
8, 47
Still Life with Fruit [W 288], *191,*
191–92
*Still Life with Profile of Charles
Laval* [cat. 7; W 207], 69–70,
70
Still Life with Pumpkin [now
lost; W 312], 220, 236
Sunflowers and Mangoes [W
606], 350, *351*
Sunflowers on an Armchair
[cat. 144; W 603], 350, *351*
*Sunflowers with Puvis de
Chavannes's "Hope"* [W 604],
350, 352, *353*
*Tehamana Has Many Parents
(Merahi metua no
Tehamana) (The Ancestors
of Tehamana [Les Aïeux de
Tehamana])* [cat. 141; W
497], 341, *341*
To Make a Bouquet or *The
Makings of a Bouquet (Pour
faire un bouquet)* [W 49], 41,
42, 350
*Les Vendanges. See "Human
Miseries"*
*Vision of the Sermon (Vision du
sermon)* [cat. 31; W 245],
134, *134,* 136–37, 144, 180,
194, 251, 274, 349
*Washerwomen at the Roubine
du Roi Canal* [cat. 41; W 303],
211, *213,* 222, 293
Washerwomen at the Roubine

du Roi Canal [cat. 44; W 302],
222–23, *225*
*Where Do We Come From? What
Are We? Where Are We Going?
(D'Où venons-nous, que
sommes-nous, où allons-
nous)* [W 561], *349,* 350
*Wine Harvest. See "Human
Miseries"*
*Winter (Breton Boy Repairing
His Sabot)* [W 258], *226,* 246
*Woman with Flower (Vahine no
te tiare)* [W 420], 338–39, *339*
*Wood Tankard and Metal
Pitcher* [cat. 1; W 47], 41, *42,*
43
Yellow Christ (Le Christ jaune)
[cat. 100; W 327], 297, *299*
*Young Breton Bathers (Petits
Baigneurs)* [cat. 4; W 272],
64, *65,* 82, 119
Young Christian Girl [W 518],
345, *345*
*Young Wrestlers—Brittany
(Jeunes Lutteurs—
Bretagne)* [cat. 29; W 273],
117, *118,* 119–20, 274
Works—Sculpture, 43
Be in Love (Soyez amoureuses)
[G 76], 297, 307
Decorated Wooden Box [G 8],
46, 68–69
*Female Nude with Flower
(known as Lust)* [cat. 130; G
88], *315,* 327
*Reclining Woman with a Fan in
a Tropical Landscape* [cat.
108; G 74], 327, *329*
Woman Strolling [G 4], 43, *44,*
47, 64
Works—Works on paper
Annotated pages from
Sketchbook from Arles and
Brittany, 232, 234–35, *235*
Apsara from Angkor Wat and
sketch after Botticelli's
Lorenzo Tornabuoni, 282
Christ, 297, *299*
Compositional study for *The
Painter of Sunflowers,* 237,
238
*Dramas of the Sea—Brittany
(Les Drames de la mer—
Bretagne)* from *Volpini Suite*
[cat. 90; Gu 8, K 3], *276,* 277
*Dramas of the Sea (Les
Drames de la mer)* from
Volpini Suite [cat. 90, Gu 7, K
2], *276,* 277
Drawing after Puvis de
Chavannes's *Hope,* 345–46,
346
Head of a Tahitian Woman, 339,
339

Ictus, 279, *279*
Landscape sketch, *230,* 236
Leda from *Volpini Suite* [Gu 1, K
1], *276,* 277
Letter to Émile Schuffenecker,
238, *239*
Madame Ginoux (study for
Night Café) [cat. 38], *184,*
186, *322,* 323
Seated Breton Woman, 66
Seated figure, inspired by
Puvis de Chavannes's *Hope,*
345–46, *346*
Seated Model, Back View, 197,
199
Seated Model, Front View, 197,
199
Self-portrait sketch, 155, *155*
Site drawing, of the Moulin
Neuf and Aven River, *64*
Sketches for *Arles Landscape
with Two Dogs,* 246, *246*
Sketches of Breton costume
and face [cat. 103], *310*
Sketches of *Christ in the
Garden of Olives* and *Be in
Love and You Will Be Happy*
[cat. 104], *308*
Sketches of Marcelle Roulin,
228, *229*
Sketches of sheep, *253*
Sketches related to
Arlésiennes (Mistral), 252,
253
Sketch for *Washerwomen,* 222,
225
Sketch of a faience jug with the
face of a youth in relief, *280*
Sketch of a girl skipping rope,
222, *225*
Sketch of Breton figures, *126,*
133
Sketch of *Her Name Is
Vairaumati,* 340
Sketch of seated Breton
woman, *66*
Sketch of van Gogh's *Path
through the Ravine,* 305
Sketch of vase with a figurine
of a nude woman, *61*
Sketch of *Vision of the Sermon*
[cat. 32], 136, *136*
Sketch of *Young Wrestlers—
Brittany* [cat. 30], *118*
Studies for *The Painter of
Sunflowers, 237,* 242
Volpini Suite, 275, *276,* 277. *See
also* Volpini show
Writings, 2, 23, 159–60
Avant et après, 332, 353
"Les Crevettes roses." *See
"Diverses Choses"*
"Diverses Choses," 239, 348–50
"Natures mortes," 344

Noa Noa, 345–45, 348
"Notes synthétiques," 45, 47
"Racontars de rapin," 352–53
"Turkish manual," 55, 202, 210
Geoffroy, Charles (after
Grandville), *Sunworshiper, 84*
Gerardin, Auguste, *Les Fêtes du
soleil au Palais de l'Industrie,* 98
Gheel, Belgium, 21, *21,* 32, 235, 321
Ginoux, Joseph-Michel, 107, 244–45
Ginoux, Marie (née Julien), 184,
186–90, 202, 253, 323
Gladwell, Harry, 32, 110
Goes, Hugo van der, 121, 153
Gogh-Bonger, Johanna (Jo) van
(Theo's wife), 97, 273, 342
Gogh-Carbentus, Anna van (moth-
er), 11, 200, 202
Gogh, Theodorus van (Theo; brother), correspondence with
Vincent, 16; as dealer, 81–82, 99,
105, 107, 153–54, 158, 213; exhibition of Vincent's work (1890),
334; opinions on contemporary
art, 55, 82; support of Arles project, 132, 153; support of Vincent,
34, 158, 331
Gogh, Theodorus van (father), 9,
11–12, 14–15, 19–21, 30, 34, 37,
40, 116
Gogh, Vincent van, *20;* analogical
thinking, 1, 16, 121, 216; on
artists collaborating, 33–34,
56–57, 107–08, 111, 120, 147, 210;
and Egyptian art, 120, 284–85; on
friendship, 32, 111, 113, 120, 144;
and Gethsemane theme, 125, 137,
143–44, 146, 197, 203, 273, 286,
291, 300, 307, 316–17, 320; identification with Christ, 138, 265, 291,
302, 323, 349; and Impressionism
and Neo-Impressionism, 71–72,
82, 111, 132, 203; and Japanese
art, 74–75, 93, 98–99, 101–02,
109, 119–20, 151, 173–74, 180,
273; painting from memory, 190,
195–98, 202–03, 233, 324; painting quickly, 129, 161, 166–67,
186–87, 203, 207; and portraiture, 90, 144, 187, 200, 222,
226–27, 232; and primitivism, 84,
117; pursuit of style, 284, 293,
306–07; signs himself "Vincent,"
3; use of tracing, 233, 240, 256,
271
Works—Paintings
*Allée des Tombeaux (Les
Alyscamps)* [cat. 72; F 568, JH
1622], 172, *174,* 176, 181
Les Alyscamps [F 569, JH 1623],
176, 180
Angel (after Rembrandt) [F
624, JH 1778], 300, 302, *302*
Anna Cornelia van Gogh-

Carbentus [F 477, JH 1600],
200, 202, *202,* 228, 256
*The Arlésienne (after Paul
Gauguin)* [cat. 132; F 540, JH
1892], *322,* 323
*The Arlésienne (after Paul
Gauguin)* [cat. 133; F 543, JH
1895], *322,* 323, 327
*The Arlésienne (Madame
Ginoux)* [cat. 74; F 489, JH
1625], 184, *185,* 186–87, *187,*
190, 202, 226
*The Arlésienne (Madame
Ginoux)* [cat. 86; F 488, JH
1624], 245–46, 256, *258*
*Arles seen from the Snowy
Plains of La Crau* [F 391, JH
1358], 102, *104*
*Arles: View from the Wheat
Fields* [F 545, JH 1477], *289*
Armand Roulin [F 492, JH
1642], 227, *227*
Armand Roulin [F 493, JH
1643], 227
*Avenue de la Gare with Plane
Trees* [F 398, JH 1366], 102,
104
*The Bedroom (La Chambre à
coucher)* [cat. 68; F 482, JH
1608], 153, *154,* 169, 181
*The Bedroom (La Chambre à
coucher)* [cat. 120; F 484, JH
1771], 300
*La Berceuse. See "Madame
Roulin Rocking the Cradle
(La Berceuse)"*
*Bowl with Sunflowers, Roses,
and Other Flowers* [F 250, JH
1166], 58, *59*
*Bowl with Zinnias and Other
Flowers* [cat. 9; F 251, JH
1142], 58, *58*
Brothel Scene [F 478, JH 1599],
195, *195,* 200
Butterflies and Flowers [cat.
114; F 460, JH 1676], 273, *274,*
284
Country Churchyard [F 84, JH
772], *39,* 39–40
A Cypress against a Starry Sky
[cat. 135; F 683, JH 1982],
323–24, *325*
Cypresses [cat. 117; F 613, JH
1746], *288,* 289, 294
The Dance Hall [cat. 87; F 547,
JH 1652], 244, 250–51, *251*
Doctor Gachet [F 753, JH 2007],
324, *326*
*Entrance to a Quarry (L'Entrée
d'une carrière)* [cat. 123; F
635, JH 1767], 302, *304,* 306
Falling Leaves (Les Alyscamps)
[F 487, JH 1621], *178,* 180–81,
224, 320, 330

Van Gogh (cont.)

Falling Leaves (Les Alyscamps) [F 486, JH 1620], *179*, 180–81, 320, 330

A Farmhouse in Provence (Un Mas de Provence) [cat. 56; F 565, JH 1443], *114*, 166

Fishing in Spring, the Pont de Clichy (Asnières) [cat. 18; F 354, JH 1270], 71, *72*

Flowering Plum Tree (after Hiroshige) [F 371, JH 1296], 102, *106*

Garden of the Hospital (Saint-Paul-de-Mausole, Saint-Rèmy) [cat. 124; F 660, JH 1849], 316, *317*

Gauguin's Chair [cat. 78; F 499, JH 1636], *209*, 209–10, 216, 268, 323

The Green Vineyard [cat. 67; F 475, JH 1595], 166, *167*, 190, 195

In the Forest (Sous-bois) [cat. 137; F 773, JH 2041], 330, *330*

Irises [F 608, JH 1691], 284–85, *285*

L'Italienne, 90

Joseph Roulin. See "Monsieur Roulin"

Lane of Poplars [F 122, JH 522], *36*, 37

Langlois Bridge [F 571, JH 1392], 102, 105, *105*

Large Plane Trees (The Road Menders)(Les Grandes Plantanes) [cat. 127; F 658, JH 1861], 320, *320*

The Lover (Lieutenant Milliet) [F 473, JH 1588], 183, *183*

Madame Roulin [F 503, JH 1646], 228–29, *231*, 232–33

Madame Roulin Rocking the Cradle (La Berceuse) [cat. 89; F 508, JH 1671], 229, 233, 245, 256–57, *261*, 270–72, 279, 284, 293, 297, 300, 316

Madame Roulin Rocking the Cradle (La Berceuse) [cat. 112; F 505, JH 1670], *271*, 272

Madame Roulin Rocking the Cradle (La Berceuse) [F 506, JH 1669], 272, *273*

Madame Roulin Rocking the Cradle (La Berceuse) [cat. 113; F 507, JH 1672], 272, *273*

Madame Roulin Rocking the Cradle (La Berceuse) [F 504, JH 1655], 272, *273*

Madame Roulin with Her Baby Marcelle [F 491, JH 1638], *228*, 228, 232–33, 348

Madame Roulin with Her Baby Marcelle [cat. 82; F 490, JH 1637], 228, *229*, 232–33, *233*,

236, 256, 348

Marcelle Roulin [F 441, JH 1641], *229*, 233, 245

A Memory of the Garden (Etten and Nuenen) [F 496, JH 1630], 196–97, 200, 202–03, *205*, 206, 222, 232, 240, 253, 257

Monsieur Ginoux [cat. 85; F 533, JH 1649], 244–45, *245*

Monsieur Roulin [F 432, JH 1522], 128, 174, 222, *232*, 233, 256, 284

Monsieur Roulin [F 434, JH 1574], *232*, 233

Moulin de Blute-fin, Montmartre [F 274, JH 1115], *60*

Mountains (Saint-Rèmy) [cat. 118; F 622, JH 1766], 290, *290*, 304

The Mousmé [F 431, JH 1519], 126, *126*, 330, 339

The Night Café (Le Café de nuit) [F 463, JH 1575], 141, 187–88, *188*, 209

A Novel Reader (Une Liseuse de romans) [cat. 75; F 497, JH 1632], 200, *201*, 236

The Old Yew Tree (Le Vieil If) [F 573, JH 1618], 161–62, *165*

Oleanders and Zola's "Joie de vivre" [cat. 60; F 593, JH 1566], *127*, 128, 132

Olive Grove [cat. 125; F 710, JH 1856], 317, *318*

Olive Grove [cat. 126; F 586, JH 1854], 317, *319*

Olive Trees in a Mountain Landscape [F 712, JH 1740], 285, *286*

A Pair of Boots (Les Souliers) [cat. 21; F 333, JH 1236], 74–75, *76*, 116

Parisian Novels (Romans parisiens) [cat. 25; F 359, JH 1332], 90, *91*, 128, 210

Path through the Ravine [F 662, JH 1804], 302, 304, *305*, 306, 323

Patience Escalier with Walking Stick [F 444, JH 1563], 128, *250*, 251

Paul Gauguin (Man in a Red Beret) [cat. 83; F 546, not in JH], 236, *236*

Pear Tree in Blossom [cat. 55; F 405, JH 1394], 102, 104, *106*

Pietà (after Eugéne Delacroix) [cat. 122; F 630, JH 1775], 300, 302, *303*, 308, 324

Plate with Onions, "Annuaire de la Santé," and Other Objects [F 604, JH 1656], 268,

269

The Poet (Eugène Boch) [F 462, JH 1574], 146, 183, *183*

The Poet's Garden (Le Jardin du poète) [cat. 63; F 468, JH 1578], 141–42, *143*, 144, 151, 171, 181, 190, 273

The Potato Eaters [F 82, JH 764], 37, *38*, 74, 128, 141

Public Garden with a Couple and a Blue Fir Tree [F 479, JH 1601], *150*

Public Garden with Newly Mowed Lawn and Weeping Tree [F 428, JH 1499], 142, *142*

The Raising of Lazarus (after Rembrandt) [cat. 134; F 644, JH 1972], 323, *324*

The Reaper [F 617, JH 1753], *289*, 289–91, 297, 308

The Red Vineyard [F 495, JH 1626], 190, *192*, *194*, 194–95, 222

Road Menders. See "Large Plane Trees (The Road Menders)(Les Grandes Plantanes)"

Road to Tarascon [destroyed; F 448, JH 1491], 116, *116*

Self-Portrait [cat. 19; F 345, JH 1249], 71–72, *73*

Self-Portrait at the Easel [cat. 54; F 522, JH 1356], *92*, 93

Self-Portrait Dedicated to Charles Laval [F 501, JH 1634], 247, *248*

Self-Portrait Dedicated to Paul Gauguin (Bonze) [cat. 64; F 476, JH 1581], 147, *148*, 151, 153, 184, 266, 342

Self-Portrait with Bandaged Ear [F 527, JH 1657], 268, *268*, 270, 277, 283

Self-Portrait with Bandaged Ear [cat. 109; F 529, JH 1658], 268, *269*, 270, 277, 283

Self-Portrait with Dark Felt Hat at the Easel [cat. 8; F 181, JH 1090], *56*, 57, 71, 93

Self-Portrait with Palette [cat. 119; F 626, JH 1770], 300, *301*

Self-Portrait with Straw Hat [cat. 20; F 526, JH 1309], 72, *74*, 114

Sower [lost], *31*

The Sower [cat. 57; F 422, JH 1470], 114, *115*, 116–17, 120–21, 132, 141, 161, 203, 266, 289, 302

The Sower [cat. 69; F 494, JH 1617], 161–62, *164*, 166, 169, *169*

The Sower [cat. 79; F 575a, JH

1596], 217, *220*

The Sower [F 450, JH 1627], 217, *218*, 220, 245

The Sower [cat. 80; F 451, JH 1629], 217, *219*, 220, 245

Spectators at the Arena [F 548, JH 1653], 198, *198*, 200, 203

The Starry Night [cat. 116; F 612, JH 1731], 285–86, *287*, 293, 323

The Starry Night over the Rhone (La Nuit étoilée) [cat. 65; F 474, JH 1592], 144, *145*, 146–47, 197, 209–10, 286

Still Life with Bible and Zola's "Joie de vivre" [cat. 3; F 113, JH 946], 6, *7*, 37, 39–40, 90, 128, 200, 310, 343, 346

Still Life with Vase and Honesty ("Judaspenningen"). See Gogh, Vincent van, Works on paper, Sketch of Still Life with Vase and Honesty ("Judaspenningen")

Sunflowers [F 453, JH 1559], *129*, 132

Sunflowers [destroyed; F 459, JH 1560], *129*, 132

Sunflowers [F 456, JH 1561], *130*, 132

Sunflowers [cat. 61; F 454, JH 1562], *131*, 132, 138–39, 169, 203, 220, 240, 242, 266, 271, *272*

Sunflowers [cat. 84; F 457, JH 1666], 240, *241*, 242, 271

Sunflowers [F 455, JH 1668], *271*

Sunflowers [cat. 110; F 458, JH 1667], 271, *271*, 272

Terrace and Observation Deck at the Moulin de Blute-fin, Montmartre [cat. 10; F 272, JH 1183], 58–59, *60*

Two Sunflowers [cat. 23; F 375, JH 1329], *77*, 77–78, 82, 85, 220, 352

Two Sunflowers [cat. 24; F 376, JH 1331], 77–78, *78*, 82, 85, 220

Van Gogh's Chair [cat. 77; F 498, JH 1635], *208*, 209–10, 216, 268

Self-Portrait with Straw Hat [cat. 20; F 526, JH 1309], 72, *74*, 114

Washerwomen at the Roubine du Roi Canal [F 427, JH 1490], *128*, 129, 132, 195, 222

Weaver near an Open Window [F 24, JH 500], *35*

Women Picking Olives [F 655, JH 1869], *318*, 320–21

The Yellow House [cat. 66; F 464, JH 1589], 144, *146*, 147, 209

The Zouave [F 423, JH 1486],

123, 124

Works—Works on paper

Anthon van Rappard [F 1297, JH 491], 207

Breton Women in the Meadow (after Émile Bernard) [cat. 88; F 1422, JH 1654], 223, *223*

Couple Strolling amonst Sunflowers [F 1720, JH 1308], 77, *79*

La Crau seen from Montmajour [F 1420, JH 1501], *163*

En Route, 116, *116*

The Garden at the Vicarage at Nuenen [F 1128, JH 466], *204*

Landscape near Montmajour with Train [F 1424, JH 1502], *163*

The Night Café (Le Café de nuit) [F 1463, JH 1576], *141*

Olive Trees, Montmajour, 124

Patience Escalier [F 1461, JH 1564], 339, *339*

Peasant Woman, Stooping and Gleaning [F 1279, JH 836], 202, *204*

The Potato Eaters [F 1661, JH 737], 37, *38*, 266, 274

The Public Garden in Place Lamartine with the Yellow House [F 1513, JH 1412], *107*

Seated Zouave [F 1443, JH 1485], *123*, 124

Sketch after Millet's Sower, *115*

Sketch of The Bedroom [JH 1610], *154*

Sketch of La Berceuse flanked by Sunflowers, *272*

Sketch of A Cypress against a Starry Sky [cat. 136; JH 1983], 324, *325*

Sketch of In the Forest [JH 2042], 330, *330*

Sketch of A Memory of the Garden (Etten and Nuenen) [cat. 76; JH 1631], 203, *204*

Sketch of The Mousmé (for Bernard) [F 1504, JH 1520], 126, *126*, 128

Sketch of The Mousmé (for Gauguin) [F 1722, JH 1521], 126, *126*, 128, 133, 339, 348, *348*

Sketch of sailboat, 331, *331*

Sketch of The Sower [JH 1472], 114, *115*

Sketch of The Sower [JH 1628], *218*

Sketch of Still Life with Vase and Honesty ("Judaspenningen") [JH 726], *36*, 37

Sketch of the Yellow House [JH

Van Gogh (cont.)
1413], 107
Sketches of The Sower and The
Old Yew Tree [cat. 71; JH
1619], 161, 164
Sorrow [F 929a, JH 130], 32, 33,
191
Sower [F 852, JH 275], 31
The Sower (after Millet) [F 830,
JH 1], 31
Stacks of Wheat near a
Farmhouse [cat. 58; F 1426,
JH 1514], 166, 168
Washerwomen at the Roubine
du Roi Canal [F 1473, JH
1405], 128
Washerwomen at the Roubine
du Roi Canal [cat. 59; F 1444,
JH 1507], 211, 212
Weeping Tree (L'Arbre
pleureur dans l'herbe) [cat.
115; F 1468, JH 1498], 273,
274
Writings
albums, 17–19, 221
letters, 2, 16, 159–60, 342, 349
sermon, 19
Gogh, Vincent van (Cent; uncle), 14,
20, 128
Gogh, Willemina van (Wil; sister),
202
Goncourt, Edmond de, 75, 121; La
Maison d'un artiste, 142
Goupil et Cie, 14–15, 19, 34, 57
Goupil, Jules (after), A Young
Citizen of the Year V, 20, 20
Goyen, Jan van, 34
Grand Bouillon, Restaurant du
Chalet, 78
Grand Boulevards, 78
Grandville, Jean-Jacques, "Soleil"
from Les Fleurs animés, 84
The Graphic, 32, 32, 33, 74, 210
Groningen School, 11, 17
Groupe des Artistes Indépendants.
See Indépendants
Guillaumin, Armand, 47, 53, 55, 59

H
Haan, Jacob Meyer de, 214, 291,
307, 309–10, 321, 333–34
The Hague, the Netherlands, 30–33
Hague School, 57–58, 102
Hals, Frans, 39, 232
Hartrick, A. S., 57, 64, 65
Haviland, 61
Heemskerck, Maerten van, Saint
Luke Painting the Virgin, 227, 228
Heine, Heinrich, 17, 147, 308
Henry, Marie, Inn of, 309–10,
312–13, 313, 315, 327, 336
Heyde, Jan van der, Still Life with
Bible, 6, 6
Heyns, Zacharias, Emblemata, 79
Hiva Oa, Marquesas Islands,

352–53
Hokusai, Katsushika, 174, 238;
People in a Shower, 179;
Wrestlers [cat. 147], 118, 119
Holbein, Hans, the Younger, The
Dead Christ, 335, 336
Holl, Frank, 32
Hoornik, Clasina (Sien), 32–33, 107,
227
Hugo, Victor, 21–22, 40, 259; Le
Dernier Jour d'un condamné,
259–60; Les Misérables, 150
Huret, Jules, 335
Huret, Juliette, 336
Huysmans, Joris-Karl, 192

I
ictus (Ichthys), 234
Impressionism, 43, 53–55, 138, 207;
as lowercase term, 53; "romantic" and "scientific," 55, 57, 68,
207. See also Neo-Impressionism
"Impressionist and Synthetist
Group," 291. See also Volpini
show
Impressionist exhibitions, 1874
(first), 54; 1879 (fourth), 40; 1880
(fifth), 41; 1882 (seventh), 43–44,
52; 1886 (eighth), 2, 52–54, 57, 71
Indépendants, 47, 53, 59, 61, 284,
304, 323, 334
Indochina. See French Indochina
insanity and creativity, 120–21,
137, 321, 333
Institut Loriol, Paris, 29
International Exhibition, 1886,
52–53, 57. See also Petit, Georges
Isaacson, J. J., 214, 294, 304, 308
Isaiah, "Servant Songs," 6
Israëls, Josef, 57, 105

J
Japanese art, 74–75, 98–99
Java. See Borobudur (central Java)
Joan of Arc, 312
John, Saint (the Baptist), 277, 280,
327
Jones, Reverend T. Slade, 19
Jossot, Henri Gustave, "They'll All
Go To Heaven," 299
jute, 2, 159, 170, 180, 209, 226, 240

K
Kahn, Gustave, 210
kampong. See Universal Exposition,
Paris, 1889
Karr, Alphonse, Voyage autour de
mon jardin, 85, 142, 142
Kate, J. J. L. ten, 11, 20
Kempis, Thomas à, 11
Kendrick, Charles, Ye Soul Agonies
in ye Life of Oscar Wilde, 79
Kinsbergen, Isidore van, The
Assault of Mara, 281; unknown

figure with four arms, 282
Khmer Museum, Paris, 279, 312
Koninck, Philips de, 34, 114
Koning, A. H., 78
Korin, Ogata, Musicians [cat. 146],
135

L
La Fontaine, Jean de, 239
Laisnay, Thérèse, 24
Lalaisse, François Hippolyte,
Breton Woman, 67
Lamartine, Alphonse de, 100
Lantier, Claude. See Zola, Émile,
L'Oeuvre
Laurillard, Eliza, 11, 20; Geen dag
zonder God (No Day without God),
18
Laval, Charles, 70–71, 83, 132, 141,
247, 291, 336; Self-Portrait
Dedicated to Vincent van Gogh
[cat. 53], 247, 247
Lavater, Johann Kaspar, 238
Leclerq, Julien, 344–45
Lenepveu, Jules-Eugène, Joan of
Arc's Vision, 312, 314
Le Pouldu, Brittany, France,
262–63, 291, 297, 307
Lima, Peru, 4–5, 24–25, 24, 26–27,
27, 85–86. See also maps
Livens, Horace M., 57
Longfellow, Henry Wadsworth, 12
Loti, Pierre, 84, 158, 183, 274, 279,
297, 343, 345
Madame Chrysanthème, 96,
126, 151, 183, 184
Le Mariage de Loti (Rarahu),
84–85, 184, 333, 341, 343–45
Mon Frère Yves, 96, 187
Pêcheur d'Islande (Icelandic
Fishermen), 158, 227,
270–71, 277
Louvre, Paris, 57
Luke, Saint, 77, 122, 137, 232
Luyken, Jan, 12; De Zedelijke en
Stichtelyke Gezangen (Moral and
Edifying Hymns), 13; Vonken der
Liefde Jesu (Sparks of Jesus'
Love), 13; De Bykorf des Gemoeds
(The Heart's Beehive), 164

M
Maaten, J. J. van der (after),
Funeral Procession through a
Field, 12, 13
Madagascar, 327, 330, 333
Mallarmé, Stéphane, 334, 336
Manet, Édouard, 34, 37, 39, 54–55,
153; Déjeuner sur l'herbe, 54
Manet, Eugène, 53
Man of Sorrows, 19, 19, 20, 254
Mantegna, Andrea, The
Resurrection of Christ, 303
maps, 20

Les Alyscamps, 173
Arles and environs, France,
102–03
La Crau, 162
France, 54
Lima, Peru, 24
The Netherlands and Belgium, 11
Peru, 23
Place Lamartine, Arles, 109
Roubine du Roi Canal, 211
Tahiti and Hiva Oa, Marquesas
Islands, 337
Zundert, The Netherlands, 14
Zundert and environs, The
Netherlands, 17
Marchais, Jean-Baptiste-Etienne,
Christ Laborer, 32
Maris, Jacob, Drawbridge, 105, 105
Marquesas Islands, 347, 352
Marseilles, 99–100
Martin Brothers, Grotesque figural
spoon warmer, 88
Martinique, 71, 83–84, 88, 99, 111
Mauclair, Camille, 341–44, 349
Maupassant, Guy de, 75, 125; Au
soleil, 97; Bel-Ami, 111, 183; "Le
Horla," 235, 270; Pierre et Jean,
101–02
Maus, Octave, 213, 274
Mauve, Anton, 32–33, 57, 104
Mauve-Carbentus, Jet, 105, 214
Mercure de France, 342, 344, 349
Méryon, Charles, 121
Michelangelo, 39
Michelet, Jules, 16–18, 21, 30, 32,
227, 242; "Les Aspirations de l'au-
tomne" in L'Amour, 16–17, 20, 37
Michel, Georges, 21, 34, 58, 114; The
Storm, 35
Midi (Mediterranean). See
Provence, France
Millet, Jean-François, 3, 20–21,
30–31, 34, 37, 39, 74–75, 82–83,
116; retrospective of 1887, 72, 90,
114
Angelus, 72
Ceres (Summer), 197, 200
Departure for the Fields, 116,
116
The Grape Harvester at Rest,
191, 193
The Sower, 30, 114, 217
Wooden Shoes, 74–75, 76
Milliet, Lieutenant Paul-Eugène,
178, 183, 189
Milton, John, Paradise Lost, 309–10
Mirbeau, Octave, 334–35, 344
Mistral, Frédéric, 100; Mireille, 172
Mochica, 88
Monet, Claude, 40–41, 43–45, 52,
55, 82–83, 207; Bouquet of
Sunflowers, 202, 203; Fishermen
on the Seine at Poissy, 71, 72;
Stacks of Wheat, 317

Monfreid, Georges-Daniel de, 338,
353
Montenay, Georgette de, Emblèmes
ou devises Chrestiennes, 18
Monticelli, Adolphe, 3, 58, 72,
98–101, 99, 111, 138–39, 166–67,
207, 217, 220, 272, 289, 321; Vase
with Flowers, 58
Montmartre, 58
Montpellier, 253. See also Musée
Fabre, Montpellier
Moréas, Jean, 274
Morice, Charles, 274, 334, 343–46,
353
Morisot, Berthe, 52
"Mother Hubbard" dress, 339
Mouret, Octave. See Zola, Émile, Au
bonheur des dames
mousmé, 126, 142, 184, 186. See
also Gogh, Vincent van, The
Mousmé
Musée Fabre, Montpellier, 253–55,
254
Musée Lapidaire, Arles, 101
Musée Réattu, Arles, 101
Museum of Comparative Sculpture,
Trocadéro, Paris, 279
Musset, Alfred de, 17; "La Nuit de
décembre," 18, 194, 254

N
Nabis, 277, 333, 341
Nanteuil, Celestin, Pietà, 300, 302,
303
Naturalist literature, 43, 56, 75, 90,
97, 128, 188–89, 200. See also
Goncourt, Edmond de;
Maupassant, Guy de; Zola, Émile
Neo-Impressionism, 53–55, 68, 71,
117, 207, 291
North Africa, 183
Noterman, Emmanuel, The Artist
and His Model, 238

O
oleander, 126, 128, 142
Orientalism, 344
Ostade, Adriaan and Isaäk, 34

P
pagode. See Universal Exposition,
Paris, 1889
Panama, 71
Pantazis, Pericles, 192; The Little
Thief, 191, 192
Papeete, Tahiti, 337, 347
Paul, Saint, 16–17, 19–21, 235,
309
Paris, 50–51, 57, 60. See also
Montmartre
Paris-Lyon-Mediterranée Railway
(P.L.M.), 100
Pension Gloanec, 64, 64, 90
Peruvian mummy, 279, 280

Petit Boulevard, 78, 81

Petit, Georges, 44, 52–53

Petit Séminaire de La Chapelle-Saint-Mesmin, Orléans, 28–29

Petrarch, 142, 151

physiognomy and phrenology, 238

Pilgrims, 83

Pissarro, Camille, 29, 40–41, 43–45, 47, 49, 52–55, 61, 64, 68, 70, 72, 75, 334, 343, 352; and primitivism, 64, 69–70

    Apple Picking, *53*

    Dance, 113, *113*

    Paul Gauguin Carving "Woman Strolling," *44*

    Peasant Women Chatting, 65, *66*

    Study for *Weeders, Pontoise*, *66*

    Weeders, Pontoise, *66*

Pissarro, Georges Manzana, *Paul Gauguin*, *342*

Pissarro, Lucien, 75

Pizarro, Francisco, 87

Politiken, 55, 63

Pomare V (king of Tahiti), 337

Pont-Aven, Brittany, France, 64, *64*, 90, *94–95*, 113, 297; School of Pont-Aven, 345

"Portraits of the Next Century," 342

Prado (Luis Carlos Frederico Linska de Castillon), 257, 259–60, 265–66, *266*, 277

Pranzini, Henri, 257, 259, *266*, 277

Praxiteles (after), *Venus of Arles*, *171*

Pre-Raphaelite Brotherhood, 139

Provence, France, 97–99. *See also* Arles, Provence; and Marseilles

Punaauia, Tahiti, 347

Puvis de Chavannes, Pierre, 88, 90, 173–74, 176, 180, 345–46, 350; retrospective of 1887, 88, 90, 120

    Hope, 88–89, *89*, 90, 126, 128, 165, 254, 272, 330, 336, 340–41, 346, 350, 352

    Pleasant Land, *118*, 120, 174

    The Poor Fisherman, 346, *346*, 350

    Portrait of Eugène Benon, 90, *91*, 200

Q

Quincey, Thomas de, 259

R

Rappard, Anthon van, 31–34, 37, 107, 110, 150, 234

Rarahu. *See* Loti, Pierre, *Le Mariage de Loti (Rarahu)*

Redon, Odilon, 53, 240, 277; *Flower-Cyclops*, 242, *243*; *Head of a Martyr*, *278*

Reid, Alexander, 99, 321

Rembrandt van Rijn, 16, 20–21, 31, 39, 144, 232, 239, 255

    The Agony in the Garden, *124*, 144

    The Angel Raphael, 289, 300, *302*

    The Descent from the Cross, *318*, 320

    Flight into Egypt: A Night Piece, 20, 116, *116*

    The Holy Family, 200, *201*, 227

    The Raising of Lazarus, 323, *324*

    Self-Portrait in Front of the Easel, *56*, 57

    Young Man with a Walking Stick (the "Lacaze Rembrandt"), 57, 255, *257*, 300, 313, 321

Renan, Ernest, 15, 18, 28, 273

Renoir, Pierre-Auguste, 41, 43–45, 52

La Revue indépendante, 210

Ricard, Gustave, 254

Richepin, Jean, 75; *Braves Gens (Roman parisien)*, 90

Rijksmuseum, Amsterdam, 39

Rimbaud, Arthur, *Tête de faune*, 63

Robert, Karl, *Le Fusain sans maître (Drawing without a Master)*, 30

Robinson Crusoe 21, 33, 84, 279

Rod, Édouard, *Le Sens de la vie*, 290

Rodin, Auguste, 61–62; *Faun and Nymph*, 62, *62*; *Head of Saint John the Baptist*, 277, *278*

Romanticism, 54, 207

Rossetti, Christina, 313

Rouen, France, 45

Roulin, Armand, 227

Roulin, Augustine, 200, 251, 272

Roulin, Joseph, 128, 166, 189, 200, 266, 270

Roulin, Marcelle, 200, 227

Rousseau, Théodore, 34

Rubens, Peter Paul, 16, 183, 320

Rugendas, Johann Moritz, *Plaza de Armas*, *27*; *Tapadas*, *27*

Russell, John, 126, 140

Ruysdael, Jacob, 34, 39

S

Saintes-Maries, 109

Saint-Paul-de-Mausole, 273, 283–84

Saint-Rémy, Provence, France, *262–63*, 283, 285, *287*

Saint-Trophîme, 101, 142

Salon, 29, 52

Salon de la Nationale, 69

Salon des Refusés, 1863, 54

Sandoz, Pierre. *See* Zola, Émile, *L'Oeuvre*

Schuffenecker, Émile, 47, 69, 246, 335

Schumann, Robert, *Berceuse*, 310

sea voyage metaphor, 16, 17, 19, 32–33, 109–10, 270–71, 277, 331

Segatori, Agostina, 74, 90, 259

Sensier, Alfred, *La Vie et l'oeuvre de J.-F. Millet*, 75, *76*, 83, 193–94

Sérusier, Paul, 277, 291, 310, 333, 341; *The Talisman*, 277

Seurat, Georges, 53, 55, 61, 72, 82, 88, 93, 224, 334; and primitivism, 69, 87–88

    Fishermen, 71, *72*

    A Sunday on La Grande Jatte—1884, *53*, 53–55, 64, 88, 223–24, 350

sexuality and creativity, 3, 85, 122, 124, 137–38, 182–83, 187, 197–98, 214, 338

Shakespeare, William, 21

Signac, Paul, 53, 61, 71, 72, 90, 111, 273, 353; *Still Life: Oranges, Apple, and Maupassant's "Au soleil,"* *91*

Silvestre, Théophile, *Eugène Delacroix: Documents nouveaux*, 289

singeries, 239

Sint Andries, Antwerp, *227*, 227–28

Sisley, Alfred, 43, 45, 52

Société de Saint Luc, 47

soleil. See sunflower

"sorrowful yet always rejoicing," 16–17, 19–21, 75, 313

Southeast Asia, 178, 283, 313

South of France. *See* Provence, France

Souvestre, Émile, 17

stella maris, *227*, 227–28, 270

Stowe, Harriet Beecher, 21, 84; *Uncle Tom's Cabin*, 323

Stricker, Johannes (van Gogh's uncle), 11, 17, 20, 30

Strindberg, August, 346, 348

Studio of the South concept, 1, 139–40, 176, 266, 327, 349, 353

Studio of the Tropics concept, conceived by van Gogh, 1, 99, 214, 216, 321, 333; transplanted by Gauguin, 256, 313, 316, 327, 333, 350

struggle, theme of, 120, 137, 144

sunflower, 75, 77, 85, 98, 139, 327, 350, 352

Symbolism, 275, 306, 334–35, 341

syncretism, 275, 277, 279

T

tableau vs. *étude*, 41, 43–44, 54–55, 64, 85, 117, 167, 180, 195, 210, 217, 233, 245, 337

Tahiti, 63, 84–85, 333; Gauguin's first trip, 336–41; Gauguin's second trip, 347–52. *See also* maps

Tambourin, 74

Tanguy, Père, 78

Tartarin. *See* Daudet, Alphonse, *Port Tarascon*, *Tartarin de Tarascon*, and *Tartarin sur les Alpes*

Tehamana, 338, 341, 345

Tehura. *See* Tehamana

Tersteeg, Herman Gijsbertus, 14, 33, 99, 104–05, 109, 214, 266, 321

Teufelsdröckh, Diogenes. *See* Carlyle, Thomas, *Sartor Resartus*

Thoré, Théophile (Willem Bürger), 16; *Les Musées de la Hollande (The Museums of Holland)*, 16, 31

Tissot, James, 77; *Behold He Standeth behind Our Wall*, 77, *79*; *Melancholia*, 191

tournesol. See sunflower

Tristan, Flora (Gauguin's maternal grandmother), 23–25, 28; *The Peregrinations of a Pariah*, 25, 306, 327

Tristán y Moscoso, Don Mariano (Gauguin's maternal grandfather), 24

Tristán y Moscoso, Don Pio, 25, 28

Tonkin (northern Vietnam). *See* Southeast Asia

Toulouse-Lautrec, Henri de, 57, 78, 109

typology, 11

U

Uhland, Ludwig, 17

Union Centrale des Arts Décoratifs, 69

Universal Exposition, Paris, 1889, 1, 280, *283*, 283–84, 312; Colonial Exhibition, 280, 313; *kampong*, 280; *pagode*, 280, 283, 312

Uribe, Juan, 71

V

Vairaumati, 340–41

Valjean, Jean. *See* Hugo, Victor, *Les Misérables*

van Gogh. *See* Gogh, van

Velázquez, Diego, 239; *Kitchen Maid with the Summer at Emmaus*, *8*

Venus of Arles, *171*, 172

Verdier, Antoine, *Christ with a Crown of Thorns: Alfred Bruyas*, *255*, 277

Vingt, Les (The Twenty), 71, 213, 274, 321, 334

Virgin Mary, 227–28, 232, 336

Vollard, Ambroise, 349–50

Volpini show, 284, 291

Vondel, Joost van den, 75, 77

Vos, Kee, 30, 110

W

Wackenroder, Wilhelm, *Outpourings from the Heart of an Art-Loving Monk*, 138

Wagner, Richard, 110–11, 116, 121–22, 231–32, 272, 310, 333, 344; *Das Kunstwerk der Zukunft*, 110; *The Flying Dutchman (Le Vaisseau fantôme)*, 110, 133, 270

Wasmes. *See* Borinage, Belgium

Wauters, Émile, *Madness of Hugo van der Goes*, 121, *121*, 153

Wentzel, Gustav, *Breakfast*, *8*

Westerhoven, Jan van, Jr., *Den Schepper verheerlijckt in den Schepselen (The Creator Praised by All Creation)*, *10*

Whistler, James McNeill, 65

Whitman, Walt, 146

Wilde, Oscar, 77

Wirgman, T. B., *Some "Graphic" Artists*, *32*

Wisselingh, Elbert Jan van, 99

Y

yellow, 21, 235, 344, 349

Yellow House, *107*, 107–08, 141, *159*, 160, 186, 268, 272–73; as *bonzerie*, 151, 289, 350; decoration and furnishing of, 132, 139, 151, 323

Z

Zola, Émile, 32, 37, 40, 43, 54–55, 82, 174, 188

    L'Assommoir, 75

    Au bonheur des dames (The Ladies' Paradise), 37

    La Faute de l'abbé Mouret, 124–25

    La Joie de vivre (Zest for Life), 6, 9, 37, 75, 128, 194, 297, 300

    L'Oeuvre, 54–55, 69, 82–83, 121–22, 137–38, 143–44, 151, 153, 197, 203, 207, 265, 334

    Le Rêve, 188, 210, 289

Zorrilla, Manuel-Ruiz, 52

Zouaves, 111, 124, 176, 178, 257

Zundert, The Netherlands, *5*, 12, 14. *See also* maps

73: Photo by Katya Kallsen—© President and Fellows of Harvard College. 79: Victor Merlhès, *Paul Gauguin et Vincent van Gogh 1887–1888: Lettres retrouvées, sources ignorées* (Taravao, Tahiti, 1989), p. 101.

Chapter 4
1: Rémi Venture, *Arles* (Marguerittes, 1989), p. 55. 4, 7, 27, 29, 56, 65, 66, 71, 78, 79, 95, 106, 107, 116, 119, 122: Courtesy of Van Gogh Museum. 5: © British Museum. 9, 13, 24, 118, 120: © Christie's Images Incorporated 2001. 10, 14, 28, 33, 73, 115: © Stichting Kröller-Müller Museum. 12: Photo by Dénes Józsa. 15, 18: Photo by John Blazejewski, Marquand Library of Art and Archaeology, Princeton University Library. 16: Photo by J. L. Mabit. 17: Alinari/Art Resource, NY. 21, 54: Scala/Art Resource, NY. 23: Photo by B. Delgado. 32, 136: RMN/Art Resource, NY. 37, 38, 59: Photo by Erich Lessing/Art Resource, NY. 46: Courtesy of Galerie Maurice Tzwern, Brussels. 48, 102, 141: © Museum of Fine Arts, Boston. All rights reserved. 50, 52, 87: Photo by Ole Woldbye—Ordrupgaard, Copenhagen. 53: © Reproduced with the Permission of The Barnes Foundation.™ All Rights Reserved. 55: Photo by Peter Willi—Courtesy of The Bridgeman Art Library, New York. 58: Giraudon/Art Resource, NY. 60: Courtesy of Alex Reid & Lefevre Ltd. 61: © Rijksmuseum, Amsterdam. 63, 93, 137: © The Metropolitan Museum of Art. 64, 88: © Museum Folkwang Essen. 69: © The National Gallery, London. 70: Ronald Pickvance, *English Influences on Vincent van Gogh* (London, 1974), p. 24. 74: René Garagnon, *Arles en photos et cartes postales anciennes, 1890–1981* (Arles, n.d.), p. 30. 75: Archivo fotográfico del Museo de Bellas Artes de Bilbao © Museo de Bellas Artes de Bilbao. 76: Courtesy of Mitchell-Innes & Nash. 77: Photo by W. Dräyer, Zurich. 80: Photo by Robert Wedemeyer. 81: Photo by Marcello Saporetti. 83: © 2001 The Museum of Modern Art, New York. 84, 96, 98, 108, 109, 127: © The Israel Museum, Jerusalem. 90, 121, 129: © 2001 Board of Trustees, National Gallery of Art,

Washington, D.C. 91: Photo P. Corbierre—Service Régional de l'Inventaire de Basse-Normandie. 92: © Frans Halsmuseum, Haarlem. 94, 103: Photo by Joe Mikuliak—Philadelphia Museum of Art. 97: © The Saint Louis Art Museum. 104, 117, 126: Raymond Cogniat, *Paul Gauguin: A Sketchbook* (New York, 1962), pp. 220–21, 20–21, 56–57. 105, 139: Ronald Pickvance, *Gauguin* (Martigny, 1998), p. 12, p. 162. 110: *Dictionary of Belgian and Dutch Animal Painters Born between 1750 and 1880* (Knokke-Zoute, Belgium, 1998), p. 370. 111, 112: Victor Merlhès, *Paul Gauguin et Vincent van Gogh 1887–1888: Lettres retrouvées, sources ignorées* (Taravao, Tahiti, 1989), between pp. 240–41, 242. 123: Photo by P. Pierrain—© Photothèque des Musées de la Ville de Paris. 124: Photo by H. Lewandowski—RMN/Art Resource, NY. 130, 133: Musée Fabre, *Le Roman d'un Collectionneur: Alfred Bruyas* (Montpellier, 1977), n. pag. 131, 132, 135: Photo by Frédéric Jaulmes—© Musée Fabre Montpellier.

Chapter 5
1: Caroline Boyle-Turner, *Sérusier et la Bretagne* (Douarnenez, 1995), p. 28. 2, 9, 15, 16, 18, 62, 64, 65, 69, 71, 72, 96, 97, 99, 105, 106: Courtesy of Van Gogh Museum. 15: Photo by Reindert Groot. 6: Photo by Ole Woldbye—The Danish Museum of Decorative Art, Copenhagen. 8, 21, 27, 48, 98: © Stichting Kröller-Müller Museum. 11: Musée du Faouët, *Cent ans d'estampes en Bretagne, 1808–1908* (Morbihan, [1996]), p. 14. 13: Photo by Graydon Wood—Philadelphia Museum of Art. 17: © The National Gallery, London. 19, 47, 89: © The Metropolitan Museum of Art. 22, 60: © Christie's Images Incorporated 2001. 28: Photo by Adam Rzepka—© Musée Rodin. 29: Courtesy of Galerie Daniel Malingue, Paris. 30: Sotheby's, *Continental Books and Manuscripts* (London, 1997), p. 112. 31: *Wallraf-Richartz-Jahrbuch* 46/47 (Cologne, 1985/86), p. 281. 32: RMN/Art Resource, NY. 33: Ziva Amishai-Maisels, *Gauguin's Religious Themes* (New York/London, 1985), fig. 21. 34: © Musée de l'Homme.

35: Photo by Arnaudet—RMN/Art Resource, NY. 41: © ND-Viollet. 44, 45: © 2001 The Museum of Modern Art, New York. 46: Jean-Paul Clébert and Pierre Richard, *La Provence de van Gogh* (Aix-en-Provence, 1981), p. 54. 49: Photo by Jean de Calan—© Musée Rodin. 50: Photo by David Heald—© The Solomon R. Guggenheim Foundation, New York. 52: Photo by H. Lewandowski—RMN/Art Resource, NY. 54: © 2001 Museum Associates/LACMA. 55, 68: © Museum of Fine Arts, Boston. All rights reserved. 56: Eugène Royer, *Les Calvaires bretons* (Rennes, 1981), p. 91. 57: Photo by Speltdoorn. 61, 75: © 2001 Board of Trustees, National Gallery of Art, Washington, D.C. 63, 100: Courtesy of The Bridgeman Art Library, New York. 66, 93: © Scala/Art Resource, NY. 70 a, b: Jean-Jacques Luthi, *Émile Bernard* (Paris, 1982), p. 39. 73: Photo by J. Lathion—© Nasjonalgalleriet 2001. 74, 86: © Museum Folkwang Essen. 76: Photo by Malcolm Varon, N.Y.C., © 2001. 77: Courtesy of Eric M. Zafran. 78: Eric M. Zafran, ed. *Gauguin's Nirvana: Painters at Le Pouldu 1889–90* (New Haven/London, 2001), p. 92. 79: Edme Casimir de Croizier, *L'Art khmer* (Paris, 1875), p. 72. 81: Photo by Claus Ørsted. 83: Maurice Malingue, *Gauguin* (Paris, 1943), p. 144. 84: Musée de l'Homme, *Le Musée Indo-Chinois* (Paris, n.d.), pl. 4. 85: Photo by Robert Wedemeyer. 88: © British Museum. 101: © Musée des Beaux-Arts de la Ville de Reims. 103: Photo by Charles Choffet.

Coda
1: Paul Gauguin, *Avant et après* (Leipzig, 1918), p. 12. 3: Photo by Martin Bühler, Oeffentliche Kunstsammlung Basel. 4: Giraudon/Art Resource, NY. 9: Courtesy of Van Gogh Museum. 11: Ader Picard Tajan, *Sérusier* (Paris, 1984), p. 55. 13: © 2001 The Museum of Modern Art, New York. 15: Galerie Dario Boccara, *Manzana Pissarro* (Paris, 1973), p. 79. 17: © Sterling and Francine Clark Art Institute, Williamstown, Massachusetts. 18: Ziva Amishai-Maisels, *Gauguin's Religious Themes* (New York/London, 1985), fig. 27. 19: Photo by H. Lewandowski—

RMN/Art Resource, NY. 22: Photo by Luiz Hossaka. 23: Réunion des Musées Nationaux. 24: © Museum of Fine Arts, Boston. All rights reserved. 28: © Christie's Images Incorporated 2001.

Map credits
Maps, cutaways, and diagrams were created by Tom Willcockson, Mapcraft, Woodstock, Illinois, in collaboration with studio blue, Chicago. Maps are based on information provided by the authors, who assume sole responsibility for their content.

The maps of Zundert, The Netherlands, and environs (ch. 1, figs. 15 and 16) were drawn up from on-site observation and informed by the following sources: *Grote Historische Atlas van Nederland*, vol. 4, *Zuid-Nederland, 1838–1857* (Groningen, 1990); Frank Kools, *Vincent van Gogh en zijn geboorteplaats* (Zutphen, The Netherlands, 1990).

The map of Lima, Peru (ch. 1, fig. 25), was informed by the following sources: Margarita Cubillas Soriano, *Lima Monumento Historico* (Lima, 1996); *Lima centro histórico* (Lima, 1998); Javier Prado Heuderbert, *Lima: Arquitectura y escultura religiosa virreynal* (Lima, 1996); David Sweetman, *Paul Gauguin: A Life* (New York, 1996). The cutaway of the Echenique residence was made possible through photographs courtesy of Ana Maria Reyes, Chicago, and Claudia Chocano, Lima.

The maps related to Arles and the Crau (ch. 4, figs. 3, 19, 72) were drawn up from on-site observation, with reference to relevant works by van Gogh and Gauguin, and informed by the following sources: an assortment of Baedeker, Joanne, and Murray travel guides from the period under consideration; *Dominique Roman: Objectif Provence* (Arles, 1997); *Charles Nègre, Photographe* (Arles, 1980); René Garagnon, *Arles en photos et cartes postales anciennes 1890–1981* (Arles, n.d.); *In Relation to Van Gogh: Photography by Contemporaries* (Amsterdam,

1990); Rémi Venture, *L'Abbaye de Montmajour: Le Temps retrouvé* (Barbentane, n.d.); Rémi Venture, *Arles: Métamorphoses* (Barbentane, 1989). The cutaways of the Yellow House (ch. 4, fig. 2) were informed by a to-scale reconstruction and by Ronald Dorn, *Décoration: Vincent van Goghs Werkreihe für das Gelbe Haus in Arles* (Hildesheim/Zurich/New York, 1990).